Individuals + organization
Nuances of positions
Day by day, year by year

- did pacifism gain the political legitimacy
  That lib, Nad, socialist, conserv in domestic
  politics?

- politics + principle - people join + leave, new
  groups formed

- top political figures shifting positions

Labour + pacificism

- detail on support for L of N

Sources -   primary on peace
              secondary on govt

SEMI-DETACHED IDEALISTS

Semi-Detached Idealists

THE BRITISH PEACE MOVEMENT AND INTERNATIONAL RELATIONS, 1854–1945

MARTIN CEADEL

OXFORD

UNIVERSITY PRESS

OXFORD

UNIVERSITY PRESS

Great Clarendon Street, Oxford OX2 6DP

Oxford University Press is a department of the University of Oxford.
It furthers the University's objective of excellence in research, scholarship,
and education by publishing worldwide in

Oxford New York

Athens Auckland Bangkok Bogotá Buenos Aires Calcutta
Cape Town Chennai Dar es Salaam Delhi Florence Hong Kong Istanbul
Karachi Kuala Lumpur Madrid Melbourne Mexico City Mumbai
Nairobi Paris São Paulo Shanghai Singapore Taipei Tokyo Toronto Warsaw
and associated companies in Berlin Ibadan

Oxford is a registered trade mark of Oxford University Press
in the UK and in certain other countries

Published in the United States
by Oxford University Press Inc., New York

© Martin Ceadel 2000

The moral rights of the author have been asserted
Database right Oxford University Press (maker)

First published 2000

British Library Cataloguing in Publication Data

Data available

Library of Congress Cataloging in Publication Data

Ceadel, Martin.
Semi-detached idealists: the British peace movement and international relations,
1845–1945/Martin Ceadel.
p. cm.
Includes bibliographical references and index.
1. Peace movements—Great Britain—History. 2. Great Britain—Foreign relations—19th
century. I. Title.
JZ5584.G7 C43 2000 327.1´72´06041—dc21 00–060681
ISBN 0–19–924117–1

1 3 5 7 9 10 8 6 4 2

Typeset in Times by
Cambrian Typesetters, Frimley, Surrey
Printed in Great Britain
on acid-free paper by
T.J. International
Padstow, Cornwall

For
Jemima

CONTENTS

ABBREVIATIONS

Add. MSS	British Library Additional Manuscripts
BLPES	British Library of Political and Economic Science
CBCO	Central Board for Conscientious Objectors
EC	Executive Committee
FoR	Fellowship of Reconciliation
FPC	Friends' Peace Committee
FSC	Friends' Service Committee
GC	General Council
HP	*Herald of Peace*
HW	*Headway*
IAPA	International Arbitration and Peace Association
ILP	Independent Labour Party
LIPL	Ligue internationale de la paix et de la liberté
LIPP	Ligue internationale et permanente de la paix
LNU	League of Nations Union
LPCR	*Labour Party Conference Report*
LUB	League of Universal Brotherhood
NLW	National Library of Wales
NMWM	No More War Movement
NEC	National Executive Committee
NPC	National Peace Council
NUWSS	National Union of Women's Suffrage Societies
PCCM	Peace Congress (or Conference) Committee minutes
PN	*Peace News*
PPU	Peace Pledge Union
PSLB	Peace Society Letter Book
PSM	Peace Society executive committee minutes
RIIA	Royal Institute of International Affairs
UDC	Union of Democratic Control
WAWSA	*War Against War in South Africa*
WIL	Women's International League
WPA	Workmen's Peace Association
WPC	Women's Peace Crusade

1

Introduction

Britain's peace activists have always been semi-detached from international relations in virtue of their location in what R. W. Seton-Watson, a perceptive foreign-policy analyst writing in 1938, called a 'hybrid, intermediate, geographical position, as part of Europe, and yet detached from it'.[1] They have been close enough to the continent to fear being drawn into any major war which breaks out there, yet distant enough not to be permanently anxious about national security. In consequence of this semi-detachment, they have had both the incentive to seek to abolish war and the serenity—reinforced by a generally reassuring experience of domestic politics—to believe that this ambitious goal might be achievable. They have thus always been idealists— or 'utopians', as E. H. Carr, a professor of international relations, famously called them in 1939[2]—in virtue of their belief that international relations can be conducted in a pacific way.

In 1854 these semi-detached idealists had, for the first time since peace associations had been established, to oppose a decision—and moreover an enthusiastically supported one—to go to war. They endured the adversity resulting from their dissent, and in the next few decades rebuilt their position as an accepted voice in public life, although by the end of the nineteenth century their associations were suffering a loss of vitality. Shocked by the First World War into reinvigorating and reconstructing their movement, they came through another period of unpopularity before enjoying unprecedented public support during the inter-war years. Finally, however, Hitler discredited many of the ideas which they had been promoting. Since 1945, when the atomic bomb and the incipient cold war reinforced the disillusioning effect of the discovery of Hitler's extermination camps, hopes for a fundamental reform of international relations have been at a low ebb. Only on the particular issue of nuclear weapons has a significant level of peace activism been achievable, and even then only intermittently.

[1] R. W. Seton-Watson, *Britain and the Dictators: A Survey of Post-War British Policy* (Cambridge, 1938), 7.
[2] E. H. Carr, *The Twenty Years' Crisis: An Introduction to the Study of International Relations* (1939).

2 *Introduction*

Having taken the British peace movement from its antenatal stage to sturdy adolescence in a previous book,[3] I here consider its age of maturity. Some research has, of course, already been done on this subject. As early as 1931 A. C. F. Beales published a pioneering and ambitious account of the period down to the 1920s;[4] but though much relied upon, it is seriously flawed: indeed, within a few years of its publication the American scholar Irwin Abrams noted in his own far superior study of continental activism that Beales's 'research is not solid, and the work is crowded with mistakes'.[5] Other, more accurate, books have tackled the British peace movement in the round for part of this period.[6] Moreover, a growing number of works have focused on particular associations, groups, or activists, though they have almost invariably done so without placing their subject-matter in the context of peace activism as a whole.[7] No study has reliably charted the rise, fall, and

[3] M. Ceadel, *The Origins of War Prevention: The British Peace Movement and International Relations, 1730–1854* (Oxford, 1996).

[4] *A History of Peace: A Short Account of the Organized Movements for International Peace* (1931).

[5] I. M. Abrams, 'A History of European Peace Societies 1867–1899', Ph.D. thesis (Harvard, 1938), fo. 473.

[6] e.g. J. A. Berkman, 'Pacifism in England 1914–39', Ph.D. thesis (Yale University, 1967); S. Frick, 'Joseph Sturge, Henry Richard and the *Herald of Peace*: Pacifist Response to the Crimean War', Ph.D. thesis (Cornell University, 1971); J. Hinton, *Protests and Visions: Peace Politics in Twentieth-Century Britain* (1989); P. Laity, 'The British Peace Movement 1896–1916: Ideas and Dilemmas', D.Phil. thesis (Oxford University, 1995); K. Robbins, *The Abolition of War: The 'Peace Movement' in Britain 1914–1919* (Cardiff, 1976); E. W. Sager, 'Pacifism and the Victorians: A Social History of the English Peace Movement 1816–1878', Ph.D. thesis (University of British Columbia, 1975); W. H. van der Linden, *The International Peace Movement 1815–1874* (Amsterdam, 1987).

[7] Examples include: J. Barnes, *Ahead of his Age: Bishop Barnes of Birmingham* (1979); D. Birn, *The League of Nations Union 1918–1945* (Oxford, 1981); L. Bisceglia, *Norman Angell and Liberal Internationalism in Britain 1931–1935* (New York, 1982); E. Bramsted, 'Apostles of Collective Security: The LNU and its Functions', *Australian Journal of Politics and History*, 13 (1967), 347–74; H.P. Cecil, 'The Development of Lord Robert Cecil's Views on Securing a Lasting Peace 1915–19', D.Phil. thesis (Oxford University, 1971); C. Cline, *E. D. Morel 1873–1924: The Strategies of Protest* (Belfast, 1980); R. J. Fielding, 'The Elimination of War: An Examination of the Work of Sir Norman Angell', Ph.D. thesis (Sussex University, 1967); H. Hanak, 'The Union of Democratic Control during the First World War', *Bulletin of the Institute of Historical Research*, 36 (1963), 167–80; G. B. Henderson, 'The Pacifists of the Fifties', *Journal of Modern History*, 9 (1937), 314–41; R. A. Jones, *Arthur Ponsonby: The Politics of Life* (1989); T. Kennedy, *The Hound of Conscience: A History of the No-Conscription Fellowship 1914–1919* (Fayetteville, Ark., 1981); D. Lukowitz, 'British Pacifism and Appeasement: The Peace Pledge Union', *Journal of Contemporary History*, 9 (1974), 115–27; R. Mayne and J. Pinder with J. C. de V. Roberts, *Federal Union: The Pioneers. A History of Federal Union* (1990); A. J. A. Morris, *Radicalism Against War, 1906–1914: The Advocacy of Peace and Retrenchment* (1972); M. Swartz, *The Union of Democratic Control in British Politics during the First World War* (Oxford, 1971); J. A. Thompson, 'Lord Cecil and the Pacifists in the League of Nations Union', *Historical Journal*, 20 (1977), 949–59; J. Vellacott, *Bertrand Russell and the Pacifists in the First World War* (Brighton, 1980); J. Wallis, *Valiant for*

mutual interactions of all the significant elements of the peace movement in this period, even though without this basic information judgements about the movement's political influence, social characteristics, or ideological approach cannot meaningfully be made. Thus, whilst acknowledging a considerable debt to previous books, articles, and dissertations—many of them of a very high standard—I feel justified in claiming to offer something new: the first properly researched long-run account and comprehensive overview.

Because it covers nine decades, a lengthy period for a work using primary sources throughout, my book has little space in which to wander from its central narrative. However, since even *histoire événementielle* necessarily has an analytical agenda, if only a tacit one, I should make mine explicit at the outset. In a nutshell, my assumption will be that, while peace movements can usefully be treated both as pressure groups and as social movements, they can even more helpfully be interpreted as ideological protagonists.

To regard peace movements essentially as pressure groups is to see them as instrumental rather than expressive organizations, existing in order to influence public opinion and preferably also public policy.[8] Peace associations have often highlighted their efforts in this direction: for example, as the Peace Society approached its seventy-fifth birthday in 1881, it emphasized how it made full use of

all the means by which any public question can be advanced; by lectures and Public Meetings; by the diligent use of the Press; by Memorials to Governments; by Petitions to, and working in, Parliament; by communication and conferences with Friends of Peace in other countries. Indeed, it would be difficult to suggest any means for the propagation of an idea which it has not tried.[9]

During the twentieth century, moreover, the Peace Society's successors devoted much effort to adding new lobbying techniques to this repertoire, including film, radio, television, the private referendum, the sit-down demonstration, and the peace camp.

However, peace movements have kept going doggedly on even when their pressure politics has failed and the best they can do is bear witness to their beliefs. Activists are often impelled by their consciences to keep propounding their opinions even when almost no one is taking any notice. Thus, on 6 December 1914, a courageous Unitarian minister, Dr Stanley Mellor,

---

Peace: A History of the Fellowship of Reconciliation 1914 to 1989 (1991); D. Wilson, *Gilbert Murray OM 1866–1957* (Oxford, 1987).

[8] An example of this approach is B. G. Buzan, 'The British Peace Movement from 1919 to 1939', Ph.D thesis (London School of Economics, 1973), the abstract of which states that its main concerns are to 'explain the movement's failure to influence the government' and to examine 'the methods of pressure open to the interwar peace organizations'.

[9] *Herald of Peace* (Mar. 1881), 198.

painfully conscious as a pacifist of being shunned by the overwhelming
majority of his fellow citizens who supported the First World War, told his
Liverpool congregation: 'I know that my voice is only one, and one with little
influence. . . . But if many will not listen, I would speak to the few. . . .
Therefore, you lonely idealists, dreamers, believers in humanity, seekers after
good . . . pursue your sincere idealistic road, dream your dreams. . . .'[10]

Moreover, even when they have found themselves working with the grain
of public opinion, peace campaigners have rarely contributed as much to political outcomes as they have understandably liked to believe. When the public
has become agitated about peace issues, it has usually done so in response to
world events rather than to the peace movement's propaganda; and when
politicians have felt pressurized to take up the peace question, they have
usually done so in response to public opinion rather than to the actions of the
peace movement. In other words, to a considerable extent international crises
have impinged directly on the public; and the political system has reacted
directly to the public's resulting anxieties: the intermediating role of peace
activists in both these responses has usually been modest. In addition, it must
be recognized that ministers have sometimes embraced peace ideas of their
own volition: the fourth Earl of Clarendon, British Foreign Secretary 1853–8
and 1868–70, is a case in point. I have therefore suggested that a suitable analogy for the peace movement when conditions are unfavourable is a pilot light,
keeping the flame of peace thinking alive yet requiring the fuel of combustible
public sentiment in order to ignite a mass campaign, and that a suitable analogy when conditions are favourable is a glider, drawing attention to the upcur-
rents of peace sentiment which sustain it yet unable either to power its own
take-off or indefinitely to extend its time aloft.[11] Such an assessment may
offend peace activists who wish to believe that their contributions are more
substantial. However, it at least exonerates them from the charge, which their
opponents have periodically made, of causing conflicts by leading the country's adversaries to believe that they could get away with aggression.

In this book I therefore try to avoid inflating the political importance of the
peace movement in order to justify writing about it. I give due recognition to
the lobbying tactics used by the movement, and attempt at the end of each
chapter to judge the effect which these, as distinct from the unmediated influence of international events, have had on its political fortunes; and I also
acknowledge those occasions on which these efforts seem to have affected
public policy. However, I do not claim to perform this last task scientifically:

---

[10] S. A. Mellor, *Five Sunday Evening Addresses delivered in Hope Street Church Liverpool,*
November 8th to December 6th 1914 (Liverpool, 1914), 58–9.
[11] Ceadel, *Origins of War Prevention*, 19.

this would require a study not just of the government's perception of domestic constraints but of all the other inputs into policy-making too, which is simply not practicable over so long a period. I have therefore not used official records at all, but have relied on secondary studies of governmental policy-making. Indeed, the fact that the latter mention the peace movement so rarely is a further reason for not judging the significance of the peace movement in exclusively pressure-group terms.

Some writers have treated peace movements essentially as social movements. This is to see them as operating outside conventional political channels and seeking to influence 'the social networks and cultural symbols through which social relations are organized'.[12] This approach has the merit of recognizing that peace movements are to some extent products of their social and cultural setting. For example, the League of Nations Union, 'that prize inter-war non-party cause' as it has been described by a leading historian,[13] is undoubtedly of interest for what it reveals about Britain's vigorous associational culture. And it is obviously true that a study of the peace movement can shed light on various aspects of the social history of the period in question, such as in this case the process of secularization, the declining influence of the provincial businessman, the increasing prominence of the journalist, the publicist, and the labour activist, and even improvements in prison conditions. Yet, as I have argued elsewhere,[14] a social-movement approach cannot be pushed too far without implying that peace activism was an obliquely expressed form of introspection about social conditions rather than a sincere attempt to tackle the problem of international war.[15] Thus to return to the example of the League of Nations Union: whatever social functions it may incidentally have fulfilled within inter-war Britain, its *raison d'être* and constant priority were to support an experiment in international organization—facts which must receive their due emphasis in any account of its activities.

---

[12] This phrase comes from S. Tarrow, *Power in Movement: Social Movements, Collective Action and Politics* (Cambridge, 1994), 1. For a sceptical view, see G. Jordan and W. A. Malone, *The Protest Business? Mobilizing Campaign Groups* (Manchester, 1997), ch. 2.

[13] B. Harrison, *Prudent Revolutionaries: Portraits of British Feminists between the Wars* (Oxford, 1987), 167.

[14] Ceadel, *Origins of War Prevention*, 88–91.

[15] An example is the—to my mind unsubstantiated—claim that the Peace Society was founded 'by men who were more concerned about crime and irreligion in society than they were about war itself': E. W. Sager, 'The Social Origins of Victorian Pacifism', *Victorian Studies*, 23 (1979/80), 211–36 at 232. The same approach tends to imply that even domestic campaigns have a real purpose other than their professed one: e.g. the French campaign against nuclear power in the 1970s and early 1980s has been defined by a social-movement theorist as 'the actor in the class war for the control of historicity' which is taking over 'the central role played by the working-class movement in the labour conflict of industrial society' in the 'post-industrial, programmed society now taking shape': A. Touraine, *Anti-Nuclear Protest: The Opposition to Nuclear Energy in France* (Cambridge, 1983), 3–4.

ideological

I therefore give priority to a third approach, which interprets peace movements above all as ideological protagonists driven by the conviction that they
have achieved fundamental insights into international relations. This is to see
them as genuinely concerned with the moral, ethical, and analytical problems
posed by war, and determined to propound solutions to them, irrespective of
whether the public or the government is interested. It has the advantage of
recognizing the visionary quality of their commitment better than the pressure-group approach and the substantive quality of their interest in international relations better than the social-movement approach. It also identifies
the main claim of peace movements to significance, which is less the
change terms of internal discussion constraining effect of their lobbying on the political process, or the transfor-
mative effect of their activism on social relations, than the cumulative effect
of their ideological claims on the terms in which international relations are
discussed. Though hard to measure in a precise way, their constant criticism
of the 'axiom that the best security for peace is to be prepared for war'[16] has
altered the way in which governments explain their foreign and defence policies and publics respond to these policies, and has contributed to the creation
of such international bodies as the Court of International Justice, the League
of Nations, and the United Nations.[17]

The ideological approach also offers the most coherent definition of the
term 'peace movement', which entered English usage as early as the 1840s
yet has been frequently criticized for appearing to imply that those who do
not support it are pro-war. This implication is undoubtedly true of the small
minority of its opponents, here labelled 'militarists', who glorify conquest on
the grounds that it advances civilization, and is partially true of another small
group, here called 'crusaders', who believe that the first use of military force
is sometimes necessary to achieve justice and thereby create the conditions
for lasting peace. But it is not true of that large majority, known here as
'defencists', who hold that the incidence of war is minimized when all countries reject aggression and maintain national defences strong enough to deter
others from attempting it. It is thus defencists who promote the axiom *si vis
pacem, para bellum* ('if you want peace, prepare for war'). In other words the
peace movement not only differs from militarists and crusaders in opposing

---

[16] *HP* (Mar. 1863), 170.

[17] This claim is made in C. Lynch, *Beyond Appeasement: Interpreting Interwar Peace
Movements in World Politics* (Ithaca, NY, 1999), an interesting work which appeared when all
but the final chapter of this book had been completed. I regard her approach, which emphasizes
the peace movement's development of 'a normative agenda that posed significant challenges to
traditional norms of state behaviour' (p. 214) as very close to mine, though she presents it as the
application of a social-movement approach to world politics. Her work is particularly impressive for not only covering two countries but looking at some governmental records as well as
primary material on certain peace associations.

aggressive war: it also differs from defencists in its conviction that it is possible to abolish war rather than merely stave it off for substantial periods. Indeed, the first edition of the *Peace Year Book* was to note in 1910: 'The object of the Peace Movement is to establish a better order in the world, a condition of International Justice and Friendship, in place of the existing condition of War and "Armed Peace".'[18] Its appropriation of the label 'peace' is therefore justified by its ideologically distinctive view that peace can exist as a positive and permanent condition rather than merely as a truce between armed and watchful antagonists.

Ideology thus unites the peace movement against militarists, crusaders, and above all defencists. Yet it also divides it, particularly between an absolutist and a reformist wing. The former, a small but dedicated minority for which the word 'pacifist' is reserved in this book, believes that war can immediately and unconditionally be repudiated. The latter, a much larger but more amorphous grouping which is here described as *'pacificist'* following a suggestion by the historian and activist for the Campaign for Nuclear Disarmament, A. J. P. Taylor,[19] argues that the abolition of war will be achieved only by improving the structure either of the international system or of its constituent states and that until this has been achieved defensive military force may be needed to protect these reforms.

Because it has always contained a *pacificist* wing, the peace movement has always in principle faced the possibility of acute ideological division if a war breaks out which some *pacificists* believe is both defensive and politically progressive: this occurred for the first time at the outbreak of the Crimean War. In such an eventuality, the peace movement has found some of its members supporting war while claiming still to be pursuing peace principles. Only when *pacificists* have managed to link their support for war to the promotion of an evidently eirenic reform, such as the creation of a league of nations, have they been able to make their predicament as pro-war members of the peace movement seem less paradoxical.

In addition to this cleavage between absolutists and reformists, there have been internal disagreements among pacifists with different creeds and *pacificists* with different political commitments. However, such ideological tensions have often proved creative: a common motive for establishing new associations has been the desire to make sure that a particular ideological voice is heard. An ideological approach thus offers an understanding both of the coherence of the peace movement and of much of its internal dynamic.

---

[18] National Peace Council, *International Peace Year-Book* (1910), 1.
[19] A. J. P. Taylor, *The Trouble Makers* (1957), 51 n: I italicize it to minimize visual confusion.

By thus confining the peace movement to pacifists and *pacificists* I exclude those who oppose wars or defence efforts for reasons other than an ideological objection to defencism. Such opponents have often been very influential: for example, it was fear of obstructive dissent on nationalist—rather than on pacifist or *pacificist*—grounds which held the British government back from introducing conscription within its Irish territory in either world war; and it was in large part 'the defence of Welsh civilization', rather than pacifism or *pacificism*, which led a university lecturer, a minister of religion, and a schoolmaster to burn down the Royal Air Force's bombing range at Penros in Wales during 1936.[20] However, such nationalists, like isolationists, appeasers, and defeatists, are better regarded as the fellow-travellers of the peace movement than as its members: I therefore use the term 'anti-war' to distinguish them from authentic 'peace' campaigners.

Mainly for reasons of manageability, I focus on the 'primary' peace movement, by which I mean those associations and individual campaigners that worked for peace as an exclusive or predominant goal: examples include the Peace Society, the Women's International League, the League of Nations Union, and Ponsonby's personal effort on behalf of his Peace Letter. However, where it is essential to understand the context in which this primary activism took place, I also take cognizance of that 'secondary' peace movement which has worked to abolish war as an expression of a broader associational purpose, whether religious, political, or social: examples include the Society of Friends, the Liberal and Labour Parties, and the Women's Co-operative Guild.

I hope my subject-matter and approach to it require no further justification. However, I am conscious of needing to explain why the research and drafting of this book have been spaced over a period of three decades. Indeed, as a sometime subject coordinator in the Research Assessment Exercises which have latterly cast their shadow over British universities,[21] I am conscious that the research autobiography which follows may smack too much of enjoyable nose-following and too little of the disciplined plan-implementation now apparently required by Britain's higher education funding councils.

When, having graduated in modern history at Oxford in 1969, I stayed on to undertake research, I was particularly interested in the process by which public opinion changed, and wished to explore how the widespread peace sentiment in Britain at the end of the 1920s transformed itself into a general public support for the Second World War a decade later. Although I soon concluded that, in the absence of sufficient survey data, little of a penetrating

[20] S. Lewis, 'Why We Burnt the Bombing School', in R. Reynolds (ed.), *British Pamphleteers* (2 vols., 1951), ii. 287–300 at 299–300.
[21] For Politics and International Studies, Oxford University, 1996.

nature could be said about this subject, I realized that the peace associations, whose attempts to influence public opinion I had *inter alia* been looking at, were of considerable interest in their own right and deserved serious and dispassionate attention. Early in 1970 I therefore switched to a study of the British peace movement during the 1930s.

My new topic proved fascinating, the only trouble being that it proved too big for Oxford's doctoral word-limit, so that after doing a considerable amount of work on them, I jettisoned the *pacificists* from my thesis (which, delayed by a succession of teaching jobs, was completed only in 1976) in order to do justice to the pacifists.[22] Nor did I reinstate them when I later revised my thesis for publication (in 1980): instead I extended its chronological scope from 1931–9 to 1914–45, and reorganized it around the theme of the rise and fall of the idea that pacifism was a practical policy rather than an unworldly creed.[23] However, my intention at that stage was to use what I had already drafted on inter-war *pacificism* in a second book that would cover the period from 1900 to the present day; and I therefore undertook further research on various aspects of this subject in the early 1980s, using it in Oxford lectures on the post-1945 peace movement, in articles and essays,[24] and in various research papers.[25]

But a distraction soon arrived in the form of an invitation from my colleague Alan Ryan to develop my conceptual interests in pacifism and *pacificism* for a book in the OPUS series. In consequence I devoted most of my limited research time to exploring these ideologies in more detail and identifying their competitors: it was in this book[26] that I identified militarists, crusaders, and defencists as the peace movement's ideological adversaries. I also tackled the question of why the popularity of the various peace-or-war ideologies has varied so considerably from country to country, and came up with an answer in terms of the different degrees of security provided by their

---

[22] M. Ceadel, 'Pacifism in Britain, 1931–1939', D.Phil. thesis (Oxford University, 1976).

[23] *Pacifism in Britain 1914–1945: The Defining of a Faith* (1980).

[24] M. Ceadel, 'Popular Fiction and the Next War, 1918–1939', in F. Gloversmith (ed.), *Class, Culture and Social Change: A New View of the 1930s* (Brighton, 1980), 161–84; 'The First British Referendum: The Peace Ballot, 1934–5', *English Historical Review*, 95 (1980), 810–39; 'Between the Wars: Problems of Definition', in R. Taylor and N. Young (eds.), *Campaigns for Peace: British Peace Movements in the Twentieth Century* (Manchester, 1987), 73–99; 'La Campagne pour le désarmement nucléaire (CND) et l'approche britannique des relations internationales', *Relations internationales* (Paris), no.53 (Spring, 1988), 83–91; 'Britain's Nuclear Disarmers', in W. Lacqueur and R. Hunter (eds.), *British Peace Movements and the Future of the Western Alliance* (New Brunswick, NJ, 1988), 218–44.

[25] One of these, presented to A. J. P. Taylor's seminar at the Institute of Historical Research in London, is mentioned in his widow's diary, where my name is given (fairly phonetically) as 'Martin Keegan': see E. Haraszti Taylor, *My Life with Alan* (1987), 184.

[26] M. Ceadel, *Thinking about Peace and War* (Oxford, 1987; OPUS paperback edn., 1989).

geo-strategic situations and the different degrees of liberalism found within their political cultures. In simplified form my argument was that acute insecurity and an illiberal culture encourage militarism; moderate insecurity and a conservative culture encourage defencism; moderate security and a moderately liberal culture encourage *pacificism* and pacifism; and considerable security and a political culture wholly dominated by liberalism encourage crusading. This analysis explained the comparative strength of Britain's peace movement: since the country was secure in respect of its insular position, but only moderately so because of its close proximity to Europe, and also possessed a political culture in which a vigorous liberalism was balanced by a strong conservative tradition, it fitted into the moderately secure and moderately liberal category.

Thereafter I resumed work on twentieth-century *pacificism*, and, after writing detailed studies of a couple of its aspects,[27] embarked on what was intended to be a brief introductory chapter on the period before 1900. However, this grew into a substantial book (published in 1996) analysing the emergence of the idea that war was preventable and tracing the history of the British peace movement, including both its pacifist and *pacificist* wings, from its origins in the 1790s. At one stage I hoped in this book to take the story down to 1900, and did considerable work on the late nineteenth century;[28] but for reasons of space I eventually terminated it in 1854, the end of Britain's long post-Napoleonic peace.

Ending as it does at the end of the Second World War, this book does not incorporate my work on the post-1945 period. Even so, it pulls together research and writing carried out in discrete bursts during the early 1970s, early 1980s, late 1980s, early–middle 1990s, and late 1990s. My research notes and early drafts therefore constitute distinct, almost archaeologically identifiable, layers reflecting these different phases. The final writing up was mainly done during a year's sabbatical and post-proctorial leave between Easter 1998 and Easter 1999 for which I am grateful to both the University of Oxford and New College, though the finishing touches were delayed by duties as the acting head of the university's Department of Politics and International Relations.

---

[27] M. Ceadel, 'The First Communist "Peace Society"': The British Anti-War Movement 1932–5', *Twentieth Century British History*, 1 (1990), 58–86; 'Supranationalism in the British Peace Movement in the Early Twentieth Century', in A. Bosco (ed.), *The Federal Idea, i. The History of Federalism from the Enlightenment to 1945* (1991), 169–91.

[28] Some of it was used in M. Ceadel, 'Sir William Randal Cremer', in K. Holl and A. Kjelling (eds.), *The Nobel Peace Prizes and the Laureates: The Meaning and Acceptance of the Nobel Peace Prize in the Prize Winners' Countries* (Frankfurt, 1994), 167–92.

Over many years I have received helpful service from the staffs of the Bodleian Library (particularly its outstanding Upper Reading Room team led by Helen Rogers, Vera Ryhaljo, and David Busby, and the staff of Room 132 led by Colin Harris), the British Library, the British Library of Political and Economic Science, Churchill College Library, Friends' House Library, Nuffield College Library, the University of London Library, and the other libraries mentioned in the bibliography. For information, interviews, or access to personal papers I am indebted to Ota Adler, Gerald Bailey, Sheila Barton, Elizabeth Bing, Lord (Fenner) Brockway, Lady Cobbold, Peter Deed, Clive R. Dunnico, Mabel Eyles-Monk, Frank Hardie, the Revd Sidney Hinkes, Sir Charles Kimber, Ethel Mannin, Leah Manning, Jan Melichar, Lucy Middleton (née Cox), Edward Milligan, Hilda Morris, Mary Murry (née Gamble), Sybil Morrison, Pamela Parkin, Myrtle Solomon, Lord (Donald) Soper, David Spreckley, Margaret Storm Jameson, Nigel Spottiswoode, Janice Ure, Roy Walker, Roger Wilson, and Lady Wilmot. I also acknowledge the courtesy of the National Peace Council, the Peace Pledge Union, and the United Nations Association (residuary legatees of the League of Nations Union). Peace activists, and their families, have been a pleasure to work with: this applies also to those whom I have consulted over events since 1945 which have not found their way into this book.

Over the same period I have been given scholarly assistance on various points by Irwin Abrams, Stephen Bird, L. R. Bisceglia, Mark Bostridge, Peter Brock, David Carlton, Chris Cook, Barry Croucher, John Davis, Michael Freeden, Sir Martin Gilbert, Lawrence Goldman, A. D. Harvey, Karl Holl, Norman Ingram, Thomas Kennedy, Anne C. Kjelling, Helen Langley, Paul Laity, Ross McKibbin, Colin Matthew, Amitabh Mattoo, Kenneth Morgan, Roland Quinault, Richard Rempel, Keith Robbins, John Rowett, Eric Schneider, Miles Taylor, Daniel Waley, John Walsh, the Revd Alan Wilkinson, Sir Duncan Wilson, and Wim van der Linden. Having suggested that Paul Laity, who was then in search of a topic, work on the late nineteenth- and early twentieth-century peace movement, and having co-supervised the resulting doctoral thesis, I regret that what I expect to be a valuable published version has not appeared in time for me to make reference to it here.

My greatest debt, as ever, is to my family. Debby and Jack having already received their dedications, this is Jemima's turn; and Dickon will just have to be patient.

M.C.

New College, Oxford
March 2000

2

Rise,
February 1793–October 1851

By the time of the Crimean War, Britain's peace movement had not merely established itself but had passed its first peak of optimism. During the eighteenth century changing attitudes towards both international relations and political activism had made possible the first known suggestion of a peace association, by the utilitarian philosopher Jeremy Bentham in 1789, and the world's first peace campaign, which began early in Britain's French wars of February 1793 to June 1815. In the aftermath of this long conflict the first peace associations had been established. As domestic politics gradually liberalized and a long peace was enjoyed, the peace movement had broadened its appeal, enjoying a moment of apparent influence during 1848–51.[1]

FROM FATALISM TO A PEACE-OR-WAR DEBATE

The emergence of a peace movement in Britain was an early symptom of the transformation in thinking about international relations which got under way between the 1730s and the 1790s. Previously, war had been regarded by many people as an evil: indeed, scholars have sometimes applied the word 'pacifism' to medieval and early modern complaints about it.[2] But it had been almost universally treated as an unavoidable fact of life: for most Christians it was a divine punishment that was beyond human comprehension, let alone human remedy. According, for example, to the historian M. S. Anderson: 'In early modern Europe almost everyone regarded war as a normal, perhaps even a necessary, part of human life.'[3] However, during the eighteenth century the combined influences of the enlightenment, evangelical

[1] The evidence on which this chapter is based can be found in Ceadel, *Origins of War Prevention*. Source notes given here are mainly for material not included in that book, although some important secondary sources are re-acknowledged.

[2] B. Lowe, *Imagining Peace: A History of Early English Pacifist Ideas* (University Park, Penn., 1997). S. Marx, 'Shakespeare and Pacifism', *Renaissance Quarterly*, 45 (1992), 49–96.

[3] M. S. Anderson, *War and Society in Europe of the Old Regime 1618–1789* (Leicester, 1988), 13.

Christianity, material improvements in political, social, and economic life, and changes in the international system began undermining this fatalistic view of international relations. In its place there developed a belief that human agency could limit the incidence of war, most Christians now concluding that this was in accordance with the divine purpose. In Anderson's words, 'war was being slowly tamed'.[4] This intellectual transformation was consolidated by the reduction in European warfare which followed Napoleon's defeat in 1815; and it made such progress in Britain by the middle of the nineteenth century that a prominent liberal intellectual, John Bowring, could, albeit unhistorically, assert: 'Peace may be deemed the *normal*—the natural state of human society. It is the state which is associated with the very earliest history of our race,— the state to which, as we believe, under the guidance of a sound philosophy, and of a pure christianity, mankind is gradually again tending.'[5]

However, an important qualification must at once be made: this new belief applied only to the relations among 'civilized' countries. In respect of the relations between such countries and 'barbarous' regions of the world, fatalism lingered until the First World War. It did so most evidently in the form of imperialism, which took it for granted that advanced states would seize more backward territories by force.

As fatalism faded in respect of the international relations of the advanced world, a public debate began on the extent to which international relations could be conducted without war. The five main viewpoints identified in the Introduction soon made an appearance. In 1796, for example, the French political theorist Joseph de Maistre, who had become an extreme anti-liberal in reaction to his country's revolutionary regime, expressed the militarist conviction that 'the true fruits of human nature—the arts, sciences, great enterprises, noble ideas, manly virtues—spring above all from the state of war. It is well known that nations reach the apex of the greatness of which they are capable only after long and bloody wars.'[6] Crusading was expounded in the 1790s by both the radical Thomas Paine and the conservative Edmund Burke, the former wanting revolutionary France to conquer and reform monarchical Britain and the latter wanting Britain to defeat and extirpate the radical regime in Paris. Defencism had been given a classic exposition in *The Principles of Moral and Political Philosophy*, published in 1785 by the influential Anglican theorist of the conventional wisdom, William Paley, and soon established itself as so dominant a viewpoint that by 1843 an American

---

[4] Ibid., 187.

[5] J. Bowring, *The Political and Commercial Importance of Peace: A Lecture Delivered in the Hall of Commerce, London* (n.d.), 2. Though the British Library catalogue estimates the year of publication as 1845, the lecture was given on 3 Nov. 1846 (see *HP* (Dec. 1846), 190).

[6] Cited in *The Works of Joseph de Maistre*, ed. J. Lively (1965), 63.

visitor could without controversy tell the world's first international peace
meeting that the doctrine 'to preserve peace, a nation must be prepared for
war' was 'the almost universal sentiment from the earliest to the present age,
and with all classes of people'.[7] A remarkable number of the arguments used
by nineteenth- and twentieth-century *pacificists* were adumbrated in
Bentham's essay 'A Plan for an Universal and Perpetual Peace', written in
1789 though not published during his lifetime. And the first expositions of
pacifism as a viewpoint for all Christians—rather than as the peculiarity of
the other-worldy sects which had intermittently espoused it since the 1170s—
appeared in 1796.[8]

Except that moralistic wars of intervention were often described by their
critics as crusades, these viewpoints were not known by the labels given here.
Defencism and *pacificism* have already been noted to be recent academic
neologisms. Militarism did not enter the language till the 1860s,[9] and was
employed to describe the maintenance of large, often conscripted, armies
even in peacetime, rather than the theory of international relations according
to which such armies were deployed. And pacifism was coined—in French,
by the peace activist Emile Arnaud—as late as 1901.[10] Despite these termi-
nological deficiencies, however, the ideological structure of the peace-or-war
debate was largely understood from the outset, at least in Britain: militarists
and crusaders were conscious of advocating extreme viewpoints; defencists
dissociated themselves from aggression and the glorification of war, and
emphasized their commitment to order and equilibrium through a balance-of-
power policy; *pacificists* did not accept defencism's assumptions that the
balance of power justified military intervention and that international relations were a zero-sum game, and also disapproved of crusading's interventionist zeal; and pacifists knew that their rejection of even defensive war
classed them as utopians in everyone else's eyes.

[7] J. Blanchard, *Preparations for War: Being One of the Papers Presented to the Peace
Convention in 1843* (Peace Society, n.d. [1843]), 1.

[8] Namely, 'A Member of the Establishment' [in the American edn. 'A Clergyman of the
Church of England'], *Thoughts on the Lawfulness of War*, and I. Scott, *War Inconsistent with
the Doctrine and Example of Jesus Christ*: both works are discussed in Ceadel, *Origins of War
Prevention*, 171–5. I. (an abbreviation for 'Iohannis') Scott was John Scott, a Calvinist whom I
have recently discovered (from J. R. Scott, *Memorials of the Family of Scott, of Scott's-Hall in
the County of Kent* (1876), 243) to have been a banker. His son, Benjamin Whinnell Scott, was
chief clerk to the Chamberlain of London; and his grandson, Benjamin Scott, a banker and
prominent Nonconformist, was Chamberlain of London himself 1858–92.

[9] N. Stargardt, *The German Idea of Militarism: Radical and Socialist Critics, 1866–1914*
(Cambridge, 1994), 19.

[10] See below, p. 158. Some writers have unhelpfully implied that it was used earlier by
employing it within quotation marks as if quoting directly from 19th-cent. sources: see Beales,
A History of Peace, 97, and R. T. Shannon, *Gladstone and the Bulgarian Agitation* (1963), 123.

The main consequence of the lack of convenient labels for these view-points was that long-winded formulations had to be used instead. Thus when during the Crimean War the Peace Society's long-serving secretary Henry Richard, himself a pacifist, wished to explain that the London daily paper he was involved in launching would be *pacificist* but not pacifist, he described it as one in which 'moral questions, and especially the principle of peace, should be steadfastly advocated. I don't mean the abstract principles of the Peace Society, but a general pacific policy, as expressed by such ideas as international arbitration, reduction of armaments, non-intervention, etc.'[11] Similarly, when his colleague on this publishing venture Richard Cobden wanted to complain that the rest of the press favoured either defencism or radical crusading, he specified that it took 'either the line of our old aristo-cratic diplomacy in favour of the "balance of power" and dynastic alliances, or the more modern and equally unsound and mischievous line on behalf of Mazzini and the "nationalities" '.[12]

The lack of a ready vocabulary did not prevent pacifists and *pacificists* from having a degree of understanding of the complexity of their respective viewpoints from the outset. Pacifists knew that they differed among them-selves as to where exactly they drew the line. Since many early pacifists objected to coercion and killing as well as war, and were therefore commit-ted to a socially subversive rejection of domestic policing and capital punish-ment as well as military service, those who did not take this extreme view made a virtue of their moderation. During the American Civil War, moreover, pacifists were to discover that some of their number did not think that non-international military conflict counted as war. And in the twentieth century, when first aerial bombardment and then nuclear warheads raised the costs of war to a level for which few if any political benefits could compensate, a new type of pacifist appeared who believed that war was wrong only under the modern technological conditions which ensured that its harmful side-effects would outweigh any good it did.

Pacifists always knew, moreover, that they could derive their position from different inspirations. To protect themselves from accusations of sedition, early British pacifists insisted that they were motivated purely by their read-ing of Christian scripture and that any worldly arguments they used were merely secondary. However, it was not until the 1840s that the possibility of non-religious pacifism was explicitly acknowledged: the American non-resister Adin Ballou noted that 'philosophical' and 'sentimental' inspirations

---

[11] Cited in C. S. Miall, *Henry Richard, MP* (1889), 115.
[12] Cobden to Bright, 11 Feb. 1855, in J. Morley, *The Life of Richard Cobden* (2 vols., 1881), ii. 171.

for pacifism were also possible (though he rejected both in favour of the Christian inspiration);[13] and the British Chartist Thomas Cooper was an avowed agnostic when he espoused pacifism in 1846.[14]

Furthermore, pacifists always took different views as to how their absolutism related to worldly politics. Particularly in Britain, most early pacifists were pessimistic in orientation, expecting the conversion of their own nation to occur only in a very remote future, and even then not seeing pacifism as a practical policy until other nations had embraced it too. Pessimists assumed that all that pacifists could do for the foreseeable future was bear witness to their faith. (Admittedly, those with a strong evangelical faith sometimes consoled themselves with the thought that divine intervention might compensate for the fact that the politics of this world were a vale of tears.) A few other early pacifists, especially in the United States, adopted an optimistic orientation, seeing the conversion of their nation as a medium-term possibility which would offer an effective means of deterring or disarming aggression. For example, in setting up his New England Non-Resistance Society in 1838, William Lloyd Garrison, the American pacifist and anti-slavery campaigner with a dedicated though small following in Britain, presented the 'non-resistance principle' as not only a Christian duty but also 'a measure of sound policy, of safety to property, life and liberty, of public quietude and private enjoyment'.[15] From the 1840s, however, the pacifist mainstream has most commonly taken a middle position, here called the collaborative orientation. Feeling unable to make claims for the efficacy of their own absolutism but wishing none the less to be political relevant, they have collaborated with *pacificist* campaigns as a step in the right direction.

When it emerged in embryonic form during the eighteenth century, *pacificism* was inspired by a rationalist or rational-Christian sense of a harmony underlying the natural order; but, as modern political ideologies developed, they offered their own diagnoses of the problem of war so that there came to be as many varieties of *pacificism* as there were progressive ideologies in domestic politics. In Britain as in the United States, many *pacificists* were avowed radicals, blaming war on élites and vested interests, and seeing popular control as the solution. (Indeed the argument that 'republican' regimes are necessary for peace, though normally attributed by modern international relations scholars to an essay published in 1795 by the German philosopher Immanuel Kant, was already a near-commonplace of Anglo-American radicalism.) Others were

---

[13] A. Ballou, *Christian Non-Resistance in All its Important Bearings* (London edn., 1848), 1.

[14] Ceadel, *Origins of War Prevention*, 334–5.

[15] 'Declaration of Sentiments adopted by the Peace Convention held in Boston, September 18, 19, and 20, 1838', in *Selections from the Writings and Speeches of William Lloyd Garrison* (Boston, Mass., 1852), 75.

liberals, seeing irrationalism in the form of a preoccupation with national or state prestige as the problem, and free trade, improved international law, or even an international organization as the remedy. Later, some were socialists, blaming war on capitalism, and predicting its abolition as a result of economic and social change. And, after the period covered by this book, the ranks of the *pacificists* were afforced by feminists and ecologists, indicting patriarchy and industrialism respectively, and predicting that their overthrow would produce peace. From a fairly early stage, therefore, *pacificists* were aware of an ideological diversity which at times inhibited their capacity to work together.

However, being reformers rather than absolutists, *pacificists* were not divided, as pacifists were, over the merits of political action. Their equivalent disagreement was over where they located the middle way between pacifism and defencism, both of which they disliked. Their debate focused on two questions: what counted as a defensive use of force and an adequate level of preparedness? and what criteria other than defensiveness did a just use of force have to satisfy?

Defencists took an expansive view of defensiveness, including for example the rendering military assistance to an ally, and partly for this reason favoured high levels of military provision. But, although some *pacificists* were sympathetic, most interpreted defensiveness more narrowly as resistance to an attack on home territory only, and therefore believed that reductions of military expenditure were usually possible. Defencists also assumed that defensiveness was not only a necessary but a sufficient justification for the use of force.

However, *pacificists* did not. For example, one of the architects of the League of Nations, Lord Robert Cecil, was to note that 'self-defence by itself may not be regarded by all as a justification for war'. And although he argued that in practice a nation defending itself against foreign aggression 'may almost always be regarded as the champion of law',[16] socialist *pacificists* would have objected that this justification was unlikely to apply to the defence of an ill-gotten colony, since this encouraged imperialism and thereby inhibited progress towards ultimate peace. These two questions— how far defensiveness could be stretched, and whether it was a sufficient condition for a just war—were often combined: when defencists called for military support to Turkey, as they did for much of the nineteenth century, *pacificists* had to decide both whether this would constitute a meaningfully defensive action for Britain and whether in the long run the propping up of the despotic Ottoman regime would do more political harm than good.

---

[16] Lord R. Cecil, *Peace and Pacifism* (Oxford, 1938), 20.

Many participants in Britain's peace-or-war debate understood that it was conditioned by the country's distinctive geo-strategic situation and political culture. For example, William Roscoe, a prominent opponent of the French war of 1793–1815, welcomed the aloofness induced by the English Channel, asking rhetorically in 1802: 'Are we not happily separated from the rest of Europe by the ocean that surrounds us, and which places us rather as spectators than as actors in the concerns of the Continent?'[17] The degree of protection from invasion afforded by insularity undermined militarism, weakened defencism somewhat, and encouraged the doctrine of non-intervention. It therefore disposed Britons towards the more generous of the two views of the peace movement identified by a detached observer in 1862: 'By the majority of mankind the advocates of peace are looked upon either as visionaries or, worse still, as traitors, who would sell the liberties of their country for the sake of preserving a theory intact.'[18] Furthermore, as the *Herald of Peace* warned on the eve of the Crimean War, when calls for a crusade against Russia were at their height: 'the accident of our insular position' had meant that 'so little is seen of the horrible realities of war . . . that we are in danger of forgetting its essentially brutal and degrading nature'.[19] In other words, insularity encouraged at least a rhetoric of crusading.

Yet, for two reasons, Britain was only moderately secure. First, the English Channel was narrow; and Britain depended for its livelihood on international trade—considerations which prompted the claim during the Napoleonic War that it was 'an abuse of language to talk of her being separated from the continent by the straits of Dover'.[20] Even with a strong navy, there was a risk of invasion or blockade if a hostile power controlled the Low Countries. In consequence, every British government felt obliged to concern itself with the distribution of power within Europe as a whole; and the public's near-isolationist complacency about the continent was periodically punctuated by defence panics which the peace movement came to regard as a national peculiarity. Secondly, Britain had acquired colonies coveted by other European countries, which gave it a further reason for paying attention to far-flung regions. An example was the 'Eastern Question', in which Britain concerned itself for much of the nineteenth century with Russian encroachment onto the territory of Ottoman Turkey because it believed that this might ultimately threaten its control of India.

[17] W. Roscoe, *Occasional Tracts Relative to the War between Great Britain and France* (1810), 116.
[18] W. Nicolson, *The Theory of a Universal Peace Critically Investigated* (1862), 62–3.
[19] *HP* (Dec. 1853), 300.
[20] *Edinburgh Review* (Jan. 1803), 355.

The fact that Britain was thus faced with the prospect of wars of contrasting kinds, continental and imperial, complicated its peace-or-war debate. Some *pacificists*, including the Baptist minister Dr John Clifford and the Positivist intellectual Frederic Harrison, were to support several European interventions but oppose most imperial ones. Because crises in Europe and the empire tended to alternate, the peace movement apparently lost and gained certain activists in a fashion bewildering both to it and to the public. Moreover, the fact that British interests faced imperial as well as continental threats helped to ensure that defencism, even if less hegemonic ideologically than in some European countries, always remained the most influential viewpoint in the peace-or-war debate. It also produced some support for militarism, particularly after imperial rivalry intensified at the end of the nineteenth century: 'English militarism is acquired rather than instinctive, and is the product of imperialism', as a radical observer was to acknowledge.[21] The prospect of being drawn into a major European conflict also obliged those who feared war to work to prevent it, rather than simply to escape it through isolationism, at least in respect of the continent. Thus, although at the start of his career as a commentator on international affairs in the mid-1830s (when he may have been briefly a pacifist) the Manchester calico manufacturer Richard Cobden believed in the possibility of 'no foreign politics'—in other words, total isolationism—for Britain, by the end of the following decade he had accepted the need for such diplomatic initiatives as arbitration and commercial treaties and also for 'moral intervention' in certain European crises. In addition, proximity to the European theatre of war stopped British crusaders completely overlooking the fact that military force was a blunt instrument for the promotion of idealistic objectives.

The main characteristics of English political culture, including the special place of peace activists within it, had been laid down in the seventeenth century. The monarchy and Anglican Church (the Church of England) were deposed as a result of the Civil War of the 1640s, restored in 1660, and circumscribed by the 'Glorious Revolution' of 1688–9, after which they had to face the countervailing influence of parliament and the 'dissenting' (later called 'Nonconformist') Protestant denominations. Even this upheaval helped to launch what turned out to be the world's most influential pacifist sect, the Quakers, who had emerged during the interregnum. Despite having been a 60,000-strong, radical-puritan movement with a strong streak of militancy, they responded to the challenge of the Restoration by committing themselves to non-resistance in January 1661. And though they dwindled into a small, disciplined, and increasingly prosperous sect, which called itself the Society

---

[21] C. E. Playne, *The Pre-War Mind in Britain: An Historical Review* (1928), 126.

of Friends, the Quakers stuck to this absolutist commitment, and refused not only to undertake militia service but also—unlike the Mennonites—to hire substitutes or pay fines either. Though still mocked because of their peculiarities of dress and speech, they won increasing respect within mainstream society; and towards the end of the eighteenth century some of their leading figures began to establish links with some of the Anglicans and dissenters who, like them, had been influenced by evangelicalism.

England's pioneering industrial revolution gave the country the confidence to reject mercantilism and interpret international commerce as a positive-sum game. Its Protestant dissenters injected a moralistic tone into public life which was later dubbed the 'Nonconformist conscience'. Although this was sometimes to favour crusading, it also made an important contribution to pacifism and *pacificism*: the Congregationalists were acknowledged as second only to the Quakers in the role they played within the peace movement;[22] and the Unitarians ran them close when allowance was made for their smaller numbers.[23] Only the Methodists, who had originated as a ginger group within the established church, offered little help before the very end of the nineteenth century. (Observers also noted that there were 'very few Jews among the members of the British peace societies',[24] and that Roman Catholics were scarce too.) The Nonconformist conscience also helped the socialist movement which developed in the later stages of industrialization: for the most part, its members either were avowedly Christian socialists or had constructed their socialism as a surrogate for their religious tradition, in either case retaining Nonconformity's progressive approach to politics, both domestic and international.[25] Though waning with secularization, dissent remained important to peace activism well beyond the period covered by this book. For example, the social historian Alan Howkins, who in his youth in Bicester was an active member of the Campaign for Nuclear Disarmament (founded in 1958), has described how the 'nonconformist conscience', rather than 'any theory of proletarian internationalism', still 'fed my town's CND group in the late 1950s and early 1960s'.[26]

On the other hand, the survival in England of crown, aristocracy, and established church, and the country's comparatively painless adaptation from élite to mass politics, ensured a conservative tradition that was confident enough

---

[22] See e.g. *Arbitrator* (Oct. 1890), 109; (May 1907), 80.

[23] See e.g. *Arbitrator* (June 1901), 93.

[24] *Concord* (May 1907), 58.

[25] e.g. the guild socialist S. G. Hobson noted that the socialist ILP filled a moral vacuum left by the decline of Nonconformity, particularly in Yorkshire: see his *Pilgrim to the Left: Memoirs of a Modern Revolutionist* (1938), 38–40.

[26] R. Samuel (ed.), *Patriotism: The Making and Unmaking of British National Identity* (3 vols., 1989), ii. 82.

to be constitutionalist in its approach to domestic politics and moderately defencist in its approach to international relations. The country was spared the reactionary or populist variety of right-wing politics which nurtured militarism. Instead, the realism of the mature conservative approach to international relations injected a dose of political scepticism into public discussion, and thereby served to inhibit the crusading tendencies of Protestant moralism.

Britain's moderately secure geo-strategic situation and moderately liberal political culture thus encouraged an outlook of engaged insularity and prudent moralism which particularly encouraged the belief that war could be abolished. When combined with the country's influence as a great power, its peace activists often implied that Britain had a special mission to preach peace to the rest of the world. In 1862, for example, the Revd Samuel Harris Booth of Birkenhead could raise cheers from his fellow members of the Peace Society by declaring:

He would have England remember the very high position she occupies among the nations of the earth. He believed that England had it in her single power to put an end to war. Had she but the moral courage to go forth and say to the world, 'I will not fight—certainly not, unless I am attacked,' she would rise to a moral dignity unexampled amongst the nations of the earth. Following in England's wake, all nations would say, 'Let there be an end to war,' and the duelling of nations would be over.[27]

Similarly, Hodgson Pratt of the International Arbitration and Peace Association claimed in 1884 that there was 'a great opportunity for England, with its munificence in great causes, with its natural aptitude for organisation, and with its insular position of comparative security, to take the first place in the inculcation of Arbitration and Peace'.[28] When the World Disarmament Conference was being planned in 1931, the National Peace Council asserted that 'no country could be more fitted to take the lead than ourselves, standing aside, as we do, from that Europe of which we are yet a part'; and four years later the League of Nations Union detected among the delegates to its general council a wish that 'the poor benighted foreigner would model his conduct upon those nice simple ideals which we, without much difficulty, profess'.[29]

The British peace movement was aware that most of Europe suffered from an insufficiency of both security and liberalism. The prevailing geo-strategic situation on the continent gave rise to pessimistic *Realpolitik* or even overt militarism, and caused peace activists, where these existed, to be viewed as

---

[27] *HP* (June 1862), 72.
[28] *IAPA Monthly Journal* (15 Jan. 1885), 63 (reporting a speech on 15 Dec. 1884).
[29] *Peace Review* (July/Aug. 1931), 1 (alluding to the views of Philip Noel Baker). *Headway* (Aug. 1935), 190.

traitors rather than visionaries. And the political culture, often influenced by Roman Catholicism or Lutheranism, further discouraged the formation of peace associations.

The United States, however, was too secure and too liberal for the good of the peace movement: its geo-strategic security was so great as to allow it to ignore the balance of power; and its model liberal constitution and puritan tradition, unchecked by a feudal élite, also contributed to a self-righteous approach to the international system which oscillated between the desire to take charge of it and the desire to wash its hands of it. American peace sentiment thus leaked away into crusading in moments of confidence and into isolationism in moments of disappointment.

THE EMERGENCE OF THE BRITISH PEACE MOVEMENT

Britain's peace movement has therefore been the oldest (except in one technical regard, shortly to be noted), the strongest, and the most durable in the world. Two years after the formation in 1787 by Quakers and other evangelicals of the Society for Effecting the Abolition of the Slave Trade, which must have served as a model, Bentham proposed a 'Pacific or Philharmonic Society'.[30] After England was drawn during February 1793 into a war with France, a spasmodic and disjointed peace campaign began, with the first petitions opposing the conflict being mounted in 1795.[31] Although the following year the first expositions of non-sectarian pacifism were published, this first peace campaign was primarily *pacificist*. It received some help from the Whig followers of Charles James Fox, who argued the non-interventionist case in parliament, and rather more from provincial businessmen, many of them Unitarians. Later in these French wars, in response to Britain's abolition in 1807 of the slave trade, the creation of an association to achieve a similar breakthrough in respect of the peace question began publicly to be discussed by both Unitarians and Quakers, though nothing was attempted while the fighting continued.

The idea crossed the Atlantic; and, indeed, because the Anglo-American War of 1812–14 ended before the Napoleonic War did, and because there was less political tension there than in post-war Britain, it bore fruit in the United States first. The one exception to Britain's claim to have the world's oldest peace movement is that the first three peace associations were American,

[30] A discovery by S. Conway: see 'Bentham on Peace and War', *Utilitas*, 1 (1989), 93.

[31] See J. E. Cookson, *The Friends of Peace: Anti-War Liberalism in England 1792–1815* (Cambridge, 1982); and E. V. Macleod, *A War of Ideas: British Attitudes to the Wars Against Revolutionary France 1792–1802* (Aldershot, 1998), chs. 3 and 4.

being founded in cosmopolitan New York City in August 1815, in the Shaker sect's stronghold of Warren County, Ohio, on 2 December 1815, and in the strongly Unitarian city of Boston, Massachusetts, on 24 December 1815.[32]

Britain's first peace association was proclaimed on 20 May 1816, when the Society for Abolishing War was launched at a meeting in the London Coffee-house by an impulsive radical and Unitarian publisher, Sir Richard Phillips, though it failed to establish itself.[33] However, on 14 June 1816 the Society for the Promotion of Permanent and Universal Peace—from the outset normally shortened to the Peace Society—was founded at a private gathering in London by a Quaker-led group of evangelicals. They had been discussing such a venture for exactly two years, their initial meeting on 7 June 1814 being probably the first serious discussion about forming a peace association anywhere in the world; but they had been delayed first by the continuation of the war and then by the upsurge of political radicalism that followed it. Their patience and prudence paid off: their society proved to be the world's first enduring peace association as well as the first with a national reach and reputation.

The Peace Society was established on a distinctive ideological basis. Its precursors had taken three different lines: the New York Peace Society, before it modified its constitution in 1818, had been exclusively pacifist; London's short-lived Society for Abolishing War had been exclusively *pacificist*; and the Massachusetts Peace Society in Boston had opened itself equally to pacifists and *pacificists* on a diversity-of-opinions basis. After much discussion, the Peace Society opted to be pacifist in respect of its top tier but to allow *pacificists* in a subordinate position. In other words, it committed itself to Christian pacifism, and formally restricted membership of its London committee (and, until a rule change in 1818, membership of the committees of its local 'auxiliary societies' as well) to those who fully endorsed that commitment; but it allowed *pacificists* to join as rank-and-file members (and after 1818 as committee members of auxiliary societies too) in the hope that they would in time undergo full conversion to the society's 'high ground' or 'grand principle'. In the long term this concession was ineffective, since by the 1850s, if not sooner, the society was so clearly identified with pacifism as to be unattractive to most *pacificists*. However, in the short term this concession may have enabled the Peace Society to attract enough non-pacifist members to help it through its difficult early years: for example, it enabled Jeremy Bentham, a *pacificist*,

---

[32] The pioneering study was M. Curti, *The American Peace Crusade 1815–60* (Durham, NC, 1929).

[33] This society was first noticed by W. H. van der Linden: see *The International Peace Movement 1815–1874* (Amsterdam, 1987), 2.

to become an ordinary member and his disciple John Bowring to remain one after recanting his pacifism and resigning as officer and committee member in 1823.

Indeed, in its early years the Peace Society faced considerable pressure, from some pacifists as well as *pacificists*, to open its doors still wider by switching to a diversity-of-opinions basis. But it feared that to do so would require the society to pronounce on the political merits of each conflict as it arose, which would be more divisive and contentious than if its hands were known to be tied in advance by religious scruple. Such a further dilution of its pacifism would also alienate the Quakers who from the start were to constitute a majority of its members—to such an extent that from 1823 the Peace Society's annual meeting was timed to coincide with the London Yearly Meeting of the Society of Friends—and who also provided virtually all its major donors. Indeed, the Peace Society was often accused of being a Quaker-run society, and presumably to rebut such a charge made sure that non-Quakers were never outnumbered on its London committee. It therefore held its ground, pointing out that those who disagreed with its top-tier pacifism were free to set up more permissive associations. This proved a shrewd decision, since despite their vast numerical superiority over pacifists, *pacificists* normally showed less commitment as activists than did pacifists, especially religious ones.

The Peace Society's major achievement in its first decade and a half was to establish itself in a difficult political climate as an organization with about 1,500 subscribers and, more important, a small but reliable core of donors. It did so by being cautious and respectable, emphasizing that it was a religious not a political body, making no claims for the practical efficacy of its ideas (except for the occasional suggestion that a truly Christian and therefore non-resisting nation could expect the protection of divine providence), and restricting its activities to the publication of the *Herald of Peace* and a carefully vetted series of tracts.

However, as the political environment liberalized after the Great Reform Act of 1832, and as the government became drawn into unpopular imperial wars (most notably in China and Afghanistan) in the late 1830s and early 1840s, the society asserted itself more, sending petitions and memorials to parliament and government, hiring travelling lecturers, holding public meetings, collecting 'peace pledges' (a tactic borrowed from the teetotal movement), and even organizing a General Peace Convention in London on 22–4 June 1843.

Another reason why the Peace Society became more active was to forestall criticism from two more outspoken pacifist groups which had grown up outside its ranks. The first, which Alex Tyrrell has labelled 'the moral radical party',[34] was a network of prosperous Quaker and dissenting businessmen from the provinces led by the remarkable Joseph Sturge, a Quaker corn merchant in Birmingham, who were active in a wide range of social-improvement campaigns, notably teetotalism and anti-slavery, and were impatient with the caution of the London-based philanthropical establishment of which they saw the Peace Society as a part. The second group, much smaller and more short-lived, comprised the followers of William Lloyd Garrison, whose hatred of the American political system for its tolerance of slavery had led him to adopt near-anarchist political views. Both Sturgeites and Garrisonians set up local pacifist bodies in Britain during the early 1840s, and at one stage seemed poised to form a joint rival to the Peace Society, to be called the British Peace Association, though this never materialized.

In addition, the Peace Society had to contend with two political movements, Chartism and the Anti-Corn-Law League, which developed in the late 1830s in response to high food prices and in protest against the Whigs' failure to follow the Great Reform Act with other progressive measures. The Chartists were radical working-class campaigners for adult male suffrage and other democratic initiatives, some of whom advocated the use of physical force in support of these objects. The Peace Society responded by urging non-violence; and there is some evidence, overlooked by historians of Chartism, that it thereby helped to curtail the Newport insurrection of 1839.[35] In doing so the society incurred the displeasure of the physical-force Chartists. However, thanks in particular to Joseph Sturge's attempts to bring working- and middle-class radicals together, it established good relations with some of the Chartists who committed themselves to the use of moral force only, notably Henry Vincent and Arthur O'Neill, both of whom became peace lecturers, though Thomas Cooper's agnosticism placed him beyond the pale.

The Anti-Corn-Law League was formed by liberal industrialists opposed to agricultural protection, such as the Manchester starch-and-gum manufacturer George Wilson. Though not challenging the Peace Society's principles, as the physical-force Chartists did, it sought to entice the society into its own campaign for free trade. Although failing to achieve this, it managed to divert Cobden away from primary peace activism for a decade (1838–48). Thus, although in 1842 Cobden attended the 'Conference of the Friends of Peace' called by the Peace Society to plan the General Peace Convention, he did so in an effort to persuade it to make free trade its priority; and, having failed to so, he absented himself from the convention itself, despite having been listed as a delegate.

[34] A. Tyrrell, *Joseph Sturge and the Moral Radical Party in Early Victorian Britain* (1987).
[35] See Ceadel, *Origins of War Prevention*, 327–8.

In addition to pursuing their chosen single issues, both the Chartists and the Anti-Corn-Law League acted at times as secondary peace associations: the former claimed that wars 'would seldom or scarcely ever occur' if aristocratic rule 'were put down';[36] and the latter deemed it 'an inevitable rule that free and equitable trade always was a bond of peace'.[37] Both these diagnoses were *pacificist*—radical and liberal respectively—and reflected a growing interest in this strand of peace thinking at the expense of pacifism. The Peace Society responded to the increase in support for *pacificism* by adopting a collaborative orientation towards it: indeed, it came to place more emphasis on policies such as arbitration than on its own doctrine of non-resistance. It held the General Peace Convention of 1843 on a diversity-of-opinions basis— a precedent followed by all subsequent national or international peace meetings—in order to accommodate British and American *pacificists* as well the handful of delegates from continental Europe where pacifism was almost unknown. The convention attracted unprecedented publicity, and stimulated the Peace Society to hold public meetings. This ideological flexibility and increased activity helped to delay the formation of a distinctively *pacificist* rival. Yet the fact that peace activism was understood to be broader based than previously, encompassing *pacificists* as well as pacifists, was reflected in the entry of 'peace movement' into the language during the first half of the 1840s.

During the second half of that decade, moreover, the peace movement began to attract significantly increased attention. Three events of 1846 gave it particular impetus. First, the government's proposal to revive the militia, which had not been called up since 1831, offended sections of a working class partially radicalized by Chartism. Second, the repeal of the Corn Laws produced a new confidence among reformers that governments were bound to yield to concerted public pressure. Third, the charismatic but ingenuous 'learned blacksmith', Elihu Burritt, arrived from New England and launched a League of Universal Brotherhood, which for a time institutionalized Joseph Sturge's moral radical party and extended its appeal into the artisan class. Reflecting the wide range of Sturgeite philanthropic concerns, the League campaigned for racial and social justice as well as pacifism; and though Burritt was a devout Congregationalist, its tone was less religious than that of the Peace Society, so Thomas Cooper was able to join it. It also promoted the more radical of the two versions of arbitration which competed for support on both sides of the Atlantic, the 'Congress of Nations' (a gathering at which international law would be codified and a 'Court of Nations' to apply it would

---

[36] *Northern Star* (10 Nov. 1838), cited in H. Weisser, *British Working-Class Movements and Europe 1815–48* (Manchester, 1975), 95.

[37] W. Cooke Taylor, cited in R. F. Spall, 'Free Trade, Foreign Relations, and the Anti-Corn-Law League', *International History Review*, 10 (1988), 405–32 at 409.

be established). The League of Universal Brotherhood established Burritt as the peace movement's best-known figure, attracting audiences of 4,000 to hear him speak. By creating a nation-wide representative structure, holding regular regional meetings, and collecting 10,000 signatures to its pacifist pledge, it for a couple of years outperformed the Peace Society. The latter was still controlled by its London committee, had only a patchy network of local auxiliaries, and was never able to raise its membership (which in principle required an annual subscription of at least half a guinea) much above the 1,500 it had achieved early in its existence.[38]

After November 1847, moreover, a panic over 'the national defences' provided a further stimulus to peace activism. In December a Peace of Nations Society was launched, a liberal-*pacificist* association which aspired to have an international membership.[39] Progressive intellectuals seemed particularly keen at this time to distance themselves from pacifism: for example, in a private letter written on 30 December 1847 the liberal philosopher John Stuart Mill, a *pacificist* like his father James Mill, went out of his way to register disagreement with the 'principles professed by the Peace Society . . . as, though I think it an effect of the progress of improvement to put an end to war, I regard war as an infinitely less evil than systematic submission to injustice'.[40] In January 1848, moreover, Sturge and Burritt set up a National Defences Committee, a shadowy front organization formed on a diversity-of-opinions basis in an attempt to mobilize *pacificists*—particularly Chartists—unwilling to associate themselves with pacifist associations. The Peace Society felt unable to cooperate with either new body, and was relieved when each faded away: the Peace of Nations Society never properly established itself, perhaps because of poor organization and lack of money, though it remained in nominal existence for at least six years; and the National Defences Committee became redundant when Louis-Philippe, the French king who had been thought to be poised to invade, became an early victim of the 1848 revolutions and arrived in England as refugee rather than conqueror. Soon afterwards the British government abandoned its renewed attempt to revive the militia—a rare retreat in the face of public hostility.

The spring of 1848 marked the start of a three-year golden age for the nineteenth-century peace movement, during which the Peace Society also

---

[38] Anonymous, block, and repeated subscriptions make computation of Peace Society membership difficult even in years when annual reports were published. My estimate for 1832 is 1,537 and for 1882, 1,625; and F. K. Prochaska gives 1,428 for 1895 in his very useful *Women and Philanthropy in Nineteenth-Century England* (1980), 231–5.

[39] Another discovery by W. H. van der Linden: see his *International Peace Movement*, 203–4.

[40] Cited in *The Letters of John Stuart Mill*, ed. H. S. R. Elliot, 2 vols, (1910), i. 133.

recovered its position as dominant association. This period began inauspiciously: in Britain Chartism prepared for what proved to be its final intimidatory mass demonstration on 11 April 1848; and in Europe revolutionary outbreaks frustrated Burritt's attempt to convene an international peace conference in Paris and precipitated violent repression in many countries. However, the Chartists' London protest passed off peacefully, and with hindsight marked the beginning of an era of political tranquillity in Britain. Moreover, the liberal regime in Belgium allowed Burritt to hold his 'congress'—a term preferred by continental opinion to 'conference'—in Brussels on 20–2 September 1848. It passed motions in favour of arbitration and the reduction of armaments, thereby establishing those policies on the peace movement's agenda, and earning an unprecedented quantity and quality of publicity.

Paradoxically, Burritt's triumphant Brussels congress marked the moment from which the end of his brief pre-eminence within the British peace movement can be traced. His preoccupation with international congresses caused him to neglect his own League of Universal Brotherhood. And he acquired two powerful rivals in Cobden and Henry Richard. Cobden could at this time have traded on his Corn-Law triumph to 'set up for a genteel politician', as he later ruefully observed,[41] yet instead he returned to primary peace activism during 1848. Richard, a Welsh-born Congregationalist minister of considerable intellectual ability, took over as secretary of the Peace Society in January 1848, and was to hold the position for the next thirty-seven years. He at once responded to the League of Universal Brotherhood's more elaborate organizational structure by designating the 'non-resident' section of the Peace Society's London committee as a 'general committee', the metropolitan section becoming the 'executive committee'. Intended to make the society look less centralized, this change was largely cosmetic: the general committee met only very occasionally; and appointments to its membership became little more than honorific recognitions of the society's provincial benefactors, almost all of them Quakers. Richard also helped Burritt organize the Brussels Peace Congress, and became joint secretary with him of the Peace Congress Committee which was established on 31 October 1848 to follow up its work and plan further such events.

The Peace Congress Committee proved to be a useful mechanism by which the pacifists of the Peace Society and League of Universal Brotherhood could provide out-of-doors support for Cobden's parliamentary efforts on behalf of arbitration and the reduction of armaments, without either compromising their own principles or embarrassing Cobden by direct

---

[41] Cobden to Richard, 2 Feb. 1862: Add. MS 43,659 fos. 146–7.

association with utopians. That Cobden felt increasingly uneasy about being associated directly with the Peace Society was evidence that its strategy of confining pacifism to its top tier and admitting *pacificists* as ordinary members had outlived its usefulness. As a free trader who did not want reductions in tariffs to be offset by increases in income taxes, Cobden had come to favour a reduction in government spending, which in turn required a less expensive defence policy and a more pacific foreign policy. He therefore came to support both arbitration, albeit in the moderate form of bilateral arbitration treaties rather than the Congress of Nations favoured by Burritt, and the reduction of armaments by international agreement. Although Cobden had not gone to the Brussels congress, he sent a message of support which Joseph Sturge read to the delegates. However, though committing himself to peace activism again, Cobden had been dissuaded by his arduous efforts for the Anti-Corn-Law League from again becoming responsible for a pressure group. He therefore made no attempt to launch a *pacificist* association, though logically one was required to balance the Peace Society and the League of Universal Brotherhood within the framework of the Peace Congress Committee.

Thus instead of being a genuine association founded on a diversity-of-opinions basis at both leadership and grass-roots levels, the Peace Congress Committee was a front for a sometimes uneasy alliance between a *pacificist* leader and a pacifist following. None the less it worked well enough and—slightly renamed, as we shall see—was to remain in existence for a decade. It offered Cobden some protection against being accused of being a pacifist; and it enabled Cobden and Richard to forge an understanding which became so close that it is now hard to determine when Cobden's speeches and pamphlets influenced Richard's contributions to the *Herald of Peace* and when the reverse occurred. Cobden's respect for Richard helped the latter supersede Burritt as the peace movement's principal organizer.

The formation of the Peace Congress Committee thus undermined not only Burritt's personal standing but also the separate identity of his League of Universal Brotherhood (whereas that of the Peace Society was secure in virtue of its much longer history, as well as of Richard's position as Cobden's confidant). Admittedly, Burritt's league still issued a monthly paper, the *Bond of Brotherhood*. Moreover, in 1849–51 his long-standing tactic of sending peace messages, which he called 'olive leaves', to the press for insertion as free copy, was taken up by a network of women's groups known as Olive Leaf Circles, which held private meetings to fund, often through sewing and embroidery, the dispatch of such messages to European newspapers. Women had constituted at least a tenth of the membership of the Peace Society from the start, and had contributed to its literature; but they had been prevented by the conventions of polite society, which only the Garrisonians had been willing to challenge, from either speaking at meetings or sitting on committees when men were present. The Peace Society had also established a few female local auxiliaries in the 1820s and 1830s, though these had lapsed. It had also considered a women-only national auxiliary in 1830, but had not proceeded after the two ladies it approached declined to cooperate. By providing a constructive purpose for all-female gatherings which were also sociable and respectable, the Olive Leaf Circles persuaded a significant number of women to make an autonomous contribution to the peace movement (albeit under the general aegis of the League of Universal Brotherhood) for the first time. The *Bond of Brotherhood* was thus justified in boasting: 'Up to 1849, they had not taken part, in separate and organized societies, in this great work of philanthropy. The Olive Leaf Mission provided a special and genial field for their quiet though invaluable sympathies and activities.'[42] Despite this new appeal to women, the League of Universal Brotherhood had all but lost its male following; and its financial position was also precarious.

The Peace Society, by contrast, was able in 1850 to build two rooms onto the premises which it had leased since 1841 from the London Missionary Society at 19 New Broad Street, and also to make regular increases in the print-run of the *Herald of Peace*,[43] mainly for the purpose of sending free copies to Christian ministers. It was thus benefiting from the prosperity of its leading Quaker donors; and it had recovered its leading position within the peace movement because of its enthusiastic support, mediated through the Peace Congress Committee, for Cobden. It raised petitions in support of his arbitration motion, which received the respectable total of 79 votes (against 176) in the House of Commons on 12 June 1849. It also worked with Burritt to organize a second continental peace congress in Paris on 22–4 August 1849, at which Cobden was the principal speaker. This fared even better than the first, despite coinciding with the final crushing by the Russians, who had come to the Habsburgs' aid, of Hungary's bid for national independence. Cobden found the congress 'an agreeable affair', particularly enjoying the sight of 'Quakers and Quakeresses' thronging the French Foreign Office for an official reception given to congress delegates

[42] *BB* (July 1855), 188. Olive Leaf Circles are mentioned in J. Liddington, *The Long Road to Greenham: Feminism and Anti-Militarism in Britain since 1820* (1989), 15, though their link to the League of Universal Brotherhood is not.

[43] Newspaper Stamp Duty returns from the appendix (pp. 52–3) to the *Report for the Select Committee on Newspaper Stamps* (Parliamentary Papers n.d.), are: 1844, 1,000 (which covers a part-year only, since it registered for the first time late in that year); 1845, 5,000; 1846, 6,750; 1848, 8,000; 1848, 9,450; 1850, 12,350. Each full-year figure is the cumulative total of twelve monthly issues. (Figures for the period from 1851 until the abolition of compulsory stamp duty in 1855 appear below at Ch. 5 n. 48.)

by the Foreign Minister, Alexis de Tocqueville, into whose ear Cobden whispered the comment: 'you have never had so large an amount of moral worth under your roof before'.[44]

Cobden also spoke at the three big meetings in Britain with which the Peace Congress Committee followed up the Paris congress, and attempted to have two further peace resolutions, on arbitration and the reduction of armaments respectively, debated in the House of Commons during 1850. Though failing to win a slot for either in the parliamentary ballot, he argued for the reduction of armaments in the supply debate on 8 March and moved an amendment calling for a gradual lowering of public expenditure to 1835 levels (which, however, received only 59 votes);[45] and on 12 June 1850 he attended the Peace Congress Committee for the first time. Sixteen days later he mounted a memorable attack on Foreign Secretary Palmerston during an ultimately unsuccessful attempt to censure him for employing a passing British fleet to blockade the Greek government into redressing some minor grievances by two British residents of Athens, one of whom, Don Pacifico, had only a tenuous claim to be regarded as a British subject. Since the Peace Society had now in effect taken over the work of the Peace Congress Committee, this debate involved it in a major party-political controversy for the first time, and made it tacitly a part of an emerging Liberal movement.

Two months after the Don Pacifico debate, Cobden was the star turn at the third continental peace congress, organized by Richard and Burritt in the initially unpromising soil of Frankfurt on 22–4 August 1850. Its most memorable moment was a visit from Julius Haynau, the Austrian general who had become notorious for his brutality in suppressing the Hungarian uprising. It was also followed up by a dramatic but unsuccessful attempt by Sturge, Burritt, and their Quaker friend Frederic Wheeler to mediate in the crisis between Prussia and Denmark over Schleswig-Holstein. Cobden disapproved of this effort, but none the less spoke at post-congress rallies in Britain. He also renewed his attempt to propose a disarmament motion in the House of Commons: a debate eventually took place on 17 June 1851, though he did not press his resolution to a vote because Palmerston, ever sensitive to the way the wind was blowing, astutely professed to agree with its objectives, thereby winning over a number of Cobden's supporters.

Cobden also played a major role in planning the London Peace Congress of 22–4 July 1851, at which he gave the major speech. Benefiting from the country's new prosperity and diminished social tension, as well as from the

---

[44] Cobden to Ashworth, 3 Sept. 1849: Add. MSS 43,653 fos. 124–5.
[45] Hansard, cix HC cols. 542–616: I omitted to mention this amendment in *Origins of War Prevention*.

success of that summer's Great Exhibition, this congress saw peace hopes rise to unprecedented heights. Richard later claimed of the mood at this time:

There seemed a prospect, not indeed of a new millennium, but of a steady increase of mutual respect and good-will among nations, and of the growth of a public opinion, under the pressure of which Governments might be obliged to seek for some more rational means of settling their differences than by recourse to the sword, and some less ruinous method of preserving peace than by an insane rivalry of armaments. . . .[46]

This proved to be the pinnacle of the nineteenth-century peace movement. In the short term, it was to face a decade and a half of adversity; and even though it was to recover some of its lost ground, it was not to reach a similar position of authority until the late 1920s.

Britain's peace movement enjoyed comparatively favourable geographical and cultural conditions. Even allowing for this, its record in its first six decades was impressive because of its willingness to face adversity, both during and in the immediate aftermath of the French war. It established pacifism and *pacificism* as significant minority viewpoints within the peace-or-war debate. Moreover, at one moment at least—when the government backed down over the militia in 1847—it combined with anti-war feeling of a prudential kind to achieve a political victory. By the summer of 1851 *pacificism* seemed to be on such a sharply rising trajectory of public sympathy as to have some prospect of eventually displacing defencism.

---

[46] H. Richard, *Memoirs of Joseph Sturge* (1864), 457. For similar observations see W. Dorling, *Henry Vincent: A Biographical Sketch* (1879), 52; and C. S. Miall, *Henry Richard, MP: A Biography* (1889), 52, 82–3.

Summary of earlier books

3

Struggle,
October 1851–December 1866

The Great Exhibition and London Peace Congress were to be remembered for decades to come as the most confident moments in the history of the peace movement.[1] Within months it was thrown onto the defensive by the rapturous reception which the British public gave to the Hungarian patriot Kossuth in the autumn of 1851 and by a French-invasion scare which led to the passing of a Militia Act in 1852. These setbacks were exacerbated by the revival of the Eastern Question, which intensified demands for an anti-Russian crusade and resulted in Britain's declaration of war in March 1854. This transition from a hard-won and only briefly tasted celebrity to an acute and lengthy notoriety tested the movement's mettle to the utmost. However, the Peace Society proved equal to the experience; and Cobden remained its loyal ally, albeit a chastened one. Moreover, the movement faced further challenges even after peace was restored, of which Palmerston's triumph in the 1857 general election and the American Civil War of 1861–5 were the most worrying. But, although depressed at being pushed back to the margins of political life, it was also reassured by the steady progress which non-interventionist sentiment was making.

SETBACKS, 1851–1856

The welcome given to Kossuth between 23 October and 20 November 1851 demonstrated how many British liberals and radicals could at this time be tempted to support crusading rhetoric because of their hatred of Russia and sympathy for 'the nationalities' which it was oppressing—sentiments which the long-serving Whig politician Lord Palmerston was particularly adept at exploiting.[2] It also revealed the limitations of non-intervention as a *pacificist* nostrum.

---

[1] See e.g. *HP* (June 1886), 74; (June 1889), 237.

[2] See G. Claeys, 'Mazzini, Kossuth and British Radicalism', *Journal of British Studies*, 28 (1989), 225–61; A. Taylor, 'Palmerston and Radicalism, 1847–1865', 33 (1994), 157–79; M. Finn, *After Chartism: Class and Nation in British Radical Politics, 1848–1874* (Cambridge, 1993); M. Taylor, *Decline of British Radicalism 1847–1860* (Oxford, 1995), ch. 8.

Precisely because it was a flagrant example of the interventionism he so disliked, Cobden had led the protest against Russia's suppression of the Hungarian rebellion against Habsburg rule in 1849, and had thereby run into the problem of how a non-interventionist punishes intervention. Cobden's initial response had been to suggest cutting off foreign loans to the aggressor,[3] though he had not persisted with this suggestion beyond 1850, perhaps because it proved hard to reconcile with his long-standing belief that all commercial contact was beneficent.

Appearing on a platform with Kossuth in 1851, Cobden claimed that a diplomatic protest by Britain and the United States would have immediately stopped the Russians. He thereby ventured into the ambiguous area of moral interventionism previously occupied only by small groups such as the People's International League, which in 1847 had attempted to build a coalition in support of Italian freedom that included both Mazzinian crusaders and non-interventionists by implying that there was a middle way between military intervention and isolationism.[4] The ambiguity concerned whether a protest to the Russians would be effective because it had intrinsic moral power or because of an implicit threat of military action if it were ignored. Cobden seems to have had a genuine confidence in the inherent persuasiveness of moral force that harked back to his apparent pacifist phase. However, his friends feared that the British public would interpret moral interventionism as a tacit military threat, with the result that his non-interventionist campaign would be compromised. This disapproving line was taken by not only by pacifists like Richard and Sturge but by his associate John Bright, who, though a Quaker, was never a pacifist and had previously played little part in the peace movement.

The Peace Society issued a statement during Kossuth's visit, implying that the Hungarians should have practised non-resistance to the Russians. The fact that this statement was signed not only by Henry Richard but also by Joseph Sturge, who as yet was neither an officer of the society nor a member of its executive or general committees, was an indication that the Peace Society had won over its former critics in the moral-radical party. The Richard–Sturge statement infuriated Cobden, who feared that his recent closeness to the Peace Society would cause him to be identified with pacifism in a context in which it was uniquely unpopular. He therefore argued that as a matter of urgency the peace movement should emphasize the distinction between the Peace Congress Committee, with which as a diversity-of-opinions body he was happy to be associated, and the Peace Society, with which as an absolutist body he was not.

---

[3] *The Times* (24 July 1849).
[4] Ceadel, *Origins of War Prevention*, 379.

Before the peace movement could thus advertise its internal divisions, it was reunited by a new danger: Louis Napoleon's *coup d'état* in France during December 1851 led to an invasion scare in Britain. The government introduced a militia bill, which was resolutely opposed in parliament by Cobden and his liberal colleague Milner Gibson and in the country by an unprecedently militant Peace Society, some of whose members were threatened with prosecution for displaying anti-militia placards that were alleged to be seditious. The bill became law in 1852, though its compulsory provisions were never implemented because voluntary recruitment—again despite the peace movement's best efforts—proved successful.

The invasion scare subsided as suddenly as it had arisen because the Eastern Question flared up again. When the Tsar sent an army across the Pruth river into Turkish territory in 1853, France was converted from potential invader of Britain into important ally against Russia. Many defencists saw the Tsar's move as challenge to Britain's vital interests, though, faced with a public which did not easily understand the geo-political case for viewing so remote an intervention as a form of forward defence, they often supplemented defencist arguments with a moralistic emphasis upon Russia's illiberal and despotic behaviour.

They were tempted to do so by the fact that during the first half of the 1850s crusading achieved its highest ever level of support in Britain. One of its leading advocates was the wood-engraver and Mazzinian polemicist, W. J. Linton, whose desire to overthrow Europe's absolutist empires caused him to rail against 'the miserable doctrine of non-intervention—the refuge or pretence of Whig knaves, the shallow subterfuge of traders who care nothing if the whole world go to wreck so they may have a percentage on the breaking up', to oppose arbitration—until, that is, '*the earth shall be divided into nations*, instead of Kingdoms'—since there could 'be no arbitration between Right and Wrong', and even to support the Militia Act on the grounds: 'The State has a right to press any for the service of the country.'[5] Admittedly, even Linton thought it impolitic to admit to favouring aggressive war. In 1851, when urging the restoration of Mazzini's short-lived Roman republic which had been overthrown by French troops two years earlier, he retreated in mid-sentence from overt military interventionism to ambivalent moral interventionism:

Our arm is long enough to reach the Vatican itself. Our arm,—indeed that is not needed: but our English word, voiced in her old heroic style, shall go forth, bidding the French Usurpation recall its Cossacks from the Eternal City, and cheering the Italian Exile with one hearty world-rejoicing shout—'England will stand by you, go in and establish your Republic.'[6]

[5] *English Republic* (1851), 30–1, 111, 288; (1852), 54–5, 112.
[6] *English Republic* (1851), 72.

And in 1852, anticipating that his assertion that men 'must fight . . . for the sake of real Peace, the Peace which can only be established upon Justice, upon the overthrow of wrong' would prompt the question, 'Can you deliberately propose that we go to war?', he offered an evasive reply: 'My dear Sir! I propose nothing of the sort. I propose only that we shall be honest, and do our duty to our neighbours, whether that lead to war or not. Peradventure, the good resolution may obviate the necessity of war.'[7] But, despite these prevarications, Linton's support for crusading was unmistakable—for example in his call in 1851 for 'War: life-long war for Right, or till Victorious Right shall become manifest as Peace . . . war against Usurpation, whatsoever it may call itself; war even to the knife rather than compromise with any incarnation of Wrong', and also in his prediction in 1853 that, 'with or without a war between the European despots, a war will come: the war between the People and the Despots'.[8]

The peace movement was thus faced with adversity of a kind to which it had grown unaccustomed. It therefore suspended its series of international peace congresses in 1852, and decided instead to attempt only national gatherings with effect from the following year. As a result the Peace Congress Committee returned to normal English usage by retitling itself the Peace *Conference* Committee in 1853. On 27–8 January of that year a 'Conference of the Friends of International Arbitration and Peace' was held in Manchester: as the explicit and prominent mention of arbitration in its title indicated, its principal organizers were self-consciously hard-headed members of the 'Manchester School' not previously associated with the peace movement—such as George Wilson, who had been chairman of the Anti-Corn-Law League—who were keen to distance their liberal *pacificism* from Christian pacifism. The Peace Society obligingly kept a low profile: when it sent its travelling agent, the Baptist pastor William Stokes, to the city to help organize the conference, it was aware that, 'as his official connection with the Peace Society is so well known . . . the more he is out of sight the better'.[9] Cobden was the main speaker, and was backed by Bright who had not previously spoken at such a gathering; and the conference, which dealt mainly with the invasion panic, passed off to the satisfaction of both the Peace Society and the Mancunian *pacificists*. The latter generously funded a follow-up campaign, and, despite efforts to coordinate with the Peace Conference Committee in London, ended up by creating a separate Manchester Peace Conference Committee. In October 1853 a second national peace conference

[7] *English Republic* (1852), 15–16.
[8] *English Republic* (1851), 274; (1853), 326.
[9] J. Sturge to G. Wilson, 7 Dec. 1852: Wilson Papers. (This letter is wrongly indexed as emanating from 'T. Slater'.)

was held at Edinburgh, this time mainly the work of the Peace Society and local Quakers and devoted to the Eastern Question. Cobden and a reluctant Bright were again the major speakers.

As the prospect of British military intervention increased early in 1854, despite the best efforts of Prime Minister Aberdeen, the various peace associations issued non-interventionist literature but attempted no public meetings. Joseph Sturge's last-gasp effort, with his fellow Quakers Robert Charleton and Henry Pease, to intercede with the Tsar in St Petersburg on 10 February was carried out under the auspices of the Society of Friends. Despite having elected the three of them to its general committee as recently as May 1853, the Peace Society dissociated itself from their initiative; and Cobden was also critical, describing it as 'positively mischievous' because it distracted from British responsibility for the crisis.[10] The one comfort which the peace movement could derive from the notoriety which had descended upon it since the autumn of 1851 was that it was being treated as a significant political actor, even to the implausible extent of being blamed for Russia's aggressive behaviour in the Near East.

Kossuth's visit, the militia crisis, and the Eastern Question had thus posed problems for the peace movement even before Britain entered the war against Russia. A few of its supporters had converted to defencism: this is what seems to have happened to the veteran radical MP J. A. Roebuck, who as late as 1849 had supported Cobden's arbitration motion in the Commons, but in 1853 praised the Royal Navy's Spithead naval review as 'a great peace exhibition',[11] and was to campaign for greater military efficiency during the Crimean War. Rather more of them had embraced crusading, *The Times* noting shrewdly on 19 August 1853 how susceptible 'peace men' were 'when it is a crusade that is preached'. One who did so was Thomas Cooper, whose abandonment of pacifism has been dated to the early 1850s, and who endorsed an appeal for a fund to help Kossuth and Mazzini in 1852.[12]

However, what caused most difficulty within the peace movement was not the recantation of pacifism or *pacificism* in order to embrace defencism or crusading but a much commoner switch from a non-interventionist to an interventionist *pacificism*. Despite Cobden's continued insistence that Russia was too backward to be a threat to Britain and Turkey too barbarous to be worth saving, many *pacificists* concluded that military action to support a victim of Russian aggression was sufficiently defensive and politically enlightened to be justifiable. Because such *pacificists* were more reluctant

---

[10] Cobden to Richard, 10 Jan. 1854: PSLB.

[11] Cited disapprovingly in *HP* (Oct. 1853), 277.

[12] J. Bellamy and J. Savile (eds.), *Dictionary of Labour Biography*, ix (1993), 53. *English Republic* (1852), 26–7.

than defencists and crusaders to give advance notice of their willingness to endorse British intervention, it was not until Britain declared war against Russia on 28 March 1854 that the numbers taking this position became apparent.

The peace movement had never previously had to face up to the fact, inherent in having a substantial *pacificist* element as well as a pacifist core, that, when confronted with a British declaration of war, it might find some of its members unable to oppose that decision while none the less insisting that their views had not changed. It had assumed that, because under Cobden's influence most of its *pacificists* were non-interventionists, this divisive situation would occur only if Britain suffered direct and unprovoked aggression: in such an event, the peace movement would in principle split between *pacificists*, who would all rally to the defence effort, and pacifists, who would all oppose it. However, the peace movement's leadership believed that unprovoked aggression was almost inconceivable, and therefore gave little thought to the possibility of such a split. It was therefore shocked in 1854 to discover how many *pacificists* felt obliged to support British intervention while insisting that their peace principles remained intact. For example, 'A Lover of Peace, though *not* a member of the "Peace Society" ' wrote to the *Nonconformist* insisting that the Crimean War was 'in its origin and aims a defensive war. It is this character that stamps it in glory ... It is a war engaged in and prosecuted "for the extinction of war".'[13] Those *pacificists* who remained non-interventionists denied that Britain's action was defensive: for example, to Liverpool's financial reformer and liberal politician Lawrence Heyworth it was 'an armed intervention to arrange the quarrels of remote and barbarous disputants'.[14] They and their pacifist colleagues found it difficult to accept interventionist *pacificists* as sincere in their professions of intellectual consistency: Richard, for example, was withering in his disparagement of what he called 'Friends of Peace—with an exception'.[15]

However, non-interventionist *pacificists* and pacifists can be forgiven for their lack of generosity towards their erstwhile colleagues, because some of these embraced pro-war propaganda with indecent enthusiasm. Thomas Cooper, a former pacifist as already noted, specialized in dramatically recreating the charge of the Light Brigade in his popular lectures.[16] The Congregationalist editor, Dr John Campbell, a former speaker at Peace

---

[13] *Nonconformist* (28 Feb. 1855), 159–60.
[14] Heyworth to Revd W. Brewster, 26 May 1855, in L. Heyworth, *Glimpses at the Origin, Mission, and Destiny of Man* (1866), 52.
[15] *HP* (Aug. 1854), 60.
[16] *The Life of Thomas Cooper, Written by Himself* (1872), 297, 340–1.

Society meetings and signatory of Burritt's pledge, used his religious papers to argue that the war was advancing the cause of Christianity, and was to be denounced at the Peace Society's annual public meeting in 1855 by a Baptist pastor, Dr Jabez Burns.[17] Another Congregational periodical, *British Quarterly Review*, published an overtly militarist article, which claimed that, if war were abolished,

the existence of man, even in a barbarous state, would be jeopardized, and in a civilized state, impossible. Nations, though preserving their vigour for a time, must at length, in the present condition of humanity, become effeminate with ease and luxury, and as their populations decline, the weaker, more barbarous states, cooped up in their own territories, would be precluded from appropriating their refinement and dominion, and from acquiring the courage, magnanimity and heroism fitted to enable them to rule, instead of the vitiated minds whom they have displaced.

Astonishingly, the editor responsible for publishing this militarist article, the prominent Congregationalist divine Dr Robert Vaughan, had once been a member of the Peace Society's London committee. He had been converted to pacifism as a newly ordained minister in Worcester 1819 as a result of a confrontation with the local auxiliary peace society which the young Joseph Sturge had helped to set up in that year, prior to his move to Birmingham. The time of what the *Herald of Peace* later called Vaughan's 're-conversion or un-conversion' from pacifism is unclear;[18] but he had come to Bright's notice as 'the fighting Doctor of Divinity' by the time of Kossuth's visit, when he appeared to be a liberal crusader.[19] Another disappointing straw in the wind was Tennyson's poetry: whereas in 1832 'Locksley Hall' had included hopeful and references to the 'Parliament of Man and the Federation of the World' which would follow the abolition of war, in 1855 'Maud' made contemptuous allusions to the materialistic corruption produced by peace.

It was a small compensation for these defections that the peace movement acquired an improbable fellow-traveller, the influential and obsessive radical crusader David Urquhart, long known for his love of Turkey and hatred of Russia. Whereas most crusaders welcomed the Crimean War as 'a war of principle—a war of Parliamentary Government against absolutism, of liberty against slavery, of civilization against barbarism', in the words of a Chartist publication,[20] Urquhart condemned it as a sham crusade, because

---

[17] *Empire* (26 May 1855), 410–11. This incident was omitted from the official account: see *HP* (June 1855), 215–18.

[18] *HP* (Aug. 1859), 234.

[19] Bright to Cobden, 4 Nov. 1851: Bright Papers Add. MS 43,383 fo. 223. *HP* (Oct. 1851), 197–8.

[20] *People's Paper* (27 Apr. 1854), cited in J. Savile, *Ernest Jones: Chartist* (1952), 213.

of his overriding mistrust of Palmerston's motives in promoting it.[21] Though Urquhart's critique of 'secret diplomacy' was half a century later to be taken up by *pacificists*, his denunciations of the Crimean War offered a prime illustration of an 'anti-war', as distinct from a 'peace', campaign.

During the two years of British involvement in the Crimean War the peace movement's campaign went through four distinct phases, the transitions coming in late October 1854, June 1855, and late February 1856. During the first seven months its goal was little more than survival. Even this was difficult for its *pacificist* wing: all non-interventionists had to accept that most of their fellow liberals, radicals, or socialists disagreed with them; and those who were active politicians had to balance loyalty to their principles against the loss of influence which would result from incurring excessive unpopularity. Bright was the lone voice against the war in the House of Commons on 31 March 1854, though even he was to tell Sturge 'to rest quiet at present' and wait for the war to end.[22] Cobden, his authority undermined by his previous underestimate of the seriousness of the Eastern Question, was even more cautious, discouraging the Peace Society from issuing 'a Final Protest', on the grounds that it would be interpreted as publicity-seeking, and because he was convinced that there were but '10 men in the House' and '120 outside', apart from the Quakers, who supported him.[23] He hoped for a war-weariness bred of early financial and commercial difficulties, which, because of the resilience of the British economy, never came. Of the other *pacificist* MPs, only Milner Gibson was to take political risks during the war. Their extra-parliamentary support was similarly muted: the Manchester Peace Conference Committee instructed its secretary, F. W. Chesson, that he should attempt no 'further service for peace [other] than to obtain reliable information upon the effect of the present war upon the commerce of this country'; and the London Peace Conference Committee met only once between February and late October 1854.[24]

In some respects pacifists were more comfortable when war broke out than non-interventionist *pacificists*. For one thing, those whose views were grounded in Christianity were treated more leniently than those whose thinking was essentially political, although at the end of the war the *Herald of*

---

[21] The best analysis of Urquhart's remarkable career is in M. Taylor, 'The Old Radicalism and the New: David Urquhart and the Politics of Opposition, 1832–67', in E. F. Biagini and A. J. Reid (eds.), *Currents of Radicalism: Popular Radicalism, Organised Labour and Party Politics in Britain, 1850–1914* (Cambridge, 1991), 23–43.

[22] Bright to Sturge, 4 Sept. 1854: Sturge Papers Add. MS 43, 723 fos. 28–9.

[23] Cobden to Richard, 8 and 22 Sept. 1854: Cobden Papers Add. MS 43,657 fos. 231–2, 233. Cobden to Bright, 14 Sept. 1854, cited in Morley, *Life of Richard Cobden*, ii. 162.

[24] Chesson Diary, 21 July 1854: John Rylands Library; for Chesson's life see *Aborigines' Friend*, NS 3/12 (Mar. 1889), 513–23. PCCM, 5 Aug. 1854.

Peace was to warn its readers that the 'sinister compliment' which many supporters of the war had 'paid to what is called the *religious* peace men, at the expense of others' merely indicated that Christian pacifists were viewed 'as harmless visionaries, who are not likely, in any practical form, to traverse the warlike policy they admire'.[25] For another thing, British territory was not in danger: it was not pacifism but non-interventionist *pacificism* which was under particular intellectual pressure.

Comfort and freedom from critical scrutiny are, however, ultimately bad for pacifism, which helps to explain why Britain's first major war for four decades produced so few additions to its literature.[26] A considerable amount of the Peace Society's publishing effort was devoted to the non-pacifist utterances of politicians such as Bright, Gladstone, and Grey; and the *Herald of Peace* gave editorial priority to Richard's learned but essentially Cobdenite analysis of the international situation. Moreover, most pacifists rejected the label 'peace-at-any-price' (and its variant 'peace-at-all-price'), which had entered common usage shortly before the war. It was understandable that they should resent a phrase which had been malevolently crafted by defencists to suggest that the peace movement as a whole—it was applied to *pacificists* too—consisted of 'spiritless timid folk, who spoke for peace because they were afraid of war', as a Peace Society official was to put it a quarter of a century later when Disraeli revived it.[27] Yet it was a not inaccurate description of pacifism: indeed, in the autumn of 1853 Richard had acknowledged a 'straightforward moral obligation to preserve the peace at whatever cost';[28] and during the war the unfailingly blunt Joseph Sturge took pride in the label.[29] The timidity of most pacifists in respect of accusations of favouring 'peace at any price' revealed to what a low level their ideological confidence had sunk.

Pacifism was in any case at a difficult transitional stage in the 1850s, partly as a result of changes in theological fashion. In its early years the Peace Society had been mainly evangelical in outlook and had consoled itself with the doctrine of particular providence according to which a truly Christian (and in its view therefore pacifist) nation could expect divine protection. In this way it achieved some of the psychological advantages of the optimistic orientation while at the same time reassuring the government that it was not making any claims about worldly politics. However, its faith in particular

[25] *HP* (Mar. 1856), 26.
[26] As noted by Frick, 'Joseph Sturge, Henry Richard and the *Herald of Peace*', fos. 177–8.
[27] W. Pollard, 'The Peace-at-Any-Price Party', *Fraser's Magazine*, 22 (1880), 490–500, at 494.
[28] *HP* (Oct. 1853), 279.
[29] As reported in *Empire* (10 Mar. 1855), 229.

providence gradually declined, particularly as it came increasingly to collaborate with *pacificism*, a product of the Enlightenment.

Moreover, in 1854 it discovered that particular providence was being widely invoked by supporters of British intervention. For example, preaching on the fast day called by the government after declaring war, the Anglican curate of Mildenhall in Suffolk insisted that 'although the war now commencing has been mainly occasioned by the evil passions of man, the hand of God is in it. The present crisis has not arisen independently of his overruling Providence.' He also presented the British empire as another beneficiary of particular providence: 'God has granted us a wonderful pre-eminence among the nations of the earth . . . Has He not given these vast tracts of country, with their teeming populations, to us as trustee for Him?'[30]

In reaction to such claims, the Peace Society tended to emphasize human responsibility, thereby troubling some of its still evangelically minded supporters. Arthur A. Rees, a dissenting minister from Sunderland, supported its stand against the war but accused it of 'continually ignoring the important scriptural truth, that though the real responsibility of governments is not to be overlooked, yet the *real source* of war, as a providential event, is the *sin* of the nations which are scourged by it'. But Richard replied emphatically to Rees: 'We do not believe that God is the author of this war';[31] and in May 1855 the Peace Society's annual report urged Christians to regard the conflict 'not . . . as a misfortune or a mysterious dispensation of Providence, but as the unmixed offspring of human wickedness'.[32] The Crimean War thus confirmed the society's leaders in their tendency to play down claims about particular providence: these were increasingly left to adventist sects, which kept them alive until at least as late as the Second World War, to the surprise of the tribunals assessing claims for conscientious objection.[33] However, the Peace Society had discarded particular providence without deciding how otherwise to combat the argument that a pacifist country would simply be enslaved by an aggressor. It was not until after the Crimean War, as we shall see, that the *Herald of Peace* belatedly made claims for 'The Safety of Peace Principles'.

Though this was to be the last war in which the government was to hold fast days, secularization and political change had not yet gone far enough to allow non-Christian inspirations for pacifism wholly to supersede Christian

[30] E. H. Lovelock, *The Penitent's Confession and Plea for Mercy and the Christian's Duties in the Present Crisis* (1854), 3–4, 21.

[31] *HP* (Apr. 1854), 47–8.

[32] *HP* (June 1855), 212. See also A Clergyman of the Church of England, *Notes from France on the War with Russia* (1855), 2.

[33] G. C. Field, *Pacifism and Conscientious Objection* (Cambridge, 1945), 5.

ones. Admittedly, consequentialist and humanitarian arguments were more commonly used than ever, as for example by Southampton's Unitarian minister Edmund Kell in a sermon on the war's second fast day:

Let trembling pity contemplate the frightful mass of human misery at Balaklava. Visit the hospitals of Scutari, made hallowed grounds by the angel-visits of Miss Nightingale and the Sisters of Mercy, through long wards of untold suffering. Oh, I could narrate to you such touching incidents of woe as could melt a heart of iron . . . And what *one single* rational object have we in view in the prosecution of the war, which will counterbalance all these enormous evils?[34]

Yet such arguments were still regarded as secondary to scriptural ones. In addition, political inspirations for pacifism remained undeveloped. The Christian anarcho-pacifism which had been vigorously propounded by Garrison and his disciples had lost credibility in Britain as its originators became preoccupied with the possibility of war against the slave-holding states instead.[35] The celebrated Russian novelist Count Leo Tolstoy, who was to revive it the 1880s, was at this time a Russian army officer on active service in Sebastopol. And socialism had yet to inspire its own brand of pacifism, although, as will shortly be seen, it was already beginning to generate its own variety of *pacificism*.

Even if they did not distinguish themselves intellectually, pacifists often showed moral courage, though the absence of conscription limited their opportunity to demonstrate this. The Society of Friends remained generally true to its peace testimony, though the London chemist Jacob Bell declared himself one of the war's 'strongest supporters' during an unsuccessful bid to get himself back into parliament at the Marylebone by-election of December 1854;[36] and 'many held their views silently', as Isichei's excellent study of Victorian Quakerism has noted.[37]

The League of Universal Brotherhood reaffirmed its pacifism, but was too weak to mount much of a campaign at any stage in the war. Because of visits to the United States, Burritt was in the country for only half the war, from 18 August 1854 to 29 September 1855,[38] so his pedestrian and easy-going Quaker assistant Edmund Fry was left in charge.[39] A hundred or so Olive Leaf

---

[34] E. Kell, *Peace, the Gift, the Injunction of Our Holy Redeemer: The Paramount Obligation of Immediate Peace* (1855), 13–14.

[35] P. Brock, *Pacifism in the United States: From the Colonial Era to the First World War* (Princeton, 1968), 669.

[36] *Manchester Examiner* (20 Dec. 1854), 3.

[37] E. Isichei, *Victorian Quakers* (1970), 150.

[38] *Bond of Brotherhood* (Sept. 1854), 26; (Nov. 1855), 63.

[39] Fry's limitations as well as his strengths were itemized in an unusually candid obituary by Richard: see *HP* (Jan. 1867), 150–1.

Circles, which almost always met in private houses, continued to function,[40] though they were so little known that one of the few newspaper reports of their activities felt obliged to explain that they constituted 'one of the numerous societies ... which are silently, but not the less efficiently, aiding the better known and more influential "peace movement", of which Cobden, Bright, Wilson and Richard are the acknowledged leaders'.[41] Burritt's journal, *Bond of Brotherhood*, lost some of its circulation but claimed to be selling 4,000 copies at the end of 1855.[42] Although 'about 400' people attended the League's annual meeting in May 1855, they were predominantly Quakers in town for their Yearly Meeting who also provided most of the 'contributors and purchasers' at the League of Universal Brotherhood's financially crucial bazaar; and Burritt was privately aware that 'the very existence of our Society hangs upon a silver thread; and the chance of its surviving is very small indeed'.[43] In the event, the League of Universal Brotherhood just outlasted the war.

The Peace Society had become so identified with 'peace at any price' that it could not plausibly have softened its pacifist stance even had it been tempted to do so. Its greater prominence in the late 1840s had not been translated into significant increases in its membership, merely into expressions of goodwill. The latter had evaporated in the immediate pre-war years and now turned to hostility; but its core subscribing membership of 1,500 or so seems to have remained surprisingly intact. After the war the society claimed to have learned not only 'how little reliance is to be placed upon those who ... join a cause in the hour of its prosperity and triumph' but also 'the far more grateful and inspiring truth that, with very rare exceptions the old and true friends of peace have maintained with unswerving loyalty, their allegiance to their principles'.[44] However, the Peace Society's leaders were depressed by the fact that many of those who in theory remained loyal interpreted their pacifism as a long-term aspiration rather than a commitment to immediate action. This was, however, partly the society's own fault: for a decade it had been paying more attention to arbitration than to non-resistance; and since the second half of the 1840s it had with increasing frequency described pacifism as an 'abstract principle'[45]—the slightly derogatory term used by Cobden and Bright when distancing their own *pacificism* from it.

[40] *Bond of Brotherhood* (Sept. 1854), 38; (Oct. 1854), 38; (July 1855), 180–1; (Aug. 1855), 16.
[41] *Empire* (10 Feb. 1855), 167.
[42] *Bond of Brotherhood* (Sept. 1854), 29; (May 1856), 152.
[43] Burritt Diary, 28, 30, 31 May, 31 July 1855: New Britain Public Library, Connecticut.
[44] *HP* (June 1855), 65.
[45] For early usages see Burritt Diary, 3 Nov. 1846, and *HP* (Dec. 1849), 410–11.

It was not surprising, therefore, that although pacifism was only rarely recanted during the Crimean War, it was only rarely acted upon either. Richard later drew attention to two justifications for inactivity which had been used by those still accepting that all war was forbidden by Christianity. One was that it was best to 'offer no opinion upon, nor employ any argument against, the actual war in hand'. This was to regard pacifism as an abstract principle in the sense of having no application to concrete circumstances. The other, resorted to by those prepared to criticize the war as having been both unchristian and impolitic in its origins, was to argue that, 'seeing that we are actually in it, we are for prosecuting it with vigour'. This was to regard pacifism as an ethic which applied only in peacetime.[46] The first signs of the gradual dilution of the Peace Society's pacifism were thus apparent in the willingness of some of its members to imply that their principles could not be implemented during the war.

Faced with intellectual evasions within its ranks as well as with what it acknowledged to be general enthusiasm for the war, the Peace Society tried 'to steer between the opposite extremes of timidity and rashness'.[47] It printed Bright's Commons speech of 31 March 1854, increased the circulation of the *Herald of Peace*,[48] and went ahead with its own anniversary meetings on 23 May 1854, including the public meeting in Finsbury chapel which followed the small and private meeting of members. But at this time it did not issue a public statement, hold other meetings, or put up placards. After three months of phoney war, William Stokes lectured experimentally in south Wales, the region thought to be most sympathetic to the peace cause: though generally successful, Stokes was shouted down at a meeting in Neath where his chairman was, ironically, the local ironfounder and co-founder of the Peace Society, Joseph Tregelles Price. However, consultations in the region thought to be the next most favourable, the north of England, resulted in a decision not to send Stokes to hold meetings there. Stokes therefore attempted to lecture in his own locality, Birmingham, but was able to do so only 'to some extent', finding 'the prevailing war mania a serious obstacle rendering it extremely difficult to secure local co-operation, or even a suitable place in which meetings might be convened'.[49]

The war briefly enjoyed a further surge of popularity in the early autumn

---

[46] *HP* (June 1856), 65.

[47] 1855 annual report, in *HP* (June 1855), 209–10.

[48] Newspaper Stamp Duty returns from the Parliamentary Papers are (covering twelve issues in a full year): 1851, 15,000; 1852, 13,500; 1853, 15,250; 1854, 24,250; and Jan.–June 1855, 9,000 (equivalent of 18,000 for a full year). The figures for 1844–50 were given above Ch. 2, n 43.

[49] Peace Society annual report, in *HP* (June 1855), 210.

of 1854, after the British and French armies had finally carried the war into the Crimea in September; but their failure to take Sebastopol, and the battle reports by W. H. Russell—which, thanks to the electric telegraph, appeared in *The Times* after only a twenty-day delay—made possible a second and less quiescent phase of the peace campaign from late October onwards. Wilson and Chesson of the Manchester Peace Conference Committee were among those who decided at this point to 'placard the walls as the best means of counteracting the war spirit'.[50] Bright responded to a request from a constituent that he support a patriotic fund for the war's widows and orphans with an unprecedentedly fierce polemic in which he accused the government of 'an imbecility perhaps without example', condemned Turkey as 'the most immoral and filthy of all despotisms', and disclaimed responsibility for the war's victims: 'I will have no part in this terrible crime. My hands will be unstained with the blood that is being shed.'[51] The London Peace Conference Committee held a 'Conference of the Friends of Peace' on 29 November, chaired by Sturge, which decided that although it was still the case that 'any attempt to hold public meetings in the midst of the present warlike excitement would be productive of more harm than good', tracts and placards were now worthwhile.[52] The Society of Friends issued 'A Christian Appeal from the Society of Friends to their Fellow Countrymen on the Present War' and presented it to the Prime Minister on 13 December:[53] helping to draft this and taking part in the deputation to Lord Aberdeen proved to be the last services to the peace cause of Joseph Tregelles Price, who developed acute bronchitis on returning to Neath and died on Christmas Day 1854, thereby breaking the Peace Society's last link with its founding committee. Sturge placarded Birmingham on 2 December with a statement blaming the war (rather than corn merchants like himself) for increased bread prices, thereby causing great local controversy. On the same day a London weekly paper, the *Empire*, appeared for the first time under the ownership of two pacifists, George Thompson, a Congregationalist ex-clerk who had achieved prominence as first a Garrisonian orator and then a radical MP for Tower Hamlets 1847–52, and John Hamilton, a young Scottish journalist who had previously been a dissenting minister. They brought Chesson to London to work for them, his secretaryship of the Manchester Peace Conference Committee passing to

[50] Chesson Diary, 21 Oct. 1854: REAS /11/2.

[51] *The Times* (4 Nov. 1854), 10. 'Brief Statement of the Labours of the Manchester Peace Conference', *HP* (Oct. 1858), 113.

[52] PCCM, 29 Nov. 1854. See also Chesson Diary, 29 Nov. 1854.

[53] Frick, 'Sturge, Richard and the *Herald*', fos. 56–60; id., 'The *Christian Appeal* of 1855: Friends' Public Response to the Crimean War', *Journal of the Friends' Historical Society*, 52 (1968–71), 203–10. *HP* (Feb. 1855), 170.

William Stokes, who moved north from Birmingham.[54] Thompson, Hamilton, and Chesson produced a newspaper which was continuously critical of the war.

On 18 December Bright survived an attempt by his opponents to censure him at a town meeting in Manchester Town Hall for his opposition to the patriotic fund: Wilson mobilized his old Anti-Corn-Law League following so skilfully in support of Bright that neither side could make itself heard; and the show of hands was too close to call. Four days later Cobden felt encouraged enough to make his first Commons speech against the war. He also resolved 'to take the bull by the horns in Yorkshire'[55] and hold a meeting in his West Riding constituency on 17 January 1855, though this went badly wrong when he was heavily defeated by a local liberal, Edward Baines, the second-generation proprietor of the *Leeds Mercury*. Baines was no crusader, and won by presenting the *pacificist* case for the war, the *Nonconformist* commenting that the motion he put forward as a challenge to Cobden was 'very pacific for a war resolution' and his speech—in which he emphasized that he 'had invariably been the advocate of peace'—even more so. Cobden blamed the lack of 'out-of-doors support for the party of peace and non-intervention' which had let him down in the West Riding on the pernicious influence of a press which propounded either defencism and crusading.[56] He therefore began work in earnest to establish a daily paper to promote *pacificism* (or, in his words, 'the politics of the "Manchester School"—peace, free trade, non-intervention, economy, & c.'),[57] a project which he had been contemplating since early in the war in anticipation of the abolition of the newspaper stamp duty.[58] After various delays, this paper was to appear, as the *Morning Star*, just thirteen days before the peace treaty.

Five days after Cobden's humiliation in his constituency, Roebuck put down a Commons motion calling for a select committee to inquire into the conduct of the war, which, after being carried on 29 January, led to Palmerston replacing Aberdeen. Cobden, who viewed the new Prime Minister as a 'great sham and not nearly so warlike as his foolish dupes and adulators have believed', persuaded himself that 'Palmerston will be anxious to steal from Aberdeen the credit of getting out of the war'.[59]

The peace movement therefore pressed on with its campaign, which was

---

[54] PSM, 18 Dec. 1854.

[55] Cobden to Richard, 1 Jan. 1855: Cobden Papers Add. MS 43,657 fo. 250.

[56] Morley, *Life of Richard Cobden*, ii. 171.

[57] Cobden to Bright, 12 Jan. 1855: Cobden Papers Add. MS 43,650 fo. 90.

[58] See Cobden to Sturge, 24 Apr. 1854: Add. MS 43,722 fo. 23.

[59] Cobden to Richard, 7 Feb. 1855, in J. A. Hobson, *Richard Cobden: The International Man* (1919), 125. Cobden to Bright, 11 Feb. 1855: Cobden Papers Add. MS 43,650 fo. 95.

now spearheaded by George Thompson, who with the support of the Manchester Peace Conference Committee undertook sixteen major meetings in Lancashire and the West Riding of Yorkshire, plus one in Birmingham, between late February and late March. He suffered occasional defeats at the hands of local crusaders, for example at Oldham on 27 February, where a Mr Quarmly argued that 'Russia aimed at universal empire, and the welfare of the working classes demanded that she should be checked and driven back' and a Peter Seville insisted that 'the peace-at-any-price party had caused the war'.[60] But 'in the majority of places', as the Peace Society noted, Thompson was well received.[61] Arthur O'Neill, the moral-force Chartist who had become a Baptist pastor in Birmingham, also embarked on a series of successful meetings in the Midlands 'under the direction of Mr Sturge'.[62] Bright became more assertive: on 25 February he made his celebrated 'angel of death' speech in the Commons;[63] on 6 March he told a Manchester Peace Conference Committee meeting that an 'association for the purpose of teaching the people of the country the doctrine of non-intervention' might be needed, a suggestion that was much commented on though never followed up; [64] and on 22 March he and Milner Gibson presented Palmerston with a petition from the Manchester Peace Conference Committee signed by 'upwards of 11,000 persons'.[65]

The Peace Society began holding meetings of its own, addressed mainly by Richard and the West-Country Quakers Samuel Bowly and Robert Charleton.[66] And Thompson made a second speaking tour in the North, this time experiencing only two defeats, which, being both by narrow margins in towns known to be unsympathetic, could be deemed moral victories: these came on 12 April at Newcastle, where he was opposed by two crusading champions of the 'nationalities' cause, the radical local newspaper proprietor Joseph Cowen, and the Chartist George Julian Harney, and on 7 May at Leeds, the scene of Cobden's more crushing setback four months previously.[67]

This second phase in the peace campaign reached a climax after

---

[60] *Oldham Chronicle* (3 Mar. 1855), 2–4.

[61] PSM, 5 Mar. 1855 (see also PCCM, 6 Mar. 1855). The meetings in Thompson's first tour are listed in *HP* (Apr. 1855), 193–4.

[62] PSM, 14 May 1855. *HP* (May 1855), 205.

[63] Hansard, cxxxvii HC col. 1757.

[64] *Nonconformist* (14 Mar. 1855), 204.

[65] *Nonconformist* (28 March 1855), 252.

[66] PSM, 9 Apr. 1855. *HP* (May 1855), 205; (June 1855), 211. A.F. Fox, *Memoir of Robert Charleton* (1873), 90.

[67] *Empire* (21 Apr. 1855), 330–1; (12 May 1855), 374. Thompson's second tour is itemized in *HP* (May 1855), 205.

Palmerston's cabinet decided to reject peace terms negotiated at Vienna. This briefly opened up the possibility that both the Peelites, who had left the government soon after Palmerston became Prime Minister, and the Conservatives, led in the Commons by Disraeli, might support the peace resolution which Milner Gibson, who had consulted Richard at the Peace Society's office,[68] proposed to introduce on 21 May.[69] Though Palmerston outmanœuvred the Peelites, obliging Gibson to drop his motion, the Peace Conference Committee held a major meeting two days later in the London house of James Bell, a Quaker MP who belonged to the Peace Society's executive committee. Attended by thirty representatives of most sections of the peace movement—including Bowly, Bright, Burritt, Cobden, Hindley, Richard, Sturge, and Thompson, though only R. H. Greg was present from the Manchester Peace Conference Committee[70]—it resolved 'to increase the number of lecturers in the field, to get up petitions for peace, and also to see about starting a twopenny or penny paper in London as an organ of the cause'; and it also established a subcommittee, on which Bright and Cobden agreed to serve, to take these matters forward.[71] On 24 May the Commons began a six-day debate on the government's rejection of the Vienna terms, in which Cobden made his first public criticism of the war since January and the Peelite Gladstone spoke 'with my whole heart in the sense of peace'.

But with Disraeli not joining them, the government survived without even a division; and the second phase of the peace campaign ran out of steam after eight months of effort. Two days later, the Peace Society's executive committee was told that Cobden, Bright, and Milner Gibson now wanted merely to 'wait upon events in the Crimea'.[72] In addition, Manchester lapsed into quiescence; Thompson's touring days were over as he faced renewed financial difficulties because the *Empire*'s opposition to the war had caused its circulation to drop; and Sturge's health was deteriorating.

The beginning of a third phase in June 1855 was the work of London-based journalists and political activists with only limited previous connections to the peace movement. Its prime movers were John Hamilton of the *Empire* and James 'Bronterre' O'Brien. The latter, an Irish barrister who had become a radical journalist and now led a London-based Chartist splinter group, the National Reform League, had from the outset opposed the Crimean War, perhaps to distance himself from other leaders of the rump of Chartism, such as Ernest Jones, who had hailed it as a crusade. In June 1855 the

---

68   Burritt chanced upon them there: see his Diary, 17 May 1855.
69   Compare *Empire* (26 May 1855), 410–11, with *HP* (June 1855), 215–18.
70   Sturge to G. Wilson, 26 May 1855: Wilson Papers.
71   PCCM, 23 May 1855. Burritt Diary, 23 May 1855.
72   PSM, 11 June 1855.

National Reform League issued a penny pamphlet containing a condemnation of the war which professed to 'speak the sentiments of at least 1,500 intelligent tradesmen and mechanics who voted for it unanimously at three public meetings' and for which a sale of 2,500 copies was claimed.[73] This pamphlet propounded an early form of socialist *pacificism*:

View it as we may, fellow countrymen, the present war is a monstrous iniquity. It is wasting the blood and treasure of the country in a struggle in which they who contribute the blood and treasure have no interest whatsoever. It is a war to enrich landlords, farmers and graziers—with high rents and famine prices—at the expense of a starving population. It is a war to build up sudden fortunes for shipowners, shipbuilders, contractors, jobbers, and army, navy and commissariat adventurers, at the expense of tradesmen falling into bankruptcy and impoverished artisans. It is a war for usurers and speculators, who, having made huge fortunes during the late 'flush of prosperity,' wish to invest their floating capital in new government securities, for which, of course, there must be new loans, new debts, new taxes—so that these voracious cormorants may feed and fatten at the expense of those who have saved nothing, while they preserve their ill-gotten hoarded capitals intact. In short it is a war to rob, impoverish and decimate the industrious classes, for the gain of feudal tyrants, usurers, and commercial vampires, speculating in the blood and calamities of their fellow creatures.[74]

This and eleven subsequent statements critical of the war were given free publicity in the *Empire*, which O'Brien, whose own meetings seem previously to have been largely ignored, congratulated for thereby showing 'due regard to the moral and material interests of the country', in contrast with a 'narrow, sordid, one-sided sickly opposition [to war] founded on more commercial considerations'[75]—a crude dig at liberal *pacificism*. The *Empire* had decided to publicize O'Brien's meetings because John Hamilton, who had taken sole charge of the paper while Thompson was away campaigning, was making an effort to persuade 'the friends of Administrative Reform'—the radicals and liberals who had previously campaigned for a more efficient war effort—to join 'an open and straightforward opposition to the war' instead.[76] From 18 June Hamilton had therefore taken part in a series of public meetings in London at which the case against continuing the war was put by speakers used to addressing working-class audiences but whose views were on the Christian and liberal end of the metropolitan radical spectrum. In addi-

---

[73] Letter from National Reform League, *Empire* (14 July 1855), 521–2.

[74] Cited from *Empire* (23 June 1855), 471. The pamphlet was entitled *The War with Russia: An Address of the Council of the National Reform League to the People of Great Britain and Northern Ireland* (n.d. [1855]): a copy survives in the University of London Library.

[75] Letter from National Reform League, *Empire* (14 July 1855), 521.

[76] *Empire* (23 June 1855), 472–3.

tion to Hamilton himself and Thompson, these speakers included: Chesson, by now Thompson's son-in-law and the part-time secretary of the Aborigines Protection Society;[77] John Passmore Edwards, a carpenter's son who had become a journalist and lecturer[78] and had first come into the peace movement as an admirer of Burritt but also supported the Peace Society; John Ingram Lockhart, a writer and translator who had stood as a Chartist candidate in the previous general election;[79] Washington Wilks, a writer of working-class origins, radical politics, and evangelical religion, who had initially supported the war;[80] and Jabez Inwards, a temperance lecturer and member of a sect called the Reformation Church who not only 'took the high ground of opposition to all war' but also was 'a foe to capital punishment and against snuff, tobacco, and opium'.[81] By the beginning of August, Hamilton was describing their efforts as constituting 'A New Peace Movement', and was seeking financial assistance from Wilson, Sturge, and even—albeit less successfully—from Gladstone.[82]

On 9 September 1855 Sebastopol finally fell to the French and British armies, producing an upsurge of pro-war emotionalism but also convincing some defencists—including Disraeli, who was later complimented by the *Herald of Peace* for his 'moderate and pacific counsels' at this time[83]—that a compromise peace could now be secured without shame. Hamilton's campaign continued, with the London merchant George Dornbusch, later a member of the Peace Society's executive committee, reporting their costs to Sturge.[84] Moreover, after completing ten 'free, crowded, and public assemblies' in as many weeks, it decided on 24 October to institutionalize itself as a 'Stop-the-War League', with Chesson as its secretary *pro tem*.[85] He issued a call for subscriptions which made clear that it was intended to be a broad-based association, since it would not 'collectively pronounce judgement upon the abstract question of peace, nor upon the origin of the present war; but leave every member to take his own ground, confining their united action to the development of a public sentiment in favour of an early termination of the conflict'.[86] The committee, which met on 17 November to draw up a constitution for the

[77] See Chesson's obituary in *Aborigines' Friend* (Mar. 1889), 513–23.

[78] See E. H. Burrage, *J. Passmore Edwards: Philanthropist* (1902).

[79] Taylor, *Decline of English Radicalism*, 255–6.

[80] See *Nonconformist* (29 June 1864), 525; and W. Wilks, *Edward Irving: An Ecclesiastical and Literary Biography* (1854), 1.

[81] *Empire* (20 Oct. 1855), 740–1. *The Life and Labours of Jabez Inwards* (n.d. [1860]), 21.

[82] Hamilton to Wilson, 20 July 1855: Wilson Papers.

[83] *HP* (Jan. 1856), 3. R. Blake, *Disraeli* (1966), 363–4. J. B. Conacher, *Britain and the Crimea, 1855–1856: Problems of War and Peace* (1987), 136.

[84] Dornbusch to Sturge, 11 Oct. 1855, and Sturge to Wilson, 17 Oct. 1855: Wilson Papers.

[85] This date is given in *Empire* (1 Dec. 1855), 848.

[86] *Empire* (27 Oct. 1855), 753, 757, 768; (10 Nov. 1855), 785, 793, 800.

Stop-the-War League, comprised Hamilton as chairman, Dornbusch as treasurer, Chesson and Lockhart as joint secretaries, and Wilks, Passmore Edwards, and L. A. Chamerovzow as ordinary members.[87] The last-mentioned had recently become secretary of the British and Foreign Anti-Slavery Society (his former post at the Aborigines' Protection Society having passed to his friend Chesson, as already noted), and was a long-standing supporter of the Peace Society, whose annual meeting of members he had attended with Dornbusch.

One notable absentee from the committee was Thompson, who faced acute financial embarrassment which he attributed to his 'losses as a peace journalist', and soon had to go into hiding from his creditors before fleeing to a job in India.[88] Another was O'Brien, who had spoken at several Stop-the-War meetings but whose outspokenness at the expense of 'Jew usurers' and insistence that 'the capitalists of Europe were the primary cause of war' were unlikely to endear the new committee to potential donors such as George Wilson, to whom its new chairman immediately appealed for financial assistance on the grounds that the Stop-the-War League could win over audiences which the Peace Society could not.[89] Cobden—who, having received 'letters from new men, clergymen and others, urging the formation of a Society to Stop the War', had temporarily recovered his belief that wartime activism could have 'good effects'—welcomed the new body while keeping his distance from it.[90]

It was, however, not the continuing campaign against the war but Austria's and France's agreement of peace terms which forced Palmerston to accept a negotiated peace. A last desperate campaign in favour of fighting Russia to a finish was launched by crusaders. It caused some peace activists to falter: even Henry Vincent—accurately described in the *Empire* as 'a once eminent preacher of absolute peace who has never made a public recantation of that doctrine'—was now reported as opposing a 'patched-up peace', information which the peace movement considered 'as surprising as it was lamentable'.[91] However, it roused Cobden into writing a pamphlet pointing out how difficult a decisive victory this would be to achieve militarily, an argument which sat uneasily with his pre-war emphasis on Russia's weakness. Published at the very beginning of 1856 under the title *What Next—and Next?*, Cobden's

---

[87] The only source for the membership of this committee is John Hamilton's letter to George Wilson, 18 Nov. 1855: Wilson Papers.

[88] Thompson to Wilson, 17 and 29 Dec. 1855, and Hamilton to Wilson, 14 Dec. 1855: Wilson Papers.

[89] Hamilton to Wilson, 18 Nov. 1855: Wilson Papers.

[90] Cobden to Richard, 15 Nov. 1855: Cobden Papers Add. MS 43,657 fos. 301–2.

[91] *Empire* (12 Jan. 1856), 937. See also Richard to Vincent, 9 Feb. 1856: PSLB.

pamphlet was of interest for declaring that it was its author's intention 'to promote a general reduction of naval establishments at the close of the war', and for claiming that the 'balance of power' sought by defencists amounted to a 'a pact or federation of the States of Europe' which ought to be 'the subject of a peaceful diplomacy', thereby providing further evidence of Cobden's move away from isolationism and towards internationalism.[92]

On 1 February 1856, a Protocol was signed at Vienna; and a diplomatic congress was summoned to Paris twenty-four days later. On 9 February the Stop-the-War League advertised in the *Empire* for the last time: it had held about thirty peace meetings, a fifth of the peace movement's total since May 1855.[93] On 25 February the Paris Congress opened, and resolved to finalize a treaty by 31 March. The fourth, briefest, and most successful phase in the peace movement's campaign now began. On 6 March the London and Manchester Peace Conference Committees held a joint meeting to discuss whether to press Palmerston to insert a clause in the treaty requiring future disputes to be arbitrated. Although ill-attended and informed that Cobden and Bell were 'decidedly' hostile to any such move,[94] the two committees went ahead with a large deputation to Palmerston on 14 March. Eighteen *pacificist* MPs took part, including a reluctant Cobden, who was pressured to do so by Gibson, and several supporters of the war, such as Lord Robert Grosvenor, George Hadfield, and Edward Miall. The remaining thirty-nine members of the deputation were mainly from the Peace Society, led by Sturge and Richard; but they also included Fry from the League of Universal Brotherhood, Chamerovzow and Wilks from the Stop-the-War League, and two representatives from the Manchester Peace Conference Committee.[95]

Sturge, Richard, and Hindley followed up the deputation by travelling to Paris in order to lobby the plenipotentiaries gathered there, and were soon joined by Chamerovzow, who was formally representing the British and Foreign Anti-Slavery Society but also acted as their interpreter. Their sojourn in the French capital was 'trying to our patience and somewhat mortifying to our pride', as Sturge later admitted, since the plenipotentiaries were understandably reluctant 'to have it known that they have any suggestions from us of the Peace party if they intend to have an arbitration clause'.[96] However, on

---

[92] Cobden to Bright, 28 Dec. 1855: Cobden Papers Add. MS 43,650 fo. 165. R. Cobden, *What Next—and Next?* (1856), 3, 48, 50.

[93] *HP* (June 1856), 63.

[94] PCCM, 6 Mar. 1856.

[95] PSM, 17 Apr. 1856. *HP* (Apr. 1856), 39–40.

[96] Sturge to Cobden, 9 Apr. 1856, cited in Frick, 'Henry Richard and the Treaty of Paris of 1856', *National Library of Wales Journal*, 17 (1971/2), 299–313 at 308–9.

25 March they were sympathetically received by British Foreign Secretary Clarendon, whose own views had a *pacificist* tinge.[97] Five days later the peace treaty was signed, its Article VIII prescribing mediation for any future dispute between Turkey and Russia. And on 14 April the Paris congress agreed 'Protocol 23', which recommended the same remedy for all future international disputes. This protocol had been Clarendon's initiative, but was claimed as a success by the peace movement which was understandably keen to find an achievement which might partially offset the two years of vilification it had suffered.[98] Thus, having credited Protocol 23 with elevating arbitration from 'an Utopian dream . . . into a practical question', Cobden praised 'the energy of Joseph Sturge and his companions of the Peace Society, who went to Paris during the Congress . . . at the risk of ridiculous failure', and went on to speculate about a 'federation plan' to help the 'old world' reduce its armaments and insecurity.[99] Even Gladstone, a defencist who remained convinced of the original justice of the war but whose support for the Vienna terms was an early sign that he was capable of working in harmony with *pacificists*, hailed the protocol as 'perhaps' the first international declaration to include 'at least a qualified disapproval of a resort to war'.[100]

The peace movement's record in 1854–6 was on balance very creditable to it. In difficult circumstances—Russia being singularly hated and the economy holding up too well to generate much social discontent—and in the face of what Richard described as 'hard, worldly, turbulent crowds, some of them drunk on gin and many of them with passion', it had been defeated by disorder or counter-resolution in 'four or five instances only' out of the approximately 150 public meetings held after May 1855.[101] None the less, the movement had been very badly bruised; and many of its members shared Cobden's conclusion that it had been a mistake to criticize a war once it had broken out.

CHALLENGES AND REASSURANCES, 1856–1866

The ending of Crimean War brought the movement only partial relief: indeed, it was afflicted by a number of personal problems and diversions at this time.

---

[97] Neither of the early studies of his career brings this out: Sir H. Maxwell, *The Life and Letters of George William Frederick Fourth Earl of Clarendon* (2 vols., 1913); G. Villiers, *A Vanished Victorian: Being the Life of George Villiers Fourth Earl of Clarendon 1800–1870* (1938).

[98] *HP* (June 1856), 61, 71.

[99] Cobden to Chevalier Bunsen, 27 Sept. 1856, cited in S. Schwabe, *Reminiscences of Richard Cobden* (1895), 282–7.

[100] Hansard cxlii HC col. 99 (6 May 1856).

[101] *HP* (Mar. 1856), 25; (June 1856), 63.

Bright, who had suffered a mental breakdown at the end of January 1856, was out of action for two years. Cobden, whose son died in April, was distracted by this bereavement and its prostrating effect on his wife, and deferred the post-war campaign for the reduction of armaments which he had promised at the start of the year. Samuel Gurney, the wealthy bill-discounter who had served as the Peace Society's treasurer for twenty-four years, died in June, though his son of the same name and occupation agreed to succeed him. The *Morning Star*, launched on 17 March 1856 and lasting until 1868, failed to deliver the expected boost to the liberal-*pacificist* cause, proving instead to be a source of frustration for all those involved with it. Its poor journalistic quality infuriated Cobden, who 'could not for some time bear the sight of the paper'.[102] In particular, its demands cruelly exposed the limited education of John Hamilton, who had moved to the paper from the *Empire*. Therefore, at the request of Sturge, who offered to fund extra 'help at the Peace Office', and with the consent, 'after long and careful deliberation', of the Peace Society's executive committee,[103] Richard was brought in on a part-time basis to supervise the paper and improve its leaders, only to be accused by Cobden of doing so to such an extent as to risk it 'sinking as a news-paper and becoming a daily Peace Herald'[104] and to find his authority undermined by the appointment of a general manager.[105]

These coincidental difficulties exacerbated the psychological letdown which, as it now discovered for the first time, a peace movement tends to experience when it is released from the discipline of standing out against a popular war. The Peace Conference Committees having lapsed into only spasmodic activity, it was the Peace Society which took the pessimistic decision that 'a Peace Congress . . . on the Continent', which Burritt had been calling for from New England since as early as 8 January 1856, was 'not expedient'.[106] Instead, the Peace Society contemplated 'a general meeting of the Friends of Peace, in some large town in this country',[107] but did not proceed even with this more modest proposal after receiving discouragement from its leading parliamentary supporters. In particular, Cobden regarded any 'general agitation for peace' as 'very delusive', and informed Sturge that 'late experience' had shown that the 'religious and timid' types 'like Baines and Ewart' who might take part in such an agitation were liable to defect at the first

---

[102] Cobden to Richard, 27 May 1856: Cobden Papers Add. MS 43,658 fo. 30.
[103] Sturge to Richard, 7 July 1856: Richard Papers NLW MS 14023D. PSM, 25 July 1856.
[104] Cobden to Richard, 15 May 1857: Cobden Papers Add MS. 43,658 fo. 326b.
[105] Miall, *Henry Richard*, 115–18.
[106] *Bond of Brotherhood* (Feb. 1856), 109. PSM, 20 May 1856. Burritt to Richard, 8 Sept. 1856: Richard Papers NLW MS 5503B.
[107] *HP* (June 1856), 68.

setback, albeit whilst still 'professing that their sole object was to conquer "an honourable peace" '. Cobden recommended that the peace movement should instead take each international crisis as it arose 'with a view to force the public to adopt some *principle* of foreign policy'.[108] He warned Richard that, 'without new blood', merely 'exhibiting a skeleton of our former selves at a public meeting would more harm than good',[109] and bluntly informed Sturge that campaigning was pointless 'unless we could get some men of mark to come fresh into the fold with us'.[110] As an example of the required calibre of recruit Cobden gave Gladstone's brother Robertson, who had offered a donation to the peace movement shortly before the Crimean War but otherwise kept his distance from it.[111]

Yet such men were not forthcoming. Indeed, even some of those who had courageously opposed the Crimean War now gave other political and philanthropic issues priority over peace. Bright concluded that 'all we have done as a "Peace Conference" or "Peace Society" of late years has been of no use' and may even have 'done a positive harm';[112] and, when he was fit enough to campaign again, chose to do so for franchise reform. Samuel Bowly, though in practice still one of the Peace Society's most active members, informed it that his temperance work left him little time to agitate on other questions.[113] Sturge temporarily turned his energies towards humanitarian work on the Finnish coast where a British blockade had caused particular distress[114]—an early instance of Quaker relief for war victims. In addition, a series of peace lectures held by the Peace Society in London over the winter of 1856–7 produced only 'very thin' attendances; and a proposed meeting in the London Tavern had to be called off.[115]

For its part, the League of Universal Brotherhood decided to abandon the struggle for survival. Even its Olive Leaf Circles were suffering, it admitted, because 'marriage has removed valuable helpers from one sphere of duty and interest to another'.[116] Early in 1857 it began talks with the Peace Society about handing over what little remained of its operations. With Richard partly occupied with the *Morning Star*, the Peace Society was prepared to engage Edmund Fry as an additional administrator and lecturer at £4 per week.[117]

---

[108] PSM, 14 July 1856. Cobden to Sturge, 29 Oct. 1856: Add. MS 43,722 fos.163–4.
[109] Cobden to Richard, 19 Nov. 1856: PSLB.
[110] As Sturge reported to Richard, 21 Nov. 1856: Richard Papers NLW MS 14023D.
[111] *HP* (Nov. 1853), 258.
[112] K. Robbins, *John Bright* (1979), 132 (citing Bright to Sturge, Oct. 1857).
[113] Ibid. 142. PSM, 9 Jan. 1860.
[114] Tyrrell, *Joseph Sturge*, 222–4.
[115] PSM, 15 Dec. 1856, 16 Feb. 1857.
[116] *Bond of Brotherhood* (Oct. 1856), 40.
[117] PSM, 24 Feb., 6 July 1857.

The *Bond of Brotherhood* continued as a free-standing publication until shortly after Fry's death in 1867. And Olive Leaf Circles appeared as a separate though dwindling item on the Peace Society's balance sheet until the end of the 1860s. Otherwise all trace of the League of Universal Brotherhood, which in 1847–8 had been Britain's first mass peace association, disappeared when it merged with the Peace Society in May 1857.

Before the peace movement could work out what level of activity was feasible in these difficult post-war conditions, it found itself at the centre of the political stage in remarkable circumstances. One of the Peace Society's former officers, Sir John Bowring, involved Britain in a war with China, in protest against which Cobden defeated Palmerston in the House of Commons, and thereby triggered a general election that proved disastrous for the 'Peace party'. As the honorary foreign secretary in 1820–3 of the Peace Society and the lecturer on free trade at Manchester in 1838 who had stimulated the formation of the local association out of which the Anti-Corn-Law League had grown, Bowring was an unlikely source of enmity for the peace movement and liberal opinion. None the less, even in his pacifist days he had exhibited Palmerstonian attitudes: as a businessman travelling widely on the continent he had been employed by the government to carry diplomatic dispatches, and after being arrested by the French while on one such mission in 1822 had published a pamphlet which, while abominating 'all war as most unwise and most unholy', also complained at the government's failure 'to obtain the reparation of grievances committed on her citizens'.[118] Subsequently, while a *pacificist* and liberal politician, he had shown enthusiasm for some uses of military force.[119]

In the 1850s Bowring had been driven by financial necessity to obtain a permanent diplomatic position; and in 1854 he had risen to become British plenipotentiary in China and governor of Hong Kong, an appointment carrying a knighthood. In October 1856—ironically just a month after the *Herald of Peace* had reprinted a *pacificist* lecture he had given eleven years previously[120]—he ordered a prolonged bombardment of Canton as punishment for the boarding by China of the *Arrow*, a ship flying the English flag, on suspicion of piracy. Bowring believed that his *pacificist* principles were not thereby contravened, because, as he later argued in his autobiography, these applied only to relations with rational countries:

---

[118] [J. Bowring], *Detail of the Arrest, Imprisonment and Liberation of An Englishman by the Bourbon Government of France* (1823), p. vi. See also G. F. Bartle, 'Jeremy Bentham and John Bowring: A Study of the Relationship between Bentham and the Editor of his *Collected Works*', *Bulletin of the Institute of Historical Research*, 36 (1963), 27–35.

[119] See S. Conway, 'John Bowring and the Nineteenth-Century Peace Movement', *Bulletin of the Institute of Historical Research*, 64 (1991), 344–58 at 345.

[120] *HP* (Sept. 1856), 104–5.

The powers of reason fail when coming in contact with the unreasoning and barbarous. No man was ever a more ardent lover of peace than I—in fact I had been the Secretary of the Peace Society, and had always taken an active part in promoting the peace-movement—but with barbarous—ay, and sometimes with civilized nations, the words of peace are uttered in vain—as with children too often the voice of reproof.[121]

In view of such a capacity for self-justification it is unsurprising that an acquaintance later described him as not only 'the busiest of busy bodies' but also 'the slipperiest'.[122]

Bowring's bombardment of Canton, news of which reached England in February 1857, confirmed Henry Richard in his conviction, expressed in response to a separate conflict with Persia, 'that we are more frequently at war than any country, *not* excepting Russia'. He therefore condemned Bowring's behaviour as 'utterly indefensible', and denounced the folly of fighting 'an Empire consisting of 350 millions of the human race'.[123] With Gibson as seconder, Cobden moved a censure motion in the Commons on 26 February with a soberly factual speech which Palmerston—who also insisted that, as a former member of the Peace Society 'distinguished for amiable qualities and the mildness of his disposition', Bowring had behaved reason-ably—accused of having an 'an anti-English feeling'. After four evenings of debate, Cobden's and Gibson's motion was narrowly carried on 3 March by 263 votes to 247. On this occasion, the peace party achieved the parliamen-tary alliance with both Peelites and Conservatives which had eluded it during the Crimean War.[124]

Though sweet, this revenge for the Don Pacifico debate eight years earlier was very short. Palmerston called an immediate general election, and issued an address to his constituents urging the nation not to 'give their support to men who have . . . endeavoured to make the humiliation and degradation of their country the stepping stone to power'.[125] In a hurried and ineffective attempt to distance itself from party politics, the Peace Society created a sepa-rate 'Electoral Committee' to carry out its campaigning against Palmerston: early in April this was reported to be 'busy at work'.[126] Yet Cobden, despite changing constituencies from the West Riding to the ostensibly safer

---

[121] *Autobiographical Recollection of Sir John Bowring* (1877), 217–18.

[122] J. Neal, *Wandering Recollections of a Somewhat Busy Life: An Autobiography* (Boston, Mass., 1869: facsimile edn., Ann Arbor, Mich., 1976), 273.

[123] *HP* (Jan. 1857), 150; (Feb. 1857), 157; (Mar. 1857), 169.

[124] Hansard, cxliv HC cols. 1391–1421, 1811–12, 1846–50. The majority consisted of 202 Conservatives, 18 Peelites, 9 Irish, and only 36 Whigs or Radicals: see C. F. Jackson, 'The British General Elections of 1857 and 1859', D.Phil. thesis (Oxford University, 1980), fo.117.

[125] Cited in Jackson, 'Elections of 1857 and 1859', fo. 166.

[126] PSM, 9 Mar., 6 Apr. 1857.

lost seats

Huddersfield, lost his seat, as did Bell, Fox, Gibson, Miall, and several other prominent liberals who had supported his motion. So too did Bright, despite having been too ill to vote for Cobden's motion, or indeed to campaign on his own behalf, though he was to be returned for Birmingham at a by-election four months later. However, Hindley—who had 'become enfeebled, both in mind and body' and ceased to 'exhibit, in his public conduct, the firmness and decision which his friends could have wished', as his pacifist colleagues candidly admitted after his death later in the year—saved himself from defeat by having abstained on the Cobden–Gibson motion on the grounds that 'the Tories were making it a party question'.[127]

At the Peace Society's annual meeting of members the following month the chairman understandably denied that those who had lost their seats had done so 'on account of their peace views', and blamed 'local influence' instead. It was true that there was considerable variation from constituency to constituency: some of Cobden's supporters, notably Hadfield and J. B. Smith, were re-elected; and the peace party was afforced by the entry into parliament of Sturge's nephew Charles Gilpin, a loyal supporter of the League of Universal Brotherhood. But Cobden was convinced that 'the most warlike returns have come from the most popular constituencies'[128]—the reverse of his analysis of the 1852 general election. And Richard also took the view that 'the people of England have pronounced against a policy of peace, and in favour of a policy of war'.[129] Moreover, the most detailed historical study of the campaign has suggested that, despite varying local conditions, the election had only the one issue, the Bowring affair.[130] The contest was thus symbolized by the defeat in Southwark of Apsley Pellatt, a long-standing supporter of the peace movement, by Admiral Sir Charles Napier, a long-standing critic who had commanded Britain's Baltic fleet before becoming a politician. The lesson of the 1857 general election was thus that the peace movement should be cautious. For that reason the Peace Society's meeting of members on 19 May 1857, which ratified the take-over of the League of Universal Brotherhood, declined to adopt Dornbusch's suggestion that it embark on a disarmament campaign.[131]

lesson of caution

However, the Indian mutiny soon showed that the peace movement was still capable of taking a courageous stand. While refusing to condone an act of violence, the *Herald of Peace* interpreted the mutiny as another harmful consequence of the Crimean War, 'though the time may not yet have come for

[127] *HP* (June 1857), 214; (Feb. 1858), 23.
[128] Cobden to Richard, 13 Apr. 1857: Cobden Papers Add. MS. 43,659 fo. 303.
[129] *HP* (May 1857), 193; (June 1857), 209.
[130] Jackson, 'Elections of 1857 and 1859', fos. 165–227.
[131] *HP* (June 1857), 209.

tracing that connection', like the financial crisis of the same year which 'brought so many proud commercial fabrics to the ground'.[132] As well as condemning 'the bitter British cry for vengeance' against the mutineers, which was 'so pitiless and furious as to have disgusted even those nations of the Continent whose military morality was supposed to be most lax and accommodating', the Peace Society blamed the mutiny on the coercive nature of British rule in India, citing the scriptural warning: 'They who take the sword shall perish by the sword'. It also demanded 'an end, once for all, and once for ever, to that system of annexation and conquest so insanely and iniq-uitously pursued in India'.[133] The peace movement's anti-imperialist stand widened the gulf between it and mainstream evangelicalism: for example, Cobden, himself once sympathetic towards that religious tendency, now wanted to ask 'so-called Evangelical Christians . . . point blank who told them that God gave us India in trust for religious purposes'.[134]

Sturge originally hoped to undertake a mission of reconciliation to India, but settled instead for a Conference of the Friends of Peace in Manchester on 13 November 1857, to coincide with a temperance convention in that city. A 'strictly private' occasion, organized by Richard in his capacity as secretary of the London Peace Conference Committee and attended by two dozen men from different parts of the country, this gathering decided in favour of a national campaign on the Indian question.[135] Fry, O'Neill, and Stokes lectured widely on this subject for the Peace Society or the Peace Conference Committee, as did Wilks under other auspices: all reported attentive audiences; and O'Neill's widely diffused placard 'Vengeance on India' was claimed to have had a particular effect on public opinion.[136] Even Dr John Campbell joined in the condemnation of British repression in India, leading to his being praised at the Peace Society's 1858 public meeting by the same speaker, Jabez Burns, who on the same occasion three years previously had vilified him for his endorsement of the Crimean War. This rehabilitation may have encouraged Campbell to reappear on the platform at the 1859 meeting.[137]

However, the Manchester meeting had drawn attention to the decline of local peace activism in the face of recent setbacks. The moribundity of the Manchester Peace Conference Committee in the aftermath of Bright's general-election defeat was particularly remarked upon.[138] A special joint meeting between the Peace Society and the London Peace Conference

[132] *HP* (Jan. 1858), 6–7.
[133] *HP* (Sept. 1857), 244, 246; (Jan. 1858), 7; (Feb. 1858), 18.
[134] Cobden to Richard, 8 Jan. 1858: Cobden Papers Add. MS 43,659 fo. 3.
[135] PSM, 5 Oct. 1857. *HP* (Dec. 1857), 276.
[136] *HP* (June 1858), 62–3.
[137] *HP* (June 1858), 70; (June 1859), 212.
[138] PCCM, 27 Nov. 1857.

Committee decided to send a deputation to George Wilson and his colleagues in Manchester on 20–1 July 1858, as a result of which it was decided to create a new body uniting the ailing local Peace Conference Committee with the Peace Society's own followers in the town (whose separate auxiliary, active in the early 1840s, had latterly been subordinated first to the League of Universal Brotherhood, because of the early bond Burritt had forged with Manchester's leading Quakers, and then to the Peace Conference Committee). A circular launching a new 'Manchester Peace Conference and Arbitration Committee', with Stokes as its secretary, was issued on 22 September.[139] Within a year, however, the new organization was reported to be 'not in a very flourishing condition' and urgently in need of a contribution from London towards Stokes's salary; and in 1860 it was to become an auxiliary of the Peace Society.[140] The Peace Conference Committee in London, whose existence as a body distinct from the Peace Society had long been an increasingly hollow pretence, was allowed to lapse at this time.[141] In 1858 the Peace Society, whose auxiliaries mostly enjoyed only a nominal existence, suffered a fall in its subscriptions and donations to their lowest level since the society's first decade. It was thus in a desperate effort to stimulate local activism and recruit 'younger men' that Richard and Sturge led delegations to the main towns of Lancashire and Yorkshire during the second half of 1858 and the early months of 1859.[142]

Sturge's devotion of such a large proportion of his fading energies to trying to mobilize the regions on behalf of the London committee marked the completion of his transition from the Peace Society's provincial gadfly into its national elder, which had been symbolized by his election in May 1858 as president of the society in succession to Hindley. However, he enjoyed the honour for less than a year, dying while preparing to attend the May 1859 meetings of the Society of Friends and the Peace Society. Not only did British philanthropy and moral protest thereby lose perhaps their most remarkable proponent ever: the peace movement was deprived of a figure crucial alike to its finances, to its relations with the Society of Friends, and to its sense of purpose. Sturge's legacy of £450 to the Peace Society[143] was no substitute for the regular subventions he had provided: indeed, much of the society's effort in the coming year was devoted to seeking financial pledges from other

---

[139] Minutes, Special Meeting of Peace Conference Committee and Peace Society, 20 Apr. 1858. PSM, 9 Aug. 1858. *HP* (Aug. 1858), 95–6; (Oct. 1858), 117–18.

[140] Richard to Stokes, 27 Oct., 4 Nov. 1859: PSLB. PCCM, 14 Oct. 1859. PSM, 24 Oct. 1859, 20 Aug. 1860.

[141] The meeting of 14 Oct. 1859 was the last recorded in its minute book.

[142] PSM, 6 Dec. 1858. *HP* (June 1858), 66; (Apr. 1859), 190–1.

[143] PSM, 11 July 1859.

members, almost all of them Quakers, to fill the financial gap left by Sturge's death.

Sturge's moral authority in the Society of Friends was reflected in the London Yearly Meeting's decision in 1859, as a posthumous tribute, to implement his recommendation that distinctive Quaker dress become optional.[144] A combination of the sect's numerical decline and its growing worldly success had produced strong internal pressure to moderate its traditional peculiarities; and in 1860 expulsion for marrying a non-Quaker—a fate which had for example overtaken Elizabeth Pease, a pacifist with Garrisonian sympathies who belonged to one of the sect's grandest families, as recently as 1853[145]—was ended.

No change was proposed to the peace testimony, on which Sturge had been an unbending traditionalist; but it was in any case beginning to be repudiated by a minority of members. One Quaker claimed in 1859 to 'have conversed with numbers of [his co-religionists], who, while actively engaged in the affairs of the Society, justify war'.[146] Some of these were prepared to do so publicly. For example, one inquired in a Quaker periodical: 'What would become of England and her numerous dependencies if she were tomorrow to adopt the ultra-peace sentiments, and all at once to disband her army and navy?', and criticized the 'impracticality of Friends' views on the subject of peace'.[147] Quakers began to expect backsliding on this issue: by 1861 an elderly member of Society of Friends who remained true to its 'peaceable principles' found the fact there were only 'a few' dissenters from the peace testimony among his young colleagues a matter for rejoicing.[148] With hindsight, the start of the slow and silent erosion of Quaker pacifism can be traced back to the late 1850s. Given the overlap of membership, this erosion was to have serious long-term consequences for the Peace Society, as will be seen.

Sturge took just over a year to be replaced as the Peace Society's president: it was not until June 1860 that Joseph Pease, who in 1832 had become the first Quaker MP, accepted the office.[149] However, this proved a sound long-term choice, since his family was to shoulder the burden of the presidency until 1903 and again from 1911 to 1914. However, Sturge was never fully replaced as a driving force, despite the valiant efforts of the Peases or such weighty and loyal Quaker manufacturers as John Priestman of Bradford, who acknowl-

---

[144] Isichei, *Victorian Quakers*, 159.

[145] A. M. Stoddart, *Elizabeth Pease Nichol* (1899), 179, 185–7. For her pacifist career see Ceadel, *Origins of War Prevention*, 316–20, 323, 474.

[146] S. Fothergill, *Essay on the Society of Friends: Being an Inquiry into the Causes of their Diminished Influence and Numbers* (1859), 180.

[147] *British Friend* (Feb. 1859), 47–8.

[148] *Private Memoirs of B. and E. Seebohm, Edited by their Sons* (1873), 401.

[149] PSM, 18 June 1860.

edged 'a special sense of obligation' towards the Peace Society following Sturge's death,[150] and Edward Smith of Sheffield. The burden of giving direction to the society now fell almost exclusively onto Richard, as was reflected in the 'somewhat unusual' resolution of 'gratitude and confidence' with which 'the Secretary and the Committee' were honoured at the 1860 meeting of members.[151] Richard showed considerable resilience at this time. Having joined the Peace Society when its prospects were buoyant, he had been dispirited by its subsequent decline; and, as a colleague was later to acknowledge, it was not surprising 'that there were times when he was somewhat cast down'.[152] In addition, the demands and power struggles of the *Morning Star* had dented his self-confidence. His health had suffered: taking a water-cure at Malvern in the autumn of 1858 he was to report to his brother that, despite being 'in better spirits than . . . for years', he had 'not lost the symptoms in the head, though . . . they are less frequent and less violent than they were last year'.[153] He was sustained not only by his deep religious faith but by his intuition that the worldly lessons of the Crimean War were gradually being learned.

As it thus reconciled itself to being once again a mere pilot light, keeping the cause of peace alive until the public again became more receptive, the Peace Society came under renewed pressure to be less absolutist and thereby cast its net more widely. Its pacifism had come under increased scrutiny since the end of the Crimean War as sympathizers felt able to pose the fundamental question about the practical consequences of a policy of non-resistance to which even some Quakers now sought an answer.[154] Prompted by a correspondent, Richard offered a somewhat overdue reply in two *Herald of Peace* editorials on 'The Safety of Peace Principles'. He admitted that 'going unarmed' would not itself 'afford any guarantee of security' for a nation which had previous practised 'long indulgence in sin', but insisted that a nation which had shown habitual regard for 'the obligations of Christianity in its conduct towards other nations . . . might without armed defence trust to the influence of its principles and the protection of Providence, even though surrounded by those that are armed'. His argument was thus two-pronged. The first was that over time Christian behaviour had an pacifying effect on neighbouring countries. The second was an appeal to 'Providence', albeit the

---

[150] As noted after Priestman's own death in 1866: *HP* (June 1867), 205.

[151] *HP* (June 1860), 69.

[152] *HP* (July 1867), 232.

[153] H. Richard to E. Richard, 1 Oct. 1858: Richard Papers NLW MS 14020D.

[154] See various letters under the name 'Pacificus' in the *Friend*: (June 1856), 109; (Oct. 1859), 188; (Nov. 1859), 208–9. See also the responses in *HP* (Nov. 1859), 268–70; (Dec. 1859), 280–2.

general providence of beneficent moral laws rather than the particular providence of miraculous rescue. Richard criticized 'man's propensity . . . to attach
exaggerated importance to physical miracles', emphasized the 'calm reliance
of God upon moral in preference to physical power in the accomplishment of
his own purposes', and argued that because God had the power to impose his
will upon his creation but chose not to, that creation must be deeply imbued
with its own capacity to reward good: 'If he [God] deigns to govern the world
by its means, we may be quite sure that it [the world] is profoundly in
harmony with the deepest principles on which the moral constitution of the
universe rest, and must therefore possess a mighty and mysterious energy,
before which all other forms of power must succumb.'[155] This approach was
immanentist rather than transcendental: it saw God as ever present within the
'secular' world rather than making occasional interventions from outside.
Indeed, Richard was later explicitly to assert: 'God *never* overrules the natural
operation of the moral laws he has established for the government of the
world.'[156] He was thus an early expositor of a theological liberalism which
was to become increasingly widespread among Protestants in the late nineteenth and early twentieth centuries.

The Peace Society's theological liberalism explains why Unitarians were
more at ease with it during the second half of the nineteenth century than during
the first. This was despite the fact that, as their rationalist approach had become
widespread within most Christian churches, Unitarians had declined as a distinct
denomination. It was also despite the fact that the Peace Society was careful not
to offend its trinitarian mainstream: as late as 1878 the *Herald of Peace* inserted
'the word "Lord" before the Saviour's name' in an article by a prominent
Unitarian contributor so as 'to avoid offence to the religious sensibilities of the
generality of our readers'. It was perhaps to compensate for this behaviour that
the importance to the peace cause of the 'intelligent Christian denomination of
Unitarians' was handsomely acknowledged the following year.[157]

However, although theological liberalism was gaining ground, it normally
led to liberal *pacificism* rather than pacifism. Even within the Peace Society,
Richard's conviction that the secular world was already invested with a
'mysterious energy' that would protect a non-resisting country was far from
universally shared. Some members favoured a revival of an umbrella organization like the Peace Conference Committee, on the grounds that such an
association would tap support which the Peace Society, being widely
regarded as utopian, could not. In particular, a prominent Quaker from York,
Joseph Rowntree, suggested to the Peace Society's executive committee in

155 *HP* (June 1857), 210–11: see also (May 1857), 198–9.
156 *HP* (Sept. 1862), 102–3.
157 *HP* (Aug. 1878), 109; (July 1879), 274; (Aug. 1879), 285.

August 1860 that it create 'a system of correspondence and cooperation throughout the country on the Peace Congress principle with a view to secure aid on practical questions connected with the Peace Movement from persons who though sympathizing with the general policy may not be prepared to adopt the full Christian position as held by the Society'.[158] Rowntree repeated his suggestion at a Conference of the Friends of Peace in London on 4 February 1861, which had been convened mainly to discuss a campaign for the simultaneous reduction of armaments; but it was merely referred back to the Peace Society.[159] There was some support for Rowntree's idea: at a private *Conversazione* during June 1862 in the Bedford Square home of the celebrated Quaker physician who had discovered Hodgkin's disease, Dr Thomas Hodgkin, both Richard and Chamerovzow argued for a revival of the Peace Conference Committee in order to make a broad-based protest against bloated armaments.[160]

The real need, of course, was for *pacificists* to take the lead in creating such a body. However, as previously, neither Cobden nor Bright was prepared to do so. Cobden had taken up the armaments issue during 1861 in belated fulfilment of his promise of five years previously; but he held to the view that a campaign which could draw only on 'names that are already known to be of our sect' was pointless.[161] He had therefore asked Samuel Morley, a wealthy London hosiery manufacturer and evangelical Congregationalist, to promote a pro-disarmament petition, insisting that it was 'of the utmost importance' that this 'should emanate from the "bankers, merchants and others of the City," and not from the Peace Society or the "Manchester School" '; but, receiving no response because Morley was preoccupied with currency reform instead, he at once became discouraged. Cobden was also prepared to lend his name to the 'Arbitration Committee' which was contemplated during the acute Anglo-American crisis over the *Trent*, the British ship from which early in the American Civil War the federal government seized two confederate agents in November 1861; but the United States climbed down before this could be formed.[162] He also initially backed the Peace Society's idea of holding a peace congress during a second Great Industrial Exhibition in London in 1862,[163] though when the time came he was recuperating in Scotland and unwilling to take part.

---

[158] PSM, 20 Aug. 1860. [159] *HP* (Mar. 1861), 165.
[160] *HP* (July 1862), 76–7.
[161] Cobden to Richard, 16 Apr. 1862: Cobden Papers Add MS 43,659 fos. 171–2.
[162] Cobden to Richard, 4 Feb., 17 Apr., 18 Dec. 1861, 30 Jan. 1862, cited in Hobson, *Richard Cobden*, 282–3, 286, 288, 294, 300. Cobden to Morley, 8 Nov. 1861, cited in E. Hodder, *The Life of Samuel Morley* (3rd edn., 1887), 151–2.
[163] PSM, 14 Oct. 1861.

Bright remained preoccupied with franchise reform, and even on that issue was losing faith in pacific methods to such an extent that by 1866—the year before a suffrage extension was eventually achieved—he was to use the menacing argument that, 'however much we may wish political questions to be settled by moral means, yet it is not more immoral for the people to use force in the last resort, for the obtaining and securing of freedom, than it is for the government to use force to suppress and deny that freedom'.[164] When asked to attend a peace congress in 1862, he bluntly refused any longer to 'cast pearls before swine'.[165] Without his or Cobden's participation the Peace Society concluded that there was 'no prospect of holding a Conference with any probability of success'.[166] However, the society's 'Address to Foreign Visitors', and its *Conversazione*, already mentioned, in Dr Hodgkin's home, 'at which a considerable number of foreign gentlemen assisted', served as partial substitutes.[167]

Left as the sole organized expression of the peace movement, the Peace Society experienced a curious mixture of discouragement and encouragement. The principal discouragement was Britain's sharpening appetite for imperial expansion. As the *Herald of Peace* put it at the start of 1859:

The constant policy of aggression carried out by combined cunning and violence, the plunder of Indian provinces; wars like those carried on in Afghanistan, in Scinde, in Burmah, in Persia, in China; annexations like those of Sattara and Oude; a traffic like that in opium; punishments so sweeping and ferocious as those inflicted on the Indian mutineers—is there any man amongst us who doubts that if such things had been told us of Russia, France, or America, we should have poured upon their heads an instant execration?[168]

The Peace Society continued to condemn further imperialist acts, most notably a third China war in 1859, the punitive destruction of the Japanese city of Kagosima in 1863,[169] and the suppression, using means 'beyond all bounds of justice or necessity', of the Jamaican rebellion of 1865.[170]

The second discouragement was the arms race. In the words of the Peace Society's annual report for 1859–60: 'It is obvious that what jeopardises the peace of Europe more than any other cause—more than all other causes combined—is that system of rivalry in armaments with which the great governments menace each others, amid perpetual professions of amity and

[164] J. Bright, *Speeches on Parliamentary Reform, & c.* (Manchester, n.d.[1866]), 20.
[165] Bright to Richard, 16 Apr. 1862: PSLB.
[166] PSM, 5 June 1852.
[167] PSM 7 and 21 July 1862. *HP* (June 1863), 205.
[168] *HP* (Jan. 1859), 145.
[169] PSM, 7 Nov. 1863.
[170] *HP* (Jan. 1866), 4.

friendship.'[171] In insular Britain defencists still needed panics about France's supposedly aggressive intentions to mobilize public support. In 1859 they exploited rumours of a Franco-Russian alliance to produce a Volunteer rifle-corps movement, which was encouraged by Tennyson's new poem, 'Riflemen form!',[172] but resented by peace lecturers as an intermittent source of disturbances at their otherwise orderly meetings.[173] The Peace Society made gestures of goodwill towards France: it went to considerable efforts in June 1860 to ensure a welcome a French working-men's choir, the Orphéonists; and it issued a friendly address to the people of France which was taken to Paris in April 1861 by Richard and Joseph Cooper, a Quaker hat-manufacturer who had worked closely with Sturge in the anti-slavery movement, where it was published in a number of newspapers.[174] The fear of a French invasion lasted until 1861, and reminded Cobden of the scares of 1847–8 and 1852–3: the one fruit of his return to the armaments issue in 1861 was his pamphlet *The Three Panics*, which, delayed ironically by the *Trent* crisis, had little impact when it finally appeared in April 1862. It had been written with information supplied by Richard, who devoted much of the *Herald of Peace* at this time to the financial burden of armaments.[175] Indeed, in the early 1860s the Peace Society often sounded as keen on retrenchment as on peace.

Of encouragement to the peace movement, however, was that arbitration was gaining wider acceptance, even if only for settling other people's disputes. Richard was struck by 'the singular unanimity with which all speakers did homage to arbitration as a safeguard against war' during the parliamentary discussion of the Franco-Portuguese dispute in 1859. He was careful to praise the contribution of Charles Buxton, son of the ultra-moderate, Quaker-descended, anti-slavery campaigner Sir Thomas Fowell Buxton, though Cobden privately saw him as 'a chip off the old block' and despaired of his inherited Whiggish caution.[176]

Even more encouraging for peace activists was the gradual decline of crusading sentiment. This first became apparent during Napoleon III's and Cavour's wars of 1859–61 to liberate Italy from Austrian rule. In the run-up

---

[171] *HP* (June 1860), 63.

[172] D. Beales, *England and Italy 1859–60* (1961), 65–7. See also I. W. F. Beckett, *Riflemen Form: A Study of the Rifle Volunteer Movement 1850–1908* (Aldershot, 1982).

[173] *HP* (June 1861), 195; (June 1862), 65.

[174] PSM, 25 and 29 June 1860; 5 and 22 Apr. 1861. *HP* (June 1861), 193–4, 197. Richard Diary, 9–12 Apr. 1861: NLW MS 10200A.

[175] *HP* (Sept. 1859), 244–6; (Apr. 1860), 42–4; (Sept. 1860), 97–8; (Jan. 1861), 133–4; (Apr. 1861), 169–72; (Nov. 1861), 255–6; (July 1862), 79–80.

[176] *HP* (Apr. 1859), 181. Cobden to Richard, 1 Feb. 1864: Cobden Papers Add. MS 43,659 fos. 292–3.

to the May 1859 general election, the Peace Society campaigned uninhibit-edly for non-intervention, and was pleased that Palmerston felt constrained to moderate his anti-Austrian stance.[177] This election was followed in June by the creation of a united Liberal Party which, though under Palmerston's lead-ership, embraced not only Peelites such as Gladstone but also some Cobdenites. Cobden himself, who had been returned unopposed for Rochdale while away in the United States, was offered a cabinet post by Palmerston, but declined on the grounds that for 'the past twelve years' he had been 'the systematic and consistent assailant' of the Palmerstonian approach to foreign policy. Bright was passed over, apparently because his attacks on the aristoc-racy made him unacceptable to Queen Victoria.[178] But Gibson and Gilpin agreed to serve.

Although Palmerston was more constrained than formerly, the Peace Society felt obliged to remind 'the friends of liberty' that it was 'as vain to attempt to destroy despotism and establish freedom by war, as it is to cast out devils by Beelzebub the prince of the devils'. The society also participated in a big meeting at Exeter Hall on 30 June 1859 and in a deputation to Palmerston twelve days later, both of which argued for 'strict non-interven-tion' by Britain.[179] However, the Liberal government acted in a prudent fash-ion: Gladstone, its Chancellor of the Exchequer, encouraged Cobden to negotiate his celebrated commercial treaty with his French colleague Chevalier; and in the Italian crisis Palmerston restricted himself to moral interventionism. Acknowledging late in 1860 that the 'sentiment of non-inter-vention . . . has of late made very considerable, not to say rapid, progress', Richard claimed that this was 'mainly attributable to the silent operation of the Peace Society'.[180] He was obviously and understandably exaggerating the peace movement's contribution: suspicion of France had played at least as big a role as principled non-interventionism; and the triumph of the Italian cause without British military help made crusading unnecessary. None the less, the peace movement's long-standing insistence that war was an ineffective polit-ical instrument must have had some effect on public attitudes.

Britain's non-intervention in the Italian wars was followed by the same policy during the American Civil War which broke out in April 1861. Despite considerable unemployment in Lancashire as a result of the North's blockade of the South's cotton exports, most working men did not contest this decision. Moreover, despite widespread British resentment at the North's boarding of the *Trent*, many Nonconformist churches supported the Peace Society's call

---

[177]   PSM, 11 Apr., 2 May 1859. Beales, *England and Italy*, 70–1, 164
[178]   Morley, *Life of Richard Cobden*, ii. 230. Robbins, *John Bright*, 146–7.
[179]   *HP* (Aug. 1859), 229, 238–9.
[180]   *HP* (Dec. 1860), 125–6.

for arbitration.[181] Although their transatlantic denominational links gave them a particular motive for avoiding war in this case, their response was particularly gratifying in view of a previous Nonconformist susceptibility to crusading which had caused an unusually downcast Sturge to tell the Peace Society's 1856 public meeting that he 'had met with more clergymen of the Church of England who sympathized with peace principles than he had met with Dissenting ministers'.[182] Indeed, the *Trent* affair marked the start of a reconciliation between Nonconformity and *pacifism*.

None the less, the Peace Society regarded the American Civil War as a cruel disappointment. It had initially hoped to avert the conflict; but its first address to the American people was overlooked because the fighting broke out before the document could be sent across the Atlantic;[183] and a second in the autumn of 1862, aimed at American Christians and suggesting mediation by a European country, 'awoke very little favourable response'.[184] Thereafter, the society was upset by the extent to which progressive opinion on both sides of the Atlantic lauded the Northern war effort. The American Peace Society, already accustomed because of its arguments with the Garrisonians to emphasizing the legitimacy of the domestic police power, now presented the federal government's action as an exercise of that power. For their part, the Garrisonians, though previously wanting the Southern states to secede in the belief that this would lead to their collapse, presented it as an anti-slavery crusade ('God's hand is in it')[185] even though as professed pacifists they declined to take part personally; and in Britain their old ally Thompson, who had returned from India, and his son-in-law Chesson did the same.[186] Bright also supported the North, arguing privately in 1863: 'I want no end of the war, and no compromise, and no reunion until the negro is made free beyond all chance of failure.'[187] And although Cobden was unwilling to go so far, his approval of the anti-slavery cause placed him in a moral dilemma which he concealed by invoking the lesson of the Crimean War: it was futile to comment on any conflict in progress.[188]

[181] See in particular the list of petitions to Palmerston in *HP* (Mar. 1862), 34.
[182] *HP* (June 1856), 71.   [183] PSM, 1 Apr. 1861. *HP* (June 1861), 197.
[184] PSM, 3 Nov. 1862. *HP* (June 1863), 209.
[185] Van der Linden, *International Peace Movement*, 537.
[186] Temperley, *British Antislavery*, 252–6.
[187] Cited in E. W. Orr, *The Quakers in Peace and War 1920 to 1967* (Eastbourne, 1974), 13. See also Robbins, *John Bright*, 161–8.
[188] He used this argument repeatedly: see Cobden to Charles Sumner, 27 Nov. 1861, in Hobson, *Richard Cobden*, 342; Cobden to Richard, 12 Oct. 1862: Cobden Papers Add. MS 43,659 fo. 306; and *Speeches on Questions of Public Policy by Richard Cobden, MP*, ed. J. Bright and J. Thorold Rogers (2 vols., 1870), ii. 314 (speech at Rochdale, 29 Oct. 1862). Cobden's thinking at this time is well analysed in van der Linden, *International Peace Movement*, 553–5.

Richard knew that he was offending many of his friends when he argued the pacifist case. He countered the American Peace Society's insistence that 'when in former times they protested against war, they meant only war between nations' with the assertion that the characteristics which made war objectionable not only applied to civil war but did so 'with far greater emphasis than . . . even to international war'.[189] He met the Garrisonian claim that the war was divinely ordained with the retort: 'How do they know it is of God? Is it simply because it has happened? Why, then, slavery is also of God.' He denied that the North was motivated primarily by anti-slavery feeling, claiming that 'the great bulk of the men who are know swelling the war cry, and rushing into the ranks to fight, are those who despise the "nigger" and hate the Abolitionists as cordially as ever'.[190] And he insisted instead that the North's 'moving impulse' was 'the preservation of the Union, the Constitution of 1787, the insult offered to the American flag'—in other words, 'the *status quo ante bellum*'.[191]

With many colleagues rejecting this analysis, Richard's mood became unwontedly tetchy: he accused those who still insisted that 'the war is of God' of exhibiting the 'singular propensity' of men, 'sometimes under the influence of a weak, sentimental pietism, to father their own crimes and those of their fellow men on the Supreme', and complained 'how few persons have the courage to adhere consistently to a principle through evil report and good report'.[192] Privately, he even wondered in a letter to a Quaker who had come out in support of the Northern cause

whether the best thing would not be to dissolve the [Peace] Society altogether. Every new war that arises detaches us from some class of our friends, as this American War seems to have detached you and John Bright. If things go on so, I expect to find myself at last standing alone in the full maintenance of principle. I am, I own, deeply discouraged and strongly tempted to throw the whole thing up.[193]

Not surprisingly, the 'wear and tear of mind, the heartbreaking discouragement' affected Richard's health during 1862–3, causing 'symptoms of the return of my old plagues'.[194]

The American Civil War not only reduced its secretary to near-despair: it brought two additional difficulties for the Peace Society. First, despite the constancy of its pacifism, it was accused of partiality towards the Northern cause, its executive committee expressing its disquiet at 'the frequent charges

[189] *HP* (May 1862), 59.   [190] *HP* (June 1861), 199–201.

[191] *HP* (Aug. 1861), 222–5; (Nov. 1861), 258–9.

[192] *HP* (Sept. 1862), 102; (Nov. 1862), 130–1.

[193] Richard to C. Sturge, 18 Dec. 1862, cited in A. Tyrrell, 'Making the Millenium [sic]: The Mid-Nineteenth Century Peace Movement', *Historical Journal*, 21 (1978), 75–95 at 95.

[194] Richard to H. E. Gurney, 17 Jan. 1862; Richard to J. Cooper, undated [1863]: PSLB.

made against the Society of having encouraged or connived at the American war'.[195] Admittedly, some of its most loyal supporters wanted it to abandon strict neutrality: for example, the long-serving Unitarian secretary of the Liverpool Peace Society, Isaac B. Cooke, urged it to 'soothe the wounded feelings of the Americans' by at least acknowledging that 'the war was commenced by the South'.[196] Second, the conflict raised the question of how pacifism was to be defined. Some members of the Peace Society claimed that its rejection of war should not apply to 'a process of justice against criminals'. Thus a Quaker speaker at a Conference of the Friends of Peace in Manchester on 10 January 1865 insisted: 'If government is to be maintained, rebellion must be suppressed', prompting Cooke to concede that 'the principle of the inviolability of human life would be a sounder principle on which to base the doctrines of the Peace Society than the one now adopted'.[197] In other words, though Britain's pacifists had already come across no-killing and no-government as well as no-war viewpoints, they were disconcerted by the problem of line-drawing as presented by the American Civil War, which was larger in scale and more ferocious in quality than many international military conflicts, yet on one constitutional reading was merely a police action against rebels, and on one moral reading was directed towards a uniquely just act of domestic reform, the emancipation of the slaves.

In principle, the war also raised intellectual difficulties for one strand of liberal-*pacificist* thinking by showing that the federal union created by the American states was no guarantee of peace. But although Cobden regarded it as 'truly an awful reverse for our peace principles to see the Federation principle provide no safeguard against war, in its most gigantic proportion',[198] most *pacificists* as yet believed that arbitration could succeed without being backed by supranational institutions. And the North's eventual success in preserving the union limited the damage which the civil war could do to the federal principle.

More encouragingly for the Peace Society, during 1863–4 crises over Poland and Schleswig-Holstein passed off without British military intervention. Sympathy for the Polish uprising of 1863—expressed for example in Congregationalist minister R.W. Dale's crusading claim to a town's meeting in Birmingham that Britain 'shall never shrink from using' both its army and its fleet 'in behalf of justice and freedom wherever our national duty and our national honour require'[199]—led the Peace Society to warn progressive opinion

---

[195] PSM, 11 Sept. 1863.   [196] *HP* (Oct. 1863), 262–3.
[197] *HP* (Feb. 1865), 162, 166–7.
[198] Cobden to Richard, 20 Sept. 1863: Cobden Papers Add. MS 43,659 fos. 235–6.
[199] Cited in A. W. Dale, *The Life of R. W. Dale of Birmingham* (1898), 253.

against expecting the British to be 'the Quixotes of universal humanity', and to condemn the 'small clique of sentimental fanatics' that favoured a crusade. However, it abandoned a memorial 'praying the Government to adhere strictly to the principle of non-intervention' after a 'wise, temperate, statesmanlike speech' by the Foreign Secretary, Russell, indicated that the government did not want to risk war.[200] The Schleswig-Holstein crisis in 1864 caused Richard to condemn the 'idea of nationality' as 'a poor, low, selfish, unchristian idea, at variance with the very principle of an advanced civilisation'.[201] But once again Palmerston's and Russell's threat of intervention was a bluff, leading both Cobden and Bright to conclude that their non-interventionist principles had again triumphed.[202]

Nor, despite the obvious similarities between the two events, did Garibaldi's visit to Britain later in 1864 occasion the difficulties for the peace movement which Kossuth's had thirteen years previously. The post-Chartist generation of London working-class leaders competed to welcome the Italian military hero, and protested when his visit was cut short, apparently to spare the government embarrassment. Because Garibaldi had expressed support for international arbitration as a long-term goal once nations had won their freedom, the Peace Society presented him in as eirenic a light as possible. Edmund Fry even claimed in the *Herald of Peace* that 'the essentially distinguishing characteristics of the Italian patriot are those, not of a man of war, but a man of peace', forcing Richard to make clear that the Peace Society was none the less opposed to Garibaldi's use of military force.[203] The society planned to present Garibaldi with a specially bound volume of essays on the Congress of Nations, though he was spirited out of the country before it could do so.[204] Moreover, Cobden did not make the ambiguous claims for Garibaldi as a moral interventionist which he had for Kossuth. And Sturge was no longer alive to insist on a forthright condemnation of the visitor's military activities. This time, therefore, the peace movement avoided painful disunity.

At the end of 1864 the *Herald of Peace* gave an unusually optimistic title, 'Gradually Coming Right', to an article which noted that on a range of issues, including the futility of the Crimean War, public opinion had come round to its views, and expressed satisfaction that the Peace Society had not agreed to the suggestion of its 'professed friends' that its flag 'be for a time, if not altogether struck down, at least lowered to half mast'.[205]

[200] *HP* (May 1863), 194; (June 1863), 210–11; (Aug. 1863), 232–4. PSM, 4 May 1863.
[201] *HP* (Feb. 1864), 18.
[202] K. Bourne, *The Foreign Policy of Victorian England 1830–1902* (Oxford, 1970), 108–9. Van der Linden, *International Peace Movement*, 506.
[203] *HP* (May 1864), 53; (July 1864), 84.
[204] PSM, 9 May 1864.   [205] *HP* (Dec. 1864), 132.

It was therefore ironic that the society had by then run into financial troubles, arising largely from a reduction in support from the Gurney family[206]—an early warning of the financial difficulties which led to Overend & Gurney's spectacular crash in 1866—and causing Richard to lament that the society had 'never had a steady, regular income of £1,500 a year'. In the summer of 1863 it briefly employed an agent to collect subscriptions on its behalf: this was Lewis Appleton, a Quaker later to become notorious within the peace movement for his devious behaviour. Appleton's early efforts having proved unsuccessful,[207] the society faced a deficit of nearly £500 at the end of the 1863–4 financial year, and resorted to an appeal. Although letters were sent 'to only a very limited number' of targets,[208] their dispatch was delayed by the 'difficulty to find friends willing to back them with a few words of private application';[209] and without Charleton's loyal assistance the society would have been in real difficulty at the end of 1864.[210] Even so, redundancies were needed: it was partly 'to relieve the Society of some part of the financial pressure which now rests upon it' that Fry retired at this time, being rewarded with membership of the executive committee.[211] (He carried on lecturing, however, and in improved financial circumstances a year later was temporarily restored to the payroll.[212]) Early in 1865 a number of wealthier members of the Society of Friends were added to the executive committee,[213] their donations having become more important to the Peace Society than its need to play down its Quaker connections. One of them, the Reading tea merchant John Horniman, proved to be a major benefactor. The series of regular regional Conferences of the Friends of Peace which the society had launched with two gatherings at Manchester on 25 October 1864 and 10 January 1865 were also designed to attract further financial support, not only from former sympathizers whom the 'untoward' events of 'the last twelve years . . . had done much to discourage and disperse' but also from 'young persons, who have risen into manhood and womanhood since the events referred to'. Though attendance at these conferences was modest, the proportion of ministers taking part in them was taken as an encouraging sign.[214]

It was thus at a moment of modest ideological recovery yet considerable institutional precariousness for the peace movement that Cobden died on 2 April 1865. The Peace Society was gratified by the tributes posthumously

---

[206] PSM, 16 Dec. 1863, 17 June 1864.
[207] PSM, 3 June, 6 July, 7 Nov., 14 Dec. 1863. [208] *HP* (June 1865), 204.
[209] PSM, 13 Dec. 1864. [210] PSM, 9 Jan. 1865, 6 Mar. 1865,
[211] PSM, 13 Dec. 1864, 9 Jan. 1865. See also Burritt's obituary of Fry in *Bond of Brotherhood* (Jan. 1867), 8–9.
[212] PSM, 4 Dec. 1865. [213] PSM, 9 Jan., 3 Apr. 1865.
[214] *HP* (June 1865), 206–7.

paid to a politician who had taken on a full share in its unpopularity: indeed, the respect in which Cobden was held showed how deeply liberal *pacificism* had embedded itself in British political culture. But the society now needed Richard to take on Cobden's role as a statesman as well as replace Sturge as an institutional motivator. Richard was already gaining a reputation as a writer: his biography of Sturge had appeared in 1864; and he was the first choice of Cobden's widow to write her husband's life, though he eventually passed the task to John Morley. His standing in Welsh and Nonconformist circles also fitted him for a more ambitious public role. Within three months of Cobden's death he was invited to stand for Cardiganshire in the general election. The Peace Society's executive committee 'fully encouraged' him to accept, despite having refused Stokes permission to lecture 'on political Reform' only four years previously.[215] In the event Richard withdrew from the contest because of a disagreement with his local backers;[216] and he was not to become an MP for another three years.

Although expecting to take only a 'very moderate' interest in the 1865 election, because the Tories and Liberals 'resemble each other so closely' particularly in their military extravagance,[217] the *Herald of Peace* was pleasantly surprised by the 'totally different tone' of the campaigning compared with 1857 in particular, and by the emphasis which the Liberals placed both on non-intervention—which even the former crusader Joseph Cowen 'strongly' endorsed when put on the spot by the local peace association—and on the Cobden–Chevalier commercial treaty; and it singled out Gladstone's contribution for special praise.[218] Admittedly, on further reflection the Peace Society was depressed by Liberal failure to condemn imperial wars and repressions, and by the fact that 238 MPs in the new parliament were 'directly connected with some form of military service, and therefore personally interested in promoting a large military expenditure'[219]—a theme that thereafter featured strongly in its propaganda. But the society was pleased by the end of the American Civil War, despite a continuing Anglo-American crisis over the *Alabama*, a British-built ship which the Palmerston government had allowed to embark on a campaign against Northern shipping, and for which the United States claimed compensation. And it was relieved when Palmerston's death in October 1865 at long last removed 'a blustering, arrogant, dictatorial spirit'[220] from British public life.

In 1866 the Peace Society cautiously hoped that its period of adversity

[215] PSM, 3 Dec. 1861.
[216] PSM, 3 July, 11 Sept. 1865. *HP* (Aug. 1865), 238–9.
[217] *HP* (July 1865), 217.   [218] *HP* (Aug. 1865), 229, 237.
[219] *HP* (June 1866), 62–3.   [220] *HP* (Nov. 1865), 265.

was drawing to a close. Its agents were confident: Stokes reported that 'the year now closed has been by far the nearest approach to national recovery' since the Crimean War; and Fry commented on a 'very marked increase of sympathy and interest in the cause of Peace shown by ministers of the Gospel'.[221] The executive committee made a second experiment with Lewis Appleton as a collector, and this time, with the economy picking up, was 'gratified' by his early takings.[222] A more obvious sign of renewed hope was that the society made a renewed effort to stage another international peace congress. Burritt had been pressing for one, still believing that it could serve as an embryonic 'Congress of Nations'. After an absence of nearly eight years he had returned to Britain in 1863 to become United States consul in Birmingham,[223] though while the Civil War continued in his native land he limited his public utterances to pious generalities because, as the Peace Society's executive committee had noted when declining his earlier offer to lecture for it, 'no American would be listened to with much favour on the Peace Question' in view of 'the peculiar circumstances of his own country'.[224] Burritt's impatience was apparent at the 1866 meeting of members when he warned of 'a prevalent impression that the Peace Society was dead, or at least in a dying condition' and argued that 'a Congress of the eminent jurists of Europe . . . to discuss practical points of international law' and perhaps also to 'concoct an arrangement for a progressive and simultaneous disarmament' would show that it 'was still alive'.[225] The Peace Society had consulted its supporters about such a congress and found them to be favourable, but dropped the idea because of the 'dark clouds'[226] which were to produce the Austro-Prussian War on 15 June. It was partly consoled, however, by the brevity of the conflict and the non-interventionist policy adopted by Britain's Conservative Foreign Secretary Lord Stanley, the son and heir of Prime Minister Derby.

At its public meeting on 22 May the Peace Society was painfully reminded by an enthusiastic evangelical from the Young Men's Christian Association who spoke from the floor that it was ending its fifth decade still in 'a hole and corner' position. Its celebration of its half-century on 14 June 1866 was appropriately restrained: having posed the question 'What has been the result of this fifty years of propagandism of Peace?', its annual report replied: 'We cannot tell', and made no stronger claim than that the society had 'attained to the dignity of being abused', was 'not dead', and did 'not mean to die'.[227]

---

[221] *HP* (June 1866), 61–2. [222] PSM, 19 May, 6 Aug. 1866.
[223] P. Tolis, *Elihu Burritt: Crusader for Brotherhood* (Hamden, Conn., 1968), 273.
[224] PSM, 10 Mar. 1862. [225] *HP* (July 1866), 84.
[226] PSM, 9 Apr., 7 May 1866. *HP* (June 1866), 64; (Sept. 1866), 97.
[227] *HP* (June 1866), 65, 70.

During this decade and a half, the peace movement had demonstrated that it was not a temporary product of unusual circumstances, namely the exhaustion produced by the protracted French wars of 1793–1815 and the optimism produced by the long peace of 1815–54. Retaining its integrity in the teeth of the emotionalism needed to justify to the public an intervention in support of so remote a country, it survived, albeit much shaken, to enjoy in the short term modest rewards such as Protocol 23 of the Treaty of Paris and Cobden's defeat of Palmerston over the *Arrow* war, and in the longer term more substantial though less tangible rewards such as a growing disillusionment with the Crimean War and the avoidance of intervention by the British government. However, when the historian G. M. Trevelyan later claimed that but for the campaign against the Crimean War waged by Bright and others Britain might have fought for Austria in 1859, for the Confederacy in 1861, for Denmark in 1864, and in other wars,[228] he was allowing his own *pacifism* to run away with his academic judgement. Even so, it is clear that at the very least the continuous insistence by the leadership of the peace movement that non-intervention was a morally superior policy made it easier for governments to resist crusading and other calls for military engagement.

[228] G. M. Trevelyan, *Life of John Bright* (1913), 217.

4

Recovery,
January 1867–May 1882

From the beginning of 1867 the peace movement enjoyed a significant recovery which lasted for a decade and a half. It acquired continental counterparts for the first time in 1867; an extended franchise helped Henry Richard enter parliament the following year; and the Franco-Prussian War of 1870–1 not only prompted the establishment of a Workmen's Peace Association but stimulated interest in arbitration and the codification of international law among the growing ranks of intellectuals, academics, and 'the leading jurists of Christendom'.[1] The ensuing 'Armed Peace', as it came increasingly to be called,[2] between France and Germany kept these ideas to the fore; a revival of the Eastern Question in the second half of the 1870s generated a vigorous campaign against British intervention; and Gladstone seemed for a while thereafter to be turning his Liberal Party into a secondary peace association. This period marked Henry Richard's heyday: 'short, stout and somewhat prosaic' though he was in the opinion of the *Pall Mall Gazette*,[3] the Peace Society's secretary became a national figure, partly as 'a sort of representative Welshman'[4] and the 'chief representative in Parliament of the English [sic] Nonconformists',[5] but principally as the 'chief and most prominent international man since the death of Cobden'.[6]

However, 'Militaryism', as the *Herald of Peace* initially called it, and the doctrine of 'the survival of the fittest' both became matters of concern during the 1870s.[7] Peace activists had to face jingo violence over the Eastern Question and the Afghan Wars later in that decade. And the founding in 1880 of an additional society, the International Peace and Arbitration Association, proved controversial because of the devious behaviour of its principal organizer. Yet until the Egyptian crisis blew up in June 1882, the movement's recovery still seemed to be making steady progress.

---

[1] *HP* (Nov. 1873), 338.   [2] See e.g. *HP* (Mar. 1876), 30.
[3] Cited in *HP* (Sept. 1888), 113.
[4] Richard to Gladstone, 7 Aug. 1885: Richard Papers NLW MS 14022E.
[5] Miall, *Henry Richard*, 356.
[6] In the words of A. J. Mundella, MP, 26 May 1876: cited in *HP* (June 1876), 79.
[7] See respectively *HP* (Dec. 1872), 161; and (Apr. 1876), 59.

EUROPE, LIBERALISM, AND ARTISANS, 1867–1871

At the beginning of 1867 the *Herald of Peace* returned to its fiftieth-anniversary question: 'What has the Peace Society Done?'. Now, however, it offered an upbeat answer: it was 'no mean fruit' of the society's 'thousands of lectures and millions of tracts' that 'war, once so popular, is now ... studiously avoided as the greatest curse of mankind', that interventionist voices had fallen silent, and that 'that empty pretence "the balance of power" ... may now be fairly regarded as being dead and buried.'[8]

A reason for this more positive tone was that the society now expected within months to hold its first continental congress for a dozen years, timed to coincide with a Universal Exhibition in Paris. On a preliminary visit to the French capital Richard had been encouraged to seek Napoleon III's personal blessing;[9] and in February 1867 Richard, Cooper, and Henry Pease, with Chamerovzow as interpreter, were favoured with what they regarded as a very satisfactory interview with the French emperor.[10]

To their great disappointment, however, the permission which they had then been led to expect was not forthcoming. The French government had changed its mind, owing to a European crisis of Napoleon III's own making: to compensate for Prussia's gains from Austria the previous year, he tried to negotiate the French acquisition of Luxemburg, thereby incurring the displeasure of Prussia. Early in May the Luxemburg issue was resolved at a great-power conference in London, which was welcomed by Richard as 'a precedent which may be of the utmost value in the future' and by a speaker at the Peace Society's public meeting as 'the first that had averted war'.[11] Thus although the executive committee had to admit its failure as yet to arrange the expected peace congress, it could express the hope that 'now the question of Luxembourg was settled, the French authorities might be disposed to reconsider'.[12]

It could also identify encouraging developments which partially compensated for delays in Paris: a 'considerable improvement' in the society's finances, which enabled the committee to raise the salary of its secretary, who had just married at the age of 54, to £400 a year;[13] the first speech at its annual public meeting, albeit from the floor, by 'A Working Man', a sign of developing artisan interest in the peace movement at an opportune moment;

---

[8] *HP* (Feb. 1867), 157–8.
[9] PSM, 31 Jan. 1867.
[10] PSM, 25 Feb. 1867.
[11] *HP* (June 1867), 212, 214.
[12] *HP* (July 1867), 232: see also (May 1867), 198; (June 1867), 207.
[13] PSM, 1 Apr. 1867. Miall, *Henry Richard*, 145–6.

and the creation by the Social Science Association, a body founded in 1857 which had become a centre of progressive and academic thinking on a wide range of issues, of a committee to codify international law.[14]

In addition, the Luxemburg crisis itself had stimulated peace sentiment in France: interacting with promising developments in French politics (already reflected in the invitation to the Peace Society to attempt a congress the previous year), it had produced two *pacificist* associations in 1867: the Union de la paix, set up among the Freemasons of the trading port of Le Havre by a local editor, Félix Santallier; and the Ligue internationale et permanente de la paix (LIPP), formed in Paris by the liberal Frédéric Passy, which drew its main support from Protestants, Jews, and secularists. Though weakened by the hostility of mainstream Catholicism, these two bodies represented the first autonomous primary peace initiatives of any significance on the European continent, and were thus a considerable source of encouragement to the Peace Society, which, having tried to establish associations there in the past,[15] observed 'with more satisfaction than they can describe' the fact that for 'the first time, the *people* of the Continent of Europe have claimed the right to have a word to say' on 'the question of peace and war'.[16]

The Peace Society duly renewed its efforts to hold a Paris congress, Richard and Cooper returning to the city with a new memorial to the French government; but they found it courteously obdurate, this time on the grounds that a Paris congress 'would be taken advantage of to make a political demonstration',[17] and were therefore forced to drop the idea. They had also sought to forge links with the new French peace movement, but found it not only handicapped by the absence of the 'unbounded freedom of association and agitation' to which Britain had grown 'so accustomed' but also fragmented by the 'sense of individuality' on the part of 'each coterie' that caused Richard later to report to the American Peace Society that, for all their enthusiasm, the originators of the new French associations lacked 'the habit, or the experience that you and we have in forming and conducting voluntary societies'.[18]

The most dynamic of France's six strands of peace organization was a group led by Charles Lemonnier, a journalist and follower of the pioneering French socialist Saint-Simon,[19] which was in Richard's words 'founded on what may be called a Democratic basis'. It was therefore too left-wing both

[14] *HP* (June 1867), 206, 214–16. L. Goldman, 'The Social Science Association, 1857–1886: A Context for Mid-Victorian Liberalism', *English Historical Review*, (1986), 95–134.
[15] See Ceadel, *Origins of War Prevention*, 274, 352, 393.
[16] *HP* (June 1867), 209 (see also 217–20).
[17] PSM, 8 July 1867.
[18] *HP* (July 1867), 227. Van der Linden, *International Peace Movement*, 640.
[19] Van der Linden, *International Peace Movement*, 675–6.

for Passy's LIPP, which took the Cobdenite view that existing governments could establish peace through free trade, arbitration, and the reduction of armaments, and for the Peace Society, which feared that its congress 'would be taken advantage of to make a political demonstration'.[20] Lemonnier and his colleagues therefore held a congress on their own, outside French juris-diction, at Geneva on 9–12 September 1867. The Peace Society publicized this in a respectful manner, but declined to participate for fear that it would be 'too political'.[21] Instead it took part in a general conference in Amsterdam of the Evangelical Alliance, a Protestant body, but found itself unable to raise 'the question of Peace . . . because the people of Holland were full of suspi-cions as respects the aggressive designs of Prussia on their country'.[22]

Lemonnier's congress at Geneva justified the Peace Society's reserva-tions: indeed, the *Nonconformist* reported that 'the crazy-brained revolution-ists who attended its sittings' could not have hit on a 'surer way of playing into the hands of military despots'.[23] It installed Garibaldi as its honorary president; 'and the first thing he did . . . was to proclaim war—war to the knife against the Pope and the Papacy', as Richard noted in disbelief. Having 'no inconsiderable experience in the management of large meetings', Richard had urged Lemonnier and his fellow organizers to require all speak-ers to adhere to a 'definite programme', and was therefore critical when instead they produced 'a speculative and controversial anarchy'. Richard blamed this on their failure to understand that 'the right of free discussion, like every right, has certain restrictions and conditions without which it will infallibly run to seed, and bear no fruit'.[24] He was to be less censorious about the congress at Berne a year later, which Lemonnier reportedly conducted in 'a far more grave, temperate, and deliberative spirit'.[25] But after Victor Hugo took advantage of the presidency of his 1869 congress in Lausanne to call for 'one last' war in order to achieve 'eternal' peace, Richard was to ask exasperatedly: 'can anything be more transparently absurd than the maxim that some of them openly avow, that universal peace is to be attained through a universal war?'[26]

At his Geneva congress of September 1867, Lemonnier formed the Ligue internationale de la paix et de la liberté (LIPL), a name which could easily be mistaken for Passy's LIPP. (In consequence, when the latter was to relaunch itself in 1872, after being suppressed during the Franco-Prussian War, it did

---

[20] PSM, 8 July 1867. *HP* (July 1867), 227.   [21] PSM, 5 Aug. 1867.
[22] PSM, 14 Aug. 1867. *HP* (June 1868), 66.
[23] *Nonconformist* (18 Sept. 1867), 766.   [25] *HP* (Nov. 1868), 127.
[24] *HP* (Oct. 1867), 257.
[26] S. E. Cooper, *Patriotic Pacifism: Waging War on War in Europe, 1815–1914* (New York, 1991), 42. *HP* (Sept. 1869), 258–9.

so under the title Société française des amis de la paix, which the *Herald of Peace* usually translated as French Peace Society.) A further source of short-term muddle was the holding of a second political congress in Switzerland only days before Lemonnier's: this was the gathering at Lausanne on 2–9 September 1867 of the International Working Men's Association—Karl Marx's 'First International', which had been created in 1864. The leadership of the International Working Men's Association promoted an anti-capitalist critique, expressed in an amendment passed at Lausanne which blamed war on 'pauperism and the lack of economic balance' and called for 'a more equitable distribution of production', and therefore wished to distance itself from the LIPL's views, which were radical rather than socialist. However, many of its followers went straight from their own congress in Lausanne to the LIPL's at Geneva,[27] thereby causing the two congresses to become conflated in some people's minds.

With its volatile mixture of *pacificist*, crusading, and revolutionist initiatives, to which pacifists struggled to make appropriate responses, 1867 thus resembled 1847–8, albeit in a minor key. In Britain the momentous political development of 1867 was the Second Reform Act, which, by giving the vote to urban artisans, made working men the largest element in the electorate. The Peace Society was aware of the significance of this change, Richard having stressed 'the extreme importance of endeavouring to imbue the minds of the working men who are about to be enfranchised in such large numbers with right views on the subject of peace and war'.[28] As a belated replacement for Edmund Fry, who had died 'literally in his work' at a meeting in the Guildhall Coffee House on 7 December 1866,[29] it therefore chose the Congregationalist minister, W. H. Bonner, for being 'favourably known as an advocate of popular rights, and possessing an aptitude for addressing the masses', having already lectured for the Reform League, a radical organization pressing for manhood suffrage. (The London-based Bonner joined the Birmingham-based O'Neill and the Manchester-based Stokes.) The society was pleased when, in the autumn of 1867, 'an important movement for peace appeared spontaneously among the working-men of Birmingham'. O'Neill did his best to encourage this movement; and Burritt, whose experience of such activity went back twenty years, drafted fraternal addresses to the French and German peoples on its behalf.[30]

The following year the Peace Society gamely renewed its efforts to hold a continental peace congress. In April 1868 Richard and Cooper travelled to

[27] Van der Linden, *International Peace Movement*, 748.
[28] PSM, 5 Aug. 1867.
[29] PSM, 4 Dec. 1865, 10 Dec. 1866. *HP* (Jan. 1867), 150–1; (June 1867), 205.
[30] PSM, 5 Aug. 1867. *HP* (June 1868), 62–4.

Brussels, location of the first such congress exactly twenty years previously, but were again frustrated: they were warned by the Belgians of 'one great distinction . . . between the Continent and England', namely that continental Catholicism favoured standing armies and distrusted English religious pacifism as 'a Protestant movement and an attempt at proselytism in disguise'; and they were reminded of the 'old objection . . . that wild and violent spirits, especially from France, would take advantage of such a meeting to launch forth into political speculation and diatribes and fanatical attacks upon the Governments'.[31] The Peace Society therefore abandoned its efforts to hold a continental gathering. Even so, its annual report took a generally favourable view of trends of popular opinion in Europe, and in respect of those in Britain was so pleased by 'the rapidity and even apparent suddenness with which public opinion has matured' as to claim that 'success may be nearer than many imagine'.[32] Richard also noted with satisfaction in the spring of 1868 that it was now conceded 'on all sides'—albeit in many cases 'reluctantly and tacitly'—that the society had been 'in the right'when it had taken a stand against 'the Russian war, the French invasion panics, the duty of British intervention in foreign, and especially in continental quarrels, and the necessity and efficacy of large armaments for the security and peace of nations'.[33]

The Peace Society also intensified its efforts to mobilize the newly enfranchised British artisans, holding discussions with the Reform League in August 1868. This had evolved since the passing of the Second Reform Act into an organization for electing working men who would support the Liberal Party in parliament,[34] a 'Lib-Lab' strategy which the Peace Society liked. The Reform League's representatives at this meeting included its president, Edmond Beales, a barrister who was an evangelical Anglican as well as a political radical, and George Odger and Randal Cremer, both trade unionists who had been early activists in the International Working Men's Association and had attended the Lausanne and Geneva congresses the previous September.[35] For Cremer, this meeting with the Peace Society was an important stage in his transition from quarrelsome artisan activist to elder statesman of the peace movement: he was in 1903 to become the first Briton to win a Nobel Peace Prize and in 1907 the first professional peace campaigner to be knighted.[36] Beales, Odger, and Cremer had all supported the Northern cause

[31] Richard Diary, 14–19 Apr. 1868: NLW MS 10205B.

[32] HP (June 1868), 67.

[33] HP (June 1868), 68–9.

[34] A. D. Bell, 'The Reform League from its Origins to the Reform Act of 1867', D.Phil. thesis (Oxford University, 1961), fo. 110.

[35] PSM, 8 Aug. 1868. The help of the Reform League was publicly acknowledged in the next annual report: see HP (June 1869), 209.

[36] For his career see Ceadel, 'Sir William Randal Cremer', 49–70 at 52–3.

in the American Civil War and also the Polish revolt, and had been involved in the creation of a British section of the LIPL, which however was stillborn. The Peace Society met them half way by paying sympathetic attention to the congress of the International Working Men's Association at Brussels in September 1868, even though this endorsed a 'strike of the people against war'[37]—an expression of socialist *pacificism* rather than Christian pacifism.

The Peace Society also welcomed the results of the October 1868 general election, the first to be held on the newly extended franchise. It was particularly pleased at Richard's success at Merthyr Tydfil, a Welsh borough whose electorate had increased tenfold and which had also acquired a second parliamentary representative. It not only allowed Richard, who held his seat until his death twenty years later, to stay on as secretary: it raised his annual salary to £500 (MPs not being remunerated by the state until 1912), and paid for more of the time of William Tallack—a Quaker who also worked for the Howard Association and had recently been engaged as a part-time helper—to assist him at 19 New Broad Street, particularly in producing the *Herald of Peace*.[38] Tallack's new terms of appointment provided a timely strengthening of the staff: Stokes had succumbed to alcohol-related collapse in 1869, and finally retired two years later after more than a quarter-century of service;[39] Bonner died suddenly on 11 October 1869;[40] and Appleton's behaviour as collector of subscriptions had been causing concern since soon after his reappointment.[41]

The 1868 election also produced the first truly Liberal government. The party no longer had to contend either with Palmerston's truculently defencist leadership, or with a militant crusading wing, or again with Cobden's isolationism (although in his last years this had in any case been somewhat moderated). It therefore began to unite behind a *pacificist* perspective which, though still wary of involvement in foreign wars, now favoured constructive engagement in the international system. For example, Richard was now more careful than formerly, when using the term non-intervention, to specify that its meaning was 'not as is sometimes most untruly alleged, non-intercourse with other nations, or want of interest in the general affairs of the world, but simply abstaining from meddling in the affairs of others'.[42]

---

[37] *HP* (Oct. 1868), 117–18; (June 1869), 211.

[38] PSM, 20 July 1868, 17 Mar. 1869, 6 Aug. 1869. Richard to Hayward, 12 Aug. 1874: PSLB.

[39] PSM, 15 June 1869, 19 Oct. 1870, 12 July 1871. Stokes's 'particular infirmity' can be inferred from Richard to Stokes, 3 Aug. 1871 (copy): PSLB. Stokes had served the society for 27 years.

[40] *HP* (Nov. 1869), 283.

[41] See e.g. PSM, 10 Sept. 1866.

[42] *HP* (June 1875), 249.

Admittedly, the new Liberal Prime Minister, Gladstone, a former Tory who still described himself as a 'liberal conservative', was a defencist: he rejected Cobdenism and, in Matthew's words, 'supported a traditional priority of the "national interest" view of international affairs'.[43] But as a devout High Churchman he also believed in the higher authority of a 'public law of Europe' which it was the duty of the Concert of Europe to defend. (His unvarying opinion was that Britain's and France's declaration of war against Russia in 1854 had been such a defence of public law.) Gladstone's moderate-defencist belief that the great powers had a right and a Christian duty to uphold public law as they understood it was easy to reconcile with the liberal-*pacificist* idea that the international community had a right and moral duty to defend peace and justice. To quote Matthew again: 'Gladstone based his position on the precedent and eirenicism of the past, but he also found himself offering, and newly associating with a popular campaign, a vision of international legitimacy and order which, as later developed and institutionalized in the League of Nations and the United Nations, represented the best hope of twentieth-century Liberalism.'[44] The *Herald of Peace* thus admired Gladstone's speech to the Lord Mayor's banquet in the City of London on 9 December 1869, which argued that free trade and improved communications were nurturing 'an international public opinion, a standard of international conduct higher than the particular standard which each nation has set for itself'; that no development was more hopeful 'than that the moral authority of all nations over each nation should grow up and be elevated from year to year'; and that, while forswearing 'impertinent interference', it was important for Britain to build 'a sentiment of true brotherhood with those countries with which we are connected by so many kind ties'.[45] The Peace Society also welcomed Gladstone's willingness to submit the *Alabama* dispute to arbitration.

Thus the Liberal party began melding diverse ideological strands into a mature liberal *pacificism*, and became something of a secondary peace association. Admittedly, implementing its *pacificist* ideas proved difficult. Indeed, the tension at this time between liberal ideals and governmental constraints was symbolized by Bright's unhappy experience in office: in 1868 he became the first dissenter to sit in the cabinet but suffered a second nervous breakdown which forced him out in December 1870, though he returned to the government in August 1873.[46]

Richard's election to parliament as a representative of a generally congenial party resulted in some changes of style and substance for the Peace

[43]   H. C. G. Matthew, *Gladstone 1809–1898* (Oxford, 1997), 186, 353.
[44]   Ibid. 272.
[45]   As cited in *HP* (Jan. 1870), 4.
[46]   Robbins, *John Bright*, 205–9.

Society. From 1869 onwards MPs reappeared on the platform of its annual public meeting—the first, other than its own leaders such as Hindley or the Peases, to do so since the society had become politically unpopular in the early 1850s. So, albeit more occasionally, did 'Lib-Lab' activists, such as Cremer, who in 1869 tried to persuade his middle-class audience that the International Working Men's Association was a proponent of 'Peace on earth and goodwill among men'.[47]

More importantly, tactics were modified. In August 1869 the society's executive committee decided that 'the idea of further Peace Congresses must, for the present, be given up'.[48] Instead, it backed Richard's proposal to visit 'many of the principal capitals of Europe' during October in an attempt to arrange for the simultaneous reduction of armaments to be 'brought before the various legislatures at or around the same time'.[49] Talk of an international disarmament agreement was also in the air, with Clarendon, Gladstone's Foreign Secretary, known to be supportive.[50] Richard's tour went well; and he reported back optimistically first to an afforced executive committee[51] and then to the annual public meeting, which attracted 'a larger audience than on any previous occasion'. The latter occasion was also significant for speeches by Passy—who observed that the operations of his own association 'appear very small by the side of yours'—and an Indian Baboo, and for what turned out be the final appearance of Burritt, who had lost his consular post in 1869 following a change of administration in Washington and was about to return home: characteristically, despite promising 'only ... a few words', the American delivered what the *Herald of Peace* called a 'massive speech'.[52]

Richard ran into delays, however, when he tried to introduce his own reduction-of-armaments resolution in the Commons. Charles Buxton, who had already put down a similar motion, had to be persuaded 'no longer to stand in the way of such a motion being made by Mr Richard'.[53] And no sooner had this been achieved than the Franco-Prussian War put an immediate stop to any talk of the reduction of armaments, though it was soon to stimulate talk of arbitration instead.

Napoleon III's provocation of a conflict with Prussia on 19 July 1870 rekindled anti-French feeling in Britain. 'We were all "Prooshians" in our village, as indeed were most English people', the radical intellectual

---

[47] *HP* (June 1869), 216. [48] PSM, 6 Aug. 1869.
[49] *HP* (June 1870), 65. See also Richard's diary of his tour, 29 Sept.–16 Oct. 1869: NLW MS 10205B.
[50] Villiers, *A Vanished Victorian*, 351–7. I. Abrams, 'Disarmament in 1870', *Die Friedenswarte*, 54 (1957), 57–68.
[51] PSM, 25 Nov. 1869. [52] *HP* (June 1870), 69.
[53] PSM, 12 Jan., 18 June 1870.

L. T. Hobhouse was to recall from his childhood.[54] Aware of their new political clout, working men started a lively debate as to whether Britain should intervene against France or remain neutral. In London their alignments reflected the factionalism of labour politics[55] more than attitudes to peace and war in general. Former members of the Reform League dominated a meeting on 21 July in Arundel Hall, which declared itself opposed to intervention, and elected a peace committee of about fifty working men with Cremer as its honorary secretary.[56] On 25 July—two days after the International Working Men's Association had drafted its first address on the war[57]—this 'Workmen's Peace Committee' (as it called itself) held a further meeting, at which several speakers, including Cremer, 'condemned the war and all wars on principle'.[58] The committee drafted an address to working men which was formally adopted at a further meeting held on 1 August,[59] and then published as a leaflet. The address made the standard radical assumption that wars were caused by 'dynastic jealousies or rivalries, court intrigues, secret treaties, diplomatic squabbles, and balances of power'; but it followed the Chartists in also stressing the pivotal role of working men: 'Why should we continue to suicidally furnish the means of our own destruction? . . . Without us wars must cease, for without us standing armies could not exist.' It implied that isolationism was a viable option for Britain: 'We are abundantly able to repel invasion, should any power be wicked or foolish enough to attempt it.' Yet it offered a constructive policy too: 'What we claim and demand—what we would implore the peoples of Europe to do, without regard to courts, cabinets, or dynasties—is, to *insist* upon arbitration as a substitute for war.'[60] Arbitration was a concept which working men understood because of its increasing use in labour disputes: indeed, the 1870s were to experience what a contemporary called an 'arbitration craze'.[61]

The Workmen's Peace Committee had ventured down a path which more established opponents of war felt unable to take. Quakers concentrated on

[54] L. T. Hobhouse, *The World in Conflict* (1915), 8.

[55] On which see H. Collins and C. Abramsky, *Karl Marx and the British Labour Movement* (1965), and R. Harrison, *Before the Socialists: Studies in Labour and Politics 1861–1881* (1965).

[56] *The Times* (26 July 1870). Sager, 'Working-Class Peace Movement', 123 n.

[57] This was published on 28 July: see *Karl Marx and Friedrich Engels: Writings on the Paris Commune*, ed. H. Draper (New York, 1971), 11.

[58] *The Times* (26 July 1870).

[59] *The Times* (2 Aug. 1870).

[60] *The Workman's [sic] Peace Committee to the Working Men of Great Britain and Ireland* (leaflet: n.d.[1870]). See also *The Times* (2 Aug. 1870).

[61] V .L. Allen, 'The Origins of Industrial Conciliation and Arbitration', *International Review of Social History*, 9 (1960), 237–54 at 240.

relief work among war victims, despite the dangers of disease.[62] The Peace Society convened 'A Special Meeting of the Friends of Peace on the War Crisis', chaired by Charles Gilpin at its office on 23 July, which however resolved that it was too dangerous to hold public meetings,[63] the explanation given to members being that 'it would be almost impossible in the present excited state of the country, to prevent the intrusion of injudicious speakers whose remarks might give rise to damaging misapprehension of the objects of the Society and so do more harm that good'.[64] Moreover, the non-interventionist statement which the society issued was addressed, cautiously, to 'the Friends of Peace' rather than to the government or the public. However, it was prepared to subsidize the activities of those with fewer political inhibitions: praising the 'very good address of a pacific nature' produced by the Workmen's Peace Committee, it gave it £250, and also offered 'pecuniary aid' to the International Working Men's Association to help it distribute a second call, issued on 9 August, for working-class solidarity and peace.[65]

By mid-August the prospect of British intervention against France had subsided, after assurances had been given regarding Belgian independence. The Workmen's Peace Committee thus began thinking of turning itself from an *ad hoc* neutrality campaign into a permanent association for educating its class about arbitration and the reduction of armaments. Before it could do so, however, the replacement of the hated Napoleon III by a new republican regime on 4 September made many British working men sympathetic towards France for the first time. This was evident by the time the Workmen's Peace Committee assembled again in Arundel Hall on the evening of 7 September to discuss its institutionalization as 'a Working Men's National Peace Association, to advocate arbitration in place of war'. Cremer and Beales reiterated the neutralist position, the latter saying 'emphatically that he would be no party to taking sides in the present war'. But Odger had succumbed to pro-France sentiment, and 'declared that if the war was continued the current of public feeling would be changed in favour of the French Republic'. For the time being these two views could be reconciled in a resolution which hailed 'with gladness the restoration of a French Republican government as calculated to lead to a speedy end of the war';[66] and a similar formula preserved harmony at the large meeting which launched the Workmen's Peace Association at St James's Hall on the evening of 10 September.[67]

[62] *HP* (Jan. 1871), 156. M. E. Hirst, *The Quakers in Peace and War: An Account of their Peace Principles and Practice* (1923), 266–70.
[63] PSM, 4 Aug. 1870.   [64] *HP* (Aug. 1870), 93.
[65] PSM, 4 Aug., 19 Oct. 1870. *HP* (Sept. 1870), 102.
[66] *The Times* (8 Sept. 1870).   [67] *The Times* (12 Sept. 1870).

This compromise was effective as long as the pro-France lobby only wanted Britain to press for peace. Increasingly, however, this lobby fell under the control of Cremer's political rivals, who wanted Britain to intervene militarily. This view was most energetically promoted by the Positivists (followers of the French thinker Auguste Comte), who though neither working-class nor numerous had under the leadership of Professor Edward Beesly won the trust of certain sections of London artisan opinion. Thus Cremer complained that Odger had fallen under the influence of 'Comtists who did not represent the interests of English working men' (a judgement which Marx loftily dismissed as 'not worth anything'[68]); and Richard claimed that Positivists were not numerous enough across the whole country to fill an omnibus.[69] Yet Beesly was able to use a meeting on 13 October 1870 of another progressive body, the Land and Labour League, to assert that 'dishonour' was worse than war, and demand the sending of 20,000 British troops to help the French.[70] Although even Beesly's old friend and fellow Positivist Frederic Harrison was initially embarrassed by this interventionist call,[71] he soon came round to the same view. And Odger signed an interventionist memorial to the Prime Minister drafted by the Positivists—a repudiation of his former neutralism to which an editorial in *The Times* drew attention.[72]

Coincidentally, within a few weeks a call for British intervention against Russia was also to be made. On 31 October the Tsar took advantage of the Franco-Prussian conflict to repudiate the Black Sea clauses of the 1856 Treaty of Paris. The International Working Men's Association, which had detected 'the dark figure of Russia' behind the Franco-Prussian War in its address of 23 July and warned of its potential for mischief in a second address on 9 September,[73] took the lead in calling for Russia to be punished.

With both a pro-France and an anti-Russia crusading spirit thus alive among working men, the Workmen's Peace Association (WPA), which formally adopted its rules and principles as a permanent organization on 3 December 1870, still had an emergency role to play.[74] Having received a further £500 from the Peace Society two days later,[75] the WPA issued a statement opposing war with Russia that same month and a leaflet, *Questions*

[68] *General Council of the First International 1870–71* (Moscow, n.d.), 102–3.
[69] National Reform Union, *Report of the Great Meeting in Support of Mr Gladstone's Government and Non-Intervention in the Free Trade Hall on Wednesday Evening, February 1st, 1871* (Manchester, 1871), 25.
[70] *The Times* (14 Oct. 1870). See also Harrison, *Before the Socialists*, 231.
[71] M. Vogeler, *Frederic Harrison: The Vocations of a Positivist* (Oxford, 1984), 98.
[72] *The Times* (4 Jan. 1871).
[73] *Karl Marx and Friedrich Engels*, ed. Draper, 35–40 (at 39) and 41–9.
[74] *HP* (Jan. 1871), 156. Van der Linden, *International Peace Movement*, 879.
[75] PSM, 5 Dec. 1870.

for the Working Men of Great Britain to Ask Themselves Before They Vote At Public Meetings in Favour of a War Policy to Assist France, in the new year. On 10 January 1871 the Positivists held a meeting for trade unionists which shouted down a non-interventionist resolution and was later admitted by Harrison to have been 'as hotly bellicose as could be imagined'.[76] Ten days later, however, a WPA deputation participated, along with Richard and two other prominent Congregationalist ministers associated with the Peace Society and sympathetic to the labour movement, G. M. Murphy and Newman Hall, in a meeting at which an interventionist resolution proposed by a group of Republicans was defeated.[77]

When France made peace and the London conference settled the dispute with Russia, the WPA found itself free of this war crisis, and able from mid-February to turn to general issues. It therefore organized some big events with distinguished guest speakers, who did not however always behave as expected. For example, on 22 February 1871 it summoned a meeting to 'oppose any extension in our military institutions or increase in our national expenditure for warlike purposes and to urge on our government the duty of taking the initiative in promoting the establishment of a High Court of Nations for the resolution of International Disputes'. But although the resolutions to this effect were passed, discordant notes were struck. In particular, Lord Amberley, a Liberal ex-MP who was to die young and be best remembered as the father of the philosopher and peace activist Bertrand Russell, insisted that, despite favouring arbitration, 'he could not agree in the view that England should reduce her armaments, as to do so would most likely lead to war'. Amberley's statement provoked 'some few cries of "No, No!" ' from the audience, though 'a considerable number present agreed and cheered the speaker'.[78] On 10 March 1871 the WPA held a similar gathering to protest against the government's proposal to increase military expenditure, inviting Amberley's friend John Stuart Mill to take the chair. Mill too was concerned about British security—it was partly for that reason that he had thought the call for war on Russia so irresponsible[79]—and had come to favour a citizen army. He therefore used the WPA's meeting to advocate 'the assimilation of our military system to that of Switzerland rather than to that of Prussia', a sentiment which considerably upset the WPA's paymaster, the Peace Society.[80]

[76] F. Harrison, *Autobiographic Memoirs* (2 vols., 1911), ii. 15.
[77] *The Times* (12 and 21 Jan. 1871). For the friendship between Murphy and Hall, see N. Hall, *An Autobiography* (1898), 221, 260–1.   [78] *The Times* (23 Feb. 1871).
[79] See Mill's letter of 18 Nov. 1870, printed in *Early Life and Letters of John Morley*, ed. F. W. Hirst (2 vols., 1927), i. 168–9, and his letter of the following day, printed in *HP* (Dec. 1870), 142–3.   [80] *HP* (Apr. 1871), 206. PSM, 22 Apr. 1871.

Such occasions proving expensive as well as unpredictable in the message they sent, the WPA stopped mounting them. Except at times of international crisis, it limited its meetings to little more than an annual *soirée* and a public meeting in connection with each year's Trades Union Congress. It had established an office, in company with other radical organizations, at 9 Buckingham Street, Strand, and employed Cremer there as its full-time secretary. As honorary treasurer it appointed Benjamin Lucraft, a cabinet-maker who had spoken in support of a popular strike against war at the Brussels congress of the International Working Men's Association in September 1868 and also carried Peace Society literature to the Basel congress of the same organization a year later,[81] though his election to the first London School Board led him in December 1872 to surrender the position to Benjamin Britten, a shoemaker.

The WPA's social composition differed significantly from that of the Stop-the-War League of 1855–6, the last body formed to mobilize the masses against war. It was class-conscious and secular where the earlier body had been dominated by men of humble origins whose careers as journalists, ministers, or entrepreneurs had taken them away from manual work and who were strongly influenced by Protestant dissent. The one prominent member of the WPA who would have fitted easily into the Stop-the-War League was Howard Evans, a journalist who had contemplated a career as a Congregational minister.[82] Only two men of wholly bourgeois backgrounds held positions in the WPA: Beales, by now a judge, was made president in recognition of his trusted position in working-class political circles over the previous seven years or so; and Hodgson Pratt, who having retired from the Indian Civil Service had established his philanthropic credentials in the Working Men's Club and Institute Union[83] and could offer special expertise as a frequent and multi-lingual traveller in Europe, was given the title of honorary international agent, albeit in his case only after considerable argument as to whether a member of the middle class was acceptable.[84]

That the WPA was 'a genuine and *bona fide* working class organization, originated, constituted and directed entirely by working men' was stressed by the Peace Society, which insisted that it always 'left them entire liberty of action and abstained from any appearance of patronizing and controlling them altogether'.[85] None the less the WPA's financial dependence on the

[81] G. H. Dyer, W. Catchpool, and A. S. Dyer, *Six Men of the People* (n.d.[1882]), 5–7. PSM, 28 Sept. 1869. *HP* (Oct. 1869), 263.

[82] H. Evans, *Radical Fights of Forty Years* (1913), 103.

[83] See B. T. Hall, *Our Fifty Years: The Story of the Working Men's Club and Institute Union* (London, 1912).

[84] *The Times* (Jan. 1872).

[85] *HP* (June 1871), 222 (July 1875), 263.

Peace Society during the 1870s made it deferential. The WPA regularly sent representatives to the Peace Society's annual meetings: for example, at the 1876 meeting of members Cremer volunteered the assurance that 'no important operation' of the WPA 'had ever been undertaken' without the 'counsel and approval' of the Peace Society or its secretary, after which Richard confirmed that he 'had never met a body of men more amenable to counsel and advice' than were 'the leaders of the Workmen's Peace Association'—a humiliating exchange that was printed not only in the *Herald of Peace* but more surprisingly in the WPA's journal too.[86] The need to propitiate Christian-pacifist paymasters also caused the association to make its objection to war sound as religious and as absolutist as its clientele would accept. Much later, when free of the Peace Society's subsidy, Cremer made clear he was not a pacifist, replying when asked whether Britain should ever defend itself: 'Yes; when danger is proved to exist; but not before. I ask where the danger is.'[87] He also made less effort to conceal his secularist tendencies: even Evans, whose piety led him to understate Cremer's dislike of Christianity, later admitted that he was 'possibly . . . a doubter'.[88]

The WPA's financial dependence reflected the smallness of its basis of support once the emergency of 1870–1 was over, and not just its members' limited financial means. Though seen by the social historian Eric W. Sager as 'the largest political organization supported and led by working men in the 1870s',[89] and though itself claiming 'some thousands of members'[90] early in its existence, it never possessed either the mass nominal membership of the League of Universal Brotherhood in its heyday or a core of wealthy subscribers like the Peace Society. It did, however, recruit working men of some local standing as 'honorary agents': these were said to number 100 within a year; were shown to exceed 400 during the 1876–8 crisis over the Eastern Question which proved to be the WPA's finest hour; and reportedly peaked at 'upward of 1,000' in the early 1880s.[91] Sager was impressed by the speed with which the WPA, few of whose founders 'were active trade union officials', acquired support 'within the trade councils and larger unions', especially 'outside the large factories' and within the craft and agricultural unions.[92]

[86] *HP* (June 1876), 78; *Arbitrator* (June 1876), 1–2.
[87] Hansard, cccxxxiv HC col. 1259 (25 Mar. 1889).
[88] Evans, *Cremer*, 338.
[89] Eric W. Sager, 'The Working-Class Peace Movement in Victorian England', *Histoire sociale—Social History*, 12/23 (May 1979) 122–41 at 122. See also his 'Pacifism and the Victorians', ch. 9.
[90] *Arbitrator* (May 1872), 3–4.
[91] *Arbitrator* (Feb. 1872), 2. *HP* (Feb. 1882), 23.
[92] Sager, 'Working-Class Peace Movement', 142–3.

The WPA did its best to attract leading trade unionists. It established a particularly close relationship with Joseph Arch, who established the National Agricultural Labourers' Union in 1872. In addition, after Beales died in 1881 it chose Thomas Burt, the Northumberland miners' leader who in 1874 had become one of the two first working-class MPs, as its president. Burt, who received 552 out of the 571 votes cast in a democratic election for this office,[93] was a noted enthusiast for the arbitration of labour disputes: in 1882 he was, coincidentally, to arbitrate a dispute between ironmasters and their employers in conjunction with his opposite number at the Peace Society, Joseph Whitwell Pease[94]—evidence of the ideological connection made by many Liberals between industrial and international conciliation. Burt was, however, the WPA's only big catch. Cremer's bad relations with 'the Junta' that dominated London labour politics ensured that only its most isolated figure, the Ironfounders' leader Daniel Guile, showed any interest in the WPA after the end of the Franco-Prussian War. The most substantial figure to join its council was James Rowlands, a watch-case maker who lectured for many progressive causes in London and was to become a Lib-Lab MP in 1886.[95]

INTERNATIONAL LAW, ARBITRATION, AND RESPECTABILITY, 1871–1875

The espousal by a group of artisans of the cause of arbitration was but one symptom of a significantly increased interest in international law among groups not previously involved in the peace movement. Increasing professionalism within the academic and legal worlds had been producing a new interest in international law even before the Franco-Prussian War gave it a boost: in particular, the American jurist David Dudley Field, who was active in the Social Science Association, had been working since 1866 on *Outlines of an International Code*, which appeared in 1872.[96]

This more widespread interest in ideas which it had come to regard as its own came as a mixed blessing to the peace movement. The Peace Society welcomed the extra attention, regarding 1871–2 as 'probably' its busiest period thitherto: it engaged additional temporary lecturers, and raised a special fund of £10,000, 'mainly contributed in the Northern Counties', to

---

[93] *Arbitrator* (May 1882), 3.   [94] *HP* (June 1882), 74.
[95] *Arbitrator* (Sept. 1880), 3; (Dec. 1882), 5.
[96] *HP* (Apr. 1872), 49. See also L. Goldman, 'Exceptionalism and Internationalism: The Origins of American Social Science Reconsidered', *Journal of Historical Sociology*, 11 (1998), 1–36 at 16–17.

enable it to exploit new opportunities 'especially in connection with the subject of International Arbitration'.[97] Shortly before his death even the discredited Sir John Bowring sent the *Herald of Peace* an article on this topic, which it duly published, billing him tactfully as a 'veteran diplomatist'.[98] In 1872–3 the society expanded its honorific general committee, and issued a number of invitations to join its executive committee.[99] In February 1872, the WPA launched a journal, which it fashionably named the *Arbitrator*; and for the next year and a half the association made the securing of support for Richard's parliamentary motion its priority.

Yet pacifists were upset by the suggestion, which was made more frequently in the early 1870s than at any other time before the First World War, that arbitral awards be enforced militarily. As Tallack admitted on 25 January 1871 during a discussion on arbitration at the rooms of the Social Science Association, some 'friends of peace' favoured 'a reserve army, furnished in quotas from each nation, to enforce, where necessary, the decrees of an international court, and to act as a police of nations'.[100] The Peace Society tried to insist that enforcement was unnecessary as well as wrong. In this claim it was able to invoke Leone Levi, an Italian Jew who, having come to Britain as a businessman, had converted to Presbyterianism and become first an academic and then a practising international lawyer with a special interest in commercial law.[101] He had first tried to interest the Peace Society in his specialism in 1851, but had made little progress until he was appointed to its executive committee ten years later,[102] and did not become influential until the decade after that.

But even with Levi's authoritative support, the society could not prevent a number of recent converts to arbitration arguing for enforcement, as was illustrated when it accepted the offer of a lecture from the Cambridge professor J. R. Seeley, who was not yet a celebrant of imperial expansion. In his address to the Peace Society on 28 March 1871, Seeley called for an international system which 'is something essentially different from, and cannot be developed out of, the already existing system by which European affairs are settled in Congress of the great powers'. Moreover, he insisted: 'We have a problem of federation before us, and not merely of constituting a law court'. And not only did he hold up the United States as a model federation, despite its recent civil war: he also insisted that any federal executive must have the power to

[97] *HP* (June 1872), 69, 73. PSM, 4 Dec. 1871, 3 July 1872
[98] *HP* (Nov. 1872), 141–2. Bowring died on 23 Nov. 1872.
[99] PSM, 3 July 1872, 15 May 1873.   [100] *HP* (Feb. 1871), 167.
[101] See L. Levi, *The Story of my Life: The First Ten Years of my Residence in England, 1845–1855* (privately published, 1888).
[102] PSM, 16 Dec. 1851, 10 June 1861.

enforce its decisions. In moving a formal vote of thanks, Richard made clear the Peace Society's opposition to enforcement, and also criticized Seeley for implying that the peace movement had never interested itself in practical measures of war prevention: indeed, Richard emphasized that the Peace Society had promoted the Congress and Court of Nations since as early as 1831, and noted that a federal scheme on the lines advocated by Seeley was being promoted in Europe by the LIPL, though 'unhappily, that body has mixed up its views on this question with other extreme and irrelevant opinions, which has compelled the London Peace Society to hold aloof from them'.[103] Seeley gracefully accepted Richard's reproof, and was not thereby discouraged either from attending a WPA discussion of a High Court of Nations on 8 July 1871 or from addressing a Ladies Peace Meeting a year later.[104]

This flurry of interest in enforcement caused pacifists to face up for the first time to the problems inherent in the collaborative orientation. When they had started giving priority to support for *pacificist* measures in the 1840s, they thereby found themselves endorsing proposals which were either less thoroughgoing than they would ideally have liked (such as the reduction, rather than total renunciation, of armaments) or undertaken for different reasons (political and economic, rather than religious). But they had not been required to endorse military force, since even *pacificists* had then assumed that public opinion would suffice to secure compliance with the decisions of a Congress and Court of Nations.

Now for the first time the Peace Society had to introduce reservations into its support for *pacificist* schemes. For example, in 1871 its executive committee found itself 'promoting the circulation' of Frederick Seebohm's book *International Reform* on account of its analytical excellence, whilst also making clear the society's inability 'to endorse the use of physical force advocated by the author in the last resort'.[105]

Fortunately for the Peace Society, however, once international lawyers came to consider what sovereign states would in practice accept, their interest in ambitious schemes diminished. There were to be some notable exceptions, such as Professor James Lorimer of Edinburgh University.[106] But the general view was to be expressed in 1896 by England's Lord Chief Justice. Addressing the International Law Association (whose founding as the Association for the Reform and Codification of the Law of Nations will

---

[103] *HP* (Apr. 1871), 197–9.

[104] *HP* (Aug. 1871), 253; (Aug. 1872), 107.

[105] *HP* (June 1871), 228.

[106] For an analysis of his ideas see H. Suganami, *The Domestic Analogy and World Order Proposals* (Cambridge, 1989), 54–9.

shortly be noted), Lord Russell of Killowen emphasized that there was no prospect of a 'League of Nations of the Amphictyonic type', able 'to coerce a recalcitrant member of the family of nations'; but he implied that this did not greatly matter since the 'sanctions which restrain the wrongdoer', namely 'dread of war and the reprobation of mankind' were 'not weak' and indeed were growing stronger by the year.[107] Ideas of federation and enforcement were thus largely to die down, reviving only after 1914 when a league of nations came to be widely advocated.

During the early 1870s, however, pacifists had an uncomfortable time. Many of the new enthusiasts for arbitration wished to distance themselves from anything which smacked of absolutism. A rank-and-file supporter, John Thomas Rice of Bentham, warned that Anglicans and Wesleyans in particular were holding back from 'associations under the name of "Peace" Societies, as being in their view rather too closely associated with Quakerism', and suggested that ' "Anti-War" Societies' should be formed to cater for them instead.[108] The Peace Society had anticipated this difficulty by creating local 'International Arbitration Associations' under its own auspices. One of the first, for Yorkshire, was established at Leeds on 26 January 1872, and later secured the patronage of the Archbishop of York and the Dean of Ripon[109]— evidence of unprecedented support from senior Anglicans for peace activism when packaged under the arbitration label. In some cases these arbitration associations were the society's local supporters redesignated: indeed, in Manchester, a city whose preference for the 'arbitration' label dated back at least to the peace conference there in 1853, the Lancashire and Cheshire International Arbitration Association—which incidentally attracted a gesture of support from both the Catholic Bishop of Salford and the Anglican Bishop of Manchester—was acknowledged in the *Herald of Peace* as 'the auxiliary association of the Peace Society in Manchester'.

However, having seemingly *pacificist* local associations focused on the single issue of arbitration as satellites of the Peace Society, a national association identified with pacifism as an ideology to be applied to the full range of war-related issues (including non-resistance and disarmament), was problematical. The executive committee in London soon recognized that it was an 'anomaly for such an Association to be collecting subscriptions for a Society whose views it does not agree with in their entirety'.[110] It also discovered that addresses given on the continent by one of its lecturers 'in the name of the International Arbitration Society' had 'given rise to some misconceptions'

---

[107] Lord Russell of Killowen, *Arbitration: Its Origin, History, and Prospects* (1896), 30.
[108] *HP* (May 1872), 64.
[109] *HP* (Mar. 1872), 30; (Jan. 1873), 179.
[110] *HP* (Nov. 1872), 151. PSM, 22 Feb. 1875.

regarding its own views.[111] Admittedly, some members of the Peace Society claimed that this problem would soon resolve itself because 'the Arbitration Societies ... will find themselves led to the root of our principle', as A. B. Hayward of the Liverpool Peace Society, one of the few auxiliaries with a vigorous local life, put it at the 1873 meeting of members.[112] But this was wishful thinking: whereas when the Peace Society had adopted its two-tier approach almost six decades previously it had been plausible to hope that defencists taking an interest in *pacificism* would be won over to pacifism once they came into contact with it, it was now clear that a considerable section of the public knew exactly what pacifism was and wanted a non-absolutist and more selective approach instead. By thus catering itself for the demand for arbitration associations the Peace Society postponed the creation of new *pacificist* rivals into the next decade, but did so at the price of doctrinal ambiguity.

Richard decided that arbitration rather than the reduction of armaments should become the subject of the Commons motion he had been contemplating since before the Franco-Prussian War. However, the timing of such a motion caused him 'great perplexity':[113] having received many welcome endorsements from representative meetings of Nonconformists, trade unionists, and Liberals, he was unsure whether to proceed while progressive opinion was so supportive or wait until a final decision had been reached in the *Alabama* dispute, the arbitration of which was causing great anxiety because of American demands for 'indirect damages'. His consultation of the 'Friends of Peace' in the spring of 1872 showed them 'very nearly balanced' on the subject.[114] Richard decided to be patient, and was gratified at the 'calm and dignified submission' of both government and public in Britain to an award in September 1872 which favoured the United States.[115]

Thereafter, like Cobden before him, Richard had to wait until he was successful in the ballot for an opportunity to introduce his arbitration motion. The extra-parliamentary campaign in his support was reassuring. The Peace Society's executive committee was told that the 'very satisfactory' local conferences on international arbitration held at Bristol and Darlington were 'very influentially attended by Members of Parliament, magistrates, clergymen, ministers, and other gentlemen; and the proceedings were well reported in the newspapers'.[116] And Richard devoted an editorial to this 'curious and altogether very encouraging' trend of public opinion.[117]

Meanwhile the secretary of the American Peace Society, the Revd James B. Miles, passed through London on a mission to invite 'forty or fifty of the

---

[111] PSM, 22 Oct. 1872.
[113] *HP* (June 1872), 76.
[115] *HP* (Oct. 1872), 130–1; (June 1873), 250.
[117] *HP* (Mar. 1873), 204–5.

[112] *HP* (June 1873), 245.
[114] PSM, 19 Feb., 8 Apr. 1872.
[116] PSM, 26 Feb. 1873.

principal jurists of the world' to codify international law. An increasingly frail Burritt, though enthusiastic about Miles's project, was unable to make the journey. Miles's encounters with the Peace Society showed the extent to which the latter had shifted from a pressure-group to a parliamentary approach since its secretary's election to parliament: Richard, backed by the future Liberal MP Frederick Pennington, emphasized that his Commons motion would treat the codification of international law as the responsibility of legislatures and governments not of peace associations and publics. However, on 29 March a compromise formula was agreed between Miles and Richard: this stated that the influence of public opinion should be brought to bear on legislatures, which, as 'the natural and legitimate organs of national sentiment and desire', would in turn invite their governments to tackle the problem in conjunction with other governments.[118]

In June 1873 Richard was finally notified of an opportunity on 8 July to debate his motion 'praying that her Majesty would be pleased to direct the Secretary for Foreign Affairs to enter into communication with Foreign Powers with a view to the establishment of a permanent system of international arbitration'. The peace movement's effort to generate petitions in Richard's support reached a climax: the Peace Society claimed a total of 1,165 petitions and 207,391 signatures, though it stressed that the latter figure was depressed by the fact that many petitions adopted at meetings or by associations had been signed only by the chairman or secretary.[119] Shortly before midnight in a sparsely attended House, Richard's motion was carried by 98 votes to 88, despite the fact that Gladstone had opposed it on the grounds that he would have preferred it to have been worded as a resolution of the House rather than a request to the sovereign.[120] Unlike in the *Arrow* debate sixteen years previously, which the government had made an issue of confidence, the Conservatives voted on ideological rather than partisan lines: including tellers, the majority comprised 92 Liberals and 8 Conservatives and the minority 42 Liberals and 48 Conservatives.

Elated by this outcome, which the Peace Society later admitted having awaited in a state of 'anxiety', Richard decided to visit the continent to press for the adoption of similar resolutions, and spent from September to December 1873 travelling through Belgium, Holland, Germany, Austria, Hungary, Italy, and France.[121] This tour bore fruit in that the legislatures of Belgium, Holland, and Italy—and also Sweden, which he had not visited—

[118] *HP* (Feb. 1873), 194–5; (May 1873), 229–30.
[119] *HP* (June 1873), 260; (Aug. 1873), 298; (June 1874), 82.
[120] Hansard, cxvii HC cols. 51–90.
[121] PSM, 26 July 1873. *HP* (Aug. 1874), 77–8.

adopted arbitration motions.[122] Richard also attended an important conference at Brussels in early October, at which the Americans Field and Miles played an influential part, and which had the same chairman, August Visschers, as the Brussels Peace Congress of a quarter of a century before. The conference established an Association for the Reform and Codification of the Law of Nations, a body designed to unite peace activists and lawyers— the latter in their specialist capacity having already been catered for by the establishment at Ghent a month previously of an Institute for International Law. The gatherings which these two organizations were to hold each summer, initially in the same European city and in succession to each other, not only proved a partial substitute for international peace congresses but also increased Richard's understanding of the legal problems involved in arbitration.

When Richard returned from the continent, the Peace Society had to turn its attention to a general election. It issued an address to its followers, urging them to seek 'distinct pledges from Candidates in support of any well-devised measure of a pacific and economical tendency', and published 'posters and handbills containing striking facts and statistics for the consideration of Electors'. But it was careful to deny 'political propagandism', and to insist that it had always recognized the contributions to peace of certain leaders of 'each great political party'.[123] However, after the Conservatives won the election and formed their first majority administration since 1846, the *Herald of Peace* admitted 'uneasiness' on account of 'the spirit which pervades the rank and file' of the victors, 'too many' of whose MPs had 'been returned in the "beer and bung" interest'.[124] The new Prime Minister, Disraeli, was to adopt a Palmerstonian style of defencism, albeit associating it with Britain's imperial greatness rather than with its supposed championship of the liberties of Europe. To the peace movement it was disappointing that the Conservatives thus committed themselves decisively to defencism, since during their long period as the minority party they had shown occasional signs of playing the peace card, as Disraeli himself had done in the latter stages of the Crimean War. But matters could have been worse: despite the Peace Society's fears that the conscript armies of the continent would be imitated in Britain,[125] the Conservatives were never to make a serious effort to introduce compulsory military service in peacetime—a sign of the strength within the political culture of liberalism (an obstacle to protectionism too) and of the sense of

---

[122] Van der Linden, *International Peace Movement*, 915.
[123] *HP* (Feb. 1874), 13. PSM, 27 Jan. 1874.
[124] *HP* (Mar. 1874), 37, 39.
[125] *HP* (June 1875), 241.

security engendered by insularity. Moreover, by the logic of adversary politics, the Conservatives' decision to trumpet their defencism was to encourage
the Liberals to commit themselves more thoroughly to *pacificism*.

The Peace Society's first initiative after the change of government was,
coincidentally, to create a Ladies' Peace Association, which was formally
constituted at the Peace Society's office on 22 April 1874. This was a
response to increasing calls for it to allow women a greater role in its activities. In December 1871 a newly appointed member of the executive committee had 'suggested the propriety of asking some ladies to speak in public on
the peace question'; but his colleagues were 'not prepared at present to take
any definite steps in that direction'.[126] In 1872 a visit to England by the
American writer Julia Ward Howe led to the creation of a 'Women's
International Peace Society', an independent body which apparently existed
in Manchester for several years;[127] and at a meeting of the Social Science
Association in the autumn Mrs E. M. King advocated an international peace
society involving women, on account of 'their greater horror of war, and from
having all to lose and nothing to gain from it'.[128] By 1873 the Peace Society's
annual report acknowledged that Mrs King and Joseph Sturge's eldest daughter Sophia, who was already established in London progressive circles
through her friendship with John Bright's sister Priscilla McLaren, had both
shown a 'disposition to enter upon a course of active propagandism in favour
of the peace cause among their own sex', and declared its own view to be that
such work was 'emphatically within the province of woman'.[129] British
women had also begun addressing mixed peace meetings: for example,
another of John Bright's sisters, Margaret Lucas, did so at the annual meeting
of the Keighley Peace Association on 31 January 1874.[130]

The offer from Mrs E. M. Southey 'to initiate organized efforts' for a
Ladies' Peace Association[131] was thus a typically belated and cautious
response on the part of the Peace Society. Although expressing pleasure that
what had been 'scattered and occasional' had been rendered 'orderly and
permanent' by the creation of the ladies' association,[132] it clearly did not think
that the role of women in the peace movement had otherwise changed. The
account in the *Herald of Peace* of the Ladies' Peace Association's first *soirée*,
held on 2 June 1875, thus began by emphasizing how 'tastefully decorated'

[126] PSM, 4 Dec. 1871.
[127] *HP* (Aug. 1874), 113; (Dec. 1874), 175.
[128] *HP* (Oct. 1872), 135.
[129] W. R. Hughes, *Sophia Sturge: A Memoir* (1940), 20–1. *HP* (June 1873), 252.
[130] *HP* (Mar. 1874), 33.
[131] PSM, 4 Mar. 1874.
[132] *HP* (June 1875), 77.

the Memorial Hall, Faringdon Street, had been for the occasion, and how the 'agreeable' choir had included five 'fair and skilful' pupils from the North London College for Ladies, Camden Road, whose principal, Miss Buss, was a leading member of the association. Richard's address on that occasion accused women of being 'too generally dazzled' by war fiction. (More to the point, Richard read a letter from Burritt reminding the new association of the 'many local ladies' committees' which had promoted his Olive Leaves 'twenty years ago'.[133]) At its second *soirée*, moreover, all but one of the speakers were male. There is no evidence that the Ladies' Peace Association felt patronized any more than the WPA, however. Like the WPA, it saw its role as mobilizing a distinctive constituency in support of the Peace Society's traditional message, rather than as offering a distinctive critique of the causes of war. In other words it existed to interest women in the peace issue—in which context it is noteworthy that A. B. Hayward regarded 'the ladies' of his locality as 'the most determined opponents that the Liverpool committee have to deal with'[134]—rather than to claim a feminist insight into it.

By the mid-1870s the Peace Society had under Richard's stewardship partially regained the position in public life which it had enjoyed at the mid-point of the century. It offset its absolutism by emphasizing its religious idealism, its willingness to collaborate with mainstream Liberalism, and its ultra-respectability on socio-moral issues such as the role of women. During the period of particular prosperity for the British economy which was drawing to a close, it had been able to use its financial strength to justify its dominant position within the peace movement despite the ever-growing strength of *pacificism*. In 1874, for example, it was able not only to give £100 to its ladies' association but also to subsidize its profligate Manchester auxiliary and Passy's Société française des amis de la paix.[135] In addition, it was not only the regular paymaster of the WPA, but willing to make an additional donation in respect of a visit on 6–7 September 1875 by a forty-seven-strong WPA delegation to a private meeting with French workers in Paris. This was a bold undertaking, which the Peace Society had initially discouraged, because a Franco-German war scare had only just ended and the atmosphere in Paris remained tense. Indeed, on his arrival in the French capital Cremer discovered that leading Republicans were boycotting the conference (in some cases because they favoured 'the one-more-war theory' which, as already noted, Victor Hugo had propounded at the LIPL's congress at Lausanne in 1869), and realized that 'the large majority of the representative working

---

[133] *HP* (July 1875), 257.   [134] *HP* (June 1876), 78.
[135] PSM, 24 June 1874.

men' whom he had known through the International Working Men's Association and other circles had 'been either shot or transported' in the interim.[136] None the less, the visit passed off well; and the WPA was to take further deputations to meet its Parisian counterparts in June 1879 and February 1885.[137]

In 1874–5 the Peace Society faced a dispute with its landlords, who wished to redevelop its premises, that required it to practise what it preached regarding arbitration. The umpire decided that the Peace Society's lease ran until 1925 but that it had to change premises within the same street.[138] After a year in temporary accommodation at 18 South Street while building work was in progress, the society moved on 15 March 1876 to 20 New Broad Street, next door to its former location. There it was to remain until the expiry of its lease, though in 1880 the road was renumbered by the Post Office so that its address became 47 New Broad Street.[139]

THE EASTERN QUESTION, BEACONSFIELDISM, PARTISANSHIP, AND NEW ORGANIZATIONS, 1875–1882

The Peace Society was thus in a serene if potentially overstretched condition when in 1875 a revolt in Bosnia-Herzegovina brought what its agent O'Neill called 'the ever-recurring Turkish question' back onto its agenda, where it was to remain for three years, raising the peace question to an unprecedented visibility in domestic politics, and forcing the Peace Society back into public controversy.

When O'Neill began lecturing on the Bosnian question in November 1875, he was struck by the fact that, because of 'heart-rending accounts . . . of cruelties perpetrated by the Turks', the announcement of this topic 'never fails to secure a large audience': at a Staffordshire factory he had an audience of 700 artisans; and he found his rural lectures, held in a central village at 'the time of full moon' to allow the audience to travel in the evening from hamlets 'five or six miles distant', 'very telling' experiences too. O'Neill's comments, which appeared in the society's annual report in May 1876, showed that the interest of working men in the Eastern Question was being catered for by the Peace Society several months before news of further atrocities against Bulgarians began to reach the country in the summer of 1876.[140] However, at

[136] PSM, 22 July, 26 Nov. 1875. *Arbitrator* (Sept. 1875), 3–8. Evans, *Cremer*, 88.
[137] *Arbitrator* (June–July 1879), 3; (Feb.–Mar. 1885), 10–12.
[138] PSM, 29 Dec. 1874, 1 Apr. 1875.
[139] *HP* (Apr. 1875), 220; (Mar. 1876), 29; (Jan. 1880), 9.
[140] *HP* (June 1876), 79.

this stage the Peace Society was not greatly alarmed: indeed it almost welcomed this further evidence that the Ottoman empire was 'the vilest tyranny on the face of the earth' as confirmation after twenty years that the Crimean War had been an 'utter failure' and that its criticisms of Turkey at that time had been 'amply vindicated'.[141]

However, it grew a little worried when Disraeli obstructed great-power pressure on the Ottoman regime in May 1876 and thereby raised the prospect of a British intervention on the Turkish side. O'Neill believed that the peace movement's efforts during the previous winter and spring had inoculated working men against Russophobia. For example, the annual conference of the National Society of Brassworkers passed a non-interventionist resolution on 30 June 1876 and sent it to the Foreign Secretary, Derby (the former Lord Stanley, who had succeeded to his father's earldom in 1869), and local MPs. And the next day the Midland Auxiliary of the Peace Society began working on a national deputation to the Foreign Secretary, whom the Peace Society knew of old to be 'eminently cautious and pacific'.[142] Great efforts were put into ensuring that by the time this took place on 14 July it had 'attained to the proportion of something like a *national* deputation': 250-strong, drawn from most parts of the country, and led by John Bright, it represented more than 'what is technically known as the peace party in this country', as Richard pointed out to the Foreign Secretary.[143] Indeed, in the terminology of this study it represented anti-war opinion, including defencists who regarded an anti-Russian stance as imprudent, as well as *pacificists* and pacifists. Derby, whose private view was that British foreign policy was most successful 'when "isolative" ', referred respectfully to the deputation in his diary and noted correctly that his address to it 'was decidedly a success as far as the audience was concerned'.[144]

After the Bulgarian atrocities were reported during the summer of 1876, however, the peace movement was confronted with the opposite risk: that progressive opinion might 'rush into an opposite extreme', as the *Herald of Peace* put it, and favour military intervention *against* Turkey.[145] This risk was increased, ironically, by Gladstone's response to events. He had retired following the Liberal defeat in 1874, but, impressed by the disinterested concern about the Balkans being shown by working men, now resumed the leadership of Liberal opinion: on 5 September he published his celebrated

[141] *HP* (June 1876), 77, 84.
[142] *HP* (June 1876), 76.
[143] *HP* (Aug. 1876), 107–8; (June 1877), 246–7.
[144] *A Selection from the Diaries of Edward Henry Stanley Earl of Derby (1826–93) between September 1869 and March 1878*, ed. J. Vincent (Camden 5th Series 4, 1994), 241, 309.
[145] *HP* (Oct. 1876), 141.

pamphlet, *The Bulgarian Horrors and the Question of the East*. Its message was moderate, yet posed some problems for the peace movement; its rhetoric was inflammatory, and caused even greater difficulties.

Gladstone called merely for Bulgarian autonomy under Turkish sovereignty, and assumed that this could in practice be achieved by diplomatic pressure from the Concert of Europe, though he believed that military force would be acceptable if what he was to call 'Coercion by menace'[146] failed. However, the peace movement, though anxious to indulge anti-Turkish feeling as far as possible, was unable to support the threat of armed intervention. The Peace Society objected on pacifist grounds, and the WPA argued more prudentially that 'nobody proposes that we should fight on the subject, as everybody believes that the withdrawal of our support from Turkey will practically settle her fate in Europe'.[147] Moreover, although liberal *pacificists* might have persuaded themselves that Turkish military action in the Balkans was a form of aggression against incipient nation-states which the Concert of Europe, as the best available international authority, would be justified in resisting, they did not do so. Perhaps they shared the reservations about the moral authority of the Concert of Europe which were to be clearly articulated in the Peace Society's annual report for the year ending May 1877: this conceded that great-power behaviour in the crisis had revealed 'an attempt, though blindly and blunderingly made, to establish an European solidarity, and an implicit acknowledgement that there ought to be something like an international tribunal', but insisted that none the less the Concert had fallen far short of the 'grave and judicial tribunal' required.[148]

The inflammatory rhetoric of Gladstone's pamphlet, particularly its much-quoted call for the Turks to leave Europe 'bag and baggage', encouraged a number of liberals and radicals to demand action against the Ottoman regime. Sometimes this took the form of an ambiguous moral interventionism: for example, a speaker seconding an anti-Turkish resolution at the Peace Society's 1877 public meeting hoped that 'the great British empire' would 'send forth a voice of no uncertain sound', and, after a member of the audience complained 'I thought this was to be a peace meeting', won applause by retorting: 'I do not know anything more pacific than public opinion.'[149] However, overt demands for a crusade were also made. The *Herald of Peace* noted sadly of some liberals and radicals: 'Their very philanthropy is bellicose and bloodthirsty', and became particularly critical of 'the clerical propensity to promote and justify war'.[150]

[146] In the Commons on 14 May 1877, cited in Matthew, *Gladstone 1809–1998*, 274.
[147] *Arbitrator* (Sept. 1876), 9.
[148] *HP* (June 1877), 250.   [149] *HP* (June 1877), 255.
[150] *HP* (Oct. 1876), 141; (June 1877), 253.

Gladstone's strong language, and the anti-Turkish crusading sentiment which it helped to stimulate, made Disraeli (who had just been created Earl of Beaconsfield) more determined than ever to stand by his own policy of defending the Ottoman empire against a possible incursion by Russia in support of its fellow Slavs. The peace movement found itself facing a fight for neutrality on two fronts, as it had during the Franco-Prussian War, but with the complication that on this occasion it had a strong ideological bias of its own, against Turkey. As later noted by the Peace Society, its duty was 'to hold an even balance between two strong opposing impulses, tending in the direction of general war'. One, mainly found among Conservatives, was anti-Russian and inspired by defencism ('the traditional policy of this country, which was supposed to bind us, for the sake of British interests, to maintain at all costs the integrity and independence of the Turkish Empire'). The other, advocated by some liberals and radicals, was anti-Turk and inspired by crusading ('the feeling of uncontrollable indignation caused in the popular heart by the revelations . . . of the hideous brutalities committed by the Turks in Bulgaria . . . which begot a desire in some quarter for armed intervention— to suppress such outrages, and to establish good Government in Turkey'[151]).

The peace movement's difficulty in adjusting rapidly to this complex new situation was apparent on 11 September when a WPA deputation talked generalities to the Foreign Secretary and gave him the impression that 'none of them seemed to have any clear idea of what they wanted'.[152] Moreover, its public meetings, though in O'Neill's words 'never surpassed as to the numbers attending them, or the strong feeling manifested', faced disruptions in some parts of the country: for example, in Liverpool a peace meeting on 21 November 1876 was 'interrupted by rowdy cheers for Beaconsfield' from 'Orangemen' and other 'rowdies' who had to be ejected by the police.[153] In an effort to demonstrate the underlying strength of anti-Beaconsfield opinion, a parliamentary committee of fifteen MPs[154] organized a National Conference on the Eastern Question in St James's Hall on 8 December 1876, attended by 1,200 people and dominated by Gladstone. Richard's speech betrayed a worry that this impressive occasion might prove more anti-Turk than anti-war: he therefore made clear that he did 'not want to go to war against Turkey any more than for it' and indeed regarded 'a war waged in the interests of philanthropy' as especially objectionable.[155] But he none the less

---

[151] *HP* (June 1877), 246–7.
[152] Stanley, *Diaries*, 325.
[153] *HP* (Dec. 1876), 179; (June 1877), 247–8.
[154] PSM, 20 Nov. 1876.
[155] Eastern Question Association, *Report of Proceedings of the Nations Conference at St James's Hall London December 8th 1876* (n.d.), 30–2, 83. Gladstone to Broadhurst 23 Nov. 1876: H. Broadhurst Papers I.

hailed it as 'the grandest public meeting of modern times',[156] and supported its decision to found an Eastern Question Association. This proved to be an inactive body; and the agitation against Beaconsfield's foreign policy lost momentum in the new year.

A new phase in the crisis was inaugurated on 24 April 1877, when Russia finally declared war on Turkey, thereby increasing the risk of British intervention. Since the attitude of working men to such an eventuality was understood to be decisive, the WPA came into its own. Urged by the Peace Society 'to be on their watch to exert their influence, on the side of peace and nonintervention as far as possible' and given a special subvention for the purpose, the association circulated 50,000 copies of *Shall We Go to War?*, an address endorsed by 217 representative working men, which warned against a war to help the 'waning power' of the Turks, 'a race whose dominion means the continued reign of vices too foul for Western civilization to name'. During June 1877 it protested against meetings held in London 'to support Lord Beaconsfield's policy of stirring up a feeling of antagonism against Russia'.[157] The crisis eased from July until early December, while the Russians were held up at Plevna; but after the fall of that stronghold demands for assistance to Turkey became more strident. When on 30 December 1877, the WPA's leaders took a brass band into Trafalgar Square for a meeting 'to protest against an unholy war to maintain the abominable tyranny of the unspeakable Turk', they 'found a large number of roughs and some hundreds of idle people awaiting them', as a sympathetic paper, the *Daily News*, reported.[158] Early in the new year the WPA began complaining of 'the nightly assurances of Music Hall singers and audiences that we have "got the ships and got the men and got the money too" '[159]—a reference to the popular song which gave the language the term 'jingoism', coined by a prominent radical, G. J. Holyoake, in a letter to the *Daily News* on 13 March 1878.[160] Fear of jingoistic violence saw the cancellation of a meeting due to have been addressed by Gladstone, whose house was attacked by a mob shortly afterwards.[161] And the 'disgraceful eruption of rowdyism' forced the Peace Society to suspend its meetings 'for some weeks . . . as drunken and disorderly men broke up the audiences by mere clamour and violence'.[162]

---

[156] *HP* (Jan. 1877), 182, 188.
[157] PSM, 18 Apr., 21 May 1877. *Arbitrator* (May 1877), 6–7, 10; (June 1877), 6–5.
[158] Cited in G. C. Thompson, *Public Opinion and Lord Beaconsfield* (2 vols., 1886), ii. 290–1.
[159] *Arbitrator* (Jan. 1878), 2: see also (June 1878), 2; (Aug. 1878), 7; (Dec. 1878), 11–12.
[160] H. Cunningham, 'Jingoism in 1877–78', *Victorian Studies*, 14 (1970–1), 429–53 at 429.
[161] *The Gladstone Diaries*, ed. M. R. D. Foot and H. C. G. Maththew (14 vols, Oxford, 1968–94), ix. 292–3.
[162] *HP* (June 1878), 80.

Tension reached its peak after a victorious Russia imposed the Treaty of San Stefano on Turkey early in March 1878 and the eirenic Lord Derby resigned. The WPA was anxious to prove that, in its treasurer's words to the Peace Society's meeting of members in May, 'the intelligent portion of the working classes, the *skilled* artisans, are generally in favour of peace, whereas the "Jingo" pro-war party is recruited from the higher and lower orders of the population, especially from the uneducated and ignorant among the masses'.[163] It had been waiting nervously for the gesture that more than anything else would justify its existence but which, as Cremer had pointed out as late as the end of March, 'must never be used except under circumstances of gravest importance'—the summoning of its 'National Council, all of whom are, more or less, men well known as possessing the confidence of their order'.[164]

On 1 April the WPA sent a representative to an emergency meeting of the Peace Society's executive committee 'to consult them as to the best course for the Working Men's body to adopt under the existing emergency'. Five days later leaders of the two organizations held a joint meeting, the proceedings of which, 'being of a confidential and at present incomplete nature', were not then recorded, but concerned an approach by the WPA through Richard to a wealthy Quaker chemical manufacturer from Birmingham, Arthur Albright, to fund a big anti-war demonstration in London on 10 April 1878.[165] Albright, who was soon revealed to have offered the remarkable sum of £1,000, attended a rare meeting of the Peace Society's general committee on 9 April, which discussed the practical arrangements;[166] and the following day, at what was claimed to be only four days' notice, a 'Workmen's National Anti-War and Arbitration Conference' took place in the Memorial Hall, Faringdon Street, attended by 470 delegates from many parts of the country. Burt took the chair; and Gladstone made the principal speech, which was rapturously received.[167] The conference was a remarkable feat of organization, perhaps the most impressive campaigning achievement so far in the peace movement's history, and was followed four weeks later by a second WPA conference in Faringdon Hall on 4 May at which 656 members of Joseph Arch's union—'genuine tillers of the soil', as the Peace Society emphasized—assembled 'for the purpose of protesting against this country being dragged into war, and to urge arbitration as a mode of settling present differences between England and Russia'.[168] Since this meeting cost £800, it is not

---

163 *HP* (June 1878), 78–9.   164 *HP* (Apr. 1878), 55.
165 PSM, 1, 6 Apr. 1878. *HP* (May 1878), 64.
166 PSM 9, 11 Apr. 1878.
167 Evans, *Cremer*, 100–3. *Arbitrator* (Apr. 1878), 3–15. *HP* (May 1878), 63.
168 *HP* (June 1878), 80.

surprising that additional contributions were required to pay for it. The most notable of these came from Samuel Morley, whose long-standing support for Arch's union probably predisposed him to help with this event, in contrast to his failure even to reply to Cobden's request for help with a disarmament petition seventeen years previously.[169]

The importance of the WPA's special conferences of 10 April and 4 May 1878 was emphasized by the limitations of the Peace Society's efforts at this time: two offers to hold a conference jointly with the Eastern Question Association in May were declined, first because the latter body feared 'an unfavourable contrast with their Conference of last year and also on account of the absence of many Members of Parliament during the Easter Recess', and then because it wanted to wait 'until the political crisis may become more threatening than at present'.[170] However, in the opening days of May 1878 peace and arbitration meetings, funded by Albright, were held in Birmingham, Leeds, Liverpool, Newcastle, Edinburgh, and Glasgow, and other northern and Scottish towns.[171] Later in May Albright proposed 'a national anti-war conference in London on June 3'; but the executive committee of the Peace Society referred the idea to its meeting of members, which expressed 'a considerable difference of opinion' and decided not to endorse it.[172] It probably feared that such a meeting would both risk disorder and appear partisan: its annual public meeting later the same day was enlivened by 'a small party of Jingoes' and reminded by its president that the society had 'nothing to do with politics'.[173]

During the summer of 1878 the crisis was brought to an end by an agreement to revise the Treaty of San Stefano at the Congress of Berlin, which the *Herald of Peace* initially hailed as 'already a virtual Court of International Arbitration'.[174] Instead of their usual visit to the annual meeting of the Association for the Reform and Codification of the Law of Nations, which that year was in Frankfurt, Richard and Levi went to Berlin in an effort to contribute to the development of international law by more direct methods. Their aim was to persuade the plenipotentiaries to build on Protocol 23 of twenty-two years previously; but they met with a firm refusal to consider any issue not covered in San Stefano. Their face was saved to some extent by the fact that Article 63 of the new Treaty of Berlin reaffirmed those decisions of

---

[169] PSM, 10 May 1878 and (for the Report of the Albright Anti-War Fund) 19 May 1879. Hodder, *Life of Samuel Morley*, 354–5.
[170] PSM, 29 Apr., 14 May 1878.
[171] *Arbitrator* (May 1878), 4–11.
[172] PSM, 20 May 1878. *HP* (June 1878), 79.
[173] PSM, Meeting of Members, 21 May 1878. *Arbitrator* (June 1878), 2. *HP* (June 1878), 87.
[174] *HP* (July 1878), 93.

the Congress of Paris which had not explicitly been modified, and could therefore be regarded as reiterating Protocol 23.[175] None the less, the Peace Society's view of the Congress became increasingly critical, as the WPA's had been from the start.[176] The limitations of the Concert of Europe as a promoter of international law were becoming more apparent than ever.

Although the Berlin Congress temporarily resolved what for nearly three years of 'incessant anxiety' had been 'the one absorbing question',[177] namely the Russo-Turkish conflict, the peace movement still had to contend with other aspects of what the government provocatively came to call its 'spirited foreign policy', such as its wars in Afghanistan.[178] It had to deal with belli-cose mobs: for example, at Birmingham, where the Peace Society's Midlands Auxiliary had held its own against the local jingoes during the previous three years, 'the war party' disrupted a town's meeting on 3 December 1878 to discuss the Afghan situation.[179]

The peace movement had also to deal with the charge that anyone who crit-icized a spirited foreign policy must be an advocate of peace at any price. Beaconsfield had borrowed this smear tactic from Palmerston: when the House of Lords debated the Afghan conflict on 10 December, he accused his opponents of being all motivated not by 'great Whig principles' but by 'that principle of peace-at-any-price, which a certain party in the country upholds', and made the remarkable assertion that this 'deleterious doctrine' had 'done more mischief than any I can well recall that have been afloat in this century. It has occasioned more wars than the most ruthless of conquerors . . . It has dimmed occasionally even the majesty of England.'[180] That the temperature of the peace-or-war debate was at an unprecedented level in the autumn of 1878 was further indicated by the appearance of Britain's first book-length exposition of militarism, by a Sandhurst lecturer, James Ram, who had been driven to take up his pen by dislike of the doctrine of peace at any price. (It should be noted, however, that Ram's militarism exhibited a revealing differ-ence from the continental variety, which reflected the liberal and secure envi-ronment in which it was produced: it rejected conscription, on the grounds that any 'nation that cannot find voluntary soldiers of her own stock deserves to be conquered by any other that can.'[181])

As during the 1850s when the 'peace at any price' label had first been

[175] *HP* (Aug. 1878), 110–12; (June 1879), 250–1. Miall, *Henry Richard*, 294–300.
[176] *HP* (Sept. 1878), 122. *Arbitrator* (July 1878), 1.
[177] *HP* (June 1878), 79, 82.
[178] See the complaints about this term in *HP* (June 1879), 252; (Oct. 1879), 312.
[179] PSM, 15 Oct., 2 Dec. 1878. *HP* (June 1879), 252–3.
[180] Hansard, ccxlii HL col. 520 (10 Dec. 1878).
[181] J. Ram, *The Philosophy of War* (1878), 72. Ram's views are discussed in Ceadel, *Origins of War Prevention*, 31.

applied, the Peace Society might have welcomed it as a tribute to its own absolutist viewpoint. But instead it worried about its unsettling effect on *pacificists*. Richard complained that Beaconsfield's tactics exploited 'ludicrous sensitivities' among Liberals, 'especially some of the younger members of that party', who in consequence 'scarcely ever make a speech without ostentatiously proclaiming that they don't belong to the peace at any price party'. He therefore played down the society's own pacifism as the belief of 'a small body of persons' which had 'never been imported into politics', and played up its determination 'to promote arbitration, or a mutual reduction of armaments, or to enforce the principle of non-intervention' based 'on those general grounds of reason, justice, humanity, and the interests of mankind, which most men are prepared, in thought at least, to admit'.[182] However, he failed to explain why the Peace Society did not avoid confusion by renouncing its pacifism and becoming officially *pacificist*.

Indeed, the society stood by its top-tier pacifism, as its dependence on Quaker support still required it to do, even while in practice treating this as more than ever an 'abstract' commitment. Thus fear of being seen to endorse defensive war caused its executive committee initially to hold back when Passy's Société française des amis de la paix announced an international peace congress to coincide with another Great Exhibition in Paris in October 1878. However, eventually it allowed Richard 'to take such part in the proceedings as his judgement may suggest'; and Henry Pease also decided to attend. They worked successfully to block a resolution approving the enforcement of international law, and also refused to support a federation of peace associations, on the grounds that continental ones mostly lacked 'an organized and independent existence'.[183] Partly because of the Peace Society's reservations, the Paris congress received little attention either at the time or subsequently, despite having been attended by as many as 150 delegates and being the only international peace meeting to be held between 1851 and 1889.

The Peace Society's insistence on remaining officially pacifist was making the formation of *pacificist* rivals ever more likely. In the autumn of 1879—during another Afghan War, which, having followed hard upon what the Peace Society condemned as a 'purely aggressive' war against the Zulus,[184] had intensified opposition to Beaconsfield's imperial policy—tentative steps had been taken in the direction of forming an Anti-Aggression League. The lead had been taken by the social philosopher Herbert Spencer, whose father

---

[182] *HP* (Jan. 1879), 184.
[183] PSM, 21 Sept. 1878, 15 Oct. 1878, 15 Jan. 1879. *HP* (Nov. 1878), 144, (June 1879), 250–1. M. H. Pease, *Henry Pease: A Short Story of his Life* (1897), 67. Abrams, 'A History of European Peace Societies', fos. 158–64.
[184] *HP* (Mar. 1879), 214.

had been an admirer of Dymond and his uncle a supporter of Sturge and Burritt. Impressed by the fact that working men and Nonconformists as well as his own circle of middle-class rationalists had 'been manifesting anti-war feelings very strongly', Spencer consulted a number of friends about an effort to resist the 're-barbarization' of Britain by 'an antagonistic agitation'. These friends included Frederic Harrison, who, though vulnerable as a Positivist to the appeal of a crusade in support of France, was opposed to British imperialism, and Arthur Hobhouse, uncle of L. T. Hobhouse and a formerly apolitical lawyer, who was incensed by Beaconsfield's Afghan policy. However, at this stage neither Spencer nor any of his associates followed up their idea.[185]

One reason for their delay in launching a pressure group was that during 1879–80 it was possible to condemn Beaconsfieldism through mainstream party politics. Indeed, Arthur Hobhouse felt that the foreign-policy crisis 'obliged him to become a party man' at this time.[186] The peace movement drew closer than ever to Liberalism. In the spring of 1879 the *Herald of Peace* published an unusually outspoken attack on the government's 'bellicose policy of theatrical Imperialism', though to avoid accusations of partisanship it claimed that this was 'not because Lord Beaconsfield is a Conservative, but because he is a tool of the Jingoes and of sycophantic Imperialists'. It also accused the cabinet of being influenced by those with 'so many vested pecuniary interests in a warlike policy, aided . . . by stockjobbing specialists',[187] thereby adopting the radical critique which the WPA had already been using, for example in its claim that the Turkish investments of London's 'Stock Exchange gamblers and financiers' explained the jingoism of 1878.[188]

More significantly, Gladstone not only broadened his critique of the Eastern Question into more general indictment of 'Imperialism'—a word he had first used in 1878[189]—but also launched an innovative political campaign with a series of speeches in his new constituency of Midlothian in November 1879. After a general election was called, he made a second series of speeches there in March and April 1880. The six 'right principles of foreign policy' which he set out in his Midlothian campaign emphasized peace and freedom, rejected 'needless and entangling engagements', and accepted 'the equal rights of all nations', whilst also stressing the Concert of Europe. Moreover, after he triumphed in the general election, he took office for the first time as a 'liberal' (as distinct from 'liberal conservative').[190] Even though Gladstone

[185] Ceadel, *Origins of War Prevention*, 387, 408. H. Spencer, *An Autobiography* (2 vols., 1904), i. 306–6; ii. 329–30. Vogeler, *Frederic Harrison*, 188.
[186] L. T. Hobhouse and J. L. Hammond, *Lord Hobhouse: A Memoir* (1905), 115.
[187] *HP* (May 1879), 233–4.   [188] *Arbitrator* (Apr. 1878), 2.
[189] Matthew, *Gladstone 1809–1898*, 307.
[190] Ibid. 353, 375.

never espoused a fully *pacificist* position, he and Beaconsfield had between them aligned their parties in such a way that the left became identified with an idealistic and pacific foreign policy and the right with a power-political and imperialistic one. Not all Liberals were happy with this alignment: Joseph Chamberlain already believed that his party was harmed 'by its connection with those who are in favour of peace at any price and others who measure everything by a pecuniary standard'.[191] But the logic of adversary politics meant that most of them, and later most Labour politicians, found themselves expounding a *pacificist* rhetoric—even though it proved difficult to turn into a distinctive policy while in office—as an alternative to the defencism expounded by the Conservatives.

The peace movement understood the 1880 general election in these ideological terms: for example, the Peace Society's annual report noted that the central issue had not been 'the justice or injustice of this or that particular war, but what was to be the fixed policy of the government'.[192] Its goodwill towards Gladstone's new government was apparent when Richard, who been waiting to introduce a reduction-of-armaments motion since the previous autumn,[193] won a chance to do so on 15 June 1880. Faced with a plea from the new Prime Minister not to press it to a division, Richard accepted an alternative formula suggested by Bright, who was a member of the new government, which Gladstone accepted and was carried without a division.[194] Indeed, for the first two years of the new administration, the peace movement had no doubts where it stood on 'the question as between war and arbitration, or as between Gladstonianism and Jingoism'.[195]

Having a government which it truly admired helped compensate the Peace Society for an institutional setback. It had been selling investments to fund its campaign over the Eastern Question, and thereafter succumbed to financial problems at the end of the 1870s as an economic recession and the deaths of key donors reduced its income. Facing a deficit, the society noticed 'the extraordinary proportion of the subscriptions, absorbed by the cost of collection under the present system', and decided to dismiss its Birmingham-based collector, Lewis Appleton, with whom it had been in dispute over his expenses claims and his tendency to issue appeals and give lectures without the society's permission. A talented though wayward man, Appleton was frustrated by a collector's lowly and limited role: he had previously applied unsuccessfully to be a lecturer for the society, had contemplated working for the 'French Peace Society', and had written Liberal political pamphlets. After

---

[191] Chamberlain to W. T. Stead, 10 Aug. 1878, cited in M. Swartz, *The Politics of British Foreign Policy in the Era of Disraeli and Gladstone* (1985), 131.
[192] *HP* (June 1880), 79.   [193] PSM, 5 Nov. 1879. *HP* (June 1880), 75–6.
[194] Hansard, cclii HC cols. 80–112.   [195] *HP* (Mar. 1882), 25–6.

the expiry of the three months notice which he had been given in February 1880, he appealed for reinstatement; but, after he had been personally 'heard at some length' by the executive committee, this was turned down at the end of July. And although on departing he handed over £577 which he owed to the society, 'at least £220 of subscriptions and donations . . . received by him' remained unaccounted for.[196]

Appleton's cleverness was shown in the speed and skill with which he founded a rival organization, the International Arbitration and Peace Association (IAPA), to provide him with employment. The process whereby he did so remains obscure because the records of this organization have not survived; and those of his co-founders who wrote accounts did so many years later.[197] Appleton seems to have acted as catalyst to individuals who were anyway thinking of starting a *pacificist* association. The veteran municipal reformer William Phillips hosted the preparatory meetings, which commenced on 16 August 1880, according to the first annual report. Dr G. B. Clark, a doctor associated with various political causes, including the Transvaal Independence Committee of which he became secretary in January 1881, was one of those taking part.[198] Herbert Spencer was consulted at one stage; but the others thought his 'anti-aggression' approach too negative, so he continued to explore it independently. It was noteworthy, however, that few with prior experience of the peace movement were involved in the foundation of the IAPA, apart from the newspaper proprietor Passmore Edwards, a former stalwart of both the League of Universal Brotherhood and the Stop-the-War League, who became a vice-president and resigned from the Peace Society's executive committee in consequence,[199] and Hodgson Pratt, honorary international agent of the WPA, who became chairman and was soon to be the association's acknowledged leader. Appleton also broke new ground for peace associations by recruiting aristocratic vice-presidents, such as the Duke of Westminster and the Earls of Derby and Shaftesbury, to add lustre to the IAPA's letterhead.

The title of the new association was shrewdly chosen, presumably by Appleton. 'Peace' evoked the long-standing Peace Society. 'International

[196] PSM, 5 Nov., 19 Dec. 1879, 29 Jan., 13 Feb., 8 June, 23 and 30 July, 14 Nov. 1880, 3 Jan. 1881.

[197] W. Phillips, *Sixty Years of Citizen Work and Play* (n.d. [1910]), 18–20. G. B. Clark, 'The Origins of the I.A.P.A.', *Concord* (Nov./Dec. 1914), 131–2. J. Frederick Green, 'The I.A.P.A.', *Arbitrator* (Apr. 1925), 30. These, the published annual reports which survive for 1881, 1882, 1887, 1891–4, 1897, 1901, and 1909, the *IAPA Monthly Journal* (July 1884–Apr. 1887), *Concord* (May 1887–Dec. 1917/Jan. 1918), and occasional reports in *The Times*, are the main sources used for this account.

[198] A. Davey, *The British Pro-Boers 1877–1902* (Cape Town, 1978), 27.

[199] PSM, 15 Nov. 1880.

Arbitration' and 'Association' evoked the local International Arbitration Associations which the society had set up only eight years previously: indeed, Appleton had briefly acted as secretary of one of these, in Manchester; and his long-serving successor in that capacity, William Pollard, was loudest in his complaints about 'the injurious effects in the North of England, of Lewis Appleton's efforts to obtain subscribers and supporters for his new association'. Richard was also alarmed that, because Appleton was well known as the Peace Society's former collector, many of its supporters would support his new venture 'under a misapprehension that it was for the support of the efforts of this Society'.[200] And the Glasgow-based Quaker journal *British Friend*, which had long been disposed to support the Peace Society's rivals, was willing to publicize the IAPA. As a result many of those who originally supported Appleton's new initiative did so on the basis of misinformation: indeed, it was notable that of the twenty-five names listed as constituting the IAPA's executive committee in 1881, no fewer than seventeen disappeared the following year.

Yet for those consciously seeking an alternative to the Peace Society, the IAPA had five plausible features. Three were reminiscent of the short-lived Peace of Nations Society thirty-three years previously. First, it was *pacificist*: its circular appealed to those 'unable to accept the abstract doctrine that all war is wrong'; and Phillips liked to quote from a favourite poem the tag: 'War if not defensive, indefensible'.[201] The Peace Society insisted that it had been promoting *pacificist* policies such as arbitration for many years, but was undeniably committed to pacifism.

Second, the IAPA did not claim to be Christian, and therefore appealed to a secularist movement that was making significant strides: indeed, 1880 marked the start of the atheist Charles Bradlaugh's six-year struggle to take his seat in the Commons; and both he and his daughter Hypatia Bradlaugh Bonner were notable late nineteenth-century peace activists. The Peace Society could not deny that its rules excluded non-Christians without offending its leading supporters.

Third, the IAPA was professedly an international association. This claim was especially resented by the Peace Society, which devoted most of its one public statement about 'Mr Lewis Appleton's Proposed New Peace Association' to the argument that it was possible to be more international than the Peace Society had been for 'thirty or forty years' only by creating 'an international committee' meeting 'in some central place like London, or Paris,

---

[200] *HP* (Nov. 1872), 151. Richard to Walter Wren, 29 Dec. 1880: PSLB. PSM, 3 Jan. 1881.
[201] In 1907 he was to use from this as the title of a pamphlet: it came Philip James Bailey's poem, *Festus*, originally published in 1839.

or Boston', which was an 'absurdity' that no 'man in his senses' could regard as practicable.[202] Nevertheless, the IAPA claimed 'adherents' in foreign countries, established relations with both Lemonnier and Passy in France, and held small conferences in Europe, notably at Brussels in October 1882 and Berne in August 1884 with a number of preparatory meetings in Paris in between. (At the Peace Society's 1884 meeting of members a harassed and perhaps also jealous Richard, facing enquiries as to why he and his executive committee had given up trying to hold European congresses, was to allude to one of the IAPA's international gatherings as having been a 'fiasco' which had 'done much more harm than good', thereby prompting a protest from Pratt.[203]) In addition, Pratt travelled widely on the continent, where he became better known than in Britain.

The fourth distinctive feature of the IAPA was that women were allowed as members of the executive committee. One of the beneficiaries of this rule, Mrs E. M. Southey, aware that the Peace Society had declined to do the same, persuaded the Ladies Peace Association, of which she was the main founder, to support Appleton's new organization. Forced by the Peace Society to choose between it and the IAPA, it opted for the latter, and therefore disaffiliated from the former in the spring of 1882.[204] The Peace Society replaced it with a new ladies auxiliary on 12 July 1882,[205] thanks to the willingness of Priscilla Peckover, a Quaker from a banking family in Wisbech, Cambridgeshire, to play a leading role in organizing it. Miss Peckover, who thereby began her rise to international celebrity within peace circles, was to prove herself an astonishingly successful mobilizer of grass-roots support.[206]

The IAPA's fifth novelty was its aspiration to become an arbitral tribunal in its own right. It intended, 'in the event of any dispute arising between two nations', to draw up 'a careful statement of the facts, which shall be published widely in the two countries', whilst at the same time it urged 'the immediate appointment of arbitrators'.[207] In other words, it wished not only to create what a peace association founded half a century later, the New Commonwealth Society, would call an 'international equity tribunal' but also to constitute that equity tribunal itself. As Sturge, Burritt, and Wheeler had already discovered in their attempt to mediate between Prussia and Denmark by personal shuttle diplomacy in 1850, such third-party initiatives led inevitably to accusations from one or other party of partiality.[208]

---

[202] *HP* (Oct. 1880), 134.   [203] *HP* (June 1884), 62; (July 1884), 85.

[204] Richard to Priscilla Peckover, 17 Dec. 1881: PSLB. PSM, 23 Dec. 1881; 14 Mar., 26 Apr. 1882.

[205] PSM, 19 June, 9 Aug. 1882.

[206] For her career see V. Grossi, *Le Pacifisme européen 1889–1914* (Brussels, 1994), 90–6.

[207] *The Times* (22 Sept. 1881).

[208] See Ceadel, *Origins of War Prevention*, 454.

As well as committing itself to an ambitious and contentious mission, the IAPA was initially saddled with the corrupt Appleton as its principal orga-nizer. Although the Peace Society never publicly announced why it had parted company with him, it privately notified his new employers of 'the extreme irregularity of his management of the funds entrusted to him', and refused to sign a letter drafted by Appleton 'exonerating him . . . from having been orig-inally dismissed on grounds of dishonesty'.[209] However, Appleton managed to hoodwink the IAPA for several years, perhaps by declaring that he would not take a salary: his 'first year's services were gratuitous' according to the IAPA's first annual report. The IAPA's initial worries concerned its financial weakness: although claiming 1,710 'adhesions' during its first year, its actual subscribers numbered no more than 450. As early as November 1881 Pratt was seeking a merger with other associations: the WPA considered this possi-bility seriously, but politely rejected it on 18 January 1882.[210]

While the IAPA was struggling to make a go of itself, Herbert Spencer had approached Richard, impressed by another parliamentary resolution that he had introduced on 29 April 1881 condemning the propensity of Britain's colo-nial officials 'to contract engagements, annex territories, and make war' on their own authority: this had been defeated only by seventy-two votes to sixty-four.[211] On behalf of Frederic Harrison, John Morley, Arthur Hobhouse, and others, Spencer urged the Peace Society to adopt 'the ground not of non-resistance but non-aggression'. Although it predictably declined this sugges-tion, its secretary attended the protracted series of meetings to set up a separate association based on the non-aggression principle. By the end of 1881 the decision had been at last taken to launch an Anti-Aggression League:[212] Richard had evidently managed to remove anything offensive to pacifists from the aims of this body, and therefore felt able to support it. So, less surprisingly, did Joseph Whitwell Pease, who had become the new pres-ident of the Peace Society upon his uncle Henry's death, despite having once been a member of the Hull Volunteers.[213]

As set out at a prominent though modestly attended public launch at Westminster Palace Hotel on 22 February 1882, at which Spencer made a rare venture into public speaking, the Anti-Aggression League's goals were to provide information on foreign and colonial relations, to increase parliamen-tary control over the executive, to curb the power of officials overseas, to limit the use of force 'in defence of every British subject, wherever he may choose

[209] PSM, 14 Feb., 6 Apr. 1881.
[210] *Arbitrator* (Dec. 1881), 8; (Jan. 1882), 8.
[211] For Richard's speech see Hansard, cclx HC cols. 1423–33.
[212] PSM, 30 May, 29 Sept., 22 Nov., 23 Dec. 1881.
[213] Beckett, *Riflemen Form*, 29.

to wander', and to promote arbitration—all policies already supported by the Peace Society and unexceptionable to progressive opinion.[214]

Despite having thus carefully protected itself from the peace-at-any-price jibe, the Anti-Aggression League foundered. To some extent this was because of its timing. The belief that Gladstonianism was an assured antidote to aggression was still strong among progressives, particularly in view of the fact that Beaconsfield had died in April 1881. Hobhouse was convinced that this was why the league 'met with no support'.[215] Richard also acknowledged that some people thought the league had 'come into existence too late', though he emphatically and presciently insisted that the snake of jingoism had been scotched but not killed.[216] And Harrison, who as a Positivist was detached from Liberalism, claimed that the league 'melted away under the poisonous solvent of the party system'.[217] To a much greater extent, however, the league failed because a potentially broad ideological base was no substitute for leadership and drive. Spencer, who had found the launch meeting a chore to organize, later acknowledged that he had assumed that if the 'large amount of anti-war feeling . . . were provided with some means of expressing itself, there would result a self-sustaining movement', and therefore expected to 'initiate such a movement, and then leave others to carry it on'. Yet he found that from neither religious nor political circles 'did there come any support worth naming.'[218]

The Anti-Aggression League had thus faltered even before a transformation in the political scene took place which might have made it but in fact broke it. Whereas as late as 23 May 1882 the Peace Society's annual report had welcomed the unusual fact 'that throughout the vast extent of the British empire there has been peace everywhere within our borders', by the beginning of June Richard was warning: 'Things are looking very ugly in Egypt'.[219] The Gladstone government's intervention in Egypt ended the peace movement's second period of comparative influence.

The additional knowledge of 'all the ghastly and horrible details of the battlefield, the ambulance and the hospitals'[220] which the Franco-Prussian War in particular had provided, and the tensions resulting from the unification of Germany, the Eastern Question, and Beaconsfieldism had helped to increase public interest in the peace question. However, the peace movement did much

---

[214] *The Times* (23 Feb. 1882), 5c.
[215] Hobhouse and Hammond, *Lord Hobhouse*, 138.   [216] *HP* (Mar. 1882), 32.
[217] Harrison, *Autobiographical Memoirs*, ii. 122.
[218] Spencer to Richard, 4 and 16 Feb. 1882: Richard Papers NLW MS 5505C. Spencer, *Autobiography*, ii. 376–7.
[219] *HP* (June 1872), 66, 72.   [220] *HP* (Mar. 1873), 204.

to ensure its own revival: although the devious Appleton had been able to exploit the reservations about the Peace Society held by a progressive mainstream which was increasingly secular as well as *pacificist* in outlook, it had energetically campaigned for arbitration, and forged a lasting though inter- mittently disillusioning connection with artisans, international lawyers, and Liberals. The peace movement depended heavily on Richard's personal ability to use the zeal and resolution of the absolutist wing to prevent the reformist wing becoming too tempted by the compromises of mainstream politics; and from the onset of the Egyptian crisis he was to find this difficult.

5

Relapse,
June 1882–August 1898

During the decade and a half between the Egyptian crisis and the summoning of the first Hague Conference, peace activism underwent a disappointing relapse. Britain's interventions in Egypt and the Sudan, the more depressing for being carried out by a Liberal government, knocked the stuffing out of much of the movement. By the 1890s, in contrast, the comparative absence of international crisis prevented its recovery, by allowing public attention to concentrate on domestic issues, including Ireland.

Pacifism was increasingly relegated to a personal sphere even by members of the Peace Society; and the reprinting by the Friends' Peace Committee of Dymond's essays,[1] in preference to issuing new literature, indicated that it was intellectually in the doldrums. The reduction of armaments disappeared from the political agenda because many British progressives thought it impractical, as for the most part did the continental *pacificists* who revived International (now called 'Universal') Peace Congresses in 1889. Indeed, even the more modest goal of the limitation of armaments increasingly seemed too ambitious. Arbitration received significant support only in its most limited forms, such as an Anglo-American treaty. And schemes for international government were, with hindsight, conspicuous by their absence.

The established primary movement faltered through financial and ideological difficulties. Individual campaigners and thinkers, *ad hoc* bodies, and secondary associations began to step into the breach, though as yet only tentatively. The most conspicuous independent publicist was to be W. T. Stead, the son of a Congregational minister and a brashly innovative journalist whose capacity to metamorphose from 'a Jingo of the Jingoes' into 'the bitterest foe of Jingoes' and back was to be one of the peace movement's biggest perplexities.[2] Despite having supported Gladstone over the Bulgarian horrors, during the 1880s Stead campaigned for naval expansion and for the sending of General Gordon's expedition to the Sudan.[3] He did not take up the peace

---

[1] Minutes, FPC, 20 July 1888.
[2] These descriptions were used by a puzzled Cremer in the *Arbitrator* (July 1890), 62.
[3] F. Whyte, *The Life of W. T. Stead* (2 vols., 1925), i. 117.

cause until 1894, and even then not consistently. The most important intellectual was Tolstoy, though his ultra-pacifist ideas took time to reach their full influence in British progressive circles. Special initiatives such as the Arbitration Alliance began to be launched, albeit only in the 1890s. And socialist societies were eventually to offer valuable support to the primary peace movement, though the most prominent of these, the Independent Labour Party (ILP), was not founded until 1893 and, despite declaring support for 'disarmament and universal peace' as early as its 1894 conference, was in the words of its principal historian 'primarily domestic' in its 'early horizons'.[4] Thus neither the primary associations nor the various potential substitutes for them made much of a mark during this period.

EGYPT, RADICALISM, AND DILUTION, JUNE 1882–MAY 1884

British involvement in Egypt enabled the older peace associations to demonstrate their mettle. The WPA summoned a protest meeting for representative working men and MPs at the Westminster Palace Hotel on 20 June, at which Sir Wilfrid Lawson was the main speaker and a broad-based Egyptian Committee was set up. The Peace Society issued a stern address to the government the following day.[5]

However, although Spencer drew up a 'circular' on the Egyptian question for the Anti-Aggression League on 16 June, his desire 'to express somewhat more sympathy with the Government in the difficulty of its position than has thus far been done' played into the hands of the Prime Minister. Gladstone invited him to breakfast on 22 June, and won him over by expressing 'very hearty sympathy' for his league and accusing the Peace Society of having 'botched the matter' by its rigid adherence to non-resistance. Spencer thereafter trusted Gladstone and Bright to ensure that the government behaved with as much restraint as possible over Egypt,[6] though the Anti-Aggression League went ahead with a meeting on 26 June at which Harrison spoke.[7]

Britain's bombardment of Alexandria on 11 July 1882 inaugurated a military occupation of Egypt, which proved successful, although it was followed by an entanglement in the Sudan where an ill-fated British expedition under

---

[4] D. Howell, *British Workers and the Independent Labour Party 1888–1906* (1983), 345.

[5] *Arbitrator* (June 1882), 2–4. *HP* (July 1882), 82.

[6] Spencer to Bright, 24 June 1882, cited in D. Duncan, *The Life and Letters of Herbert Spencer* (1908), 224. *Gladstone Diaries*, x. 284. Spencer to Richard, 25 June 188: Richard Papers NLW MS 5505C.

[7] *HP* (July 1882), 91–2. D. Wiltshire's reference to the League's 'first meeting' being on '16 June 1882' seems to be an error: see *The Social and Political Thought of Herbert Spencer* (Oxford, 1978), 91–2.

General Gordon was sent in 1884. During this period progressives had thus to make painful choices between their political support for Gladstone and their moral opposition to aggression.

Most chose the former, a reality which killed off the Anti-Aggression League. Its leaders met the Egyptian Committee in an attempt find a basis for cooperation, but were accused by Cremer of being merely 'an anti-*Tory* Aggression League'.[8] By the time Spencer took himself off to lecture in the United States in August, his League was reported to have 'died of sheer inanition'.[9]

However, a minority chose the latter option. Bright resigned from the cabinet on 15 July, though his loyalty to his former colleagues prevented him from speaking out against their policy.[10] The Congregationalist theologian Dr Samuel Davidson, an outspoken opponent of the Crimean War and a veteran vice-president of the Peace Society, concluded that the Egyptian campaign 'must be condemned by every true disciple of Christ', and noted sadly: 'The Liberals are better in opposition than in office.'[11]

Despite its alliance with Gladstone during the Eastern crisis of the late 1870s, the WPA had preserved a degree of detachment from his government,[12] and therefore felt uninhibited about campaigning on the Egyptian issue. However, it was financially constrained in consequence of a 'very considerably diminished' subvention from a financially embarrassed Peace Society.[13] The WPA believed that real responsibility for the Egyptian imbroglio lay with the bondholders who had duped Gladstone into protecting their special interests. (In fact Gladstone was himself a bondholder, holding a third of his personal portfolio in Egyptian Tribute Loan.[14]) By seeing financial interests as harmful, the WPA helped to push radical thinking further away from Cobdenism and towards the analysis which J. A. Hobson was to make famous twenty years later. For example, Cremer argued in 1882: 'The men who formerly made wars were generally monarchs and unscrupulous statesmen, but our modern warmakers are financiers';[15] and he also vented his anger upon 'Army Contractors, Unprincipled Speculators, and Unscrupulous Journalists', as well as 'our aristocratic Foreign Office officials'.[16] At times the WPA's propaganda sounded incipiently socialist, as

---

[8] *Arbitrator* (July 1882), 4–7.   [9] *Arbitrator* (Aug. 1882), 4.
[10] As noted by M. E. Chamberlain, 'British Public Opinion and the Invasion of Egypt, 1882', *Trivium*, 16 (1981), 5–28 at 20.
[11] Diary entry for 27 Nov. 1882, cited in *The Autobiography of Samuel Davidson, D.D., Ll.D. Edited by his Daughter* (Edinburgh, 1899), 134.
[12] See e.g. *Arbitrator* (Feb. 1881), 3–4.   [13] *Arbitrator* (Sept. 1883), 1.
[14] Matthew, *Gladstone 1809–1898*, 387–8.
[15] *Arbitrator* (Sept. 1882), 2: see also (Nov. 1882), 2.
[16] *Arbitrator* (July 1884), 3; (Jan. 1885), 2.

when it denounced 'the powerful and selfish class of capitalists'. Too often, however, it was merely anti-Semitic, as when it condemned 'the pernicious influence wielded by stockjobbers and the whole tribe of Shylocks'.[17]

The Peace Society also condemned the Egyptian and Sudanese adventures—the last time it was to take a robust stand against a major British military involvement. It took pride in having protested 'before actual hostilities had commenced' in Egypt,[18] condemned the 'national conceit' which had persuaded Britain it could 'manage the affairs of every people better than they can themselves', and pronounced itself humiliated by the fact that a Liberal Party which had gone to the country with an anti-jingo cry only two years before 'should now try to rehabilitate what some think its waning popularity, on a foundation of pure Jingoism'.[19] Richard spoke out four times in parliament, although the paucity of his support from fellow Liberal MPs, including Quakers, caused him 'surprise and regret' and led to complaints at the Peace Society's next meeting of members.[20] The tightening of party discipline was making it harder for the ordinary Liberal MP to stick his neck out, with the result that individualists such as Sir Wilfrid Lawson and Henry Labouchere were left to articulate what others presumably thought. With the Liberal press often leaving their criticisms of the Egyptian involvement unreported, both the Peace Society and the WPA were accused of being soft on the government for partisan reasons, an accusation that was extremely hurtful to those who had in fact made themselves very unpopular by criticizing their political friends. When even Harrison—who opposed the Sudanese War under the auspices of the Positivist Society following the collapse of the Anti-Aggression League—took this line at the beginning of 1884, Richard expressed bitter resentment at the 'disposition in this country to sneer at the Peace Society and to condemn it whatever it does or abstains from doing'.[21]

Its opposition to the Egyptian and Sudanese interventions took a heavy toll on the Peace Society. In personal terms Richard found unpopularity harder to take than during the Crimean War: this was partly because of his age (being now in his seventies, he was less resilient) but also because of his position (having become a national figure, he now had more to forfeit in the way of public affection).

The criticism incurred by the Peace Society reduced its capacity to uphold its own absolutism in a rigorous fashion, particularly as it was aware that to do so would merely advertise a cleavage within an increasingly beleaguered

---

[17] *Arbitrator* (July 1883), 8; (Oct. 1883), 3.
[18] *HP* (June 1883), 235.
[19] *HP* (Nov. 1882), 142; (Dec. 1882), 154.
[20] *HP* (Aug. 1882), 100–4; (June 1883), 233.
[21] Richard to Harrison, 5 Jan. 1884: PSLB.

peace movement. Demands that it abandon pacifism became more insistent: even one of its most active supporters, James Henderson, called for this at the 1883 meeting of members.[22] Through constant use, the society's standard reply—that such a step was unnecessary because the Peace Society collaborated with *pacificists* in any case—became so well honed as to become double-edged: it implied that the society's top-tier pacifism had lost all practical meaning because the society already behaved as if it was *pacificist*. Thus, while refusing formally to abandon its pacifism, the society seemed increasingly willing after 1882 to concede that it was of little real significance.

Moreover, some of its members were weakening in their personal absolutism. As early as the autumn of 1880 its employee William Pollard had published an article claiming that pacifism was a 'counsel of perfection' which the Peace Society had never urged upon 'governments only nominally Christian' like those of modern Britain.[23] Pollard was a leader of the liberal, anti-evangelical faction within the Society of Friends which was beginning to present the peace testimony as a peculiarity of the devout which need not be recommended to those exercising political responsibilities.[24] And Appleton had justified his involvement with the *pacificist* IAPA by arguing that his own pacifism applied 'only to Christian men and communities' and not 'in the international sense', since 'in the world's present degenerate state' the lion would not lie down with the lamb, as in Isaiah's prophecy; rather, 'the lamb would be inside the lion'.[25] It was not surprising therefore that one of the rising stars of the Society of Friends, J. W. Graham, then an undergraduate at King's College, Cambridge, responded to the occupation of Egypt by disputing the proposition 'that for any Christian government to make war is a sin', while insisting that as a Quaker he was personally committed to the peace testimony.[26]

Pollard's, Appleton's, and Graham's approach was compatible with true pacifism provided that those who held it genuinely wanted their fellow citizens all to come round to their own absolutist faith. If they did not—because they wanted enough people without pacifist scruples always to be available to defend their country—they were 'exemptionists' rather than pacifists. (I have discussed the difference between pacifism and merely seeking exemption from military service for oneself more fully elsewhere.[27]) During the

[22] *HP* (June 1883), 234.

[23] *Fraser's Magazine* (Oct. 1880), 490–500, at 492, 496.

[24] See D. M. Blamires, 'Towards a Biography of William Pollard', *Journal of the Friends' Historical Society*, 55 (1983–9), 112–23.

[25] *British Friend* (Feb. 1881), 45.   [26] *Friend* (Dec. 1882), 304.

[27] See Ceadel, *Pacifism in Britain 1914–1945*, 9–10, 20–1, 43–6 (where it is called 'quasi-pacifism'), and *Thinking about Peace and War*, 139–41.

Egyptian and Sudanese Wars it was apparent that an increasing number of Quakers did not know where they stood on this point, their general 'luke-warmness' towards the peace testimony at this time prompting an acknowledgement that never in its history had their sect been 'so divided' on the subject.[28]

With backsliding on the increase within the Society of Friends, it was not surprising that even the executive committee of the Peace Society was affected. In 1882, for example, one member resigned because he could not accept pacifism. He was not forced out by a society which still demanded high standards of absolutism of its leading members: instead, Richard expressed regret at his departure and informed him that 'if you had continued amongst us you would never have found any measure proposed by us which you could not have cordially supported'.[29] No concern was expressed that a non-pacifist had been elected to the executive committee in the first place. Indeed, the society seems to have tacitly relaxed its requirements for committee members at this time. In an editorial in the *Herald of Peace*—which, bowing to the *pacificist* wind, added 'and International Arbitration' to its title with effect from May 1883—Richard argued that the principles they were required to endorse 'amount to no more than this "that war is inconsistent with the spirit of Christianity and the true interests of mankind"'.[30] Though technically accurate, his statement ignored the fact that since the society's inception that phrase had been understood to refer to *all* war.[31] The dilution of the Peace Society's top-tier pacifism, which was matched by an increasing tendency for the WPA to deny being 'a peace-at-any-price party',[32] was thus well under way before Richard relinquished the secretaryship.

By the spring of 1884 retirement seemed an attractive prospect to Richard, especially after the particularly bruising experience of supporting Labouchere's criticism of the government's policy in the Sudan with an uncompromising speech condemning the killing of Arabs 'for no offence . . . except that they were defending their families against invasion',[33] and being subsequently vilified for his pains. The previous two years had seen his hopes dashed for the second time in a long career. Just as the society's own pressure-group efforts had collapsed after seeming to influence public opinion during 1848–51, so the Gladstonian Liberal Party had succumbed to imperialism after

---

[28] *Friend* (Mar. 1883), 115; (Apr. 1884), 91
[29] PSM, 26 Apr. 1882. Richard to W. G. Snowdon Gard, 18 May 1882 (copy): PSLB.
[30] *HP* (July 1883), 254.
[31] Ceadel, *Origins of War Prevention*, 226–30.
[32] *Arbitrator* (Oct. 1883), 4.
[33] Aberdare to Richard, 19 March 1884: Richard Papers NLW MS 14021D. Hansard, cclxxxv HC col. 1670.

seeming admirably *pacificist* during 1879–81. Although at the executive committee on 17 May 1884 Richard agreed to stay on for a while, he told the meeting of members three days later that this was because he did 'not wish to leave the ship in a storm, or to abandon his post at a period of trial or danger'; and he drew attention to 'symptoms of declining health, which warn him he must not put too much strain upon his strength'.[34] His monument in the Congregational cemetery at Abney Park in north London, unveiled five years later, was to give 1884 as the end of his secretaryship of the Peace Society:[35] though an error, this accurately identified the year in which he lost his appetite for the job.

In its attempt to be a new kind of peace association, the IAPA did not take a stand against the intervention in Egypt; and in any case its lack of a periodical (until July 1884) ensured that its profile was low. Instead, it worked at its European links, soon discovering how difficult the role of international equity tribunal was going to be. In particular, it found that even peace activists were divided on national lines over contentious issues. The worst of these was Alsace-Lorraine, which Germany had seized from France in 1870–1. Thus Jean Dollfuss of Strasbourg—an early supporter of Passy's association but, following his enforced change of nationality as a result of the Franco-Prussian War, a deputy in the German Reichstag—'disturbed' the 'calmness' of the IAPA's Brussels conference with a letter demanding the return of this province.[36] And a similar demand at the IAPA's third annual conference, by a renegade French Catholic priest who had also supported Passy, Père Hyacinthe Loyson, provoked a strong letter of dissent from Karl Blind, a German refugee active in London's progressive politics.[37]

None the less the IAPA continued to offer practical solutions to international questions, neutralization becoming its particular favourite. It tried with French colleagues 'to arrive at an understanding on the subject of Egypt and the Suez canal'. And on 22 December 1884, it recommended that a friendly mission be sent to the Sudanese rebels who were laying siege to General Gordon's forces, instead of another military expedition, having been persuaded to take this emollient line by the pro-Egyptian poet and traveller Wilfrid Scawen Blunt.[38]

---

[34] PSM, 17 May 1884. *HP* (June 1884), 61–2.

[35] I am grateful to Dr A. D. Harvey for a photograph of this memorial, as I am to Professor Keith Robbins for a postcard of Richard's statue in Tregaron (for which see PSM, 30 Aug. 1893).

[36] *The Times* (18 Oct. 1882).

[37] *IAPA Monthly Journal* (1 July 1884), 10; (1 Aug. 1884), 17–18. For Loyson, see V. Grossi, *Le Pacifisme européen 1889–1914* (Brussels, 1994), 188–93.

[38] *The Times* (12 July 1883). *IAPA Monthly Journal* (Sept./Oct. 1884), 26; (15 Jan. 1885), 59.

INSTITUTIONAL INTROSPECTION, 1884–1889

The mid-to-late 1880s were marked by severe organizational problems which forced the primary associations to consider their very future. A number of controversies occurred in 1884–5: a naval scare, largely fomented by Stead, which prompted the Cobden Club to reissue its hero's *The Three Panics* and was later counted as the fourth of six panics in an updated version of that work by the editor of the *Economist*, F. W. Hirst;[39] the killing of General Gordon in January 1885, causing national outrage and resulting in General Wolseley's punitive expedition to the Sudan; a Franco-German war crisis; and an Anglo-Russian confrontation over Afghanistan.

In responding to these controversies, peace activists found themselves more isolated than ever from their Liberal colleagues yet still accused by defencists of applying 'one moral standard to the conduct of Conservatives and another to the conduct of Liberals'.[40] Richard steered a courageous middle course: when the Commons debated a Conservative motion censuring the government, he repeated his condemnation of the Gladstonian military interventions, but insisted that 'the heaviest measure of guilt is at the door of the party opposite' for having inaugurated the spirited foreign policy, and voted with the government.[41] The result was that he offended both sides of the chamber.

The primary associations were afflicted by financial weakness and uncertainty about their futures. The Peace Society reported 'no ordinary difficulties' to its annual meetings in May 1884; and despite a fundraising drive by William Jones, a Quaker who had been engaged in 1882 as financial and organizing secretary, it reported a deficit of £450.[42] The WPA also acknowledged a 'most unsatisfactory' financial position at the end of the year.[43] And the IAPA, over £700 in debt, admitted that its belated launching of a periodical was 'a bold thing, in the present state of our finances'.[44]

The Peace Society's loss of confidence was such that it was even willing during the autumn of 1884 tentatively to consider a merger with the IAPA. Following a 'friendly and courteous' overture from Pratt, it established a subcommittee to explore the possibility with IAPA representatives, though it insisted that its own religious basis was not negotiable.[45] The two sides met on 5 December, Pratt offering that 'in case of an amalgamation any unpleasant

---

[39] *HP* (Nov. 1884), 125; (Dec. 1884), 142. F. W. Hirst, *The Six Panics* (1913), 41–8.
[40] For this charge against the Peace Society and Richard's reply to it, see *Christian Commonwealth* (5 Feb. 1885), 225, and (19 Feb. 1885), 252. For a similar charge against the WPA see *Arbitrator* (Oct. 1885), 3.   [41] Hansard, ccxxciv HC cols. 1665–74 (27 Feb. 1885).
[42] *HP* (June 1884), 61, 62, 76.   [43] *Arbitrator* (Dec. 1884), 1.
[44] *IAPA Monthly Journal* (1 July 1884), 3, (31 July 1885), 136.
[45] PSM, 17 Oct., 27 Nov. 1884.

personal element now on the staff of his association could be got rid of'—an indication that the IAPA already regarded Appleton as expendable. But Pratt wanted 'Jews, Freethinkers, and others' still to be welcome. When the Peace Society's executive committee met to discuss the negotiation, which to its annoyance had been publicized by Cremer in the *Arbitrator*, Arthur Pease, its president's brother and himself a Liberal MP, pointed out that 'the majority' of its subscribers were Quakers who, if offended by an amalgamation, might set up a peace association of their own.[46] (A Friends' Peace Committee was shortly to be established in any case, as will be seen.) A further meeting of the two sides on 16 December considered what alterations in the Peace Society's rules would be needed to allow it to absorb IAPA members. It agreed that the commitment to 'Christian principles' could be replaced by one to 'morality and religion'—a significant concession on the society's part. However, on the subject of 'defensive war', a long discussion ended unsatisfactorily in ambiguity: it concluded that the existing requirement for committee members merely to oppose 'war'—which, as has just been noted, Richard had recently been interpreting in an unprecedentedly permissive manner—need not be changed, since IAPA members could 'put upon it their own interpretation which was probably not that of the Founders of the Peace Society'.[47] However, after consulting the rank and file, the executive committee decided in February unanimously to heed the advice of its president: 'We must not, now, lower our standard; or we drift into an unknown sea.'[48] It therefore rejected a merger with the IAPA.

There is no evidence that Richard opposed this decision; but at the next meeting of the executive committee he gave notice of his retirement.[49] His successor, chosen by a special general conference of members on 8 May 1885, was the financial and organizing secretary, William Jones. His varied career had included relief work in France after the Franco-Prussian War and in Bulgaria after the atrocities. However, his Quakerism and period of service as a tutor to the Pease family made his appointment look somewhat inbred: Sir Joseph Whitwell Pease (as he had become since accepting a baronetcy) expressed concern that it would 'give to the Peace Society too much the character of a Quaker society'. Perhaps to minimize this perception, Richard was given the title of honorary secretary and made permanent chairman of the executive committee;[50] and he continued to write the editorial in the *Herald of Peace* each month.[51]

---

[46] *Arbitrator* (Dec. 1884), 1. PSM, 8 Dec. 1884. Richard to Pratt, 9 and 10 Dec. 1884 (copies): PSLB. [47] PSM, 2 Jan. 1885.
[48] PSM, 10 Feb. 1885. [49] PSM, 25 Mar. 1885.
[50] PSM, 8 May, 23 July 1885. *HP* (June 1885), 233–4
[51] As acknowledged after his death: *HP* (Sept. 1888), 116.

Richard was also returned unopposed to parliament in the general elections of November–December 1885 and June–July 1886, the second necessitated by Gladstone's espousal of Home Rule, which led to defections from his party and allowed the Conservatives to hold office for all but three years (1892–5) of the next two decades. The *Herald of Peace* returned to the view that there was 'little difference' the parties, since both were regrettably predisposed towards jingoism, and lamented that the 'noble motto' peace, retrenchment, and reform had ceased to be 'a party-cry', so that those interested in the peace question had to press every candidate as to his particular views.[52]

Between the two elections, on 19 March 1886, Richard introduced a variant of his resolution of five years previously, protesting at the ability of Britain's imperial officials to involve the nation in conflict. This time he defeated Gladstone on a procedural vote, an outcome which embarrassed some of his supporters, including Alfred E. Pease (the son of the president of the Peace Society), who as loyal Liberals reversed themselves on the substantive motion and thereby helped to defeat it by 115 votes to 109.[53] Richard also addressed the Association for the Reform and Codification of the Law of Nations when it met in London in July 1887, having urged Peace Society members to attend as at previous meetings he had felt 'at a disadvantage, because he was not supported by a sufficient number who held to the same views'[54]—an indication that the burgeoning profession of lawyers was now taking a greater interest in such occasions than a faltering peace movement.

Meanwhile the Peace Society was at best marking time as an organization. Its financial position remained poor: in 1887 ordinary subscriptions and donations were reportedly 'the smallest ever received'; and in 1888 the society was £330 in the red.[55] In terms of institutional energy it was being outperformed by its Ladies' Peace Association, which in the summer of 1885 was claiming 9,217 members,[56] 4,000 of them in the local association at Wisbech run by the dynamic Priscilla Peckover, who deserved the plaudits she received in every annual report at this time. Three years later Miss Peckover turned her organization into a 'Local Peace Association Auxiliary':[57] that a national organization to encourage local activism was needed was a tacit rebuke to the Peace Society.

William Jones was proving an indifferent secretary. Indeed, his memoirs suggest that he was by temperament a traveller and lecturer rather than an

---

[52] *HP* (Jan. 1886), 8; (July 1886), 81.
[53] See Hansard, ccciii HC cols. 1386–96. Sir A. E. Pease, *Elections and Recollections* (1932), 114.
[54] *HP* (July 1887), 242; (Aug. 1887), 249, 254–7.
[55] *HP* (June 1886), 73; (June 1887), 230; (June 1888) 69.
[56] *HP* (July 1885), 262.   [57] *HP* (June 1889), 230.

organizer.[58] In 1887 he was given nearly four months of leave to attend an international Quaker conference in the United States. This had been summoned to discuss doctrine, in particular the growing challenge to evangelicalism from theological liberalism; but a separate meeting on arbitration was also to be held.[59] Jones had just been widowed, and may also have been unsettled by his American visit, which persuaded one of his British co-delegates, George Gillett, that a new peace campaign was needed. On his return Gillett persuaded London Yearly Meeting in May 1888 that 'this would be better done by this Society than by the Peace Society because we should speak as Christians to our fellow Christians'[60]—a comment which suggested a declining regard for the Peace Society among Quaker activists. A Friends' Peace Committee was duly established the following month, with Gillett as its principal secretary. (It initially called itself 'the Joint Committee' because it was appointed by the Women's Yearly Meeting Committee as well as the Meeting for Sufferings Committee.[61]) Jones also decided to devote himself to a specifically Quaker mission. On 25 June 1888 he told the Peace Society's executive committee of a projected visit to Australia under Quaker auspices for which he sought 'prolonged leave of absence'. His employers received this news 'with much concern';[62] and shortly afterwards Jones tendered his resignation, having decided to remarry and settle in Sunderland after his long journey.

Less unexpected than Jones's departure, but more upsetting because it deprived the Peace Society of the man still regarded as 'their leader and shepherd',[63] was the death in Wales on 20 August 1888 of Henry Richard, who three months before had missed the annual meeting for only the second time since becoming secretary forty years previously. (Surprisingly, he had outlived his predecessor by only six years: although John Jefferson had retired suddenly in 1848 because of severe illness, he had lived for a further thirty-four years, during which he was an obscure and inactive vice-president of the society.[64]) Acknowledging nine days after Richard died that 'the Peace Society was what his ability and sagacity had made it',[65] the executive committee knew that without him the society's future could not be taken for granted, and therefore summoned a special conference of members. This met on 19 November, with twenty-two members present and others having written in with their views.

---

[58] W. Jones, *Quaker Campaigns in Peace and War* (1899).
[59] Isichei, *Victorian Quakers*, 9–10, 226.
[60] Cited in *Friend* (June 1888), 165.
[61] It met first on 21 June 1888 and was not described in its minutes as the Peace Committee until 1893.
[62] PSM, 25 June 1888.
[63] *HP* (June 1889), 226.
[64] Ceadel, *Origins of War Prevention*, 324.
[65] PSM, 29 Aug. 1888.

'One or two speakers suggested the desirability of amalgamating the Peace Society with one or both of the Arbitration Associations with which the names or Mr Hodgson Pratt and Mr Cremer, M.P. are respectively associated'; but the majority disagreed, emphasizing their desire to preserve 'the distinctly religious basis of this organisation'.[66]

The IAPA gained unexpected breathing space when its large debt was dramatically written off at its annual meeting on 22 July 1885.[67] This was done in style by the Scottish-American steel magnate Andrew Carnegie, whose father had emigrated from Britain when Chartism failed in 1848. In his adoptive land Carnegie had become a conservative and patriot who wished to absorb Canada; but on his regular visits to his home country he patronized radical and peace causes. While in Britain during 1884 he had bought a progressive newspaper, the *Echo*, from Passmore Edwards,[68] who presumably introduced him to the IAPA.

Having thus been rescued, the association was able to offer Appleton a two-month extension of his contract, which was due to expire, whilst warning him that any further renewal 'shall have to be on some more satisfactory basis as regards to expenses'. Appleton declined, however, and was deemed on 30 July to have severed his connection with the IAPA, which duly asked for subscriptions and donations to be sent directly to its office in future.[69]

Appleton took his revenge on IAPA, as he had on the Peace Society, by launching another association. This was 'British and Foreign Arbitration Association', of which he was purportedly 'honorary secretary'. In the circular announcing its existence in the spring of 1886, Appleton claimed to have been the creator of the IAPA but to have resigned because of its 'mischievous interference' in national policy and in particular its assumption that 'in every quarrel England must always be in the wrong'.[70] This claim was taken seriously in an editorial in *The Times*, which was ever on the look out for stories damaging to the peace movement.[71] The IAPA responded by denying that Appleton had been its sole creator, noting that 'from the outset he received the aid and co-operation of Mr William Phillips' who 'has always claimed to be the principal founder'. It also pointed out that Appleton had been 'a paid officer, at a very liberal remuneration'.[72]

Appleton had again named his new organization artfully: 'British and

---

[66] PSM, 19 Nov. 1888. *HP* (Dec. 1888), 149.

[67] *IAPA Monthly Journal* (31 July 1885), 139.

[68] J. F. Wall, *Andrew Carnegie* (New York, 1970), 431.

[69] *IAPA Monthly Journal* (25 Aug. 1885), 142; (Aug./Sept. 1886), 94–5. *The Times* (20 and 29 May 1886).

[70] *The Times* (17 May 1886).

[71] *The Times* (17 May 1886).

[72] *IAPA Monthly Journal* (30 June 1886), 64–5.

Foreign', long used as a prefix by Bible, anti-slavery, and temperance societies, must have been designed to strike a chord with older philanthropists; and 'Arbitration Association' caused 'misapprehension'[73] within the similarly titled IAPA, which was still having to repeat its disavowals of a connection with Appleton more than a decade later.[74] However, the British and Foreign Arbitration Association was a pseudo-society: none of Appleton's collaborators was known to the peace movement or prominent in public life; its greater expenditure on its premises than on its meetings soon attracted unfavourable public comment;[75] and, presumably in an attempt to curry favour with defencists, it was to oppose the call for arbitration in the Fashoda crisis and support Britain's war against the Boers.[76] None the less Appleton's ability to produce plausible pamphlets, letters to the newspapers, and even a quick and sycophantic biography of Richard,[77] ensured that for at least a decade he retained a vestige of credibility. He was even listed as a Fellow of the Royal Historical Society in 1889—wrongly, it later emerged, because he had never paid the necessary subscription.[78]

However, in 1895—the year the British and Foreign Arbitration Association published only its second multi-year *Report*—Appleton began a six-year spell of being pilloried in the radical MP Henry Labouchere's muckraking paper *Truth*, for sending begging letters (including one seeking help with the cost of applying for the newly established Nobel Peace Prize), misrepresentation, and even an assault on a servant.[79] Eventually, Appleton sued: in 1902 the Peace Society was asked by Labouchere's lawyers to release its minutes relating to him so that they could defend a legal action.[80] It was indicative of Appleton's genuine though misdirected intellectual energy that only a couple of years before his death in 1912 he was, without obvious pecuniary motive, writing learned historical letters to an officer of the British Museum.[81]

Without Appleton to sour relations between the two bodies, the IAPA made a further proposition to the Peace Society in the autumn of 1885: that

---

[73] *IAPA Monthly Journal* (30 Mar. 1886), 29.

[74] See *Concord* (Nov. 1897), 81.

[75] *Echo* (13 June 1888).

[76] As noted in *Concord* (Jan. 1899), 14; (Nov. 1899), 180.

[77] L. Appleton, *Henry Richard: The Apostle of Peace* (1889): several historians have taken this seriously as a historical source.

[78] *Truth* (16 May 1901), 1220; (30 May 1901), 1362. I am grateful to Dr R. Quinault, secretary of the RHS at the time of my inquiry in 1992, for checking its records.

[79] *Truth* (26 Dec. 1895), 158; (22 July 1897), 210; (16 June 1898), 1497; (22 Sept. 1898), 710–12; (8 Dec. 1898), 1431; (16 Dec. 1899), 1190; (7 Feb. 1901), 315; (25 Apr. 1901), 1013; (2 May 1901), 1090–1; (23 May 1901), 1293.

[80] PSM, 21 Feb. 1902.

[81] See the H. J. Ellis Papers: Add. MS 41319 fo. 233.

both associations join a 'federation of Peace societies', of which Richard would be the first president. The IAPA had decided upon this scheme at an international meeting in Basel on 17 September 1885[82] in an effort to make its international-equity-tribunal strategy appear less arrogant. At its next annual meeting, on 16 July 1886, the Bishop of London was to warn it from the chair of 'the temptation that will constantly beset it to behave as if it were already appointed a Court of Arbitration'; and Pratt was to acknowledge: 'Mistakes may have been made as to the time and method of applying the principles of the Association.'[83] Pratt hoped that if a federation of peace societies 'throughout Europe' were achieved, it could claim that any substantive recommendation it made had been arrived at 'in co-operation and consultation with the Societies which represent the nations concerned in any particular dispute'.[84] In other words, a collectivity of European peace associations would be more legitimate as an international equity tribunal than a solitary national one. To arrive at a single British arbitral voice in such a federation, the Peace Society and the IAPA would presumably have had either to merge or to create a joint committee: predictably, therefore, the Peace Society turned the proposal down in April 1886, though it did so 'with a courteous letter' and an invitation to Pratt to address its own public meeting the following month where he 'was loudly cheered'. The society also cooperated with the IAPA over a scheme for an international court prepared by Levi, though this was to receive disappointingly little support from his fellow international jurists.[85]

Despite being aware that 'most Continental nations' lagged far behind Britain 'in the spirit of independent organization for public objects', Pratt continued to work in Europe to found a federation of societies, or 'League of Peace', which would have the international legitimacy to tackle the causes of war. He attempted to establish component associations even in Germany, where 'the fear of doing anything to offend the authorities is strong', but had little success once the locals realized that his federation or league would want to pronounce on Alsace-Lorraine too.[86]

Meanwhile at home the IAPA had to face the fact that, until it established a federation, it was merely a national association and one moreover that lacked the Peace Society's Quaker core and established reputation. Admittedly, in 1885 Dr G. B. Clark was elected as a Liberal MP, at the same time as Cremer of the WPA, causing the association to note with satisfaction:

[82] *IAPA Monthly Journal* (30 Nov. 1885), 179, 186–8. PSM, 12 Jan. 1886.
[83] *IAPA Monthly Journal* (31 July 1886), 76, 79.
[84] *IAPA Monthly Journal* (6 Nov. 1886), 106.
[85] PSM, 9 Apr., 26 May., 15 Dec. 1886. *HP* (June 1886), 76–7.
[86] *IAPA Monthly Journal* (1 Nov. 1884), 35; (25 June 1885), 118; (30 Jan. 1886), 2. R. Chickering, *Imperial Germany and a World without War* (Princeton, 1975), 42–4.

'All the executives will be directly represented in the House of Commons (as the Peace Society has been in previous Parliaments).'[87] But Clark's election had been partly funded by the Boers, who from 1886 to 1892 retained him as their honorary consul,[88] thereby reducing his usefulness on other issues.

At the end of 1886, having moved into cheaper premises at 40–1 Outer Temple, the IAPA chose the secretary who was to serve it until its demise thirty-nine years later. This was J. Frederick Green, an Anglican curate who was in the process of leaving the church as he moved to the left politically. (During the First World War, as will be seen, he was to move to the right.) Green developed the association's *Monthly Journal* into the principal means of drawing attention to its existence, declaring it 'a medium for the expression of all reasonable and temperate opinions respecting international politics' rather than 'the advocate of one set of opinions in preference to another', and renaming it *Concord*.[89]

Meanwhile, the WPA was responding radically to its 'very discouraging position for want of funds', which the Peace Society had decided early in 1886 it could no longer even try to rectify.[90] In response to a recommendation of its financial committee, the WPA resolved after 'mature deliberation' on 13 October 1886 to call itself the 'Workmen's Peace Association and International Arbitration League'.[91] This restyling reflected Cremer's decision to campaign for an Anglo-American arbitration treaty, a decision made possible by his election in 1885 as a Lib-Lab MP for Haggerston, a constituency in London's East End which had been created by that year's electoral redistribution. Previously only three working men had entered the Commons, including Burt: now Cremer was able to announce that eleven artisan MPs would attend the WPA's fifteenth anniversary meeting in February 1886.[92]

Characteristically, Cremer devoted his maiden speech in the Commons to opposing votes for women, a deeply held conviction which led the historian of his trade union to summarize his political outlook as being 'in favour of international peace and of the subjection of women'.[93] But he first made an impact when on 30 August 1886 he moved an amendment critical of the Burma War which, though easily defeated, attracted 127 votes. Since only one of these was from a Tory (Burdett-Coutts, who, having been asleep when the division was called, had gone through the wrong voting lobby), this

[87] *IAPA Monthly Journal* (30 Jan. 1886), 2.

[88] A. Davey, *The British Pro-Boers 1877–1902* (Cape Town, 1978), 31, 35–6.

[89] *IAPA Monthly Journal* (25 Feb. 1887), 14. It was renamed *Concord* with effect from its 27 May 1887 issue.

[90] PSM, 12 Jan. 1886.   [91] *Arbitrator* (Nov. 1886), 8.

[92] *Arbitrator* (Jan. 1886), 1.

[93] R. W. Postgate, *The Builders' History* (1923), 292 n.

respectable level of support from Liberals showed, the *Arbitrator* claimed, that though 'nearly dumb' while their party was in power, they could be expected to do 'a great deal of barking for economy' now that they were 'unmuzzled'.[94]

Cremer was to continue to introduce radical motions: on 4 February 1887, for example, he divided the House on an amendment calling on the government to evacuate Egypt.[95] But he was aware that an Anglo-American arbitration treaty offered the best chance of mobilizing widespread support. As he later acknowledged, such a treaty had been suggested several years earlier by Walter Hazell, the London printer who in 1885 became treasurer of the Peace Society; and it was reported by the autumn of 1886 to have supporters in Congress.[96]

To help with his campaign, Cremer approached Carnegie (presumably via his colleague Howard Evans, who worked on the *Echo*), encouraged by an optimistic comment in a book he had published in the United States during 1886, *Triumphant Democracy*: 'A league of peace to which each country will send delegates to decide international difficulties is not quite so far in the future as may at first sight appear.'[97] When Carnegie came to Britain in the spring of 1887, on a visit during which he sold the *Echo* back to Passmore Edwards, he attended a meeting at Anderton's Hotel, London, on 16 June, chaired by Burt, with the WPA council, sympathetic Liberal MPs, and others such as Pratt.[98] This occasion seems to have increased Carnegie's interest in arbitration: he expounded its virtues, for example, in his speech accepting the freedom of the city of Edinburgh a month afterwards.[99]

Meanwhile Cremer, 'a wonderful "whipper-in" ' in the words of a WPA colleague,[100] persuaded 232 of his fellow MPs to put their names to an address to the President of the United States welcoming the introduction into the United States Congress of a resolution supporting an Anglo-American arbitration treaty. Despite the comparatively uncontentious nature of the issue, only thirteen of these signatories were Conservatives, a matter of regret to Cremer; and the fact that 175 were Gladstonian Liberals and forty-four Liberal Unionists illustrated the ideological quality of parliamentary voting on foreign policy at this time.[101] In August 1887 he announced that a deputation, which was 'to be introduced to President Cleveland by Mr Andrew Carnegie', would

[94] Hansard, cccii HC col. 702 (19 Feb. 1886); ccviii HC cols. 807–9 (30 Aug. 1886). *Arbitrator* (Sept./Oct. 1886), 1, 3–8.
[95] Hansard, cccx HC cols. 656–60.   [96] *Arbitrator* (Dec. 1886), 8; (June 1887), 2.
[97] Cited in Evans, *Cremer*, 124.   [98] *Arbitrator* (June 1887), 2–4.
[99] *The Times* (9 July 1887).
[100] F. W. Soutter, *Fights for Freedom* (1925), 233–4, 245.
[101] *Arbitrator* (Aug. 1887), 2; (Sept./Oct. 1887), 4. W. C. Lubenow, *Parliamentary Politics and the Home Rule Crisis: The British House of Commons in 1886* (Oxford, 1988), 84–7.

visit the United States in October 1887 to present the address in person.[102] Shortly before it did so, however, the Peace Society's secretary William Jones, *en route* for his Quaker conference, received a personal interview on the same issue with Cleveland on 23 September.[103] Fearing that others were stealing his thunder, Cremer wrote a letter to *The Times* insisting that his parliamentary petition was 'solely the action of the Workmen's Peace Association' (as he still called it).[104] His own deputation of ten MPs, one peer, and three representatives of the Trades Union Congress, plus Carnegie, handed its petition, afforced by two belated signatures, to the President on 31 October 1887. Hostility to Britain from Irish-Americans following the rejection of Home Rule made a positive response from Cleveland impolitic; but a resolution urging the President to negotiate arbitration treaties with any friendly country desirous of doing so was passed by the Senate in 1888; and a concurrent resolution of the two Houses of Congress to the same effect was adopted two years later.[105]

In the aftermath of this high-profile campaign, the WPA completed its rebranding: on 13 June 1888, to coincide with a move into new offices at 23 Bedford Street, it dropped the original part of its title to become simply the International Arbitration League. The explanation given was that 'the movement in favour of "Treaties of Arbitration" has now assumed such proportions that it has been deemed advisable to concentrate all our energies in that direction', and its previous name, being 'exclusive', had 'led many friends of "Treaties of Arbitration" to misunderstand our objects, and it is of the utmost importance to secure their cooperation'.[106]

Not only its name but its style changed. Where it had previously had only five vice-presidents, all Lib-Lab MPs, it soon acquired seventy-three, many from the middle or upper class; and within a few years it had nine peers, among them the Duke of Westminster and Marquis of Ripon, and 136 MPs.[107] However, the composition of its decision-making body, the council, was left unaltered. And, unsurprisingly in view of Cremer's anti-feminist views, advantage was not taken of the abandonment of the restrictive label 'workmen' to open its membership to women such as Mrs Ann Ellis of the Weavers' Society, who had spoken for peace at the WPA's meeting in connection with the Trades Union Congress of 1883.[108]

---

[102] *The Times* (23 Aug. 1887).
[103] *HP* (Oct. 1887), 278; (Nov. 1887), 285.   [104] *The Times* (24 Sept. 1887).
[105] Evans, *Cremer*, 129. H. M. Cory, *Compulsory Arbitration of International Disputes* (New York, 1932), 28–9. D. S. Patterson, *Toward a Warless World: The Travail of the American Peace Movement 1887–1914* (Bloomington, Ind., 1976), 18–21.
[106] *Arbitrator* (June/July 1888), 1.
[107] *Arbitrator* (Aug. 1888), 12; (July 1891), 76–7.   [108] *Arbitrator* (Sept.1883), 5.

Cremer's league also declared itself *pacificist* rather than pacifist at this time. Released from its financial subservience to the Peace Society, it could dissociate itself from the condemnation of 'all war as anti-christian', and emphasize its intention to 'start on a broader basis and welcome the co-operation of all who "seek peace and pursue it" whatever their opinions on war in the abstract'.[109]

It is possible that the WPA changed its name and distanced itself from absolutism at this time because Cremer wanted to join forces with the IAPA. Negotiations about a merger reached an advanced stage: early in 1889 the International Arbitration League denied 'inaccurate and unauthorized' press reports that it had already concluded a deal with the IAPA whereby Burt became president, Pratt chairman of council, and Cremer secretary of the combined body—but only on the grounds that its council had yet formally to ratify this deal. Its leadership was therefore embarrassed when the council, which was still all-artisan, declined to sacrifice its distinctive identify in this way.[110]

The IAPA was irritated by this snub, but at a special meeting of supporters on 7 August 1889 made a virtue of necessity by deciding that it too 'filled a special place not occupied by other societies of the same kind', and therefore should continue in its present form.[111] Thereafter, although cooperation was occasionally attempted—as for example when all three primary associations held a joint meeting on 12 February 1890 in connection with the Anglo-Portuguese dispute[112]—talk of mergers ended. An excessively inward-looking phase in the movement's history was over.

EUROPEAN INITIATIVES AND BRITISH STAGNATION, 1889–1898

Having decided on 19 November 1889 to maintain its independent course, the Peace Society advertised its vacant secretaryship. The salary of £300, soon raised to £400, though lower than Richard's, was competitive, and the field of applicants strong.[113] The one selected was the Revd William Evans Darby, a 45-year-old Camarthenshire-born Congregationalist, who had ministered at chapels in Chippenham, Bath (where his flock included a veteran Peace Society member, Handel Cossham), and Watford.[114] He shared Richard's

---

[109] *Arbitrator* (Nov. 1888), 4.
[110] *Arbitrator* (Feb. 1889), 1; (Mar./Apr. 1889), 17. *HP* (Apr. 1889), 202. *Concord* (16 Mar. 1889), 25; (17 July 1889), 4.
[111] *Concord* (15 Aug. 1889), 89.   [112] *HP* (Mar. 1890), 29.
[113] PSM, 29 Nov., 28 Dec. 1888, 20 Feb. 1891.
[114] For biographical details see *HP* (May 1893), 223–4, citing *At Home* magazine.

willingness both to defend Christian pacifism and to develop a specialist interest in arbitration, and was to serve a twenty-six-year stint.

Darby began energetically, making a number of internal changes: the number of vice-presidents was immediately expanded to compete with the arbitration societies; the *Herald of Peace* introduced illustrations in an attempt to widen its appeal; the cost of the three major auxiliaries, at Birmingham, Liverpool, and Manchester was queried; and, on the grounds that raising money depended 'almost entirely for success upon direct *personal* visitation and solicitation',[115] another collector was hired. Darby devised 'Peace Sunday'—an invitation to clergymen and ministers to devote their pre-Christmas sermons to condemnations of war—which began in December 1889 and became one of the most economical means whereby the society drew attention to itself.[116] He also introduced a more welcoming attitude to women: Priscilla Peckover was invited to join the executive committee, though she preferred to become one of the new vice-presidents, along with Richard's widow and Margaret Lucas—this last appointment a mark of respect following the death of her brother, John Bright, in March 1889; and Ellen Robinson, an active member of the Friends' Peace Committee who was also to serve as secretary of the Local Peace Association Auxiliary from 1894 to 1904, spoke at the annual public meeting.[117]

But outside the society itself Darby inevitably lacked the stature not only of Richard but also of Cremer, Pratt, and established continental *pacificists* such as Lemonnier and Passy. The Peace Society thus played no part in the institution in 1889 of inter-parliamentary conferences: this was the achievement for which Passy and Cremer were both to be awarded Nobel Peace Prizes. Passy had been elected to the French parliament in 1881, serving for eight years,[118] and in early 1887 had tabled a motion in favour of arbitration treaties which, following Cremer's example, he retabled in April 1888 with particular reference to a treaty with the United States.[119] Passy seems to have suggested a meeting of the British and French parliamentary supporters of arbitration; and at the council meeting on 13 June 1887 at which it also adopted its new name, Cremer's association responded favourably; Cremer then visited Paris; and on 6 August Passy issued invitations for a meeting in that city on 31 October. However, the event was disappointingly ill-attended:

---

[115] 'Secretary's Paper on the General Work and Organization of the Society': PSM, 29 Mar. 1889.

[116] PSM, 18 Oct. 1889.

[117] PSM, 15 and 29 Mar. 1889. *HP* (June 1889), 90.

[118] F. Passy, *Pour la paix* (Paris, 1909), 80.

[119] Y. Zarjevski, *The People have the Floor: A History of the Inter-Parliamentary Union* (Aldershot, 1989), 38.

Cremer had attempted to postpone it 'to suit the convenience of English M.P.s'; and in the event only nine of these, including himself and Burt, were present, and only twenty-five French deputies.[120] None the less the meeting made plans for a repeat performance in Paris the following summer during that city's celebrations for the centenary of the French Revolution. Held on 29–30 June 1889 at the Hôtel Continental and attended by ninety-six parliamentarians (twenty-eight of them from Britain), this instituted the organization which eventually became known as the Inter-Parliamentary Union for Arbitration.[121] The dropping of the last two words from its title in 1908, the year of Cremer's death, reflected the fact that by then its real function proved to be the bringing together of legislators to discuss any issue, not just peace.

Nor did the Peace Society play a leading role in the simultaneous revival of international peace conferences. On 23–7 June 1889 310 activists attended the first of what became an almost annual series of Universal Peace Congresses in Paris, just before the gathering of parliamentarians. The principal organizer was Lemonnier, with help from Passy and Pratt who at that time merged their Paris-based organizations: in other words, the Société française des amis de la paix joined with the French *comité* of Pratt's IAPA to form the Société française pour l'arbitrage entre nations.[122] After Darby visited Passy in May to find out about the congress, the Peace Society agreed to present, jointly with the IAPA, the scheme for a High Court of Arbitration which Levi had revised shortly before his death the previous year. Six of its members attended, being encouraged by what they saw, except for the 'sadly ominous' absence of German participation.[123] And a delegation of Quakers also took the view that the resolutions adopted in Paris 'were satisfactory'.[124]

Thereafter the Peace Society and IAPA collaborated, with Quaker approval, on the organization of the next congress of activists, which was arranged for 14–19 July 1890 in London so as again to precede the inter-parliamentary conference, which Cremer was organizing. The 'Universal Peace Congress Committee' which they formed for the purpose was notable for including significant representation from their affiliated women's associations.[125] Pleased at getting 'the Christian aspect of peace' onto the agenda, though having to settle for a prayer meeting before each session rather than as an integral part of proceedings, the Peace Society considered the London

---

[120] *Arbitrator* (Oct. 1888), 1; (Nov. 1888), 4–5.
[121] J. Douglas, *Parliament Across Frontiers: A Short History of the Inter-Parliamentary Union* (1975), 5–9.
[122] Abrams, 'European Peace Societies', fo. 203.
[123] PSM, 26 Apr., 17 May, 14 June 1889. *HP* (July 1889), 241; (Aug. 1889), 264.
[124] Minutes, Friends' Peace Committee [FPC], 3 July 1889.
[125] See *HP* (Feb. 1890), 23.

congress to be 'one of the most successful gatherings of the kind' ever held.[126] None the less, fewer than 180 delegates—including wives, who were now listed as full participants—actually attended.[127] And even allowing for the lack of a Great Exhibition as a backdrop the congress did not achieve the public impact of its precursor in 1851.

The International Arbitration League had reservations about the new Universal Peace Congresses. Standing on his dignity as an MP far more than Richard ever had, Cremer regarded conferences of activists as less important than those of parliamentarians. He avoided complaints of ingratitude from the peace association which paid his salary by crediting it with the foundation of inter-parliamentary conferences: he thus described the first of these in the *Arbitrator* as 'the fifth gathering of our League in Paris',[128] thereby treating it as analogous to the conferences with French workers which the WPA had intermittently organized since 1875. Cremer also criticized the timing of the conferences of activists, which he regarded as a ruse not only for sharing the publicity attracted by the conference of parliamentarians but also for setting the latter's agenda.[129] He saw to it that after 1892 the two events were geographically separated.

Even the Peace Society developed concerns about the direction which the Universal Peace Congresses seemed to be taking. At Rome in 1891 the congress decided to form a secretariat, or International Peace Bureau, in Berne. The Peace Society regarded this as 'an out-of-the-way continental town',[130] and feared that on account of its location it would be dominated by Lemonnier's Swiss-based LIPL and also seek to exercise a centralizing influence over other associations. Even though this worry proved unfounded, partly because of Lemonnier's death in 1891, the Peace Society's attitude towards the European movement became increasingly negative. It feared that Britain was 'to be looked to almost exclusively for the supply of funds'.[131] This was because continental associations, though increasingly numerous, were often tiny and impoverished. For example, the very establishment of the Deutsche Friedensgesellschaft (German Peace Society) in 1892 by Alfred Fried, a Viennese Jew working in Berlin as a publisher, was a notable achievement in a country in which defencism was more seriously challenged by militarism than by *pacificism*; but the association itself proved very weak.[132]

---

[126] PSM, 21 Feb. 1890. *HP* (Sept. 1890), 129; (June 1891), 250.

[127] They are listed in *HP* (Aug. 1890), 117–18.

[128] *Arbitrator* (July/Aug. 1889), 2.

[129] See e.g. his complaint in *Arbitrator* (Nov. 1891), 122.

[130] *HP* (Apr. 1892), 39.   [131] PSM, 16 Jan. 1891.

[132] Abrams, 'European Peace Societies', fos. 266, 277.

Continental associations also had three ideological drawbacks from the Peace Society's point of view. First, they had a higher proportion of non-Christian supporters, and therefore wanted to keep religion out of the congresses, so that at the Rome congress they blocked even an anodyne Anglo-American resolution declaring that 'the war spirit is essentially opposed to the precepts, example and spirit of Christ'.[133] Secondly, they lacked a significant pacifist tradition but possessed a stronger juridical one, which, under the slogan 'peace through law', favoured the enforcement of arbitral awards. For example, in France the Société française pour l'arbitrage entre nations lost support in the 1890s, and was replaced as the dominant French peace association by the Association de la paix par le droit (which had been formed in 1887 by a group of young protestants in Nîmes and was known until 1895 as the Association des jeunes amis de la paix).[134] At the 1892 congress at Berne the continental associations passed a resolution, 'entrusting to Arbitrators some means of enforcing their decision', which the Peace Society found itself virtually alone in opposing.[135] Thirdly, continental peace activists were less puritanical, and could see no problem in holding the 1902 congress in Monaco, whereas the Peace Society, reluctant to offend Quakers and other Nonconformists, stayed away from what it described as 'one of the blackest and most deadly moral plague spots in the whole world'.[136]

The relationship between British and continental peace activists had subtly but significantly changed. Whereas during the first two-thirds of the century the former had always taken the lead, during the 1880s and 1890s the latter became the innovators. In 1889, for example, Bertha von Suttner, a Prague-born Austrian aristocrat, pioneered the popular anti-war novel with *Die Waffen Nieder*, which the *Arbitrator* found 'almost painfully exciting' in places.[137] She went on to found the Österreichische Friedensgesellschaft (Austrian Peace Society) in 1891, to inspire the creation of the Nobel Peace Prize, and to win one for herself in 1905. Similarly, Jacques Novikow, the cosmopolitan son of a Russian manufacturer, launched what would later be called 'peace biology'[138] by insisting in a book published in Paris in 1893, *Les Luttes entre sociétés humaines et leurs phases successives*, that contrary to the views of militarists and defencists, Darwin's thinking had anti-war

[133] *HP* (Dec. 1891), 370.
[134] Abrams, 'European Peace Societies', fo. 284. Chickering, *Imperial Germany*, 337–8. N. Ingram, *The Politics of Dissent: Pacifism in France 1919–1939* (Oxford, 1991), 20–2.
[135] *HP* (Sept. 1892), 129.
[136] PSM, 20 Dec. 1901. *HP* (Feb. 1902), 183; (Apr. 1902), 209.
[137] *Arbitrator* (Feb. 1893), 19.
[138] See P. Crook, *Darwinism, War and History* (Cambridge, 1994).

implications because the highest forms of struggle were non-military. And Ivan Bloch, a Russian banker, railway constructor, and Tsarist adviser of Polish-Jewish origins, whose six-volume *The War of the Future* was published in Russian and French in 1898, was the first to argue that changes in military technology had made war suicidal.[139]

Even pacifism, previously a virtual peculiarity of the English-speaking world, was losing intellectual vitality there,[140] while being redefined and reinvigorated by Tolstoy. The former soldier was reacting against his past life and the repressive Russian political system, though he was also influenced by reading Garrison and Ballou. An inveterate compiler of 'rules for life',[141] Tolstoy began in the 1880s to set out a no-force regimen of such rigour that the Peace Society found it hard to take seriously. The *Herald of Peace*'s comment on his first pacifist work, *What I Believe*, which appeared in 1885, was that its conclusions were 'so decidedly pronounced in favour of absolute non-resistance to evil that perhaps only a minority even of the members of the Peace Society, or of the Society of Friends, would be prepared to endorse them in all their breadth'.[142] Gradually, however, Tolstoy's reputation for trying to live up to his principles caused his ideas to gain influence. In the 1890s the Peace Society came to recognize him as 'the foremost and most uncompromising Peace advocate in the world',[143] and even sent him copies of its periodical.[144] When his second pacifist book, *The Kingdom of God is within You*, which was banned in Russia, appeared in Britain and France in 1894, the *Herald of Peace* welcomed the 'considerable' and 'respectful' press attention which it received in the light of the fact that it expounded 'what are usually deemed very ultra views'.[145]

Being derived from Christianity, Tolstoy's 'law of love' appealed to intensely devout Christians. For example, it influenced both Stephen Hobhouse, L. T. Hobhouse's saintly cousin who converted to Quakerism and became a celebrated conscientious objector, and C. J. Cadoux, a clerical officer in the Admiralty who became prominent both as a Congregationalist scholar and a pacifist.[146] However, because of its universalistic quality it also

---

[139] The sixth volume was published in English as I. S. Bloch, *Is War Now Impossible?* (1899).

[140] e.g. Brock has noted that 'only three books dealing with the question of pacifism were published in the United States' between the Civil War and the First World War: *Pacifism in the United States*, 931.

[141] See H. Troyat, *Tolstoy* (New York, 1967), tr. N. Amphoux from the French original (Paris, 1965).

[142] *HP* (June 1886), 93.   [143] *HP* (June 1895), 220.

[144] *HP* (Dec. 1893), 325.

[145] *HP* (Mar. 1894), 26, though see also (Aug. 1894), 101.

[146] S. Hobhouse, *Forty Years and an Epilogue* (1951), 59–61. E. Kaye, *C. J. Cadoux: Theologian, Scholar and Pacifist* (Edinburgh, 1988), 10–11.

appealed to anarchists, humanitarians, rationalists, and socialists. For example, one of Britain's leading Tolstoyan pacifists, Edward G. Smith, was a rationalist; and the explicitly socialist pacifism which gradually appeared within the ILP owed much to Tolstoy. The extremism of Tolstoy's creed made it more memorable than that of the Peace Society or Society of Friends. By the Boer War even a Quaker could label 'the Christianity which rejects war' as 'Tolstoi Christianity'.[147] And by the First World War a critic of the peace movement could write that, although pacifism had 'long found its strongest expression among the Society of Friends—or "Quakers" . . . during recent years it has been based largely on the teachings of Tolstoi'.[148]

The comparative intellectual stagnation of the British peace movement at this time can partly be attributed to a blurring of the difference between the foreign policies of the two main parties and a comparative international calm. The Liberals having been discredited by their Egyptian intervention, the Conservatives under the leadership of the third Marquess of Salisbury adopted a moderate style of defencism which prompted Cremer to ask in 1892: 'What has become of the Jingoes of England? Twelve or fourteen years ago they were everywhere.'[149] Even though there were still 'very few Conservatives among the ranks of the Peace Society',[150] or for that matter in the other associations, the Liberal electoral victory of 1892, which brought Gladstone back to power, aroused little enthusiasm within the peace movement. When the 'Grand Old Man' of British politics retired from the prime ministership aged 84 in 1894 after a dispute with his colleagues about what he saw as excessive naval expenditure, he was succeeded by Rosebery, a 'Liberal Imperialist' who, as a worried Cremer noted, 'sometimes talks as though he were a Jingo'.[151] The resignation of the Liberal government after the 1895 election caused peace activists little grief, though the fact that 'a number of the warmest and most active friends of Peace' lost their seats was upsetting.[152]

Salisbury's new government largely avoided foreign-policy controversy until 1898. Indeed, during the 1890s generally the international situation, which at the start of the decade the secretary of the Friends' Peace Committee described as ' "a truce," certainly not a peace',[153] turned out to be more stable

---

[147] Cited in E. H. Jones, *Margery Fry: The Essential Amateur* (1966), 54.
[148] F. Ballard, *The Mistakes of Pacifism or Why a Christian can have Anything to Do with War* (n.d. [1915]), 16.
[149] *Arbitrator* (June 1892), 71.
[150] *HP* (May 1885), 224.
[151] *Arbitrator* (Dec. 1894), 86. See also H. C. G. Matthew, *The Liberal Imperialists: The Ideas and Politics of a Post-Gladstonian Elite* (1973).
[152] *HP* (June 1896), 73.   [153] *HP* (June 1890), 91.

than expected. In May 1891 the Peace Society's annual report noted that the gloomiest prognostications about the arms race had not been fulfilled: the 'armed peace' coexisted with the best 'pacific understanding' among the governments of Europe for twenty years.[154] Three years later it expressed its puzzlement at a 'peculiar' aspect of the times which was to be frequently commented on over the next two decades: 'Never, in the history of civilisa-tion, were there more men under arms than at the present time; never was there a more universal and genuine shrinking from the idea of war.'[155] And a further four years later it divided its review of the year into two sections: a 'reverse' section which commented on depressing though distant develop-ments (including British military action on India's North-West Frontier, in South Africa, and against the Sudanese); and an 'obverse' one which claimed: 'The gain to Peace has been immense . . . Even the reasons given by bellicose nations for their actions . . . are a concession to the morality and majesty of peace.'[156] As these comments tacitly recognized, defencists could claim surprising success for their policies.

Moreover, because for most Englishmen, comparatively secure on their island, 'the prospect of war at present carries no terror', as a peace activist noted in the spring of 1899,[157] it was in any case hard to interest them in inter-national questions. Indeed, the only such issue to catch their imagination during the decade was Turkey's treatment of its Armenian subjects, particu-larly the massacres of 1895–6. The outraged response which these atrocities provoked in Britain, particularly from the Nonconformist conscience, resem-bled that over the Bulgarian atrocities two decades before, except for two slight differences which had contradictory effects. First, Salisbury distanced himself from Turkey: this reduced the partisan dimension of the crisis. Second, Russia was now seen as less of a threat to Turkey: this made inter-vention to help the Armenians seem more like forcible domestic reform than international war.

In consequence, although the crisis was less politicized, there were more calls for the use of force. One came from a leading Baptist pastor, John Clifford.[158] Another came from Gladstone, who, at what turned out to be his last great public meeting, in Liverpool on 24 September 1896, urged that Britain should suspend diplomatic relations with Turkey and inform 'the Sultan that she shall take into consideration the means of enforcing, if force alone is available, compliance with her just, legal, and humane demand'[159]—

---

[154] *HP* (June 1891), 248.   [155] *HP* (June 1894), 68.
[156] *HP* (June 1898), 66.   [157] *Concord* (Apr. 1899), 59–60.
[158] Laity, 'British Peace Movement 1896–1916', fo. 169.
[159] *The Times* (25 Sept. 1896), 5.

a bellicose declaration which, ironically, resulted in the resignation of Rosebery, whose defencism inclined him to caution on this issue, from the Liberal leadership. And even within the Society of Friends there was sufficient interest in a crusade for Ellen Robinson to warn London Yearly Meeting 'not to give way to the terrible temptation of desiring to overcome evil in the East by means which we had consistently recognised as wrong in themselves'.[160] Though the Peace Society had from the outset insisted that 'compassion needs to be carefully directed into wise and pacific channels',[161] it found it hard to condemn those who disagreed with it. Its annual report for 1896/7, after reaffirming that 'it could not favour war, by whomsoever it is pursued', admitted that, in view of the failure of diplomatic pressure to restrain the Ottomans, 'it was perhaps not to be wondered at that some of the warmest friends of humanity and of Peace should lose heart and hope, and . . . agitate for more decisive and vigorous action, even though it should involve, as urged by Mr Gladstone, the single-handed appeal to force by this country.'[162]

For the three primary peace associations, the 1890s were a decade of institutional underperformance. The International Arbitration League was suffering from an erosion of the artisan base which had been its real asset during its first decade. That Cremer had played down its class identity so soon after being elected to parliament as a spokesmen for working men was indicative of the ambivalent position in which he and his generation, who had entered politics in the late 1850s, were starting to find themselves in the 1880s because of social and ideological change. The members of the league's council knew that they needed 'young men to take their places', and were increasingly self-consciousness about their 'artizan' character and their status as 'Officers of organized bodies, such as Trades, Friendly, Religious, Temperance, and Political Societies . . . School Boards and Town Councils', who in some cases had been 'rewarded with municipal honours'.[163] During its previous incarnation as the WPA, it had discovered in the Eastern crisis of 1875–8 how deep was the attitudinal gulf between its network of honorary agents and the mainly unskilled workers who supported jingoism and Conservatism. Moreover, during the 1880s and 1890s changes within the trade-union movement were transferring influence to more militant activists within the craft unions and to some extent also to the new unions of unskilled workers: as a result, Thomas Burt was aware by 1891 of being regarded as 'a back number'.[164] And the Lib-Lab MPs, who had once seemed to constitute

[160] *British Friend* (June 1897), 158.
[161] *HP* (1 Jan. 1895), 154–5.
[162] *HP* (June 1897), 250.
[163] *Arbitrator* (Mar. 1883), 5, 6; (Apr. 1883), 7; (July 1883), 1.
[164] T. Burt, *An Autobiography* (1924), 288.

the vanguard of a significant political force, numbered only twenty-four in total:[165] the Liberal Party was adopting fewer working-class candidates; and independent-labour strategies and socialist ideas were developing as alternatives to Liberalism. Linked as it thus was to an obsolescent political tradition, the league was to face worsening financial difficulties 'owing to the death of several old subscribers and the falling away of others'[166] from which only a regular subscription from Andrew Carnegie after 1892[167] as well donations from individual Quakers rescued it. The dropping of the name WPA had thus taken place at a time when the artisans who had created the association were beginning to lose their authority as spokesmen for workmen generally.

Its major asset now being Cremer's position as an MP, the International Arbitration League expressed satisfaction that 'the lead in regard to parliamentary action has passed to us since the death of Mr Richard'.[168] In parliament Cremer continued to make an Anglo-American arbitration treaty his priority. He put down a House of Commons resolution in its support in 1891, but experienced a long wait for an opportunity to introduce it, during which his ungracious complaint of lack of support from the Peace Society stung Darby into a forthright protest.[169] By the time Cremer's chance came on 16 June 1893, 1,348 petitions had been submitted in his support; and after he had accepted a minor amendment from Prime Minister Gladstone, his resolution was passed without opposition, while Andrew Carnegie watched from the public gallery and Conservative MPs mostly stayed away.[170] During 1894 Cremer pressed ahead with a second address to President Cleveland, for which he whipped in no fewer than 354 British MPs as signatories (only twenty-one of them Conservatives, however),[171] and which he presented in person at the White House on 18 January 1895. Later that year, moreover, a crisis with the United States over British Guiana's frontier with Venezuela made Anglo-American arbitration a real issue for the first time since the *Alabama* crisis.[172]

Although Cremer was delighted by the publicity which the crisis brought, he was cast down when the Olney-Pauncefote treaty which ended it on 11 January 1897 was mutilated by the Senate, and when the United States went

---

[165] See J. Shepherd, 'Labour and Parliament: The Lib.-Labs as the First Working-Class MPs, 1885–1906', in E. F. Biagini and A. J. Reid (eds.), *Currents of Radicalism* (Cambridge, 1991), 187–213.
[166] *Arbitrator* (Mar. 1892), 39.
[167] Laity, 'British Peace Movement, 1896–1916', fo. 58.
[168] *Arbitrator* (Dec. 1889), 1.
[169] *Arbitrator* (Mar. 1892), 34. *HP* (Apr. 1892), 38–9.
[170] *Arbitrator* (June/July 1893), 65, 79. Hansard, xiii HC cols. 1240–73.
[171] *HP* (Dec. 1894), 138.
[172] Laity, 'British Peace Movement 1896–1916', fo. 152.

to war with Spain the following year. He was also upset at having for financial reasons to convert the *Arbitrator* from a monthly into an 'occasional publication' appearing about four times a year.[173] In addition, he had narrowly lost his seat at the 1895 general election, attributing the result to corruption by his opponents. He was increasingly out of sympathy with urban mass culture, on the frivolity of which by July 1898 he was blaming his league's inability to recruit new members: 'Every progressive organization is suffering from the blight which seems to have settled upon our countrymen, the great bulk of whom appear to care very little for anything but football, cycling, racing, and betting.'[174] If ever a peace activist needed the lifting of the spirits which the Tsar's Rescript was imminently to provide, it was Cremer.

Although no longer needing to sound pacifist, Cremer had become, like most radical *pacificists*, an isolationist, telling the Commons that he supported disarmament because he took 'the common sense view, and had asked himself whether there was any real fear of attack if we minded our own affairs', and repeatedly asking: 'Where is the danger? Where is the foe?'[175] The International Arbitration League's response to the Armenian crisis, though sympathetic to 'oppressed minorities', was therefore opposed to intervention,[176] its isolationist instincts being reinforced in this case by secular distaste for the evangelicals who favoured a crusade.

The IAPA, too, was faced with a struggle to survive once its merger hopes had fallen through. It retained a public-relations flair, attracting audiences to its annual meetings by inviting famous names such as the writer Arthur Conan Doyle (who was later, however, to embarrass it by his support for the Boer War).[177] It continued to pronounce upon substantive international problems, being irritated when the Universal Peace Congresses, with the Peace Society's support, declined to do the same.[178] Occasionally, these pronouncements offended its own members: an example was a decision of its executive committee on 17 December 1895 that Britain might in certain circumstances relinquish Cyprus.[179] It also continued to promote its European mission, though this remained largely a personal effort by Pratt, who because of frequent absence from Britain as well as declining health resigned as chairman of the executive committee in 1897 aged 73, though he retained an active

[173] *Arbitrator* (July–Nov. 1897), 31.
[174] *Arbitrator* (July 1898), 46.
[175] Hansard, cccxxvi HC col. 405 (15 May 1888); cccxxxiii HC cols. 1541–5 (7 Mar. 1889); cccxxxiv HC col. 1259 (25 Mar. 1889); xxxi HC cols. 1312–6 (18 Mar. 1895).
[176] Laity, 'British Peace Movement 1896–1916', fo. 172.
[177] *Concord* (July 1893), 122; (Feb. 1902), 23–6.
[178] *Concord* (18 Jan. 1893), 4. Laity, 'British Peace Movement 1896–1916', fo. 83.
[179] *Concord* (Feb. 1896), 22.

involvement in the association for the remaining ten years of his life. He was replaced by the artist Felix Moscheles: the London-born son of a distinguished Bohemian pianist, the godson of the composer Mendelssohn, a former member of Mazzini's People's International League, and later a keen esperantist, he was self-consciously a 'cosmopolitan' by 'descent, birth, and convictions'.[180] Moscheles also constituted a personal link with the Peace Society, whose executive committee he had sat on since 1883: this was useful in securing its support for his proposal, which both the International Peace Bureau and the Universal Peace Congress at Budapest had endorsed, for a 'Peace Day' on which all peace associations would hold simultaneous annual gatherings to discuss an agreed theme. Peace Days were held from 1896 onwards, initially on 22 February, George Washington's birthday, but after 1910 on 18 May, the day on which the 1899 Hague conference had opened. In Britain, the Peace Day gatherings were normally held in Moscheles's London studio. They proved a useful forum for activists, who were usually afforced by an eminent guest such as the playwright George Bernard Shaw.[181]

The IAPA's survival owed much to J. Frederick Green's willingness— helped presumably by his private income and sense of humour[182]—to remain its secretary. Moreover, Green's joining of the Fabian Society, the Society of Friends of Russian Freedom, and, later, the Social Democratic Federation (a Marxist political party founded in the 1880s) helped to steer the association towards a new role: as a bridge between the primary peace movement and the socialist or advanced-radical politicians for which the rigidly Lib-Lab International Arbitration League refused to cater. At this time the Second International, launched in Paris in the same year as the Universal Peace Congresses, was using a series of international socialist congresses to promote its view that capitalism caused war. However, its powerful German contingent, though prepared to advocate opposition to all armaments expenditure, obstructed attempts to commit the Second International to a general strike against war.[183]

In line with his previous involvement with organizations for working men, Pratt wanted to broaden the IAPA's base in a democratic direction, being convinced that no peace association could 'rest satisfied with having brought together a few men and women of the middle or bourgeois class'.[184] The

---

[180] *IAPA Monthly Journal* (31 July 1886), 78. See also F. Moscheles, *Fragments of an Autobiography* (1899), 31, 246, 253. His portrait of Pratt is mentioned in the latter's *DNB* entry.

[181] *Concord* (Mar. 1896), 28. *HP* (June 1896), 74.

[182] For a portrait see Hobson, *Pilgrim to the Left*, 124, 127–8.

[183] D. Newton, *British Labour, European Socialism, and the Struggle for Peace 1889–1914* (Oxford, 1985), 50–7.

[184] *Concord* (Oct. 1894), 119.

IAPA's key recruit among Green's new left-wing contacts was G. H. Perris, the journalist son of a Unitarian minister, who had helped to found the Society for Friends of Russian Freedom in 1890 and subsequently became fascinated by Tolstoy's thought. In January 1898 Perris, who at that time was trying to give the word 'paxist' to the language,[185] assumed the editorship of a restyled *Concord*, which began calling for 'a distribution of parties' on the grounds that 'since the disaster of Mr Gladstone's retirement and the succession of Lord Rosebery, there has been, so far as foreign and Imperial questions are concerned, no Liberal Party at all'.[186] However, Perris's first issue as editor showed that he was fully aware of how 'few in number' were the members of peace associations; and 'small but very much alive' was the most favourable comment on the IAPA which his journal could make on the basis of its annual meeting on 14 June 1898.[187]

The IAPA was thus in ideological transition during the 1890s. Its veteran leader Pratt was still essentially a liberal, albeit an advanced one; but its new recruits were taking the organization down a socialist path. In this it was unique among primary associations: the International Arbitration League remained defiantly Lib-Lab as already noted; and the Peace Society was anti-socialist, and described as 'wild and unwarranted' the claim of the Second International's London congress of 1896 that 'the socialisation of the means of production, distribution, and exchange is the only way to secure Peace'.[188]

The Peace Society still professed to be 'beyond comparison, the most active and effective of all associations having for their object the advocacy of International Arbitration and Peace'.[189] Its Quaker financial bedrock ensured that this was true: even at its lowest ebb during the decade its income was, at £2,400, more than twice the incomes of its two rivals combined. Even so, and despite Darby's effort both to increase income and reduce expenditure, it for three years ran a deficit of £800, which it blamed on the 'multiplication of other agencies' and the 'prevalent commercial depression'[190] and which it cleared in 1895–6 only because of unexpectedly large legacies. Its need to use such windfalls as income rather than endowment was clearly unfortunate: when the wealthy Quaker tea-merchant John Horniman bequeathed it £10,000 in 1893, his will prudently stipulated that the principal could not be touched,[191] with the ironic consequence that the society found itself worse off in the short term, since the donations Horniman had made during his lifetime had yielded as much as the interest on his legacy, and news of his munificent bequest

[185] *Concord* (Dec. 1897), 90; (Jan. 1898), 9.   [186] *Concord* (Apr. 1898), 50.
[187] *Concord* (Jan. 1898), 5; (July 1898), 99.   [188] *HP* (Aug. 1896), 108.
[189] *HP* (Oct. 1889), 290.   [190] *HP* (June 1895), 211–12, 214.
[191] PSM, 30 Aug. 1893.

apparently caused other members to feel they could give less.[192] In the long term, the income from the Horniman endowment was probably the main reason why the society was not formally wound up after it became moribund during the First World War but was instead preserved in a state of nominal existence.

The Peace Society's appetite for making unpopular protests was further declining in the 1890s: for example, the executive committee's discussions of the Matabele War in 1893, the Cretan crisis in 1897, and the Spanish–American War in 1898 all had a defeatist tone which would have been unthinkable during the Richard era;[193] and it admitted a sense of 'despondency' in the spring of 1898 when it concluded that 'the time for permanent treaties of Arbitration or proposals of mutual disarmament is not yet'.[194]

Even where its pacifism remained strong, it seemed to belong to a bygone era. For example, when in 1894 its long-serving employee William Tallack wrote to *The Times* expressing surprise that in all the recent public discussion about armaments no reference had been made 'to a most important element in our national defence—the protection and overruling of Providence',[195] his argument seemed quaint as well as, by Tolstoyan standards, complacent. The society's old guard of indomitable absolutists was in any case disappearing. William E. Corner, a Unitarian who had joined the executive committee in April 1858 and been one of its most active members for thirty-five years, resigned in June 1896 at the age of 80. Moreover, through death the society lost Arthur O'Neill, its agent in the Midlands for over forty years, in 1896, and Elizabeth Pease Nichol, the sometime Garrisonian who had been expelled from the Society of Friends for 'marrying out' but in her last months became one of the society's new breed of female vice-presidents, in 1897.

Faced with the difficulty of justifying pacifism, other than in terms of an excessively demanding Tolstoyan perfectionism, an increasing number of the Peace Society's committee members solved the problem either by holding back from doing so (thereby infringing its rules, as previously understood) or took the collaborative orientation to such an extreme as to push their own pacifism into a very private sphere. This became particularly apparent during the naval panic of 1894–5, when the society's treasurer, Walter Hazell, who had recently entered parliament at a by-election, was asked by a woman's magazine why on 18 March 1895 he had been one of thirty-two MPs to vote for a Commons motion proposed by Sir Wilfred Lawson in favour of a reduction of armaments. Hazell's reply was that he had done so merely to make 'a formal protest', that he was not a 'Little Englander', and that he wanted the

---

[192] *HP* (Nov. 1893), 315.
[193] PSM, 17 Nov. 1893, 19 Mar. 1897, 15 Apr. 1898.
[194] *HP* (Apr. 1898), 42.
[195] Cited in *HP* (Feb. 1894), 14.

Royal Navy to be 'strong' and in 'a high state of efficiency'. More remarkable than Hazell's remarks themselves was the fact that the *Herald of Peace* reproduced them with the tolerant comment: 'There is room in the Peace Society and its Executive for varying shades of personal opinion.'[196] Hazell not only repeated his remarks on other occasions but also advocated the use of force in support of the Armenians.[197] Growing uncertainty as to what the society stood for was exacerbated by remarks made by non-members: thus a Liberal MP who had been invited as a guest speaker told the Peace Society's 1895 public meeting that, although he had 'not hesitated to vote for the increase in the navy', he had also wanted 'to give two votes, if possible, to the views of the Peace Society'.[198]

As the three primary associations began to find their traditional activities less rewarding during the 1890s, *ad hoc* bodies began to be created in an attempt to mobilize support on particular issues from those reluctant to commit themselves to the peace movement on a more general or permanent basis. An early example was the Arbitration Alliance, created in 1894 to win support on this specific issue from the churches. It arose out of an ecclesiastical meeting held during the 1893 Universal Peace Congress at Chicago, where the Anglo-American religious approach to peace was given unwonted prominence, and was officially launched in London on 9 February 1894, with the Peace Society providing its secretariat. Three months later it became the focus of the first and most modest of Stead's eruptions into peace activism. Until recently known as an ultra-defencist, he now pressed the Arbitration Alliance into promoting a Memorial calling for an agreement by the great powers not to increase their armaments before 1900, and within a year received 130,729 signatures.[199] However, in 1895 he suffered 'something like a nervous breakdown of health', and the following year supported the Jameson Raid.[200] Two more *ad hoc* bodies appeared in 1896: an Anglo-American Arbitration Committee, of which Stead was secretary, notwithstanding his ultra-imperialism, and which he used not merely to promote reconciliation between Britain and the United States but also to urge every nation to appoint a 'Lord High Arbitrator';[201] and an Increased Armaments Protest Committee, of which G.H. Perris was a co-founder.[202]

[196] *HP* (May 1895), 199–200.
[197] Laity, 'British Peace Movement 1896–1916', fo. 170. [198] *HP* (June 1895), 211, 219.
[199] See its first annual report: *HP* (July 1895), 227–9.
[200] Whyte, *Life of W. T. Stead*, ii. 67, 88.
[201] W. T. Stead, *Always Arbitrate Before You Fight: An Appeal to English Speaking Folk* (1896), 4, 6, 8.
[202] Laity, 'British Peace Movement 1896–1916', fo. 76, 153.

This period was perhaps the most disappointing in the peace movement's history. After the disillusionment of Gladstone's support for intervention in Egypt, which involved the Peace Society and WPA in much acrimony, the primary associations had spent too much time on their internal problems and too little on promoting their ideas; but alternative agencies for campaigning were only starting to take up the slack. The peace movement as a whole was in urgent want of the stimulus which in their different ways the Tsar's Rescript, the Boer War, and the Anglo-German naval race were all to bring.

6

Quickening,
August 1898–August 1914

The Tsar's Rescript of 29 August 1898 inviting other countries to a peace conference 'has quickened interest in the peace movement', as the *Herald of Peace* soon noted.[1] Its ideas suddenly became prominent: the Hague conference of 1899 created an international court of arbitration, and was followed by a second gathering in 1907; the word 'pacifist' entered the language after 1901; regular National Peace Congresses began in 1904; and an exposition of a 'New Pacifism' by an obscure Paris-based journalist, Norman Angell, became the first mass-selling peace book on its publication in 1910. But these developments reflected a greater breadth of interest in war-prevention as more people became anxious about the international situation rather than an increased depth of commitment to peace activism. Indeed, before the end of this period, 'the weakening of enthusiasm through the more general conventional acceptance of its principles' was being complained of by the Peace Society.[2]

The balance within the peace movement changed significantly. Individuals, such as Stead, Hobson, and Angell, played leading roles. So did *ad hoc* bodies as various the International Crusade of Peace, which supported the Tsar's Rescript, a Stop-the-War Movement, which courageously opposed the conflict in South Africa, and assorted 'vigilance committees', as G. H. Perris called them,[3] which agitated on the pressing foreign-policy issues of the moment. And socialist societies developed into useful secondary associations. By contrast, the primary associations again failed to rise to the occasion.

THE FIRST HAGUE CONFERENCE AND THE BOER WAR,
1898–1902

The Tsar's Rescript was hailed by the Robert Spence Watson, a Quaker solicitor and prominent Gladstonian Liberal from Newcastle, as 'the greatest event

[1] *HP* (Dec. 1898), 145.   [2] *HP* (Jan. 1909), 208.
[3] G. H. Perris, *Our Foreign Policy and Sir Edward Grey's Failure* (1912), 215.

of my life'.[4] Though interpreted by defencists as a sign of Russia's inability to cope with the economic strain of the arms race, it led to the arranging of the first Hague Conference for 18 May 1899. In Britain many progressives were suspicious of any idea emanating from so authoritarian a source; and some Quakers succumbed to their traditional anxiety about appearing 'to accept the principle of gradual disarmament'.[5]

More than anyone it was Stead, whose indomitable drive had not been felt in the peace movement since Joseph Sturge's death forty years previously, who insisted that the Hague Conference be treated by the British peace movement as a major opportunity. Admittedly, Stead did so to some extent because of a partiality towards Russia which can be traced back to the early 1870s:[6] this, along with his spiritualism, his imperialism, and his tendency to make eccentric suggestions, such as that the Pope be made arbitrator-in-chief, made most peace activists suspicious of him. Indeed, although they no longer regarded him as the 'madcap' of the mid-1880s,[7] they found him 'delightfully outrageous'.[8] Stead embarked on a tour of European capitals in the autumn of 1898; and although this was only partially successful, it encouraged him to call for 'a great pilgrimage of peace throughout all Nations, beginning in San Francisco and ending at St Petersburg', as well as for the raising of £10,000.[9] In Britain his campaign struck a chord, as was evidenced by the widespread convening of town's meetings in the months following the Tsar's initiative[10]—the last time, it seems, that this traditional form of political self-expression was used in Britain on a significant scale.

Stead persuaded the three established peace associations to join him in forming an International Crusade of Peace, their 'narrow fear that the permanent machinery of the Peace Movement may be weakened by this large and sensational appeal' being been overcome by an assurance that this special campaign would last only three months.[11] The crusade was publicly launched at a meeting in St James's Hall on 'Peace Sunday', 18 December 1898, Stead claiming it to be different 'from all previous Peace agitations in being directed to a single definite aim, the excellence of which is recognized by all'.[12] In fact, Tolstoy was to dismiss the proposed conference as a futile

---

[4] P. Corder, *The Life of Robert Spence Watson* (1914), 278.
[5] *Friend* (9 Sept. 1898), 575.
[6] Whyte, *Life of W. T. Stead*, i. 44.
[7] *Arbitrator* (Oct. 1884), 1.
[8] *Concord* (Apr. 1899), 59.
[9] Whyte, *Life of W. T. Stead*, ii. 129–45. PSM, 18 Nov. 1898.
[10] See e.g. *The Czar's Manifesto on Disarmament and Peace: Great Town's Meeting in the Winter Gardens, Harrogate, September 18th 1898* (Harrogate, 1898)
[11] *Concord* (Jan. 1899), 5.
[12] *War Against War!* (13 Jan. 1899), 1.

diplomatic palliative, prompting Stead, who regarded Tolstoy's belief that the Sermon on the Mount required the rejection of all force as absurd extremism, to condemn the Russian writer for carrying 'an absolutely impossible interpretation of his text to an absolutely impossible conclusion'.[13] The crusade's provisional committee first met on 21 December. It published twelve issues of a special campaign magazine largely written by Stead, *War Against War!*, between 12 January and 31 March 1899. It also sent out speakers to the local gatherings at which delegates were chosen for a National Convention in London on 21 March: Stead travelled to as many of these as he could; and Darby, who chaired the organizing committee, spoke at 'four meetings a week in connection with the Peace Crusade'.[14]

The crusade had to drop its ambitious idea of an international pilgrimage because, as Stead ruefully noted, no similar campaign could be mounted in the United States, because of its size, or on the continent, because of its lack of a tradition of public demonstration. Even in Britain the crusade did not attract quite enough support to hold its National Convention in the Albert Hall as originally envisaged.[15] Yet nearly 400 delegates filled St Martin's Town Hall, Charing Cross; the crusade was recognized by the arbitration societies as 'absolutely unique in the history of popular agitation';[16] and even Darby compared it favourably with the agitation following the Bulgarian atrocities.[17] Admittedly, no sooner was the crusade over than the Peace Society complained that, although its own members had 'formed the backbone of the movement, and had done much of the work', its position as 'the leader of the popular Peace propaganda of the country' had been ignored by Stead for fear of being branded 'Peace at any price'.[18] But the society recovered its good humour when the Hague conference resulted in the formation of a permanent court of arbitration and raised its hopes of 'a complete reform in international diplomacy'.[19]

However, while the Hague conference was lifting the spirits of the British peace movement, a looming confrontation with the Boers was starting to depress them. On 12 June 1899 Chamberlain's Liberal critics, including Dr G. B. Clark of the IAPA, formed a Transvaal Committee; but the extent of the imperialist sentiment against which it was pitted became apparent on 24 September when its meeting in Trafalgar Square was broken up by jingoes,

[13] *War Against War!* (24 Feb. 1899), 99.
[14] PSM, 17 Mar. 1899.
[15] *War Against War!* (17 Mar. 1899), 145.
[16] *Concord* (Mar. 1899), 49. See also *Arbitrator* (Apr. 1899), 75.
[17] *Concord* (Apr. 1899), 60; *HP* (Mar. 1899), 181.
[18] *HP* (Apr. 1899), 200–1.
[19] *HP* (Aug. 1899), 258–9.

with Moscheles, who was among the speakers with Pratt and Cremer, being struck under the left ear by a penknife thrown from the crowd.[20] Moreover, the Transvaal Committee's work was rendered even more difficult on 9 October when the Boers pre-emptively issued their own ultimatum, which enabled the British government to claim that it was forced to fight in self-defence.[21]

The first eight months of the South African War, which included the Boer victories of 'Black Week' in December 1899 and the much vaunted reliefs of Ladysmith and Mafeking (the latter celebrated by the memorable public 'mafficking' of 18 May 1900), were comparable in adversity for the peace movement to the Eastern crisis of 1875–8: once again, elements of the working class were prominent among the jingoes;[22] and a peace paper commented in March 1900 that 'the history of this movement during the past week has been little but accounts of one riot after another'.[23] Even though hostility abated somewhat thereafter, as Boer fighters were gradually hunted down by the British army and many of their compatriots were moved into concentration camps, the peace movement 'suffered terribly' in the general election of October 1900.[24] None the less, what now seems remarkable is not that opponents of the war were vilified as 'pro-Boers', or that the visiting British South African, Samuel Cronwright-Schreiner (husband of the writer Olive Schreiner) eventually had to abandon his speaking tour, but that they had expected to be able to hold meeings and invite perceived apologists for the enemy during a conflict.

The Transvaal Committee soon lapsed into inactivity. The League of Liberals against Aggression and Militarism, formed in February 1900, was a secondary association intended to save the Liberal Party from the Liberal Imperialists: it reminded Arthur (now Lord) Hobhouse of the Anti-Aggression League of two decades previously,[25] and had as negligible an impact on the public. However, two important groups were formed: the South Africa Conciliation Committee, and the Stop-the-War Movement.

The South Africa Conciliation Committee was established at a private meeting in Westminster Palace Hotel on 1 November 1899, although it did not issue a public declaration until 17 January 1900.[26] It was a moderate body which campaigned for a just peace rather than a halt to the war, though this

[20] *Concord* (Oct. 1899), 163–7.

[21] Davey, *British Pro-Boers*, 43, 49–51. This book provides the best account of the *ad hoc* associations created during the war: see ibid. 77–88.

[22] See the corrective in Newton, *British Labour*, 118–23, to the attempt to underplay working-class support for the war in R. Price, *An Imperial War and the British Working Class* (1972).

[23] *War Against War in South Africa* (16 Mar. 1900), 350.

[24] *HP* (Nov. 1900), 130.

[25] Hobhouse and Hammond, *Lord Hobhouse*, 223.

[26] G. P. Gooch, *Life of Lord Courtney* (1920), 393, 420, 428.

did not prevent some of its meetings being broken up.[27] Its leading light was Leonard Courtney, who, though sitting in parliament as a Liberal Unionist since breaking with Gladstone over Home Rule, has been identified as an exemplar of 'the older Liberalism'.[28] It mostly attracted Liberals, such as the veteran Herbert Spencer and the classicist Gilbert Murray; but Keir Hardie of the ILP was also a member.

The South Africa Conciliation Committee's most interesting supporters were Emily Hobhouse, the first controversial female peace activist, and J. A. Hobson, the celebrated critic of imperialism. The former, sister of the progressive Liberal theorist L. T. Hobhouse, was co-organizer and main speaker at the first public meeting for women during a major war, held on a ticket-only basis at Queen's Hall on 13 June 1900 under the auspices of the committee's women's group; and she afterwards made a well-publicized visit to South Africa to help war victims and expose the concentration camps.[29] Whereas Peckover had shown herself an outstanding organizer, Emily Hobhouse had a talent for controversy: she was refused entry by the British authorities when she attempted a return visit to South Africa, and was to cause outrage during the First World War when she paid an unauthorized visit to Germany and German-occupied Belgium.

J. A. Hobson, an Oxford-educated economist who had been denied academic preferment on account of his heterodox opinions, reported on South Africa for the *Manchester Guardian* and published three books on the conflict. The first, the unsold copies of which were bought up by the Conciliation Committee to lend to supporters, was a survey of the local origins of the war. It emphasized the role of 'a small confederacy of international financiers working through a kept press'. Although Hobson was embarrassed by the fact that many of these were Jewish, noting the difficulty of stating 'the truth about our doings in South Africa without seeming to appeal to the ignominious passion of *Judenhetze*',[30] some other opponents of the war, including the budding writers G. K. Chesterton and Hilaire Belloc, welcomed the chance the war offered to indulge in anti-Semitism.[31] Hobson's second book asked why Britain's 'lay multitude' at home had succumbed to jingoism. Although this question reflected a growing contemporary interest in psychological theories of political behaviour, Hobson initially offered a

[27] See e.g. *Concord* (Aug. 1900), 119.

[28] See D. A. Martin, *Pacifism: An Historical and Sociological Study* (1965), 79–82.

[29] J. Liddington, *Long Road to Greenham*, 47. J. Fisher, *That Miss Hobhouse* (1971), 99–110.

[30] J. A. Hobson, *The War in South Africa: Its Causes and Effects* (1900), 189, 229.

[31] G. K. Chesterton, *Autobiography* (1936), 114–17. See also C. Hirschfield, 'The Anglo-Boer War and the Issue of Jewish Culpability', *Journal of Contemporary History*, 15 (1980), 19–31.

mainly sociological explanation in terms of the 'bad conditions of town life in our great industrial centres' which, along with a 'biassed, enslaved, and poisoned press', had harmed the nervous systems of the working class.[32] However, the third and most famous book, *Imperialism: A Study*, adopted an economic approach, rejecting 'the merely sentimental diagnosis which explained wars or other national errors by outbursts of patriotic animosity or errors of statecraft', and insisting that war, though irrational 'from the standpoint of the whole nation', was 'rational enough from the standpoint of certain classes in the nation'. Where the previous generation of radicals, such as Cremer, had assumed greed to be a motive, Hobson argued that underconsumptionism—the insufficient purchasing power of an unequal society—drove financiers to invest abroad and demand that the state use force to help them. This was a step towards Lenin's diagnosis of imperialist war as a systemic product of capitalism, and therefore received the support of many avowed socialists. But Hobson remained a radical who believed that democratic control rather than the abolition of capitalism was the remedy. He thus argued: 'Secure popular government, in substance and in form, and you secure internationalism: retain class government, and you retain military Imperialism and international conflict.'[33]

The Stop-the-War Movement was launched by Silas K. Hocking, a former Methodist minister who had become a novelist and an aspiring Liberal politician. Hocking took action after receiving many private expressions of agreement with a letter to the press criticizing the war; but, as a newcomer to peace activism, he was 'not prepared for the abuse' he was to receive. Indeed, he feared for his life for 'many months', was forced to stand down as a parliamentary candidate, and suffered a boycott of his novels.[34]

Hocking's initiative might have been stillborn but for Stead's unexpected but characteristically wholehearted support. The former apologist for the Jameson Raid astonished his imperialist friends by coming out with a weekly paper on 29 October 1899 under the title *War Against War in South Africa* and a masthead beseeching: 'Deliver us from Bloodguiltiness, O Lord!' It was to lambast the British government in the most outspoken terms, accusing it in one issue alone of 'lying', 'fraud', 'bad faith', and 'wholesale murder'.[35] On 10 November it published an address to the Queen, calling for peace, and asked for signatures in its support to be sent to the 'Stop the War Secretary' at 40 Outer Temple (the IAPA's address).

---

[32] J. A. Hobson, *The Psychology of Jingoism* (1901), 1, 7, 125.

[33] J. A. Hobson, *Imperialism: A Study* (1902), 52, 171.

[34] S. K. Hocking, *My Book of Memory: A String of Reminiscences and Reflections* (1923), 178–9, 183–7.

[35] *WAWSA* (12 Jan. 1900), 193.

Soon afterwards a Stop-the-War Committee came into existence: it included Hocking as chairman, the Revd John Clifford—who opposed imperialist conflicts despite his propensity for European crusades—as president, and Cobden's daughter Jane Cobden Unwin as head of its women's section. Among its sympathizers were Passmore Edwards, whose experience of the peace movement now stretched back more than fifty years, and the rising star of Welsh Liberalism, David Lloyd George.[36] One its first tasks was to arrange 'a conference of the Friends of Peace'.[37] Billed as a 'Stop-the-War Conference', this took place, shortly before the Conciliation Committee had publicly declared itself, on 11 January 1900 in Exeter Hall. Though an invitation-only gathering, it was attacked by a mob at the incitement of the jingo press, and was able to proceed only because stewards from the Social Democratic Federation, which played a leading role in opposition to the war until a change of policy in August 1901, held the rowdies at bay while Cremer prevailed upon the police to intervene.[38]

After this conference, the Stop-the-War Movement, as it now called itself, hired larger premises, and by the end of March was claiming to have received nearly 4,000 signatures for a new petition against the conflict.[39] But although attracting considerable publicity, it had a short life: at the end of April regular publication of its loss-making paper was suspended; and its big, ticket-only meeting on 24 May 1900, at which a number of members of the Social Democratic Federation criticized it for complacency and ignorance of the underlying causes of imperialism and war,[40] marked the end of its active life. By August, the Stop-the-War Movement was admitting that its 'chief work . . . has been for some time past the distribution of literature'.[41]

Stead's personal peace campaign continued, however. In August 1900 he used the final issue of *War Against War in South Africa* to campaign, albeit unavailingly, for an International Union of Peace, an idea which he had been discussing with sympathizers in London.[42] He also promoted it at a major meeting in Paris on 3 August attended by Cremer, Pratt, Lawson, Ivan Bloch, and several Boer delegates. Stead was aware that his proposed union would duplicate the work of the International Peace Bureau, which was attempting at this time to improve its coordination of the peace movement; but he regarded the Berne-based organization as unable 'from impecuniosity and

---

[36] *WAWSA* (19 Jan. 1900), 212–13.
[37] *WAWSA* (29 Dec. 1899), 167; (5 Jan. 1900), 179.
[38] B. C. Croucher, 'British Working Class Attitudes to War and National Defence, 1902–1914', Ph.D. thesis (Swansea University, 1992), fo. 362. *WAWSA* (9 Mar. 1900), 322–7.
[39] *WAWSA* (30 Mar .1900), 379.
[40] *WAWSA*, 1 June 1900, supplement, 3–4.
[41] *WAWSA* (Aug. 1900), 30.
[42] A 'general council' is listed in *Review of Reviews* (June 1901), 549–51.

general lack of support' to do its job. However, he seemed unaware that the role he envisaged for his International Union of Peace was that originally envisaged by Pratt for his IAPA, namely to act as an international equity tribunal. Stead conceived the 'special business' of his proposed new body as being 'to know where friction is arising in the bearings of the international machine, and to proceed to apply oil betimes'. He was even more sanguine than Pratt in claiming that 'at least one-half' of all disputes 'would be resolved into thin air if the facts were but distinctly ascertained and clearly stated'.[43]

Moreover, in September of the following year Stead made a public nuisance of himself at the Universal Peace Congress at Glasgow. This had been allocated to a British city in the mistaken belief that the Boer War would be over by then; and the decision to proceed with it, even though fighting was still going on, worried the Peace Society.[44] A compromise was negotiated whereby the Glasgow congress would mute its criticisms of the host country: it would note that Britain had refused arbitration whereas the Boers had accepted, but would not otherwise condemn British behaviour. Characteristically, however, Stead rejected this deal. Repudiating all such 'namby-pamby resolutions', he demanded 'an explosion of pacific sentiment' against his own government, and—albeit unsuccessfully—proposed a motion which declared his country 'in effect incommunicate of Christianity'.[45]

The 1901 Glasgow peace congress was of interest for a reason other than Stead's outburst: it was the first public occasion at which Emile Arnaud of the LIPL uttered his new word 'pacifisme'. He had coined it the previous month to distinguish the programme of the peace movement as a whole from the 'federalisme' to which a minority of activists, led by Novikow, wished to restrict it.[46] It took five years for 'pacifism' (or, for English-language purists, 'pacificism') to catch on in Britain: it was not until the autumn of 1903 that the word began appearing even in peace journals;[47] and Moscheles, who as late as 1905 was still using 'paxist' as an alternative, did not succumb to it until 1906.[48] Moreover, it took more than a decade for the word's ambiguity—since it was applied to both absolutists and reformists—to become a matter for

[43] *WAWSA* (10 Aug. 1900), 17–19.

[44] PSM, 21 June, 19 July 1901.

[45] *Proceedings of the 10th Universal Peace Congress St. Andrew's Hall, Glasgow, 10–13 September 1901* (1901), 82–90. *HP* (Nov. 1901), 150–1.

[46] *Proceeding*, 74, 79. Arnaud had first used 'le Pacifisme' in an article in *L'Indépendance belge* which he immediately reprinted in *États-Unis d'Europe: Journal de la Ligue internationale de la paix et de la liberté* (Aug. 1901), 1: I am grateful to Irwin Abrams for a copy of the latter.

[47] Laity, 'British Peace Movement 1896–1916', fo. 5.

[48] *Concord* (May 1905), 71; (Mar. 1906), 37.

comment. It was in 1913, for example, that the *Arbitrator*, complaining that a recent life of Lloyd George had denied that he was a pacifist, commented: 'The error of the biographer is to make the term "pacificist" equivalent to "non-resistant".'[49] When the *Concise Oxford Dictionary*, which had overlooked the word in 1911, included it in a supplementary addendum to its 1914 edition, it agreed with the *Arbitrator* and defined it broadly: as 'the doctrine that the abolition of war is both desirable and possible'.

During the Boer War the two arbitration associations were content to play second fiddle to the *ad hoc* groups. The IAPA noted the difficulties of doing otherwise with 'but an average income of four or five hundred pounds' to work with.[50] None the less it dispatched an early memorial of protest to the Prime Minister with 58,833 signatures collected in a fortnight;[51] it repeatedly condemned the 'mob rule' to which critics of the conflict were subjected; and it issued a statement blaming the war in South Africa on a 'capitalist conspiracy' and urging 'the two extreme wings' of the peace movement—'those of the Liberal culture tradition on the one hand and the Labour-Socialist leaders on the other'—to work together.[52] It allowed its office to be used as a temporary address by the Stop-the-War Movement, presumably on the urging of Green and G. H. Perris. However, in respect of the attitudes of Pratt and the association's moderate mainstream, Paul Laity is correct to characterize the IAPA's approach as 'essentially that of the South Africa Conciliation Committee'.[53]

The International Arbitration League acknowledged that, because its 'resources were altogether insufficient to undertake an anti-war campaign', it had supported the 'temporary organizations' instead.[54] None the less, having rediscovered the artisan radicalism which had been somewhat submerged since its change of name, it declared that Britain stood 'condemned by the whole civilized world', and admitted having latterly 'relied too much upon the pacific tendencies of Lord Salisbury'.[55] It also condemned the 'monetary interests of a few powerful men', notably 'newspaper proprietors'—a recognition of the power of the new mass press—and 'gold speculators'. Its council issued a formal protest signed by seven Lib-Lab MPs,[56] its new array of socially elevated vice-presidents apparently proving of little service to it. Aligning itself firmly with Stead's Stop-the-War Movement, Cremer's league

---

[49] *Arbitrator* (June 1913), 65.
[50] Cited in *WAWSA* (24 Nov. 1899), 49.
[51] *Concord* (Nov. 1899), 182–3.
[52] *Concord* (Apr. 1900), 53–6; (May 1900), 77; (Oct. 1900), 147.
[53] Laity, 'British Peace Movement 1896–1916', fo. 105.
[54] *Arbitrator* (June 1902), 68.
[55] *Arbitrator* (Oct. 1899), 105.
[56] *Arbitrator* (Jan. 1900), 1, 5.

suffered attacks on its meetings reminiscent of those it had endured during its WPA days twenty-four years previously. Its annual meeting on 21 March 1900 was reduced in size because 'very many of our friends were fearful that Jingoes would storm the building'. And by the end of 1901 it was acknowledging that 'the defection of weak-kneed supporters has left us financially crippled'.[57]

However, the Peace Society stayed largely aloof from the campaign against the Boer War, thereby demonstrating how much more of its nerve and sinew had been lost since it had made a last effort during the Egyptian and Sudanese interventions. Initially it rejected as 'not expedient' both its president's suggestion of 'a protest, or something similar' and Priscilla Peckover's suggestion of a memorial to the government, while the *Herald of Peace* answered its own question negatively: 'Is there anything we can do? Sadly, for the present, we must confess there is not.' Throughout the autumn and winter of 1899–1900, moreover, the society continued to insist that 'the time was inopportune' for such initiatives.[58] By the time it issued a memorial, the war was well into its second year.[59] It even criticized those who campaigned actively against the conflict, insisting: 'Misdirected zeal . . . may easily become harmful, and there has been a great deal attempted . . . in the name of peace which has nothing pacific about it but the motive'—a clear dig at the Stop-the-War Movement, which Darby had been instructed not to 'identify himself with'.[60] The society's main aim in respect of the Glasgow congress was to avoid controversy, Darby being in his element calming the delegates down after Stead's provocative intervention.

caution

The Peace Society hastily invented a couple of doctrines to justify this caution. The first was that in wartime it should continue its 'ordinary' activities but not undertake 'special' ones.[61] It thus continued with 'Peace Sunday' and appealed for £600 to do 'good work at the Paris Exhibition',[62] but declined to collaborate with *pacificists* in their campaign. Defending this view after the war, the *Herald of Peace* argued that since 'actual war is simply the . . . direct application of the forces that are associated with an Armed Peace', it should not matter to the society 'so far as its work is concerned, whether the nations are at war or only preparing for war'.[63] However, the society did not even maintain all its ordinary activities. Indeed, it argued that because it had consistently criticized Chamberlain's policy in previous years,

---

[57] *Arbitrator* (Apr. 1900), 32–4; (Dec. 1901). 37.
[58] PSM, 20 Oct., 17 Nov., 15 Dec. 1899; 19 Jan., 16 Feb., 16 Mar. 1900. *HP* (Nov. 1899), 290.
[59] *HP* (Jan. 1901), 7.   [60] *HP* (Mar. 1900), 30. PSM, 19 Jan. 1900.
[61] *HP* (Mar. 1900), 30.   [62] *HP* (Jan. 1900), 1; (Apr. 1900), 38.
[63] *HP* (Sept. 1902), 286.

it had 'no need to repeat these protests' in wartime.[64] And, although it held its annual meetings in London as usual, it abandoned the autumnal conferences it had recently begun holding in the provinces. The second new doctrine was that its 'non-partisan tradition' stopped it protesting.[65] However, as has already been noted, a much less restrictive view had been taken throughout Richard's long secretaryship.

The Peace Society resorted to these excuses for avoiding protest not merely from fear of public hostility and to avoid embarrassing its local supporters, as had been the case during the early months of the Crimean War, but also from fear of splitting its executive committee and alienating its core supporters. Illustrative of an ever-increasing laxity at the top was the attitude of Thomas Snape, the Methodist president of the Liverpool Peace Society, a former MP, and a sometime scourge of 'apologies for war'.[66] His decision to accept the Liberal nomination for South East Cornwall in the 1900 general election caused him to be accused of 'secession to the war party' since this was Leonard Courtney's seat.[67] Snape insisted that Courtney had lost all chance of readoption: his Liberal Unionist supporters and their Conservative allies had repudiated him because of his opposition to the war; and the Liberals did not want him because he had left them in protest against Home Rule fourteen years previously. Even so, Snape had undoubtedly expressed support for the war: indeed, he admitted having assured the local Liberals that he himself took the view that 'there was no alternative but to drive the Boers back to their own land'.[68] And he had started tolerating apologists for war, as became apparent when Hugh Price Hughes, a Wesleyan minister who had opposed the Sudanese War a decade and a half previously,[69] 'nonplussed the general expectation and showed himself an Imperialist, and a supporter of what he regarded as an inevitable conflict', as his daughter later put it.[70] When Hughes's expulsion from his vice-presidency was proposed, for a second time, at the Peace Society's meeting of members, Snape blocked it from the chair with the comment: 'There is a great deal of difference of opinion about this war; even the Peace Society itself has not been united in regard to it.'[71]

Since the Peace Society was still 'largely a Friends' Association', as a

---

[64] *HP* (Mar. 1900), 30.   [65] e.g. *HP* (June 1900), 66.

[66] See his intervention at the Peace Society's 1877 meeting of members: *HP* (June 1877), 245.

[67] *HP* (Oct. 1900), 118. See also PSM, 21 Sept. 1900.

[68] *Speaker* (20 Oct. 1900), 66.

[69] *HP* (May 1885), 220.

[70] [D. P. Hughes], *The Life of Hugh Price Hughes by his Daughter* (1904), 542.

[71] *HP* (June 1902), 238.

Quaker periodical had recently put it,[72] its interpretation of its pacifism was affected by that of the Society of Friends. As already noted, this had become steadily more latitudinarian since the late 1850s, as the Egyptian crisis had revealed. The creation of the Friends' Peace Committee in 1888 was thus less a sign of increased zeal than a recognition that attitudes which could once have been taken for granted within the sect now required special nurturing. By the 1890s a significant number of birthright Quakers stopped pretending that they accepted all the peculiarities of the sect into which they had been born, as a result of which the Society of Friends was obliged to acknowledge that it had 'a great many nominal members'.[73] Although, this in turn stimulated a 'Quaker renaissance' which tried to bring the society as a whole back to a belief its traditional principles, it could not prevent some of its leading members having doubts about the practicality of the peace testimony. For example, the most celebrated Quaker by convincement of the late nineteenth century, Caroline E. Stephen, had been unable to shed her pre-conversion belief that 'certain wars appear to be not only inevitable but justifiable' and that 'there are treaty obligations requiring us to take up arms for the protection of weaker nations, from which we could not suddenly recede'. She had solved the dilemma by adopting an exemptionist view, regarding the peace testimony as binding only on 'thorough-going Christians', such as the Quakers, who in consequence should decline all political responsibility: 'Our place surely still is mainly to leaven, not to govern, the world.'[74] And even the Friends' Peace Committee's most prominent lecturer, Samuel J. Capper, had advocated the use against Turkey of what he called 'police force' during the Armenian crisis.[75]

Unsurprisingly, therefore, the response of the Society of Friends to the Boer War was timid. Even the Friends' Peace Committee decided in April 1900 that it was still 'not advisable at the present time' to issue an address, although by December 1900 it believed that 'some protest should be made . . . against the methods that are being employed in prosecuting the war'.[76] A leading light of the Quaker renaissance thought such an attitude 'lamentably weak . . . I have been appalled at the falling away among our younger people especially';[77] and *Reynold's Newspaper* commented that 'the sect is no longer to be regarded as a strenuous and united peace organization'.[78] For the first

---

[72] *British Friend* (July 1892), 145.   [73] *British Friend* (June 1893), 146.

[74] C. E. Stephen, *Quaker Strongholds* (1890), 129–31, 138–40.

[75] *British Friend* (Mar. 1896), 76.

[76] Minutes, FPC, 4 Apr. and 6 Dec. 1900.

[77] S. Allott, *John Wilhelm Rowntree 1868–1905 and the Beginnings of Modern Quakerism* (York, 1994), 69. See also R. A. Rempel, 'British Quakers and the South African War', *Quaker History*, 64 (1974/5), 75–95.

[78] Cited in Isichei, *Victorian Quakers*, 151.

time a significant number of prominent Quakers backed a war publicly. John Bellows, a prominent lexicographer who had just returned from lobbying the Hague conference and was a friend of Tolstoy, endorsed the government's reasons for going to war.[79] And Robin Hodgkin, who had just graduated from Balliol and was later to become Provost of the Queen's College, Oxford, went so far as to join the army.[80] Indeed, Hodgkin and his father Dr Henry Hodgkin both concluded at this time that many Quakers were guilty of suppressing their doubts about the peace testimony because it was convenient for them to do so. Hodgkin senior argued that, if all war was really unlawful, 'we ought without a single day's delay to abandon all our defensive armaments, accepting all the disastrous consequences of such a step'. But he noted that he and many other Quakers did not really want this to happen, and pointed out that it was deceitful 'to profess to wish our rulers to disarm, while in our inmost heart we are hoping that they will do nothing of the kind'.[81]

In effect the Hodgkins were accusing some of their co-religionists of being exemptionists rather than true pacifists (who, even if they accept that most people do not yet share their conscientious objection, none the less want them all to come round to it as soon as possible). Pondering her cousin Robin Hodgkin's decision to enlist, Margery Fry, the future Principal of Somerville College, agreed that exemptionism was indefensible, and that those accepting traditional Quaker pacifism must accept that 'it was a creed not only for those of spiritual genius but capable of being held by the most commonplace and mundane people too'. Although not yet prepared to repudiate it, she doubted that as a mass faith it would 'work as well even for this world as common sense'.[82]

Quakers were thus starting to make up their own minds about their religious inheritance as the twentieth century began. For example, the Fry sisters took different paths: Isabel rejected pacifism and Quakerism as early as 1913; Margery remained troubled but orthodox until 1935, as will be seen; and Joan M. and A. Ruth Fry were to remain serene pacifists and loyal Quakers for the rest of their lives. Likewise, although as the First World War approached some Quakers grew increasingly embarrassed by the peace testimony, others wished to propagate it more effectively, which was why an additional organization, the Northern Friends' Peace Board, appeared in 1913.

Because of the loss of confidence on the part of the Peace Society and

---

[79] B. D. Phillips, 'Friendly Patriotism: British Quakerism and the Imperial Nation', Ph.D. thesis (Cambridge University, 1989), fos. 70–2.

[80] H. H. Hewison, *Hedge of Wild Almonds: South Africa, the 'Pro-Boers' and the Quaker Conscience* (1989), 119, 129.

[81] L. Creighton, *Life and Letters of Thomas Hodgkin* (1917), 239, 241–3.

[82] Jones, *Margery Fry*, 54, 179.

some members of the Society of Friends, the Boer War proved to be the first conflict in which Christian pacifists proved generally less resilient in the face of adversity than many secular *pacificists*, who had to face the fact that most of their fellow progressives—for example, those belonging to the Fabian Society, which felt unable to condemn the conflict—rejected their political judgement. Despite its much vaunted insistence on not lowering its 'Christian standard of Peace . . . down to the standard of mere expediency, or political economy', as Sir J. W. Pease had expressed it as recently as 1895,[83] religious pacifism emerged from the war as a very insipid and *attentiste* faith. The Peace Society's sensitivity on this score was evident in its overdefensive assertion, in the annual report which appeared as the conflict ended, that despite having avoided 'the promotion of peace by bellicose methods . . . its attitude has never been more uncompromising than during the period under review'.[84]

CONFRONTATION WITH GERMANY, 1902–1914

The excitement of the Tsar's Rescript and the shock of the Boer War gave way to a dozen years of mounting international tension. As Germany increased its armed forces, fear of war could be detected in Britain for the first time since the Napoleonic Wars. Defencism was the principal beneficiary; but peace activism was also stimulated, despite the limited capacity of the established peace associations to raise their game. Even so, insularity limited the extent to which the peace-or-war debate impinged on the country. Much of the population ignored European affairs as late as July 1914. And even some members of the peace movement were less engaged with the cause than they would have been had they not complacently assumed that Britain could in practice opt out of a Franco-German conflict.

The war in South Africa had alerted defencists to the vulnerability of Britain's far-flung imperial possessions: for example, G. F. Shee, the secretary of the National Service League which was formed in 1901 to press for conscription, judged correctly that future historians would be astonished 'that a fabric of Empire so vast should have reposed on a foundation so precarious'.[85] At the same time Germany's fleet-building programme had started to give rise to an alarmist literature predicting the invasion of the British Isles, including the novel *The Riddle of the Sands* (1903), the news-

---

[83] *HP* (June 1895), 217.
[84] *HP* (June 1902), 241–2.
[85] G. F. Shee, *The Briton's First Duty: The Case for Conscription* (1901), 1.

paper serial *The Invasion of 1910* (1906), and the West End play *An Englishman's Home* (1909).[86] The country's sense of insecurity produced movements and propaganda emphasizing the positive aspects of warfare and presenting the international system as a Darwinian struggle. Admittedly, there was a striking absence of calls for aggressive or preventive war: the emphasis was overwhelmingly on defensiveness, as when Shee claimed to be 'as ardent a devotee of Peace as any member of the Peace Society' and insisted that conscription 'would render peace absolutely certain'.[87] But even though faced with militarized defencism rather than authentic militarism of the kind which could be found in Germany, the peace movement felt its values to be under assault from every quarter. For example, Silas Hocking found himself deploring 'the way thousands of boys were being trained for military service in the Boy Scouts movement',[88] which had been set up by the celebrated defender of Mafeking. The American philosopher William James thought that the peace movement should roll with the punch, telling the Universal Peace Congress at Boston in 1904: 'The plain truth is that people *want* war . . . We do ill, therefore to talk much of universal peace or of a general disarmament.' His advice to his fellow activists was therefore: 'We must cheat our foe, circumvent him in detail, not try to change his nature.'[89] Six years later James elaborated this strategy in an essay which came to be one of the most widely cited in peace literature: *alternative*

Pacifists ought to enter more deeply into the aesthetical and ethical point of view of their opponents . . . So long as anti-militarists propose no substitute for war's disciplining function, no *moral equivalent* of war, analogous as one might say to the mechanical equivalent of heat, so long they fail to realise the full inwardness of the situation.

James suggested that this moral equivalent of war could be found in a military-style conscription of youth for exacting work of a socially constructive nature.[90] This was beyond the power of the peace movement to deliver; and it was not until after the First World War that anti-militarist alternatives to the Boy Scouts were attempted. (The most notable of these were the Kibbo Kift Kindred, established in 1920 by John Hargrave, who was of Quaker descent and served at Gallipoli as a stretcher-bearer in the Royal Army Medical

[86] For this genre see I. F. Clarke, *Voices Prophesying War 1763–1884* (1966), ch. 4.

[87] Shee, *The Briton's First Duty* (1901), pp. xiii, 214.

[88] Cited in *Friend* (24 May 1912), 332.

[89] W. James, 'Remarks at the Peace Banquet', in his *Memories and Studies* (1911), 299–306 at 304.

[90] James, 'The Moral Equivalent of War' in *Memories and Studies*, 267–96 at 283, 290.

Corps, and its offshoot the Woodcraft Folk, formed in 1925 by Leslie Paul, a pacifist and socialist.[91])

The peace movement had to accept that in this pre-war atmosphere there was little chance of promoting its traditional policies of arbitration and the reduction of armaments. The second Hague conference, which met in 1907, thus raised few of the expectations of the first, and gave rise to 'a feeling of disappointment'.[92] Stead had again done his best to champion it, his efforts on its behalf turning out to be his final contribution to the peace cause: during what F. W. Hirst called 'The Fifth or Dreadnought Panic', which began in 1908,[93] he reverted to ultra-defencism; and he had not changed his mind again by the time he went down with the *Titanic* in 1912.

Progressive opinion could have responded to this loss of confidence in arbitration and the limitation of armaments by proposing an international organization that would enforce international law and provide security against aggression—the 'peace through law' approach long supported by the largest French peace association. However, most lawyers had grown sceptical about such schemes during the last decades of the nineteenth century. As the First World War drew closer, a few calls for 'federation',[94] 'juridical order',[95] or a 'Peace League'[96] came from peace activists; and the enforcement of international law also featured increasingly on the agenda of Universal Peace Congresses. However, in Britain there was no advanced indication of the enthusiasm for a league of nations which was soon to be manifested. One reason was that peace activists still believed that, in the words of a Quaker MP, 'there were obvious ways of enforcing decisions', by which he meant pressure from public opinion.[97] Another reason for the lack of British support for an international organization was that it would involve burdensome commitments for a country accustomed to considerable freedom of manœuvre. Prior to the educative experience of being drawn into a war which had erupted out of a seemingly remote Balkan crisis, progressives were not persuaded that the benefits of belonging to an international organization would justify the costs. Although the engaged strand in *pacificist* thought had made considerable inroads on the detached strand as Gladstone's influence on liberalism had superseded Cobden's, it had not won a complete victory.

[91] See L. Paul, *Angry Young Man* (1951), 28–9, 53–63.
[92] *HP* (June 1908), 140.
[93] Whyte, *Life of W. T. Stead*, ii. 293. Vogeler, *Frederic Harrison*, 264, 274–6. Hirst, *The Six Panics*, 59–102 (the sixth panic being false sightings of airships over Britain early in 1913).
[94] *HP* (Mar. 1906), 186; (Jan. 1911), 76.
[95] See *HP* (June 1910), 68; and H. G. Alexander, *Joseph Gundry Alexander* (1920), 182.
[96] Advocated in A. Carnegie, *War as the Mother of Valour and Civilization* (Peace Society, 1910), 5–6.
[97] A. T. Bassett, *The Life of the Rt. Hon. John Edward Ellis, M.P.* (1914), 240.

The belief that neutrality in a Franco-German conflict might in practice again be possible for Britain helps to explain why 'appeasement' and 'peaceful change', as they would be called in the 1930s, received only a modest amount of support in the years before 1914. It is important to distinguish clearly from the outset between these two policies for achieving accommodation rather than confrontation. Appeasement is best understood as an attempt to seek a *modus vivendi* with an adversary on the realist grounds that the concessions needed to bring this about are less damaging to the national interest than the likely costs of a policy of containment. Appeasers thus belong to the anti-war rather than the peace movement. Peaceful change is best reserved for an attempt to achieve reconciliation with another country in accordance with the perception, arising from either pacifism or *pacificism*, that there is never any true conflict of interest between countries. Advocates of peaceful change are thus authentic members of the peace movement.

Appeasement was the main objective underlying the formation in 1905 of an Anglo-German Friendship Committee. Peaceful change was the motivation for J. Allen Baker, a Quaker MP who was president of the Metropolitan Free Church Federation, to try to bring together the Protestant churches of Britain and Germany a few year later. His efforts began at the 1907 Hague conference; and his four interviews with the Kaiser were in the best tradition of peace missions by British Quakers to continental autocrats. Baker was assisted by his friend and fellow Liberal MP W. H. Dickinson, a diffident Anglican who was after 1914 to play an important role in the movement for a league of nations.[98] Baker and Dickinson instigated an exchange of delegations in 1908–9 which led to the formation in 1910 of the Associated Council of Churches in the British and German Empires for Fostering Friendly Relations between the Two Peoples. Its journal *Peacemaker*, launched the following year, indicated that the new body attempted to cater for the full spectrum of accommodationist opinion: it welcomed those who sought improved relations with Germany 'without committing themselves to absolute condemnation of war' as well as 'doctrinaire advocates of peace'. Even so, its exposition of peaceful change—for example, its assertion that Anglo-German disagreements 'are without exception susceptible of adjustment if only goodwill be available'[99]—was too ingenuous for some peace activists. It must have been this organization which Norman Angell had in mind when he ridiculed that 'whole school of person who . . . would have us believe that all international differences would disappear if only we can have

---

[98] H. C. White, *Willougby Hyett Dickinson 1859–1943: A Memoir* (Gloucester, 1956), 49, 64–71.
[99] *Peacemaker* (July 1911), 1–2.

enough Anglo-German junketings, dinner-parties, exchange visits of clergy-men, and what not'.[100] Undeterred, the Associated Council expanded itself to become the World Alliance for Promoting International Friendship Through the Churches, though the place and time of the conference to launch this new phase of its existence—Constance in Germany on 1 August 1914—could scarcely have been more unfortunately chosen.[101]

The peace movement's strongest card was thus not the public's desire to accommodate Germany, which was less marked than in the prelude to the Second World War, but its suspicion of the alliances, formal and informal, which successive British governments concluded. The Conservatives signed a treaty with Japan in 1902, which was directed against Russia, and made an informal entente with France in 1904. And despite having won their landslide electoral victory of 1906 on a platform of peace, retrenchment, and reform, the Liberals signed a convention with Russia in 1907 (and renewed it three years later), continued the expansion of the Royal Navy so as maintain its lead over the German fleet, and introduced army reforms. However, both govern-ments failed to make clear why between them they had abandoned isolation and aligned themselves with their former imperial rivals, France and Russia. Admittedly, their explanatory task was complicated by two factors. First, Britain was drawn by its alignment with Russia into a competition with Germany and Austria for influence in the Balkans, where a British vital inter-est was hard to identify. Second, much of the British public judged allies by their political congeniality or otherwise. Most progressives disliked the Russian convention because they hated the Tsarist regime. A much smaller number favoured alignment with France out of sympathy with its republican principles: however, the aged Frederic Harrison still took this view, and became an anti-German crusader, as he had done during the Franco-Prussian War.[102]

The British government was notably poor at explaining its alignment with France and Russia, partly because of its own lack of geo-strategic awareness. As late as the end of July 1914 it became apparent that some cabinet ministers had not understood that *Realpolitik* provided a case for standing by France irrespective of any legal or moral commitments which Britain had made.[103] In the event, the government was able to cover its confusion by invoking Germany's violation of respect for Belgian neutrality as the principal

---

[100] N. Angell, *The Great Illusion* (Sept. 1912 edn.), 356.

[101] Robbins, *Abolition of War*, 17–18. E. P. and P. J. N. Baker, *J. Allen Baker Member of Parliament: A Memoir* (1927), 186, 218–26. Phillips, 'Friendly Patriotism, fos. 267–9, 272–83.

[102] Vogeler, *Frederic Harrison*, 364.

[103] See G. C. L. Hazlehurst, *Politicians at War July 1914–May 1915: A Prologue to the Triumph of Lloyd George* (1971), ch. 6.

justification for intervening. As a question of morality rather than national interest, this pretext was 'useful for bringing in Liberals', as an opponent of the war soon noted.[104] What thus became evident only after the First World War broke out was that, except in regard to naval competition, Britain had a cultural aversion to thinking in power-political terms. Indeed, in the autumn of 1914 a professional soldier, Frederick Hammond, was moved to issue a pamphlet in order to complain that

the average Englishman does not even now, after three months of war, fully understand either the imminence of the danger or what, primarily, England is fighting for. . . . With all due deference to the distinct and chivalric reasons for England's participation in this greatest of wars, it is still necessary to insist that the struggle is not, primarily, an essay in national knight-errantry. . . . The possession by an enemy of the coasts of Belgium and France would mean our destruction as a nation.[105]

And later in that conflict, the perceptive radical writer on foreign affairs, H. N. Brailsford, was to acknowledge how much the pre-1914 international thinking of Britons like himself had been weakened by an unconscious 'horror of talking and writing in terms of power'.[106]

However, the established peace associations proved ineffective in exploiting public incomprehension of Britain's new diplomatic alignment. *Concord* recognized this when it complained how few prominent men 'care to throw in their lot definitely with the bodies which exist to oppose militarism and to advocate international arbitration, although peace ideas are more popular than they have been for a generation past'. Significantly, it also acknowledged the greater influence of secondary peace associations 'like the TUC, Women's Liberal Federation, the chief Socialist bodies, and the Cobden Club'.[107] In this period, radical critics of the Liberal government's foreign policy preferred to work through vigilance committees: these included the Congo Reform Association, of which the former shipping clerk E. D. Morel was the leading light;[108] the Balkan Committee, in which two of Sir Thomas Fowell Buxton's great-grandsons, Noel Buxton and Charles Roden Buxton, were active;[109] the short-lived Foreign Policy Committee, which L. T. Hobhouse organized in 1911 and of which Courtney acted as president;[110] and, catering

---

[104] 'Memorandum re Causes of the War, Aug. 10 1914': C. R. Buxton Papers, box 1(1).

[105] F. Hammond, *War—and the Average Man* (1914), 5, 7, 11.

[106] H. N. Brailsford, *A League of Nations* (1917), 5.

[107] *Concord* (July/Aug. 1904), 104; (Mar. 1905), 48.

[108] C. A. Cline, *E. D. Morel 1873–1924* (Belfast, 1980), ch. 4.

[109] T. P. Conwell-Evans, *Foreign Policy from a Backbench 1904–1918: A Study Based on the Papers of Lord Noel-Buxton* (1932), 4.

[110] Gooch, *Life of Lord Courtney*, 572–4. P. F. Clarke, *Liberals and Social Democrats* (1978), 164.

for Liberal parliamentarians, the disarmament committee and the foreign affairs group which were constituted in 1908–9 and 1911–14 respectively.[111]

The Peace Society's declining appeal was reflected in its difficulty in finding a new president when Sir J. W. Pease died in 1903. Only a year before, he had been personally embarrassed by a banking failure: his family had been saved from bankruptcy only by the intervention of another bank of Quaker origin, Barclays.[112] His son Alfred E. Pease could no longer afford to remain an MP and had taken an administrative post in South Africa, and in any case had 'voted men and money' for the Boer War.[113] Courtney and six others declined the post before Robert Spence Watson accepted.[114] His commitment to the peace movement had caused his house to be attacked during the Boer War; and when later he was sworn in as a privy councillor he was excused, 'as a Quaker and President of the Peace Society', from wearing the ceremonial sword.[115] The society's financial difficulties led it to bid unsuccessfully for the lucrative Nobel Prize following the success of the Institute of International Law in 1904,[116] and to reduce the *Herald of Peace* to a quarterly during the depression of 1907–8 and again from 1913 onwards.

It was presumably to raise money that the society introduced life membership at this time; but only sixty-nine names appeared on the first list, three-quarters of them Quakers. Interestingly, the non-Quaker minority included Bertrand Russell, of whom it had once been thought that he 'never joined any of the main many pacifist organizations' in Edwardian Britain.[117] Russell had enthusiastically supported the Boer War before undergoing a change of attitude which he later attributed to seeing his friend Evelyn Whitehead in agonizing pain because of a heart attack in 1901. His claim that the insight he thereby gained into the nature of suffering made him a pacifist[118] is probably an oversimplification: his conversion was almost certainly more gradual,[119] and at this stage, his life subscription to the Peace Society notwithstanding,

---

[111] H. Weinroth, 'Left-Wing Opposition to Naval Armaments in Britain before 1914', *Journal of Contemporary History*, 6 (1971), 93–120. There is additional material in H. Weinroth, 'British Pacifism 1906–14: A Study in the British Peace Movement during the Early Years of the 20th Century', Ph.D. thesis (Cambridge University, 1968).

[112] M. W. Kirby, *Men of Business and Politics: The Rise and Fall of the Quaker Pease Dynasty of North-East England, 1700–1943* (1984), 107–8, 124.

[113] Pease, *Elections and Recollections*, 12, 296.

[114] PSM, 18 Dec. 1903, 15 Jan., 18 Mar., 15 Apr., 13 May 1904.

[115] Corder, *Life of Robert Spence Watson*, 281, 303.

[116] PSM, 25 Jan., 23 June 1905.

[117] B. Russell, *Prophecy and Dissent, 1914–16: The Collected Papers of Bertrand Russell*, xiii (1988), p. xxxi. The list of life members which includes Russell's name is in the Peace Society's archive which was not available to the editors of this excellent volume.

[118] *The Autobiography of Bertrand Russell* (3 vols., 1967–78), i. 145–6.

[119] See A. Ryan, *Bertrand Russell: A Political Life* (1988), 35.

went only as far as *pacificism*. Having already expanded its number of vice-presidents, the society converted its general committee into a council in 1910: this purely honorific body began with 182 members, of whom fourteen were women (including Caroline Playne, later a prominent writer on peace issues).

That this new body included many non-pacifists was one sign that the society's absolutist message was being compromised. Another was that, at least according to his widow, the former headmaster of Sedbergh School, Henry Hart, had become 'a member of the Peace Society and also of the National Service League, believing that the work of the latter was needed until the ideals of the former could be realized'.[120] The society also failed to make overtures to the new and dynamic elements within the pacifist movement, such as the Tolstoyans or the socialist and Christian-socialist absolutists who were beginning to emerge as a significant minority within the ILP. Its increasing defeatism was evident when Priscilla Peckover suggested that it make a special effort to combat 'the Militarist and Conscriptionist propaganda': the society's leaders replied wearily that they were 'fully alive to the extent, character, utility and obligation of the counter-efforts which this evil calls for. At the same time they do not, at the moment, see their way to any effective action . . .'[121]

The Peace Society's loss of momentum partly reflected the flagging energy of its secretary. By 1910 the executive committee knew that it needed 'a young educated gentleman, with journalistic experience' in the additional post of Organizing Secretary to help it 'get into political, religious and social circles where hitherto it has had but small influence'; but a mounting deficit—including £1,167 owed to its printers—prevented such an appointment.[122] The creation in December 1910 of the Carnegie Endowment for International Peace did not bring the hoped-for financial relief: the new foundation initially distributed its funding to peace associations via the Berne bureau, which spent much of it on a notably lacklustre journal, the *Peace Movement*, initially published in three languages.[123] In 1911, moreover, Watson's death reopened the problem of the presidency. Alfred E. Pease, back in England, declined: he was out of sympathy with pacifism and was to leave the Society of Friends five years later. J. W. Wilson, a Liberal MP and Quaker, also turned it down. But J. A. Pease, Alfred E.'s younger brother, accepted: although he had voted for war credits in the Boer War he had tried not to

---

[120] Cited in G. G. Coulton, *A Victorian Schoolmaster: Henry Hart of Sedbergh* (1923), 174–5—a reference I owe to the late Colin Matthew.
[121] PSM, 19 June 1908. For a similarly negative response, see 25 Feb. 1909.
[122] PSM, 27 Oct. 1910, 26 Jan. 1911.
[123] The English edn. appeared between 15 Jan. 1912 and 15 July 1914.

offend the peace movement either.[124] The society's diminished public standing was exposed when the Prime Minister and Foreign Secretary refused to
receive deputations during the Italo-Turkish War of 1911 (which, embarrassingly, much of the Italian peace movement supported, despite its country's
obviously aggressive behaviour).[125]

The International Arbitration League might have collapsed altogether in
this period had not Cremer—back in the Commons since 1900 but an increasingly reclusive figure living alone in the league's office—won the Nobel
Peace Prize for 1903. This new award had created jealousies within the peace
movement: Passy's sharing of the first prize in 1900 had annoyed Cremer,
who gave himself the main credit for founding the Inter-Parliamentary Union;
and Passmore Edwards was soon to complain that 'nobody was working for
Peace nowadays, but everybody for the Nobel Prize'.[126] However, it enabled
Cremer to live down an early reputation for mercenariness by donating
£7,000 (virtually the entire prize) to his peace association, on condition that
working men should always constitute two-thirds of its national council.

Cremer hoped that the International Arbitration League would be able to
raise the same sum in matching contributions, and thereby buy itself a building; but only £1,700 was raised, mostly from Carnegie.[127] Cremer's Nobel
Prize was therefore invested; and like Horniman's bequest to the Peace
Society, it yielded an income which was substantial enough to enable its
beneficiary to outlive its real usefulness. After 1906, moreover, Cremer
became a political fossil: although that year's general election was a triumph
for his party, it also resulted in the appearance in the Commons of a block of
thirty MPs from the new Labour party which outnumbered the Lib-Labs;
although Cremer was consoled by a knighthood, his group of ageing and anti-
socialist artisans was thereafter marginalized. After Cremer died in 1908, he
was succeeded as secretary by another Lib-Lab MP, Fred Maddison, who was
to lose his Commons seat in January 1910, depriving the league of its last
remaining political asset, parliamentary representation.

Maddison lacked his predecessor's acerbic courage—during the Boer War
his caution had caused him to be booed at a peace meeting[128]—and under his
leadership the International Arbitration League lost such radicalism as it still

---

[124] 27 Apr., 11 May 1911. C. Hazlehurst and C. Woodland, *A Liberal Chronicle: Journals and Papers of J. A. Pease, Lord Gainford 1908–1910* (1994), 7–10.
[125] PSM, 28 Dec. 1911, 15 May 1913. For the Italian peace movement's pro-war views, see Grossi, *Le pacifisme européen*, 280–4; and Cooper, *Patriotic Pacifism*, 173–4.
[126] *HP* (Feb. 1907), 13.
[127] *The Times* (5 May 1904). *Arbitrator* (May 1904), 160; (May 1905), 193; (Apr. 1906), 263. Evans, *Cremer*, 273–7.
[128] *WAWSA* (Aug. 1900), 26.

retained. Its annual *soirée* had already become a formal dinner; and in 1911 the Foreign Secretary, Sir Edward Grey, was the guest of honour. But, although it had thus become liberal rather than radical in its *pacificism*, because of its frequent affirmations of confidence in Grey and his colleagues, the league lacked the intellectual edge to advance this strand of thought from 'arbitration' towards 'federation', even to the extent that the Peace Society did. Nor, despite its move away from pacifism, did it discuss enforcement. Indeed, in 1930 Maddison was revealingly to admit to a leading campaigner for an international police force: 'In Cremer's day the question of sanctions was not very much to the front, and I hardly ever heard him mention it.'[129]

The most creative of the primary associations at this time was the IAPA. Admittedly, it lost the services of G. H. Perris for a while. After a pilgrimage to Tolstoy in 1904, he had finally decided that he could not accept non-resistance, though this did not affect his hostility to British foreign policy. It was the opportunity to become foreign-news editor of *Tribune*—a radical paper launched in 1906, following the demise of the *Echo*, by a grandson of Cobden's loyal ally Thomas Thomasson[130]—which caused him to leave *Concord* that year. After *Tribune* folded, Perris worked for the Foreign Policy Committee, before returning to the editorship of *Concord* in 1914. During his absence, the IAPA concentrated on wooing those in agreement with Keir Hardie's assertion in a letter of 7 March 1907 to Moscheles: 'I see no hope for the triumph of peace principles until society has been reorganized on the communistic non-competitive basis. It is for this, amongst other reasons, that I am a Socialist.'[131]

Such socialist *pacificists* were a minority even with the labour movement, most members of which were radical or even liberal *pacificists*, and a handful of which, mainly to be found in the ILP, were pacifists. Moreover, while waiting for society to be reorganized on a socialist basis, this minority was divided over what interim policy to adopt. A few socialist *pacificists* favoured socialist patriotism, the belief that Britain, though not yet socialist, was sufficiently progressive to be protected enthusiastically against reactionary foes. This was the line taken by the Social Democratic Party, as the Social Democratic Federation had become in 1906, and by its successor body after 1911, the British Socialist Party. It had called for a citizen army since 1884, and although it had opposed the Boer War (until August 1901), it had subsequently become hostile to Germany. Only a rank-and-file rebellion in

[129] Maddison to Davies, 11 Nov. 1930: Davies of Llandinam Papers.
[130] A. J. Lee, 'Franklin Thomasson and the *Tribune*: A Case-Study in the History of the Liberal Press, 1906–1908', *Historical Journal*, 16 (1973), 341–60.
[131] Hardie to Felix Moscheles, 7 Mar. 1907, cited in *Concord* (Mar. 1907), 38.

December 1912 forced it to tone down its increasingly chauvinistic message.[132]

However, the vast majority of socialists criticized 'militarism' and supported what later became known as 'war resistance'—the policy of meeting any attempt on the part of a capitalist government to declare war with a general strike. The ILP mounted an anti-armaments campaign in the autumn of 1910 and a 'No Conscription' protest in November and December 1913 which attracted financial support from the Friends' Peace Committee.[133] It also argued for war resistance. Even though the Second International had decided in 1907 that a general strike was impractical, Keir Hardie, who had supported the idea since 1896, still favoured it as a propaganda weapon which, even if essentially a bluff, might stimulate peace sentiment among the working class and perhaps make governments more cautious. Hardie's call for the investigation into the feasibility of an anti-war strike was accepted by the ILP in 1910, and—having been given impetus by syndicalist propaganda and a wave of economic strikes in Britain during 1911–12 and by the progress of the Social Democrats at the 1912 German election—by the Labour Party (of which the ILP was a component) in 1912, and, in modified form, by the Trades Union Congress the following year.[134]

Encouraged by this socialist-*pacificist* enthusiasm, confined to a minority of the labour movement though it was, the IAPA completed the move to the left which had begun when Green became its secretary. Even the septuagenarian Moscheles embraced socialism.[135] *Concord* endorsed the general strike against war, in contrast to the *Herald of Peace*, which regarded it as 'the method of force still', and the *Arbitrator*, which rejected it as an incursion into the domain of trade-union leaders who 'know their own business best'.[136] By 1912 'Are we Socialists or Syndicalists or Pacifists?' was a question which the IAPA admitted it was 'often asked'.[137] Because it thus shared the preoccupations of the left, it did not focus on the case for arbitral sanctions and an international authority to organize them, even though as the one extant primary association which had from the outset been anti-pacifist it was best placed to have done so. Nor did it anticipate the radical supranationalism which was to be advocated by Brailsford, Hobson, and others after 1914 as a left-wing variant of the league-of-nations idea. Indeed, though Hobson was to

[132] Newton, *British Labour*, 152. Croucher, 'British Working Class Attitudes', fo. 391.
[133] Minutes, FPC, 5 June and 6 Nov. 1913.
[134] Newton, *British Labour*, 59, 250–9, 265–9, 279, 282. Croucher, 'British Working Class Attitudes', fos. 413–26.
[135] *Concord* (Jan. 1904), 8, and (Dec. 1908), 142.
[136] *Concord* (Feb. 1911), 17. *HP* (Sept. 1910), 105–6. *Arbitrator* (May 1913), 53.
[137] *Concord* (Apr. 1912), 37.

write an article on world government a few months before the First World War broke out, it was notable that he did not publish it in *Concord*.[138]

The second main thrust of the IAPA's efforts, its campaign to improve the coordination of the peace movement, at last bore fruit in the form of a National Peace Council. This first appeared as a secretariat for arranging national peace congresses, an event pioneered by the French in 1902 and taken up by the Friends' Peace Committee after some of its members had learned about it at the Universal Peace Congress in Rouen the following year. The IAPA immediately welcomed it; and a meeting at Quaker headquarters on 9 February 1904 appointed Green as honorary secretary of a committee to organize a British equivalent. The first 'National Peace Congress' was duly held at Manchester on 22–3 June 1904.[139] Both the primary and secondary movements were represented: the latter included religious bodies (Quaker, Congregationalist, and Unitarian), socialist societies (the ILP and Social Democratic Federation), and women's groups (including the Women's Co-operative Guild, which had been formed in 1883 to help working-class women and had involved itself in political and social questions under its dynamic general secretary, Margaret Llewelyn Davies, who served from 1889 to 1921[140]). National Peace Congresses became almost annual events down to the outbreak of the Second World War.[141]

Following the first such gathering, the organizing committee was kept in being as a National Council of Peace Societies, Green being joined as co-secretary by Mary Cooke, an activist for both the Peace Union (as the mainly female Local Peace Association Auxiliary had been renamed in 1902) and the Friends' Peace Committee. Its main role was to organize subsequent congresses, the fourth of which, at Scarborough in 1907, resolved to increase the number of participating societies. To bring this about, H. W. Perris, a former Unitarian minister who had worked with his brother G. H. on *Tribune* and was unemployed after its collapse, was brought in as a full-time secretary early in 1908.[142]

A further reason for appointing H. W. Perris was to prepare for the Universal Peace Congress which was to be held in London in July of that year. This proved to be a social success, demonstrating the remarkable respectability which the British peace movement had by then achieved. King

---

[138] It appeared in *War and Peace: A Norman Angell Monthly* (Mar. 1914), 155–6.

[139] *Concord* (Nov. 1903), 162; (Apr. 1904), 49. The best account is in Laity, 'British Peace Movement 1896–1916', ch. 5.

[140] J. Gaffin and D. Thoms, *Caring and Sharing: The Centenary History of the Co-operative Women's Guild* (1983), 113, 266.

[141] They are listed in Appendix 1.

[142] *Concord* (Aug./Sept. 1908), 88–9. *HP* (Feb.–Apr. 1908), 128.

1910
formal acceptance
universal
Peace
Congress

Edward VII received a deputation from the congress, 'thereby setting a strik-
ing example to the rulers of the civilized world', as the council later noted.[143]
The 450 delegates were given a banquet by the government at which Prime
Minister Asquith toasted 'the International Peace Movement'. And Lloyd
George, the erstwhile 'pro-Boer' radical who was now Chancellor of the
Exchequer, addressed the congress, although he was interrupted by
suffragettes chanting: 'Peace must begin at home by giving votes to
women.'[144] Darby, who had attended all but two of its eighteen precursors,
was impressed. 'No previous Congress has evoked such general interest or
received such influential support', he noted, concluding that 'the peace movement has not only entered the sphere of practical politics, but has become
exceedingly popular'.[145]

In the afterglow of the London congress the National Council of Peace
Societies was made a permanent body under the title National Peace Council,
meeting for the first time as such on 5 August 1908. It began under favourable
conditions: because the Peace Society was no longer emphasizing its pacifist
purity, and because few *pacificists* were pressing for the enforcement of arbitral awards, it was not paralysed by disagreements over the issue of enforcement as it was to be in the 1930s, though it rejected its secretary's attempt to
define an agreed policy on the subject in 1913.[146] The most divisive issue in
its early years was the socialist-*pacificist* call for an anti-war strike. In 1911
a motion in favour of such a policy was proposed by Hardie and G. H. Perris
at the National Peace Congress; but a decision was deferred. The following
year a similar motion, this time proposed by W. C. Anderson of the ILP and
G. H. Perris, was defeated by eighty-nine votes to forty-seven after a 'very
interesting' discussion.[147]

At the end of 1909 H. S. Perris left the National Peace Council to work for
the Shakespeare Memorial Committee, having been refused permission to
continue on a part-time basis.[148] He was replaced in January 1910 by Carl
Heath, who had been persuaded to apply for the post by Hobson: raised as a
Baptist but tempted by Anglicanism while a volunteer worker at Toynbee
Hall, Heath was a handicraft teacher by profession and a humanitarian activist
by inclination.[149] During his secretaryship the National Peace Council began

---

[143] Minutes, NPC Council, 1 June 1910.
[144] *Concord* (Aug./Sept. 1908), 111. *HP* (Sept. 1908), 166, 170, 173–4.
[145] *HP* (Sept. 1908), 161. This was officially only the 17th congress because the gatherings in
1899 and 1900 were merely 'general assemblies': see Cooper, *Patriotic Pacifism*, 219.
[146] Minutes, NPC Council, 2 July 1913.
[147] *Concord* (July 1911), 80; (June 1912), 74. Minutes, FPC, 6 June 1912.
[148] Minutes, NPC Council, 7 July 1909.
[149] See Heath's unpublished autobiography in the Reginald A. Smith papers: Friends House
MS 516/2/10.

issuing a *Peace Year Book* which gave the names and addresses of affiliated associations and the country's leading activists: 850 were included in the first edition. Although the council was to be shaken to its foundations by the First World War, it was the one pre-1914 primary association to play a significant role in the inter-war period, thereby eclipsing its founder, the IAPA.

The limitations of the established associations, even as coordinated through the National Peace Council, were demonstrated by the remarkable propaganda success of a previously unknown journalist, Norman Angell (full name: Ralph Norman Angell Lane), who became the star of a one-man peace campaign. Angell's education had been limited and had taken place mainly in France and Switzerland; and his early career had included ranching in the United States as well as work for numerous local newspapers.[150] He had settled in Paris where his experience of chauvinistic outbursts during the Dreyfus affair, coupled with his knowledge of similar American and British behaviour during the Venezuelan frontier crisis and the Boer War respectively, as well as his reading of Gustave Le Bon's *Psychologie des foules*, had led him as early as 1903 to write a book (as Ralph Lane) challenging Hobson's proposition 'that if financial influence is kept well in hand by democratic control, nothing is to be feared', and to insist instead on the role of 'non-economic factors' such as the emotionalism of the 'mass mind' in causing war.[151]

Six years later, with the Anglo-German naval race and Balkan crisis both in full swing, Angell's main worry as a liberal *pacificist* was no longer the jingoism of the masses but the assumption of Europe's élites that they could take the confrontation between their alliances to the point of fighting without economic disaster. Like Hobson a decade earlier, he shifted from a psychological to an economic explanation. In November 1909 he published a pamphlet, *Europe's Optical Illusion*, to warn that 'the complex financial interdependence of the capitalists of the world'[152] made even a successful war of conquest ultimately counterproductive because any territorial gains would be more than offset by losses caused by financial dislocation. Since by then he was working as general manager of the continental edition of Northcliffe's *Daily Mail*, he adopted his middle names as a *nom de plume* to avoid identifying his employer with his views. The pamphlet, which was sent to influential people, impressed Lord Esher, and was well enough received for Angell to expand it into a book a year later with the addition of a section rebutting social-darwinist claims about human nature and a new title suggested by Northcliffe, *The Great Illusion*.

---

[150] A. Marrin, *Sir Norman Angell* (Boston, Mass., 1979), 19–30.
[151] R. Lane, *Patriotism under Three Flags: A Plea for Rationalism in Politics* (1903), 3.
[152] Norman Angell, *Europe's Optical Illusion* [1909], 44.

Boosted by a deteriorating international situation, it sold two million copies in four years, was translated into twenty-five languages, and became the basis of a 'New Pacifism'.[153] Its remarkable success transformed Angell's life: in 1912 he moved to London, adopted his *nom de plume* as his everyday identity, and became a full-time peace propagandist. His work was supported by the specially created Garton Foundation, of which Esher, the Conservative former Prime Minister A. J. Balfour, and the industrialist Sir Richard Garton were trustees, and Esher's son Maurice Brett was secretary: it thus constituted a classic anti-war movement of defencists who hoped that Angell's peace ideas would have an influence on the Germans. But success brought with it some difficulties for a highly sensitive and intelligent yet under-educated man: for much of the rest of his life Angell found himself required to defend or gloss a hastily written journalistic tract as if it had been a considered academic treatise.

'Norman Angellism', as his thinking was often called, resembled early Cobdenism but with a significant difference: hope (that commercial intercourse would improve international political relations) had given way to fear (that war would damage the international financial system). Angell also differed from most *pacificists* in not emphasizing political reform: instead of advocating arbitration, let alone an international organization, he criticized the Hague conferences for seeking 'to modify by mechanical means the political machinery of Europe' rather than working 'through the reform of ideas'.[154] In emphasizing attitudinal rather than structural change, he sounded somewhat like a pacifist: indeed, Darby had just published a collection of sermons delivered during the 1908 Universal Peace Congress which similarly argued that any political union 'which is not the federation of the hearts and minds of men, will not amount to much'. However, whereas pacifists such as Darby understood such a reform of opinion to require an 'enormous moral change',[155] Angell gave the impression that it required only 'hard thinking', after which 'a process of rationalization' would begin[156] and the merits of *pacificist* policies would soon be perceived.

All propagandists who invoke rationality have to explain why they expect intellectual blinkers which have remained in place for so long suddenly to be shed: Angell's argument was that the peace movement had previously 'failed

---

[153] These figures are given by H. Weinroth, 'Norman Angell and *The Great Illusion*: An Episode in Pre-1914 Pacifism', *Historical Journal* 17 (1974), 551–74. Other accounts give lower sales, however.

[154] Angell, *The Great Illusion* (Sept. 1912 edn.), 350.

[155] W. E. Darby, *Beneath Bow Bells: Addresses on International Peace* (1909), 18, 31.

[156] N. Angell, 'War as the Failure of Reason', in J. M. Robertson, *et al.*, *Essays Towards Peace* (1913), 67–75, at 70, 74.

largely because it has not put (and proven) the plea of interest as distinct from the moral plea', whereas he had shifted 'the plane of discussion . . . to that of policy and interest'.[157] It was partly because he thus made the reform of opinion sound so easy that he was widely interpreted as arguing that war was 'unlikely' (as the *Herald of Peace*'s review of the original pamphlet had put it[158]) and perhaps even impossible because the financial authorities would put a stop it. Indeed, *The Great Illusion* must have owed much of its success to the easy reassurance which it was believed to offer its readers, and which was moreover confirmed by certain incautious interviews which its author and his disciples gave while promoting it.[159] Within a short time Angell was having to correct the misapprehension he had created, by insisting that he had all along argued that it was 'not the likelihood of war which is the illusion, but its benefits'.[160] He was to spend much of his subsequent career repeating this correction, and was to justify his acceptance of a knighthood two decades later as a way of salvaging his reputation.[161]

Angell prided himself on the hard-headedness of his approach. He dissociated himself from the absolutism to which the Peace Society was still formally committed: indeed, in the light of Angell's subsequent flirtations with this viewpoint, it is noteworthy that he stated explicitly: 'I am not a non-resister; I believe that aggression should be, and must be resisted, and I would vote any sum necessary to that purpose—to the last penny and the last man.'[162] His 'New Pacifism' rejected 'altruism' as a basis for its propaganda, opposed 'the reduction of our war budget by a single sovereign',[163] and presented itself as a 'scientific' rather than political doctrine. In Britain, 'International Polity', 'War and Peace', 'Right Understanding of International Relations' and 'Norman Angell' clubs, leagues, and societies were formed, many of them at universities—most notably Cambridge, where enthusiasts included the economists Hubert Henderson, Dennis Robertson, and Gerald Shove. In the opinion of the secretary of the National Peace Council these bodies constituted 'a new type of society . . . which aimed rather at the study of the problems than at any definite peace propaganda'.[164] Indeed, they have

[157] Angell, *The Great Illusion* (Sept. 1912 edn.), 306–7, 315–22. I quote from this edn. because by then Angell had become more explicit about his methods.

[158] *HP* (Mar. 1910), 26.

[159] J. D. B. Miller, *Norman Angell and the Futility of War: Peace and the Public Mind* (1986), 6–7.

[160] N. Angell, *Peace Theories and the Balkan War* (1912), 9. He had issued a similar denial to the *Daily Mail* as early as 15 Sept. 1911: see N. Angell, *After All* (1951), 152; and he also incorporated one in the preface to the 3rd edn. of *The Great Illusion* (Sept. 1912).

[161] N. Angell to Cecil and others, 31 Dec. 1930: Cecil Papers, Add. MS 51140.

[162] N. Angell, *The Foundations of International Polity* (1914), 165.

[163] Angell, *Europe's Optical Illusion*, 5, 105.

[164] H. Martin (ed.), *The Ministry of Reconciliation* (1916), 91–2.

some claim, in common with the vigilance committees, to be regarded as the forgotten pioneers of the academic study of international relations. A periodical, *War and Peace: A Norman Angell Monthly*, was also launched, albeit by a separate company and with Angell as a regular contributor rather than editor. Predictably, however, Germany showed scarcely greater enthusiasm for the 'New Pacifism' than for the old: Angell undertook a lecture tour there early in 1913, and in some places suffered from the unwelcome attention of patriotic societies.[165]

Angell's self-consciously tough-minded approach was less novel than he thought. As we have seen, versions of it had already been adopted by the Manchester Peace Conference Committee in the 1850s, by Pratt's IAPA in the 1880s, and by Stead at the turn of the century. Similar arguments had also been used by Novikow, as Angell was embarrassed to discover when asked to write the foreword to a English edition of his work.[166] Indeed, continental peace activists, operating in less congenial environments than their British counterparts, had always been forced to emphasize non-altruistic argument: they understandably resented the fact that, despite having spent thirteen years in Paris, Angell was ignorant of their writing; and they also disliked the fact that he shunned their Universal Peace Congresses.[167]

For all its claim to be scientific, Angell's 'New Pacifism' increased the ideological content of the peace-or-war debate. Although strongly supported by Sophia Sturge,[168] its materialism provoked many moralists to register their disapproval. Christians led the way: Canon W. L. Grane, one of the hundred or so members of a Church of England Peace League which had been established in 1910,[169] argued that the reform of opinion could best be achieved by appealing to 'the conscience and imagination and affections' as well as to 'their calculative facilities';[170] and Darby endorsed Grane's emphasis on religion and altruism as 'the Newest Pacificism'.[171] But the Tolstoyan pacifist Edward G. Smith was no less hostile to what he regarded as Angell's lowering of the campaign against war 'to the level of the stockbroker', even though he and Angell were both supporters of

[165] P. D. Hines, 'Norman Angell: Peace Movement 1911', D.Ed. thesis (Ball State Teachers' College, 1964), fos 105, 111–12.

[166] J. Novikow, *War and its Alleged Benefits* (1912), pp. xii–xv.

[167] Grossi, *Le Pacifisme européen*, 148, 157–60, 163–4.

[168] Hughes, *Sophia Sturge*, 120–2.

[169] A. Wilkinson, *The Church of England and the First World War* (1978), 21.

[170] W. L. Grane, *The Passing of War: A Study in Things that Make for Peace* (July 1912 edn), 85. The 1st edn. had appeared four months previously.

[171] W. E. Darby, *The Claim of 'The New Pacificism': A Paper Read at the Autumnal Conference of the Peace Society, Dundee, October 14th, 1912* (1912), 5, 11.

Hypatia Bradlaugh Bonner's Rationalist Peace Society, another small association established in 1910.[172]

Similarly, Angell's reassertion of the claims of the liberal approach at a time when this had been losing ground to its socialist and radical competitors stimulated the latter to further effort. The socialist campaign for an anti-war strike, which has already been discussed, gained momentum after *The Great Illusion* was published, partly because some socialists believed that they must offer their own policy of war prevention. Radicals were provoked into reaffirming the Hobsonian thesis. In his review of Angell's 1909 pamphlet, for example, Brailsford insisted that 'the enemy is not so much the faulty reasoning of the many as the shrewd self-interest of the few'. He was a former *Tribune* journalist, who had already joined the ILP but had not yet concluded that the overthrow of capitalism, as distinct from the establishment of democratic control, was essential to the abolition of war. Brailsford's writing at this time, by arguing that 'the potent pressure of economic expansion is the motive force in an international struggle', did much to extend Hobson's analysis of Britain's position in South Africa into a general critique of great-power relations.[173] Similarly, a barrister and political writer, J. A. Farrer, criticized *The Great Illusion* for overlooking the fact that, though 'contrary to the economic interest of the nation as a whole', war remained 'the distinct interest of ... the capitalists who finance war loans, of the companies or firms whose capital is sunk in providing the material of war, of journalists and newspapers to whom war means employment, excitement, and promotion'.[174] And Hobson himself reminded the 1912 National Peace Congress: 'The forces of international finance are not wholly beneficial.'[175]

In addition, radicals extended their analysis in the immediate pre-1914 period to include two additional threats to peace: secret diplomacy and the international armaments trade. With respect to the first of these, it was not surprising that suspicion of the inbred thinking of foreign-service officials developed at this time: backbench MPs were resentful at the reduction in the information given to them as a consequence of the increase of parliamentary business and the tightening of party discipline; the Diplomatic Service and Foreign Office were still exempted from the meritocratic system of recruitment long used by the Home Civil Service; and the Liberal government was encouraging an anti-aristocracy rhetoric for the purposes of its confrontation with the House of Lords on domestic issues.

---

[172] *Concord* (Oct. 1913), 93. For the Rationalist Peace Society, see Robertson *et al.*, *Essays Towards Peace.*

[173] F. M. Leventhal, *The Last Dissenter: H. N. Brailsford and his World* (Oxford, 1985), 96, 108, 113, 124, 131.   [174] *Concord* (Oct. 1910), 140.

[175] J. A. Hobson, *The Importance of Instruction in the Facts of Internationalism* (1912), 2.

The leading critic of the Britain's foreign-service officials was a former member of the caste, Arthur Ponsonby. An intense and idiosyncratic courtier's son who struggled for much of his life against 'the debilitating belief that he was helpless in the fact of predetermined universe', Ponsonby had spent eight unsatisfying years as a diplomat and had even considered going into the theatre before entering politics and becoming principal private secretary to Sir Henry Campbell-Bannerman, the Liberal Prime Minister. Taking over the latter's parliamentary seat on his death in 1908, he became particularly interested in the peace question, apparently after a chance meeting with Moscheles.[176] Ponsonby's refusal, despite that interest, to become chairman of the National Peace Council when approached in October 1910[177] was further evidence of the low status of the primary peace movement. But as a Liberal backbencher he gained a reputation as an influential *pacificist*: for example, after the Agadir crisis he published a pamphlet warning that the British Foreign Secretary, stuck 'in an official groove and an atmosphere created by the conventions of official secrecy', was 'taught to value the opinion of the expert diplomatic world higher than the often inarticulate but far more profound sentiments of his fellow countrymen'. But, despite this attack on his previous profession, Ponsonby was also aware that part of the problem lay with his present one: modern politicians were 'less conversant with world politics and the intricate details of foreign relations' than they were with 'social reform, domestic relations, and the condition of the people'. He apparently assumed that a better informed House of Commons would find a way to resolve Anglo-German antagonism: 'Many think that a better understanding with Germany would be the surest foundation for securing the establishment of European peace. We do not understand what obstacles lie in the way . . .'[178]

If Ponsonby's approach to international relations was already marked by ingenuousness, which was to become even more evident after the First World War when he became a pacifist, that of his fellow scourge of the Foreign Office, E. D. Morel, was marked by a belief in conspiracy worthy of the pioneering scourge of 'secret diplomacy', David Urquhart. Either in spite or because of being himself 'the offspring of a Franco-British alliance', in that his father was French and mother English,[179] Morel had become convinced that the British and French foreign services were jointly obstructing his agitation for reform in the Belgian Congo. The eventual success of that agitation early in 1911 freed him to take his revenge on the Anglo-French *entente*. The

[176] R. A. Jones, *Arthur Ponsonby: The Politics of Life* (1989), 7, 18, 34, 67–8.

[177] Laity, 'British Peace Movement 1906–1916', fo. 204.

[178] A. Ponsonby, *Democracy and the Control of International Affairs* (1912), 5, 7–8, 13, 15.

[179] As noted by H. Hanak, 'The Union of Democratic Control during the First World War', *Bulletin of the Institute of Historical Research*, 36 (1963), 167–80 at 168.

following year he published a well-researched book on the Moroccan issue, which was dedicated to 'those who believe the establishment of friendlier relations between Britain and Germany to be essential' and warned of the danger of Britain 'backing the wrong horse' in its choice of ally. But though his hostility to France made him in a sense pro-German, Morel was more fundamentally an isolationist, and denied that Britain needed an ally at all: 'Let us, on the contrary, keep our hands free, unfettered by alliances or under-standings of a compromising character from which our partners may profit but from which, as John Bright said long ago, we stand in the long run to lose. ...'[180] Morel's trenchant volume has been credited by A. J. P. Taylor with turning progressive opinion decisively against the French republic.[181]

The 'armaments ring', which had previously escaped criticism to a surpris-ing extent, was widely denounced after a German deputy, the Social Democrat Karl Liebknecht, exposed its cross-border collusions in the Reichstag on 18 April 1913.[182] G. H. Perris took the issue up in Britain, telling that year's National Peace Congress that the cosmopolitanism of the arms trade made its exploitation of nationalist sentiment 'rank humbug'.[183] So too did two young members of the ILP: the journalist Fenner Brockway and J. T. Walton Newbold, a young Quaker embarking on a left-wing career that was to take him into parliament as a Communist (though he would end up as a supporter of the National government).[184]

Yet despite its identification of so many short-term pressures for war, progressive opinion was complacent about containing them. In 1912 G. H. Perris, while acknowledging that the arms race increased 'the danger that the guns many suddenly go off as it were, by themselves', was none the less confident: 'The day of warfare is passing . . . The earth is indeed plotted out', and insisted both that rulers and peoples 'now see and admit that war would mean economic ruin for the victor as well as the vanquished, for capitalists as well as labour', and that 'in a rudimentary form, the United States of Europe is an accomplished fact'.[185] In 1913 William E. Wilson, a Quaker lecturer, believed that war was 'already playing a decreasing part in international affairs', and that it was 'unlikely that any modern nation will become a martyr'.[186] As late as March 1914 Brailsford predicted in a major work, *The*

---

[180] E. D. Morel, *Morocco in Diplomacy* (1912), v. 215–16.
[181] Taylor, *The Trouble Makers*, 120–1.
[182] Weinroth, 'British Pacifism 1906–1916', fo. 139. See also C. Trebilcock, 'Radicalism and the Armament Trust', in A. J. A. Morris (ed.), *Edwardian Radicalism 1900–1914* (1974), 180–201.   [183] G. H. Perris, *The War Traders: An Exposure* (1913), 31.
[184] Newton, *British Labour*, 308–10.
[185] Perris, *Our Foreign Policy and Sir Edward Grey's Failure*, 115–16, 193, 197.
[186] W. E. Wilson, *Christ and Peace: The Reasonableness of Disarmament on Christ, Humanitarian, and Economic Grounds: A Peace Study Text-Book* (1913), 155, 188.

War of Steel and Gold, that 'there will be no more wars among the six Great Powers'.[187] And shortly after the First World War broke out a Presbyterian minister, Richard Roberts, was to attribute the underdeveloped state of Christian thinking to the fact that, in the previous decade, 'the possibility of war between the great European powers had seemed so remote that it was felt to be hardly worthwhile to take the trouble' to clarify it.[188]

The slow-burning fuse lit by the assassination of the Austrian archduke at Sarajevo on 28 June 1914 caught the peace movement unawares. As late as 23 July the Peace Society's executive committee showed little unease at its regular monthly meeting. On 28 July Austria–Hungary declared war on Serbia, making the situation acute, but generating only a modest degree of concern among the primary associations. The Peace Society did not reconvene its executive committee. The International Arbitration League summoned its council for 31 July and its committee for the following day; but the August issue of its journal optimistically reaffirmed its long-standing 'confidence in Sir Edward Grey's influence for peace'.[189] And the British delegates to the foundation meeting of the World Alliance for Promoting International Friendship Through the Churches departed as planned for Constance on 31 July,[190] the day before Germany went to the war.

Belatedly, radicals established two short-lived *ad hoc* groups to campaign for British neutrality. One was set up by Angell, for whom the outbreak of war was a particularly galling experience. Predictably, he was accused of having denied the possibility of such an eventuality, even though his supporters pointed out that they would not have wasted their time 'attempting to prevent something they believed to be impossible'. Alternatively, he was charged with having wrongly predicted a financial crash at the outbreak of war, to which he replied he had merely claimed that aggression would not prove economically beneficial overall, a judgement to which he still adhered.[191] But he was soon to admit that his early thinking had suffered from a different weakness: it had pursued the strategy of 'modifying general opinion' without considering the question of 'political machinery'.[192] In consequence, as he was to put it in his autobiography, he had failed to ask: 'How shall a political truth, once established, be translated into workable policy?'[193] Forced by the war to come up with a policy, he initially embraced neutralism. He therefore formed

---

[187] H. N. Brailsford, *The War of Steel and Gold: A Study of the Armed Peace* (1914), 35. The preface was dated Mar. 1914.
[188] J. M. Fry (ed.), *Christ and Peace: A Discussion of Some Fundamental Issues Raised by the War* (n.d. [1915]), 17–18.
[189] *Arbitrator* (Aug. 1914), 86; (Sept. 1914), 100.
[190] White, *Willougby Hyett Dickinson*, 136–7.
[191] *War and Peace* (Sept. 1914), 347, 350.
[192] *War and Peace* (Oct. 1914), 9.   [193] Angell, *After All*, 318.

a Neutrality League, based on his own peace movement, which had just concluded a successful ten-day conference in the Quaker centre at Jordans near Beaconsfield. His Cambridge disciple Dennis Robertson became secretary; and his journal argued in its August issue that 'this country must in no case be drawn into the conflict'.[194] Angell's outspoken letter in *The Times* of 2 August showed how strongly he and his colleagues disliked siding with Russia's 'very rudimentary civilisation' against a 'highly civilised' Germany. The Neutrality League's manifesto, published on 3 August, argued that Britain had no interest in going to war, partly because it risked having its role as 'financial centre of the world . . . transferred to the other side of the Atlantic.'[195]

Meanwhile Hobson and Graham Wallas, a lecturer at the London School of Economics best known for his 1908 work *Human Nature in Politics*, began putting together a separate British Neutrality Committee. This sent a letter to the press on 2 August, signed among others by Courtney, L. T. Hobhouse, Murray, G. M. Trevelyan, and the chairman of the Labour Party, Ramsay MacDonald. The committee formally constituted itself on 4 August, eleven hours before Britain's ultimatum to Germany expired. Those present when it did so included C. R. Buxton, Bertrand Russell, and Goldsworthy Lowes Dickinson, a fellow in political science at King's College, Cambridge, who was also on the staff of the London School of Economics. The British Neutrality Committee formally dissolved itself the following day.[196]

Socialists and suffragists also acted as secondary peace movements. The British section of the Second International staged a large anti-war rally in Trafalgar Square on 2 August, addressed by Hardie and other representatives of the Labour and socialist movements, including the prominent Anglican socialist George Lansbury.[197] Women had played only a limited role in the peace movement while concentrating on their suffrage campaign: the Women's Co-operative Guild did not take up the peace issue in a major way until after war broke out; the Peace Society's predominantly female offshoot, the Peace Union, was almost exclusively Quaker and made little impact;[198] and the 'curious' under-representation of women in peace associations generally had been commented on by Moscheles.[199] But the International Women's Suffrage Alliance, which was meeting in London on 31 July, adopted a manifesto

---

[194] *War and Peace* (Aug. 1914), 309.
[195] P. C. Hafer, 'Two Paths to Peace: The Efforts of Norman Angell 1914–1918', Ed.D. thesis (Ball State University, 1972), fos. 53–6, 252–4. N. Angell, 'War and Peace, 1914', in J. Bell (ed.), *We Did Not Fight* (1935), 43–60.
[196] Clarke, *Liberals and Social Democrats*, 165–7.
[197] Newton, *British Labour*, 327–9.
[198] Its minute book for 1907–21 survives with the Peace Society's minute books
[199] *Concord* (Feb. 1912), 13–14.

calling for mediation and sent it to the major embassies in London. And several women's organizations united to arrange a meeting for the evening of 4 August, though by the time it met the expiry of Britain's ultimatum was only three hours away and crowds were gathering on the streets of the capital to celebrate the start of the war.[200]

The 'enormous increase of interest in Peace questions'[201] in this period was largely the result of an anxiety about an impending clash with Germany which made some inroads into Britain's insular complacency. A number of individuals, *ad hoc* bodies, and secondary associations responded with energy. But the established associations added little value to the peace campaign, partly because they were now 'vegetating on the edge of insolvency', according to one historian's astringent assessment.[202] Even allowing for the greater urgency generated by fear of aerial bombardment, a comparison with the pre-1939 period shows how much the peace movement underachieved institutionally in the prelude to the First World War. However, its latent strength, which arose from the extent to which its values were embedded in British political culture, was demonstrated by the fact that, despite the ineffectiveness of the neutrality movement, the government was in August 1914 to explain the *casus belli* in essentially *pacificist* terms.

[200] Liddington, *Long Road to Greenham*, 59, 77–9. A. Wiltsher, *Most Dangerous Women: Feminist Peace Campaigners of the Great War* (1985), 15–23.
[201] *HP* (June 1911), 169.
[202] Marrin, *Sir Norman Angell*, 108.

7

Reconstruction,
August 1914–December 1918

Britain's involvement in its first great-power conflict for fifty-eight years produced 'a shock of incredulity, then a feeling of "Never again! This must be the war to end war" ', in G. L. Dickinson's words,[1] and 'struck us with surprise as the thing it is, an anachronism, an obsolete barbarity, a blot on civilisation', in Brailsford's.[2] The peace movement's response to the unexpected conflict went through three distinct phases. First, in 1914–15 the old primary associations proved unequal to the challenge, and were supplanted, not by *ad hoc* bodies, but by durable new ones, namely the Union of Democratic Control, the No-Conscription Fellowship, the Fellowship of Reconciliation, the League of Nations Society, and the Women's International League. Secondly, in 1916 conscientious objectors challenged conscription; and a section of the movement began campaigning for a negotiated peace. Thirdly, in 1917–18 war-weariness, the Russian revolutions, and American intervention combined to create a climate in which the movement was able to inject certain of its ideas, most notably the league of nations, into the political mainstream.

AUGUST 1914 TO DECEMBER 1915

The public was as excited by war in 1914 as it had been in 1854 or 1899. With British involvement being justified more on moralistic than on jingoistic grounds, the First World War was closer in atmosphere to the Crimean War than to the Boer War, albeit without the anticipatory crusading zeal of sixty years previously. Admittedly, as the costs of the conflict became more apparent, its supporters became ever more insistent that it was a crusade against Prussianism, in line with the principle noted by Irene Cooper Willis: 'The greater the sacrifice, the holier the war, the more Satanic the enemy.'[3] Yet the

[1] C. R. Buxton (ed.), *Towards a Lasting Settlement* (1915), 11.
[2] Brailsford, *A League of Nations* (1917), 2.
[3] I. C. Willis, *England's Holy War: A Study of English Liberal Idealism during the Great*

most commonly voiced justification for British intervention was *pacificist*, the moral obligation to come to the aid of a helpless victim of lawlessness. Indeed, as Angell noted, the violation of Belgian neutrality was accepted by 'ninety nine Britons out of a hundred . . . as the reason why we entered the war'.[4]

Public excitement also involved a higher ratio of anxiety to arrogance than at the outbreak of the Crimean and Boer conflicts, since the First World War was both on a larger scale and closer to home. Consequently, in 1914 most supporters of the war felt morally obliged for to volunteer for military service—a very significant, though largely unheralded, change since previous conflicts. At least some of those who had believed until 4 August that insular Britain had the option of neutrality suddenly felt vulnerable. For example, L. T. Hobhouse privately argued on 6 August 1914: 'We cannot continue criticism of the policy which has led to this war as we did in the case of South Africa, for our safety is at stake. We can none of us now think of anything but this one object.'[5] And in a series of *Manchester Guardian* articles published during the spring of 1915 and later issued in book form, he publicly acknowledged his arrival at the view—reinforced by the menace of submarines to the country's shipping—that Britain 'can no longer pursue her own course in internal security regardless of the fate of Europe'.[6]

Although in the emotion of the hour it did not always keep them separate in its mind, progressive opinion had to ask itself two questions in August 1914. The first was political: did the wrong committed by Germany on Belgium outweigh the contributory negligence of British foreign policy in consequence of its imperialism, irrationalism, secret diplomacy, arms trading, and capitalism about which peace activists had been complaining since the turn of the century? Most *pacificists*, especially those trustful of the Liberal government, concluded that it did. They included Gilbert Murray, who abandoned neutralism after watching the Foreign Secretary defend his policy in the Commons on 3 August: he thereupon published both pro-Russian and pro-war pamphlets and eventually also a book-length vindication of *The Foreign Policy of Sir Edward Grey*.[7] Most who took this view were keen to show that they did so on *pacificist* rather than defencist grounds, by supporting it as 'The War That Will End War', a phrase coined by the novelist and progressive intellectual

War (New York, 1929), p. xix. This work, a compilation of studies first published in 1919, 1920, and 1921, grew out of her work for Russell: see R. Monk, *Bertrand Russell: The Spirit of Solitude* (1997), 387–94.

[4] *War and Peace* (Oct. 1914), 24.
[5] Cited in Robbins, *Abolition of War*, 39.
[6] L. T. Hobhouse, *The World in Conflict* (1915), 16–17.
[7] D. Wilson, *Gilbert Murray OM 1866–1957* (Oxford, 1987), 218–20, 222–5.

H. G. Wells in the first few days of the conflict.[8] They therefore supported the 'League of the Nations of Europe' for which G. L. Dickinson was calling by September,[9] even if only a few of them were to be early members of the League of Nations Society.

The second question for progressive opinion was theological or ethical: even if the war was politically justifiable, was it also right on religious or moral grounds? This too was overwhelmingly answered in the affirmative, the Christian churches giving a strong lead to this effect. For example, although on 4 August John Clifford returned from the abortive Constance conference minded to oppose British intervention as in the Boer War, he immediately changed his mind and assisted with army recruitment. The council of his Baptist Union declared that 'the call of God has come to Britain to spare neither blood nor treasure in the struggle to shatter a great anti-Christian attempt to destroy the fabric of Christian civilisation'.[10] Even the once sceptical Unitarians mostly supported the war: one of their most influential figures, L. P. Jacks, insisted that to do so was 'a religious act'; and the Bing family, Tolstoyan pacifists whose son Harold became a conscientious objector, were required to withdraw from the congregation of which they had been long-standing members.[11] Only a handful of Unitarian ministers became pacifists, such as Stanley Mellor of Liverpool, who was cited in the introduction to this book as an example of a peace activist aware of his lack of influence, and Basil Martin of Finchley, a convert from Congregationalism who experienced 'loneliness' in his new denomination because so few of its members shared his opposition to the war.[12]

The peace movement was thus faced with its biggest test to date. The primary associations, which had held their nerve in the Crimean and Egyptian Wars and been bailed out by *ad hoc* initiatives in the Boer War, were now found wanting. Indeed, the Peace Society, the IAPA, and the International Arbitration League were all mortally wounded by the First World War, though each showed some capacity to linger on. Moreover, the National Peace Council came close to disintegration before ultimately pulling through.

The Peace Society's response to the outbreak of war was to reaffirm its pacifism in principle but not act upon it in practice. It fell between the two

[8] N. and J. MacKenzie, *The Time Traveller: A Life of H. G. Wells* (1973), 298.

[9] *War and Peace* (Sept. 1914), 345–6.

[10] A. Wilkinson, *Dissent or Conform? War, Peace and the English Churches 1900–1945* (1986), 24–5. For the timing of the delegates' return from Constance, see White, *Willoughby Hyett Dickinson*, 66, 136–7.

[11] A. Ruston, 'Unitarian Attitudes to World War 1', *Transactions of the Unitarian Historical Society*, 21 (1995–8), 269–84 at 274. C. Moorehead, *Troublesome People: Enemies of War 1916–1986* (1987), 30.

[12] B. Martin, *An Impossible Parson* (1935), 143.

stools of formal acquiescence in and resolute condemnation of British intervention, thereby losing support on two fronts. This ambivalent stance cannot be understood without noting the divided state into which the Society of Friends, to which most of its members still belonged, had fallen. The traditional peace testimony, though never formally to be abandoned, had continued to lose its authority. On the society's own figures, during the First World War as many as a third (33.6 per cent) of its males of military age undertook military service; and fewer than a half (44.5 per cent) became conscientious objectors.[13] Moreover, some of the Quakers who remained loyal to the testimony did so 'with too little searching of heart', as Wilson Harris later admitted in respect of himself.[14] Others did so on exemptionist rather than truly pacifist grounds. An example was J. W. Graham, whose doubts while an undergraduate three decades previously about whether non-Quaker Christians should renounce war have already been noted. He now published a book in which, while purporting to expound orthodox Quaker pacifism, he insisted that 'the fleet and army could not be disbanded tomorrow', refused to condemn his fellow citizens for acting 'on current standards' that differed from Quaker ones, and approvingly cited the exemptionist views of Caroline E. Stephen.[15] Moreover, at least according to the much later recollection of a co-religionist who knew him well, Graham also argued privately that 'it was a good thing that there were not too many pacifists, as that might seriously undermine the strength of the Allies and lead to a German victory'.[16] It was revealing that Graham's standing as an interpreter of the peace testimony was unaffected by his drift into exemptionism: he was thus to chair the Friends' Peace Committee from 1923 to 1931. And it was unsurprising that a private meeting of leading Quaker pacifists midway through the war was 'reminded that many members of our Society require to be brought into a different mind on this peace question'.[17]

None the less, though pacifism could no longer command the sincere assent of the Society of Friends as a whole, it inspired a zealous minority. In January 1915 the Friends' Peace Committee established a War Sub-Committee, which seems to have attempted to do for Quakers what the newly established Fellowship of Reconciliation was doing for Christian pacifists

[13] J. Rae, *Conscience and Politics: The British Government and the Conscientious Objector to Military Service 1916–1919* (1970), 73.

[14] W. Harris, *Life So Far* (1954), 98.

[15] J. W. Graham, *War from a Quaker Point of View* (1915), 67–9.

[16] H. Alexander to M. Graham, 15 Aug. 1960: Graham Papers—a citation I owe to Thomas Kennedy.

[17] Minutes of a Conference between the Peace Committee and the Service Committee, 2 Nov. 1916 (FPC minute book).

more generally.[18] More importantly, in May 1915 London Yearly Meeting established a Friends' Service Committee, which though initially set up to help Quakers of military age, some of whom had lost their jobs because of their pacifism, became a doughty fighter against conscription.[19] Its mainstays were A. Barratt Brown, a Quaker with a strong social conscience, and (after Wilson Harris resigned) J. P. Fletcher, who as an envoy from London Yearly Meeting had helped to mobilize his Australian colleagues against the Defence Act of 1910 which had introduced compulsory military training within the dominion.[20] The Friends' Service Committee was to become the most intransigent of all peace organizations, urging conscientious objectors to reject offers of alternative service and on one occasion defying government censorship rules. The emergence of this zealous pacifist minority had several causes. It was a continuation of the Quaker renaissance which had begun in the 1890s: in other words, it was in part a fundamentalist reaction against the sect's loss of enthusiasm for its traditional principles. It reflected the exposure of younger Quakers to socialist and Tolstoyan ideas. And it was reinforced by the conversion to Quakerism during the First World War of a number of dedicated pacifists—including Walter Ayles and Carl Heath, as will shortly be noted—who saw the Society of Friends as the quintessential peace sect.

Disliking the choice between tacit support for the war effort and intransigent resistance to it, many Quakers sought a middle way in humanitarian activity, the Friends' Peace Committee expressing 'warm sympathy with those Friends who are giving themselves to Red Cross work'.[21] The most celebrated outlet for humanitarianism was the Friends' Ambulance Unit which first left England for the front on 31 October 1914,[22] having been improvised by J. Allen Baker's Cambridge-educated son, Philip Baker. Always a *pacificist* rather than a pacifist, he was to become well known, having added his wife's maiden name, Noel, to his surname,[23] as a supporter of the League of Nations and a Labour politician. The ambulance unit was an unofficial body, which some pacifists criticized as a cog in the war machine.

[18] For this body see H. Alexander, 'A Nearly Forgotten Chapter in British Peace Activity—1915', *Journal of the Friends' Historical Society*, 55 (1983–9), 139–43.

[19] T. C. Kennedy, 'Fighting about Peace: The No-Conscription Fellowship and the British Friends' Service Committee, 1915–1919', *Quaker History*, 69 (1980), 3–22.

[20] Minutes, FSC, 3 Nov. 1915. Brock, *Quaker Peace Testimony*, 279–81.

[21] Minutes, FPC, 5 Nov. 1914.

[22] M. Tatham and J. E. Miles, *The Friends Ambulance Unit 1914–1919: A Record* (n.d.[1919]), pp. ix 3.

[23] He did so in 1922, presumably as an act of reconciliation following the marital crisis of that year described in D. J. Whittaker, *Fighter for Peace: Philip Noel-Baker 1889–1982* (York, 1989), 26–7. He added a hyphen in 1943: see his *Who's Who* entries.

More acceptable to the generality of Quakers was the Friends' War Victims Relief Committee, soon dubbed the 'Warvics', which was organized by A. Ruth Fry.[24]

The Quakers connected with the Peace Society were for the most part from the respectable mainstream which, though unwilling to repudiate the peace testimony, was also unwilling to act on it. This helps to explain why its attitude to the war fell between the two stools of supporting and defying the war effort. Because the Peace Society formally retained its pacifism it lost a number of important members. Its Quaker president J. A. Pease decided to remain in the Liberal government even after it declared war, and therefore gave up his office in the society, announcing that this was 'not because my views on peace principles have altered a tittle but because I might be regarded as being in a false position'.[25] The Peace Society accepted his resignation because it felt obliged 'under present circumstances' to 'hold an absolutely detached outlook'.[26] The Congregationalist chairman of its executive committee, Hazell, wanted the society 'to present a motor ambulance for the benefit of the wounded' and resigned after his colleagues decided—presumably for the same reason that the Society of Friends decided not to adopt the Friends' Ambulance Unit as an official body—that 'the Society should not undertake work of that kind'.[27]

But the Peace Society was so cautious in the implementation of its pacifism as to leave Vera Brittain with the recollection that it 'accepted the war as inevitable'.[28] On 5 August its executive committee called on the society's members 'to hold themselves in check' while waiting for an opportunity to work for peace. Although at its next meeting on 1 October it agreed to draft a manifesto 'reaffirming its principles', it decided not to publish this until after the end of the conflict, which it still expected to be short. And its disapproval of the newly formed Union of Democratic Control was evident in its criticism of 'so-called pacifists' for 'remaking the world and laying down the law as to what *must* and *shall* be'.[29]

To succeed Hazell as chairman of the executive committee the society chose the patent lawyer Herbert Sefton-Jones, despite the fact that he was a leader of the faction within the Society of Friends which did not wish to condemn the war.[30] This choice alienated sincere pacifists: it was almost

---

[24] Jones, *Margery Fry*, 93–4. A. R. Fry, *A Quaker Adventure: The Story of Nine Years' Relief and Reconstruction* (1926).

[25] Pease to J. B. Hodgkin, 4 Aug. 1914 (copy): Gainford Papers.

[26] PSM, 22 Oct. 1914.   [27] PSM, 1 and 22 Oct. 1914.

[28] V. Britain, *The Rebel Passion: A Short History of Some Pioneer Peace-Makers* (1964), 34.

[29] PSM, 5 Aug., 1 Oct. 1914. *HP* (Oct. 1914), 105, 107.

[30] PSM, 26 Nov. 1914. I owe my information about his role in the Society of Friends to Thomas Kennedy.

certainly no coincidence that the meeting of the executive committee which elected Sefton-Jones also recorded the resignation after thirteen years' service of Harold J. Morland, an accountant with Price Waterhouse and a third-generation Quaker member of the Peace Society, whose subsequent service on the Friends' Service Committee (and, later, in the No More War Movement) indicates that he remained a staunch pacifist. In the summer of 1916, the new chairman published an anti-German pamphlet, *German Crimes and our Civil Remedy*, on the strength of a close acquaintanceship with that country, including residency there as early as the Franco-Prussian War. Though insisting he was a 'Free Trader', Sefton-Jones called for 'the restriction of German commercial activities for at least five years' after the war by means of an allied boycott and discriminatory tariffs. And, though claiming to be 'a Pacifist', he expressed the wish that 'not only the Kaiser himself and his sons, but also the assassins through whom his will has been carried out, should answer with their lives for the misery they have caused' and that 'the entire German garrison in our midst' should be permanently repatriated. He also made explicit how far he had pushed his own pacifism into the private sphere by attacking 'professed Pacifists' who, on account of 'impracticable idealism' and 'confused thinking', were unable to 'recognize any distinction between the idea of conduct for the individual in . . . the "Sermon on the Mount", and that incumbent on the Rulers of States to whose peoples they stand in a fiduciary relation'.[31] Not surprisingly, this pamphlet caused a member of the Peace Society's executive committee—J. E. Hodgkin, who had succeeded Hazell as treasurer—to question its author's suitability to be chairman. But Sefton-Jones met Hodgkin's complaints by emphasizing that he had written 'in his personal and not in his official capacity', and was allowed to keep his chairmanship.[32]

Admittedly, the Peace Society made some effort to reinvigorate itself following the first wartime meeting of members in May 1915. To encourage local activism, it changed its rules to allow auxiliaries to send a delegate to the executive committee, an incidental effect being that women attended this body for the first time in its ninety-nine-year history. However, its key decision was to press Darby to make way for 'a younger man'.[33] Darby's departure was later explained to the National Peace Council as the consequence of his appointment as 'legal adviser to the Imperial Japanese Foreign Office',[34] though this was presumably to save his face.

The Peace Society's new secretary with effect from January 1916 was the

---

[31] H. Sefton-Jones, *German Crimes and our Civil Remedy* (1916), 8, 16–18.
[32] PSM, 27 July 1916.
[33] PSM, 22 July 1915.
[34] Minutes, NPC Council, 2 Feb. 1916.

Revd Herbert Dunnico, a Welsh-born Baptist in his late thirties who had ministered in Warrington and Liverpool for fourteen years.[35] Briefly a factory-worker and a coal-miner in his youth, and still an active ILP member, he was more forthright than his immediate predecessors, showing real anger when newly founded associations failed to give his venerable organization what he considered to be its due respect.[36] Dunnico did his best to revive the Peace Society during its centenary year by involving it in the work of the Peace Negotiations Committee, a body whose work will shortly be discussed.

However, the society's decline proved inexorable. For example, it had held its annual public meeting, albeit more unobtrusively than usual, in 1915; but it was refused the Memorial Hall for what would have been the commemoration of its centenary in 1916, and thereafter attempted no wartime gatherings. This decision reflected the executive committee's timidity: of its members only the Quaker Robert O. Mennell—whose peace work was mostly carried on through the Friends' Service Committee, of which he became secretary, and as a conscientious objector[37]—seems to have suffered for his beliefs. The boast of the society that for a time the *Herald of Peace* was 'the only British pacifist publication dispatched to neutral countries'[38] was an ambivalent one: though intended to imply that the periodical in question was particularly enterprising, it could be read as indicating that it was particularly anodyne. In any case, the society could afford to publish it only spasmodically after October 1917.

Once the war was over, an already moribund Peace Society suffered further from Dunnico's preoccupation with his political career: he stood for Labour in 1918, and was elected for Consett in 1922, though he lost in 1931; thereafter he supported the National government, standing unsuccessfully as a National Labour candidate in 1935, and receiving a compensatory knighthood three years later. The society's enforced move from New Broad Street after eighty-four years in 1925, when its lease expired, symbolized its inability to live up to its comparatively illustrious past. It started using the name 'International Peace Society' in an effort to claim a distinctive role for itself; but the younger generation of peace associations still ignored it, causing one of the occasional issues of the *Herald of Peace* to comment: 'It would not be an ungracious act if the new organizations now working for peace (whose lives have fallen in more pleasant places by reason of the pioneer work done) recognized a little more fully the debt they owe to "The Peace Society".'[39]

---

[35] PSM, 24 June, 22 July, 25 Nov. 1915.   [36] *HP* (Jan. 1927), 34–5.
[37] PSM, 25 Feb. 1915. *HP* (Oct. 1918), 88.   [38] *HP* (Sept. 1919), 104.
[39] *HP* (Jan. 1927), 34–5.

Universal—or International, as they once again tended to be called—Peace Congresses continued to be held, the thirty-third and apparently the last taking place apprehensively at Zurich during last days of August 1939;[40] but they too were almost completely ignored by the dynamic elements of the peace movement.

The Peace Society's sole public impact during the inter-war period was achieved when politicians addressed its annual meetings. In the early 1920s there were still a few Christian opponents of the First World War who saw value in such occasions. An example was Lord Parmoor: though a devout Anglican with strong family ties to the peace movement—by his first marriage he was Leonard Courtney's brother-in-law, for example—and with a strong commitment to the World Alliance for Promoting International Friendship through the Churches, he was not a quite a pacifist and was thus served better by the Peace Society than by its more absolutist competitors.[41] And Dunnico's party connections ensured the attendance of Labour parliamentarians, even though their views did not sit easily with those of the society's traditional membership. The most prominent of these was MacDonald, who even consented to be a vice-president for a time, though he probably did so in order better to snub the League of Nations Union, for reasons to be noted. The last time the Peace Society hit the headlines was during the 1935 general election when the Conservative leader, Stanley Baldwin, gave a speech justifying rearmament at its annual meeting, presumably choosing this occasion so as to give his politically controversial message an eirenic aura without risking the critical reception which an active association might have provided.[42] 'No other peace organization in the world can take greater pride in the representative character of its platform', the society boasted in 1938. By then it was in effect admitting that its pacifism had become purely formal: 'If we decline to advocate the abolition of the army, navy, air force as a practical policy today, it is not that we have lost faith in the ultimate ideal or that we have ceased to work and pray for it, but for other reasons, that seem to us sound.'[43] The final issue of *Herald of Peace* covered January–April 1939; and the final committee meeting, according to the long run of surviving minute books, took place on 5 July 1939. Thereafter the society's existence was within the bosom of the Dunnico family, which still keeps its records.

[40] See the brief note by Caroline Playne in *Peace* (Jan. 1940), 65.

[41] See Lord Parmoor, *A Retrospect: Looking Back over a life of More than Eighty Years* (1936), pp. xi, 175–6, and ch. 9.

[42] It was presumably Baldwin's speech on 31 Oct. 1935 that misled C. L. Mowat into claiming of the 1930s: 'The Peace Society was strong, and held large meetings, addressed by men of eminence': *Britain between the Wars 1918–1940* (1955), 422.

[43] *HP* (Oct.–Dec. 1938), 1, 5.

In August 1914 the IAPA was paralysed by indecision as to the political merits or otherwise of the war: that month's issue of its journal was pulped because it had been overtaken by events; and the next, in October, was non-committal. This was because G. H. Perris, who had recently returned as *Concord*'s editor, was 'evading the main question for three months', as he later admitted. Having previously come close to accepting Tolstoyism, as already noted, he understandably experienced 'agonizing pain' when in November he felt obliged to endorse the war.[44] However, what destroyed the IAPA was not this decision but its failure to realize that not arbitration but an international organization was becoming the principal goal for liberal *pacificists*: as a result, it was superseded by the movement for a league of nations. It went into steep decline, ceasing to issue *Concord* after the December 1916/January 1917 issue. Moscheles and Perris died in 1917 and 1920 respectively. Green, still its secretary, moved to the right, defeating MacDonald in the 1918 general election on behalf of the National Democratic Party (an anti-socialist body set up to rally working-class opinion behind the Lloyd George coalition), and ending his career as a Conservative Party worker. Without an endowment to prolong its half-life excessively, the IAPA was to expire with dignity in 1925.

The International Arbitration League was to be the recipient of the IAPA's modest residual balance of £123.[45] Despite having urged neutrality as late as 4 August, it too came out in favour of the First World War, doing so on the *pacificist* grounds that Britain was fighting 'above and before all things a war against militarism' and that modern history offered 'no parallel to the German crime in Belgium'.[46] Despite having so abruptly reversed itself, it still wanted to be regarded as 'pacifist': while recognizing that a 'distinction should be made between pacifists who hold the extreme doctrine of non-resistance and those who do not', it insisted that the latter had an equal right to that name, and objected to the efforts of 'some pacifists to rule us out of the household of faith'.[47] However, this was a lost semantic cause, as its veteran president Thomas Burt grudgingly conceded in 1917 when he claimed that, despite endorsing the war, he remained 'a peace man', though 'not a pacifist in the narrow improper sense in which the word is now used'.[48]

Like the IAPA, the International Arbitration League missed the opportunity

---

[44] *Concord* (Nov./Dec. 1914), 125.

[45] J. F. Green to F. Maddison, 28 Feb. 1925: International Arbitration League Papers.

[46] *Arbitrator* (Oct. 1914), 111; (Nov. 1914), 122.

[47] *Arbitrator* (June 1915), 62–4; (Aug. 1915), 86. The journal took the same view in the Second World War: see (Oct.–Dec. 1941), 116.

[48] Cited in T. Burt, *An Autobiography with Supplementary Chapters by Aaron Watson* (1924), 312.

to put itself at the forefront of the movement for a league of nations. Unlike that body, however, it possessed the income—the interest from Cremer's donation plus a grant from Carnegie—to eke out a lengthy twilight existence. It published occasional issues of the *Arbitrator* until as late as 1956; and only in 1963 did it finally merge itself into another minuscule internationalist organization, the Mondcivitan Republic, with some of its funds going to the headquarters of the Inter-Parliamentary Union for the foundation in 1967 of a Randal Cremer Memorial Library.[49]

The National Peace Council almost went the way of the associations which had set it up. Its original response to the outbreak of war was one of caution, its chairman, the Liberal MP Gordon Harvey, 'expressing himself strongly against any immediate action'.[50] Thereafter, deep divisions emerged. A motion to condemn Germany and Austria–Hungary was supported even by Joseph Gundry Alexander, a Quaker active in the Peace Society and on the Friends' Peace Committee, but opposed by a pacifist minority.[51] The council's president, Lord Channing of Wellingborough, supported the war, 'crying out . . . for the blood of Germans' in the later recollection of Carl Heath, its secretary, but resigned in June 1915.[52] Heath himself resolved his previous uncertainties in a pacifist direction: he published an absolutist book,[53] a move which 'somewhat alarmed' some of his colleagues, and became a Quaker and conscientious objector. Disagreements became very bitter during 1916, when a motion declaring the war 'righteous', which had been proposed by Ethel Behrens of the Jewish Peace Society and seconded by Maddison of the International Arbitration League, was blocked. Several associations, including the IAPA, the Rationalist Peace Association, and the International Arbitration League, subsequently withdrew; but the No-Conscription Fellowship joined. During the period in which the National Peace Council 'showed signs of increasing paralysis, if not of completely breaking up', Heath 'suffered from a real sense of despair'; but his tenacity and the support he received from leading Quakers helped it to survive long enough for it 'to renew itself' on the basis of a revised constitution.[54] In January 1917 and May 1918 it was even to hold National Peace Congresses, albeit of a minimal and self-effacing kind compared with those before the war.

[49] Interview with Mr Peter Deed, 31 Mar. 1993. Douglas, *Parliament across Frontiers*, 2.

[50] Minutes, NPC Council, 9 Sept. 1914.

[51] Alexander, *Joseph Gundry Alexander*, 185–6, 189.

[52] FPC, *Friends and International Peace* (1924), 5. Minutes, NPC Council, 2 June 1915.

[53] See C. Heath, *Pacifism in Time of War* (n.d.[1915]).

[54] Heath, unpublished autobiography: in R. A. Smith Papers, Friends House Temp MS 516/2/11, fos. 69, 73–7, 81. Minutes, NPC Council, 5 July 1916, 10 Jan., and 11 July 1917. Minutes, FPC, 6 Sept. and 1 Nov. 1917.

The period from September 1914 to October 1915 was one of exceptional institutional creativity, with five significant new primary associations being launched. Two of them, the Union of Democratic Control and League of Nations Society, were *pacificist*, radical and liberal respectively. One, the Women's International League, was organized by gender rather than ideology. And two, the Fellowship of Reconciliation and the No-Conscription Fellowship, were pacifist, Christian and socialist respectively.

The Union of Democratic Control (UDC)[55] was formed by a hard core of unrepentant neutralists. Though much weakened because of Germany's violation of Belgian neutrality, non-interventionist *pacificism* could still tap three veins of support. The first was a still significant residue of isolationism. John Burns recorded his motives for resigning from the cabinet when it decided to enter the war as: 'Splendid Isolation, no Balance of Power, no incorporation in the Continental system'.[56] And an assumption that national security was not really at risk was a factor in Bertrand Russell's opposition to British intervention: he had no doubts about the 'ultimate victory of our side',[57] and was to admit in his autobiography that it was not until the invasion crisis of 1940 that he 'realised that, throughout the First War, I had never serious envisaged the possibility of utter defeat'.[58] The second was the left's enduring hatred of Tsarism. Dislike of fighting alongside Russia was to be the main reason why Herbert Morrison, the future Labour minister, was to plead a conscientious objection to the war.[59] And the third was a cultural partiality among intellectuals towards Germany. The veteran Liberal statesman John Morley, who resigned from the cabinet at the same time as Burns, had always disliked the *entente* with France because of his preference for Germany.[60] A perception of German superiority over the Russians reinforced Russell's opposition to British intervention: on 1 August 1914 he had privately described Germany as 'wholly disinterested', and thereafter wrote a pamphlet representing the war as 'a great race-conflict, a conflict of Teuton and Slav'.[61]

The decision to organize neutralist sentiment was taken by the politician C. P. Trevelyan, who, unlike his historian brother G. M., had been unable openly to support the British Neutrality Committee because he was a junior minister in the Liberal government. He resigned on 5 August, and drew up a statement

---

[55] Unless otherwise indicated my account is derived from the definitive study by M. Swartz, *The Union of Democratic Control in British Politics during the First World War* (Oxford, 1971).
[56] Cited in K. D. Brown, *John Burns* (1977), 176.
[57] Russell to H. Flexner, 7 Sept. 1914, cited in Russell, *Prophecy and Dissent*, p. xiii.
[58] Russell, *Autobiography*, ii. 191.
[59] H. Morrison, *An Autobiography* (1960), 61–2. B. Donoughue and G. W. Jones, *Herbert Morrison: Portrait of a Politician* (1973), 40–1.
[60] D. A. Hamer, *John Morley: Liberal Intellectual in Politics* (Oxford, 1968), 362–7.
[61] Monk, *Spirit of Solitude*, 372–3.

calling for parliamentary control over foreign policy and for fair peace terms. On 10 August a small private gathering discussed a campaign to promote this statement: those present were likened by Russell, who was one of them, to 'eight fleas talking of building a pyramid'.[62] Four of them—Angell, MacDonald, and Morel, plus Trevelyan—agreed to create a new association, and were joined shortly afterwards by Ponsonby as a fifth co-founder. The UDC was initially intended as a behind-the-scenes ginger group to keep the government and the Liberal party alive to the possibilities and prerequisites of peace. But its existence was revealed on 10 September, after one of the recipients of its circular to potential sympathizers had leaked it to the ultra-patriotic *Morning Post*.

The UDC therefore went public in a letter to the press, dated 17 September, announcing the four cardinal points that should govern any post-war settlement. First, no territory was to be transferred without a plebiscite. Secondly, foreign policy was to be brought under democratic control. Thirdly, an international council was to be established. And, fourthly, drastic international disarmament and the nationalization of the armaments industry were to be proposed. On 2 May 1916 an additional point was to be added at the insistence of Hobson, an active supporter who became alarmed at 'a vigorous campaign in favour of converting our existing war-alliance into a fiscal and commercial alliance to continue the conflict upon the economic plane after the military operations are concluded'.[63] Hobson's fifth point specified that commercial warfare was to be avoided through the extension of the principle of the open door for trade.

These cardinal points—and, indeed, the organization's very name—indicated that the UDC was squarely in the radical-*pacificist* tradition as elaborated since the beginning of the century. Even its third point, an international council, differed significantly from a league of nations as conceived by liberal *pacificists*. Whereas the latter soon decided upon an international organization that would concentrate on conflict resolution and collective defence, radicals preferred one that was either more limited or more ambitious. The UDC's international council fell into the former category: it was almost certainly conceived of as a simple forum in which diplomacy could shed its secrecy rather than as an elaborate body with supranational powers. By 1917, as public interest in the league idea increased, the UDC felt obliged to make a more specific proposal for a 'Community of Nations'; but, as a recent study has shrewdly noted, this was 'largely a public relations exercise' whose

---

[62] Russell, *Prophecy and Dissent*, p. xlix.
[63] *The U.D.C.* (June 1916), 57. S. Harris, *Out of Control: British Foreign Policy and the Union of Democratic Control, 1914–1918* (Hull, 1996), 132–3.

'vagueness betrayed a lack of any real interest in a League of Nations on the part of most of the Union's leadership'.[64] Individual UDC supporters, notably Hobson and Brailsford, advocated a much bolder type of international organization: they wanted a federation on the grounds that it alone would have the legislative authority to tackle war's economic and colonial causes. But Morel was unmoved by such an ambitious scheme, so radical federalism never became UDC policy.

In its letter of 17 September 1914, the UDC's founders were careful to insist that it was not 'a "stop-the-war" movement' and that it offered no suggestion 'as to the stage in the military operations at which peace should be urged'. It was also circumspect in its tactics, attempting no public meetings until March 1915, when Morel spoke in Cambridge, and suspending them during the period of strong anti-German feeling which greeted the sinking two months later of the *Lusitania*. Russell, who had established the Cambridge branch which invited Morel, felt that the UDC's 'eagerness to disclaim any lack of patriotism or of determination that victory must be ours' meant that it was virtually useless until 'after the war'.[65] The UDC refused to campaign against conscription, and did not launch a negotiated-peace campaign until 1916, which it was even then very careful to avoid calling a stop-the-war campaign.

For many activists, this early caution was founded purely on the tactical consideration that if it behaved too provocatively, its ideas would be ignored. Privately they still regarded British involvement in the war as unnecessary. This was most obviously true of Morel, who became its full-time secretary and—thereby arousing MacDonald's political jealousy—its acknowledged leader. Morel's opposition to the war caused him to proffer his resignation as a Liberal parliamentary candidate on 4 August 1914, though he was taken aback at the alacrity with which this was accepted.[66] He reissued his pre-war volume condemning Anglo-French policy over Morocco, and made regular contributions to the ILP's *Labour Leader* which were republished in book form during 1916 under the title *Truth and the War* and caused considerable offence to the authorities.[67] Though frequently accused of pacifism, Morel was merely an isolationist: he refused to allow opposition to conscription to be added to the UDC's cardinal principles, on the grounds that he personally would find it 'impossible to resist' the call to enlist for genuine home defence;

[64] Harris, *Out of Control*, 164.

[65] Russell to Lady O. Morrell, 8 June 1915, cited in Russell, *Prophecy and Dissent*, 1.

[66] Cline, *E. D. Morel*, 98–100.

[67] E. D. Morel, *Ten Years of Secret Diplomacy: An Unheeded Warning (Being a Reprint of 'Morocco in Diplomacy'* (1915). Swartz, *Union of Democratic Control*, 122–6.

and the official history of the UDC later confirmed that Morel was 'not . . . a "pacifist" in the absolute sense'.[68]

MacDonald, who resigned as chairman of the Labour party on 7 August 1914, also opposed the war so emphatically as at times to give a misleading impression of pacifism. He claimed in a book published in 1917: 'If we once admit that force is necessary for national defence, then every other militarist evil follows.' And he was to tell a meeting of the Peace Society in 1919: 'National Defence and the security of a political system never could be perfected by force, and never could be secured by war.'[69] That in fact he too was merely an isolationist was made clear in September 1914 when the prospect of a rapid German military advance that would threaten British security caused him to waver from his previous neutralism. He sent a message to a recruiting meeting which, albeit in characteristically convoluted language, insisted: 'Victory must . . . be ours.'[70] Germany's failure to break through enabled him to revert to neutralism almost immediately.

Brailsford, who was elected to the UDC's general council in November 1914, was also hostile to the war. He had been, in his biographer's words, 'formerly more a Gladstonian than a Cobdenite'—having indeed fought for the Greeks in 1897—but 'came down on the Cobdenite side' in August 1914. His opposition to the war led some of his radical colleagues, such as L. T. Hobhouse, to accuse him of pro-Germanism. Yet he too would have supported a war which he considered to be genuinely defensive, as he made clear by drilling at a volunteer club and later enrolling as a private in a volunteer regiment.[71]

However, some UDC members showed a more consistently positive attitude towards the war than Morel, MacDonald, and Brailsford. Ponsonby voted for war credits in 1914, claiming to want 'the war to be well conducted and no effort spared',[72] though because he continued to attack the Foreign Office as a narrow caste with 'a distorted perspective, a narrow vision, and a false sense of proportion',[73] this did not save him from considerable unpopularity. C. R. Buxton, a UDC supporter who emerged in the summer of 1915 as a leading Liberal advocate of peace negotiations, initially backed the war

---

[68] Morel to Trevelyan, 27 May 1915, cited in Swartz, *Union of Democratic Control*, 236. H. M. Swanwick, *Builders of Peace: Being Ten Years' History of the Union of Democratic Control* (1924), 188.

[69] J. R. MacDonald, *National Defence: A Study in Militarism* (1917), 46. *HP* (Sept. 1919), 110.

[70] Cited in D. Marquand, *Ramsay MacDonald* (1977), 175.

[71] Leventhal, *The Last Dissenter*, 124–7.

[72] Jones, *Arthur Ponsonby*, 90.

[73] A. Ponsonby, *Democracy and Diplomacy: A Plea for Popular Control of Foreign Policy* (1915), 66.

effort to the extent of undertaking a mission with his brother Noel to try to prevent Bulgaria aligning itself with Britain's enemies.[74] And Arthur Henderson proved even more supportive of the war, despite his election to the UDC's general council in November 1914: having succeeded MacDonald as chairman of the Parliamentary Labour Party, he was to become a member of war cabinet.

Angell soon lost his absolute confidence in neutralism, and was for at least a decade to waver between it and internationalism. His magazine immediately accepted that the war was 'now a fact to be accepted', and even carried a 'Your King and Country need you' recruiting appeal.[75] Angell declined Russell's request that he write an indictment of pre-war British policy, obliging Russell to write *The Policy of the Entente, 1904–1914: A Reply to Professor Murray* himself, with research assistance from Irene Cooper Willis.[76] Angell's changing approach was apparent in the appendix which, evidently as an afterthought, he added to the partially reworked version of *The Great Illusion* that he published late in 1914 in an attempt at self-vindication. Noting that seven nations had combined to fight Austria and Germany, he now wondered: 'Why for the purpose of a permanent peace should not eight, or for that manner eighteen, undertake to combine against any one nation that commits aggression upon its neighbours?' And he went on to make the significant acknowledgement that

this means the abandonment of certain Radical doctrines which have been held very tenaciously in the past: non-intervention, no military alliance with foreign countries, etc. But those doctrines, defensible as they were before the war, have, for good or ill, by our act been abandoned. We have become an integral part of the European system and it is outside the domain of practical politics to go back.[77]

In the spring of 1915 Angell crossed the Atlantic, and made contacts with circles close to President Woodrow Wilson. He came to doubt whether, in view of German attacks on neutral shipping, complete neutrality was possible even for the United States. On 31 May he published an article in the American magazine *New Republic* suggesting that the United States and certain other neutrals join with the allies in 'an international control of the world's supplies for the purpose of withholding them from Germany', which might prove to be 'the beginnings of the world organization of our common resources'.[78] He was thus evidently tempted to support the war as a means towards reforming the international system.

[74] Robbins, *Abolition of War*, 56.

[75] *War and Peace* (Sept. 1914), 341 and inside back cover.

[76] Russell, *Prophecy and Dissent*, p. xxiv. Monk, *Spirit of Solitude*, 383–9.

[77] N. Angell, *Prussianism and its Destruction: With which is reprinted Part II of the 'The Great Illusion'* (1914), 236, 239.

[78] N. Angell, 'A New Kind of War', reprinted in *War and Peace*, (Sept. 1915), 185–6.

However, as an ambitious public figure with the common touch, he could also imagine himself returning to Britain to lead the peace campaign on which, as will shortly be seen, the ILP had embarked in June 1915. Indeed, when the Garton Foundation finally severed its connection with him in October 1915, he toyed briefly with the idea of a 'straight-out anti-militarist campaign among the more revolutionary of the Labour people—with a possible capture of the ILP', even though aware that this 'would amount virtually to a preaching of non-resistance',[79] the policy which he had previously repudiated. A very similar line was taken by one of his Garton Foundation colleagues, B. N. Langdon Davies, who, having joined the UDC, was converted to socialism in 1915 and eventually became a conscientious objector.[80] For the moment, however, Angell resisted pacifist and leftist temptations, and not only briefly returned to Britain to offer himself for military service but on subsequently returning to the United States supported that country's entry into the war. It was thus because of doubts about isolationism as well as long periods in the United States that Angell played only a limited wartime role in the organization which he had helped to found.

Despite losing Angell's wholehearted support, the UDC made steady progress as the war went on. It appealed increasingly to progressives disillusioned by both the military deadlock and the Liberal party, yet for the most part not ready for a fully pacifist or socialist position. By the end of 1917 it had a hundred branches and a membership which has been estimated at 100,000,[81] though this is probably a considerable exaggeration. The UDC itself publicized only its indirect membership—the aggregate size of the bodies affiliated to it—which had reached 650,000 by the end of the war. It was aware that the real source of its influence was the support it received from an increasingly confident political left.

The League of Nations Society, established in May 1915, was slower into the field than the UDC because the merits of international organization, unlike the evils of secret diplomacy, had received little attention from the peace movement. This neglect was soon acknowledged. For example, Darby admitted:

Of the two parts of the political machinery of peace, greater attention has been given to International Arbitration which has sometimes been treated by Pacifists as if were the whole case, and, as *The Times* expressed it, a kind of white magic. But the other, and really more important section, International Union or Federation, has been overlooked.[82]

---

[79] Angell to Harold Wright, 15 Oct.[1915], cited in Hafer, 'The Paths to Peace', fo. 161.
[80] See his essay in J. Bell (ed.), *We Did Not Fight* (1935).
[81] Swanwick, *Builders of Peace*, 52. Swartz, *Union of Democratic Control*, 48.
[82] *HP* (Jan. 1915), 124.

L. T. Hobhouse attributed this oversight to the fact that pre-war peace schemes had all 'presumed a general will for peace'.[83]

However, within months of the outbreak of war the demand for 'some sort of international authority' was 'continually upon the lips or pens of a large number of more or less intelligent persons of every variety of political belief', in the words of Leonard Woolf, who was commissioned by the Fabian Society, previously aloof from such issues, to write the first systematic study of the subject.[84] Leading the way was G. L. Dickinson, who has the greatest claim to be the intellectual progenitor of the League of Nations as eventually created. Although he had lectured on international issues before the war, and even contributed articles to Norman Angell's journal in the spring of 1914, his commitment to peace was greatly intensified through anguish at the departure of his beloved university pupils to the trenches.[85] Before the war was a month old he was advocating a 'League of the nations of Europe'.[86] He also joined the UDC, and on 17 October convened a meeting of intellectuals, including Hobson, Keynes, Russell, to discuss his ideas. A few days later he approached the veteran Liberal statesman, jurist and diplomat Lord Bryce, who had been persuaded of the necessity of British intervention by the violation of Belgian neutrality.

Although declining either to join the UDC or to become president of the Peace Society in succession to J. A. Pease,[87] Bryce agreed to chair Dickinson's private committee while it formulated an internationalist scheme. The Bryce Group, as this committee came to be called, consisted of G. L. Dickinson, W. H. Dickinson, Hobson, Ponsonby, Wallas, and E. R. Cross— this last a solicitor employed by the Rowntree family, who did most of the drafting. None was a pacifist. Although Ponsonby did not want 'a specific obligation to use force to be part of any international agreement', he still believed that 'force might eventually be used on certain occasions'.[88] And although Cross had converted from Wesleyanism to Quakerism in 1898, he

---

[83] Hobhouse, *The World in Conflict*, 89.

[84] Woolf's work first appeared as supplements to the *New Statesman* on 10 and 17 July 1915 and then as L. S. Woolf, *International Government* (1916), 7. See also Woolf, *Beginning Again: An Autobiography of the Years 1911–1918* (1964), 183–9; and D. Wilson, *Leonard Woolf: A Political Biography* (1978), 62–73.

[85] *War and Peace* (May 1914), 221–2; (June 1914), 252–3. Dickinson acknowledged his homosexual feelings in a moving memoir which was not published until nearly forty years after his death: *The Autobiography of G. Lowes Dickinson and Other Unpublished Writings* ed. D. Proctor (1973).

[86] G. L. Dickinson, *The War and a Way Out* (1915), 41, 42.

[87] K. G. Robbins, 'Lord Bryce and the First World War', *Historical Journal*, 10 (1967), 255–78 at 257. PSM, 28 Jan. 1915.

[88] Mr Ponsonby's Note on the Suggested Amendment to the Proposals for the Avoidance of War': W. H. Dickinson Papers, MS Eng.Hist. c.402, fo. 112.

had, as he pointed out in 1907, 'never felt quite able to subscribe to the proposition . . . that war is under all circumstances unlawful'.[89]

Prior to the Bryce Group's report, league schemes had been generally very ambitious. G. L. Dickinson's original proposal had been for countries to 'hand over their armaments' to a league which would then enforce international law. Brailsford's thinking reflected the ambitious version of the radical approach to international organization, as already noted. In a new edition of *The War of Steel and Gold*, which omitted the embarrassingly erroneous assertion regarding the unlikelihood of war, he argued that the problem was 'larger' than 'the prevention of war', namely 'to provide for international change without war'. And he sketched out a federal league with powers to tackle the economic causes of war.[90] Hobson made similarly far-reaching proposals, as did Woolf, whose personal ideas went beyond those of the Fabian Society.[91]

However, on grounds of practicality Aneurin Williams, a Liberal MP, advocated a limited league;[92] and this approach was adopted by the Bryce Group. Its report, which was available in a first draft for private circulation to interested intellectuals as early as February 1915, had only a very limited supranational content. The league would force members to observe a cooling-off period while their disputes were considered by a third party, but not require them to accept the third party's ruling. It would also offer them defence against attack, though, because an international police force was impractical, it expected other members to provide this.

The Bryce Group's draft proposals helped to produce a liberal consensus in favour of what Brailsford called 'the moderate minimum' for any league.[93] G. L. Dickinson immediately fell into line, declaring: 'I do not imagine a federation of Europe to be possible in the immediate future. What I do believe to be possible, as soon as the war is over, is a League of Powers to help the peace of Europe.'[94] He now accepted that the league should 'have no executive power, only the power to recommend the best solutions', and expressed the hope 'that after meeting the opposition of the sceptics and the practical

---

[89] M. D. Dubin, 'Toward the Concept of Collective Security', *International Organization*, 24 (1970), 288–318. Dickinson, *Autobiography* 190. M. Wilkinson, *E. Richard Cross* (1917), 35, 40–1, 49–50.

[90] (3rd edn., June 1915), 318, 333–7.

[91] For an analysis of the various League schemes, see M. Ceadel, 'Supranationalism the British Peace Movement during the Early Twentieth Century', in A. Bosco (ed.), *The Federal Idea*, i. *The History of Federalism from the Enlightenment to 1945* (1991), 169–91.

[92] A. Williams, 'Proposals for a League of Peace and Mutual Protection among Nations', *Contemporary Review* (Nov. 1914), 628–36

[93] Buxton (ed.), *Towards a Lasting Settlement*, 159 n.

[94] Dickinson, *The War and a Way Out*, preface to 2nd edn.

men, I shall not have to meet that of the idealists'.[95] By April 1915 he was privately arguing to Ponsonby that the 'worst enemies' of a league were 'men like Brailsford and Hobson, who go for federation. They won't get that; but they may easily prevent our getting what we ask for'.[96]

Shortly before the Bryce Group produced its first draft, an association to promote a league was mooted at a gathering hosted by the wife of Liberal MP Walter Rea on 5 February 1915 when W. H. Dickinson, Wallas, and Williams were among those present.[97] At the time of a second such gathering, on 10 March, the association was proposing to call itself the 'Union of States Society';[98] but by the time of its formal launch on 3 May it had settled for 'League of Nations Society'. (Its American counterpart, established the following month, chose the crusading-tinged title 'League to Enforce Peace'.) With an eminent lawyer, Lord Shaw of Dumfermline, as president and W. H. Dickinson as chairman of its committee, the League of Nations Society was a notably more respectable body than the UDC. Its first appeal for support ruled out not only 'any "stop the war" programme' but also 'disarmament or criticism of foreign policy'; and the society eschewed public meetings until 1917.[99]

The society did not require its members to endorse a particular league blueprint: its leaders favoured the moderate-minimum approach; but Brailsford, Hobson, and Woolf joined in order to keep alive the radical-federal alternative. However, it is important to note that moderates and radicals were agreed on the need for the league to use military force in certain circumstances. Admittedly, there was a faint ambiguity in the society's original statement of basic principles. Point three ('That the states which are members of the League shall unite in any action necessary for insuring that every member shall abide by the terms of the treaty') did not explicitly rule out the possibility that 'any action necessary' might be understood to mean moral pressure only. Two years later this point was made watertight by adding an explicit reference to the obligation to use 'economic and military forces'. However, from the start point four made it very difficult for pacifists or isolationists to become members by requiring member states to 'make provision

[95] G. L. Dickinson, *After the War* (1915), 33, 37.

[96] G. L. Dickinson to Ponsonby, 2 Apr. 1915, cited in E. M. Forster, *Goldsworthy Lowes Dickinson* (1934), 165.

[97] The best account is a memorandum by D. H. Mills, enclosed in his letter of 25 May 1938 to W. H. Dickinson: Dickinson MS Eng.Hist. c.406, fos. 100–48. The Dickinson papers supplement what is otherwise the standard work: H. R. Winkler, *The League of Nations Movement in Great Britain, 1914–1919* (New Brunswick, NJ, 1952).

[98] See the draft constitution in the Dickinson Papers: MS Eng.Hist. c.404, fos. 8–9.

[99] Birn, *League of Nations Union*, 6–8. See also H. R. Winkler, *The League of Nations Movement in Great Britain 1914–1919* (New Brunswick, NJ, 1952).

for Mutual Defence, diplomatic, economic, or military, in the event of any of them being attacked'.[100] In consequence, those who opposed military sanctions even in a last resort seem to have stayed out of the society. Ponsonby did not join; Russell, who thought it politically unwise rather than wrong on principle to equip a league with powers of enforcement, also kept his distance; and a surviving membership list is notable for the absence of identifiable absolutists. It thus seems that Murray's recollection in old age that the League of Nations Society had 'contained a good many real pacifists' was a confusion with the early years of the society's successor body, the League of Nations Union.[101] Indeed, its lack of appeal to anti-sanctionists helps to explain why the League of Nations Society had recruited only 148 members by the time of its first general meeting on 29 November 1915, making it the smallest of the peace associations formed early in the First World War.

The Women's International League, formally established at the very end of September 1915, was an offshoot of the suffragist movement. 'Suffragists' sought the vote for women by constitutional means only: they comprised the majority of the women's movement, and were represented by the National Union of Women's Suffrage Societies (NUWSS). By contrast, 'suffragettes', whose heckling of Lloyd George at the 1908 Universal Peace Congress has already been mentioned, were prepared to use violence: though highly publicized, they were a minority catered for by the Women's Social and Political Union led by Emmeline Pankhurst, whose late husband Richard Pankhurst had, among various progressive activities, been a vice-chairman of the IAPA's executive committee.[102] Mrs Pankhurst's suffragettes mostly became ultra-patriotic on the outbreak of the war, with the notable exception of a splinter group led by her left-wing daughter Sylvia.[103] The more judicious NUWSS supported British intervention too, but did so in moderate language, and called for efforts to increase international goodwill. Initially, therefore, the minority who disagreed with this line felt disposed to remain loyal.

The parting of the ways within the NUWSS came after a Dutch feminist, Aletta Jacobs, proposed a Women's International Congress in neutral Holland. A meeting in The Hague in February 1915, which arranged the

---

[100] The principles are most conveniently set out in G. W. Egerton, *Great Britain and the Creation of the League of Nations: Strategy, Politics, and International Organization* (1979), 12. For the 1917 amendment, see Winkler, *League of Nations Movement*, 66.

[101] B. Russell, *Pacifism and Revolution, 1916–18 The Collected Works of Bertrand Russell*, xiv (1995), pp. xl–xli. The membership list is in the W. H. Dickinson Papers. Murray made his claim in the David Davies Memorial Lecture for 1955, published as *The League of Nations Movement: Some Recollections of the Early Days* (1955).

[102] See *HP* (Aug. 1883), 219; and *Concord* (16 Jan. 1888), 156.

[103] See B. Winslow, *Sylvia Pankhurst: Sexual Politics and Political Activism* (1996), 80–9, 103–4.

congress for late April in that city, was attended by five NUWSS members opposed to the war. Three were to become prominent in the peace movement. Kathleen D. Courtney was later a leading member of the League of Nations movement. (Understandably, she has sometimes been confused with Leonard Courtney's wife, Kate, who was also a peace activist at this time.[104]) Catherine Marshall was to administer the No-Conscription Fellowship and be hailed as 'probably the ablest woman organizer in the land' by the ILP weekly *Labour Leader*.[105] And Theodora Wilson Wilson, a Quaker and a novelist, was to be active in the Fellowship of Reconciliation, the *Crusader* group, and the No More War Movement. (The other two were Emily Leaf and Chrystal Macmillan.) However, on 18 March the NUWSS's executive committee decided by eleven votes to six not to be represented at The Hague. Opponents of the war then seceded on the grounds that the NUWSS's professed desire to promote international goodwill had been shown to be insincere.[106] They included Isabella Ford, a Quaker socialist who insisted that the 'women of Europe, meeting in solemn conference at the Hague, were not going to ask for a peace-at-any-price, but for a worthy peace',[107] and Maude Royden, a Oxford-educated university extension lecturer who was one of the first women to attend the Peace Society's executive committee.[108]

That the secessionists had a reasonable degree of support is indicated by the fact that 180 women wished to go to the Hague congress even without the blessing of the NUWSS. Twenty-four of these were granted passports, but were then stranded at Tilbury by a last-minute Admiralty ban on crossings of the North Sea. Because of this underhand move, only three British women managed to attend: Kathleen D. Courtney and Macmillan, because they were

---

[104] For Catherine ('Kate') Potter, Lady Courtney of Penwith, see S. Oldfield, *Women Against the Iron Fist: Alternatives to Militarism* (Oxford, 1989), ch. 2. Her eight sisters included Theresa Cripps (the first wife of Lord Parmoor), Margaret Hobhouse (mother of the absolutist objector Stephen Hobhouse), and Beatrice Webb (the Fabian intellectual): for a family history see S. Hobhouse, *Margaret Hobhouse and her Family* (privately printed, Rochester, 1934). It was presumably confusion with her that caused D. Birn to misname Kathleen D. Courtney 'Katherine' in his otherwise excellent *The League of Nations Union 1918–1945* (Oxford, 1981). When the two Courtneys sat together on the WIL's executive committee, they were distinguished in the minutes by the titles 'Lady' and 'Miss'.

[105] Cited in J. Vellacott, *Bertrand Russell and the Pacifists in the First World War* (Brighton, 1980), 51: this book gives a full account of Marshall's contribution to the NCF. For her previous suffragist career see J. Vellacott, *Liberal to Labour with Women's Suffrage: The Story of Catherine Marshall* (Montreal, 1993). Vellacott's next volume is eagerly awaited.

[106] Copies of their letters of resignation and the rejoinder by NUWSS president Mrs Fawcett are in the WILPF collection, file 4/1, British Library of Political Economic Science.

[107] Cited in *Labour Leader* (1 Apr. 1915), 1. See also J. Hannam, *Isabella Ford* (Oxford, 1989).

[108] PSM, 12 Aug. 1915. See also the excellent biography by S. Fletcher, *Maude Royden: A Life* (Oxford, 1989).

already in Holland, and Emmeline Pethwick Lawrence, because she travelled direct from the United States. The Hague congress of 27–30 April had 1,136 official delegates, and passed resolutions which echoed the UDC's policies: it was thus 'not a "Stop the War" or "Peace at any Price" demonstration', as a sympathetic account emphasized.[109] Even so, it attracted considerable publicity—far more than the smaller conference which G. L. Dickinson and J. Allen Baker apparently attended in the same city around the same time, which created an obscure society dedicated to the establishment of a durable peace.[110]

The Women's International Congress launched an International Committee of Women for Permanent Peace. Its British section, which prudently dropped the mention of 'peace' and simply styled itself the Women's International League (WIL), was formed at a conference in London on 30 September and 1 October 1915.[111] It soon attracted nearly 3,000 members, and proved an enduring body; yet through its existence its impact was lessened by its lack of a clear doctrinal identity. Its leading members mostly believed, with Royden, that on issues of peace and war there was 'no cleavage of opinion on sex lines'.[112] The Women's Co-operative Guild, which took up the peace-negotiations issue in 1916 and lent its support to the otherwise ailing Peace Union,[113] took the same view. Admittedly, a distinctively maternal interest in peace was sometimes asserted, for example, by both Isabella Ford and the Women's Peace Crusade, an informal campaign centred on the Glasgow ILP in 1916 and 1917, in both cases as a supplement to a mainly socialist analysis.[114] But a fully articulated feminist *pacificism* was not to find expression within the British peace movement until after the women's liberation movement developed in the 1970s.

The WIL was thus driven not by a desire to propound a gender-based analysis of war but by a belief that a section of the population which had previously taken comparatively little interest in the mainstream peace movement should be mobilized to do so. It did so with modest success, although

---

[109] *Concord* (July/Aug. 1915), 199–200.

[110] It was described as the 'Society for a Durable Peace' in Forster, *Goldsworthy Lowes Dickinson*, 165, but was listed as the 'Central Organization for a Durable Peace', with an address in The Hague, in *Peace Year Book 1921*, 64.

[111] H. Ward, *A Venture in Goodwill* (1925), 4–15. G. Bussey and M. Tims, *Women's International League for Peace and Freedom 1915–65* (1965), 17–21. J. Vellacott Newbury, 'Anti-War Suffragists', *History*, 62 (1977), 411–25. Wiltsher, *Most Dangerous Women*, 88–9. Hannam, *Isabella Ford*, 166–74.

[112] M. Royden, 'War and the Women's Movement', in C. R. Buxton, *Towards a Lasting Settlement* (1915), 131–41 at 136.

[113] Gaffin and Thoms, *Caring and Sharing*, 109. For an acknowledgement of the Peace Union's dependence on the guild see *HP* (Oct. 1923), 2.

[114] Hannam, *Isabella Ford*, 169–70. Liddington, *Long Road to Greenham*, 129.

by attempting to mobilize all women irrespective of the kind of pacifist or *pacificist* views they held, it could speak out only in general and therefore often bland terms on divisive issues. In this, it resembled the National Peace Council, without the excuse of being a coordinating body. Its main resource was the personal quality of its leading members: their services were soon in demand from other peace associations as they lost manpower to military service or imprisonment as conscientious objectors. Indeed, during the First World War women took on administrative roles for which Mary Cooke's short-lived co-secretaryship of the National Council of Peace Societies had been one of the few pre-war precedents. The WIL's first chairwoman, Mrs Helena M. Swanwick, the Danish-born sister of the artist Walter Sickert and an active suffragist but not previously a peace activist, worked for so many peace associations that she joked to a colleague about 'stomping the country again quite a lot for the UDC ILP WIL WPC (Do you know your alphabet?)'.[115] Royden had devoted herself to the Fellowship of Reconciliation until an unfortunate experience on its behalf reduced her appetite for peace work, as will be seen; and in any case personal differences with Swanwick limited her enthusiasm to keep working for the WIL.[116] Kathleen D. Courtney's role in the League of Nations movement and Marshall's in the No-Conscription Fellowship have already been alluded to. Although the WIL itself was given priority by some of its activists—including Swanwick, who declined Russell's attempt to poach her for the No-Conscription Fellowship,[117] and Ford[118]—it must have suffered from the dispersion of the energies of its most talented members.

The No-Conscription Fellowship (NCF), founded in November 1914, was the first peace association intended to appeal above all to socialist pacifists. It was a primary association that was created by a minority within a secondary association, the ILP, that wished to give priority to the peace question. The Labour Party endorsed the war; but the ILP, though affiliated to it, issued a separate manifesto on 13 August which took a very different position. The ILP's opposition to the war had three distinct strands: the radical *pacificism* of older members, such as MacDonald, who blamed the war on élites and vested interests and who therefore supported the UDC; the socialist *pacificism* of young militants, such as James Maxton[119] and his fellow Clydesiders,

---

[115] H. M. Swanwick, *I have been Young* (1935), 254–64. Swanwick to Marshall, 5 Feb. 1918, cited in Wiltsher, *Most Dangerous Women*, 193 ('WPC' being the Women's Peace Crusade).

[116] Fletcher, *Maude Royden*, 113–14, 129–32, 136–7.

[117] Russell, *Prophecy and Dissent*, p. lii.

[118] Hannam, *Isabella Ford*, 173–4.

[119] See his contribution to Bell (ed.), *We Did Not Fight*, 213–22; and G. Brown, *Maxton* (Edinburgh, 1986), 63–6.

who had little or no connection with any peace association; and the pacifism of young intellectuals, such as Fenner Brockway.[120] Its leadership having been weakened by the illness of Keir Hardie, who was to die in September 1915, the ILP succumbed to ideological confusion when these strands tangled with each other and with a pro-war minority during its annual conference at Norwich in April 1915.[121] At Newcastle the following year, however, the ILP conference endorsed, with only three dissenters, a resolution from the Bermondsey branch calling on socialists of all nations to 'refuse to support every war entered into by any government, whatever the ostensible object of the war, and even if such war is nominally of a defensive character'. This wording was pacifist, though socialist *pacificists* could support it on the assumption that for the foreseeable future 'any government' would be a capitalist one so there was no need to specify that in future a socialist state would be entitled to defend itself. Even so, a leading ILP politician, Fred Jowett, who believed that international obligations entered into by a discredited system of secret diplomacy had none the less to be honoured, insisted that the Bermondsey resolution was binding on the party as a collectivity but not on its members as individuals, and continued to speak up for 'national defence'.[122]

The ILP's pacifist element was of particular interest because it was for the most part of explicitly political inspiration. More than other socialist societies, the ILP had filled a social and ideological vacuum left by the decline, through secularization, of the Nonconformist denominations;[123] and in consequence its socialism provided an ostensibly non-religious substitute for Nonconformity's minority pacifism as well as for its mainstream *pacificism*. For example, Brockway was the son of a Congregationalist missionary in India,[124] and had been attracted by the socially conscious 'New Theology' preached during his Congregationalist phase by the Revd R. J. Campbell, whose belief in the divinity of man must have influenced Brockway's decision to become a pacifist. On becoming an ILP socialist he adopted an explicitly secular outlook,[125] though when gaoled as a conscientious objector he

---

[120] A. Marwick, 'The Independent Labour Party (1918–32)', B.Litt. thesis (Oxford University, 1960), fo.7. R. E. Dowse, *Left in the Centre: The Independent Labour Party 1893–1940* (1966), 21–2.

[121] The best account is in Robbins, *Abolition of War*, 44–5, 66–7.

[122] Marwick, 'The Independent Labour Party', fos. 11–12. F. Brockway, *Socialism over Sixty Years: The Life of Jowett of Bradford (1864–1944)* (1946), 130–3.

[123] As noted by S. G. Hobson, *Pilgrim to the Left: Memoirs of a Modern Revolutionist* (1938), 38–40.

[124] J. H. Brown, *Frances E. Brockway* (1905), 7.

[125] e.g. he emphasized the difference between his non-religious approach and Alfred Salter's Christian socialism: F. Brockway, *Bermondsey Story: The Life of Alfred Salter* (1949), p. vii.

compromised to the extent of describing himself for prison purposes as a Unitarian.[126] Similarly, Arthur Creech Jones, raised as a Methodist, had abandoned his religious affiliation on becoming a socialist, as he made clear to a tribunal hearing his claim for conscientious objection. He therefore described war as 'a denial of human brotherhood', and claimed: 'My motive in working in the Labour movement is because I regard life as sacred.'[127]

Admittedly, not all socialist pacifists went so far towards secularism as Brockway and Jones. A number were Tolstoyans whose anarchism had an evident religious dimension: an example was the journalist and first historian of the NCF, Will J. Chamberlain, who was to join the Society of Friends while imprisoned as a conscientious objector. Others were avowedly *Christian* socialists, such as three future Labour MPs: Walter Ayles, a trade-union official and former engineering apprentice, who during the war was active in the Fellowship of Reconciliation and joined the Society of Friends; James H. Hudson, a schoolteacher and temperance campaigner, who was already a Quaker;[128] and Alfred Salter, a medical practitioner in Bermondsey (where he initiated the local-branch resolution, just mentioned, at the ILP's 1916 conference), who had become a pacifist while going through an agnostic phase but had already returned to the Christianity he had learnt from his parents, members of the Plymouth Brethren, and now grounded both his pacifism and his socialism on that faith.[129]

The NCF grew out of a request by the ILP's political (or politico-religious) pacifists that men of military age who were determined to resist military service if it became compulsory should at once register their names 'so we may know our strength'.[130] It was prompted by a number of letters to the *Labour Leader*, which Brockway was editing, that asked: 'What are we socialists *going to do*?'[131] At the suggestion of his then wife, Lilla, Brockway issued an appeal in his paper on 12 November 1914, and received 'more than 150 names in six days'.[132] They included two intense and dedicated members of the ILP who represented the two extremes of political pacifism: Clifford Allen, a charming Cambridge graduate who had moved from evangelical Anglicanism to agnostic socialism and whose worst fault was excessive charity towards German propa-

---

[126] F. Brockway, *Inside the Left* (1942), 15–16, 91.

[127] 'Report of Case of Arthur Creech Jones held at the Spring Gardens (London) Appeal Tribunal on Friday, May 5, 1916': A. C. Jones Papers 1(2), fos. 41–7.

[128] Brockway, *Bermondsey Story*, 6, 17–19.

[129] Ibid. 1, 6, 14, 19, 71.

[130] *Labour Leader* (12 Nov. 1914), 6. See also T. Kennedy, *The Hound of Conscience: A History of the No-Conscription Fellowship, 1914–1919* (Fayetteville, Ark., 1981), 42–3: unless otherwise indicated, my account of the NCF derives from this definitive study.

[131] *Labour Leader* (5 Nov. 1914), 6.

[132] *Labour Leader* (19 Nov. 1914), 6.

ganda;[133] and C. H. Norman, an anarchist-influenced shorthand writer in the Law Courts, whose minoritarian temperament led him to quarrel with his fellow pacifists as willingly as with the state.[134]

At the end of November 1914, Brockway, Ayles, Hudson, Allen, and Norman had a meeting with Leyton Richards, a Congregationalist minister who had witnessed the workings of the 1910 Australian Defence Act while working in Melbourne and on returning to his home country had taken an interest in the ILP.[135] Along with a Glasgow supporter, A. Sutherland Campbell, they announced the existence of the NCF in the *Labour Leader* for 3 December. The name harked back to the ILP's 'No Conscription' campaign of exactly a year before,[136] and was chosen to appeal to voluntarists as well as opponents of the war. Even so, the NCF was from the outset explicitly pacifist. Its first statement of principles specified that its members 'refuse from conscientious motives to bear arms, because they consider human life to be sacred and cannot, therefore, assume the responsibility of inflicting death'.[137] Moreover, the manifesto which it was to issue in the summer of 1915 reiterated this creed and acknowledged that some of its supporters had 'reached it through the Christian faith' and others 'by association with international movements'.

The 1915 manifesto was also to insist that all NCF members were 'prepared to sacrifice as much in the cause of the world's peace as our fellows are sacrificing in the cause of the nation's war'.[138] When the government registered the population to find out how many men were in principle available for military service, the NCF's attitude was expressed in Ayles's comment: 'Are we desirous of skulking away unseen? Surely not.'[139] Even so, some who regarded themselves as principled opponents of the war tried simply to evade it. Arthur Horner, a former Baptist lay preacher who had joined the ILP under the influence of Brailsford's *The War of Steel and Gold* and was later to become a Communist and general secretary of the National Union of Mineworkers, escaped to Ireland, where he served in James Connolly's Citizen Army, though he eventually returned and was imprisoned.[140] And Fred Messer, a future Labour MP, managed to elude the authorities, partly by

[133] See A. Marwick, *Clifford Allen: The Open Conspirator* (Edinburgh, 1964).
[134] See Kennedy, *Hound of Conscience*, 46 n., 174, 276; Russell, *Pacifism and Revolution*, 67–8, 136–7; and F. Goodall, *A Question of Conscience: Conscientious Objection in the Two World Wars* (Thrupp, Glos., 1999), 6.
[135] E. R. Richards, *Private View of a Public Man: The Life of Leyton Richards* (1950), 44–8, 58–61. See Richards's letter in *Labour Leader* (26 Nov. 1914), 6.
[136] Croucher, 'Working Class Attitudes', fo. 492.
[137] *Labour Leader* (6 May 1915), 2.   [138] *Labour Leader* (9 Sept. 1915), 3.
[139] *Labour Leader* (12 Aug. 1915), 10.
[140] A. Horner, *Incorrigible Rebel* (1960), 9–13, 24–9.

changing addresses, until virtually the end of the war.[141] There must have been other cases, which in the nature of things passed unrecorded; but it is none the less striking that in neither world war was 'draft dodging', as it was to become known during America's war in Vietnam fifty years later, either condoned by the British peace movement or regarded by the British government as a significant problem.

The NCF recruited nearly 350 members by February 1915, and three months later had formed branches in London (where the future Labour MP Reginald Sorensen was local secretary), Birmingham, Sheffield, and Glasgow. Crucial to its growth was the appointment in July 1915 of Edward Grubb as treasurer: despite a lapse into crusading over the Armenian issue in the mid-1890s, he felt that a Quaker over military age had a moral obligation to help the generation at risk from conscription, and proved skilled at persuading his co-religionists to contribute generously in order to show that their 'particular form of religion' had not 'become for them a means of escape from suffering'.[142] By October 1915 the NCF was claiming a membership of 5,000, which was to increase significantly when conscription was introduced and a large proportion of conscientious objectors joined.[143]

The Fellowship of Reconciliation (FoR) was launched at the very end of December 1914 to cater for Christian pacifists. Since this had in effect been the Peace Society's brief when first mooted a century previously, the creation of a new fellowship was proof that the veteran association had long ceased to be effective. Having increasingly devoted itself to collaborating with *pacificism*, the Peace Society had failed to expound what Christian pacifists should do when confronted with a war. Many of those who joined the FoR had long been attracted to the absolutist position but had crystallized their views only after August 1914. For example, the Revd Richard Roberts was shocked into doing so only by the sudden disappearance of the German worshippers from his North London congregation. This made him realize: 'The conviction that war is essentially sinful had been for many years establishing itself in the Christian conviction of the country. But it had not been analysed far enough to provide the mass of people with a set of definite principles which they could apply to the situation that had arisen.' Roberts was convinced that between 'the uncompromising pacificist' and those 'at the opposite pole who did not feel that war in itself was unchristian' remained 'a great mass of people' who had yet to work out their views. For most of this mass 'the case

[141] See the entry by J. Bellamy in J. Bellamy and J. Savile (eds.), *Dictionary of Labour Biography* (9 vols., 1972–93), ii. 260–4.

[142] Bell (ed.), *We Did Not Fight*, 143. J. Dudley, *The Life of Edward Grubb 1854–1939: A Spiritual Pilgrimage* (1946), 66–7, 95, 107–8.

[143] Kennedy, *Hound of Conscience*, 55–6.

of Belgium was decisive'; but, he noted, after much agonizing a minority concluded that even the undoubted fact of Germany's and Austria's 'immediate responsibility' for the war in political terms did not render it compatible with Christianity.[144] A case in point was E. W. Barnes, a mathematics fellow at Trinity College, Cambridge, who was also ordained as Anglican clergyman: he became a pacifist a month into the war after being invited to give a Christian address to a gathering of soldiers and finding the task intellectually impossible.[145]

The credit for mobilizing this minority belongs mainly to Henry Hodgkin, a Quaker medical missionary who, having attended the abortive Constance conference, had been upset on his return to find some of his delegates supporting British intervention.[146] Hodgkin chaired a small and mainly Quaker gathering at Llandudno on 25–30 September 1914, which was marked by great spiritual intensity, as Darby, who attended it, reported to the Peace Society.[147] Then—with the assistance of a local mathematics don of Congregationalist faith, Ebenezer Cunningham—Hodgkin organized a meeting of 130 Christian men and women in Cambridge during the last four days of 1914.

Although some of those present, including a future Archbishop of Canterbury, William Temple, took a different view, the Cambridge gathering arrived at a majority verdict in favour of pacifism. It adopted a five-point statement which became the lasting basis of the FoR: this insisted that Christians were 'forbidden to wage war', being called instead 'to a life service for the enthronement of love in personal, social, commercial, and national life'—a hazardous vocation 'in a world which does not yet accept it'.[148] Several of the papers read to the conference were published in a book, *Christ and Peace*, edited by Joan M. Fry. A general committee was formed, with Hodgkin as chairman and Lucy Gardner, another ecumenically minded Quaker, as honorary secretary: this met for the first time on 13 January 1915, adopted the name Fellowship of Reconciliation a week later, and held weekly meetings which were notable not only for their length (all-day or even two-day) but also for their open-mindedness (Temple and a Presbyterian minister, A. Herbert Gray, being invited along, as non-pacifists, to help the FoR 'avoid schismatic ways').[149] It was a further indication of the growing importance of

---

[144] Fry (ed.), *Christ and Peace*, 17–19.
[145] J. Barnes, *Ahead of his Age: Bishop Barnes of Birmingham* (1979), 59.
[146] J. Wallis, *Valiant for Peace: A History of the Fellowship of Reconciliation 1914 to 1989* (1991), 3–4: unless otherwise stated my account of the FoR is based on this official history.
[147] PSM, 1 Oct. 1914.
[148] For the five points see Wallis, *Valiant for Peace*, 7–8.
[149] Minutes, FoR general committee, 19 and 23 Mar. 1915.

women in the peace movement that they filled six of the fifteen committee places and eighteen of thirty-seven places on the council which was created in the autumn when the fellowship completed its organizational structure and opened an office at 47 Red Lion Square.[150] Richard Roberts became full-time secretary in April 1915, but was called to a congregation in the United States in September 1916, and therefore replaced by Leyton Richards. Membership grew steadily, passing 2,000 within six months and reaching 6,983 by the armistice of November 1918.[151]

Unlike the Peace Society, the FoR understood that, in the light of Tolstoy's influential example of personal asceticism and the fact that many supporters of war were volunteering for military service, pacifists had to be seen to be suffering for their convictions too. As Roberts put it: 'Our Christian service must cost us at least what national service costs the soldier.'[152] The FoR also differed from the Peace Society in arguing that war could not be isolated from the social and international order which gave rise to it. It therefore insisted, again in Roberts's words, that 'simple pacifism is bankrupt. As well try to grow figs on thistles as endeavour to impose peace on the existing international system'; and it called for 'a "transvaluation of values" on a stupendous scale'.[153]

Defining what 'Christian service' and 'transvaluation of values' meant in practice, however, proved difficult. Some FoR members equated them with socialism; but neither its founders nor the majority of its members could accept so political an interpretation. Royden, a founding committee member, initially believed that they could be expressed by taking personal risks in furtherance of Christian ideals. Early in 1915 she published a pamphlet, *The Great Adventure*, which preached 'the heroism not of the battle but of the cross; the adventure not of war but of peace', and argued that Britain should have 'disarmed in the first week of last August' whatever the danger. She was already exhibiting signs of the tension between optimism and pessimism which was to cause her views on the peace question to fluctuate during the next quarter of a century. Her pamphlet thus began with the seemingly confident assertion that 'there would have been no war' had Britain disarmed unilaterally with the support of its people, because such a gesture 'would have had its effect'; but it concluded less reassuringly by likening such an action to 'the crucifixion' and claiming that the 'truest victory' was achieved only through 'outward failure'.[154]

---

[150] Minutes, FoR council, 11–12 Oct. 1915.
[151] Minutes, FoR general committee, 2–3 Mar. 1922 (appendix).
[152] Cited in Wallis, *Valiant for Peace*, 23.
[153] Fry (ed.), *Christ and Peace*, 30.
[154] A. M. Royden, *The Great Adventure: The Way to Peace* (1915), 7, 9, 12.

During its early months of existence the FoR was in its most activist frame of mind, holding a number of peace meetings, albeit mostly in the relative safety of churches. In June 1915, however, it decided for proselytizing purposes to acquire a horse-drawn caravan, which Royden offered to lead on a 'Pilgrimage of Peace' around the midlands. This great adventure resulted in a near-disaster at Hinkley where a hostile crowd burnt the caravan and menaced its occupants. After this terrifying experience Royden understandably 'wished to have time for thought and not do public speaking': in fact, she drifted out of peace activism altogether for several years, devoting herself instead to the role of pioneering woman preacher which was to make her name. And the FoR's committee complained of 'the definite deterioration' in public opinion in recent months, and after 'some divergence of opinion' decided to avoid 'indiscriminate propaganda'.[155] This act of prudence was largely attributable to Hodgkin, as his biographer, himself a distinguished pacifist, was to acknowledge:

The Fellowship attracted to its ranks the thoroughgoing pacifists who had no misgivings and no perplexities who wanted to commit the movement to a Stop-the-War Campaign. It also included many more who had reached and who held their convictions with difficulty, and still others who believed that their propaganda must be humble and constructive, free from negation and protest. . . . Largely through the guidance of the chairman the Fellowship concentrated on the higher, the harder task of conciliation.[156]

The FoR consequently became too quietist for a minority of its supporters, who looked for more engaged alternatives. For example, Theodora Wilson Wilson protested at 'the inaction of the General Committee'[157] and was therefore to associate herself with the more activist *Crusader* group. The latter grew up around a magazine, originally called the *New Crusader*, launched in March 1916 by Wilfred Wellock of Nelson in Lancashire, an Independent Methodist and ILP socialist who developed the tradition of respect for craftsmanship and dislike of industrialism associated with William Morris to an intensity of personal commitment comparable to Gandhi's. After Wellock was imprisoned as a conscientious objector, Theodora Wilson Wilson assisted the magazine financially and editorially, shortening its name to *Crusader*.[158]

---

[155] Minutes, FoR general committee, 21 July, 21 Sept. 1915; FoR council, 11–12 Oct. 1915. S. Fletcher, *Maude Royden: A Life* (Oxford, 1989), 125–6, 132–3, 156–84.
[156] H. G. Wood, *Henry T. Hodgkin: A Memoir* (1937), 154. See also Wallis, *Valiant for Peace*, 11.
[157] Minutes, FoR general committee, 18 Apr. 1916.
[158] W. Wellock, *Off the Beaten Track: Adventures in the Art of Living* (Tanjore, 1961), 39–44. Ceadel, *Pacifism in Britain*, 50–1, 71–2. A. Rigby, *A Life in Peace: A Biography of Wilfred Wellock* (Bridport, 1988), 25–38.

The FoR's short-lived Pilgrimage of Peace of June 1915 was one symptom of an increase—albeit slight and tentative—in peace activism which began in that month. A 'British Stop-the-War Committee' was formed by C. H. Norman and a young solicitor friend of Wesleyan faith, J. Scott Duckers. When the latter was brought to court in April 1916 for refusing even to register as a conscientious objector, his supporters attended wearing 'Stop the War' badges;[159] but in general the British Stop-the-War Committee had a negligible impact. At the same time the ILP launched its own campaign for peace negotiations, which the *Labour Leader* reported from 10 June to 19 August under the heading 'Towards an Early and Enduring Peace', but which seems to have elicited only a modest response. On 24–5 June the Friends' Peace Committee convened a representative private meeting of peace activists in the belief that 'the fact of the Conference being called by the Society of Friends should ensure that it is held under a spirit of divine guidance'.[160] Attended by Trevelyan, Ponsonby and MacDonald of the UDC, G. L. Dickinson of the League of Nations Society, Allen of the NCF, Heath of the National Peace Council, and interested individuals such as Russell, it in effect endorsed the UDC's principles as a basis on which the peace movement could unite; but although it established a committee to take its work forward, nothing substantial was achieved.[161] On 8–9 July a similarly cautious Conference on the Pacifist Philosophy of Life was held 'to deal with the permanent principles and enduring factors which are not affected by any transitory political situation'. Its speakers included Darby, Heath, Hobson, Playne, Ponsonby, and Russell; and it resulted in the establishment of a League of Peace and Freedom, with Edward G. Smith as its honorary secretary, which offered a socio-psychological critique of war as 'the result of a false attitude towards life in the individual and the community'.[162] This was one of many small associations enjoying a largely nominal existence at this time—the War Office claimed in 1915 to know of as many as 115[163]—and was still in existence in 1922, by which time its most distinctive features were its appeal to rationalists and Jews and its dislike of the League of Nations.[164] Finally, C.

---

[159] Kennedy, *Hound of Conscience*, 46 n., 65 n.. *Labour Leader* (3 June 1915), 9. Minutes, FoR general committee, 23 June 1915. J. S. Duckers, *'Handed Over': The Prison Experiences of Mr J. Scott Duckers, Solicitor of Chancery Lane, under the Military Service Act* (n.d.[1917]), 15, 20. After the war Duckers was to be secretary of the Wesleyan Methodist Peace Fellowship: Minutes, NPC Council, 13 Apr. 1921.

[160] Minutes, FPC, 3 June 1915.

[161] *Friend* (9 July 1915), 536–7. Vellacott, *Bertrand Russell and the Pacifists*, 23.

[162] League of Peace and Freedom, *Towards Ultimate Harmony: Report of Conference on Pacifist Philosophy of Life, Caxton Hall, London, July 8th and 9th, 1915* (1915), 171–2.

[163] Swartz, *Union of Democratic Control*, 117.

[164] See its journal *The Flame*, which first appeared in Mar. 1920; the issue for May 1922 is the last in the British Library.

R. Buxton, whose wife Dorothy was to contribute 'Notes from the German Press' to the *Cambridge Magazine*, made an individual effort to persuade public figures to advocate the exploration of peace terms. His first attempt in June 1915 failed; and when he tried again in September he found that even radicals did not think the time ripe, MacDonald replying that it was 'too soon' for such a campaign which was likely in present circumstance to 'have a hardening effect on opinion'.[165]

In the autumn of 1915 conscription became a more pressing issue, following the introduction in October of the 'Derby Scheme', the government's last attempt to make do with voluntary recruitment. The NCF held its first national convention on 27 November, at which it reaffirmed its pacifism by easily defeating a socialist-*pacificist* amendment from the Glasgow branch which, with the class struggle in mind, called for 'the omission from the Statement of Faith of the words "because they consider human life to be sacred, and cannot therefore assume the responsibility of inflicting death" '.[166] With legislation imminent, a National Council Against Conscription was formed at the end of 1915, to coordinate opposition to it, including from voluntarists who supported the war but opposed compulsion.[167] Its secretary was B. N. Langdon-Davies, whose move to the left since his days in the Garton Foundation has already been mentioned. After the battle against compulsory military service was lost, it renamed itself the National Council for Civil Liberties, though it was to be overshadowed by the NCF.

JANUARY 1916 TO MARCH 1917

A new phase of peace activism began when conscription became law on 27 January 1916, with effect from 10 February. It was accompanied by a provision for conscientious objection that was remarkably generous—not being matched even by the United States for over fifty years[168]—in two respects. First, it recognized non-religious objectors, instead of only Christians or, even more restrictively, only members of historic pacifist sects. Secondly, it allowed unconditional exemption: in other words, it did not always require either non-combatant service in the armed forces or alternative civilian service. The only group for which it did not apparently cater for were voluntarists objecting to

---

[165] MacDonald to Buxton, 8 Oct. 1915: C. R. Buxton Papers, box 1(2). See also K. G. Robbins, 'The Abolition of War: A Study in the Organisation and Ideology of the Peace Movement, 1914–19', D.Phil. thesis (Oxford University, 1964), fo. 149.
[166] Cited in Kennedy, *Hound of Conscience*, 70–1.
[167] Ibid., 80–1.
[168] Ibid., 83.

conscription rather than to war: one of these later admitted having pretended that his objection was 'ethical' in order to 'bump up' his claim;[169] and he was presumably not the only one to do so.

This generosity on the part of a coalition government that included Conservatives was an effort to appease Liberal opinion after the Home Secretary had resigned on voluntarist grounds.[170] It testified to the way in which generations of Quakers and members of the leading Nonconformist denominations had seen their various challenges to the British state as principled demands for liberties for all rather than as selfish requests for special treatment for themselves. Had the tone been set by the Mennonites, as to a considerable extent was the case in the United States, or by more recent sects such as the Christadelphians, the Seventh-Day Adventists, and the Plymouth Brethren, which were to provide a substantial proportion of Britain's 16,500 conscientious objectors but had contributed virtually nothing to the peace movement, parliament would have been less understanding of the case for conscientious objection. The government's appeasement of Liberal opinion worked: only thirty-four Liberal MPs voted against conscription, along with eleven Labour and sixty Irish members.

None the less many conscientious objectors were to feel hard done by. The government's desire to present conscription as following seamlessly on from the Derby Scheme led it to entrust its operation not to the courts but to tribunals which, initially under the control of the War Office, often reflected the less tolerant attitudes of society in general. In addition, the tribunals faced a genuinely difficult task for three reasons: conscientious objectors turned out to be more confused, more political, and more absolutist than expected.

First, the sheer incompetence with which objectors presented their cases to their tribunals frequently made it hard for the latter to recognize their sincerity. This was not surprising in view of the fact—privately acknowledged within both the FoR and the NCF[171]—that by far the largest category were ill-educated Christian sectarians who based their objection on biblical literalism and accepted non-combatant or alternative service. However, it has rarely received sufficient attention in popular histories of the subject, which have preferred to dwell on the shortcomings of the tribunals.

Secondly, socialist objectors, who were at least 1,191-strong according to the NCF's records and therefore outnumbered the 750 Quaker objectors, were harder than religious objectors for tribunals to evaluate. For one thing, political

---

[169] Goodall, *A Question of Conscience*, 7.

[170] Rae, *Conscience and Politics*, 26–32. My account of conscientious objection in the First World War derives mainly from this important book, but also from J. W. Graham, *Conscription and Conscience: A History 1916–1919* (1922).

[171] Wallis, *Valiant for Peace*, 20. Kennedy, *Hound of Conscience*, 94–5.

pacifism was a recent phenomenon. For another, socialist pacifists were easy to confuse with socialist *pacificists*, for whom the conscience clause was not intended. Admittedly, the Central Tribunal, which gave guidance to local tribunals, understood this distinction, directing correctly that a socialist who had 'a genuine belief that the taking of human life in any circumstances is morally wrong' was entitled to claim a conscientious objection, unlike one who 'would fight in defence of a State organised in a way he approves'. But it is unlikely that most local tribunal members grasped it.

Thirdly, an unexpectedly large minority of objectors, religious as well as secular, sought unconditional exemption rather than alternative service. They sometimes did so spontaneously, on the grounds, as one of them put it in private letter to his spiritual adviser, 'that this is the only logical stand to take, otherwise one allows oneself to be used in the organization "for the effectual prosecution of the war" '.[172] They were also encouraged to take this absolutist line by the NCF, which had become the peace association of the hour. Its second national convention, held at Devonshire House, the headquarters of the Society of Friends, on 7–8 April 1916, while a hostile crowd roared its disapproval from the street and attempted to break in, attracted 2,000 supporters, including an enthralled Russell, who was shortly afterwards reported by Catherine Marshall to be 'working night and day'[173] for the fellowship, despite being neither a pacifist nor a socialist. With Russell's approval, the convention endorsed a pro-absolutist policy,[174] though it did not follow through the logic of this position, as C. H. Norman thought it should, and declare itself a stop-the-war organization.[175] The Friends' Service Committee, which worked with the NCF and FoR in a joint advisory council, adopted a similar line.

However, the tribunals took the view, which the government had probably intended them to do, that unconditional exemptions should be exceptional. The future editor of the *New Statesman*, Kingsley Martin, was given one because he was assumed to have inherited the well-known pacifist views of his father, the Unitarian minister Basil Martin, though he subsequently chose to serve in the Friends' Ambulance Unit.[176] Otherwise most such exemptions went to Quakers,[177] whose pacifism thus reached a peak of public recognition at the time when it was being repudiated by an unprecedentedly large minority

---

[172] W. Bligh to Cadoux, 23 Feb. 1916: Cadoux Papers Box 18.
[173] Marshall to G. Cannan, 20 Apr. 1916, cited in Russell, *Prophecy and Dissent*, p. lviii.
[174] Kennedy, *Hound of Conscience*, 115–18.
[175] I owe this point to Kennedy, *Hound of Conscience*, 118.
[176] C. H. Rolph, *Kingsley: The Life, Letters and Diaries of Kingsley Martin* (1973), 44 and ch. 4.
[177] Rae, *Conscience and Politics*, 113, 130.

within the Society of Friends. But since the tribunals granted only about 350 unconditional exemptions, they were insufficient to satisfy even all Quaker objectors. Thus although Jack Catchpool received one, enabling him to work for the Friends War Victims' Relief Committee, his brother Corder, with whom he had served in the Friends' Ambulance Unit before the two of them developed qualms about thereby helping the war effort, received exemption from combatant service only—a ruling he could not accept.[178]

For these three reasons, therefore, although the tribunals granted some form of exemption to four-fifths of those who came before them—a higher proportion than during the Second World War—they none the less failed to satisfy at least a third of objectors.[179] There was thus a large pool of disgruntled applicants who had to decide whether to accept an unsatisfactory ruling. In the end over three-quarters of them decided to do so, a fifth undertaking non-combatant service in the armed forces and two-thirds alternative service of a non-military kind. Therefore only at most a tenth of all objectors—even including the fortunate 350 like Kingsley Martin and Jack Catchpool—were absolutists. Yet they caught the public imagination: they were respected for their courage in undergoing imprisonment (as, for example, Corder Catchpool did for more than two years), or, if inducted into the army, by resisting the military authorities (like the thirty-four who were famously taken to France and sentenced to death for disobeying orders until Murray's protest to Asquith led to their reprieve and the army's abandonment of this tactic, which was probably only a bluff).[180] By their well-publicized suffering, the absolutists did much to raise the profile of pacifism, which therefore acquired equality with *pacificism* as a meaning of the increasingly common word 'pacifism' (or 'pacificism', as purists still insisted). However, compared with the numbers of volunteers and conscripts serving in the army, the 16,500 objectors comprised only 0.33 per cent of their cohort; and their lack of political leverage was to become painfully apparent in the final phase of the war.

Initially, many absolutists, particularly those of socialist inspiration, were optimistic in their outlook. When asked by his tribunal if he would stand by while Britain was invaded, Allen replied: 'No civilised country would think of attacking another country unless that country was a source of danger owing to its being armed.'[181] Allen was also an optimist in respect of the domestic impact of conscientious objection, claiming before going into prison that the

---

[178] E. St J. Catchpool, *Candles in the Darkness* (1966), 22–4.

[179] Rae, *Conscience and Politics*, 131–2.

[180] For an emotive account, see D. Boulton, *Objection Overruled* (1967), 164–76. More sober assessments are offered by Rae, *Conscience and Politics*, 144–7, and Kennedy, *Hound of Conscience*, 142–3.

[181] Cited in Marwick, *Clifford Allen* 29.

conscription issue 'has given the socialist movement its chance'.[182] Similarly, Morgan Jones, a schoolteacher whose Baptist and socialist principles had made him a conscientious objector, insisted: 'Our fellowship is dealing smashing blows to militarism in this country.'[183] For a time, moreover, absolutists could take comfort in the fact that their suffering either in prison or in the army was earning them the status of martyrs. In particular, the Tolstoy-influenced Quaker-by-convincement Stephen Hobhouse, who had refused his tribunal's requirement that he serve in the Friends' Ambulance Unit, became the subject of an well-connected campaign for his release. A book was published about his case, which, though ostensibly the work of his mother Margaret (Lord Parmoor's sister-in-law by his first marriage), was in fact ghost-written by Russell.[184]

[margin annotation: nothing on Catherine Marshall]

The NCF's leadership soon came to realize that the treatment which absolutists faced was too demanding for all objectors to face; and it therefore gave increasing support to those accepting alternative service instead. Allen took this view despite his own unflinching absolutism, and was supported by Russell, who, being conveniently above military-service age, was to become acting chairman of the NCF while Allen and the other founders of that body were in prison. However, not only many NCF members led by Norman but also the Friends' Service Committee remained dogmatically anti-alternativist, thereby involving the conscientious-objection movement in much wearisome internal strife.

The challenge to conscription stimulated peace activism more generally in 1916: Wellock launched the *New Crusader*, as has been noted; a Unitarian Peace Fellowship was created by Basil Martin and Stanley Mellor;[185] the National Peace Council began to recover from its early paralysis;[186] and the British Socialist Party was captured by opponents of the war.[187] Most significantly, the UDC decided to launch a negotiated-peace campaign.[188] It was instrumental in the creation on 31 March 1916 of a Peace Negotiations Committee, which was to meet twenty-one times over the next two years, and did not officially wind itself up until after the armistice.[189] Two UDC members, Swanwick and C. R. Buxton, became chairwoman and treasurer

---

[182] Cited in Rae, *Conscience and Politics*, 84.

[183] Jones to Allen, 29 May 1916, printed in K. Robbins, 'Morgan Jones in 1916', *Llafur*, 1/4 (1975), 38–43 at 39.

[184] Vellacott, *Bertrand Russell and the Pacifists*, 210.

[185] Ruston, 'Unitarian Attitudes to World War 1', 276.

[186] As noted in Alexander, *Joseph Gundry Alexander*, 199.

[187] Croucher, 'Working Class Attitudes to War', fos. 111–14.

[188] For this campaign, see H. Weinroth, 'Peace by Negotiation and the British Anti-War Movement, 1914–1918', *Canadian Journal of History*, 10 (1975), 369–92.

[189] PSM, 23 Jan. 1919.

respectively, with Dunnico of the Peace Society as secretary. The new committee professed that its object was neither 'to end war at any price' nor to 'embarrass the government' but merely to explore whether acceptable terms were possible,[190] though this did not stop the windows of the Peace Society, which acted as its base, being broken following press condemnation of the campaign. Its main activity was to promote a petition which by the autumn of 1917 received 221,617 individual signatures and endorsements from Labour organizations with a total of 900,000 members.[191]

In addition to the UDC and the Peace Society, the National Peace Council, the WIL, the Women's Co-operative Guild, the Friends' Peace Committee, the ILP, the League of Peace and Freedom, the British Socialist Party, and the NCF were all represented on the Peace Negotiations Committee. The FoR also sent delegates but 'did not wish to cooperate officially', a sign of its intensifying quietism which irritated Dunnico when it was combined with criticism of his own association: in the autumn of 1916 Cadoux, who had previously 'had some minor connection' with the Peace Society, tactlessly pointed out that it 'had not condemned the present War' and had thereby failed 'to rope in the thorough pacifists, before the F.o.R. got hold of them'; Dunnico not only denied that this was true, but counter-charged that 'even now the F.o.R is making no organized stand against the War'.[192] The World Alliance for Promoting International Friendship Through the Churches indicated that it could not support the committee's petition.[193]

The formation of the Peace Negotiations Committee was a symptom of growing doubts about the war. Another, already mentioned, was the Women's Peace Crusade in Glasgow, a city where social, ethnic, and industrial tensions had spilt over into anti-war sentiment. It was started by Helen Crawfurd, a WIL member who had been politicized by Glasgow's 1915 rent-strike, and Agnes Dollan, wife of the city's prominent Irish-Catholic journalist and ILP activist Patrick Dollan. The two of them organized a women's peace conference on 10 June 1916, out of which a 'Women's Peace Negotiations Crusade' was launched. Though short-lived in its first manifestation, this crusade had a significant working-class following and was to revive the following year.[194] A further sign of loss of enthusiasm for the war was the disenchantment, albeit stoical, of H. G. Wells's novel *Mr Britling Sees it Through*: the UDC could not resist claiming that its celebrated author had 'very largely changed his view', on the grounds that 'Mr Britling writes pure U.D.C. doctrines.'[195]

---

[190] *HP* (Aug./Sept. 1916), 46.

[191] *HP* (Oct. 1917), 78.

[192] Kaye, *C. J. Cadoux*, 51. Dunnico to Cadoux, 5 and 7 Dec. 1917: Cadoux Papers, box 19.

[193] Minutes, Peace Negotiations Committee, 31 Mar., 14 and 28 Apr. 1916.

[194] Wiltsher, *Most Dangerous Women*, 148–52. Liddington, *Long Road to Greenham*, 115–17.

[195] *The U.D.C.* (Dec. 1916), 13; (Jan. 1917), 13.

This changing mood prompted the authorities to apply some pressure to the peace movement. The NCF faced several prosecutions for leaflets deemed prejudicial to military discipline. Almost its entire national committee was fined in May 1916, although five of its members—Ayles, Brockway, Barratt Brown, Chamberlain, and Fletcher—opted for imprisonment instead. Russell was fined soon afterwards and also refused to pay, though his goods were distrained so as to deny him the chance, which he then sought out of solidarity with the NCF's absolutists, to go to prison. In June, moreover, Russell was refused a passport; in July he was dismissed from his lectureship by Trinity College, Cambridge, which had previously shown generosity in allowing him two terms leave to undertake political activities; and in September he was banned from visiting militarily sensitive parts of Britain. In addition, the NCF's office was raided on 5 June;[196] and the Peace Negotiations Committee had some of its petition forms confiscated by local police forces later in the summer.[197]

Having been dissociated as far as possible by its leading advocates from opposition to the war, the idea of a league of nations made some progress during 1916. G. L. Dickinson hit on a way of presenting it which was acceptable to those who believed that Britain intervention had been the right decision in the circumstances. He admitted: 'For the actual outbreak of this war . . . a few powerful individuals in Austria and Germany were responsible.' But he went on to insist that 'the ultimate causes of war lie much deeper. In them all states are implicated.' His message was that 'the European anarchy is the real cause of European wars',[198] thereby identifying defencism with disorder and the league of nations with stability. Ten years later he was still promoting his conviction 'that whenever and wherever the anarchy of armed states exists, war does become inevitable', in the influential history of the pre-war epoch, *The International Anarchy 1906–1914*, for which he is best remembered.

Some members of the government, a three-party coalition after May 1915, were won over to a league. The most notable was an independent-minded Conservative, Lord Robert Cecil, who was persuaded by his experience of organizing the blockade that economic sanctions were a powerful weapon for a new international authority.[199] Another was a junior minister from the Labour Party, G. N. Barnes, who accepted the chairmanship of the League to Abolish War, a small association founded on 18 May 1916 to promote a

[196] Monk, *Spirit of Solitude*, 414, 463. Kennedy, *Hound of Conscience*, 126–31.
[197] Minutes, Peace Negotiations Committee, 16 Aug. 1916 (see also 15 Nov. 1916).
[198] G. L. Dickinson, *The European Anarchy* (1916).
[199] P. Yearwood, ' "On the Safe and Right Lines": The Lloyd George Coalition and the Origins of the League of Nations, 1916–1918', *Historical Journal*, 32 (1989), 131–55 at 132–5.

league of nations equipped with its own armed forces. Created by W. T. Stead's younger brother F. Herbert Stead, a community worker in Walworth, in an attempt to maintain his family's commitment to the Hague-conference ideal, it had only 170 adherents,[200] though its creation was a straw in the wind.

Much more important, on 27 May 1916 President Wilson endorsed 'an universal association of nations' at a meeting of the League to Enforce Peace. Since both Angell and G. L. Dickinson had expounded their views in the United States, British peace activists claimed some of the credit for Wilson's new thinking.[201] Moreover, when on 10 December 1916 the American president sent a note about war aims to the allied powers, G. L. Dickinson was convinced that it 'contained actual chunks from a memorandum by Angell'.[202] When the allies replied to the American president on 10 January 1917 they prudently claimed to support a league of nations too. Wilson's speech also encouraged Brailsford to write a pro-league book aimed at British and American liberals rather than a more left-wing readership: though still expressing the hope that a league would eventually evolve into 'an international organization which will unite nations as well as Powers',[203] Brailsford's internationalist message had thus become markedly more realistic in tone since the beginning of the war.

MARCH 1917 TO NOVEMBER 1918

The third and final phase of the conflict was inaugurated by the overthrow of the Tsar. 'At last, something good had come out of the war' was how Mary Agnes Hamilton remembered the almost universal response of the progressive circles in which she moved.[204] A rally to celebrate the event and call for a British 'charter of freedom' packed the Albert Hall on 31 March 1917, Russell observing: 'A meeting of the kind would have been utterly impossible a month ago.'[205] It set up a United Socialist Committee, dominated by the

---

[200] G. N. Barnes, *From Workshop to War Cabinet* (1923), 136–7. F. Herbert Stead, *To Abolish War: At the Third Hague Congress: An Appeal to the Peoples* (Letchworth, 1916), 1–3, 49. It last appeared in the *Peace Year Book* in 1932.

[201] Swartz, *Union of Democratic Control*, 135. L. W. Martin, *Peace without Victory: Woodrow Wilson and the British Liberals* (New Haven, 1958), 111, 124. Marrin, *Sir Norman Angell*, 161.

[202] Egerton, *Great Britain and the Creation of the League of Nations*, 45. G. L. Dickinson to Woolf, 25 Oct. [1916]: Woolf Papers.

[203] H. N. Brailsford, *A League of Nations* (1917), 311–12 (written in the summer of 1916). Leventhal, *Last Dissenter*, 136–9.

[204] M. A. Hamilton, *Remembering my Good Friends* (1944), 79.

[205] Vellacott, *Bertrand Russell and the Pacifists*, 157.

ILP and the British Socialist Party, which began to plan a convention to consider the implications for the British left.[206] In May the new Russian government announced that it sought a post-war settlement without annexations or indemnities, causing the *Bradford Pioneer* to claim: 'Russia has adopted a U.D.C. Programme', and C. R. Buxton to note: 'A year ago we were treated with contempt, as a negligible minority. Today we have become strong enough to be feared . . .'[207] And on 3 June the United Socialist Committee held a prominent convention in Leeds.

However, though socialist *pacificism* was given a boost by events in Russia, socialist pacifism learnt the lesson that a political revolution was doing more to challenge militarism than conscientious objection—a fact symbolized by the fact that, to Allen's dismay, the NCF as an organization was not invited to participate in the Leeds convention. Allen's instinctive response was to call in April 1917 for a work-strike by imprisoned absolutists in order to demonstrate that conscientious objectors had political clout too; but he failed to carry the NCF with him. Thereafter even he showed the first signs of losing faith in pacifism as a political method, starting to distinguish 'the merits of wise aggressiveness from violence' and to warn his fellow absolutists that the consequence of 'keeping ourselves unsullied from the world' was political impotence.[208]

Similarly, Russell drafted a letter of resignation from his acting chairmanship on 18 May. It explained that he was doing so because the NCF was

not a suitable body for action in general politics, because thousands desire an end to the present war for every one who accepts the extreme pacifist position. I think we ought as individuals to do what we can to help those who aim at ending the war, even if they do not accept the view that war is always wrong.[209]

Although he thought better of sending this letter, during the summer of 1917 he warned NCF members that the campaign in support of Russia 'will not be an out and out pacifist movement, and if it were it is not likely it would succeed in securing peace'.[210] He also declared his willingness to join the ILP.[211]

The popularity of the first Russian revolution in Britain was attributable less to revolutionary sentiment than to the hope that it might hasten the end

---

[206] Russell, *Pacifism and Revolution*, p. xxxiv.

[207] Cited respectively in S. White, 'Soviets in Britain: The Leeds Convention of 1917', *International Review of Social History* 19 (1974), 165–93 at 167; and Swartz, *Union of Democratic Control*, 157.

[208] Cited in Robbins, *Abolition of War*, 145.

[209] Russell, *Pacifism and Revolution*, 163.

[210] Cited in Kennedy, *Hound of Conscience*, 237. See also Monk, *Spirit of Solitude*, 496–9.

[211] Russell, *Pacifism and Revolution*, p. xxxvi.

of the war. At home, growing fatigue helped the Leeds convention to stimulate a revival of the Women's Peace Crusade, which, albeit still on a very
modest scale and with peace negotiations as only a part of its programme,
now spread from Glasgow to Lancashire, the West Riding, the Midlands, and
London.[212] At the front, though the British army escaped the mutinies which
were troubling its French counterpart at this time, the strains which were not
far below the surface were evident in the behaviour of the writers Siegfried
Sassoon and Mark ('Max') Plowman, who were both later to be 'Sponsors' of
the Peace Pledge Union.

In June 1917 Sassoon, already well known as a war poet and recovering
from a wound sustained at the front, contacted Russell with the intention of
stating publicly that the war, begun as 'a war of defence and liberation, has
now become a war of aggression and conquest'. Though encouraged by
Russell to do so, Sassoon was persuaded by his friend Robert Graves and a
sympathetic commanding officer to accept treatment for shell-shock rather
than press his protest to the point of a court martial.[213] Indeed, despite appearing on pacifist platforms in 1935–6 and becoming a Sponsor of the Peace
Pledge Union, Sassoon was never an activist, but expressed his views about
war through his creative writing.

By contrast, Plowman, who had been invalided home twelve months
previously with concussion and treated by the same psychologist as Sassoon,
went through on 17 January 1918 with a long-contemplated decision to
resign his commission. When facing his court-martial he prudently maxi-
mized the religious content of his thinking, arguing that 'while I cannot
believe in a transcendent God, I believe that God is incarnate in every human
being . . . From which it follows that killing men is killing God.'[214] But the
pamphlet he soon had published by a sympathetic bookshop manager
showed that his pacifism was essentially a political protest against industrial
society. He interpreted the western front as the catastrophic culmination of a
process which within sixty years had turned ordinary Britons into 'conscripts
of industrialism':

From suburbs and from hovels, from the tenements of industrial prisons, from the pig-
sties of the countryside, they came in their thousands . . . They have been shot and
starved to death. They have been blown to pieces. They have been burned with liquid
fire. They have been poisoned with phosgene. They have been mutilated beyond

---

[212] Liddington, *Long Road to Greenham*, 122–9. See also Mrs P. Snowden's article in *The U.D.C.* (Sept. 1917), 130.

[213] J. S. Roberts, *Siegfried Sassoon (1886–1967)* (1999), 107–8.

[214] His statement to his court-martial was published in *Labour Leader* (11 Apr. 1918), 5. I am
grateful to A. D. Harvey for showing me copies of Plowman's War Office file (Public Record
Office WO 339/50680). See also Ceadel, *Pacifism in Britain 1914–1945*, 57–8.

description. They have slowly drowned in mud. They have endured modern war . . . Suddenly, and almost against its will, the tyranny of western commercialism over-stepped the mark. Suddenly men awoke to the nemesis of unrestricted national competition, and tyranny allowed its headlong greed to push its victims into the mani-fest violence of actual war.

However, although thus blaming the war on western civilization's substitution of 'the ideal of national wealth for the ideal of national happiness', Plowman insisted that the ordinary soldier was not a revolutionary but wanted merely 'to live'.[215] He went on to expand his views in one of the first post-war books to advocate pacifism, and also wrote about his war experiences, albeit much less successfully than Sassoon.[216]

It was thus understandable that, from the summer of 1917, supporters of the war became concerned about morale. On 5 June the war cabinet discussed the need to combat peace propaganda. The following month, conscientious objectors began to be 'denounced in every music hall', as J. P. Fletcher of the Friends' Service Committee noted with concern.[217] As a result of press incite-ment, mobs launched particularly brutal attacks on meetings to follow up the Leeds convention: Russell only narrowly escaped serious assault on 28 July at the Brotherhood Church in Hackney, and was deeply shaken by the violence he witnessed;[218] and the next day Arthur Horner had his teeth knocked out in an even more unpleasant episode in Swansea.[219] The authori-ties also began to harass the peace movement. In August the UDC's account books were seized in a fruitless search for German funding. At the same time a warrant was issued to search Morel's house, resulting in his conviction for a purely technical offence: he had sent material to Romain Rolland, without realizing that the French anti-militarist was living in neutral Switzerland rather than his own country. It was with some justification that the UDC described Morel's imprisonment, which broke his health, as 'the most discreditable and mean persecution in modern British political history'.[220] Moreover, although a scrutiny of the records of the various peace associations

---

[215] M. Plowman, *The Right to Live* (1918), 3–4, 5, 10. The circumstances of its publication are mentioned in a book of the same title, edited by Plowman's wife Dorothy after his death, which included a reprint of this pamphlet: see M. Plowman, *The Right to Live* (1942), 24.

[216] See M. Plowman, *War and the Creative Impulse* (1919), and 'Mark VII', *A Subaltern on the Somme in 1916* (1927).

[217] See the handwritten note to that effect on the agenda paper for the meeting of the Joint Conference of Conscientious Objector Bodies, 14 July 1917: FPC minute book.

[218] K. Weller, *'Don't be a Soldier': The Radical Anti-War Movement in North London 1914–1918* (1985), 85–8. Monk, *Spirit of Solitude*, 501–2.

[219] D. Egan, 'The Swansea Conference of the British Council of Soldiers' and Workers' Deputies, July 1917: Reactions to the Russian Revolution of February 1917, and the Anti-War Movement in South Wales', *Llafur*, 1/4 (1975), 12–37 at 22–3.

[220] *The U.D.C.* (Feb. 1918), 188.

discovered nothing incriminating, the government decided to insist that all leaflets and pamphlets about the war or the ensuing peace settlement must be cleared by the press bureau before publication.[221] Although the UDC and NCF complied with this regulation, the Friends' Service Committee refused, as a result of which three of its officials—including Edith Ellis, the identical twin of Lord Parmoor's second wife—were imprisoned.[222] On 14 November 1917, moreover, the offices of the FoR and the Peace Negotiations Committee were both searched by the police, as part of a concerted series of raids on peace activists.[223] A week later parliament passed a clause disfranchising conscientious objectors for five years after the end of the war.[224]

Adding to the government's concerns was the fact that the Labour Party qualified its support for the war effort during the second half of 1917. It did so largely out of concern at the precarious hold which the new Russian government, in which the moderate socialist Kerensky was a key figure, had on power. Labour's representative in the war cabinet, Arthur Henderson, had visited Russia to try to persuade it carry on fighting and not to take part in a conference at Stockholm organized by the Second International in case socialists from Germany and Austria were also present. But, having discovered the weakness of Kerensky and his associates, who faced challenges from both reactionaries on the right and Bolsheviks on the left, he returned in late July convinced that they would not survive unless their opposite numbers in Britain and France were seen to be making constructive efforts for peace of the kind which the Stockholm conference symbolized.[225] Henderson therefore wished to go to Stockholm himself, and secured Labour's backing at a party meeting on 10 August. When his cabinet colleagues refused to let him attend, he resigned in order to develop Labour into a political force strong enough to stop British politics succumbing to a crisis like Russia's. Since Henderson undertook this party-reconstruction work in conjunction with MacDonald, who had only recently spoken at the Leeds convention, Labour's divisions over the war were beginning to be healed.

In November 1917 the Bolsheviks seized power in Russia. Their action had many consequences: it justified Henderson's strategy for the Labour Party; it forced the British and American governments to clarify their peace aims; it alarmed conservative opinion about the effects of the war on British society; and it made imprisoned conscientious objectors worry more than ever that the march of events was passing them by.

---

[221] Swartz, *Union of Democratic Control*, 178–90.
[222] Kennedy, *Hound of Conscience*, 242–3. Parmoor, *A Retrospect*, 123.
[223] Wallis, *Valiant for Peace*, 29. Minutes, Peace Negotiations Committee, 16 Nov. 1917.
[224] Russell, *Pacifism and Revolution*, p. xlvi.
[225] J. M. Winter, *Socialism and the Challenge of War* (1974), 243–63.

The second Russian revolution helped Labour settle on a policy satisfactory to both supporters and opponents of the war: the party in effect adopted the approach of the UDC, even though this had once been thought too pacifist by its moderate mainstream of the party and too bourgeois by its left wing.[226] The new consensus was approved at a special conference on 28 December 1917,[227] from which Dunnico came away gratified by the 'changed attitude towards the war' and the 'evidence on all sides of a sincere desire to find the basis of a democratic and enduring peace'.[228] The party retained representation in the war cabinet, G. N. Barnes replacing Henderson, and could not therefore be attacked as pacifist. But its slight distancing of itself from the war effort increased its political leverage in the short term and was to help it reap the benefits of post-war disillusionment in the long term.

The new Russian government also took a leaf out of the UDC's book by declaring in favour of self-determination, open diplomacy, and the avoidance of annexations and indemnities, and also by publishing the secret treaties which the Tsarist government had entered into. In an effort to keep Russia in the war, its military partners had to demonstrate that their own reasons for fighting were not 'imperialist'. Lloyd George therefore announced Britain's war aims on 5 January 1918, doing so, significantly, in front of a trade-union audience. And three days later President Wilson set out his idealistic 'Fourteen Points'. The Bolsheviks thus won the admiration of the British peace movement. The Peace Negotiations Committee's last significant act was to inform the Russian commissar for foreign affairs that it approved his 'object of securing a peace on the basis of no annexations and indemnities'.[229] And the WIL sent a telegram with a similar message, though it was somewhat offended at Trotsky's failure to reply.[230]

The Bolshevik revolution also intensified such worries—which with hindsight seem to have been surprisingly understated—as the right had been experiencing about the effect of the war on Britain's social fabric. Lord Lansdowne had been privately urging moderate war aims since October 1916, and went public with his worries in a letter which appeared in the *Daily Telegraph* on 29 November 1917.[231] The Lansdowne letter was an anti-war rather than a peace initiative: Lansdowne was a defencist, having been

---

[226] Brockway remembered UDC members as 'bourgeois to their fingertips': *Inside the Left*, 54.

[227] G. W. Shepherd, 'The Theory and Practice of Internationalism in the British Labour Party (with Special Reference to the Inter-War Period', Ph.D. thesis (London University, 1951), fo. 67. Swartz, *Union of Democratic Control*, 147, 163–9.

[228] PSM, 31 Jan. 1918.

[229] Minutes, Peace Negotiations Committee, 14 Jan., 17 Mar. 1918.

[230] Minutes, WIL Executive, 10 and 31 Jan. 1918.

[231] Swartz, *Union of Democratic Control*, 192–3.

Foreign Secretary in the Conservative government which had established the *entente* with France. But he received enthusiastic support from *pacificists*: in particular, the veteran Cobdenite F. W. Hirst, who had been ousted from the *Economist* in 1916 because of his belief in a negotiated peace and now campaigned for this cause through a new periodical, *Common Sense*, formed a Lansdowne Committee. This called for the former Foreign Secretary to be made Prime Minister, and—again significantly—looked primarily to the Labour movement for support for this proposal. On 25 February 1918 the committee arranged a large meeting, billed as a 'Lansdowne/Labour Conference'; and on 6 March it organized another, timed to follow up a second Lansdowne letter which was published the previous day.[232]

However, the success which the newly peace-minded Labour Party and the Russian revolutionaries had apparently enjoyed in forcing the British government to formulate its war aims showed up the lack of real impact achieved by Britain's conscientious objectors. The NCF was in any case debilitated by a deep-seated division between those who saw it as a welfare organization for objectors, and therefore felt obliged to negotiate with the authorities with a view to ameliorating the lot of the imprisoned objector, and those who saw it as an implacable subverter of 'militarism', and therefore opposed anything which smacked of collusion or compromise. And it had lost Russell's services: the dispute between absolutists and alternativists within the NCF had made him so jaded that he handed the acting chairmanship to Salter on 12 January 1918.[233] Ironically, before he could return as planned to academic philosophy an injudicious sentence in an article published in the NCF's journal for 3 January 1918 led the following month to Russell's conviction for sedition. No longer seeking martyrdom as in 1916, and fearful for his health after seeing what gaol had done to Morel, he ensured that he obtained the most lenient prison conditions available.[234]

On top of these problems came the evidence that Britain's labour and socialist movements had much greater potential for reforming international relations than a small primary association like the NCF ever could. The leading socialist absolutists, who had in effect been putting their pacifism before their political affiliation, now began doing the opposite. By February 1918 Allen was recording in his diary that he and Brockway now felt that the 'Socialist Movement has first claim on us'. Morgan Jones had come to the same conclusion and was becoming so preoccupied with his own parliamentary candidature that Allen, notwithstanding his own changed priorities, noted regretfully that 'everyone has lost heart in the usefulness' of the conscientious

[232] Robbins, *Abolition of War*, 151, 157–8.
[233] Russell, *Pacifism and Revolution*, p. li. Brockway, *Bermondsey Story*, 66, 69.
[234] Monk, *Spirit of Solitude*, 521–4.

objector's stand.[235] Understandably in view of the fact that he had wrecked his health on its behalf, Allen never publicly renounced pacifism as a private faith. But he was to devote himself to domestic issues through the ILP in the 1920s, and on taking up the peace issue again in the 1930s was to emphasize the political inefficacy of an absolutist rejection of military force and to urge pacifists to collaborate with *pacificist* measures. For his part, Brockway tried valiantly to combine his pacifism with support for revolutionary socialism, although this was to prove difficult by the late 1920s. And Morgan Jones, who was to have the distinction of being the first former conscientious objector returned to parliament, played no significant part in the peace movement after his release from prison.

On 3 March 1918 the Bolsheviks made a separate peace with the Germans at Brest-Litovsk. In contrast with their previous political initiatives, which had helped the peace movement in Britain, this greatly hindered it. First, the Brest-Litovsk agreement violated UDC principles, despite C. R. Buxton's attempt to argue that 'contrary to the usual belief, it does not contain any annexations or any indemnity'.[236] Second, the ending of the war in the east enabled Germany to launch an offensive in the west on 21 March which destroyed all chance of an immediate peace. The meeting of the Peace Negotiations Committee on 17 March thus proved to be its last.[237] And by the time the German offensive faltered in June 1918 public had become very intolerant of calls for a negotiated settlement. Official pressure on the peace movement was again increased. Police visited the offices of the Friends' Service Committee to search for unauthorized publications, as a result of which Edith M. Ellis served three months in gaol.[238] And the WIL suffered both the prohibition of a demonstration planned for Hyde Park on 21 July and the violent disruption of the open-air religious service which it was allowed to hold in Manchester.[239] However, a third Lansdowne/Labour Conference passed off peacefully on 31 July.[240]

During the spring and summer of 1918 the only peace activists who were working with the grain of official and public opinion were the supporters of a league of nations. Their period of influence had begun a year earlier: it was only when the United States entered the war in April 1917 that the League of Nations Society began to assert itself. Its first public meeting took place on

---

[235] M. Gilbert, *Plough my own Furrow: The Life of Lord Allen of Hurtwood* (1965), 108–9.

[236] *The U.D.C.* (Sept. 1918), 257.

[237] However, on 15 July 1919 it was to hold a 'final meeting' as a public commemoration of its work: see *HP* (Sept. 1919), 115.

[238] Minutes, FSC, 1, 21, 22, and 28 May 1918 and 3 Oct. 1918.

[239] Minutes, WIL Executive, 18 and 25 July 1918.

[240] Robbins, *Abolition of War*, 161.

14 May, soon after its second birthday: it was chaired by Bryce and addressed among others by the Archbishop of Canterbury—a sign of growing support for the league even within the Church of England—and by the South African General Smuts, the South African statesman who was shortly to join the British war cabinet and who favoured a league capable of tackling social and economic as well as security issues. At its annual meeting on 20 July, attended by forty-seven leading members, the society removed the faint ambiguity from point three of its original principles, committed itself explicitly to economic and military sanctions, and decided that a league of nations should be given a legislative competence.[241]

The League of Nations Society also collected signatures from public figures for a manifesto, which was sent privately to the Prime Minister on 8 August 1917, calling for an Anglo-American group to draft a league scheme. Cecil pressed the Prime Minister to commit himself, as did Barnes,[242] though Lloyd George declined to do so, apparently from a concern that discussion of specific proposals would distract attention from winning the war. The society set up an office, and expanded its membership from about 400 at the time of its 1917 annual meeting to 2,000 a year later. It benefited from the discussion of war aims early in 1918: for example, Lord Parmoor proposed a motion in its favour in the House of Lords on 19 March, and was backed by Lansdowne, although this debate was interrupted by the German offensive and did not resume until 26 June.[243]

The increasing likelihood that some kind of league of nations would be set up, if only to placate Wilson, caused some supporters of the war to see advantage in creating one immediately, taking as its basis the existing alliance. This was not a new idea: as early as the spring of 1915 L. T. Hobhouse had advocated 'the conversion of the existing alliance into a permanent League';[244] and although by the following year he been converted to the view of his radical associate Hobson that 'there is no final guarantee of a permanent peace except in the formation of the Liberal state', he still thought that a start might be made through the 'existing Alliance'.[245] Late in 1917, following the creation in November by the allies of the Supreme War Council, a league of allies began to find favour within governing circles. The cabinet secretary, Maurice Hankey, and a member of his staff, Philip Kerr (the future Marquess of Lothian), both became interested in this approach in December.[246] One of

---

[241] Winkler, *League of Nations Movement*, 66.
[242] Egerton, *Great Britain and League of Nations*, 77–9.
[243] Hansard, 29 HL cols. 476–570; 30 HL cols. 383–430.
[244] Hobhouse, *World in Conflict*, 93–4.
[245] L. T. Hobhouse, *Questions of War and Peace* (1916), 198, 223.
[246] Egerton, *Great Britain and League of Nations*, 69–70.

their former colleagues, Major David Davies, a millionaire coal-owner and Liberal MP whose wealth and impulsiveness was to make him one of the peace movement's quirkiest figures, took it up in January, along with his parliamentary colleague Charles McCurdy. Murray, Wells, and the journalists J. A. Spender and Wickham Steed also lent their support.[247] And by the spring of 1918 Lord Northcliffe's committee for propaganda in enemy countries was also persuaded that the immediate creation of a league would help to undermine the legitimacy of the governments of the Central Powers as well as find favour with progressive opinion at home.[248]

Some long-standing members of the League of Nations Society, notably W. H. Dickinson, were won over to an immediate league of allies. They were aware that their own society was thought mainly to consist of people 'still babbling of our former friendship with Germany', in McCurdy's words,[249] and that it had been shunned by Cecil out of distaste for some of its activists.[250] Davies, who made a large donation to the society, was therefore thought by colleagues to be 'getting control of the society' at the end of April 1918.[251]

But Davies underestimated the extent to which 'people like Wickham Steed . . . who want to turn it into an anti-German jusqueauboutisme society' incensed people like G. L. Dickinson, who knew from his colleagues on the Labour Party's new advisory committee on international questions that in left-wing circles 'the idea of a league now between the allies is treated by everybody as destroying the very idea of a true league'.[252] At the League of Nations Society's annual meeting on 14 June 1918 the 'jingoes were defeated by the cranks', as the novelist Virginia Woolf, who attended with her husband and fellow 'crank' Leonard, recorded approvingly.[253] Although Arthur Steel-Maitland, one of the sympathetic Conservative politicians whom W. H. Dickinson had been wooing as a potential member, assumed that the society had been 'practically collared by the Pacifist section of it', his former leader A. J. Balfour was more understanding of its reservations about an international organization confined to the allies, warning league supporters in the

---

[247] Winkler, *League of Nations Movement*, 71. See also the memorandum by D. H. Mills in the W. H. Dickinson Papers.

[248] Yearwood, ' "On the Safe and Right Lines" ', 145.

[249] C. A. McCurdy, *Freedom's Call and Duty: Addresses Given at Central Hall, Westminster, May and June 1918* (1918), 9.

[250] Cecil to Dickinson, 13 Apr. 1918: W. H. Dickinson Papers, MS Eng.Hist c.403, fo. 109.

[251] *Thomas Jones: Whitehall Diary*, ed. K. Middlemas (3 vols., 1969–71), i. 61–2 (entry for 30 Apr. 1918).

[252] G. L. Dickinson to Woolf, 14 May [1918]: Leonard Woolf Papers. G. L. Dickinson to W. H. Dickinson, 4 June [1918]: W. H. Dickinson Papers, MS Eng.Hist c. 403, fo. 118.

[253] *Diaries of Virginia Woolf*, ed. A. O. Bell (5 vols., 1977–84) i. 157–8.

Commons on 1 August: 'do not call your Allied combination a League of Nations; otherwise you will never have a League of Nations at all'.[254]

The unexpected rebuff from the 'cranks' stung Davies into launching a separate and conspicuously different body, the League of Free Nations Association, on 24 June. This established an office at 22 Buckingham Gate, engaged a former army officer as a full-time secretary, and later hired a prominent journalist, William Archer, as the salaried secretary of its research committee. Murray became the association's chairman, with Davies, McCurdy, Spender, and Wells as the other members of its provisional executive committee.[255] Though seeing itself as a more realist version of the League of Nations Society, it was in some respects the more utopian of the two: in proposing that the league of nations should enforce the decisions of the international court in justiciable cases it was closer to the recommendations of the Fabians and Hobson than to those of the Bryce Group;[256] and neither Wells's hopes for world government nor Davies's calls for an international police force stood much chance of implementation.

No sooner had Davies's new association been formed than the League of Nations Society, though for some time to come experiencing 'justifiable irritation over the circumstances attending Davies' secession',[257] reconsidered its refusal to cooperate. The failure of the German offensive improved the chances of the war ending soon and thereby reduced the significance of creating a league sooner rather than later. In addition, the new body had an access to the press and financial backing which the older one lacked. But the argument used by the League of Nations Society to justify its change of heart was that, with so many countries involved in the post-war settlement when it came, it would be helpful 'if there existed a league, the main lines of which had been accepted as providing a method whereby some powers at any rate have found it possible to secure peace among themselves'. On 26 July representatives of the two sides met over dinner at the National Liberal Club to discuss a compromise. Davies still objected to a number of League of Nations Society members as 'pacifists', causing W. H. Dickinson to insist in defence of his own organization that, 'whatever that word may mean', the pacifist label did not fit any member of its committee 'except perhaps Lowes Dickinson and Noel Buxton . . . although neither of them are among the "Stop the War" crowd'. When Murray hinted that W. H. Dickinson should 'leave

---

[254] Steel-Maitland to Dickinson, 19 June 1918: W. H. Dickinson Papers. Hansard, 109 HC col. 722.

[255] LFNA, minutes of informal conference, 24 June 1918; minutes, LFNA executive, 2 and 16 July 1918: LNU papers, 2/1.

[256] Its programme is set out in Winkler, *League of Nations Movement*, 73.

[257] W. H. Dickinson to Murray, 19 Aug. 1918: Murray Papers.

this League of Nations Society to Brailsford and Hobson' and join Davies's new association instead, he was rebuffed with the emphatic statement that these radical federalists had never 'been in any sense prominent in our affairs'.[258]

But Grey, whom the League of Free Nations Association wished to recruit as its president, urged the two bodies to overcome their differences; and Lord Shaw agreed to stand down if an amalgamation occurred. A referendum of the 2,230 members of the older society produced 1,330 votes for a merger and only 89 against—a decisive outcome which confirms its lack of a significant pacifist element. None of the 987 members of the newer one, all of whom were consulted, demanded a ballot to contest the decision. On 10 October, a week after the Kaiser appointed a liberal as Chancellor with a mandate to extricate Germany from the war, a successful joint meeting of the two societies was held with Grey in the chair. And on 8 November, just three days before the armistice, the League of Nations Union was born. The new body retained the chairman, the acting secretary (the original appointee having resigned through ill health), the headquarters, and largely also the programme of the League of Free Nations Association.[259]

It was not only liberal *pacificism* which ended the war with its expectations high: radical *pacificism* also hoped that its policies would influence the peace settlement. Although aware that the public wanted an outright victory, the UDC derived some comfort from the fact that the fighting was terminated by an armistice based on the Fourteen Points. Taking credit for Wilson's ideas, Morel now boasted that 'the Union's Policy has become the World's Peace-programme'.[260]

Even if these high hopes had proved justified, there would have been a period of controversy within the peace movement as liberals and radicals fought for ownership of Wilson's legacy. The most thoughtful *pacificists* were already aware that two contrasting inferences could be drawn from his critique of the old diplomacy and balance of power. For example, as the war ended Murray published a liberal attack on the radical view that democratic control would bring peace by bringing vested interests under control. His basic argument was: 'Wars spring just as much from national passions and ignorance as from selfish scheming. And in most wars of recent times you could find as much war frenzy in the Jingo mob as in the most plutocratic club or drawing room.' What was needed was improved international legal machinery, backed by 'the sanction of an economic boycott, of excommunication, and ultimately

[258] W. H. Dickinson to Murray, 24 Aug. 1918: Murray Papers.
[259] Mills document. Minutes, LFNA executive, 26 July, 25 Oct. 1918. Minutes, LNU informal conference, 9 Nov. 1918.
[260] *The U.D.C.* (Nov. 1918), 276. See also *Foreign Affairs* (July 1919), 4.

of a crushing war'. He summed up his rejection of the radical case with the pithy assertion: 'The principle that will solve the problem of war is not Democracy but Internationalism.'[261]

In the event, a much more pressing problem for *pacificists* than their own disagreements was the public's vindictive mood as soon as the war was won. It had endured much in the previous four years: contrary to some claims, information about the horrific nature of trench warfare had been in the public domain from the start.[262] It now expected to be rewarded for having, like Wells's Mr Britling, seen it through. In the first flush of victory, it welcomed the government's promises of a punitive post-war settlement. The general election called for December 1918 therefore brought defeat not only for almost all the opponents of the war but for many of its half-hearted support-ers too. There was, for example, no member of the UDC in the new House of Commons.[263] Thus, although both liberal and radical *pacificists* were more confident than ever of the relevance of their agendas, they were obliged to wait until the government and the public were prepared to listen to them.

The peace movement had faced the biggest crisis in its history, but had almost completely restructured itself and thereby survived. Its past efforts had paid off in the legislative recognition of conscientious objection, and in the will-ingness of a section of progressive opinion to embrace democratic control and a league of nations. Admittedly, the strains of war, the political progress made by the labour movement, and the need to placate the United States were more important than the peace movement's own efforts in propelling ideas into the political mainstream during the last phase of the war and securing conces-sions such as the specification of war aims. But the conscientious objectors, though much vilified at the time, had through the willingness of their abso-lutist minority to suffer hardship won much respect. Long a part of the British public scene, the peace movement had at last acquired fame, as symbolized by the transition of 'pacifism' (and, of course, its variant 'pacificism') from being a slightly self-conscious neologism to being a workaday word. However, it ended the war rather as it began: facing widespread hostility and intolerance.

---

[261] G. Murray, *The League of Nations and the Democratic Idea* (1918), 12, 23, 28.

[262] The view commonly put forward by literary historians that censorship and failures of communication prevented realistic accounts being published until after the war is refuted in E. Schneider, 'What Britons were Told about War in the Trenches', D.Phil. thesis (Oxford University, 1997).

[263] Harris, *Out of Control*, 221.

8

Revival,
January 1919–September 1931

The long decade from the beginning of 1919 to the eve of the Manchuria crisis saw a spectacular revival in the fortunes of the peace movement. Having experienced a major rebuff in the immediate aftermath of victory, it benefited from growing public disillusionment with the post-war world. The success of the Labour party gave a boost to the Union of Democratic Control in the early 1920s. But as the international situation improved in the second half of the decade, an overcoming of initial doubts about the League of Nations contributed to the unprecedented success of the League of Nations Union, which developed into the world's most substantial peace association.

THE HEYDAY OF THE UNION OF DEMOCRATIC CONTROL, JANUARY 1919–OCTOBER 1924

As Caroline Playne later observed, it was 'the aftermath of war which produced the most difficult years for the supporters of the Peace Movement'.[1] That there was genuine popular resentment towards those thought to have shirked their wartime duties was illustrated by the experience of Arthur Horner, as recorded by the historian Stuart Macintyre: in 1919 he 'encountered fierce opposition' within his South Wales mining community 'because of his anti-war record, opposition that was hardly softened when he explained to a lodge meeting how he "repudiated the rumours of his not being willing to fight," and stated that he was "willing to shoulder a rifle to fight for the working class, but not for the enemies of the workers" '.[2] Having joined John Connolly's Citizen Army in Ireland, as already noted, Horner had indeed shown himself to be prepared to fight in what he deemed a socialist cause.

Despite such a climate of opinion, the peace movement protested against the maintenance of the blockade until Germany had accepted final peace terms. The WIL was particularly incensed, its honorary secretary, Barbara

[1] NPC, News Bulletin (Mar.1928), 2.
[2] S. Macintyre, *Little Moscows: Communism and Working-Class Militancy in Inter-War Britain* (1980), 29. See also A. Horner, *Incorrigible Rebel* (1960).

Ayrton-Gould being first arrested for fly-posting handbills blaming the government for starvation in Europe and then fined for failing to submit a pamphlet, 'Our Blockade has Caused This', to the censor.[3] And Brailsford argued that future historians would regard it 'as the most brutal and the least excusable' of the war's crimes.[4] Peace activists also complained loudly when the Treaty of Versailles, signed on 28 June 1919, proved much harsher than the UDC in particular had wanted, and the League of Nations, which came into existence in January 1920, turned out to be more limited in its powers than even the League of Nations Society had wanted. They were also disappointed by the absence from League membership of Germany, Soviet Russia, and—as a result of a post-war retreat into isolation—the United States.

A degree of public disenchantment with the war soon began to set in for domestic and international reasons. At home, industrial unrest and economic depression undermined wartime promises of social harmony and prosperity to come. George Edwards, a veteran trade unionist who had spoken at recruitment meetings in 1914, was typical of many in becoming 'bitterly disappointed at the result of the war'; and he was elected as a Labour MP at a by-election in August 1920 after campaigning on the theme: 'The foreign policy of the Government stands condemned.'[5] Opponents of the war were soon rehabilitated: Morgan Jones entered parliament in August 1921 despite having been a conscientious objector; and on returning to the Commons at the November 1922 general election, MacDonald was restored as Labour leader, his stand against the war having suddenly become an asset. Labour was well placed to benefit from this change of mood since it had won over most of the leading Liberal critics of the First World War, including Angell, C. R. and Noel Buxton, Morel, Ponsonby, Swanwick, and Trevelyan. It was further assisted politically by the Liberal split between the followers of Lloyd George and of Asquith which was not repaired until 1923. Labour thus became the principal opposition party in 1922. And in January 1924 it took office, albeit briefly, with no fewer than fifteen UDC members among its ministers, nine of them in the cabinet, including MacDonald who was both Prime Minister and Foreign Secretary.[6] Most remarkably, in the general election which led to this first Labour government the most saintly of conscientious objectors, George M. Ll. Davies of the FoR, was elected as an independent but avowedly 'Christian

---

[3] Minutes, WIL Executive, 14 Apr., 12 May 1919: surprisingly, Liddington does not mention these episodes.

[4] H. N. Brailsford, *After the Peace* (1920), 41.

[5] G. Edwards, *From Crow-Scaring to Westminster: An Autobiography* (1922), 190, 192, 216.

[6] Swartz, *Union of Democratic Control*, 221.

pacifist' MP, albeit for the atypical University of Wales constituency and with only 35.7 per cent of the vote in a three-cornered contest.

The main international cause of disenchantment in Britain was the lack of progress towards the general reduction of armaments which was supposed to follow the almost complete disarmament of Germany. France felt too insecure to reduce its military strength substantially: it regarded the League of Nations Covenant as offering inadequate protection; and the American retreat into isolation had deprived it of an additional military guarantee. Yet there was little enthusiasm in Britain for offering France additional security. The peace movement was united in regarding a military alliance as a return to the discredited old diplomacy. Most defencists, aware that Britain's imperial commitments had increased and that its military, economic, and diplomatic resources had diminished, were very reluctant to commit an army to the continent again: even Winston Churchill was to refuse in a February 1925 cabinet paper 'to accept as an axiom that our fate is involved in that of France'.[7] Defencists were also encouraged by the development of the military aeroplane, a weapon whose potential had been glimpsed in the war without its limitations being demonstrated, to believe that a strong air force could deter attack on Britain and maintain some influence over western Europe. As a result, although Britain had by signing the Treaty of Versailles accepted an obligation to uphold the European order, it none the less hoped to avoid sending troops there.

As Franco-German tension mounted and the prospect of disarmament receded, all sections of British opinion became concerned. Pacifists preached Franco-German reconciliation; socialist *pacificists* insisted that this could occur only if capitalism were ended; and radical *pacificists* argued that Britain and France should both make concessions to Germany. However, others concluded that a measure of reassurance to France could no longer be avoided. Most liberal *pacificists* wanted to achieve this by enhancing the collective-defence and arbitration capacity of the League of Nations. Since amending the Covenant was difficult, they proposed a supplementary treaty whereby as many member states as possible would accept additional obligations to each other. However, their first choice, a multilateral security pact known as the Draft Treaty of Mutual Assistance, was rejected by the first Labour government, and their second, the Geneva Protocol, by its Conservative successor under Baldwin. Most defencists wanted either to offer France an alliance without specific military commitments or merely to guarantee a non-aggression pact between it and Germany: Baldwin's government rejected the former but implemented the latter in the form of the treaties initialled at Locarno in October 1925.

[7] M. Churchill, *Winston S. Churchill Volume, v. Companion*, part i. (1979), 415.

League supporters and defencists both hoped that if France could be reassured sufficiently to moderate its behaviour then Germany would respond positively. The former pinned their faith on admission to the league, which admitted Germany to full membership and began preparing for a World Disarmament Conference; the latter pinned theirs on great-power diplomacy to exploit the spirit of Locarno. Both assumed that improved Franco-German relations and a consequential reduction of armaments would mean that British pledges to France, whether made through the league or a conventional treaty, would not in practice be called upon. When the international situation improved for a while after the Locarno agreement, this strategy of making an essentially bluffing offer of security to France seemed to be paying off.

However, the delay in turning *détente* into disarmament soon worried the public again. Almost exactly ten years after the armistice, it became receptive to naturalistic accounts of trench warfare: previously such books—for example, the one written by Max Plowman—had flopped. The breakthrough was achieved by Edmund Blunden's memoir *Undertones of War* (published in August 1928), R. C. Sheriff's play *Journey's End* (premiered in December 1928), and Erich Maria Remarque's novel *All Quiet on the Western Front* (serialized in Germany during November and December, and published in an English translation in March 1929); and their success led to the reissuing of earlier works and the rapid concoction of many new ones.[8]

In addition, exaggerated predictions about a future war became commonplace. In response to France's plan to expand its air force in 1923, Ponsonby had warned the Commons:

In future a declaration of war will be followed in two hours by a shower of bombs on your capital and principal buildings, and by the time the next war comes we cannot foresee what diabolical engines of destruction are going to be constructed to devastate humanity and all the possessions of mankind. This is an appalling prospect, and I do not thinking that anything I have said is at all exaggerated.[9]

This scenario began to appear widely in popular fiction. For example, in 1926 the second Earl of Halsbury, a former officer in the air force, published a book, *1944*, in which the dictator Kernin bombed Britain with a colourless, odourless gas and reduced it to anarchy and cannibalism: this was one of at least eighty next-war novels published in inter-war Britain.[10] Halsbury hoped

---

[8] I have examined the response to war literature in the 1920s in M. Ceadel, 'Attitudes to War: Pacifism and Collective Security', in P. Johnson (ed.), *Twentieth-Century Britain: Economic, Social and Cultural Change* (1994), 221–41 at 229–34.

[9] Hansard, 167 HC col. 110 (23 July 1923).

[10] They are analysed in M. Ceadel, 'Popular Fiction and the Next War, 1918-39', in F. Gloversmith (ed.), *Class, Culture and Social Change: A New View of the 1930s* (Brighton, 1980), 161–84.

to encourage the country to strengthen its own bombing force; but, as Baldwin was to discover after famously predicting that 'the bomber will always get through',[11] the public's understandable first reaction to such warnings was to want disarmament more than a deterrent. It was because the government wanted to please public opinion, and not because it believed the problem tractable, that in December 1930 a draft disarmament convention was finally agreed and the following month the date for a World Disarmament Conference was finally fixed for 2 February 1932. By then, ironically, the world slump had greatly undermined such chances of success as disarmament had ever had.

Because during this decade of growing disenchantment with the First World War security issues were still being fudged and general disarmament was the focus of so many hopes, the peace movement was to a considerable extent still able to avoid the polarization over the issue of sanctions which was to overtake it in the 1930s. Pacifism was therefore unable to make its mark to the same extent as during the war. It thus failed as yet to complete its capture of the word 'pacifism', with the consequence that the phrase 'absolute pacifism' came into occasional use as a means of distinguishing it from an increasingly influential *pacificism*.[12] Socialist pacifism had the additional disadvantage of having its thunder stolen by socialist *pacificism*, which developed significantly at this time. On the other hand, the National Peace Council and Women's International League, which attempted to keep pacifists and *pacificists* in step with each other, enjoyed modest success. The intellectual currents which did best in the 1920s were first radical and then liberal *pacificism*. Thus during the first half of the decade the UDC dominated peace thinking, mainly because of its ideas were congenial to the rising Labour Party, though as an organization it was already past its peak. And during the second half the League of Nations Union, which had developed an unprecedented institutional base, came into its own as progressive opinion swallowed its initial reservations about the league.

Pacifists found the transition to peace particularly difficult. Having been braced to face the greatest unpopularity during wartime, they suffered the biggest psychological letdown at its end. The FoR, which had considered its future in the summer of 1918 when Richards accepted a call to a congregation in Liverpool in the summer of 1918, discussed 'a dissolution of the countrywide organization ... and the perpetuation only of a small nucleus committee' in September 1919.[13] However, it decided to carry on as before,

---

[11] Hansard, 270 HC col. 632 (10 Nov. 1932).

[12] See the National Peace Council's *News Bulletin* (June 1926), 5, where it was used to describe the position of the NMWM.

[13] Minutes, FoR general committee, 3–4 June 1918, 15 Sept. 1919.

albeit aware that its membership had fallen. Some former supporters had resigned, including Royden, who now preferred working for the League of Nations and accused the FoR of focusing too narrowly on 'the purely pacifist position';[14] others had lapsed; and in the autumn of 1920 the inspirational Hodgkin was to depart on a medical mission to China. A 'recount of the "live" membership' later in the decade was to show that it stood at not much more than 3,000.[15]

The fellowship still agonized over social issues, and was urged by a Christian-socialist minority 'to relate pacifism to specific issues', though a majority thought that the 'genius of the Fellowship was that it was not merely a propaganda body but something like a religious order'—a view promoted by its most influential inter-war figure, Percy Bartlett, a Quaker who worked first as secretary of its London Union and then as general secretary of the FoR as a whole.[16]

The NCF decided to take the plunge from which the FoR had drawn back: on 29 November 1919 it wound itself up, apart from three watchdog committees.[17] The NCF took this step because its basic *raison d'être* no longer applied: by then the conscientious objectors had all been released; and peacetime conscription had not been attempted. Domestic politics seemed to offer a more constructive opportunity for socialists, particularly with Labour making such rapid progress. Allen for one favoured the NCF's disbandment so he could concentrate on work within the ILP, which had become Labour's principal left-wing ginger group. His disenchantment with absolutism (though, as already noted, he continued to profess himself a pacifist) was soon to be made evident in a somewhat inappropriate preface to J. W. Graham's tribute to the conscientious objectors of 1916–19 in which he insisted that 'we should not exaggerate the value of resistance to conscription, judged as a method of spreading Pacifist or Socialist opinions'.[18]

The winding up of the NCF occurred at a time when socialist *pacificism* was attracting significant support for the first time. Lenin's *Imperialism*, published in 1916, had borrowed much of Hobson's economic analysis but insisted that the overthrow of capitalism itself, rather than democratic control, was the only solution. Though rarely cited directly in British peace propaganda, it indirectly influenced the claim, heard with increasing frequency as disenchantment set in, that the First World War had been an 'imperialist' conflict. Socialist *pacificism* was also stimulated by the fact that, after it had made a separate peace with

[14] Fletcher, *Maude Royden*, 212–13, 219. Minutes, FoR general committee, 2–3 Mar. 1922.
[15] Minutes, FoR general committee, 20–2 Feb., 30–1 July 1928.
[16] Minutes, FoR Council, 8–9 Sept. 1924. See also Wallis, *Valiant for Peace*, 35–52.
[17] Kennedy, *Hound of Conscience*, 274–81.
[18] J. W. Graham, *Conscription and Conscience* (1922), 13–23 at 15.

Germany, Soviet Russia had suffered military intervention at the hands of its former allies, who initially wished to retrieve some of their own stores from the country and hoped, if possible at low cost, to install a more helpful regime there too. The intervention continued for a while after the end of the war, but was unpopular in Britain, especially on the left: at its conference in June 1919 the Labour Party passed a resolution calling on the national executive committee and the leadership of the Trades Union Congress to make 'unreserved use of their political and industrial power' to oppose it.[19]

Britain rapidly terminated its involvement in Russia; but a newly restored Poland went to war with the Bolsheviks in a dispute over their unresolved border. In a celebrated incident London dockers refused to load a merchant ship, *Jolly George*, with supplies for Poland in May 1920. And the following month's Labour Party conference passed a resolution calling for a special congress to organize 'a general strike that shall put an end once and for all to the open and covert participation in attacks on the Soviet Republic'.[20] However, the Bolsheviks managed to turn the war round and launch their own revolutionary crusade westward. When Britain and France discussed a possible rescue of Poland, the Labour Party and the Trades Union Congress formed a Council of Action on 5 August 1920 to mobilize 'the whole power of the organized workers' to prevent British involvement in a conflict with Russia; and 350 local councils were almost immediately formed. Although intervention was rendered unnecessary by Poland's halting of the Red Army's advance on 16 August, rather than made impossible by efforts of the Council of Action,[21] this episode provided a rare example of British trade unions offering their industrial muscle as a secondary peace movement. Even Ernest Bevin, who was to become famous for helping to wean the labour movement away from pacifism and war resistance in the mid-1930s, supported this policy, and was to do so throughout the 1920s.[22]

Thus whereas before 1914 the labour movement had been overwhelmingly radical or liberal in its approach to international relations, after 1918 a considerably larger minority embraced socialist *pacificism*. One who had made this transition was Brailsford, whose first post-war book argued that 'by its greed and imperialism, Capitalism has evolved on suicidal lines',[23] and who for the next two decades was to insist that the overthrow of capitalism was the essential prerequisite of peace. The growing strength of socialist *pacificism* in the

---

[19] *LPCR* (1919), 156–61.
[20] *LPCR* (1920), 138–41.
[21] The best analysis of this episode remains L. J. Macfarlane, 'Hands off Russia: British Labour and the Russo-Polish War, 1920', *Past and Present*, 38 (Dec. 1967), 126–52.
[22] Ceadel, *Pacifism in Britain 1914–1945*, 55.
[23] Brailsford, *After the Peace*, 185. See also Leventhal, *Last Dissenter*, 163.

Labour Party was evident at its 1922 conference: Richard Wallhead managed without a vote to commit the delegates 'to oppose any War entered into by any Government, whatever the ostensible object of the War'; and when some of them attacked Wallhead's motion as 'purely Utopian and purely . . . pacifist', he defended it as both socialist and *pacificist*.[24] However, the prospects of socialist *pacificism* becoming the official policy of the labour movement were small. For one thing, radical and liberal *pacificism* remained powerful rivals. For another, socialist *pacificism* was favoured by Communists, with the consequence that it was viewed with great suspicion by the leaders of the Labour Party and the trade unions.

This increased interest in a socialist diagnosis of international relations, *pacificist* rather than pacifist though it mostly was, caused some socialist pacifists to feel that the winding up of the NCF had been premature. By the beginning of 1921 the inactivity of the Pacifist Union Committee, one of the NCF's three supposed residuary watchdogs, provoked Wilfrid Wellock's and Theodora Wilson Wilson's *Crusader* group to launch an 'Affirmation Against War', for which it collected 558 signatures. As a result of this modest initiative a No More War International Movement was established at a meeting in London on 24 February 1921. Beatrice C. M. Brown, a former activist in the Free Church Suffrage League who had joined the Wellock–Wilson group, became secretary: she was later to express annoyance that the *Crusader* group's role was overlooked and the NCF's former leaders were given all the credit for creating this new organization.[25] Even so, the No More War International Movement drew its leaders from the NCF: thus Chamberlain became its first chairman, and Brockway the first editor of its journal, *No More War*, which was launched in February 1922.

The new movement's choice of name was unfortunate. From July 1921 'No More War' was adopted as the title of a series of annual peace demonstrations held in several European countries on the anniversary of the outbreak of the First World War. A rare case of peace initiatives that were genuinely international—being supported even in Germany where the Weimar Republic was providing a liberal political framework for the first time—these 'No More War' demonstrations were originally organized in Britain by a broad-based *ad hoc* committee. The 'representative character' of the 1922 demonstrations, extending as they did 'from the League of Nations Union on the right, to the "War Resisters" on the left', was their 'most remarkable feature' in the UDC's eyes.[26] The co-organizers of those demonstrations were Major Clement Attlee,

[24] *LPCR* 1922, 200–3.
[25] See her letter to *Peace News* (27 Feb. 1937), 10.
[26] *Foreign Affairs* (July 1922), 14.

the future Labour Prime Minister but then a UDC supporter and rising politician whose address for that year's general election was to assert: 'I stand for
NO MORE WAR AND NO MORE SECRET DIPLOMACY',[27] and John Beckett, then an
ILP activist though later a member of the British Union of Fascists.[28] In 1924,
the final year of these 'No More War' demonstrations, the National Peace
Council took responsibility for them. Confusion between these two 'no more
war' activities was bad for both: the No More War International Movement
pointed out that it was no less hard on the *pacificist* associations participating
in the all-inclusive demonstrations 'to mix us up with them' than it was on a
pacifist association such as itself to confuse its 'purpose with anything less
than the absolute boycott of war'.[29]

Despite this confusion, the No More War International Movement retained
its name, except for one slight modification: it dropped the word 'International' on affiliating to the War Resisters' International. The latter had been
founded at The Hague in March 1922 under the name 'Paco', but moved to
Britain early in 1923, changing its name to War Resisters' International. In
relocating, it had narrowed its horizons from being an international campaign
against conscription to being an information service about conscientious
objectors. It was run from his Enfield home by a builder, Herbert Runham
Brown, a former absolutist conscientious objector with Congregationalist and
ILP affiliations. From the time that it became the British section of the War
Resisters' International, the NCF's successor called itself the No More War
Movement (NMWM), a name it retained until, broken by the Spanish Civil
War, it was absorbed into the Peace Pledge Union in 1937.

The NMWM's ideology was shaped both by the experiences of the absolutist objectors and by the utopian hopes to which events in Russia had given
rise among a section of the left. Its original membership pledge, a hundred-
word formula derived from the *Crusader* group's affirmation, began with the
absolutist requirement to hold that 'all war is wrong', whether 'offensive or
defensive, international or civil', and therefore to abstain from 'bearing arms,
making or handling munitions, voluntarily subscribing to war loans, or using
my labour for the purpose of setting others free for war service'. It then added
the positive requirement 'to strive for the removal of all causes of war and to
work for the establishment of a new social order based on cooperation for the
common good'.[30] Except that it did not mention Christianity, merely asserting

---

[27] 1922 election address, cited in R. Jenkins, *Mr. Attlee: An Interim Biography* (1948), 99. In
his autobiography Attlee was to describe his involvement in the 'general campaign for "No
More War" ' as having been 'in tune with the prevailing sentiment': *As it Happened* (1954), 97.
[28] Attlee and Beckett led a deputation to persuade the LNU to participate: minutes, LNU
executive, 4 May 1922.
[29] *No More War* (July 1922), 4.　　　　　[30] Ceadel, *Pacifism in Britain 1914–1945*, 73–4.

that war was 'treason to the spiritual unity and intelligence of mankind', this pledge could have been accepted by a member of the FoR, provided that the abstention from war was understood as an act of individual conscience and the establishment of a new social order as an essentially moral enterprise.

In practice, however, the NMWM was very anxious to dissociate itself from what might be interpreted as an individualistic conception of pacifism. It therefore insisted that it was committed to mass action against war and to fundamental social reconstruction. As Brockway was to put it, the movement 'repudiated "bourgeois" pacifism, wished to extend individual resistance to a general strike against war, and stood for "revolution by non-violence" '.[31] However, in thus trying to make socialist pacifism seem as efficacious, both internationally and domestically, as socialist *pacificism*, the NMWM, like the ILP to which it was closely linked, created a major difficulty for itself. Unless it grew into a movement strong enough to have some prospect of stopping war and making revolution, it was doomed to suffer a yawning gulf between aspiration and reality: it could not rest content with being a redemptive minority, as the FoR could. In the event it struggled even to survive. In its early days at 304 High Holborn it even had to beg and borrow its office furniture and equipment. And, despite the elaborate democratic procedures adopted in December 1922, including an annual conference and elections for its national committee, its membership—which even by 1927, when the next edition of the *Peace Year Book* appeared, was claimed to be a mere 3,000—was smaller than the FoR's. Its income, at £3,500 or less, was also disappointing. And although it managed to secure the services as honorary treasurer of Harold J. Morland, whose wartime resignation from the Peace Society's executive committee has already been noted, these were to prove an embarrassment during the summer of 1931 when he was tried for allowing false statements to appear in the report of a company he had audited: however, although the chairman of the business concerned was sent to gaol, Morland himself was acquitted.[32]

Being in effect the pacifist offshoot of an increasingly left-wing ILP, the NMWM was too doctrinaire to exploit the consequentialist inspiration for pacifism which was beginning to emerge in response to exaggerated expectations about aerial warfare. Russell urged it to try this line, contributing an article to *No More War* which set out the case for pacifism of a contingent rather than an unqualified variety. (Contingent pacifism does not assert that the next war will necessarily do more harm than good, merely that it is sufficiently

[31] Brockway, *Inside the Left*, 131–2.
[32] *The Times* (15 May 1931), 16; (31 July 1931), 12–13.

likely to do so that the safest course of action is to refuse to support it.[33])
Russell therefore argued that those concerned to preserve peace should

publicly and solemnly pledge themselves to take no part in war, no matter what the
issue may be. It is not implied logically that all war, always, is on balance harmful.
What is implied is (a) that most wars are harmful; (b) that the outbreak of war
produces an excitement which clouds people's judgement as to whether this particular war is harmful; (c) that no one can know that a war which is in progress will not
be harmful on the whole; (d) that therefore it is better to make a rule of abstaining
from war, to guard against war hysteria.

Yet despite so lucidly expounding contingent pacifism of utilitarian inspiration, Russell was neither a pacifist nor even a peace activist at this time: he
did not join the NMWM, support Ponsonby when he began advocating pacifism on explicitly 'utilitarian' grounds in 1925, or work for any other peace
association. It was not until 1936 that he was to commit himself—and then
only for four years as it turned out—to pacifism.

The National Peace Council also found the early post-war period a considerable struggle, though it managed to keep its national congresses going.
Heath left at the end of 1919 to work for the Society of Friends, and was
succeeded in April 1920 by another Quaker pacifist, Francis E. Pollard, who
was soon bemoaning 'the disappearance of societies and branches' from the
peace movement for which 'neither the Labour Party nor the League of
Nations Union' provided a satisfactory substitute.[34] By the autumn of 1921
financial difficulties made the council consider closing down.[35] In the event
it decided merely to release Pollard,[36] whose salary it could no longer afford,
and carry on with a part-time secretaryship, which for the rest of the decade
provided pocket money for a series of Labour politicians, beginning with Ben
Spoor.

Even so, in 1923–4, after J. H. Hudson had succeeded Spoor, the council
attempted to relaunch itself with a subsidy from the Cadbury family. That
Quakers were taking such an interest in the council reflected the fact that, as
a result of having lost several *pacificist* bodies during the war and of having
been unable to persuade the League of Nations Union to affiliate, it had tilted
in a pacifist direction. Indeed, the committee set up to relaunch it evidently
considered making it exclusively so; and although ultimately concluding,
'Absolute pacifist doctrine should not be the only condition of entrance', its
reason for doing so was: 'The development of pacifist feeling could be

---

[33] See Ceadel, *Thinking about Peace and War*, 145–6.
[34] Minutes, NPC Council, 29 Sept. 1920.
[35] K. Ingram, *Fifty Years of the National Peace Council 1908–1958* (NPC, n.d. [1958]), 12.
[36] Minutes, NPC Council, 26 Oct. 1921.

expected as a result of membership within the peace council.'[37] After much discussion, all the council changed was its name: persuaded by Hudson that 'the word "PEACE" is a stumbling block in some quarters', it decided in February 1924 to become the National Council for the Prevention of War, a title already used by its American counterpart.[38] However, since it was to reverse this decision with effect from November 1931, it will for the sake of simplicity here be referred to throughout as the National Peace Council.

The council's relaunch was effective for a while. Affiliations increased; and the ambitious Oswald Mosley—later notorious as the leader of the British Union of Fascists but then a Labour MP with strong interests in the peace movement—regarded it as having sufficient potential to be worthy of his services as chairman of its executive committee for a year. Mosley had served on the League of Nations Union's executive committee but disliked its timidity and collective responsibility.[39] He took on the chairmanship wanting the National Peace Council 'to take Executive action' on behalf of affiliated societies.[40] Yet this centralising aspiration failed; and Mosley soon lost interest. Moreover, although the council cleared its deficit, it failed to achieve the additional subscriptions for which it had hoped, its income being at best £3,000 a year. It was therefore unable to issue a *Peace Year Book* between 1921 and 1927. Moreover, some of its new affiliates were purely nominal associations, such as the League to Abolish War, which joined the council upon the death of its founder and was represented there by his widow.[41]

At the end of 1925 Hudson left to help Ponsonby promote his Peace Letter, and was replaced by Rennie Smith, a former Independent Methodist lay preacher who had been educated at Ruskin College, Oxford, and had worked as a Workers' Educational Association tutor before becoming a Labour MP. The new secretary experienced 'astonishment that so many peace societies existed in England', and 'toyed with the idea of reduction and concentration' before concluding that because each represented a distinct tradition nothing would thereby be gained.[42] He was to discover, however, that these traditions could still be brought together on certain issues. One was support for the 'Optional Clause', the proposal that Britain accept the compulsory arbitration of judicial disputes.[43] Though a minor measure, it became the principal focus of pro-league idealism following the defeat of the Geneva Protocol. The

[37] Minutes, Special Reconstruction Committee, 20 Dec. 1923, in NPC Council Minutes.

[38] NPC Council Minutes, 23 Oct. 1923, 7 Feb. 1924.

[39] Mosley to Murray, 25 July, 14 Nov. 1923: Murray Papers.

[40] Minutes, LNU executive, 22 May 1924.

[41] NPC Council Minutes, 30 Sept. 1928.

[42] 'Autobiography': Rennie Smith Papers, MS Eng.Hist. d. 296–7, fos. 204–5.

[43] For a full account, see L. Lloyd, *Peace through Law: Britain and the International Court in the 1920s* (1997).

National Peace Council hailed it 'as a very considerable advance',[44] and along with the WIL and the League of Nations Union collected 488,000 signatures on a joint petition during the summer and autumn of 1925.[45] Later, as will be seen, general disarmament was to prove a similarly consensual issue for the council to tackle.

The Women's International League enjoyed a relatively smooth transition into peacetime life, having been energized by the issue of the continuing blockade, as already noted. It decided not to change its name when, following a second international congress in May 1919, its parent body, the International Committee of Women for Permanent Peace, retitled itself the Women's International League for Peace and Freedom. (Only in 1950 did the WIL fall into line and add 'for Peace and Freedom' to its name.) None the less, its membership fell: having been 4,200 at the end of the war, it was given as 'about 3,500' in the yearly report for 1923 and 'over 3,000' a year later, and may in reality have been lower. In 1923 it partially concealed this problem by altering its constitution so to permit institutional affiliations: this enabled it to acquire a substantial indirect membership, notably from branches of the Women's Co-operative Guild.[46] Like the National Peace Council the WIL was to find the Optional Clause and disarmament useful as issues which its pacifist and *pacificist* wings could both support.

The main problem for the League of Nations Union (LNU) was that it had to establish itself at a time when the League of Nations itself was an object of considerable suspicion. In addition to being associated with an unpopular peace settlement, it had been constructed in such a way as to disappoint most progressives. The LNU did its best to distance itself from the Versailles Treaty: in May 1919 the chairman of its executive committee, Professor Gilbert Murray, was among twenty prominent members to sign an open letter criticizing it; and revision of the peace settlement was prominent on the list of objectives which the LNU published in its journal, *Headway*, until late in 1920. More controversially, the LNU was tempted also to campaign for amendment of the League Covenant: it established a special committee on reorganization which concluded in July 1919 that this should be a primary goal for the LNU. However, in the next few months the LNU decided that criticism of the league itself would give the impression that the institution was unworkable; and it therefore postponed the issue of Covenant reform until a

---

[44] Minutes, NPC Council, 9 Dec. 1924.
[45] Minutes, NPC Council, 11 Nov. 1925. WIL, *10th Yearly Report Jan.-Dec.1925*, 4. *HW* (Nov. 1925), 207.
[46] Bussey and Tims, *Women's International League for Peace and Freedom 1915–1965*, 29–33. WIL, *Yearly Reports*: WIL Papers. Liddington, *Long Road to Greenham*, 133–40.

more favourable moment.[47] Inevitably it thereby aroused the suspicions of other peace associations. For example, when in January 1920 the WIL invited Lord Robert Cecil to speak at one of its meetings it felt obliged to warn him that its members 'would need to be assured that the League of Nations Union would earnestly advocate the amendments to the Covenant and the Revision of the Treaty necessary to make the League a reality'.[48]

It had been Cecil who had persuaded the LNU not to demand reform of the League of Nations: having been one of its principal architects, he believed that it could be made to work as it stood, and knew the practical difficulties of changing its Covenant. Cecil's importance for the LNU can scarcely be exaggerated. He had resigned from the government at the time of the armistice in protest at the disestablishment of the Welsh church, though this did not stop him representing it at the peace congress. On his return from Paris he was therefore able to give considerable time to the LNU. He took over from Murray as chairman of its executive committee with effect from 25 June 1919,[49] and made his first public appearance on its platform at a big rally, also addressed by the Archbishop of Canterbury, on 13 July.

As Lord Salisbury's son and an established Conservative politician, Cecil provided reassurance to right-of-centre supporters. Yet his liberal views on many issues and his evident disagreements with a party dominated by what he later disparaged as 'a Blimp section'[50] made him acceptable to progressives. He was also at the height of his personal influence: with British politics in flux owing to the coalition government, the Liberal split, and the rise of Labour, he was central to speculation about the creation of a new centre party, though this proved to be just political froth.[51] Cecil's authority rescued the LNU from possible domination by the idiosyncratic David Davies, who at this time was campaigning not only for an international police force but also to locate the league's headquarters at Constantinople rather than Geneva.[52] Admittedly, Cecil himself had two significant flaws. First, he was temperamentally headstrong: as his nephew Lord David Cecil later pointed out, he 'lacked his father's melancholy and scepticism', being instead 'sanguine and positive and impetuous like his mother'.[53] Second, his privileged but segregated upbringing at Hatfield House had not equipped him

---

[47] Birn, *League of Nations Union*, 17–19.
[48] Minutes, WIL Executive, 22 Jan. 1920.
[49] Minutes, LNU executive, 25 June 1919.
[50] Viscount Cecil of Chelwood, *All the Way* (1949), 220. Colonel Blimp was a cartoon figure, created by the socialist David Low, who represented instinctive ultra-patriotism.
[51] See M. Cowling, *The Impact of Labour 1920–1924* (Cambridge, 1971), ch. 3 ('The Conspiracies of Lord Robert Cecil').
[52] See his circular letter of 22 Dec. 1919: Murray Papers.
[53] Lord D. Cecil, *The Cecils of Hatfield House* (1973), 294.

easily to understand the preoccupations of others.[54] For example, he never grasped how deeply suspicious the leadership of the labour movement was towards anything it regarded as Communist infiltration, a lack of empathy which produced serious ructions within the LNU in the second half of the 1930s. Moreover, like Mosley, who had experienced similar early isolation, Cecil found it hard to compromise or accept rebuffs, tending to threaten resignation if his suggestions were not accepted. None the less there was no doubt that he was a remarkably positive net asset for the LNU.

Cecil established a crucial working relationship with the LNU's other key figure, Professor Murray. The latter stood down to allow him to chair the executive committee but continued to make regular trips from Oxford to 15 Grosvenor Crescent, where the LNU's office was located from 1920 to 1939, as vice-chairman; and two of Murray's children—Agnes and Basil, both of whom were to die young—worked for a time on its staff. Moreover, Murray resumed the chairmanship in May 1923, when Cecil returned to government and was made LNU president jointly with Grey, and was to hold it for fifteen years. Cecil's and Murray's temperaments were complementary, the former being the motor and the latter the brake, as was shrewdly noted by the Spanish diplomat and academic Salvador de Madariaga, who knew both from his time as a League of Nations official.[55] They also shared the same liberal perspective on international relations: Cecil later admitted to a member of the Labour Party that he felt intellectually 'more at home with the Liberals' than with either of the other two parties;[56] and his admission to Murray early in 1939 that he had 'never believed that alliances and armaments are any real solution to the international position'[57] was an indication of how *pacificist* his instincts were.

Cecil and Murray steered the LNU towards becoming a body which appealed to Conservative and non-party opinion as well as to the more usual clientele of peace associations. It was because it did not wish to 'become identified in the public mind with a body composed mostly of pacifist and Labour organizations'[58] that the LNU did not affiliate to the National Peace Council, though it eventually agreed to co-opt one of the council's members onto its own executive committee, albeit in an individual capacity; and it also cooperated with it on specific issues, notably the Optional Clause and disarmament.

---

[54] See H. P. Cecil, 'The Development of Lord Robert Cecil's Views on the Securing of a Lasting Peace 1915–1919', D.Phil. thesis (Oxford University, 1971), fo. 15; and Lord D. Cecil, *Cecils of Hatfield House*, 294–6, 305.

[55] G. Murray, *An Unfinished Autobiography with Contributions by his Friends* (1960), 179.

[56] Cecil to Noel Baker, 27 Apr. 1932: Cecil Papers, Add. MSS 51107.

[57] Cecil to Murray, 9 Feb. 1939: Murray Papers.

[58] Minutes, LNU executive, 22 May 1924.

The LNU also offered the 'No More War' demonstrations 'watchful co-operation'[59] rather than uncritical support. When it set up local branches, it did its best to enlist the support of local élites: instructions from headquarters emphasized the importance of approaching the mayor and other dignitaries at an early stage.[60] Some pioneer advocates of the league idea found the LNU too concerned with its image. G. L. Dickinson soon resigned from its executive committee because he felt increasingly out of place, though he remained loyal to the league cause.[61] Wells soon left the union altogether, having rejected the league as 'not sufficiently Utopian'.[62] As for the more left-wing league pioneers, Brailsford played no part in the LNU, and Hobson and Woolf only very marginal ones.

The union's staff, initially inherited from the League of Free Nations Association, was different from that of the general run of societies. Its early acting general secretaries were right-wing former officers under whom headquarters became 'a happy hunting ground for retired Lieutenant Colonels', as Davies, who himself had risen to major, remarked.[63] The first permanent general secretary, who started work in February 1919, was Colonel H. F. T. Fisher, who was later described in *Headway*, apparently uncontroversially, as an imperialist and a Conservative.[64] He proved to lack organizational capacity, however, and was obliged to resign in May 1920, but was later re-engaged as a fundraiser with a brief to target Conservative donors.[65] During Fisher's tenure of office the person appointed to manage the editorial department was, astonishingly, Captain Francis Yeats-Brown, a professional soldier later famous for his autobiographical story *Bengal Lancer* and his near-militarist tract *Dogs of War!*.[66]

In July 1920 the LNU opted to replace Fisher by a high-powered administrator rather than a retired soldier and appointed Maxwell Garnett as general secretary with effect from October 1920. A brilliant Cambridge-educated mathematician who for the previous eight years had been a youthful and opinionated Principal of the Manchester College of Technology before resigning over a policy disagreement, Garnett conformed to A. J. P. Taylor's observation that league supporters were 'men of the Establishment, not Dissenters'.[67]

---

[59] Minutes, LNU executive, 20 Mar. 1923.   [60] *HW* (Apr./May 1920), 111–15.

[61] Forster, *Goldsworthy Lowes Dickinson*, 172.

[62] H. G. Wells, 'An Apology for a World Utopia', in F. S. Marvin (ed.), *The Evolution of World Peace* (1921), 165. See also Wells to Murray, 'Wednesday' [Dec. 1919]: Murray Papers. Wells does not seem to have attended the LNU executive after 14 Jan. 1919.

[63] Davies to Murray, 8 Oct. 1919: Murray Papers.   [64] *HW* (Oct. 1934), 196.

[65] Minutes, LNU executive, 6 May 1920, 15 Apr. 1925.

[66] This is apparent from Murray Papers file 182 fo. 195. There is however no reference to this in J. E. Wrench, *Francis Yeats-Brown 1886–1944* (1948).

[67] Taylor, *The Trouble Makers*, 171.

His commitment to the peace cause arose from his devout Congregationalism and his loss of two brothers and a brother-in-law in the war. He brought not only administrative order but an elaborate committee system to the LNU, drawing on his early experience in the Board of Education. But he had strong views about policy too, warning of the danger of the union being perceived as 'a party political organization', and constantly pushing the line: 'Education is the main business of the League of Nations Union.'[68] The LNU's pulling back from criticism of the peace treaties followed hard upon Garnett's arrival; and it was not long before his distaste for pressure politics caused Cecil to warn the executive committee that it was 'just possible' that the LNU might have to 'take strong action in becoming definitely opposed' to a government which became 'definitely hostile to the League', and to confide to Murray that he was 'beginning to be seriously disquieted by the want of a political sense in our staff'.[69] After four years of resisting what he regarded as partisan actions by LNU activists, Garnett was regarded as so 'tiresome' as to cause leading members of the executive committee to hope that he could be returned to a university headship.[70]

None the less, Garnett's anti-political strategy helped the union present itself as all-inclusive and respectable. More than half the members of the House of Commons joined the LNU's parliamentary committee. Party leaders all agreed to be honorary presidents, except MacDonald, who, believing that he had been blackballed in 1920 as a member of an LNU advisory committee, took pleasure in snubbing the union in return.[71] (MacDonald's willingness to become a vice-president of the Peace Society has already been identified as an illustration of the lengths to which he was prepared to go in this vendetta.) The LNU's executive committee even had Conservative members, even though sincere enthusiasts for the league—such as J. W. Hills, an MP who became a loyal vice-chairman—were probably outnumbered by those sitting on it in order to rein it back. Most remarkably, gross membership (that is: the total of subscriptions taken out, less actual resignations but ignoring non-renewals) grew so rapidly—from just over 3,000 in November 1918 to 60,000 by the end of 1920 and 432,478 four years later—that the LNU hoped that it would soon reach a million.[72]

However, Cecil in particular believed that there was little point in a sound

---

[68] Minutes, LNU executive, 16 June 1921. *HW* (July 1925), 130.

[69] Minutes, LNU executive, 16 June 1921. Cecil to Murray, 26 Aug.1921: Murray Papers.

[70] Cecil to Murray, 28 Oct. 1924: Murray Papers.

[71] Minutes, LNU executive, 26 July 1923, 26 June 1924. W.H. Dickinson to Murray, 12 and 15 July 1924: Murray Papers. Birn, *League of Nations Union*, 51.

[72] Birn, *League of Nations Union*, 25. Membership figures appeared regularly in the LNU's journal *Headway* until they started to decline in 1932.

reputation and a mass membership unless these were used to defend the league at a time when British governments were mostly treating it as at best an additional diplomatic mechanism rather than as the principal forum for a new kind of international relations. The LNU thus began to behave as a pressure group, albeit a moderate one, in addition to maintaining the educational role which Garnett always preferred to promote. In 1921 it took up the issue of general disarmament, its arms limitation committee producing a report that was generally well received in Whitehall.[73] In 1922, moreover, it was persuaded by Cecil to oppose Lloyd George's proposed bilateral pact with France as a relapse into the old diplomacy.

Initially, Cecil and other league enthusiasts had hoped on the basis of the wartime blockade that economic pressure had largely solved the security problem. In 1920, for example, Will Arnold-Forster—an intense young internationalist who had been trained as a painter and was married to Virginia Woolf's friend Ka Cox—had told the National Peace Congress: 'Blockade is to be the weapon, and the compulsory weapon, of the League of Nations, while military co-operation is optional.'[74] However, having subsequently concluded that France needed military reassurance to persuade it to disarm and that this must be provided multilaterally, Cecil and the LNU promoted the Draft Treaty of Mutual Assistance. They also showed great reluctance to condemn the French occupation of the Ruhr in 1923, thereby causing the LNU's own German sub-committee to resign in protest. Cecil continued to press for the Draft Treaty after joining Baldwin's Conservative government in May 1923.[75] This appointment proved short-lived, however: Baldwin failed to receive the mandate for protection which he sought in a general election in December, and resigned the following month. Cecil, who as a principled free trader refused to stand on a protectionist programme, went to the House of Lords as Viscount Cecil of Chelwood.

Cecil's wooing by Baldwin reflected the Conservative leader's need at that time for experienced politicians to replace recently departed coalitionists more than any desire to appease pro-league opinion. Indeed, despite its carefully constructed organizational strength, the LNU was working against the tide of popular sentiment in the early 1920s. Even if the *New Statesman* overstated the case when on 28 January 1922 it claimed that 'instinctive dislike of the even the most harmless "foreign entanglements" is only a little less deep in this country than in the United States', public sentiment was undoubtedly tinged with isolationism. The left accused the LNU of 'whitewashing' the

---

[73] Birn, *League of Nations Union*, 36–8.

[74] NPC, *Monthly Circular* (June–July 1920), 290. For a sketch of Arnold-Forster, see P. Gibbs, *Ordeal in England* (1937), 67–70.

[75] Birn, *League of Nations Union*, 36–48.

league—a charge it felt obliged to contest, whilst also insisting: 'Enthusiasm is a virtue.'[76] The right saw the league as at best an ancillary instrument only, Balfour insisting in a contribution to *Headway*: 'The "old diplomacy" is necessary, and the League is never likely to replace it.'[77] Admittedly, the Nonconformist denominations could be relied on: in August 1922 a member of the league secretariat attributed a pro-league speech by the Prime Minister to 'fear of the League of Nations Union as embodied in the Ministry of the Free Churches';[78] and characteristically it was a local Free Church Council which two months later convened the meeting in the Cyclone Works Welfare Room at which a Swinton and Pendlebury branch of the LNU was launched.[79] Liberals, for whom the LNU was in Michael Pugh's perceptive words 'a surrogate political party',[80] were no less supportive: indeed, Viscountess Gladstone, the late Liberal leader's daughter-in-law, thought it impossible 'to find any enemy of the League in the Liberal Party'.[81] But both Nonconformity and Liberalism were in decline. The LNU also found it difficult to recruit 'representative Labour Members of Parliament to serve on the Executive Committee'.[82] Mainstream opinion did not become optimistic about the league until the middle of the 1920s.

A comparison of the UDC with the LNU in the early post-war period 1920s shows that institutional strength does not necessarily correlate with intellectual influence. The UDC had become organizationally fragile. Although still quoting impressive figures for indirect membership, which apparently peaked at 1,418,075 in 1922,[83] it had lost much of its real support at the end of the war as affiliated organizations concentrated on their primary functions. Although gaining some new activists, such as Attlee, the union's real membership dwindled, probably falling from thousands to hundreds. Its annual meeting in November 1921 was acknowledged to be 'smaller than usual', with a mere 'score of men . . . and a few women' present.[84] Although perhaps as many as thirty[85] of its members were elected as Labour MPs in

---

[76] *HW* (June 1924), 111.

[77] *HW* (Jan. 1924), 4.

[78] F. P. Walters to P. Noel Baker, 2 Aug. 1922: Cecil Papers, Add. MS 51140.

[79] Minutes, Swinton and Pendlebury LNU, 9 Oct. 1922.

[80] M. C. Pugh, 'British Public Opinion and Collective Security 1926–1936', Ph.D. thesis (University of East Anglia, 1975), fo. 6. For a similar sentiment, see H. A. L. Fisher *et al.*, *Essays in Honour of Gilbert Murray* (1936), 18.

[81] Dorothy Gladstone to Murray, 30 Nov. 1923: Murray Papers.

[82] Minutes, LNU executive, 14 Feb. 1924 (see also 18 Feb. 1926).

[83] Minutes, 20th General Council, 10 June 1922: UDC Papers.

[84] *Foreign Affairs* (Jan. 1922), 102.

[85] Its official history claimed thirty: see Swanwick, *Builders of Peace*, 192. But its journal consistently claimed only seventeen, though its Scottish federation also claimed sixteen: see *Foreign Affairs* (Dec. 1922), 122–3; (Jan. 1924), 134.

November 1922, they were thereby diverted away from foreign-policy preoccupations, except for Morel who was content to be virtually a single-issue
politician.

Yet the UDC's message continued to be heard far beyond its shrinking
activist core. For example, its periodical, previously called *The U.D.C.*
but relaunched in July 1920 under the title *Foreign Affairs: A Journal of International Understanding*, enjoyed an authoritative reputation within the labour
movement, despite Morel's tendency as editor to allow leading UDC
members to puff each others' books;[86] and at its peak it attracted nearly
10,000 direct subscribers, with an equivalent number of copies being distributed through affiliated organizations and trade unions.[87] In the early 1920s,
for all its institutional weakness, the UDC was Britain's most significant
peace association.

The UDC's influence arose from the fact that its policies caught the popular mood. Morel told its general council in March 1919 that, although they
had 'not become effective in the new settlement of the world', the 'principles
of the Union had won hands-down in one sense'.[88] Its next annual meeting,
held on 17 October, adopted a new programme, this time containing six
points: democratic control, disarmament, free trade, self-determination, the
democratization of the League of Nations, and the revision of the peace
treaties.[89] As the public grew increasingly disenchanted with the post-war
settlement without yet taking the view that the war had been wholly in vain,
these policies—which indicated a scepticism about the outcome of the war
that fell short of complete repudiation—struck a chord. By the autumn of
1921 Morel was noting with satisfaction: 'Many to whom its name is still
anathema . . . are to-day upholding the very precepts which the Union was the
first to preach, blissfully ignorant of their source.'[90] Even so, he was aware
that this growing ideological acceptability was accompanied by a diminishing
organizational clout: when asserting early in 1923 that the UDC had for eight
years been 'the most active and creative medium' for effecting 'something
like a revolution of thought among enormous masses of our fellow-countrymen and women', he acknowledged that, even so, 'in most of the newspapers
. . . it is usually referred to in the past tense, as though it were
. . . dead'.[91]

Angell's post-war return to advocacy of UDC principles was a straw in the
intellectual wind. In the latter part of the war he had seemed to be moving

---

[86] In the course of three summer issues in 1921, Trevelyan reviewed Morel and Angell;
Ponsonby reviewed Hobson; and MacDonald reviewed Ponsonby.

[87] Cline, *E. D. Morel*, 122.   [88] *The U.D.C.* (Apr. 1919), 320.

[89] *Foreign Affairs* (Nov. 1919), 16.   [90] *Foreign Affairs* (Dec. 1921), 82.

[91] *Foreign Affairs* (Feb. 1923), 169.

towards liberal internationalism. However, after the armistice he left America for Paris in order to cover the peace conference. Disillusioned by what he saw, he returned to Britain to attack the Versailles Treaty in terms similar to Keynes, who praised his efforts,[92] and to help with a 'Fight the Famine Council'.[93] He also joined the Labour Party and became a parliamentary candidate in 1920 (though he failed to win an election until 1929), thereby making the commitment to the left from which he had drawn back in 1915. Indeed, he seems also to have made some sort of commitment to the pacifism which he had contemplated in 1915. In the early 1920s he was thus to make remarks in support of the efficacy of non-resistance which were too much for Mrs Swanwick, who was an extreme isolationist but not a pacifist.[94] As will be noted in the next chapter, he was to assert explicitly in 1933 that he was a pacifist in his personal beliefs. But it is clear that he later regretted such comments: in 1939 he was to insist that he 'never took the pacifist position of non-resistance';[95] and in his memoirs, in which he depicted his 'left turn' during the years after 1918 as a mistake, he omitted all reference his flirtations with absolutism.[96]

The failure of the post-war settlement to deliver either stability or prosperity enabled Angell to insist that *The Great Illusion* had been essentially correct in its analysis of the war's effect on the international financial system. In a 'sequel' published in 1921 he thus argued: 'Our minds are still dominated by the medieval aspect of wealth as a "possession" of static material such as land, not as part of a flow. It is that oversight which probably produced the war; it certainly produced certain clauses of the Treaty.' His renewed conviction that as 'interdependence increases, the limits of coercion are narrowed'[97] turned him into an opponent of French attempts to pressurize Germany into paying reparations. This criticism of both Versailles and France brought him into harmony with much of UDC policy, though not to the extent of becoming wholly isolationist or anti-league. In 1924, for example, Angell did his

---

[92] Angell, *After All*, 153.

[93] N. Angell, *The Peace Treaty and the Economic Chaos of Europe* (1919), 122. For this phase in Angell's career see also F. G. Miller, 'Norman Angell: Peace, Politics, and the Media 1919–24', Ph.D. thesis (Ball State University, 1969) and P. J. Gavigan, 'Ralph Norman Angell Lane: An Analysis of his Political Career, 1914 to 1931', Ph.D. thesis (Ball State University, 1972).

[94] For her disagreement with Angell, see Swanwick, *I have been Young*, 371. Swanwick later wrote: 'I am not the sort of pacifist who lays chief stress on the absence of force, though I hope I desire the minimum of force always' (copy of letter by Mrs Swanwick to Lord Allen of Hurtwood, 13 Nov. 1933: Noel-Baker Papers 5/147).

[95] N. Angell, *Must it be War?* (1939), 106.

[96] N. Angell, *After All* (1951).

[97] N. Angell, *The Fruits of Victory: A Sequel to 'The Great Illusion'* (1921), pp. xi, 7.

best to persuade MacDonald of the merits of the Draft Treaty of Mutual Assistance,[98] though it was anathema to most UDC members.

Morel had become more extreme since his ordeal in prison had left him susceptible to what he called 'nervous breakdowns'.[99] In an obituary Ponsonby was to admit: 'The fire consumed him; whether it disrupted his sense of perspective or dislocated his sense of proportion is not the point. There was one aim and one only. Before it all else must be sacrificed.'[100] To discredit France, the erstwhile champion of the Congolese was prepared in 1920 to publish a pamphlet attacking the inclusion of African troops in the French army of occupation in the Rhineland[101] and to pursue this pruriently racist theme in *Foreign Affairs*, admittedly with the support of other *pacifi- cists* such as Ben Spoor.[102] To discredit Britain, the parliamentary candidate and future MP was prepared to argue that 'the Constitution is not democratic but oligarchic, and the vote means—just nothing at all'.[103] And to discredit the Treaty of Versailles, the self-styled exponent of 'truth' was prepared to describe its war-guilt clause as 'the most disgusting falsehood which has ever polluted the pages of history'.[104] Indeed, his rhetoric was matched only by that of a still outspoken C. H. Norman, who in a book drafted in 1919 and published five years later accused Grey of treasonably fomenting a world war against Germany, and went on to insist: 'A crooked War ended in a twisted peace.'[105] Morel's sympathy was reserved for the Weimar Republic: after an interview with its Chancellor, Stresemann, he pressed the German case strongly in a private interview with the British Prime Minister, Baldwin, on 20 October 1923.[106]

Under Morel's increasingly intense leadership, UDC propaganda focused in the early 1920s on three themes. The first was that it was wrong to support France—a policy neatly summed up in the formula that 'security for Europe' should be the goal of British policy, not 'security for France'.[107] The second, arising out of hostility to the Treaty of Versailles, was that mechanisms of peaceful change were needed. On 25 January 1923, for example, the UDC's executive issued a statement calling for a 'world conference' which would among other things revise the peace treaties and establish 'machinery to ensure free access to mineral deposits in areas of the globe still undeveloped

---

[98] Angell, *After All*, 242.   [99] Cline, *E. D. Morel*, 145.
[100] *New Leader* (21 Nov. 1924), 4.
[101] The best discussion is in Cline, *E. D. Morel*, 126–8.
[102] *Foreign Affairs* (Dec. 1921), 81.   [103] *Foreign Affairs* (Feb. 1922), 124.
[104] *Foreign Affairs* (July 1922), 12.
[105] C. H. Norman, *A Searchlight on the European War* (1924), pp. xiii–xv, 152.
[106] S. Spear, 'Pacifist Radicalism in the Post-War British Labour Party: The Case of E. D. Morel, 1919–24', *International Review of Social History*, 23 (1978), 224–41 at 206–7.
[107] *Foreign Affairs* (Mar. 1923), 193.

... and thus put an end to a fruitful cause of war'.[108] It thus anticipated ideas which were to become commonplace in the second half of the 1930s. The third theme was that the League of Nations needed reforming. As soon as the League Covenant was drafted, Hobson insisted that it had been 'poisoned by the vices of autocracy, chauvinism, conservatism, and futility. The structure and composition of the League are thoroughly bad.'[109] In July 1919 Morel privately warned Murray that because 'the League falls very short of the essential of what we consider a real League of Nations ought to be', the UDC would 'point out where and why this League fails'.[110] And in October 1919, as already noted, the democratization of the league became part of the UDC's new six-point programme.[111]

Of these themes, criticism of the league was the most controversial because it was offensive to the LNU. The UDC was motivated in part by resentment at the way in which many league supporters had uncritically endorsed the war and abused the UDC in its vulnerable early days. Its bitterness on this score was apparent in its supercilious report on the LNU's second summer school, which met in Balliol College during the summer vacation of 1921:

Not in this Hall, perhaps, will you find a single man or woman whose vision pierced the machinery of the war, and perceived beneath the mask of falsehood and dishonest appeals to sentiment and chivalry the competing lusts, the vicious and selfish patterns, the mass of poisonous half-truths, which led the peoples to their dooms.[112]

Moreover, when its disparagement of the league and its supporters moved LNU members to protest, the UDC replied by noting that its own call for an 'international council' in September 1914 made it arguably the earliest public advocate of the league idea, and suggested: 'Those who charge us with hostility to the League may be reminded of this.'[113]

Ever since 1917 the UDC's principal organizational asset had been its close connections with Labour, which found the negativity—anti-France, anti-Versailles, and anti-league—of so much UDC policy well suited to its new role as principal opposition party. The formation of MacDonald's first administration in January 1924, ostensibly a breakthrough for the UDC as well as for the Labour Party, undermined this identity of interests. The union's executive and general council lost the services of those joining the

---

108 *Foreign Affairs* (Feb. 1923), 161.
109 *The U.D.C.* (Mar. 1919), 305.
110 Morel to Murray, 2 July 1919: Murray Papers.
111 It appears on the programme as printed on the cover of *Foreign Affairs* (Apr. 1922).
112 *Foreign Affairs* (Sept. 1921), 46.
113 *Foreign Affairs* (Oct. 1923), 71.

government. Morel remained its secretary and a mere backbencher, MacDonald having denied him the foreign secretaryship he coveted; and his resentment at his exclusion from office led him to take initiatives which irritated his former colleagues. For example, he tried to introduce a Commons resolution in favour of parliamentary control over foreign policy, thereby annoying even Ponsonby, who had accepted a junior post in the Foreign Office and had already agreed the compromise measure whereby the ratification of a treaty would be delayed by twenty-one days to give MPs a chance to scrutinize the text. Morel also criticized the government's main foreign-policy achievement, the Dawes Plan, for failing to end the reparation payments by Germany which the UDC executive described as 'morally wrong, politically unwise, and morally disastrous'.[114]

Most damagingly for the union's future, MacDonald realized on taking office that Franco-German tension had to be tackled by a more engaged policy than that favoured by the viscerally detached UDC. Although willing to kill off the Draft Treaty of Mutual Assistance, on the grounds that it was too similar to an old-style alliance, he felt obliged to give serious consideration to an alternative, the Geneva Protocol, which tried to reassure France through a compulsory-arbitration scheme. The misgivings which many UDC members felt about the Geneva Protocol were publicly admitted by Mrs Swanwick, whom MacDonald sent as a delegate to the League of Nations Assembly in Geneva; but, albeit 'shrieking all the way' (as she later told Angell) and speaking up for its arbitral but not its sanctionist features, she argued that the protocol should be given further consideration in order to avoid a diplomatic impasse which would destroy all prospect of disarmament.[115] Whether the Labour government would ultimately have accepted the Geneva Protocol is a contested question:[116] all that can be said for certain is that defeat in the Commons and loss of the ensuing general election in October 1924 saved MacDonald from a particularly difficult decision.

---

[114] Jones, *Arthur Ponsonby*, 142–3. *Foreign Affairs* (June 1924), 244.

[115] *Foreign Affairs* (Oct. 1924), 76; (Nov. 1924), 100–1. Angell, *After All*, 242. Swanwick, *I have been Young*, 403–4.

[116] D. Carlton thought it 'extremely doubtful' that the Protocol would have been ratified: *MacDonald versus Henderson: The Foreign Policy of the Second Labour Government* (1970), 27; and S. Schuker claimed that there was 'not the slightest chance': *The End of French Predominance in Europe* (Chapel Hill, NC, 1976), 356; but Marquand argued that there was a 'high probability' that MacDonald 'would have fought in its support': *Ramsay MacDonald*, 356.

THE HEYDAY OF THE LEAGUE OF NATIONS UNION, NOVEMBER 1924–SEPTEMBER 1931

The change of government in November 1924 proved to be a significant watershed for the peace movement: progressive opinion in general and the Labour Party in particular became more appreciative of the League of Nations; the UDC plunged into steep decline; pacifism enjoyed a modest increase in support; and—most spectacularly—the LNU came into its own. By the start of the next decade the peace movement was enjoying unprecedented unity and popularity as it prepared for the World Disarmament Conference.

In 1925 the second Baldwin government repudiated the Geneva Protocol and concluded the Locarno agreements as an alternative way of reassuring France. With Cecil again in the cabinet (though still not based in the Foreign Office, as he wished to be), every effort was made to make Locarno as compatible with the League of Nations as possible. Labour's advisory committee on international questions was persuaded that Locarno's final version introduced the league 'at every point'; Noel Baker concluded that it was '*simply* the Treaty of Mutual Assistance—minus, alas, Disarmament';[117] and the LNU's Chelsea branch claimed in its annual report for 1925 that 'the signature of the Treaty of Locarno testifies to the triumph of the League spirit', noting also that during the past twelve months it had for the first time become 'easy to proclaim openly and confidently one's support' for the league.[118]

By the logic of adversary politics, the fact that the Geneva Protocol had been rejected by the Conservatives made it posthumously popular with progressives who had until then had reservations about it. Swanwick accused the Foreign Secretary responsible for the protocol's demise, Austen Chamberlain, of having 'gravely injured something dear to us'.[119] And MacDonald told a journalist that the issue was now 'the Protocol against the Pact of 1914'.[120] He also wrote an article conceding that sanctions could be useful 'in so far as their presence on paper is a harmless drug to soothe the nerves'[121]— a remarkably explicit acknowledgement that he saw security assurances to the French as bluffs designed to induce a more conciliatory attitude towards Germany.

---

[117] ACIQ Memorandum on Locarno Pact, Nov. 1925: Lansbury Papers. Noel Baker to Murray, 30 Oct. 1925: Murray Papers.

[118] The Chelsea branch was one of a handful which regularly published its annual reports (in 1921 and 1923–40).

[119] Swanwick, *I have been Young*, 430.

[120] Cited in Shepherd, 'The Theory and Practice of Internationalism', fo. 303.

[121] Cited in Carlton, *MacDonald versus Henderson*, 27.

By the same token, the fact that the Conservatives could be accused of reverting to the old diplomacy led some formerly sceptical progressives to discover merit in the League of Nations itself, even as it stood. For example, while admitting that 'when the scheme of the League was launched, we did not all join in a chorus of hallelujahs', Francis E. Pollard noted in 1925 that 'things have moved on since 1919', and that the League Covenant and the Geneva Protocol, though 'marred . . . by the ultimate appeal to arms', should now be recognized as 'steps on the right road'. (Since Pollard specified that this analysis applied to his fellow pacifists as 'citizens acting corporately', when 'a very second best solution' was normally all that was available, and that in respect of their 'peculiarly personal action' their 'highest convictions' still applied, he was urging them to adopt a collaborative orientation rather than recant their faith.[122])

The Labour Party also became less critical of the league. The destruction of the Liberals as a major party in the October 1924 general election took much of the sting from the far left's constant refrain, repeated at the 1925 party conference: 'The policy of the League of Nations was the policy of Liberalism and not of Socialism'.[123] Admittedly, socialist *pacificism* was briefly stimulated by the general strike of May 1926. This prompted Bevin to write an article for the NMWM arguing that 'each individual Trade Unionist . . . must himself be a war resister'.[124] It also helps to explain why Labour's 1926 conference passed a resolution, proposed by Brockway and seconded by Ponsonby, calling on workers to resist 'any threat of war, so-called defensive or offensive' (though since this resolution also called for 'concerted action' with socialist movements abroad, it left unclear whether in a last resort unilateral war-resistance was being advocated).[125] However, even at that 1926 conference a new tolerance towards the league was apparent: for example, Russell's second wife Dora 'did not think it denoted a reactionary state of mind to endeavour to modify the League of Nations instead of perpetually tearing it to pieces and putting nothing in its place'.[126]

A leading role in the party's conversion to the league was played by Henderson, despite his early membership of the UDC. A Liberal at the start of his political career—indeed, he had been Sir J. W. Pease's election agent— and a Wesleyan all his life, Henderson was ideologically closer to liberal *pacificism* than to its socialist or radical counterparts. He also had acquired an understanding of European realities through his contacts in the Second

---

[122] F. E. Pollard, *Pacifism and the League of Nations* (FPC, May 1925), 4, 13.
[123] *LPCR* (1925), 255.
[124] *No More War* (Sept. 1926), 1.
[125] *LPCR* (1926), 256.
[126] *LPCR* (1926), 254–5.

International. Significantly, he had supported the Geneva Protocol, coercive provisions and all, even before the Conservatives rejected it.[127] Henderson was helped by two middle-class intellectuals who had known each other as undergraduates at King's College, Cambridge: Philip Noel Baker and Hugh Dalton. After launching the Friends' Ambulance Unit, the former had assisted Cecil at the Paris peace conference and worked for the League of Nations Secretariat before becoming became professor of international relations at the London School of Economics in 1924. And while serving in the First World War, Dalton had developed strong anti-German sentiments which he had been forced to conceal as an aspiring Labour politician in the early 1920s. He became enthusiastic about the league after a visit to Geneva in the autumn of 1925,[128] and published a sympathetic study three years later.

Thanks largely to Henderson, Noel Baker, and Dalton, Labour could claim in the 1929 general election that its policy was based 'firmly on the foundation of the League of Nations'.[129] When after that election Henderson became Foreign Secretary in a second Labour government, with Noel Baker and Dalton as his junior ministers and Cecil as a league delegate with his own room in the Foreign Office, a cleavage could be detected between their internationalism and the residual isolationism of the Prime Minister, MacDonald, and the Chancellor of the Exchequer, Philip Snowden, a former UDC member who regarded the LNU, of whose executive committee he had briefly been a nominal member, as 'a most harmful organization' and Cecil as 'just a Tory Jesuit'.[130] Angell, elected to the Commons at last, sat uneasily between the two factions, being increasingly pro-league in his views yet still personally close to MacDonald and loyal to the UDC; but he was left on the backbenches, causing a local newspaper to complain of the missed opportunity to make 'a Ministering Angell' of him.[131]

Having lost its special relationship with Labour when it became a party of government, the UDC was in crisis. By the autumn of 1924 even Morel was contemplating its disbandment in order to concentrate on *Foreign Affairs*;[132] and his unexpected death in November of that year made disbandment more

---

[127] F. M. Leventhal, *Arthur Henderson* (Manchester, 1989), 128–30.

[128] B. Pimlott, *Hugh Dalton* (1988), 104–5, 184–7.

[129] Labour Party, *Labour and the Nation* (1928), 41. See also H. R. Winkler, 'The Emergence of a Labour Foreign Policy in Great Britain, 1918–1929', *Journal of Modern History*, 78 (1956), 247–58 at 254–7; and id., *Paths Not Taken: British Labour and International Policy in the 1920s* (Chapel Hill, NC, 1995), ch. 4.

[130] Carlton, *MacDonald versus Henderson*, 19. Minutes, LNU executive, 10 and 17 May 1923.

[131] *Huddersfield Examiner* (13 Jan. 1931), cited in L. Bisceglia, *Norman Angell and Liberal Internationalism in Britain 1931–1935* (New York, 1982), 29.

[132] Cline, *E. D. Morel*, 122.

likely. However, the UDC resolved to stay in existence 'on a strictly economic scale', with Morel's daughter Stella serving as secretary until her health collapsed.[133] Its journal was kept going by Swanwick, who tried to make it less polemical. The UDC even attracted some new activists, including the novelists and close friends Vera Brittain and Winifred Holtby. But it was affected by the general erosion of support for its brand of near-isolationism. In 1925 it could not even agree to condemn the Locarno treaties. In 1928 it was split by an attempt to restrict its membership to anti-sanctionists only: when Hobson persuaded it not to, it lost the support both of Swanwick, who, having also quarrelled with the committee over her editorial policy, accused it of having 'no coherent policy', and of Ponsonby, who thought it had 'fallen rather badly between two stools'.[134] Its membership, in steady decline since 1918 and showing 'a heavy drop' in 1927, was down to 400 in 1929 and 200 three years later.[135]

By the spring of 1931 the UDC could no longer afford to issue *Foreign Affairs*, which Angell had edited for the three years since Swanwick's resignation, except as a supplement to *Time and Tide*. The union again contemplated winding itself up, but continued because Dorothy Woodman, who had been appointed its secretary in 1928, wished to use its name for her activities. Formerly an activist in both the WIL and the NMWM and later Kingsley Martin's common-law wife, she was close to Communism (and also to an aide of the brilliant Comintern agent, Willi Münzenberg, deviser of the front-organization strategy).[136] The high point of Woodman's stewardship was the publication in 1932 of *The Secret International*, a pamphlet on the arms trade which was followed up by the private purchase of shares in arms firms in order that its members could ask awkward questions at shareholders' meetings.[137] Woodman's exposé of the arms industry attracted so much attention as to give a misleading impression of the UDC's institutional significance: when a young peace activist sought out what he expected to be 'a formidable organization', he discovered that 'in fact it was largely Dorothy herself, aided by a few faithful fellow spirits, most of them obscure and humble'.[138] Although it maintained a nominal existence until as late as 1967, when it

---

[133] Minutes, 23rd general council, 17 Dec. 1924; 10th annual meeting, 13 Mar. 1925: UDC Papers.
[134] Minutes, 25th general council, 23 Oct. 1925, 13th annual meeting, 9–10 Mar. 1928; Ponsonby to Miss Webb, 9 May 1928: UDC Papers. Swanwick, *I have been Young*, 428–9, 461–3.
[135] Minutes, 30th meeting, 18 Nov. 1927; 33rd meeting, 13 Mar. 1929, 37th meeting, 8 July 1932: UDC Papers.
[136] Rolph, *Kingsley*, 214.
[137] P. Berry and M. Bostridge, *Vera Brittain: A Life* (1995), 352.
[138] B. Nichols, *All I could Never be: Some Recollections* (1949), 213.

donated its archive to the University of Hull, the UDC's demise as an important association can be dated to the mid-1920s.

By contrast pacifism found some crumbs of comfort in an improving international climate. The NMWM moved into larger premises, at 11 Doughty Street, in March 1925. Ayles, who had managed to raise money for the movement from his fellow Quakers, was appointed as an additional secretary in 1926, joining Lucy A. Cox, a former schoolteacher who had succeeded Beatrice Brown on her retirement. Under their joint leadership the NMWM shortened its unwieldy membership pledge, launched a petition in favour of total disarmament which attracted 40,000 signatures,[139] and expanded the monthly circulation of *No More War* to 12,000. Morale was further raised by the ILP's re-endorsement of pacifism at its 1925 and 1926 conferences. The NMWM's growing optimism was reflected in the way it presented its pacifism: for example, Wellock now made the bold claim that 'given a rational Foreign Policy, a nation might not only disarm, but rest assured that its deed would inspire such confidence as to render it and its belongings sacrosanct'.[140]

However, the movement's non-violent message was compromised by the enthusiasm which a minority showed for the class struggle. When an editorial in *No More War* described the 1926 general strike as 'the greatest and most impressive demonstration of passive resistance this country has ever witnessed', a vigorous debate ensued in which Harold Bing, who had been one of the First World War's youngest absolutists and was to remain a pacifist throughout his life, argued that the strike had differed from conscientious objection in being 'an attempt to coerce others'. This view was shared by Ayles, even though he praised the strike as 'a marvellously pacific demonstration'. However, Brockway retorted that a strike against war, which all socialist pacifists supported, would also be coercive, and further insisted: 'A strike in protest against social evils which destroy human life can be as much an act of pacifism as a strike against war.'[141] The seeds of Brockway's repudiation of pacifism during the Spanish Civil War were thus being sown in the second half of the 1920s. In 1927 he announced that he supported both 'social revolution' at home and the Kuomintang's revolution in China, 'even if they sometimes use methods of violence to which I am opposed',[142] thereby reopening the controversy over the general strike. And in 1928 he stepped down from the NMWM's chairmanship, playing a reduced role in its activities as revolutionism gradually separated itself from, and gained priority over,

---

[139] *No More War* (Nov. 1926), 2.
[140] *No More War* (June 1925), 2.
[141] *No More War* (July 1926), 4, 7. 'The Coal Crisis', by P. W. Bartlett (28 May 1926): minutes, FoR executive committee.
[142] *No More War* (Sept. 1927), 5.

pacifism within his thinking. Leftism of the kind embodied by Brockway was one reason why the NMWM benefited so little from the general anti-war mood which developed in the late 1920s.

The FoR's quietism ensured that its own progress was similarly modest. Its main claim to significance was the Christian-pacifist literature produced by its members, which was the most thoughtful since the Peace Society's early tracts a century before: for example, in 1926 Cadoux, who was to be the fellowship's chairman from 1927 to 1933, issued an enlarged version of a study of early Christianity which he had first published in 1919;[143] and in 1928 Richards published a theological work which, for all the criticisms which can be made of it, had few competitors.[144] The FoR's major organizational initiative was the 'Christ and Peace' campaign, to be noted later. It had the incidental benefit of converting Canon Charles Raven to pacifism. Having been passed over for the Deanship of Liverpool, this ambitious Anglican seems to have decided that he could make more of an impact as the expositor of a purifyingly pristine Christianity rather than as a conventional churchman. He therefore joined the FoR in June 1931, and as Regius Professor of Divinity at Cambridge after 1932 was to be the most prominent British pacifist theologian of the 1930s.[145]

The FoR's membership grew slowly, though the formation of the Congregational Pacifist Crusade in 1926 indicated that there was potential for organized Christian pacifism to expand. The FoR acknowledged in 1928 that its branch life was 'very feeble', and the following year that 'the rate of increase of its membership was very slow compared with the spread of pacifism'.[146] It was notable that when in 1927 the well-connected Anglican priest and celebrated 'radio parson' H. R. L. ('Dick') Sheppard—whose father had supported the Peace Society during its declining years[147]—declared himself a pacifist, he did not join the FoR, presumably because he found it too unworldly. Nor did he join the NMWM, presumably because it was too left-wing: Sheppard was to vote for the National government in 1931. Both established pacifist associations thus failed to mobilize all their potential support in the second half of the 1920s.

Indeed, the leading pacifist of that period remained independent of them: this was Ponsonby, who launched a pacifist campaign in 1925. As early as the First World War he had at times seemed close to pacifism, as when he

---

[143] Kaye, *C. J. Cadoux*, 117–18.

[144] L. Richards, *The Christian's Alternative to War: An Examination of Christian Pacifism* (1928). For a critique, see Ceadel, *Pacifism in Britain 1914–1945*, 68–70.

[145] Minutes, FoR executive committee, 6 May 1931; general committee, 15–16 June 1931.

[146] Minutes, FoR general committee, 8–9 Oct. 1928, 10–11 Dec. 1929.

[147] See PSM, 22 Sept. 1921.

opposed the grant of coercive powers to a league of nations, argued (in October 1915) that 'by negotiation we could get just as much as we shall ever get by military action', and persuaded himself that many people had supported British intervention only because they had been duped by false propaganda.[148] However, he had also endorsed the war, denied a principled objection to military force, and publicly announced in July 1915 that he did 'not adopt the attitude of one who is a believer in immediate and general disarmament and the effective organization of passive resistance'.[149] After the war, however, he had painfully parted from Liberalism as well as from Christianity, and had secured election as a Labour MP. In doing so, he had become more extreme in his opposition to war: in July 1923, for example, he addressed the National Peace Council on 'the uncompromising pacifist position'.[150] Even so, his views were still moderate enough for MacDonald to appoint him as a junior minister in the Foreign Office, where he observed the government's agonizing over the Geneva Protocol at close quarters.

It was after the first Labour government fell that Ponsonby seems to have finally committed himself to pacifism. His peculiar philosophical views required him to do so emphatically: long troubled by an inability to comprehend the conception of eternity and indeed by more general doubts about the notion of time, Ponsonby had concluded that individuals must have the courage immediately to press for what they believed to be right.[151] Early in 1925, therefore, he began writing *Now is the Time: An Appeal for Peace*, an emphatically absolutist book which was published in the autumn of the same year.

This proclaimed a pacifism which was optimistic in orientation and—its main claim to originality—utilitarian in inspiration. Rejecting not only defencist policies ('No so-called adequate armaments . . . will give security against war') but also liberal-*pacificist* ones ('A League of Nations war will not just be a tidy little police affair'), it insisted that by contrast pacifism was 'intensely practical'. This optimism rested on two assumptions. The first was that 'in the world as we find it to-day, aggression, except perhaps on the part of the great powers against backward and weaker tribes on other continents, may be ruled out as a motive for war': he assumed that wars were caused by mistakes alone. The second was that no pacifist movement which reached 'proportions which really count, could be confined to one nation alone', so that disarmament would in practice be exemplary rather than unilateral.

---

[148] Jones, *Arthur Ponsonby*, 104–6, 116–17.

[149] A. Ponsonby, *A Basis of International Authority* (Peace and Freedom Pamphlet, 10; 1915), 7: this was his address to the founding conference of the League of Peace and Freedom, 8–9 July 1915.

[150] Minutes, NPC Council, 12 July 1923.

[151] See Ceadel, *Pacifism in Britain*, 237–8.

Ponsonby believed that he had located a 'neglected' inspiration for pacifism in 'the scales of the balance of reason applied to war', as distinct from
deriving it from 'religious', 'humanitarian', or 'socialist' principles.[152]
Russell, in an otherwise favourable review, insisted that this 'commonsense
argument', as he called it, was 'by no means new'.[153] But Ponsonby's claim
to novelty was justified in that it was being used as the central plank of a
major pacifist tract for the first time. Whereas the Christian and socialist
inspirations had little prospect of mass appeal, there was a chance that consequentialist pacifism would strike a chord with a public that was becoming
increasingly aware of the costs of the last war and the greater damage to be
expected in the next.

Despite its general boldness, however, Ponsonby's book contained a qualification of its absolutist message which gave rise to some confusion. Its
author insisted that he 'would neither vote for, nor advocate, the abolition of
the standing army and the scrapping of the navy' because public opinion was
'not ready for such a step' and would be alarmed by being presented 'with the
ultimate and concluding state of our policy' at any early stage in the
campaign.[154] He did not explain why advocating a mass refusal to fight would
not alarm the public in the same way. Nor did he subsequently clarify his
varying attitude to arms estimates: in 1927 he was to argue in the Commons
for 'the practical abolition of the Air Force', on the grounds that exemplary
disarmament of this kind would soon be reciprocated;[155] yet in 1929 he was
to annoy his some of his constituents by refusing to vote against Labour's
arms estimates.[156]

At the same time as Ponsonby published *Now is the Time*, he also launched
his 'Peace Letter', a petition which pledged those endorsing it to 'refuse to
support or render war service to any Government which resorts to arms'.[157]
He chose not to work under the auspices of any peace association, relying
mainly on his own public meetings as a way of collecting signatures—a tactic
he later thought mistaken.[158] He received some help from individuals and
organizations, including J. H. Hudson, whose resignation from the National
Peace Council for the purpose has already been noted;[159] George Lansbury,
who addressed meetings on Ponsonby's behalf; the NMWM, which publicized the Peace Letter in its journal; and the Women's Co-operative Guild.

[152] A. Ponsonby, *Now is the Time: An Appeal for Peace* (1925), 85–9, 101–3, 109, 137, 139,
153.
[153] *No More War* (Oct. 1925), 5.   [154] Ponsonby, *Now is the Time*, 173.
[155] Hansard, 203 HC cols. 2227, 2231 (17 Mar. 1927).
[156] Jones, *Arthur Ponsonby*, 171.
[157] Ceadel, *Pacifism in Britain 1914–1945*, 80–2.
[158] See his column in *Peace News* (23 Jan. 1937), 2.
[159] NPC *Monthly Circular* (Sept. 1925/Jan. 1926), 476.

And Ponsonby's seconding of Brockway's motion at the Labour Party conference in October 1926 must have helped draw attention to his campaign. In general, however, it attracted so little publicity that when he first approached the Prime Minister in November 1926 about receiving a deputation, Baldwin's advisers had not heard of the Peace Letter at all.[160] There was little press coverage of Ponsonby's Albert Hall rally on 5 December 1926, which was addressed by Brockway, Morrison, and Margaret Bondfield, as well as by Hudson and Lansbury, and attracted an audience of 9,000.[161]

Ponsonby therefore extended his Peace Letter campaign into a second year. In March 1927 he persuaded the Cambridge Union to pass by 213 votes to 138 the resolution 'That lasting peace can only be secured by the people of England adopting an uncompromising attitude of pacificism',[162] though his success attracted much less attention than the Oxford Union's 'King and Country' debate six years later. He also began developing his critique of allied propaganda into a book, *Falsehood in Wartime*, with the assistance of the Marquis of Tavistock,[163] a Christian pacifist whose unwillingness to criticize Hitler was later to make him notorious. Finally on 8 December 1927 Ponsonby presented Baldwin with 128,770 signatures to his Peace Letter.[164] The Prime Minister replied by arguing that the policy favoured by the petition would undermine the league and Locarno and encourage aggression:

England totally disarmed and an easy prey to hostile forces! Can you think of anything more likely to excite cupidity and hostile intention? We should sink to the level of a fifth rate Power, our Colonies would be stripped from us, our commerce would decline, famine and unemployment would stalk the land.. . . I share your longing for peace. God forbid that it should be again disturbed! The constant and undivided effort of the Government is for its preservation. But I have yet to learn that the cause of peace can be served by rendering our country impotent . . .[165]

Ponsonby was further rebuffed the following year when, as already noted, the UDC declined to adopt his policy of unconditional opposition to sanctions.

One reason why the increase in support for pacifism was only modest in the second half of the 1920s was competition from the LNU, whose status was enhanced by the award of a Royal Charter in October 1925. Indeed, it probably recruited more pacifists than the FoR and NMWM combined and

---

[160] G. H. Villiers, memorandum, 11 Nov. 1926, Baldwin Papers, vol. 134.
[161] *No More War* (Jan. 1927), 1–2. Jones, *Arthur Ponsonby*, 171. See also Ponsonby's reminiscences in *Peace News* (2 May 1941), 3.
[162] *Granta* (11 Mar. 1927), 345.
[163] Jones, *Arthur Ponsonby*, 168. Ceadel, *Pacifism in Britain 1914–1945*, 281–3 (where I wrongly give the name British Peace Party).
[164] *No More War* (Jan. 1928), 3.
[165] Baldwin to Ponsonby, 16 Dec. 1927 Ponsonby Papers.

perhaps even more than signed the Peace Letter. It also recruited large numbers of *pacificists*. As the socialist intellectual Richard Crossman was later to note, 'after 1925' the LNU capitalized upon the public's dislike of war 'with ever growing success' to become 'the most successful organization of its kind since the Anti-Corn-Law League.'[166]

Admittedly, the union still had its problems. Behind the scenes Garnett's relations with Cecil and others deteriorated to such an extent that in October 1929 he signed a secret agreement to leave the general secretaryship if a knighthood, a job at Geneva, or the headship of a university could be obtained for him.[167] However, MacDonald, doubtless enjoying another chance to revenge himself on the LNU, refused the first of these; and the other two were not forthcoming either. Moreover, Garnett's need for a serious operation in the spring of 1930 made it hard to dismiss him: instead Murray reminded him that staff were entitled to six months of sick leave and informed him that in his case he 'ought to take at least that amount', the executive committee even being prepared to 'consent to a year'.[168] In the event Garnett returned to his desk in the autumn, and stayed until finally forced out in 1938.

In order to maximize its support the LNU had set its minimum subscription at only a shilling, which was too low to free it from dependence on wealthy donors, in view of the fact that it had a well-remunerated bureaucracy of over a hundred to pay for. Even so, it did not reach its target of a million members by the time of the opening of the World Disarmament Conference. Indeed, before it eventually did so, thirteen months late, on 17 March 1933,[169] the LNU had ceased to highlight its gross as distinct from paid-up membership because, as the non-renewal of subscriptions became an increasing problem, it became seriously misleading to ignore them. None the less, the LNU was a triumphant success. Even its gross membership figure indicated that almost a million people had passed through subscription-paying membership during a decade in which the population aged over 18 was approximately thirty millions. Paid-up membership increased steadily from 255,469 in 1925 to a remarkable 406,868 in 1931. And its annual income of nearly £40,000 made it undoubtedly the most substantial peace association in history.

With 3,040 local (plus 295 junior and 1,452 corporate) branches at its 1931 peak, the LNU played a significant role in British associational life at a time

---

[166] E. F. M. Durbin and G. Catlin (eds.), *War and Democracy: Essays on the Causes and Prevention of War* (1938), 278.

[167] 'Comments on Lord Cecil's Memorandum dated 24th October concerning my interview with him on 16th October 1929', initialled and dated 'J.C.M.G, October 30th, 1929' and marked 'Confidential': Cecil Papers, Add. MSS 51136 fo. 5.

[168] Minutes, LNU executive, 3 July 1930.

[169] *HW* (Apr. 1933), supplement, i.

when 'a new structure of sociability based upon formal organizations', as Ross McKibbin has described it, was emerging among the middle class.[170] It offered women an easy introduction into an uncontentious type of political activism.[171] Likewise, it provided a secular substitute for a declining Protestant Nonconformity: the future Conservative Foreign Secretary Samuel Hoare was struck by the way the LNU's disarmament meetings of the late 1920s 'became semi-religious services . . . They began and ended with prayers and hymns, and were throughout inspired by a spirit of emotional revivalism';[172] and Salvador de Madariaga described Cecil and Murray as 'monks' of a 'civic religion'.[173] It was thus understandable that the LNU was sometimes satirized for its earnestness: for example, the novelist Evelyn Waugh was to make his character Sebastian Flyte, a dissipated 1920s Oxford undergraduate facing repeated injunctions to improve his behaviour, ask himself: 'How does one mend one's ways? I suppose one joins the League of Nations Union . . .'[174]

The LNU's capacity to recruit the social élite also attracted comment in the late 1920s. Dalton asserted that its branches were 'decorated by Elder Statesmen, Peers of the Realm, Bishops, retired Admirals and Generals and philanthropic ladies of the middle class. To be a "supporter of the League", especially when it is doing nothing in particular, has become a sign of respectability.'[175] And Noel Buxton even claimed that LNU branches consisted 'mainly of the [Baldwin] Government's supporters'[176]—a much exaggerated perception which was perhaps caused by the contrast between the LNU audiences he had begun addressing during the disarmament campaign and the more left-wing ones he had previously been accustomed to, for example at meetings organized by the National Peace Council.

Because Conservative supporters were a rare resource for a peace association, yet were in danger of being alienated by the more numerous left-wing supporters, the LNU was anxious to protect them as far as possible. Eventually, after discussions with senior party officials, the LNU introduced county or federal councils at which it hoped Conservatives would be more strongly represented than in local branches where progressive opinion often predominated.[177] Indeed, when in consequence a Hampshire federation was formed,

---

[170] R. McKibbin, *Classes and Cultures: England 1918–1951* (Oxford, 1998), 192: see also 86–90.
[171] As noted by M. Pugh, *Women and the Women's Movement in Britain* (1992), 106.
[172] Viscount Templewood, *Nine Troubled Years* (1954), 113.
[173] Murray, *An Unfinished Autobiography*, 178.
[174] E. Waugh, *Brideshead Revisited* (1945), 93.
[175] H. Dalton, *Towards the Peace of Nations* (1928), 89.
[176] N. Buxton to Murray, 14 June 1928 Murray Papers.
[177] Memorandum by Sir P. Gower to G. Lloyd, 10 July 1931: Baldwin Papers. Birn, League of Nations Union, 78–9.

in the headmaster's study at Winchester College, its organizing committee consisted of four knights, two colonels, a canon, and a titled woman.[178] But since the Conservative Party was so often in government, its politicians had many opportunities to incur the LNU's displeasure. Thus when in 1926 Austen Chamberlain proposed to bring Poland into the league council to balance the admission of Germany, the LNU mounted an overt and successful campaign of protest which the permanent under-secretary at the Foreign Office, William Tyrrell, described as a 'League of Nations Union debauch'[179] and which damaged relations between the Conservatives and the LNU for some time.

More dramatically, the Baldwin government's cautious approach to arbitration and disarmament antagonized Cecil. As early as 21 March 1926 he had complained to the Prime Minister: 'I cannot remain as a kind of guarantee to supporters of the League in the country, that the policy they so much desire is safe, unless I am given some means of delivering the goods.'[180] On 9 August 1927, upset by the his colleagues' approach to the Geneva Naval Conference, he resigned; and, though in response to entreaties from Chamberlain his letter to the Prime Minister explaining his decision was progressively toned down in the course of five drafts, it none the less embarrassed his party.

Cecil's resignation was followed in late October by the LNU's launch of a six-month campaign for disarmament and the Optional Clause which even Murray feared might seem anti-Conservative. Cecil, however, considered it essential if the union was not to lose support to more militant rivals.[181] Following a special council meeting on 14 October 1925 the WIL had launched a 'Peacemakers' Pilgrimage' in support of the optional clause and disarmament: its marchers overcame the disruption caused by the general strike to converge on Hyde Park for a successful final rally on 19 June 1926;[182] and the following year it revived the label 'Women's Peace Crusade' for a continuation of this campaign involving a number of other women's organizations.[183] However, the competitor that Cecil professed to fear was the National Peace Council, which had benefited from the effective demise of the UDC and from Rennie Smith's appointment as its secretary. Smith suggested 'progressive general disarmament down to the German level, as a policy on

[178] Minutes, Organizing Committee, LNU Hampshire Federation, 24 May 1932.
[179] Birn, *League of Nations Union*, 63–4.
[180] Cited in K. Middlemas and J. Barnes, *Baldwin* (1969), 360.
[181] Birn, *League of Nations Union*, 60–72.
[182] WIL, *11th Yearly Report*, Jan.–Dec. 1926, 3.
[183] Liddington, *Long Road to Greenham*, 147. This body remained nominally in existence until 1940 when it merged with the LNU's Women's Advisory Committee: see Minutes, WIL executive, 9 Jan., 13 Feb., 3 Apr. 1940.

which all the affiliated Peace Societies could agree and co-operate';[184] and the council mounted a vigorous campaign on this theme. For the LNU's disarmament campaign Cecil arranged for Will Arnold-Forster to transfer from the National Peace Council to the union, where he encountered Garnett's 'deep-seated loathing of anything in the nature of a campaign'.[185] Partly to minimize such internal difficulties, the LNU gave its disarmament campaign its own office and separate funding.[186]

Conservatives interpreted this initiative as an instance of 'the anti-government bias which permeates the activities of the League of Nations Union', and launched a counter-attack.[187] When Cecil introduced a motion in favour of the Optional Clause in the House of Lords on 15 February 1928, his successor as minister responsible for league affairs, Lord Cushendun, criticized the LNU 'for pressing on a particular policy', rather than merely inculcating general principles; and a vigorous exchange on the subject took place in the correspondence columns of *The Times*. But Baldwin did not seek a showdown: still shaken by his failure to convert the electorate to protectionism in 1923, he was reluctant to make similar attempts at political education in respect of the difficulties of arbitration and disarmament; and his strategy in relation to the union since 1925 had therefore been publicly to encourage it to stimulate 'the will to disarm'.[188] Nor did the LNU want an all-out confrontation. On 29 June 1928 fences were mended when Baldwin and Chamberlain cordially received an LNU deputation led by Cecil and Murray;[189] and on 26 October Baldwin addressed the public meeting to celebrate the union's tenth birthday.

The special campaign also had the effect of causing the LNU to play down security issues. At no stage in its history had it had shown moral scruples about military force: as already noted, even the League of Nations Society had accepted the need for enforcement; and the League of Free Nations Association had been positively enthusiastic about it. Admittedly, it allowed pacifists as members provided they could endorse the somewhat general terms of its Royal Charter. In 1926 it even co-opted A. Ruth Fry onto its executive committee, albeit largely in the interest of cordial relations with the National Peace Council, although ill health restricted her attendances and led to her resignation five years later.[190] Its co-option three years later of

---

[184] 'Autobiography', fo. 207.
[185] As Arnold-Forster later recalled in a letter to Cecil on 11 Jan. 1938: Cecil Papers, Add. MS 51140.
[186] NPC, *New Bulletin* (Sept./Oct./Nov. 1927), 4.
[187] P. Wicks to A. Chamberlain, 4 Jan. 1928, cited in Lloyd, *Peace through Law*, 77–8.
[188] Cited in *LNU Annual Report 1925*, 5. See also Middlemas and Barnes, *Baldwin*, 360.
[189] Lloyd, *Peace through Law*, 79–86.
[190] Fry to Murray, 27 Apr. 1926: Murray Papers. Minutes, LNU executive, 23 Apr. 1931.

Kathleen D. Courtney of the WIL worried J. W. Hills 'because she is a pure pacifist and repels the sort of people we have to convert'.[191] However, it was not the influence of pacifists but the desire not to muddy its pro-disarmament message that led the LNU to present moral sanctions as its primary weapon. Characteristic of its propaganda in the late 1920s was Murray's assertion that the league attacked international anarchy

by a method which is calculated to stir up the very minimum of opposition. Its normal sanction is the public opinion of the world; its most effective weapon publicity. You cannot punish a nation; you cannot even coerce by force any moderately strong nation. But you can exert a very strong pressure on even the strongest by simply putting a question to its representatives at the Assembly, or at one of the permanent commissions, and publishing its reply.[192]

Similarly, when the Ealing LNU debated with the Imperial Fascist league on 19 February 1930, it relied 'in the main on the moral force of public opinion to preserve peace and the other side on armed force'.[193]

In addition, for reasons of party harmony, Labour's League enthusiasts had no wish to advertise their disagreements with their pacifist colleagues. Therefore Noel Baker protested against *Headway*'s refusal to carry an advertisement for Ponsonby's Albert Hall meeting. And Dalton went so far as to send a public message of support to the NMWM.[194]

Only a few voices were raised in support of a greater emphasis upon sanctions. The loudest was that of David Davies, who, having loyally devoted himself to building up the LNU in Wales, decided 'by 1925', as a member of his staff later recalled, to revive his campaign for an international police force.[195] Davies had long been calling for 'a standard work dealing with the organization of sanctions' which would rival Clausewitz;[196] and, after retiring from the Commons in 1929, he wrote one himself, which was published in 1930 under the title *The Problem of the Twentieth Century*.[197] A Welsh reviewer shrewdly observed: 'The most obvious criticism ... is that if the confidence of the various states in each other ever becomes sufficiently strong to make Mr. Davies's plan feasible, the necessity for it will cease to exist.'[198] Davies was supported by a retired professional soldier who had turned his

[191] Hills to Murray, 4 Feb. 1929: Murray Papers.
[192] G. Murray, *The Ordeal of this Generation: The War, the League, and the Future* (1929), 131. This was the published version of Halley Stewart Lectures for 1928.
[193] LNU Ealing and District Branch, *11th Annual Report, Feb. 1929–Feb. 1930*, 11: Ealing Public Library.
[194] Noel Baker to Murray, 4 Feb. 1927: Murray Papers. *No More War* (Feb. 1927), 6.
[195] *New Commonwealth* (Nov. 1944), 293.
[196] Davies to Cecil, 20 Mar. 1923: Cecil Papers Add. MS 51138.
[197] An abridged version was published in 1932 under the title *An International Police Force*.
[198] Cited in G. J. Jones, *Wales and the Quest for Peace* (Cardiff, 1969), 122.

hand to graphic war memoirs, Brigadier-General F. P. Crozier, who denied that 'order-keeping' counted as war, and called for an international police force.[199] But otherwise Davies found the response to his book disappointing.

During the 1930s the LNU's leaders were privately to concede that they had been guilty during the previous decade of 'not grasping firmly this nettle of security': Murray did so to Allen in 1933, for example.[200] Consciences were thus troubled even before E. H. Carr made his famous accusation—first hinted at in his inaugural lecture as Woodrow Wilson professor at Aberystwyth in 1936 and definitively articulated three years later in his classic book *The Twenty Years' Crisis*—that league supporters were 'utopians' who had systematically ignored the problem of power. Even so, Carr's critique was to prompt Cecil to remind Murray of the LNU's sins of omission in the post-war decade: 'There is no doubt at all that for ten years we practically evaded the problem of sanctions. I remember perfectly doing it myself and I think others did the same.'[201] Admittedly, some LNU activists always denied such charges: most notably, the unshakeably sanguine Noel Baker convinced himself that he had never pulled his punches, though this was later to bring him into conflict with historians familiar with what he had actually argued prior to Hitler's coming to power.[202] Of course, it was not only league enthusiasts who obfuscated the issue of security in the pre-Hitler era: governments did the same by supporting projects as vacuous as the Kellogg–Briand pact and Briand's European Union scheme.

From the autumn of 1928, moreover, disarmament propaganda was assisted by a change in the public mood which was made evident by a two-year boom in literature about trench warfare. 'The enormous sales of these books should give great encouragement to all lovers of peace', the National Peace Council observed.[203] The peace movement had not known such rhetorical ascendancy since the brief *pacificist* bubble of 1848-51. The LNU thought that practically every politician now paid at least lip-service to the league 'unless he be a Communist'.[204] The defence establishment grew concerned: in January 1929 the permanent under-secretary at the War Office

---

[199] *HW* (June 1931), 118–19. For Crozier's early career, see Ceadel, *Pacifism in Britain 1914-1945*, 98–100.

[200] Murray to Allen, 18 Feb. 1933 (copy): Murray Papers.

[201] Cecil to Murray, 14 Nov. 1938: Murray Papers.

[202] D. Carlton has informed me that Noel-Baker denied him permission to cite his contemporary writings in *MacDonald versus Henderson* because they did not accord with his recollections of what he had written. Similarly, C. Thorne noted the difficulties of using oral history 'in some instances, and notably where Mr Noel-Baker is concerned', in *The Limits of Foreign Policy* (1972), p. xv (see also 383 n.).

[203] NPC, *News Bulletin* (June 1930), 7.

[204] *HW* (Nov. 1928), 211.

complained to the Prime Minister's principal private secretary that the LNU was conducting 'a rather bitter and unfair campaign against the Army and so-called "militarism". This causes us some concern because we have no obvious means of dealing with such unfair propaganda.'[205]

Moreover, at the May 1929 general election—during which Cecil urged voters, 'disregarding all party ties', simply to support pro-league candidates[206]—many Conservative candidates suppressed their doubts about the league and disarmament in an effort not to lose votes.[207] Indeed, looking back from the adversity of the second half of the 1930s, Cecil was to claim that this period, during which the LNU faced 'practically no opposition', had been 'unwholesome' and 'unreal' because the 'many people who disagreed with us . . . did not venture to say so' and only later came 'out into the open'.[208]

The Labour government which was returned to power after the May 1929 election was anxious to signal its support for the league, disarmament, and peace. In addition to making Cecil a league delegate, as already noted, it made a point of signing the Optional Clause, and adhered to the General Act, a further arbitral scheme. It also appointed a veteran trade unionist of known anti-militarist views, Tom Shaw, as its Secretary of State for War: through his private secretary he soon informed an official in his department, who wished to brief him on an emergency reinforcement of British troops in Palestine, that he was 'a pacifist' who did 'not wish to have anything to do with war or military operations'.[209]

In October 1929, moreover, an ecumenical 'Christ and Peace' campaign was launched within the churches—mainly at the behest of the FoR, as has been mentioned—and ran for seventeen months, its main achievement being the Church of England's *pacificist* declaration at its 1930 Lambeth Conference: 'War as a method of settling international disputes is incompatible with the teaching of our Lord Jesus Christ'.[210] In the same year even the sceptical NMWM concluded that a new era was dawning in which negative propaganda against war could give way to positive promotion of peace: it therefore changed the title of its journal from *No More War* to the more positive-sounding *New World*, claiming: 'Those who today defend war are very hard to find. As a means of settling differences war is entirely discredited in the minds of the common people.'[211] Indeed, war's one prominent British defender at this time

[205] Sir H. Creedy to R. Vansittart, 15 Jan. 1929: Baldwin Papers.

[206] *HW* (May 1929), 85.

[207] J. Ramsden, *The Age of Balfour and Baldwin 1902–40* (1978), 341.

[208] *Report of LNU General Council Dec. 1937* (1938), 53.

[209] Maj.-Gen. A. C. Temperley, *The Whispering Gallery of Europe* (1938), 118–9.

[210] Ceadel, *Pacifism in Britain 1914–1945*, 67–8.

[211] *No More War* (Mar. 1930), 4; (Apr. 1930), 5. The new title was adopted with effect from May 1930.

was himself to be discredited, albeit much later: this was the anatomist Sir Arthur Keith, who described war as nature's pruning hook in a much reviled rectorial address to Aberdeen University in June 1931, and who was long afterwards shown to have helped to fabricate 'Piltdown man'.[212]

Finding itself in tune with the public mood, the peace movement embarked on a remarkable campaign of support for the World Disarmament Conference. Organizations which depended for their effectiveness on consensus were particularly energetic. Despite feeling unable to stage national peace congresses during the four depression years of 1929–32, the National Peace Council felt confident enough to appoint a full-time secretary after Smith resigned in 1930 because of his duties as Dalton's parliamentary private secretary. It chose Gerald Bailey, a Quaker pacifist and former Liberal parliamentary candidate who was to hold the post for eighteen years. The WIL's campaign centred on an international petition, launched in 1930, which was eventually to claim a remarkable 1,517,000 signatures in Britain (thanks in large part to a sympathetic newspaper, the *News-Chronicle*) and 2,600,000 in the world as a whole.[213] Shortly after the date of the World Disarmament Conference was set, disarmament campaigners met in the Queen's Hall in London on 9 February 1931 to prepare themselves for the final push, and were told by Henderson, who was to preside over the conference: 'If the people want disarmament, they can have it. If they will exert their will they can compel results.'[214] An enthusiastic meeting of Christian organizations was held in Central Hall, Westminster, on 15 June. And a major rally in the Albert Hall, with an overspill meeting across the road in Hyde Park, took place on 11 July 1931 at which the party leaders and other politicians spoke, attracting eighty-three column inches of attention in *The Times*, though only five in the *Daily Express*.[215]

So strong had pro-disarmament feeling become that Conservatives dared not voice their doubts about its achievability. Baldwin, who had reversed his initial decision not to attend the Albert Hall meeting after being warned by an aide 'to be careful to avoid giving your opponents . . . the chance of saying that the Conservative Party are less devoted to the League and to international peace than are the other two parties',[216] revealed his true scepticism only in a whispered aside to Dalton on the platform of the Albert Hall as the audience's cheering reached its height: 'Rather pathetic, isn't it?'[217] At that stage,

[212] Ceadel, *Thinking about Peace and War*, 39, 200.
[213] *Peace Review* (Nov./Dec. 1931), 5.
[214] *The Times* (10 Feb.1931). *HW* (Mar. 1931), supplement, p. i.
[215] These calculations were made by the LNU: see HW (Aug. 1931), 142.
[216] G. Fry to Baldwin, 4 Apr. 1931: Baldwin papers, file 133.
[217] H. Dalton, *Call Back Yesterday: Memoirs 1887–1931* (1953), 341.

because Labour was in office, he did not expect to be held politically account-
able for the outcome of the World Disarmament Conference. Unexpectedly,
however, the financial crisis of August 1931 brought the Conservatives back
to power, as the dominant element within a National government that was
conceived as an emergency measure but was to rule Britain until May 1940.

At the end of the summer of 1931 defencists seemed to be under unprecedented pressure from the peace movement. They had allowed inflated hopes
about disarmament to develop, and risked being blamed when they were not
achieved. The peace movement, experiencing remarkable internal unity and
domestic support, was relieved that the international horizon seemed to be
clear of crises which might compromise the case for disarming. Cecil was
therefore glad to be able to tell the League of Nations Assembly on 10
September 1931: 'There has scarcely ever been a period in the world's history
when war seems less likely than it does at present.'[218] His speech marked the
peak of *pacificist* optimism: in less than a fortnight the post-war era was to
give way to the pre-war one.

In this period the peace movement had been a beneficiary of the failure of the
First World War to deliver the promised international improvements, which
caused opinion to turn against it. It had also had made a substantial contribution in its own right: in particular, the fashioning of the LNU into a new kind
of peace association—respectable yet vigorous—had helped to develop
public support for the league. Yet because there was no real threat to British
security during the 1920s, the peace issue had not reached its peak of intensity. Despite its remarkable revival, the peace movement had not yet had the
chance to show all that it was capable of.

[218] Cited in Thorne, *The Limits of Foreign Policy*, 4.

9

Stimulation,
September 1931–December 1935

consensus on L.g.N.
+ disarmament
ends

On 19 September 1931 Japan began the process of converting the Chinese province of Manchuria into its own puppet state of Manchukuo, thereby calling into question Cecil's sanguine pronouncement about the prospects of peace just nine days before. However, peace movements fare best when optimism is seasoned with a dash of pessimism: although the former gives their ideas plausibility, the latter is needed to give them urgency. In the early 1930s the mixture was therefore ideal: the optimism carried over from the post-Locarno period ignited with the pessimism generated by Japanese, Germany, and Italian behaviour to stimulate the most intense phase of peace activism ever, of which unquestionably the highlight was the extraordinary Peace Ballot of 1934–5.

However, the strain on all those caught up in the peace-or-war debate was considerable. In less than a decade the near-consensus in favour of the league and disarmament was to give way to a near-consensus in favour of fighting Hitler, a change of such rapidity and magnitude as to confound those who were affected by it. Dates were misremembered very quickly: as early as 1937, Baldwin's 'the bomber will always get through' speech of 1932 was being remembered as having occurred in 1935;[1] the East Fulham by-election of 1933, won on a massive swing by a Labour candidate making use of peace propaganda, was commonly post-dated by two years;[2] and a widespread misapprehension developed to the effect that Hitler's remilitarization of the Rhineland had occurred in 1934 instead of 1936.[3] Campaigns were confused even by participants: Edward Hyams, who had written a tract for the Peace Pledge Union, later muddled up its membership pledge with the Peace Ballot, as did Lord Eustace Percy, despite having sat on the LNU's executive committee at the time.[4] Such mistakes were often a subconscious rewriting of

---

[1] *Spectator* (19 Nov. 1937), 876.

[2] 'Cato', *Guilty Men* (1940), 35 (an error corrected in later edns.); K. Martin, *Editor* (1968), 171; Sir C. Petrie, *A Historian Looks at his World* (1972), 113; and C. Thorne, *The Limits of Foreign Policy* (1972), 379.

[3] As pointed out in R. Graves and A. Hodge, *The Long Week-End: A Social History of the Great Britain 1918–1939* (1940), 7.

[4] E. Hyams, *The New Statesman: The History of the First Fifty Years* (1963), 149; his tract was E. Hyams, *Few Men are Liars* (PPU, 1937). E. Percy, *Some Memories* (1958), 171.

history: peace activists who eventually concluded that Hitler had to be stopped rationalized their intellectual autobiographies in order to bring forward their conversion to this view. Thus a draft internal history produced by staff members in 1939 wrongly implied that the LNU had adopted a resolute attitude with effect from the Manchuria crisis;[5] and a letter from Noel Baker to Leonard Woolf at the height of the military crisis of 1940 erroneously claimed the East Fulham by-election as evidence that widespread support for sanctions existed as early as 1933.[6]

Progressive opinion largely convinced itself that it had been converted to containment either by the Manchuria crisis in September 1931, or by Hitler's appointment as German Chancellor in January 1993, or again by the German walk-out from Geneva in October 1933, or at the very latest by Mussolini's attack on Abyssinia in October 1935. However, it was largely deceiving itself: in 1931–2 the peace movement and the left were generally reluctant to jeopardize the World Disarmament Conference by talking of sanctions; in 1933 they were in many cases affected by a 'never again!' reflex; and although in 1934–5 they increasingly supported collective security, they did so for the most part as a policy which did not require rearmament and might be implemented through economic pressure alone. For most progressives, a continued belief in a middle way based on economic sanctions applied through the League of Nations stood in the way of their conversion to containment. Thus although the peace movement experienced increasing friction over the use of force in this period, it did not polarize.

THE MANCHURIA CRISIS, SEPTEMBER 1931—DECEMBER 1932

Japan's aggression in Manchuria came to be accepted as the watershed between the optimistic 1920s and the pessimistic 1930s. Yet the Manchuria crisis was too confused, remote, and protracted, particularly as it competed for public attention with an economic crisis in Britain, to produce significant conversions to containment. Japan's intentions towards China were initially hard to judge, causing some league supporters, most notably Grey and Murray, to argue for pacific settlement rather than a punitive approach at the LNU's general council on 10–11 December.[7] The United States was best placed to exercise leverage in the Far East; but after the league powers had waited to see whether it would cooperate with them, it merely refused diplo-

---

[5] Birn, *League of Nations Union*, 95.
[6] Noel Baker to Woolf, 29 Aug. 1940: Leonard Woolf Papers, University of Sussex Library.
[7] *The League, Manchuria and Disarmament* (LNU publication 312a; Dec. 1931), 8, 17–18.

matic recognition to Manchukuo. Thereafter, the league's procedures were operated in the most cautious way compatible with not discrediting them altogether: a commission of inquiry under the second Earl of Lytton was established in March 1932; it reported in October; and the League Assembly declared Japan an aggressor in February 1933. In response Japan gave notice of its departure from the league.

A rare manifestation of increased support for containment as a result of this crisis was the formation by David Davies of a small association to promote an international police force. Having taken up this cause again in the mid-1920s, as already noted, Davies refused to let go of it, admitting to Keynes: 'I suppose I am a fanatic. One really has to be if one is to do anything.'[8] Cecil later observed that Davies's 'defect as a reformer was that it was difficult for him to accept half a loaf'.[9] And Wells more waspishly commented that, whenever asked searching questions by his fellow internationalists about his 'international policeman', such as how he 'was to be created and sustained', Davies 'just went on saying "international policeman" ' and, eventually finding such interrogation uncongenial, 'went off with his great idea, like a penguin which has found an egg, to incubate it alone', using his wealth to create a new organization in which his thinking was 'elaborated rather than developed'.[10]

During the autumn and winter of 1931–2 Davies became convinced both that the Manchuria crisis 'pointed out . . . unmistakably the necessity of organising an international force' and that France's inclusion of such a force in its proposals to the World Disarmament Conference 'brought to life the project'.[11] In May 1932, therefore, he floated the idea of the New Commonwealth Society. The following month he obtained from MacDonald, now heading the National government, the title, Baron Davies of Llandinam, which he had long believed essential if his campaigning efforts were to be taken seriously, particularly abroad.[12] In October the official launch of the New Commonwealth Society took place. It presented itself as an élite international association dedicated to producing information and research, rather than a rival to the LNU, though Garnett pertinently questioned how a study group could commit itself in advance to certain solutions.[13] It remained small,

---

[8] Davies to J. M. Keynes, 27 Feb. 1932: New Commonwealth files, Davies of Llandinam Papers.

[9] *HW* (July 1944), 7.

[10] H. G. Wells, *The New World Order* (1940), 105–6.

[11] The quotations are from the letter dated 20 Nov. 1931 in Davies's *Letters to John Bull and Others* (1932), 107, which he published under the pseudonym Robert the Peeler. See also his address to Chatham House on 15 Oct. 1931, published in *International Affairs* (Jan./Feb. 1932), 76–90.

[12] See Davies to J. Herbert Lewis, PC, 7 Nov. 1931 (copy): Davies of Llandinam Papers.

[13] Garnett to Horsfall Carter, 17 Oct. 1932: Davies of Llandinam Papers.

its British membership having reached only 1,384 by mid-1936.[14] However, its real value was as a ginger group within the LNU, where it became a major nuisance at the twice-yearly meetings of the policy-making general council. This body had already discussed the international police force in June 1932; and when the New Commonwealth Society raised it again six months later it remitted the issue to the executive committee for guidance. The international police force was to remain a problematical item on the LNU's agenda for much of the rest of its existence.

By thus focusing attention upon so ambitious a scheme, the New Commonwealth Society may in the long run have hindered rather than helped the sanctionist cause. With hindsight what was needed in the 1930s was a strengthening of the League Council's formal powers to require member states to use their own forces for collective action against aggression, combined with an effort to prepare them politically and militarily for such an eventuality. Admittedly, the failure of the Draft Treaty of Mutual Assistance and the Geneva Protocol the decade before showed how difficult this constitutional and psychological change would have been to bring about. But an international police force posed so much more drastic a challenge to state sovereignty and conventional assumptions as to be quite utopian.

So, to an even greater extent, did a second plank in New Commonwealth Society's platform, the creation of an international equity tribunal. The society included this to forestall the charge of seeking to freeze the status quo, and placed little emphasis upon it in its propaganda at this time. Yet, by being empowered to adjudicate international disputes, including territorial ones, this tribunal would have had many of the powers of a world legislature, and was thus constitutionally more controversial even than an international police force. Although he did not realize it yet, Davies was a federalist who in his enthusiasm for the police and judicial functions of a world federation overlooked the need for a constitutional and political framework too. Sir John Fischer Williams, an international jurist who had worked for the Reparations Commission, made this point when he warned Davies in a Chatham House discussion that lawyers were not the right people 'to preside over the general march of the world'.[15] The New Commonwealth Society could thus be accused of injecting an unnecessary degree of supranationalism into the campaign to strengthen the league, as some Conservatives were soon to complain. Its sheer utopianism ironically alienated many of those whom it had been keenest to attract: those who prided themselves on being realists in respect of the role of power in international relations.

---

[14] New Commonwealth, *Annual Report 1935–36*, 40.
[15] *International Affairs* (Jan./Feb. 1932), 90–9.

None the less, during 1932 there was an unprecedented degree of interest in an international police force. The LNU seriously considered whether it might be worth establishing one in some form as a way of inducing the French to disarm: Cecil was therefore willing to support 'something of that kind', whilst acknowledging that 'the practical difficulties are very great';[16] and so, more surprisingly, was Garnett. The public found the idea much more comprehensible than previous security schemes, and, exaggerating the potency of air bombardment, assumed that such a force would consist primarily of aeroplanes. While there seemed to be a chance that the World Disarmament Conference would abolish all national military aviation, it was possible to hope that such an international air force would need merely to offer protection against the misuse of civil aviation. Indeed, if civil aviation were internationalized as part of a drastic disarmament package, the resultant pool of aeroplanes could constitute the international force.

Using this argument, which made its policy seem only minimally coercive, the New Commonwealth Society tried to secure support from pacifists. Many were unimpressed, including A. Ruth Fry who insisted that 'the analogy with the policeman does not hold good' and continued to assert that 'the real sanction required is a growth of world conscience, not of world force'.[17] But some were won over, either because they were beginning to having doubts about the absolutist viewpoint, or because they had yet to clarify their own position, or again because they had adopted a collaborative orientation. Kathleen D. Courtney informed Cecil that, although 'the idea of an international bombing force is an odious one', she did not 'personally have any objection to an international air police force consisting of the smaller fighting planes':[18] she was moving away from pacifism. Dick Sheppard endorsed the New Commonwealth Society for a while: he was an intuitive rather than systematic thinker who had yet to work out his attitude to sanctions.

Clifford Allen also supported an international police force as part of a major change in his political outlook. Having supported MacDonald's decision to head the National government, he had been ennobled as Baron Allen of Hurtwood. But he was soon disappointed at not being appointed to the cabinet as a 'National Labour' replacement for Philip Snowden, and decided instead, as he informed Davies, his new colleague in the House of Lords, to devote himself to a campaign for 'world security' as a way of breaking the disarmament deadlock.[19] This was Allen's first involvement with international issues for many years. He still claimed to be a pacifist, but now adopted

[16] Cecil to K. Courtney, 25 Sept. 1932 (copy): Cecil Papers Add. MS 51141.
[17] A. R. Fry to G. N. Barnes, 20 Dec. 1932: Davies of Llandinam Papers.
[18] K. D. Courtney to Cecil, 30 Sept. 1932: Cecil Papers Add. MSS 51141.
[19] Marwick, *Clifford Allen*, 122. Allen to Davies, [?] Dec. 1932: Davies of Llandinam Papers.

a collaborative orientation, campaigning for the internationalization of civil aviation and a league air force as the most practical means of preventing war.

However, such stimulus as the Manchuria crisis thus gave to sanctionist opinion was offset by the reaction against the League Covenant's enforcement provisions to which it also gave rise. Within the LNU the crisis exposed a previously latent disagreement over sanctions: members began to discover that their organization 'includes in its membership two groupings, for whom it is often hard to find a common platform', as one of them put it in the autumn of 1932.[20] It also helped to bring the LNU's seemingly inexorable expansion to an end: annual subscriptions fell for the first time in 1932, and, apart from a partial recovery in 1934 as the result of energetic recruiting, continued to do so throughout the decade,[21] although the union's position as the country's largest peace association was never in jeopardy.

Meanwhile, the difficulties which soon beset the World Disarmament Conference stimulated some demands for a unilateral initiative by Britain in order to start the ball rolling. For example, in the autumn of 1932 an economist who had lost an arm and won a Military Cross in the First World War, J. R. Bellerby, created an Association of the Peace Ballot of Great Britain.[22] Though wholly unconnected with the much better known Peace Ballot of 1934–5, Bellerby's association used the same methods, albeit in miniature: having issued 34,000 questionnaires, half of which were returned, it reported 57 per cent support for unilateral disarmament—Bellerby's own preferred policy—and 43 per cent opposition.[23]

Some of those reacting against sanctions or the disarmament deadlock during 1931–2 espoused pacifism or socialist *pacificism*. Pacifism had been given a boost when, by coincidence, Gandhi had arrived in London for talks about India just six days before the Manchuria crisis began. Leading British peace activists took the opportunity to discuss the non-violent techniques with which he had been resisting British rule in India, a subject that had interested the NMWM for several years—indeed, since before it had learnt to spell his name.[24] Gandhi mostly disappointed Christian quietists by presenting non-violence as a method of political confrontation rather than spiritual reconciliation.[25] But he thereby encouraged those in search of a policy which could either boost or supplant a faltering *pacificism*.

[20] *HW* (Oct. 1932), 184.
[21] The figures were: 1932, 388,255 (down 4.6% from the previous year); 1933, 374,012 (down 3.7%); 1934, 390,630 (up 4.4%); 1935, 377,824 (down 3.3%); 1936, 353,769 (down 6.4%); 1937, 314,715 (down 11.0%); 1938, 264,180 (down 16.1%); 1939, 193,366 (down 26.8%).
[22] Its early results were discussed by the WIL's executive committee on 13 Dec. 1932.
[23] Bellerby reported the final results to the next Labour conference: *LPCR* 1933, 192–3.
[24] For articles on 'Ghandi', see *No More War* (Dec. 1924), 3, and (Sept. 1926), 5.
[25] Ceadel, *Pacifism in Britain 1914–1945*, 88–90.

Maude Royden had admired Gandhi since visiting him in India in 1928. He may have been a reason for the renewed interest in absolutism which had caused her to suggest in the summer of 1931 that the FoR follow up the 'Christ and Peace' campaign with 'a retreat meeting of 100% pacifists'.[26] It was almost certainly a talk Gandhi gave on 23 September 1931[27] which inspired her to suggest what became known as the 'Peace Army'. This was non-violent resistance as third-party intervention: a force of Christian pacifists who would interpose themselves between the Japanese and Chinese in Manchuria. It was also a tangible version of the 'great adventure' for which she had yearned in 1915 but been unable to find acceptable expression. After consulting Sheppard and A. Herbert Gray, a Presbyterian minister who had recently become a pacifist and joined the FoR, Royden informed her congregation at the Guildhouse, the Congregational church in Eccleston Square, Pimlico, where she carried on a popular ecumenical ministry, of her intention 'to enrol people who would be ready if war should break out to put their bodies unarmed between the contending forces'.[28] In February 1932, after fighting had flared up again, she, Sheppard, and Gray publicly proposed to lead a Peace Army to China. It was never mobilized; but 800 men and women had responded to the idea, including the young Wesleyan minister Donald Soper, who thereby began a very long career as a prominent pacifist; and a Peace Army council was established, which remained in existence for several years.[29]

Royden's initiative was open to obvious objections. As the fashionable writer Beverley Nichols observed a decade later: 'The prospect of a horde of elderly ladies, clergymen, earnest authors, rampageous undergraduates, presenting themselves at the headquarters of ... a Japanese general and demanding facilities for self-immolation in some rocky and shell-scarred valley from which in all probability, the enemy had long fled ... it doesn't bear thinking about.' However, he admitted that he had not only volunteered for it at the time but that this was 'not a memory of which I am ashamed. At least we showed goodwill.'[30] Moreover, Royden's proposal attracted more publicity for pacifism than at any time since the gaoling of conscientious objectors in the First World War, and has subsequently received academic recognition as the blueprint for all subsequent 'unarmed interpositionary peace forces'.[31] However, she seems to have regarded the Peace Army as

---

[26] Minutes, FoR general committee, 15–16 June 1931.   [27] Fletcher, *Maude Royden*, 258.
[28] Cited in *New World* (Nov. 1931), 7.
[29] Ceadel, *Pacifism in Britain 1914–1945*, 94–8, 277–8.
[30] B. Nichols, *Men Do Not Weep* (1941), 13.
[31] T. Weber, 'From Maude Royden's Peace Army to the Gulf Peace Team: An Assessment of Unarmed Interpositionary Peace Forces', *Journal of Peace Research*, 30 (1993), 45–74.

supplementing rather than superseding *pacificist* methods: like both Brigadier-General Crozier, who joined the Peace Army council, and Sheppard, she not only continued to support the LNU but even joined the New Commonwealth Society.[32]

For the most convinced pacifists of an optimistic cast of mind, Gandhi-style non-violence was an alternative to the dangerous compromises of *pacificism*. Ponsonby, who had become a peer in 1930 as partial compensation for not receiving a cabinet post in the second Labour government, had discussed peace issues with Royden, Sheppard, and Gray in September 1931, and claimed early in 1932 that, had China been disarmed, Japan 'would never have attempted' what would have been blatant aggression. Ponsonby also criticized the World Disarmament Conference for pursuing the unsatisfactory 'half-way house' of partial disarmament, doing so on visit to Geneva in the company of the distinguished German theoretical physicist Albert Einstein, who at that time was a committed pacifist.[33]

Pacifism was also winning a new kind of convert at this time, exemplified by Beverley Nichols, whose *faux naïf* literary persona was able to draw upon authentic political ingenuousness. His pacifism was first placed in the mouth of the hero of one of his plays, performed in July 1931. He did not publicize his application to join the Peace Army, and only owned up to his new conviction in a women's magazine in September 1932.[34] Influenced by war books and disarmament propaganda, Nichols was explicitly reacting against the pain and suffering caused to individuals by war, and therefore expounded a distinctively humanitarian inspiration. Others who began to do the same during 1932 included the novelist Margaret Storm Jameson and the philosopher C. E. M. Joad.[35]

However, although the NMWM had been an early admirer of Gandhi and an exponent of optimistic pacifism for several years, it was unable to contribute much to the cause at this time because of an acute internal quarrel. The replacement of the second Labour government by the National government was interpreted by many socialists as the first sign of a revolutionary crisis in Britain. The Labour Party expelled MacDonald and moved to the left. One symptom of this was that when its new leader, Henderson, lost his seat at the October 1931 general election, Lansbury replaced him: since Ponsonby was leading the party in the House of Lords, Labour's two senior leadership posts were, remarkably, both held by pacifists from 1931 to 1935. The ILP lurched even further leftwards, disaffiliating from Labour in July 1932 so as

---

[32] Royden to Davies, 11 Oct. 1932: Davies of Llandinam Papers.
[33] Jones, *Arthur Ponsonby*, 190, 202. Ceadel, *Pacifism in Britain 1914–1945*, 91–3.
[34] *Good Housekeeping* (Sept. 1932), 16, 103.
[35] Ceadel, *Pacifism in Britain 1914–1945*, 102–8.

better to prepare for the impending struggle (though in the event it merely consigned itself to the political wilderness, except in Glasgow where its local power base was strong enough to delay this process for a decade and a half). The NMWM, already becoming more intolerant of parliamentary pacifists who had voted for Labour's arms estimates, became caught up the ILP–Labour rift. In the spring of 1932 it split not only over the extent to which pacifists could support a possibly violent revolution but also over issues of personal probity.

In particular, one of the NMWM's two secretaries and the leader of its pro-Labour faction, Ayles, was a strong personality who had always inspired mixed reactions, and, after losing his parliamentary salary following his defeat at the 1931 election, was suspected by his political foes of cultivating the movement's donors for his own purposes. When in April 1932 the NMWM's national committee established a commission to investigate its finances, Ayles immediately resigned, announcing he would shortly take up a new post in the peace movement. This proved to be the secretaryship of the British Commonwealth Peace Federation, a specially created pseudo-association which resembled Lewis Appleton's British and Foreign Arbitration Association of thirty-six years previously, both in its calculated attempt to woo patriotically minded Quakers and in its lack of an obvious function other than to provide its secretary with a salary. It claimed to want 'the British Empire to be the imperial pioneer for world peace and co-operation';[36] but the only significant figure it could recruit for this was Ayles's former absolutist colleague, Morgan Jones, whose detachment from the post-war peace movement has already been commented on. Following his resignation from the NMWM, Ayles refused to cooperate with a financial audit, and attempted to have the Post Office redirect office mail to his private address; and when a private apartment containing the NMWM's minute books for the spring and summer of 1932 caught fire, Ayles's critics suspected an attempt to destroy incriminating evidence.[37] Lucy Cox also left the NMWM, and later took a job with the Labour Party. She and Ayles were both to become Labour MPs in 1945.

With ideological disagreement thus compounded by a sense of personal betrayal, the NMWM swung sharply to the left in imitation of the ILP. It appointed an austere but abrasive zealot, the left-wing Quaker Reginald Reynolds, as its secretary, instead of E. D. Morel's daughter Stella, who, having recovered from the illness which had forced her to stop working for the UDC, had applied for the post. And it subordinated its pacifism to the

[36] *Peace Review* (July/Aug. 1832), supplement p. ii.
[37] Information from Mrs Mabel Eyles Monk.

ILP's revolutionary policy. This was to prove a disastrous move: the NMWM's support dwindled at a time when pacifism in general was benefiting from the difficulties facing the league.[38]

The stimulus which the Manchuria crisis also gave to the socialist-*pacificist* policy of war resistance became apparent with the formation of the World Anti-War Movement. This was a front organization for international Communism, devised by Willi Münzenberg and launched by him at a congress in Amsterdam during August 1932. The Soviet Union had interpreted Japan's seizure of Manchuria as the start of a probe towards its own territory. Not yet belonging to the League of Nations, and suspecting the other league states of colluding in an anti-Soviet policy, it did not urge the league to impose sanctions against Japan but hoped instead that the European labour and socialist movements would practise mass resistance against any attempt by their governments to start a war. Because the Comintern was officially in a phase of instructing Communist parties to attack all other political parties, even left-wing ones, the World Anti-War Movement was set up outside its structure as a covert means of enlisting the support of non-Communists on this urgent issue.

However, the new front organization only slightly toned down the Comintern's dogmatic hostility to 'bourgeois pacifism' which had only recently led T. H. Wintringham, the future commander of the British battalion of the International Brigade in Spain, to make the startling claim: 'The struggle against war is first a struggle against pacifism.'[39] The Amsterdam congress made minimal concessions to what it called 'futile pacifism', and was no less disparaging about the League of Nations. Moreover, the British Anti-War Movement, publicly launched in November 1932, was so blatantly under Communist control that the Labour Party and its affiliated trade unions were able to stifle its growth by refusing to let their members support it.[40] The one non-Communist recruit of any status was W. J. Brown, a former Labour MP and the leader of the Civil Service Clerical Association, who was persuaded to become chairman. Having been forced by his union to back out of a promise to support Mosley's New Party the previous year, Brown may have been seeking to re-establish his left-wing credentials; his resignation as chairman in 1934 and his condemnation of subsequent front organizations suggest that he had been deceived as to the degree of Communist control

---

[38] Ceadel, *Pacifism in Britain 1914–1945*, 109–20. Jones, *Arthur Ponsonby*, 197.

[39] *Labour Monthly* (May 1932), 290. For similar sentiments see R. D. Charques, *The Soviets and the Next War* (1932), 13.

[40] For a detailed study see M. Ceadel, 'The First Communist "Peace Society"': The British Anti-War Movement 1932–5, *Twentieth Century British History*, 1 (1990), 58–86.

when he agreed to serve.[41] Otherwise support was confined to fellow-travellers, such as Reginald Bridgeman, a disgraced diplomat active in the Communist-controlled League Against Imperialism,[42] and John Strachey, an intellectual just converted to Marxism after experimenting with the New Party.[43] Only when the tide of opinion turned in favour of war resistance during 1933 did the British Anti-War Movement enjoy a brief spell of modest influence.

The mainstream of the peace movement responded to the Manchuria crisis by seeking a middle way between the military sanctions advocated by one minority and the pacifism and war resistance advocated by two others. As Birn has shown in detail,[44] the LNU did not call for action against Japan in the resolute way it later wished it had. Its caution had many explanations: it did not wish to lose more members; it did not want to criticize the league at a difficult time; it was loyal both to Cecil, a delegate to the League Assembly and its co-president, and to Lytton, the chairman of the league's commission of inquiry and a member of its executive committee; and, above all, it feared that demanding sanctions against Japan would compromise the case for disarmament, which remained its first priority.

The World Disarmament Conference opened in Geneva on 2 February 1932 to considerable acclaim from the British peace movement. On that day, for example, an audience of 10,000 'not only enthusiastic but deeply moved' people attended a churches' disarmament meeting in London addressed by the Archbishops of Canterbury and York and other religious leaders.[45] And with Cecil as its guest the WIL mounted a 'send-off ceremony' for its petition, though Vera Brittain found it 'a great waste of time'.[46] The LNU hoped for a 25 per cent cut in armaments budgets and the prohibition of the aggressive weaponry already denied to Germany. However, the failure of the conference to make progress had by June moved Murray to jest grimly about the delegates raising 'clouds of dust about the offensive walking stick and the defensive submarine'[47] and the French politician Edouard Herriot to observe that the verb to disarm needed urgently to acquire a first person plural ('We

---

[41] See his comments on the People's Convention in W. J. Brown, *What have I Got to Lose?* (1941), 19.

[42] G. Waterfield, *Professional Diplomat: The Life of Sir Percy Lorraine* (1973), 57–8, 66–8. Bridgeman papers, in the possession of Mrs Olwen Bridgeman.

[43] H. Thomas, *John Strachey* (1973), 125.

[44] Birn, *League of Nations Union*, ch. 5.

[45] Minutes, LNU Executive, 4 Feb. 1932; *The Churches' Call for International Disarmament* (LNU No. 317, Jan. 1932).

[46] *Vera Brittain: Chronicle of Friendship: Diary of the Thirties 1932–1939*, ed. A. Bishop (1986), 30.

[47] Murray to Laurie, 6 June 1932, Murray Papers.

are disarming') instead of being conjugated only in the second person singular ('Thou shalt disarm').[48] For his part an increasingly anxious Cecil was to quip that disarmament was 'like a social function: no one wants to arrive until everyone else is there'.[49] Meanwhile pro-disarmament propaganda was adding to public worries by predicting that, should war break out again, 'London, Paris or New York could easily be reduced to the worst shambles the world have ever seen in the space of a few hours', in the words of one of many well-intentioned studies of the subject.[50]

Although the Manchuria crisis constituted only one of many difficulties for the conference, its timing was so unfortunate that Noel Baker later found it 'impossible to dismiss as absurd' the view that it had been contrived by the Japanese army in collusion with the armament manufacturers of Europe in order to sabotage the conference.[51] He therefore began writing an exposé of the arms industry to add to that produced by Dorothy Woodman of the UDC, though it was to appear too late to have a significant impact.[52] To minimize damage to the disarmament cause, progressive opinion tended to take the line that financial or economic sanctions would suffice against Japan. For example, the Labour Party and the Trades Union Congress, meeting in their national joint council on 23 February 1932, supported 'whatever cooperative and graduated measures of financial and economic constraint may be needed—in association and agreement with the United States and the Members of the League—to restore peace and to ensure a just settlement'.[53] An emergency meeting of the LNU's general council four days later called for 'whatever pressure of a diplomatic or economic character might be needed to re-establish peace'; and, in response to a question about the risk of such action producing a military backlash, Cecil answered soothingly that they would 'be applied gradually. No country was bound to take action that would expose it to grave danger. In the present case it was absolutely essential to have the co-operation of the United States. Application of economic pressure did not necessarily involve military action.'[54] The WIL, predictably experiencing 'a difference of opinion' over the role of military force, adopted a similar solution.[55] Moreover, five young dons, including the future ambassador to Washington Oliver

---

[48] Cited in P. J. Noel Baker, 'Disarmament', *International Affairs* (Jan./Feb. 1934), 3.

[49] Cited in L. Richards, *The Christian's Contribution to Peace* (1933), 107.

[50] V. Lefebure, *Common Sense about Disarmament* (1932), 123.

[51] Cited, from *Recovery* (10 Nov. 1933), in J. W. Wheeler-Bennett, *The Disarmament Deadlock* (1934), 12.

[52] P. Noel Baker, *The Private Manufacture of Armaments*, i (1936). No further volume was published.   [53] *LPCR* (1932), 68.

[54] *Minutes of an Emergency Meeting of the General Council of the L.N.U., 27 Feb. 1932* (LNU Pamphlet No. 318; Mar. 1932), 4; see also Minutes, LNU executive, 11 Feb. 1932.

[55] Minutes, WIL Executive, 9 Feb., 15 Mar. 1932.

Franks and the future Nobel-Prize-winning economist James Meade, issued
'A Letter From Oxford' in October 1932 which argued: 'The less there is of
organised military power, the greater will be the strength of moral and
economic weapons'; and they embarked upon a study of 'The Nature and Use
of Economic Sanctions', on the assumption that these represented the 'only
alternative to drifting into war' as well as offering valuable 'common ground'
between pacifists and sanctionists.[56]

HITLER'S ACQUISITION OF POWER,
JANUARY–SEPTEMBER 1933

On 30 January 1933 Hitler became German Chancellor and within two
months established his political authority. Even without this worrying development, the early months of this year would have been a time of international
crisis. The World Disarmament Conference faced breakdown because of the
long-standing incompatibility between Germany's demand for equality and
France's demand for security, and Japan's attack on China's Jehol region,
using air power in the process, exacerbated the Far Eastern crisis. Together
these events provoked alarmist comparisons with the summer of 1914.[57]
Hitler's accession to power thus added urgency to the peace-or-war debate but
in the short term produced more repudiations of containment than conversions to it.

In the form of near-isolationism and appeasement, the 'never again!' reflex
of early 1933 affected defencists as well as *pacificists*. Even the Foreign
Secretary, Sir John Simon, told the Commons on 27 February: 'However, we
handle this matter, I do not intend my own country to get into trouble'—
thereby provoking a protest from Murray.[58] Near-isolationism enjoyed its
first revival since the rejection of the Geneva Protocol, though the UDC was
no longer in a fit state to spearhead it. The Labour leadership was conscious
of the popular mood but did not wish to encourage it: in a pamphlet of July
1933 Henderson acknowledged the unpopularity of both the League
Covenant and Locarno on the grounds that by 'their terms this country is
committed to "intervene in other people's quarrels" whether its own interests

---

[56] A copy of 'The Letter from Oxford' can be found in the Murray Papers. For 'The Nature
and Use of Economic Sanctions', see *HW* (May 1934), 93. See also *Spectator* (3 Mar. 1933),
304.

[57] Such a comparison was made e.g. by Victor Gollancz (cited from Mar. 1933 in V. Brittain,
Testament of Experience (1957), 86), Norman Angell (*New Statesman*, 18 Mar. 1933, 318), and
Wickham Steed (*Listener*, 26 Apr. 1933, 654), but denied by Winston Churchill in the Commons
(Hansard, 275 HC col. 1815: 14 Mar. 1933).

[58] *Spectator* (10 Mar. 1933), 334.

are involved or not', but argued strongly against such an interpretation.[59] Calls for the revision of Versailles were suddenly revived because of a new fear of Germany. For example, in July 1933 Sisley Huddleston, a pro-German journalist who eventually became a naturalized citizen of Vichy France, wrote a deliberately alarmist book which argued that 'if there is no peaceful revision, there will be a warlike revision . . . The choice is not between revision and non-revision.'[60]

The 'never again!' reflex also took pacifist form. For example, both the prominent Methodist minister Henry Carter and the popular writer A. A. Milne were converted to an absolutist position at this time; and, in the words of its historians, the Women's Co-operative Guild introduced 'a Peace Pledge Card in 1933, which committed those who signed it to take no part in war or any preparations for war'.[61] Most famously, on 9 February the Oxford Union passed the resolution 'That this house will in no circumstances fight for its King and Country', following a brilliant speech by an outside speaker, Joad. It was often subsequently rationalized as merely *pacificist*, because it was verbally compatible with support for either a pro-league or an anti-capitalist war, and might indeed have been debated as such if either Angell or Strachey had been able to accept the invitation to propose it. But it was understood by Joad—the Oxford Union's fifth choice as proposer, since Russell and Nichols had also been asked—and by all the other speakers on the night as 'a declaration of passive resistance in any circumstances', in the reproving words of Christ Church's history tutor Keith Feiling to his former pupil, Frank Hardie, who was president of the Union at the time.[62] There were several reasons why this pacifist motion proved so much more controversial than the one Ponsonby had carried at Cambridge six years before: it occurred at a more newsworthy university; its tacit allusion to the 'Your King and Country Need You' recruiting slogan of 1914 implied that the First World War had been a futile sacrifice; it showed apparent disrespect for the crown; and, above all, it took place at a time of heightened international tension. Even so, it might well have received little attention had its critics simply ignored it: instead, they denounced it in the national press, leading certain former members of the Union, including Winston Churchill's son Randolph, into an ill-advised and ill-fated attempt to have it expunged from the record at a much-publicized second debate. Although it was his son who had thus done much to create publicity for it, Churchill was after the Second World War to lend his authority to the view that

---

[59] A. Henderson, *Labour's Foreign Policy* (1933), 10, 13.

[60] S. Huddleston, *War Unless* (1933), 65, 71. See also his *In my Time* (1938), 310.

[61] Ceadel, *Pacifism in Britain 1914–1945*, 126, 131. Gaffin and Thoms, *Caring and Sharing*, 110.

[62] Feiling to F. Hardie, 17 Feb. 1933: Hardie Papers.

no real to evidence to blame actors for failure to deter Hitler

the 'King and Country' debate bore significant responsibility for Britain's failure to deter Hitler from provoking that conflict. This allegation, for which no supporting evidence has ever been found, conveniently distracted attention from the record of Churchill's own party during the six and half years between the passing of the Oxford resolution and the outbreak of war.[63]

'Never again!' sentiment was also expressed as socialist *pacificism*. The British Anti-War Movement's campaign for war resistance thus increased its support during 1933. The congress which it held at Bermondsey on 4–5 March claimed an attendance of 1,510 delegates, of whom supposedly only seventy-three were Communists, and declared its goal to be the registration of 10,000 supporters, issuing pledge forms for this purpose. Although nothing was heard of this target again, by the beginning of July W. J. Brown was claiming that since holding its Bermondsey congress, the movement had 'grown with great rapidity, until today there is hardly a town in the country which has not either an established Anti-War Committee or a group of registered supporters of the Anti-War Movement'.[64] Moreover, its influence was apparent at the National Peace Congress at Oxford on 7–10 July—the first such gathering since 1928 and the best attended and publicized ever. The 'rather vociferous contingent from the new Anti-War Council, much skilled at the art of "getting in" by means of points of order' irritated the FoR's general secretary, though he acknowledged that its interventions had the advantage of making clear that 'the so-called Anti-War Council is opposed only to what it chooses to call "imperialist war" and is certainly not prepared to oppose war that it regards as a revolutionary weapon'.[65] Richard Crossman sympathized with the British Anti-War Movement—unsurprisingly in view of the fact that he was then married to a German who had worked as a courier for Münzenberg[66]—and therefore urged Frank Hardie, who was covering the National Peace Congress for a local journal, to 'distinguish Pacifism of the Quaker Type which if it got a majority in England would only lead to "non-cooperation in War" but would not prevent war with the Genuine Pacifism of the Anti-War Congress which says "I *fight* Fascism and Monopoly for the sake of peace" '. Even though he had recently returned from a trip to Germany which had convinced him that 'they will rearm whatever happens',[67] Crossman, like the Communists, still saw 'fighting fascism' as an internal problem for

---

[63] For a comprehensive study, see M. Ceadel, 'Student Politics, Pacifism, and the Dictators: The Oxford Union's "King and Country" Resolution, 1933', *Historical Journal*, 22 (1979), 397–422.

[64] *New Statesman* (1 July 1933), 10–11.

[65] *Reconciliation* (Aug. 1933), 155.

[66] A. Howard, *Crossman: The Pursuit of Power* (1990), 33–4.

[67] Crossman to Hardie, 3 Aug. 1933: Hardie Papers.

Britain, arising from the supposedly proto-fascist nature of the National government and manifesting itself in an anti-Soviet foreign policy, rather than as an external problem, arising out of Nazism and manifesting itself in German expansionism.

The tide of pacifism and war resistance was strong enough to pose problems for both the LNU and the Labour leadership. At the former's general council on 20–3 June 1933, the organizer for the Manchester district, C. E. Clift, argued that 'the Oxford resolution has served its purpose, and ... should be replaced by a more carefully worded declaration'. He therefore proposed a motion to the effect 'that individuals would be justified in refusing to fight or assist in any war waged in contravention of the Covenant'. This motion alarmed the LNU's executive committee, which declared that it was 'not the function of the Union to decide questions for the individual conscience but to influence, as far as possible, the policy of H. M. Government'; and Cecil had to use his personal prestige to substitute a version stating merely that members should use 'all constitutional means to prevent the Government acting in contravention of that principle'.[68]

Clift's motion was taken up, however, by some of Labour's league enthusiasts as a way of diverting war resistance into a comparatively safe channel. Its most enthusiastic exponent was Konni Zilliacus, one of the party's most exotic figures. Born in Japan, of mixed Scandinavian and American parentage, and educated in America, Finland, Sweden, and Britain, Zilliacus was ideally qualified for the job he held for nearly nineteen years in the information section of the League of Nations Secretariat at Geneva. He also had the energy to produce a stream of personal books and pamphlets on league affairs, using a series of pseudonyms until his resignation from the Geneva secretariat in October 1938 freed him to publish under his own name. In the 1920s, as 'Roth Williams', his outlook had been relatively sanguine and orthodoxly liberal-*pacificist*. After 1933, however, as 'Vigilantes', he became alarmed at a world crisis which he traced back to the coming to power of the National government,[69] and moved to the left. As he was to put it later in the decade: 'Beginning as a straight Norman Angellite, I have evolved under the impact of events since 1931 into a socialist.' But, having retained his political loyalty to the league despite adding an economic commitment to Marxism, Zilliacus had become only 'a partial heretic', as he put it.[70] In other words, he believed he could reconcile liberalism with socialism by arguing that it was capitalism which produced the nation-state and therefore inter-

---

[68] *Report LNU General Council June 1933*, 40–7. Minutes, LNU executive, 29 May 1933.
[69] Vigilantes, *The Dying Peace* (*New Statesman* pamphlet; 29 Sept. 1933), 5.
[70] Vigilantes, *Between Two Wars?* (1939), 29–30.

national anarchy.[71] Zilliacus was thus attracted to the Clift resolution as a way of combining the rejection of capitalist wars with support for league sanctions. In July 1933 he circulated a memorandum to his acquaintances in the party, 'giving my idea of the way in which the idea of direct resistance to the war might be linked up with loyalty to the League and the whole policy "put across" on public opinion and the Labour Party'.[72]

Zilliacus managed to stop some socialists going all the way to war resistance. They included Lord Parmoor's son Stafford Cripps, whose views had recently undergone a dramatic change. Formerly a Labour moderate whose initial response to the 1931 political response was sympathy for MacDonald, and a keen member of the World Alliance For Promoting International Friendship Through the Churches who was optimistic about the league and disarmament,[73] Cripps had suddenly adopted a Marxist perspective and helped to found the Socialist League in October 1932 to fill the vacuum within the Labour Party left by the ILP's disaffiliation. Early in 1933 he began expounding a left-wing view of international relations too, condemning the league and the World Disarmament Conference as 'broken reeds' unable 'to prevent capitalist nationalism plunging the world again into war', and calling on the left 'to counter the war hysteria by a general strike'.[74] However, though apparently poised on the brink of unconditional war resistance, he was persuaded by Zilliacus to step back, and to oppose only wars in contravention of the League Covenant.[75] Even so, Cripps was sufficiently uncertain about how much positive support he could show to a league run by capitalist governments that Labour's league enthusiasts regarded him as muddled.[76]

Zilliacus's strategy was taken up in modified form by the party's leadership. Henderson's pamphlet of July 1933 proposed to pass a Peace Act enshrining Britain's international obligations, such as those under the League Covenant and Kellogg–Briand pact, thereby placing 'our national legislation in full accord with our international obligations'.[77] The implication was that war resistance would become legitimate if a government flouted this statute: a Labour Party statement the following year was thus to claim that the Peace Act would make it 'impossible for any British Government to use force as an instrument of national policy without violating the law of the land'.[78]

---

[71] See, e.g. Vigilantes, *Why the League has Failed* (1938), 12.

[72] Zilliacus to Cripps, 7 July 1933: Cripps Papers.

[73] E. Estorick, *Stafford Cripps: A Biography* (1949), 60. S. Burgess, *Stafford Cripps: A Political Life* (1999), 36–41, 51. Speech notes, Bristol 28 June 1931, Bridlington 21 Jan. 1932: Cripps Papers.   [74] *New Clarion* (25 Mar. 1933), 301, 309.

[75] See Cripps's speech at Whitehaven on 29 July: *The Times* (31 July 1933).

[76] Noel Baker to Viscount Cecil, 3 Nov. 1933: Cecil Papers Add. MSS 51108.

[77] Henderson, *Labour's Foreign Policy*, 20.

[78] Labour Party, *For Socialism and Peace* (Dec. 1934), 13.

In addition to thus creating a 'never again!' mood that stimulated near-isolationism and appeasement as well as pacifism and war resistance, and which forced league supporters into damage-limitation exercises, Hitler's accession produced a few conversions in support of containment. The most dramatic was that of Rennie Smith, who had seemed close to pacifism or war resistance while working for the National Peace Council. However, he later claimed to have harboured a suspicion of Germany ever since had been trapped in that country at the outbreak of the First World War. Having gone to Berlin in mid-July 1914 to work for the International Federation of Trade Unions, Smith had been interned on the outbreak of war. Though soon repatriated, because as an Independent Methodist lay preacher he counted as a minister of religion, his sojourn in Germany had been long enough to convince him of that country's bellicosity. His subsequent marriage to a German—one of the few he had met who shared his opposition to the war as well as his socialism—failed to shake this view. On his return home he found British peace activists ill-informed about the attitudes of ordinary Germans. He was particularly irritated, or so he later claimed, by Brockway's 'naive, ignorant conception of a massive war-resistance movement in Germany, which only wanted a little encouragement from the British side, by simple fools like himself, to bring the war to an end'.[79]

However, there is no evidence that Rennie Smith took a stand on this issue at the time. Indeed, because of the terms on which he had been released by the Germans, he was excused military service and counted technically as a conscientious objector. Spending much of the war at Woodbrooke, the Quaker college near Birmingham, he enjoyed close relations with some of the most absolutist of Quaker pacifists, including A. Barratt Brown. Subsequently, as both a Labour MP and secretary of the National Peace Council he campaigned for disarmament. In 1926, 'trusting to the higher forces of human nature instead of dissipating our strength in naval and other ways that can only lead to disaster', he seconded an amendment to the naval estimates which—as its proposer, Lansbury, admitted—in effect called for the destruction of the Royal Navy.[80] And in 1929 he was claimed by the NMWM as one of 'our MPs'.[81]

However, by 1930, when Smith left the National Peace Council to work for Dalton, his underlying anti-pacifism had begun to surface, perhaps as a result of reading *Mein Kampf* during 1929. After losing his parliamentary seat at the 1931 general election, moreover, he was freer to express heretical beliefs; and

[79] 'Autobiography', fo. 162.
[80] Hansard, 192 HC col. 2765 (11 Mar. 1926).
[81] *No More War* (June 1929), 7.

he undertook voluntary work for the Inter-Parliamentary Union which kept him in touch with developments in Germany. He later claimed that it was on the 'same day' as Hitler became Chancellor that he resolved to expose German militarism.[82] With the help of J. L. Garvin, the veteran editor of the *Observer* who condemned the Nazi regime from the start,[83] and William Tyrrell, a critic of the LNU as already noted, who helped him raise money, Smith prepared a series of pamphlets about the Nazi regime, many of them his own translations of German texts, under the imprint 'Friends of Europe'. The first batch appeared in October 1933, during which month he also sent confidential memoranda to the LNU on German war preparations, and endorsed Henderson's views at Labour's 1933 conference.[84] With encouragement from Churchill and Wickham Steed, Smith was to continue with this work until the Second World War when he accepted a post on the pro-Czech *Central European Observer*. Predictably, however, his sudden change of tack in 1933 caused him to be 'often accused, by political friends who should have known better, of being a warmonger'.[85]

In addition, a handful of pacifists whose first response to Hitler's accession had been to reaffirm their absolutism began rethinking their position almost immediately. It was while he was still writing *Cry Havoc!*, which was published in July 1933 and marketed as a pacifist work, that Nichols realized that in principle he supported an international army. The 'collapse of faith in pure pacifism' which 'led automatically to the less picturesque step of devotion to the League of Nations', as he later described it, thus began in 1933.[86] Similarly, Joad soon admitted that it was 'useless' to urge conscientious objection alone and began advocating an international army too.[87] He made clear that his scruples would not allow him personally to serve in it, a seemingly contradictory position which he tried to justify, without managing to dispel the suspicion that he was essentially an exemptionist.[88] Since both Nichols and Joad were to reaffirm their absolutism before finally accepting the need to fight Hitler, their second thoughts in mid-1933 are most coherently interpreted as a retreat from optimistic to collaborative pacifism. More decisively as well as more famously, Einstein revoked his support for conscientious objection in a letter to the King of the Belgians which was published in August, and subsequently announced his support for

---

[82] 'Autobiography', fo. 253.
[83] D. Ayerst, *Garvin of the Observer* (1985), 243–4.
[84] Murray Papers, file 218, fos. 116, 126–30. *LPCR* (1933), 194.
[85] 'Autobiography', fo. 253 (see also fo. 270).
[86] B. Nichols, *Cry Havoc!* (1933), 242. Nichols, *Men Do Not Weep* (1941), 15.
[87] *Peace* (May 1933), 9. *New Statesman* (25 Nov. 1933), 653.
[88] See Ceadel, *Pacifism in Britain 1914–1945*, 160.

the New Commonwealth Society. However, in the English-speaking world the effect of Einstein's emphatic recantation was somewhat spoilt by the almost simultaneous publication of an edition of his collected pacifist assertions.[89]

Some of those already supportive of the case for international law and order spoke up for it early in 1933. The most influential was Allen, whose letter in *The Times* of 8 February 1933 argued that 'there may yet arise some case in which military sanctions may have to be considered as an extreme measure', and that an international civil-aviation authority could, 'if finally and absolutely necessary, be also resorted to for world police purposes'. He later criticized the negativity of the 'King and Country' motion,[90] and argued for sanctions in the LNU's journal.[91] In addition, he addressed the National Peace Congress at Oxford in July: his message was that the peace movement should not should not hold back from supporting 'security, law and order', which the world so urgently needed, simply 'because of a doctrine called Pacifism'; that this doctrine 'is not and never can be a political method so long as it is chiefly concerned with abstaining from the use of force'; and that its exponents should therefore either redefine their belief 'as something emphasising the power of reason' or 'go out of politics'.[92] However, his value to the cause of containment was somewhat reduced by his insistence that he remained a pacifist and a believer in the value of conscientious objection.[93]

Allen was supported at the Oxford congress by Angell, whose political position had also recently undergone a significant change, although his knighthood had come while MacDonald was still a Labour Prime Minister and he never formally broke with the Labour Party. Having come to dislike the personal and ideological demands of being a MP, Angell had stood down at the 1931 general election; and as Labour flirted with Marxism in reaction to that year's crisis he gradually came to the conclusion that he had never been a wholehearted socialist. Indeed, in 1940 he was privately to admit to Murray that 'having tried to make the best of all the Socialist slogans and Marxist incantations, I have been pushed more and more to the conviction that it is your type of Liberalism which alone can save us'.[94] It was understandable that, as an increasingly orthodox liberal-*pacificist* advocate of 'pooled power',[95] Angell was willing to endorse Allen's sanctionist argu-

---

[89] Ibid. 125.
[90] *New Statesman* (25 Feb. 1933), 219. He did so again in Lord Allen of Hurtwood, *Britain's Political Future* (1934), 92–3.
[91] *HW* (July 1933), 138.
[92] His speech was published in G. P. Gooch (ed.), *In Pursuit of Peace* (1933), 16–27: see especially 18–19.
[93] He was to reiterate this claim in 1935: see Bell (ed.), *We Did Not Fight*, 37.
[94] Angell to Murray, 13 July 1940: Murray Papers.
[95] See, e.g. his contribution in *HW* (Oct. 1932), 184–5.

ments in 1933. But it was more surprising that he too felt obliged to insist, in his writings at this time as well as at the National Peace Congress, that non-resistance and unilateral disarmament were his preferred policies.[96]

The LNU began to grasp the nettle of security in 1933, despite its wish to nurture the World Disarmament Conference, which had almost collapsed late in 1932 because of the contradictions between France's demand for security and Germany's demand for equality, and its fear of scaring off more members. Murray was prompted by Allen's letter in *The Times* to admit to Cecil that 'L.N.U. speakers as a whole have rather funked the question of security because audiences don't like it'.[97] Although when the league belatedly condemned Japan in March 1933 it did not consider punitive measures, the practical issues involved in the imposition of sanctions could no longer be ignored. The Royal Institute of International Affairs set up a study group on the subject under the chairmanship of Fischer Williams, though its deliberations were to be very protracted.[98] And Noel Baker informed Murray that 'we have got to have a great sanctions campaign in England in the near future, and in such a campaign lies the chief hope for the survival of the League': indeed, he envisaged that his own 'main occupation in life during the next two years' would be 'to get the Labour Party tied up to a sanctions policy so tightly that it cannot possible wriggle out of it'.[99] From this time Noel Baker was undoubtedly an enthusiastic sanctionist, albeit one who exaggerated the extent to which others were of a like mind.

The LNU's attempt to work out a sanctions policy was complicated by the divisive issue of an international police force. On 30 March 1933 the LNU's executive committee, to which the issue had been remitted by the general council, voted by sixteen votes to ten in favour of supporting such a force as a means of providing the security necessary to a disarmament agreement. But its Conservative members—led by Austen Chamberlain, who had joined the executive committee in February 1932 as a restraining influence,[100] but including J. W. Hills, whose genuine support for the league has already been acknowledged—protested that an international force 'would change the whole character of the League, perverting it from an instrument for preserving the peace into an engine for waging war'.[101] Since the LNU leadership

---

[96] Ceadel, *Pacifism in Britain 1914–1945*, 141–4.
[97] Murray to Cecil, 18 Feb. 1933 (copy): Murray Papers.
[98] The RIIA group produced an interim report in Oct. 1935 and, reconvening after the Abyssinia crisis, issued a substantial study, *International Sanctions*, in 1938.
[99] Noel Baker to Murray, 28 Mar. 1933: Murray Papers.
[100] *The Austen Chamberlain Diary Letters: The Correspondence of Sir Austen Chamberlain with his sisters Hilda and Ida, 1916–1937*, ed. R. C. Self (Camden 5th series 5; Cambridge, 1995), 411.
[101] Minutes, LNU Executive, 30 Mar. 1933. Chamberlain to Cecil, 3 Apr. 1933 Cecil Papers, Add. MSS 51079.

did not wish to jeopardize its all-party status by losing Chamberlain and Hills, and since it had its own reservations about an idea pressed on it by the New Commonwealth Society, it decided to drop the international police force. It thus found it expedient to reaffirm its confidence in economic pressure instead. As Murray explained to Noel Baker on 2 April 1933: 'We are having a grave and deep-seated difference in the L.N.U. about the Air Force . . . and I think we must concentrate on (1) the need of sanctions and (2) the effectiveness of diplomatic, financial, and economic sanctions.'[102] In June Cecil managed, by reiterating his own long-standing belief in economic pressure, to persuade the general council to accept this strategy.[103] This decision irritated the New Commonwealth Society but was the best outcome which the LNU leadership could achieve. In any case the Clift motion was shortly to reveal that a substantial section of the rank and file was at this time more interested in resisting non-league wars than in equipping the league with its own armed force. In these circumstances, endorsing economic sanctions was a reasonable compromise.

THE DISARMAMENT CRISIS, OCTOBER–DECEMBER 1933

The crisis at Geneva in the autumn of 1933 produced a greater impact on British thinking than the installation of the Nazi regime earlier in the year. It had been brewing for weeks because of the depth of Franco-German disagreements. On 28 September, the president of the World Disarmament Conference, Henderson, who had just been re-elected to the Commons at a by-election, admitted privately to the National Peace Council that 'it almost baffles me how we can bring closer together these two Powers'.[104]

In the short term the crisis was to stimulate the 'never again!' reflex in its varying forms. Near-isolationism was preached with increased vigour by both the Beaverbrook and the Rothermere press, which called for rearmament and intensified their attacks on the league. It was also acknowledged in a study of the Christian view of war which appeared at this time and identified 'Keep Britain out of war' as 'the one rallying cry which seems to unite all shades of opinion'.[105]

War resistance enjoyed its finest hour on 4 October when the Labour Party's conference at Hastings passed by acclamation a resolution 'to take no part in war'. This had been proposed by C. P. (now, having inherited a

---

[102] Murray to Baker, 2 Apr. 1933 (copy) Murray Papers.
[103] *Report, LNU General Council June 1933*, 57.
[104] NPC council minutes, 28 Sept. 1931.
[105] E. N. Porter Goff, *The Christian and the Next War* (1933), 41.

baronetcy, Sir Charles) Trevelyan, who exulted: 'The declaration can never be gone back on. The Labour Party without compromise is committed to war resistance.'[106] He had been backed by the Socialist League—his own membership of this body being a further indication of how attitudes had moved leftwards since 1931—and had also received support from the British Anti-War Movement, whose influence within the labour movement reached a modest peak at this time.

Trevelyan's motion was adopted without a vote because Labour's league supporters, who controlled the national executive committee even though the party was led in parliament by pacifists, had felt that the tide in favour of war resistance was running too strongly to be met head on. Instead, they attempted to circumvent it. Through their spokesman, Dalton, they argued disingenuously that the failure of Trevelyan's motion to exempt league sanctions from its rejection of 'war' was a mere oversight.[107] They also tried to counter the imputation, to which the left had returned with some enthusiasm, that the League of Nations was a liberal rather than a socialist idea: Henderson emphasized that it 'was set up largely in response to the pressure of the Labour and Socialist Movement, and under the influence of Socialist thinkers. Its fundamental idea is precisely that for which we socialists stand.'[108] And above all they concentrated on securing the adoption of an additional motion, which probably escaped the left's critical notice because it was a long 'composite' of different themes, which included support for an international police force. Their strategy had some success: Cripps was privately persuaded that Trevelyan's was 'a ridiculous resolution' which 'fails to meet the issue of national defence and ignores the international obligation to refuse help to a peace breaker',[109] and proposed loyally that Henderson's speech be printed as a party pamphlet; and Ponsonby acknowledged to Lansbury that the 'resolutions at Hastings, good in some respects, were not logically watertight' and that the party was divided.[110] Even so, Trevelyan's motion was a major embarrassment for a party which later wished to present itself as having taken a resolute stand against the Nazi regime from the outset.

Moreover, when, just eight days after Labour's delegates left Hastings, Hitler withdrew his country from both the World Disarmament Conference and the league, his skill in presenting his move as a response to intransigence by Britain and France meant that many progressives agreed with Brailsford's

---

[106] *Adelphi* (Nov. 1933), 121.
[107] H. Dalton, *The Fateful Years: Memoirs 1931–45* (1957), 45–6.
[108] *LPCR* (1933), 190.
[109] Cripps to H. Lauterpacht, 27 Oct. 1933 (copy): Cripps Papers.
[110] Ponsonby to Lansbury, 22 Oct. 1933: Lansbury Papers.

initial assessment: 'Germany has a Case'.[111] For example, Will Arnold-Forster of National Peace Council, who after a late-summer visit to a concentration camp in Bavaria had condemned the Nazi revolution as 'a more cold-blooded, deliberate denial of the fundamentals of justice and mercy than the great denial that comes with war', was now persuaded that 'we must win Germany's loyal collaboration as a partner' and that 'to use now the language of menace to Hitler, when his case is as good as it still is, is to . . . postpone indefinitely the necessary healing process'.[112]

The need to accommodate German demands was also the message of the talk broadcast from Geneva on the evening of the German walk-out by the BBC's popular pundit on international affairs, Vernon Bartlett,[113] who ironically was to be best remembered for winning the Bridgwater by-election five years later as an anti-appeaser. Blame thus immediately fell on the National government, which belatedly paid the political price for the decision of successive cabinets not to risk unpopularity by pointing out the obstacles to general disarmament.

It was understandable that Labour responded to this political opportunity by playing the peace card. At a by-election on 25 October in the normally safe Conservative seat of East Fulham its candidate, John Wilmot, achieved a sensational victory which he attributed to his emphasis on

peace and the Labour Party programme . . . The withdrawal of Hitler from the League and the tense international situation which developed occurred in the middle of the election campaign. The effect of this war scare was the exact opposite of previous experience. Instead of a stampede to Toryism and armaments, the electors calmly turned to the Labour Party as the people who mean peace, disarmament and cooperation.[114]

Baldwin reacted by sending an open letter to his party's candidate at Skipton, the next in a series of by-elections being held that autumn, which insisted that the opposition's imputation that 'the Conservative Party does not believe in Peace and Disarmament' was a 'calculated and mischievous lie'.[115] Simon, the Foreign Secretary, was so worried that, upon receiving a letter from Murray congratulating him on his Commons speech of 7 November, he at once telegraphed back: 'Don't you think letter on similar grounds over your

---

[111] For Brailsford's article under this title see *New Clarion* (21 Oct. 1933), 317–18.
[112] *Peace* (Sept. 1933), 3–4; (Nov. 1933), 1–2, 5.
[113] *Listener* (18 Oct. 1933), 570. V. Bartlett, *This is my Life* (1937), 188–92.
[114] *New Clarion* (4 Nov. 1933). For a full account of East Fulham see M. Ceadel, 'Interpreting East Fulham', in C. Cook and J. Ramsden (eds.), *By-Elections in British Politics* (2nd edn., 1997), 94-111.
[115] *The Times* (28 Oct. 1933), cited in J. P. Kyba, 'British Attitudes toward Disarmament and Rearmament 1932–5', Ph.D. thesis (London University, 1967), fo. 337.

signature to *Times* might be useful to show that Government have the support of the Chairman of the League of Nations Union?'[116] Although Labour won no more seats, its tactics in the by-elections of November and December 1933 brought about an average swing of 14.8 per cent in its favour.

That Labour's propaganda, though positive towards disarmament, was negative towards Britain's international obligations began to worry league supporters. A senior LNU official, John Eppstein, complained to Noel Baker that

Labour candidates are joining in the chorus against the Locarno Treaty, apparently in the hope of profiting by the isolationist campaign of the Express Newspapers. Wilmot, who was elected at East Fulham, though admirable from our point of view in his enthusiasm for disarmament, is credited with having renounced Continental commitments, including Locarno, and the Reverend G. S. Woods, Labour candidate at the Rusholme Bye-Election, is reported to have said: Locarno must go ... If we are not making any mistake, what is attacked in this reckless campaign is the whole spirit of British participation in collective defence against aggression.

Although, characteristically, Noel Baker denied that Eppstein's information was accurate,[117] Labour's candidates at several of these by-elections— Skipton, Rusholme, and Kilmarnock—were indeed professed pacifists. (In addition, the local physics don who stood for the party in Cambridge early in the new year, Alex Wood, was to be the chairman of the Peace Pledge Union for most of the Second World War.) Attlee admitted privately to his brother Thomas, a former conscientious objector who had been active in both the NCF and FoR,[118] that the labour movement 'has not really made up its mind as to whether it wants to take up extreme disarmament and [an] isolationist attitude or whether it will take the risks of standing for the enforcement of decisions of a world organisation against the individual aggressor states'.[119] Attlee shared many of the left's instinctive reservations about a pro-league policy, having not only supported the UDC but even, as he was to admit to the party's 1934 conference, having once favoured 'unilateral disarmament';[120] and he was still anxious to criticize those willing 'to follow Liberal instead of socialist solutions'.[121] The *Spectator*—under the stewardship of Wilson Harris, the former member of the Friends' Service Committee who had gone

[116] Simon to Murray, 9 Nov. 1933 (telegram): Murray Papers.

[117] J. Eppstein to P. Noel Baker, 7 Nov. 1933, and reply, 8 Nov. 1933 (copy): Murray Papers.

[118] See *Labour Leader* (6 May 1915), 2; and Minutes, FoR general committee, 14 Dec. 1915.

[119] C. Attlee to T. Attlee, 6 Nov. 1933, cited in W. Golant, 'The Emergence of C. R. Attlee as Leader of the Parliamentary Labour Party in 1935', *Historical Journal*, 13 (1970), 318–32 at 327. For a similar acknowledgement of Labour's ambiguity at this time, see G. R. Mitchison, *The First Workers' Government* (1934), 310.

[120] *LPCR* (1934), 174.

[121] Geneva Institute of International Relations, *Problems of Peace*, 9th series (1935), 114.

on to edit *Headway*—was of the opinion that, although peace and disarmament were 'very nearly a winning card in most constituencies', it was impossible to know 'whether the average voter means peace through a precarious isolation or through a world-organisation'.[122]

The German withdrawal from Geneva turned some peace activists against sanctions. Royden immediately withdrew her blessing from the New Commonwealth Society, having realized that, with the abolition of national military aviation now unlikely, an international police force would almost certainly have to be armed 'with the most terrible of modern weapons'.[123] She was not to join a pacifist association until the Munich crisis; but others did so at this time. The absolutist covenant of the Methodist Peace Fellowship which Henry Carter launched on 3 November 1933 was accepted by 500 ministers and the burgeoning of denominational groups of this kind led soon afterwards to the formation of a Council of Christian Pacifist Groups to coordinate them.[124]

Other peace activists were driven to espouse peaceful change. Allen qualified his recent emphasis on law and order by adding a parallel commitment to this policy. Even before the German walk-out he had been planning to hold 'a private conference of the National Peace Council . . . on October 20th . . . attended by about fifty peace experts, ranging from Cecil down to Hardie of Oxford', as he put it to Kingsley Martin.[125] He now used this gathering to put forward a fourteen-point plan to rescue the World Disarmament Conference, which Hardie and a journalist friend, Jonathan Griffin, agreed to help promote. This would require all nations to achieve total disarmament within 'a final 10 or 20 years' period' and to establish a security system based on the internationalization of civil aviation. Crucially, however, Germany was in the interim to receive 'special treatment' by being allowed 'to have prototype weapons or to rearm', while other powers were required to destroy 'all arms denied to Germany under the Treaty of Versailles'.[126] Bellerby, Joad, Noel Baker, Wilmot, and Leonard Woolf agreed to endorse a version of this plan.[127] But Murray's response to Griffin was to dismiss the goal of total disarmament as wholly unrealistic, and warn that it was 'rather important not to give occasion for any accusation that we are utopian or are crying for the

---

[122] *Spectator* (24 Nov .1933), 754. For Harris's time on the LNU staff see Harris, *Life So Far*, 200–7.

[123] Royden to Davies, 27 Oct. 1933: Davies of Llandinam Papers.

[124] *Reconciliation* (Dec. 1933), 234.

[125] Allen to Martin, 12 Oct. 1933: Kingsley Martin Papers 49. The largest collection of material relating to Allen's conference is in the Noel-Baker Papers 5/147.

[126] Allen's plan was printed in a weekly news digest edited by Griffin: *Essential News* (28 Oct. 1933), 1–5.

[127] Griffin to Murray, 13 Dec. 1933: Murray Papers.

moon'.[128] Cecil's telling response to Hardie was to note that 'your points are almost entirely what Germany desires, and very little indeed is given to the French point of view'.[129] Cecil had correctly identified where Allen's sympathies ultimately lay. Although continuing to advocate an international police force, for example at the LNU's general council in December 1933, Allen did so as part of a dual policy in which accommodation became increasingly the more important strand. Hitler sensed this, and rewarded him with a personal interview on 25 January 1935. As the two components of the dual policy became more difficult to keep together, Allen was to tilt further and further in the direction of peaceful change, until finally he crossed the line into appeasement.

Cecil countered with a plan of his own which was more acceptable to France because it offset the abolition within five years of the arms denied to Germany with 'a reaffirmation of the obligations of mutual assistance against aggression contained in the Covenant and Treaties of Locarno'.[130] However, he too failed to secure sufficient signatures to issue it as a collective manifesto.[131] The left was less willing to beat the sanctionist drum in the autumn of 1933 than it later cared to remember. Admittedly, the international Communist movement showed the first sign of moving towards an anti-fascist position when the World Anti-War Movement's student congress in Paris on 25–6 September described itself as 'Against War and Fascism' instead of merely 'Anti-War';[132] but its British supporters still advocated war resistance. Similarly, the outspoken All Souls historian and Labour activist A. L. Rowse argued that 'the object of a truly Socialist foreign policy' must now be 'to help bring down and destroy the Hitler regime';[133] but his views were unusual. More typical of progressive attitudes was Michael Foot, who at this time was known for his 'genuine pacifism and conscientious objection to the use of arms',[134] although this fact could not have been inferred from the ferocious indictment of the National government for its failure to prepare for a war against Hitler that he was to co-write in 1940.[135] Similarly, although the chairman of the LNU's Olton branch, Colonel Docker, argued that the time had come to exclude pacifists, the executive committee at Grosvenor Crescent ruled against him.[136]

[128] Murray to Griffin, 12 Dec. 1933: Murray Papers.

[129] Cecil to Hardie, 29 Nov. 1933: Hardie Papers.

[130] Cecil's memorandum, dated 27 Nov. 1933, was enclosed in his letter to Cripps, 30 Nov. 1933: Cripps Papers.

[131] Cecil to Murray, 2 Dec. 1933: Murray Papers. Noel Baker to Hardie, 2 Dec. 1933: Hardie Papers.

[132] Ceadel, 'The First Communist "Peace Society" ', 83.

[133] *New Clarion* (4 Nov. 1933), 356. [134] *Isis* (18 Oct. 1933), 7.

[135] 'Cato', *Guilty Men* (1940). [136] Minutes, LNU Executive, 16 Nov. 1933.

It was only as Hitler's first year in office came to an end that the 'never again!' reflex subsided and what was then called the 'collective peace system' came to be more generally accepted. For example, it was while writing his contribution to *Young Oxford and War*, a collection of essays published early in 1934, that Foot's views began to change. His essay began with the case for non-violence but, without betraying any awareness of inconsistency, concluded with the case for 'a collective force'.[137]

Foot's friend Hardie arrived at the same view at the same time, but by a more complex route which illustrates the intellectual turmoil in which many young activists found themselves during 1933. Though an orthodox league supporter as a teenager, Hardie regarded himself as a pacifist by the time he presided over the 'King and Country' debate on 9 February, asserting in the *New Statesman* nine days later that 'the best method of ending war was one of individual resistance to any future war'. However, after being accused by A. E. Zimmern, Oxford's first professor of international relations, of blurring 'the vital distinction between Individual Resistance . . . and Resistance in the name of a law superior to that of the individual State',[138] Hardie began to shown a greater awareness of other strands of peace thought, arguing in the *Manchester Guardian* for 29 May: ' "Pacifism is not enough." To be in favour of peace as opposed to war is only a first and small step. The next step is to think out clearly what are the means to peace.' By now he was claiming that the Oxford resolution could in principle be endorsed not only by Quakers (in other words, as a statement of pacifism), but also by league supporters (as liberal *pacificism*) and Marxists (as the socialist-*pacificist* strategy of war resistance).

Soon afterwards, despite being cautioned against 'Marxist assumptions' by Angell,[139] he transferred his support to the last of these remedies, which he was anxious to distinguish from his previous allegiance by describing it as 'not merely the resistance of individual pacifists basing their action on humanitarian or religious motives but the mass resistance of the working classes basing their action on economic motives'.[140] He thus found himself in agreement with the speech made by the Cambridge economist Maurice Dobb, a Communist who supported the British Anti-War Movement, to the National Peace Congress in Oxford.[141] However, in the autumn of 1933 his enthusiasm

---

[137] M. Foot, R. G. Freeman, F. Hardie, and K. Steel-Maitland, *Young Oxford and War* (1934), 19–70.

[138] Zimmern to Hardie, 22 (also 16) Mar. 1933: Hardie Papers. For the immediate effect of this letter on Hardie's thinking see the *New Statesman* (1 Apr. 1933), 412.

[139] Angell to Hardie, 4 May 1933: Hardie Papers.

[140] *New Statesman* (4 Nov. 1933), 547.

[141] Dobb acknowledged Hardie's support on that occasion in a letter of 26 July 1933: Hardie Papers.

for war resistance waned under the influence of Allen, by now a critic of the view that capitalism caused war, as the two of them tried to resuscitate the World Disarmament Conference. By November Hardie had therefore become critical of 'isolationism', both 'in a militarist form on the right' and 'in a Communist or semi-Communist form on the left', and instead advocated 'the middle course of internationalism'.[142] Finally, in December he set out his new and enduring support for the collective peace system in his contribution to *Young Oxford and War*.

Hardie's voyage of intellectual self-discovery during 1933 had swept him from pacifism to war resistance before taking him back to the pro-league views of his adolescence. It was difficult for him to chart this journey because a key linguistic signpost was itself in transition. At the beginning of 1933 'pacifism' (like its purist variant 'pacificism', though this had become very rare) was still often used in a non-absolutist sense: indeed, Hardie used it as an umbrella term covering liberal and socialist *pacificists* as well as pacifists in his piece for the *Manchester Guardian* of 29 May. However, the more precise meaning rapidly gained ground during the year. By November, for example, Hardie was claiming: 'There would be less confusion if the word "pacifist" were always to be taken to mean one who, on account of certain principles, philosophical or religious, will, in no circumstances whatever, take part in war.'[143] Ironically, just at this time the older, broader, and increasingly less popular sense of the word was entrenched by the publication of a supplement to the main *Oxford English Dictionary*, which retained the same meaning as in the concise version which, as already noted, had first included it in 1914. This perpetuation of an obsolescent meaning was soon criticized by the LNU's Colonel Fisher,[144] and a decade later was infuriating R. B. McCallum, one of the five Oxford dons whose special study of economic sanctions has already been mentioned, who went out of his way to complain that there was 'no excuse for anyone who has lived through the past twenty years, whether dictionary makers or others', to overlook the word's 'extreme or narrower meaning'.[145] Despite the obstinacy of the *Oxford English Dictionary*, the primary meaning of 'pacifism' in the English-speaking world has since late 1933 been the absolutist one.

---

[142] Memorandum from Mr Frank Hardie, 4 Nov. 1933: Noel-Baker Papers 5/147.

[143] *New Statesman* (18 Nov. 1933), 630.

[144] *HW* (Nov. 1934), 217.

[145] R. B. McCallum, *Public Opinion and the Last Peace* (1944), 173. See also Ceadel, *Pacifism in Britain 1914–1945*, 144–6.

THE COLLECTIVE PEACE SYSTEM, JANUARY 1934–JUNE 1935

During 1934 the balance of progressive opinion tilted decisively in favour of the collective peace system, which was beginning also to be called 'pooled security' and was from the summer of the following year to be almost universally known as 'collective security'. Germany was rearming; and the French note of 17 April 1934 put paid to the idea that the World Disarmament Conference could be reconvened. One indication of evolving attitudes was Kathleen D. Courtney's withdrawal from the executive committee of the WIL, which had become paralysed on the issue of the international police force: she had left her pacifism behind and was becoming convinced, as she was to put it during the Second World War: 'Security is . . . the essence of world co-operation.'[146] Another was the *Spectator*'s observation in July 1934, the month in which Britain's first rearmament programme was to be announced, that some former supporters of the 'King and Country' resolution 'have since said that they did not mean thereby to declare themselves unwilling to fight in defence of the collective peace system'.[147]

Significant impetus was given to this process by the LNU, which boldly launched its National Declaration on the League of Nations and Armaments, better known as the Peace Ballot.[148] This originated in resentment at the claims of the right-wing press, whose intensified attacks on the league during the autumn of 1933 have been mentioned, to speak for the public generally. As early as November 1933 C. J. A. Boorman, the editor of the *Ilford Recorder* and a vice-chairman of the local LNU branch, had convened a public meeting to consider how to combat the 'misrepresentation' of British opinion. This had established a committee to conduct a local poll. It is conceivable that Bellerby's pioneering effort, which he had reported to Labour's Hastings conference the previous month, had given Boorman the idea. The Ilford committee drew up a questionnaire with four questions: about the League of Nations, the World Disarmament Conference, Locarno, and the private arms trade. Volunteers from fifty-six local organizations took it from door to door, securing 26,000 returns. The results showed over 80 per cent support for the league, disarmament, and the prohibition of the arms trade, but 75 per cent opposition to Locarno. Cecil was guest of honour at the public announcement of these results on 8 February 1934, which coincided with the

---

[146] See WIL, *19th Yearly Report Mar. 1934–Feb. 1935. HW* (Nov. 1943), 11.

[147] *Spectator* (6 July 1934), 5.

[148] This episode is most fully analysed in M. Ceadel, 'The First British Referendum: The Peace Ballot, 1934–5', *English Historical Review*, 95 (1980), 810–39. See also Birn, *League of Nations Union*, ch. 8, and J. A. Thompson, 'The "Peace Ballot" and the "Rainbow" Controversy', *Journal of British Studies*, 20/2 (Spring 1981), 150–70.

launching by some local Rothermere papers of polls with a different set of questions and using postcards rather than house-to-house visits. These were to produce similar levels of support for the league and the abolition of the private arms trade, though slightly less opposition to Locarno, and majority approval of an increase in the Royal Air Force 'if a continental power within air reach of London arms intensively in the air'.

Without waiting for the Rothermere results, Cecil pressed the LNU executive committee on 1 March to mount a nation-wide version of the Ilford ballot. He was confronted with considerable scepticism: many of the union's officers, both national and local, were worried about the cost and the disruption to the house-to-house canvass for new members which was being launched in a bid to stem the decline in subscriptions; and even Murray feared that press hostility would make it hard to generate the necessary volume of responses. However, Cecil's confidence in his own judgement and his expectation that the LNU would defer to it made him hard to gainsay. He managed, moreover, to interest other organizations, so that a national declaration committee was established on 11 April: like the disarmament campaign committee of seven years previously, this was kept separate from the LNU, being placed under the control of Dame Adelaide Livingstone, a formidable American who during the First World War had risen to the rank of major-general, making her reputation through her work for prisoners of war. And at the LNU's general council in June 1934 Cecil overcame grass-roots apprehensions about so ambitious and expensive an undertaking.

The Conservative Party's reservations about the questions to be posed by the national declaration committee were more difficult to deal with. It detected anti-capitalist bias in the question about the prohibition of the private arms trade. It was uneasy that questions were asked about disarmament in general and the abolition of military aviation in particular but not about the need for rearmament. But its principal objection of detail was that the question about sanctions was split into two parts, (*a*) and (*b*), which asked about economic and military sanctions respectively. Conservatives were convinced that these could not be separated from each other since effective economic pressure risked military retaliation. This is what Baldwin had meant when on 18 May 1934, in answer to a question from Eleanor Rathbone, a keen advocate of economic sanctions whose Quaker-turned-Unitarian forefathers from Liverpool had been prominent in the peace movement a century before, he had told the Commons that there was 'no such thing as a sanction that will work that does not mean war'.[149]

---

[149] Hansard, 289 HC col. 2139. See also M. Stocks, *Eleanor Rathbone: A Biography* (1949), 221–8; and Harrison, *Prudent Revolutionaries*, 113–14.

More generally, Conservatives also disliked the pretence that the ballot was an objective measurement of public opinion. Admittedly, this was still an undeveloped science: in 1934 George Gallup was only beginning to develop quota-sampling techniques in the United States. But the national declaration committee was not trying to be scientific: it wished to secure as many affirmative answers to its questions as it could. Its bias was particularly evident in the simplistic green leaflet, headed 'Peace or War?', which it proposed to issue with the ballot forms. The Conservatives objected strongly to this, Austen Chamberlain planning a dramatic resignation from the LNU's executive committee on the issue. The national declaration committee promptly offered the Conservatives a 'blue' leaflet of their own devising, to be issued with the green one. Recognizing that this timely concession 'did not leave me good ground for a breach', Chamberlain was left privately seething with resentment both at Cecil, whom he regarded as 'a fanatic . . . whose actions are always on the edge of hysteria', and at the national declaration committee, which he saw as 'entirely unscrupulous in their determination to steal a verdict'.[150] In the event, most ballot workers objected to issuing the blue leaflet, particularly on account of its comment on the two-part sanctions question: 'To answer question (a) with a yes, and (b) with a no would be to adopt a policy of bluff while openly proclaiming it to be a bluff and no more.'[151] This phrase also incensed the WIL,[152] whose continued survival as a coalition of pacifists and *pacificists* required it to believe in the efficacy of unaided economic sanctions. Local committees were therefore allowed to substitute a purely factual yellow leaflet for both the blue and green leaflets, the young Conservative MP Lord Cranborne commenting only half-jokingly to Cecil, his uncle, that 'these coloured papers are becoming more dangerous than coloured shirts'.[153]

Relations with the Conservatives—and also with pacifists—would have been even worse had the National Declaration Committee not omitted a question about an international air force. This had developed into a painfully divisive issue for the peace movement as a whole. Mrs Swanwick lambasted it (and argued for an economic embargo instead) in a series of pamphlets which the WIL published early in 1934, and when asked by Angell if she preferred national air forces to an international one replied that these at least presented themselves 'honestly' and were 'not camouflaged'.[154] Lord Davies published

---

[150] *Austen Chamberlain Diary Letters*, 465–8.
[151] Minutes, LNU Executive, 26 July 1934.
[152] Minutes, WIL Executive, 14 Aug. 1934.
[153] Cranborne to Cecil, 12 Nov. 1934: Cecil Papers Add. MSS 51087.
[154] H. M. Swanwick, *Pooled Security: What does it Mean?* (1934), 23. This pamphlet was a successor to *New Wars for Old (A Reply to the Rt. Hon. Lord Davies and Others)* (1934); and *Frankenstein and his Monster: Aviation for World Service (A Sequel to 'New Wars for Old')* (1934).

another book on the subject, forthrightly entitled *Force*, which criticized the LNU for having 'clung to the apron-strings of the Foreign Office or the skirts of the peace-at-any-price pacifists'.[155]

The New Commonwealth Society finally succeeded in pressing the issue to a vote at the union's June 1934 general council. It gained approval for an international police force in principle by 102 votes to 75, though an unlimited force with a bombing capacity (as distinct from a limited force with an interception role only) was endorsed by only seventy-six votes to seventy. However, to avoid splitting the LNU, Cecil later interceded to ask for a noncommittal resolution instead. As the Revd. Gwilym Davies, the secretary of the LNU's Welsh national council, reported to Lord Davies, Cecil was 'trembling with emotion', spoke movingly of the risk of 'a disastrous split', and, in 'the emotional, almost religious atmosphere' thereby created, got his way, the official report acknowledging 'a remarkable demonstration of loyalty to the President'.[156] However, the issue merely returned, via the union's aviation subcommittee, to its executive committee, where on 1 November Allen and Austen Chamberlain argued its pros and cons respectively, the former carrying the day by twenty-three votes to eight. The general council therefore had to reconsider the matter in December 1934. Allen again spoke as if the issue was the legitimacy of force. But Chamberlain reiterated that it was constitutional—the conversion of the league from 'an assembly of equal States' into 'a super-State put above us all'; and his fellow Conservative Lord Eustace Percy expressed regret that 'none of those who support Lord Allen's resolution seem to realize what, from our point of view, the issue of principle is'.[157] Once again, however, Cecil averted a divisive decision, the LNU agreeing that the practicalities of the question should be examined in the new year by a special conference on aviation. In these circumstances it was understandable that the national declaration committee did not saddle its ballot with a question on so controversial a topic.

Trial local ballots during the summer of 1934 indicated that, whereas securing the desired answers was unlikely to be a problem, recruiting sufficient volunteers across the country to make it a truly 'national' declaration might well be. Crucial to the ballot's success, therefore, was the accession of support it received from the left as polling got under way in the autumn.

By then the Labour Party had repudiated war resistance and unambiguously endorsed the collective peace system: its national executive committee had taken this decision as early as February; and left-wing intellectuals such

[155] Lord Davies, *Force* (1934), 207.
[156] G. Davies to Lord Davies, 28 June 1934 (copy): Gwilym Davies Papers. *Report, LNU Council June 1934*, 53.
[157] Minutes, LNU Executive, 1 Nov. 1934. *Report, LNU General Council Dec. 1934*, 58, 69.

as Crossman had turned against war resistance during the spring.[158] In October the party conference at Southport accepted 'the duty unflinchingly to support our Government in all the risks and consequences of fulfilling its duty to take part in collective action against a peace-breaker'.[159] In an attempt to deny that Labour had thereby reversed itself, Henderson invoked the composite resolution which the leadership had managed to pass the previous year in addition to Trevelyan's: 'At Hastings there were two resolutions that were carried. Some people seem to have forgotten that there were two and not one only.'[160]

Henderson was fully aware that many socialists still believed that the league should at best be regarded, in Brailsford's words, as 'the supreme creative effort of liberalism to save its maimed civilization from another war'.[161] He therefore again presented it instead as a 'revolutionary break with the traditions of international anarchy' which was based on 'the socialist principle of co-operation'. Bevin used similar tactics to rebut the pacifist objection to the league, likening Wellock, who had unavailingly proposed the deletion from the party's policy statement of the reference to the duty of collective action against a peace-breaker, to 'a man joining a Union on condition that under no circumstances will you ever ask him to strike'.[162] Even so, some left-wing delegates still complained that 'the League of Nations has been put into our programme instead of our own policy on peace and war', and attempted to make the party's policy statement more left-wing by replacing its reference to the 'brotherhood of man' by one to the 'international solidarity of the workers'.[163] And Brailsford continued to accuse league supporters of neglecting capitalism's role in causing war, thereby starting an exchange of views with Angell in the *New Statesman* that was eventually reissued in pamphlet form.[164]

However, socialist war resisters had decisively lost Communist support when the Soviet Union joined the League of Nations in September 1934. The British Anti-War Movement thereafter became the British Movement Against War and Fascism, and was allowed to fade away as the party decided to support the collective peace system despite its bourgeois provenance. Communist activists were therefore encouraged to bestow their energies and organizational skills upon the Peace Ballot and to become active in the LNU.

---

[158] *LPCR* (1934), 17. *New Oxford Outlook* (May 1934), 88–91.
[159] J. F. Naylor, *Labour's International Policy: The Labour Party in the 1930s* (1969), 74–5.
[160] *LPCR* (1934), 153.
[161] H. N. Brailsford, *Property or Peace* (1934), 132.
[162] *LPCR* (1934), 155–7, 170–1.
[163] *LPCR* (1934), 11, 172.
[164] H. Brinton (ed.), *Does Capitalism Cause War?* (n.d.[1935]).

Like the Geneva Protocol a decade previously, the Peace Ballot endeared $\times$
itself to progressive opinion the more it was denounced by the right. During
the autumn of 1934 *Daily Express* mounted a sustained campaign against it.
And in the Commons on 8 November the politically inept Foreign Secretary,
Simon, accused the LNU of a socialist bias on the strength of a signed article
in *Headway* by Noel Baker. Angell considered these attacks 'of great benefit'
to the ballot.[165] They certainly encouraged Labour to throw its weight behind
it. For example, at a by-election in Putney on 28 November the Labour candidate Dr Edith Summerskill exploited the fact that her Conservative opponent
had initially condemned the ballot; and she not only accused the government
of 'warlike intentions' in a manner reminiscent of Wilmot at East Fulham, but
also brought in 'large numbers' of helpers who had worked in that by-election
campaign.[166] However, late in the campaign the Conservative candidate
prudently experienced an emotional conversion to the cause of the ballot, and
managed to win narrowly, despite a 26.6 per cent swing against him.

In addition, attacks by defencists helped overcome the doubts of some
pacifists about the enterprise. Like the international police force, which had
divided Quakers during the first half of 1934,[167] the ballot put pressure on the
absolutist strand of the peace movement to clarify its attitude to collective
security. Accepting that the international use of force offered the best practical hope for war prevention, some pacifists felt able to adopt a collaborative
orientation. One who did so Leyton Richards: in 1932 he had declined to
support the New Commonwealth Society because, though persuaded that an
international army was a step in the right direction, he was not prepared to
support such a step 'when I think I know a better one'; but a book he
completed in November 1934 showed that he had changed his mind, since it
claimed that a league force 'equipped for military operations . . . would be a
striking and significant step towards the realisation of a Christian world
order'.[168] Charles Raven's views went through a similar change at this
time.[169] It was notable that both Richards and Raven made a serious effort to
explain how they could support a military force to which they personally had
a conscientious objection.[170] Supporters of the collaborative orientation were
becoming unprecedentedly aware of the dangers of being thought merely
exemptionist. For example, Allen now made clear that his support for 'the use

---

[165] Angell to Cecil, 13 Nov. 1934: Noel-Baker Papers 2/27.
[166] *The Times* (27 Nov. 1934). E. Summerskill, *A Woman's World: Her Memoirs* (1967), 48–9.
[167] Ceadel, *Pacifism in Britain 1914–1945*, 158–9.
[168] Richards to Davies, 2 Jan. 1932: Davies of Llandinam Papers. L. Richards, *The Christian's Contribution to Peace: A Constructive Approach to International Relationships* (1935), 142.
[169] See in particular *Reconciliation* (Jan. 1934), 4–5; (Mar. 1934), 66.
[170] Ceadel, *Pacifism in Britain 1914–1945*, 161–3, 167–8.

of collective force to restrain an aggressor by judicial process' (which, he was even prepared to claim, 'should not be called war' because this term was better reserved for 'the use of force by a nation pursuing its own self-interest and declining third-party judgement'), was contingent on 'the machinery of world government' proving effective. If that machinery broke down, however,

the personal testimony of the pacifist would again become inevitable. As before, we should find combined in a common movement the Quaker pacifist who under no conditions will use force, the socialist who is anti-capitalist, and even those who might accept force if it were an instrument of international policy, but who would decline if it were used in a nationalistic and disorderly policy.[171]

By thus insisting that his support for collective security was contingent on favourable political conditions and that his default position was absolutist, Allen made clear that he was not a *pacificist* with exemptionist instincts but in a meaningful sense still a pacifist.

However, other pacifists disliked the collaborative orientation, either because they felt unable to justify the double standard seemingly involved, or because they did not believe collective security was an effective policy. They therefore insisted that pacifism had a distinctive message to offer. This explains the formation in 1934 of a Presbyterian Pacifist Group, a Baptist Pacifist Fellowship, a Church of England Peace Fellowship (the creation of Canon Stuart Morris of Birmingham, whose bishop was E. W. Barnes, still a pacifist and the only one on the episcopal bench),[172] which swelled the ranks and increased the importance of the Council of Christian Pacifist Groups.[173] It also explain's Dick Sheppard's decision to launch his celebrated 'peace pledge' in the autumn of 1934. This appeal to men—not women, because they were not expected to undertake military service—to pledge their pacifism in a future war appeared in the national press on 16 October. Within days, 50,000 postcards arrived at the home of Brigadier-General Crozier, who had now opted decisively for pacifism and had offered to act as secretary. Since Sheppard disclaimed any intention of founding a new pacifist association, his initiative was interpreted as a test of opinion to rival the Peace Ballot.[174]

Pacifists who could not support the collaborative orientation were known to be unhappy with the ballot's sanctions question. Its first part raised the divisive issue of economic sanctions. Some Quakers had long been willing to

[171] Bell (ed.), *We Did Not Fight*, 32–3, 34.
[172] See *Reconciliation* (Dec. 1934), 317–18; and also Barnes, *Ahead of his Time*.
[173] Ceadel, *Pacifism in Britain 1914–1945*, 174.
[174] e.g. by J. H. Hudson in the *Manchester Guardian* (19 Oct. 1934).

support these: for example, the Friends' Peace Committee was prepared to do so short of 'starvation methods'.[175] But others were unhappy at the coercion involved, yet felt unhappy about answering 'no' because this seemed to accept the question's premise that a nation might 'insist on' attacking another even if unprovoked.

Pacifist dislike of the ballot caused problems for the National Peace Council, which because of the prominence of the sanctions issue was passing through a very difficult phase. Its president in the mid-1930s, the historian G. P. Gooch, was later to acknowledge: 'Interminable debates took place without changing anybody's views'.[176] Vera Brittain privately found its members 'dull' and 'very elderly', being thereby considerably more polite than her husband George Catlin, who was later publicly to disparage the council as 'a kind of eunuch organization, unable to take a decision one way or another'.[177] Hardie blamed its paralysis on its influential contingent of Christian pacifists, concluding that 'nothing is to be hoped from the National Peace Council until it is split and the religious maniacs (for that is what they really are) form their own organization'.[178] The council therefore initially decided that the Peace Ballot was too divisive to support, causing Joad, who at that time was prepared to support sanctions, to complain of 'the absurdity' of its being thereby 'precluded from taking part in one of the most effective moves for peace made for many years past'.[179]

However, when in November 1934 the right came out publicly against the Peace Ballot, the pacifists rallied loyally to it.[180] Sheppard endorsed it warmly and took no further action in respect of his own peace pledge until polling was complete. Quakers accepted a compromise suggested by the Northern Friends' Peace Board[181] whereby 'I take the Christian pacifist option' became an approved answer to the sanctions question, though in practice few local committees were to advertise its availability. And the National Peace Council dropped its opposition. In the end, therefore, the quietist FoR and ultra-leftist NMWM were the only constituents of the peace movement which failed to give the ballot their enthusiastic support.

With its critics giving it the necessary publicity and progressives mostly uniting behind it, the ballot proved a remarkable success from the declaration

---

[175] Minutes, FPC, 2 Aug. 1934.

[176] G. P. Gooch, *Under Six Reigns* (1958), 292.

[177] Brittain, *Chronicle of Friendship*, 185. Sir G. Catlin, *For God's Sake, Go! An Autobiography* (Gerrard's Cross, 1972), 286.

[178] Hardie to Noel Baker, 24 Nov. 1933: Noel-Baker Papers 5/147.

[179] Minutes, NPC Council, 9 Oct. 1934.

[180] Ceadel, 'The First British Referendum', 824–6.

[181] See the letter by Helen Byles Ford and Robert J. Long, 6 Nov. 1934, published in *Reconciliation* (Dec. 1934), 326.

of the first results in November 1934 right through to its triumphal final rally in the Albert Hall on 27 June 1935, which was addressed by dignitaries as diverse as the Archbishop of Canterbury and the general secretary of the Trades Union Congress. As a social researcher was to note of its reception on a new housing estate: 'The Ballot provided an opportunity for co-operation by the local societies, churches, voluntary organizations and political parties, uniting their efforts.'[182] The fact that half a million volunteers helped distribute and collect the forms was more impressive than the fact that 11,640,066 people, an estimated 38.2 per cent of the UK population aged over 18, were persuaded to fill them in.[183]

As expected, the quality of the results was as satisfactory as their quantity. Expressed as percentages, the answers were:

1. Should Great Britain remain a Member of the League of Nations?
   Yes: 95.9   No: 3.1   Doubtful: 0.1   No answer: 0.9
2. Are you in favour of the all-round reduction of armaments by international agreement?
   Yes: 90.6   No: 7.5   Doubtful: 0.1   No answer: 1.8
3. Are you in favour of the all-round abolition of national military and naval aircraft by international agreement?
   Yes: 82.5   No: 14.6   Doubtful: 0.1   No answer: 2.8
4. Should the manufacture and sale of armaments for private profit be prohibited by international agreement?
   Yes: 90.1   No: 6.7   Doubtful: 0.1   No answer: 3.1
5. Do you consider that, if a nation insists on attacking another, the other nations should combine to compel it to stop by,
   (*a*) economic and non-military measures?
        Yes: 86.8   No: 5.5   Doubtful: 0.2   No answer: 7.4   Christian Pacifist: 0.1
   (*b*) if necessary, military measures?
        Yes: 58.7   No: 20.3   Doubtful: 0.4   No answer: 20.4   Christian Pacifist: 0.2

Despite being the result of an overtly propagandist exercise, these figures enable some judgements to be made about the state of British opinion. The allegation made later by some critics of the peace movement that the ballot

---

[182] R. Durant, *Watling: A Survey of Social Life on a New Housing Estate* (1939), 95. I owe this source to Ross McKibbin.

[183] These figures are from National Declaration Committee, *The National Declaration on the League of Nations and Armaments: Results in Each Constituency of the United Kingdom* (1935), a little known publication which includes 80,901 problematical ballots referred to London for interpretation. Most secondary works cite the earlier and less complete figures given in the 'official history': A. Livingstone, *The Peace Ballot* (1935).

was an expression of pacifism[184] was refuted by the fact that only 20.3 per cent of respondents said 'no' to military sanctions, as well as by the very small numbers—14,169 for (*a*) and 17,536 for (*b*)—who availed themselves of the 'Christian pacifist' answer to question 5, even after allowance is made for the lack of publicity given to it. On the other hand Cecil's claim a decade later that the ballot 'proved' that 'the great majority of the people . . . would have been ready to make any sacrifices that were necessary' to support the League[185] was also called into question by the fact that only 58.7 per cent of voters said 'yes' to military sanctions.

What the ballot thus manifested was a widespread belief in 'collective security', a term which according to the pacifist Henry Carter had 'almost ousted "international co-operation" from its proper primacy' among 'the watchwords of our movement', and which the *New Statesman* thought to be 'in some danger of becoming a catchword'.[186] Yet as presented in the Peace Ballot, collective security assumed that 'a boycott on trade and credit would in practice almost always be enough to stop any nation starting a war', as the National Declaration Committee's original green leaflet had put it. The 28.1 per cent of respondents who answered the first part of question 5 affirmatively but the second negatively were clearly of the view that economic pressure could be effective without the backing of military force. This view had not been discouraged by LNU propaganda;[187] and a former rector of Imperial College, Sir Thomas Holland, who had argued since the late 1920s that an aggressor's capacity to make war would be greatly restricted if it were merely denied access to a few key minerals, had brought out a well-timed and widely noticed book in its support.[188] As already noted, the ballot made no reference to rearmament, which indeed LNU branches 'had been adopting violent resolutions against' as its executive committee noted,[189] and which the Labour Party also opposed. Indeed, most ballot workers would probably have agreed with the WIL's observation: 'The argument that we need to be as heavily armed for the collective system as if we stood in isolation is, we believe, untenable.'[190] Moreover, the ballot was more a statement of abstract opinion than a judgement on the impending crisis between Italy and Abyssinia: only in the last month of polling, June 1935—when, admittedly, two million votes were cast and support for military sanctions dipped slightly but revealingly—did this become a prominent issue.

[184] e.g. by F. A. Walker, *The Blunder of Pacifism* (1940), 107.
[185] *HW* (Oct. 1945), 10.
[186] *Peace* (May 1935), 19. *New Statesman* (1 June 1935), 795.
[187] e.g. *Economic Sanctions* (LNU No. 371, Aug. 1934).
[188] Sir T. Holland, *The Mineral Sanction as an Aid to International Security* (1935): for an enthusiastic response, see *Spectator* (21 June 1935), 1052–3.
[189] Minutes, LNU executive, 21 Mar. 1935.
[190] WIL, *20th Yearly Report, Mar. 1935–Mar. 1936*, 12.

The ballot's short-term effect was considerable. Within the league movement, it helped to suspend the controversy over international police force. At the special conference on aviation, eventually held on 3–4 April 1935, some speakers had argued that preoccupation with this issue had led to a neglect of the more practical question of economic sanctions, a position endorsed by the LNU executive.[191] As a result, well in advance of the summer's general council, supporters and opponents of the international force agreed a compromise whereby the government would be urged to consider an international force only if it proved to be an essential precondition for the internationalization of civil aviation as part of a disarmament agreement[192]—by then a very unlikely eventuality.

The LNU's morale was greatly increased, despite the fact that its fall in membership, temporarily reversed in 1934, had resumed in 1935 while members were concentrating on the ballot rather than on collecting subscriptions. At the general council in June 1935 Eppstein even detected 'a touch of smugness'.[193] Particularly gratifying was the fact that the ballot had intimidated some of its Conservative critics, such as the Hampshire MP who soon felt it prudent to 'explain . . . unfortunate remarks on the Peace Ballot' to his local LNU branch in order to retain his vice-presidency.[194] Moreover, the ballot became a factor influencing the National government's strategy for dealing with Italy's aggression towards Abyssinia.

THE ABYSSINIA CRISIS, JULY–DECEMBER 1935

By 23 July 1935, when a deputation from the national declaration committee formally presented the ballot results to Baldwin, who had just succeeded MacDonald as Prime Minister of the National government, the Italo-Abyssinian dispute had become acute. Opinion began to divide increasingly on the issue of sanctions, though this process was still limited by the fact that opinion formers continued to believe that non-military sanctions would work: as late as September, for example, Keynes could insist on 'the efficacy of a comparatively mild "economic" sanctions'; and Arthur Greenwood, a leading Labour politician, could assert: 'There were ways of stopping wars without bloodshed. There were such things as sanctions.'[195] Vera Brittain, a *pacificist*

---

[191] LNU, *The Problem of the Air* (1935), 31–2, 35. E. Rathbone to Cecil, 3 May 1935: Cecil Papers Add. MSS 51141. Minutes, LNU Executive, 16 and 30 May 1934.
[192] *HW* (June 1935), 108.
[193] *HW* (Aug. 1935), 190.
[194] Minutes, LNU Southampton branch, 24 Sept. 1935.
[195] *New Statesman* (28 Sept. 1935), 401. *The Times* (17 Sept. 1935).

beginning to be tempted by pacifism, could thus assert in all sincerity during the summer of 1935 that the 'differences the peace-loving people have among themselves' were still only 'slight'.[196]

Even so, peaceful change came suddenly to the fore as a section of the peace movement took at face value Italy's claim to need the raw materials and outlets for its population which only colonies like Abyssinia could provide. It therefore urged that the economic and colonial demands of what it called the 'have not' nations should be conceded at a new peace conference. Despite still being Labour leader, Lansbury took this line in an influential personal letter published in *The Times* of 19 August, which called for a world conference in the Holy Land.[197] The FoR was so enthusiastic about Lansbury's initiative that, notwithstanding its reiterated insistence that pacifism was not a 'stop-the-war trick',[198] it adjourned a meeting of its general committee while a deputation consulted him on how best it could support his campaign.[199] The National Peace Council, which much preferred debating 'problems of economic access and control' to those of sanctions, also welcomed 'the recognition of the importance of these issues which has arisen in consequence of the Italo-Abyssinian dispute'.[200]

There was also an upsurge in pacifism. Having stayed his hand during the Peace Ballot, Dick Sheppard summoned the signatories of his peace pledge to an Albert Hall meeting on 14 July 1935, where Siegfried Sassoon read his war poetry and the Sheppard Peace Movement was launched. This soon claimed 'well over 50,000' supporters, including Nichols, whose support for the league had turned first 'to distrust, and then, during the sanctions crisis, to active hostility' and who had therefore re-embraced pacifism, and Leslie Weatherhead, a prominent Methodist minister who had just been converted to absolutism, partly because Sheppard was 'almost impossible to disagree with'.[201] The size of this new movement's support exposed the limitations of the other pacifist associations. Even after an 11 per cent increase in membership during 1935, the FoR had only 3,700 members. The denominational fellowships coordinated by the Council of Christian Pacifist Groups remained small; and the Church of England Peace Fellowship foundered after Morris threw in his lot with Sheppard instead. The NMWM was so weak that its secretary, Reginald Reynolds, took another job to save it money. In addition,

[196] Cited in Berry and Bostridge, *Vera Brittain*, 352–3.
[197] Ceadel, *Pacifism in Britain 1914–1945*, 179–88.
[198] *Reconciliation* (Aug. 1935), 145–7.
[199] Minutes, FoR general committee, 26–7 Aug. 1935.
[200] Minutes, NPC Council, 19 Sept. 1935.
[201] Nichols, *Men Do Not Weep*, 15. For contemporary evidence of Nichols's return to pacifism in 1935–6 see e.g. A. Campbell Johnson (ed.), *Peace Offering* (1936), 132–3. L. Weatherhead, *Thinking Aloud in War-Time* (1939), 21–3.

although the Peace Army council declared itself willing to interpose itself between Italians and Abyssinians,[202] this offer received no publicity.

War resistance also gained support. For many members of the Socialist League, suspicion of the League of Nations got the better of worries about fascism: for example, Cripps, who had drawn back from being a war resister in the summer of 1933, went ahead with a vengeance during the Abyssinia crisis, having become deeply concerned at 'the definite recession to Liberalism of the Labour Party', as he described it to Kingsley Martin.[203] The disaffiliated ILP, which proved to be unshakable in its support for war resistance, also opposed any action against Italy as an imperialist squabble.

Furthermore, an anti-war movement of a new kind emerged, consisting of sympathizers with fascism who did not want to confront the regime which had pioneered their ideology. In the autumn of 1935 the Catholic intellectual Douglas Jerrold, who the following year was to become famous as the sympathizer who supplied General Franco with an aeroplane at a critical juncture in his rebellion against the Spanish government, wrote a book attacking the league for failing to cope with 'those real forces of virility and dynamic energies which determine the current of history'.[204] Similarly Yeats-Brown was, according to his biographer, 'anxious to undo the impression of *Dogs of War!*, his anti-peace polemic of the previous year, because he opposed a conflict with Italy'.[205] The reversal of roles whereby much of the right was increasingly reluctant to fight and much of the left was increasingly keen to uphold international law and order became conspicuous for the first time during the Italo-Abyssinian dispute.

On the other side of the debate, the need for league sanctions was increasingly accepted. The socialist intellectual G. D. H. Cole, who had opposed the First World War, was now prepared 'to urge upon the League, with a full determination to honour any obligations which may ensue, a decisive condemnation of any covenant breaker or imperialist adventurer who disturbs the peace, and to declare complete willingness to join in any measures against aggression that the League can be induced to take'. However, despite his subsequent assertion, 'Hitler cured me of my pacifism',[206] Cole still claimed to belong to the 'tiny minority' of 'pure pacifists', and expressed the wish that 'the entire human race could be brought to share this view of mine'. He recon-

[202] Minutes, WIL executive, 5 Nov. 1935.

[203] Cripps to Martin, 25 Sept. 1935: K. Martin Papers.

[204] D. Jerrold, *They that Take the Sword: The Future of the League of Nations* (1936), 4. See also his article 'The League and the Future', *Nineteenth Century and After* (Dec. 1935), 657–74, and his memoir *Georgian Adventure* (1937), 371–3.

[205] Wrench, *Francis Yeats-Brown*, 208.

[206] In Oct. 1940: cited in A. W. Wright, *G. D. H. Cole and Socialist Democracy* (Oxford, 1979), 244 n.

ciled this apparent contradiction by declaring his pacifism to be 'an idiosyn-
crasy' rather than 'a necessary accompaniment of Socialist faith' and 'not
practical policy ... in the circumstances of today',[207] thereby showing
himself consciously to have adopted the collaborative orientation. Just as he
was doing so, Margery Fry was going further, abandoning collaborative pacifism for liberal *pacificism*. As already noted, her doubts about pacifism dated
back to the Boer War. Now, faced with the Abyssinia crisis, she found herself
'driven to saying (in imagination) to the government, "I think the upholding
of the League of Nations by force if need be is *your* right action, but I would-
n't lift a finger to help you with it" ', and concluded: '*that* seems a fairly
untenable position, doesn't it?' She therefore abandoned not only her pacifism but her membership of the Society of Friends too.[208]

Some established sanctionists were growing bolder too. When the LNU's
executive committee discussed how best to apply economic sanctions, Cecil
found that the main opposition to his claim that these were best applied gradually came not from pacifists opposing any form of pressure but from the
former league official Sir Arthur Salter, who favoured tough immediate
measures against Italy, such as 'denial of access to the Suez Canal and the
Straits of Gibraltar'.[209] In December 1935 the LNU's general council was
with only six dissentients to call for the cutting of Italy's communications
with Africa if necessary.[210] And even the WIL came out in favour of an oil
embargo.[211]

Despite the absence of the ailing Henderson, who was to die on 20 October, Labour endorsed collective security at the party conference which opened
at Brighton on 30 September 1935. It also changed its leaders. Lansbury, who
in August had promised never to accept 'an office in which I have to vote for
arms of any kind', was savagely criticized by a now strongly pro-containment
Bevin for pleading a conscientious objection to his own party's policy, and
resigned within days of the conference.[212] Ponsonby had already relinquished
his leadership in the Lords because of his opposition to sanctions.[213] A further
indication of Labour's changing attitude was the fact that even C. R. Buxton,

[207] G. D. H. Cole, *The Simple Case for Socialism* (1935), 101–2, 108–9—a book which went
to press in Sept. 1935. See also M. Cole, *The Life of G. D. H. Cole* (1971), 65.

[208] Jones, *Margery Fry*, 54, 179.

[209] Minutes, LNU executive, 29 Aug. 1935. Cecil and Salter published their differing views in
the *Spectator* (30 Aug. 1935), 315–6, and (6 Sept. 1935), 347–8.

[210] *Report, LNU General Council Dec. 1935* (1936), 57.

[211] Minutes, WIL executive, 10 Dec. 1935.

[212] *Daily Herald* (26 Aug. 1935), cited in S. Davis, 'The British Labour Party and British
Foreign Policy 1933–1939', Ph.D. thesis (London University, 1950), fos. 324–5. A. Bullock,
The Life and Times of Ernest Bevin (2 vols., 1960–7), i. 566–71.

[213] Ponsonby to Lansbury [17 Sept. 1935]: Lansbury Papers, vol.,28.

never a league enthusiast and already an advocate of 'remedying the proved grievances of the "dissatisfied" Powers', now insisted that 'though we fully recognize the relative weakness of the League as it is, and the danger of the misuse of its machinery for Capitalist ends, we still support sanctions'.[214] Likewise, Brailsford, whose thinking was entering a phase of extreme volatility, dropped war resistance in order to endorse league sanctions.[215]

In view of what the Peace Ballot had revealed about public opinion, the National government decided it could not risk seeming anti-league. As early as 22 August the cabinet decided to apply at least token economic sanctions against Italy if it attacked Abyssinia; and on 11 September the new Foreign Secretary, Samuel Hoare, made a speech at Geneva whose support for collective security was welcomed by league supporters, though its references to peaceful change appealed to appeasers and pacifists too. The government's attitude seemed sufficiently satisfactory for the LNU to cancel an Albert Hall meeting planned for 24 September.[216] Italy went to war on 3 October; and with Britain's support the league took mild economic measures against it eight days later. Before his party's reservations about the league became apparent, particularly its reluctance to proceed to sanctions which might hurt Italy, Baldwin called a general election, thereby enabling the National government to claim pro-league credentials and preventing Labour from repeating its East Fulham and Putney tactics. A friend, the former deputy secretary to the cabinet Thomas Jones, noted admiringly that Baldwin had thereby 'reconciled the Party to the League by supporting rearmament, and reconciled the pacifists to rearmament by supporting the League'.[217] We have already noted that, as an additional way of neutralizing the 'latent suspicion that the Conservative Party is linked up with the theory of large armaments', about which a party official had recently warned him,[218] Baldwin chose the moribund Peace Society's annual meeting as the audience for a major campaign speech on 31 October, endorsing the league whilst also promising 'no great armaments'.[219] These tactics helped the National government secure re-election comfortably on 14 November.

Baldwin's duplicity was exposed when the leaking by French Foreign Minister Laval of his discussion with Hoare on 7–8 December revealed that,

[214] *HW* (Nov.,1935), 209.
[215] Leventhal, *The Last Dissenter*, 241–2.
[216] Minutes, LNU executive, 19 Sept. 1935.
[217] T. Jones, *A Diary with Letters 1931–1950* (1954), 155 (diary entry for 5 Oct. 1935).
[218] Sir P. Gower to Baldwin, 1 Aug. 1935: Baldwin Papers.
[219] His speech was published in S. Baldwin, *This Torch of Freedom: Speeches and Addresses* (1935), 319–39.

despite its professions of support for the league, his government had engaged in secret diplomacy intended to buy Italy off with some Abyssinian territory. The resultant public outcry in Britain was such that Hoare resigned on 18 December, the only instance of a cabinet minister with the confidence of his colleagues being sacrificed to save a government from a protest led by a peace association. Well might the LNU, which cancelled a planned protest meeting in the Albert Hall after Hoare left office,[220] talk triumphalistically, while reviewing its December 1935 general council, of 'the part the Union is called on to play in shaping the future of Britain and the world'.[221] However, its period of exceptional influence was ending. And the bubble of collective security as understood in the first half of the 1930s was shortly to burst: for example, before the year was out a leading member of the WIL, Lady Layton, resigned from its executive committee because she had realized that economic sanctions would not work on their own.[222]

An Anglican clergyman noted during this period that 'never before has the cause of peace so captured the imagination of the world'.[223] Japanese, German, and Italian foreign policy were largely responsible for this. Yet the peace movement had done an unprecedented amount to influence the political process. Admittedly, its absolutist wing was in disarray, partly because of the NMWM's flirtation with revolutionism, so that it was left to the Peace Army, the Oxford Union, and Dick Sheppard to fly the pacifist flag most effectively. However, without the LNU's courageous and energetic challenge to the isolationist press, anti-league feeling would have been considerably stronger. As a detailed study of the British response to the Abyssinia crisis has acknowledged: 'In crystallising opinion, in organising its expression, in providing a "climate", its work and influence were gigantic.'[224] Indeed, the LNU managed to talk up collective security to such an extent that there was to be considerable disillusionment in 1936 when the realities of the international situation could no longer be ignored.

---

[220] Minutes, LNU executive, 21 Dec. 1935.

[221] *HW* (Jan. 1936), 8, reporting the general council of 4–5 Dec. 1935.

[222] Minutes, WIL executive, 10 Dec. 1935. For her involvement in the peace movement, see Lord Layton, *Dorothy* (1961), 87–97, 113–23.

[223] Canon F. L. Donaldson, 'The Things that Belong unto Peace', *Listener* (12 Apr. 1933), 578.

[224] D. Waley, *British Public Opinion and the Abyssinian War 1935–6* (1975), 113.

10

Polarization,
January 1936–March 1939

The triple crisis of 1936—the remilitarization of the Rhineland in March, the final defeat of Abyssinia in May, and the outbreak of the Spanish Civil War in July—was inter-war Britain's major watershed in respect of thinking about international relations. What the WIL's next annual report was to call 'the resultant loss of faith in the efficacy of economic sanctions'[1] destroyed the belief that there was a middle way between containment and accommodation. 'A certain crystallisation of opinion has broken up—the crystallization that believed in the League and supported collective security, and no crystallisation had as yet formed in its place' was how Joad saw it by the end of the summer.[2]

Both the peace movement and public opinion had started to polarize. One current of opinion was drawn to the pole of accommodation: many *pacificists* advocated peaceful change; many defencists supported appeasement; unprecedented numbers of pacifists threw in their lot with the Peace Pledge Union and other new associations; and a section of the far left still favoured war resistance. Another current of opinion was attracted by the opposite pole of containment: the leaders of the LNU still supported collective security even though they now understood that it required rearmament; many socialist *pacificists* came to advocate a 'peace front'[3] of the progressive states against the fascist ones; and those defencists who shared the concerns of Winston Churchill, since 1929 a backbencher, called for more energetic rearmament. Albeit to a lesser extent in socialist circles, where the Spanish Civil War in particular caused a crisis for pacifists and a real difficulty for war resisters, the accommodationists heavily outnumbered the containers. As Mary Agnes Hamilton was to point out during the Second World War: 'Don't let us try, in the 40's, to pretend that in the 30's appeasement was not a popular policy. Peace at pretty well any price, paid by anybody, was what everybody wanted. The Left was, up to 1938, as bad, and as sentimental, as the Right.'[4]

---

[1] WIL, *21st Yearly Report, Mar. 1936–Feb. 1937*, 3.

[2] *Peace* (Sept. 1936), 91.

[3] For an early use of this term, at the National Peace Congress in late June 1936, by Lord Marley, a former member of the British Anti–War Movement, see *Peace* (July/Aug. 1936), 59.

[4] M. A. Hamilton, *Remembering my Good Friends* (1944), 304.

Admittedly, not all shifts of opinion confirmed to this polarizing pattern. For example, Beverley Nichols renounced pacifism without being converted to collective security or the peace front. Six months after restating his absolutist position in a chapter of a book published in April 1936, he was admitting a 'change of view', and in a later work was to confirm his arrival at the view that 'there are some things worth fighting for'.[5] But instead of coming out in support of containment he was attracted instead to Mosley, as not only a political strong man but 'a potential bridge-builder who might span the gulf which was rapidly widening between this country and Germany', and to the Anglo-German Fellowship, an organization formed late in 1935 to promote appeasement.[6] In other words, Nichols remained on the accommodationist side of the polarizing debate, having merely transferred from the absolutist wing of the peace movement to the new anti-war movement of the right.

Less idiosyncratically, other peace activists tried to stave off polarization by combining collective security and peaceful change in a consciously dualistic package of threat and inducement. In other words, either a carrot could be proffered to help an adversary retreat in face of a deterrent threat, or a stick could be brandished in an attempt to negotiate a reduction in the size of the concession which would eventually have to be made. However, during the winter of 1937–8 this package fell apart; and a choice between its constituent elements had to be made. As was indicated by the level of support for Neville Chamberlain, who succeeded Baldwin as Prime Minister in May 1937, accommodation still proved more popular than containment prior to Hitler's seizure of Prague in March 1939.

DIVISION AND DUAL POLICY, JANUARY 1936–AUTUMN 1937

Once its true implications became clear, collective security rapidly lost much of its following. Thus when on 7 March 1936 Hitler took advantage of the Anglo-French preoccupation with the Italo-Abyssinian War to remilitarize the Rhineland, the public mostly favoured inaction because it did not wish to defy a major power within air-bombing range. Both at the smart London parties attended by Blanche Dugdale, cousin of former Tory Prime Minister A. J. Balfour and member of the LNU's executive committee, and in the depressed area where the writer and ILP supporter George Orwell was collecting material for *The Road to Wigan Pier*, sympathy for Germany was

---

[5] B. Nichols, *The Fool hath Said* (1936), 238–75. B. Connon, *Beverley Nichols: A Life* (1991), 196. B. Nichols, *News of England or A Country without a Hero* (1938), 296–9, 306.
[6] Nichols, *Men Do Not Weep*, 19–23.

uppermost.[7] And Brailsford, though recently prepared to support sanctions against Italy, now wished to propitiate Germany, and called once again for mass resistance to 'any capitalist-imperialist war, even if Geneva should bless it'.[8]

When the National government, by failing even to introduce an oil embargo, tacitly allowed Mussolini to crush Abyssinia, there was nothing approaching the outcry there had been over the Hoare–Laval pact. Newly aware of the German danger, the public mostly did not now want to risk even a naval war with Italy. The league having thus lost much of the political protection given by a sympathetic public for the past decade, Conservatives felt able to round on it. Austen Chamberlain finally resigned from the LNU's executive committee in May because it did not favour the lifting of the mild sanctions which remained in force against Italy. His younger half-brother Neville declared provocatively on 10 June that the continuation of these sanctions was 'the very midsummer of madness'. The league duly terminated them with effect from 14 July, thereby signing its own death warrant as a credible institution.

When just four days after the league's decision, General Franco's reactionary rebellion began in Spain, there was general acceptance that Britain should not become involved in a civil war which, on account of its highly ideological character, threatened to embroil much of Europe. Despite the decision of some Communists and other left-wing socialists to fight against Franco in the International Brigade, there was no crusading sentiment comparable to that aroused by the Eastern Question and the Armenian massacres. The belief that Britain could intervene with impunity had been a casualty of the First World War.

The triple crisis of 1936 produced intense public debates about Britain's vital interests in Europe and the purpose of the League of Nations, which resulted in upsurges of support for peaceful change, appeasement, pacifism, and even to some extent war resistance. The LNU faced a membership crisis, which it tried to stem by working with Allen to produce a dual strategy of collective security plus peaceful change; but its troubled relations with the New Commonwealth Society and, more especially, a new continental initiative, the International Peace Campaign, weakened the collective-security movement.

Belatedly, the public woke up to the extent to which air power had weakened

---

[7] *Baffy: The Diaries of Blanche Dugdale 1936–1947*, ed. N. A. Rose (1973), 8, 10 (entries for 12 and 19 Mar. 1936). *The Collected Essays, Journalism and Letters of George Orwell*, ed. S. Orwell and I. Angus (4 vols.; Penguin edn., Harmondsworth, 1970), i. 225 (entry for 9 Mar. 1936).

[8] Leventhal, *The Last Dissenter*, 243.

Britain's geo-strategic position. There was thus both an instinctive desire to escape entanglement in European quarrels and a realization that complete isolationism was more than ever impossible. Surveying British opinion for the *Political Quarterly*, Kingsley Martin was initially struck by how many of his compatriots 'really believe that another great war may mean, to use the hackneyed phrase, the end of civilization, and are unwilling to assume that this country must share in the general catastrophe'.[9] Yet he soon realized that although, in emotional terms, 'the whole Right and much of the Left would like "isolation" ', Lord Beaverbrook 'remains almost alone in thinking it practical politics'.[10] The very fact that Britain could be bombed from western Europe prevented it from turning its back on that region. As W. Horsfall Carter of the New Commonwealth Society put it during a discussion at the Royal Institute of International Affairs: 'We are now, whether we like it or not, essentially part of Europe', and attributed this to 'one factor: Air Power'.[11]

The serious public debate about Britain's vital interests in Europe, which had been notable for its absence both before and after the First World War, now took place.[12] It was marked by strong support for the view that Britain had to defend France and the Low Countries as well as its own territory, but by considerable disagreement as to whether its vital interests were confined to these areas or extended into central and eastern Europe. A Conservative MP who like many of his colleagues put the empire before the continent, Sir Edward Grigg, was an exemplary exponent of the case for a limited obligation towards Europe. Acknowledging that the country was 'being torn by two powerful and conflicting currents of opinion', namely those for 'limited and unlimited liability in the matter of going to war', he identified himself as part of the former current, and argued that Britain should limit itself to the defence of its homeland and empire and 'a zone west of the eastern frontier of France, Belgium and Holland'.[13]

The contrary view was expressed with great clarity by the LNU in a pamphlet which expounded what eighteen years later President Eisenhower would call the 'domino' theory. It rejected the 'France and the Low Countries but no further' school of thought by insisting: 'Limiting obligation does not limit risks', and by arguing:

[9] *Political Quarterly*, 7 (1936), 573.

[10] *Political Quarterly*, 7 (1936), 587.

[11] RIIA, *What Should We Fight For?* (1936), 116.

[12] See e.g. the five Chatham House discussions, 29 May–7 July 1936, published as RIIA, *What Should We Fight For?*; the *Spectator* series 'What Should We Fight For?', 24 July–14 Aug. 1936; and the BBC radio discussion 'Limited or Unlimited Obligations?', printed in the *Listener* (2 Dec. 1936), 1071–2, 1106–8.

[13] Sir E. Grigg, *The Faith of an Englishman* (1936), 7, 199, 303.

If—in concrete terms—a Central European combination is to have a 'free hand' in Eastern Europe, if the West is to be indifferent to the 'elimination', in one form or another, of Russia, Poland, Czecho-Slovakia, what will be the position of, say, France when the result has been achieved? The defence of France would then be all but impossible . . . If, in truth, the security of the Low Countries and France is indispensable to our own, we simply cannot afford to see allies indispensable to that defence destroyed.

The LNU pamphlet also noted that, in contrast with their reluctance to defend potentially valuable allies in Europe, advocates of limited liability were, because of imperial sentiment, willing to defend 'some distant Pacific Island of no particular value, but which is our territory'.[14]

In fact, because the cross-over of traditional attitudes to defence was continuing, the right was becoming increasingly complacent even about threats to the empire. Charles Raven noted soon after the Rhineland crisis that the letters which as a pacifist he regularly received 'from the haunts of retired military and naval officers' suddenly began omitting the 'favourite adjectives "snivelling" and "white-livered" '.[15] By contrast, progressive opinion discovered a concern about the safety of the empire: for example, Aneurin Bevan, a rising star of Labour's left, emphasized the threat to Britain's 'undisputed power in the Mediterranean' posed by Franco's rebellion.[16] In some cases it overcame its distaste for military matters: thus Esmond Romilly, who while a schoolboy at Wellington College had conscientiously objected to the officers training corps and co-founded a public-school anti-militarist magazine, was obliged to pretend that he had in fact undergone military training there in order to gain entry to the International Brigade in Spain.[17]

For public and peace movement alike the debate over where Britain's vital interests lay in Europe produced a clear majority view in favour of limited liability. F. W. Hirst could thus note with satisfaction, as a Cobdenite, that 'the year 1936' had been marked by 'a growing opposition to quixotic projects which might engage us in wars on the Continent of Europe for the support of "collective security" in conformity with the new hypothesis that peace is indivisible and that consequently Great Britain must take part against the aggressor whenever and wherever the war might break out'.[18]

The debate over the purpose of the League of Nations was similarly one-sided. Following its abandonment of sanctions against Italy, demands for its

---

[14] *The League and the Crisis: Making Collective Defence Effective* (LNU No. 397; Sept. 1936), 20–1, 30.

[15] *Spectator* (27 Mar. 1936), 572.

[16] M. Foot, *Aneurin Bevan* (2 vols., 1962), i. 219.

[17] E. Romilly, *Boadilla* (1937), 35. For his previous anti-militarist exploits see G. and E. Romilly, *Out of Bounds* (1935), 135, 141, 176, 191, 218–23, 239–40, 245–7.

[18] F. W. Hirst, *Armaments. The Race and the Crisis* (1937), 77, 78–9.

'reform' proliferated. A few of these called for the replacement of its intergovernmental constitution with a federal one in order to strengthen its capacity to defeat aggression. For example, when Lord Davies called for 'a reformed and revitalized League', he wanted to equip it with an international police force and equity tribunal.[19] However, in most cases 'reform' was a euphemism for stripping it of the power to impose sanctions and turning it into a mere forum for discussing international problems.[20] In Sir Arthur Salter's words: ' "Reform" of the League, as now commonly advocated, really means euthanasia with an epitaph of mingled reproach and regret. A League without coercion . . . is no League at all.'[21] Even so, many of the leading professors of international relations favoured the league's emasculation. Most famously, a newcomer to their ranks, E. H. Carr, did so: his inaugural lecture at Aberystwyth on 14 October 1936 was a major irritation to Lord Davies, the benefactor of his chair, since, in addition to identifying 'the problem of peaceful change' as the key to the prevention of war, it criticized military sanctions.[22]

In parallel with the debates about Britain's vital interests and the league's future there was an upsurge of interest in what the diplomat-turned-pundit Harold Nicolson called the policy of 'creating peace, or peaceful change, or concessions, or revisionism, whatever you like to call it'.[23] By 1937 'peaceful change' had become sufficiently established as a term to appear in the title of academic studies.[24] And *Headway* was to acknowledge with grudging respect: 'Peaceful change is a word of power. It is becoming a word of fashion.'[25]

From the beginning of 1936 the case for a new peace conference which had been made the previous summer in response to Italian grievances was now generalized so as to cover those of Germany and Japan too. Even the LNU issued a pamphlet in January 1936 which highlighted the demands of 'the three nations—Italy, Germany, and Japan—which are now variously referred to as "dissatisfied", "rampant", "unsatiated", or "have nots" ',[26] although it

[19] Lord Davies, *Nearing the Abyss: The Lesson of Ethiopia* (1936), pp. vii, 124, 130, 144–5, 150–3.

[20] For an extreme case see H. Rowan-Robinson, *Sanctions Begone!: A Plea and a Plan for the Reform of the League* (1936).

[21] *The Times* (16 June 1936), 12.

[22] E. H. Carr, 'Public Opinion as Safeguard of Peace', *International Affairs* (Nov./Dec. 1936), 846–62 at 860. B. Porter, 'David Davies and the Enforcement of Peace', in D. Long and P. Wilson (eds.), *Thinkers of the Twenty Years' Crisis* (Oxford, 1995), 58–78.

[23] RIIA, *The Future of the League of Nations* (1936), 135.

[24] C. A. W. Manning (ed.), *Peaceful Change: An International Problem* (1937). C. R. M. F. Cruttwell, *A History of Peaceful Change in the Modern World* (1937). H. F. Angus, *The Problem of Peaceful Change in the Pacific Area* (1937).

[25] *HW* (Aug. 1937), 144.

[26] L. Birch, *The Demand for Colonies: Territorial Expansion, Over-Population, and Raw Materials* (LNU No.0346; Jan. 1936), 3.

contained a disclaimer indicating that the executive committee had not approved its suggestions. The Marquess of Lothian, a long-standing advocate of the removal of sanctions from the Covenant (albeit initially in the interests of attracting American support for the league), took up the cause of the revision of the 1919 peace treaties. He did so despite having, in the words of a Foreign Office official who opposed appeasement, 'hands dripping with guilt for the Versailles settlement' on account of his role at that time as Lloyd George's private secretary.[27] In a letter published in *The Times* on 11 February Lothian warned that, unless it remedied 'the economic suffocation of certain nations possessed of inadequate natural resources . . . the League will eventually become no more than one-half of the new Balance of Power in which the other half will be the so-called suffocated powers'. By the end of March Lord Davies was being warned by the Welsh LNU that a new world conference was 'a popular item' with local branches in the principality.[28]

The National Peace Council was particularly enthusiastic about 'a policy of appeasement'[29]—by which it meant peaceful change—largely because this avoided the divisive issue of military force. It was so reluctant to criticize the remilitarization of the Rhineland in the policy statement it issued on 19 March that it included a reference to Germany's breach of Locarno only after a vote of twenty to nineteen. Vera Brittain was in this narrow majority: she still supported collective security, though she was already aware of having begun to 'fear war more than fascism' and of feeling 'much more nervous than most anti-fascists seem to be of our being dragged in the name of the League into a purely military alliance with France of the old nationalistic type, *called* the collective system but actually the Balance of Power all over again'.[30] Encouraged by the fact that the National Peace Congress at Leeds in June 1936 was able to agree a thirteen-point programme, the council produced a 'Statement of Minimum Policy' at the end of the summer: both documents emphasized the need to remedy the economic and colonial grievances of the have-not powers.[31]

All socialists liked aspects of the agenda of peaceful change: Attlee, the new Labour leader, was attracted by its emphasis on 'the wide economic causes which, we hold, lie at the back of this unrest',[32] and also found it easy to support a new colonial order based on international trusteeship. A few swallowed it whole: Attlee's precursor, Lansbury, who as a backbencher again

[27] *The Diplomatic Diaries of Oliver Harvey 1937–49*, ed. J. Harvey (1970), 259.
[28] G. Davies to Lord Davies, 30 Mar. 1936: Davies of Llandinam papers.
[29] Minutes, NPC council, 19 Mar. 1936.
[30] Brittain, *Chronicle of Friendship*, 256, 257 (entries for 16 and 19 Mar. 1936).
[31] See respectively *Peace* (July/Aug. 1936), 58; (Sept. 1936), 103.
[32] Hansard, 310 HC col. 848 (20 Mar. 1936).

was free to act 'even though dreadfully old, on intuitive guidance', as he informed the Prime Minister,[33] went on a mission to Germany in September 1936 in an attempt to find out what the Nazis wanted. He took with him Percy Bartlett, who immediately afterwards left the FoR to become secretary of 'Embassies of Reconciliation', a new organization, mooted at the International FoR conference at Cambridge in late July, which was designed to support Lansbury in his personal diplomacy. It helped the former Labour leader secure interviews with both Hitler and Mussolini in 1937.[34]

While progressive opinion mostly favoured peaceful change, defencists mostly favoured its realist counterpart, appeasement. Aware of the risks of war, they wished to test whether Hitler's aims were modest enough to be accommodated within a revised European settlement that reflected the military realities of 1936 rather than those of 1919. Some hoped that even if they were not, the outcome would merely be a Russo-German war from which Britain could remain aloof. On 28 July 1936 Baldwin thus sought to reassure a deputation of Tory backbenchers worried about defence by observing: 'If there is any fighting in Europe to be done, I should like to see the Bolshies and the Nazis doing it.'[35]

The most extreme form which repudiation of collective security could take was the espousal of pacifism. With the exception of its socialist strand, which was virtually destroyed by the Spanish Civil War, British pacifism now entered its golden age. It had latterly been in the shadow of the League of Nations, and tempted to support sanctions as a step in the right direction. When the league lost its authority, most pacifists repudiated this collaborative position: for example, a member of the FoR insisted that it was 'an utter denial of all moral consistency to advocate a method which you are not yourself ready to employ'.[36] One of the few pacifists who continued to support a collaborative orientation towards collective security after 1936 was Joad, who as late as mid-1937 was prepared to argue: 'It is at least certain in the long run that in international government lies our only defence against war. It can never be right to abandon the advocacy of a long-run method of salvation merely because circumstances are unfavourable to its short-run application.'[37] However, he was aware of being in a minority on this point and steered clear of the various pacifist associations.

Most pacifists were determined to show what they themselves had to offer.

---

[33] Lansbury to Baldwin, 11 Mar. 1936 (copy): Lansbury Papers.
[34] Ceadel, *Pacifism in Britain 1914–1945*, 275–6. D. C. Lukowitz, 'Percy W. Bartlett', *Journal of the Friends' Historical Society*, 55 (1983–9), 175–7.
[35] PRO Premier 1/193/7439: reference kindly given to me by Sir Martin Gilbert.
[36] *Reconciliation* (Mar. 1936), 73: this was a protest at the position taken by Allen.
[37] *Peace* (June 1937), 41.

ppu

On 22 May 1936 Sheppard met Crozier, Hudson, Storm Jameson, Ponsonby, Raven, and Soper and relaunched the Sheppard Peace Movement as the Peace Pledge Union (PPU), which rapidly developed into the strongest pacifist association in history. Having been told in detail elsewhere,[38] the PPU's story need only be outlined here. It was the creation of a remarkable man, 'the living contrary of the modern intellectual' in the words of Max Plowman, who after more than a decade and a half as a pacifist was attracted into organized peace work for the first time by Sheppard's extraordinary, aristocratic, and asthmatic charisma.[39] Others persuaded to become 'Sponsors', as the members of the original governing body were called, included Aldous Huxley, Storm Jameson, Rose Macaulay, John Middleton Murry, Bertrand Russell, and (though he never attended a Sponsors' meeting) Siegfried Sassoon. Moreover, they were joined early in 1937 by Vera Brittain, who, having wavered for many months, made a decisive and enduring commitment to pacifism after reading Russell's *Which Way to Peace?*.[40] Never had there been so distinguished a group of writers and thinkers on the committee of a peace association, still less a pacifist one.

The PPU appealed because of its simplicity. Rank-and-file membership required only the dispatch to its office—located initially at Grand Buildings, Trafalgar Square, and from August 1936 to March 1939 on the fifth floor of 96 Regent Street—of a postcard subscribing to the proposition: 'I renounce war and never again, directly or indirectly, will I support or sanction another.' Although some weeding out of inactive pledgers intermittently took place by a staff which eventually numbered thirty, no subscription was required. From July 1936 membership was available to women. With a substantial number of pledges carried forward from the Sheppard Peace Movement, membership reached six figures in August and stood at 118,000 at the end of 1936. In addition, local groups were formed, although they never managed to cater for all postcard-senders. To maintain links with members outside groups and with potential recruits the PPU opted for *Peace News*, an independent weekly 'designed after the model of the daily sensational press', as Plowman was

[38] The first account based on original sources was the useful series of articles by D. Lukowitz in the PPU's journal *Pacifist* (June/July 1971), 15–17; (Aug. 1971), 10–12; (Sept. 1971), 10–12; (Nov. 1971), 7–9; (Feb. 1972), 7–9. The first full account was Ceadel, *Pacifism in Britain 1914–1945*, chs. 11–16. See also Y. A. Bennett, 'Testament of a Minority in Wartime: The Peace Pledge Union and Vera Brittain 1939–1945', Ph.D. thesis (McMaster University, 1984); and A. Rigby, 'The Peace Pledge Union: From Peace to War, 1936–1945', in P. Brock and T. Socknat (eds.), *Challenge to Mars: Essays on Pacifism from 1918 to 1945* (Toronto, 1999), 169–85.

[39] *Adelphi* (Oct. 1938), 3.

[40] Brittain, *Chronicle of Friendship*, 303 (entry 5 Jan.1937). She filled a vacancy left by the Welsh writer Eiluned Lewis, whose brief period as a Sponsor has not previously been noticed: see Sheppard to Brittain, 27 Jan. 1937 (copy from Brittain Papers shown to me by Mark Bostridge).

later to describe it,[41] which was launched on 6 June 1936 by Humphrey S. Moore, a young Quaker journalist who had been active in the NMWM, FoR, and National Peace Council. Although still published by a separate company, this became the PPU's official mouthpiece on 25 July, with Moore remaining its editor and becoming a Sponsor.[42] The PPU also used new propaganda techniques, such as making films and showing them in a mobile van, though it felt disadvantaged by the BBC's reluctance to allow pacifists more than an occasional radio broadcast.[43]

In addition to the converts it made, Sheppard's organization attracted considerable attention from progressive opinion. For example, Kingsley Martin gave it advice on publicity and spoke at its summer camp, giving Murry the impression that he was 'shivering on the brink' of absolute pacifism.[44] Martin's interest in the PPU was in part family loyalty: as well as his father, his brother-in-law (John Barclay, the PPU's group organizer) was a prominent pacifist. It was also in part psychological compensation for his own rejection of the absolutist position during the Abyssinia crisis.

With an unprecedented level of support and publicity, the PPU began with high hopes which were later to embarrass it. In the darkest days of the war its initial belief that it had a 'sporting chance of creating a mass movement on the broadest political basis in the hope that through its very clamour and strength of numbers national policy could be so influenced as to stem the tide flowing towards total war' was recalled by an activist with a mixture of nostalgia and disgust.[45] By the time the Nazi death camps had been discovered, another activist was arguing that the early PPU 'now makes one blush by reason of its naiveté. One remembers . . . our pride in the hundred thousand signatories of the Pledge, and our belief that if these were increased two-fold or three-fold there would be no war.'[46] These memories were accurate: the PPU's aspirations in the summer of 1936 were expressed in Morris's claim that 'a million members for the Union was no idle dream'.[47] Morris's mentor in the diocese of Birmingham, Bishop Barnes, also expected the PPU to become very influential, though in his case he privately worried that, when

[41] Minutes, PPU sponsors, 27 Oct. 1937.
[42] For Moore's career see *Peace News* (5 Mar. 1938), 10.
[43] For the PPU's film unit, see Minutes, PPU Executive Committee, 24 Jan. 1938. Pacifist broadcasts reprinted in the *Listener* are listed in M. Ceadel, 'A Legitimate Peace Movement: The Case of Interwar Britain, 1918–1945', in P. Brock and T. Socknat (eds.), *Challenge to Mars: Essays on Pacifism from 1918 to 1945* (Toronto, 1999), 134–48 at 148.
[44] *PN* (1 Jan. 1938), 7.
[45] Andrew Stewart, addressing the PPU national council in May 1941: *PN* (20 June 1941), 3–4.
[46] *PN* (29 June 1945), 2.
[47] *PN* (8 Aug. 1936), 2.

this occurred, 'pacifism in England would be taken as sign of weakness by the dictators and lead them to make increasingly extravagant demands';[48] and he chose to work for the National Peace Council, of which he became president in 1937, rather than for a pacifist association. Barnes thus stood on the brink of abandoning pacifism for exemptionism, since he apparently still believed Christianity to be a pacifist religion whilst not wanting too many of his countrymen to take the same view. However, the overwhelming majority of pacifists were delighted that, at least for an eighteen-month period from the spring of 1936 to the autumn of 1937, their movement seemed to have a chance of attaining what Ponsonby had once described as 'proportions which really count'.[49]

Three other pacifist organizations, plus one that was as near-pacifist as its religious affiliation allowed, were created at this time, albeit without achieving anything like the PPU's impact. In the summer of 1936 a Parliamentary Pacifist Group was formed by three Christian-socialist Labour MPs, Hudson, Alfred Salter, and Cecil H. Wilson. This last, formerly a Liberal and a Congregationalist, had been active in the South Africa Conciliation Committee and the FoR before transferring his allegiances to the Labour Party and the Society of Friends.[50] The Parliamentary Pacifist Group consisted of Labour MPs (approximately twenty in number) and peers who were disillusioned with the party's repudiation of pacifism and wished to mobilize public opinion generally rather than campaign only among party members, though it drew the line at running independent pacifist candidates. It issued a National Manifesto for Peace and Disarmament in September, and was to hold a number of 'pacifist conventions'.

Also in September 1936 it was noted in Roman Catholic circles that an association called Pax was 'now being formed'. Its president was a prolific religious writer, Edward Ingram Watkin, who favoured an international police force but believed that 'until it comes into being—and there are no signs of its speedy advent—we must take no part in national wars'.[51] Pax argued that 'under the conditions of today in all wars between nations for national ends the moral and physical evils involved must enormously exceed any possible legitimate gains by either side', and insisted that, such wars being 'morally unjustifiable', Christians had 'the right and duty to refuse to take part in wars'.[52] Because Ingram and Pax were both careful to condemn only *national*

---

[48] Cited in Barnes, *Ahead of his Age*, 350.   [49] Ponsonby, *Now is the Time*, 180.

[50] Bellamy and Savile (eds.), *Dictionary of Labour Biography*, vi. 272–5 (entry by H. Mathers).

[51] *Colosseum*, 3 (1936–7), 188.

[52] Cited in H. Beevor, *Peace and Pacifism* (1938), 111–12. See also *Blackfriars*, 17 (1936), 854–5.

wars, they stopped short of pacifism even as an interim ethic. They knew that their church believed some wars to have higher than national ends and to be justifiable therefore. Only a few very independently minded Roman Catholics—most famously Eric Gill, the bohemian sculptor who became a Sponsor of the PPU[53]—took an absolutist position. As a cautiously orthodox body, Pax was unable to contribute much to peace activism at this time.

In October 1936 a Christian Pacifist Party was started by Howard Ingli James, a Baptist minister in Coventry. Its aim was to create a single-issue parliamentary party—a forlorn hope under the British electoral system—which helps to explain why after eighteen months it had only 140 supporters[54] and soon faded from view. Even so, by seeking to hijack the Parliamentary Pacifist Group's conventions, it briefly caused some embarrassment to Labour's pacifist parliamentarians[55] who knew that their own party, tolerant though it was of conscientious objection to certain of its policies, could not countenance an electoral challenge to party candidates.

Finally, in June 1937 an Anglican Pacifist Fellowship was formed, replacing the defunct body formed three years previously by Canon Morris and establishing itself on an enduring basis. Its principal founder was the Revd C. Paul Gliddon, an Anglo-Catholic long active in the FoR. The Revd R. H. Le Messurier, also an Anglo-Catholic, acted as its secretary. And the Marquess of Tavistock agreed to be its chairman. It had acquired 400 communicants of the Church of England as members by the end of the year.[56]

Of the two long-established associations, only the FoR benefited from pacifism's golden age, though it did so fairly modestly. It engaged Leslie Artingstall, a Congregationalist minister on the staff of the London Missionary Society, as its secretary in succession to Bartlett.[57] It enjoyed further increases in membership of a fifth in 1936 and of more than a third the following year, though it acknowledged that it could not match the 'wider' appeal of the PPU.[58] Christian pacifism was hampered in the second half of the 1930s not only by the country's continuing secularization but by a major change in Protestant theological fashion. Dependent since the 1850s on an immanentist and liberal interpretation of Christianity which had been steadily gaining support in Britain's churches, it found itself facing two powerful challenges. The first was from the transcendental emphasis on the mystery of God and the

---

[53] For Gill's extraordinary behaviour, including sexual abuse of his daughters, see F. McCarthy, *Eric Gill* (1989).

[54] *PN* (23 Apr. 1938), 16.

[55] See the plea for restraint by the organizer of the parliamentary pacifist conventions, Douglas J. J. Owen, in *PN* (14 Aug. 1937), 9.

[56] Wallis, *Valiant for Peace*, 39. *PN* (25 Dec. 1937), 12. Anglican Pacifist Fellowship Papers.

[57] *PN* (12 Dec. 1936), 8.

[58] Minutes, FoR general committee, 15/16 Mar. 1937.

sinfulness of man of the German theologian Karl Barth, whose major works were first translated into English in 1933 and who paid his first visit to Britain in March 1937. The second was from the 'Christian realism' of the American ethicist Reinhold Niebuhr, an evangelical pastor and former member of the American FoR who renounced non-violence in respect of the class struggle in 1933 (during which year he visited the general committee of the British FoR and explained how 'the social issue was to the fore' in his country[59]) and did the same in respect of international relations four years later. Having for decades prided themselves on taking their faith more seriously than co-religionists who believed in just wars, Christian pacifists were disconcerted to find themselves accused of having fallen for an essentially secular utopianism.[60] Even if their rank and file generally lacked the intellectual sophistication to be affected by this charge, their leading scholars, such as Cadoux, Raven, and Garth Macgregor, the Glasgow University professor who was the president of the Church of Scotland Peace Society and a member of the FoR, were obliged from the mid-1930s to face up to Barth's and Niebuhr's strictures in their writings.[61]

The NMWM was destroyed by the crisis into which socialist pacifism was plunged by Franco's rebellion, the suppression of which was regarded by the left as a uniquely just cause. Unlike the American Peace Society three-quarters of a century before, the NMWM did not seek refuge in the distinction between civil and international war: its pledge had always rejected both; and in any case it interpreted the Spanish conflict as a continental war-by-proxy that was in danger of escalation. With leading figures such as Brockway and Reynolds decisively putting their socialism before their pacifism, the NMWM held a conference in October 1936 to discuss changing its basis so as to meet 'such situations as that which exists today in Spain'.[62] It decided not to do so, causing its staff to resign in protest. It consulted its members about throwing in its lot with the PPU, despite the latter's 'bourgeois' tendency to view war as unconnected to the exploitative characteristics of the capitalist countries which resorted to it and also despite its undemocratic deference towards Sheppard and the Sponsors. Because the PPU was undeniably 'a much larger child than its parent had ever been', as one NMWM activist put it, and therefore stood a much greater chance of preventing war, the members supported

[59] Minutes, FoR general committee, 12/13 June 1933.

[60] M. Ceadel, 'Christian Pacifism in the Era of Two World Wars', in W. J. Sheils (ed.), *The Church and War* (Studies in Church History, 20; Oxford, 1983), 391–408 at 406–7.

[61] See C. J. Cadoux, *Christian Pacifism Re-examined* (1940); C. Raven, *Is War Obsolete? A Study of the Conflicting Claims of Religion and Citizenship* (1935) and *The Theological Basis of Christian Pacifism* (1952); G. H. C. Macgregor, *The New Testament Basis of Pacifism* (1936) and *The Relevance of the Impossible: A Reply to Reinhold Niebuhr* (1941).

[62] *PN* (17 Oct. 1936), 1.

a merger 'by a majority of about three to one'.[63] In return the PPU offered modest concessions: it made Bing and Wellock Sponsors, and in order to improve its organizational coherence created an executive committee and a general secretaryship, to which Plowman was appointed.

Political pacifism did not die out altogether with the NMWM: for example, Reynolds's outspoken and bohemian wife, the novelist Ethel Mannin, was to espouse it as late as January 1939.[64] But much of what subsequently passed for it was in reality Christian-socialist pacifism which was dependent for its repudiation of violence on the religious element within that compound. It was notable that the most effective anti-pacifist literature to be published in the second half of the 1930s was written from a socialist perspective: a leading example was the powerful riposte by the poet Cecil Day Lewis, then a Communist.[65]

The PPU outperformed other pacifist associations largely because it exploited humanitarian and utilitarian arguments for pacifism rather than Christian or socialist ones. Huxley, whose pamphlet *What are You Going to Do about it?* proved to be the PPU's most successful publication by far (and prompted Day Lewis's riposte), was influenced by the humanitarian inspiration. He had espoused pacifism the previous autumn, having been particularly impressed by *The Power of Non-Violence*, a work by an American disciple of Gandhi, Richard B. Gregg, which had been published in a British edition during September 1935.[66] Huxley's thesis was: 'Mankind is one, and there is an underlying spiritual reality. Men are free to deny or affirm their unity in the spirit. Acts and thoughts which tend to affirm unity are right; those which deny it are wrong. War is the large-scale and systematic denial of human unity, and is therefore wrong.'[67]

Russell became the leading exponent of utilitarian pacifism, setting out his beliefs in a book, *Which Way to Peace?*, which he had sent in draft to Ponsonby for his approval. Russell still accepted the justice of military force used by a legitimate world government because: 'The evil of war is quantitative, and a small war for a great end may do more good than harm.' But he no longer believed that the league had either the legitimacy or the preponderance

---

[63] Ceadel, *Pacifism in Britain 1914–1945*, 199–200. *PN* (13 Feb. 1937), 2.

[64] Ceadel, *Pacifism in Britain 1914–1945*, 229.

[65] C. Day Lewis, *We're Not Going to Do Nothing: A Reply to Aldous Huxley* (1936): see also his autobiography, *The Buried Day* (1969), 208–223.

[66] The best source on Huxley pending the publication of David Bradshaw's biography is D. Bradshaw, 'The Flight from Gaza: Aldous Huxley's Involvement in the Peace Pledge Union in the Context of His Overall Intellectual Development', in B. Nugel (ed.), *Now More than Ever: Proceedings of the Aldous Huxley Centenary Symposium Münster 1994* (Berlin, 1996), 9–27.

[67] *Nash's Pall Mall Magazine* (July 1936), 77.

of military strength to fight and win such a conflict. He had also come to believe that air power had dramatically raised the costs of a major war, and that since even a limited conflict was likely to escalate it was too risky to go to war in any circumstances. Thus, after many years either working with or observing pacifism, he finally joined it. He made clear that his approach was of the contingent kind which he had recommended to the NMWM fourteen years previously: 'What is right and what is wrong depends, as I believe, on the consequences of actions, in so far as they can be foreseen; I cannot say simply "War is Wicked," but only "Modern war is practically certain to have worse consequences than even the most unjust peace." '[68]

The PPU thus flourished because it catered for the generality of war haters shocked into absolutism by the horror and destructiveness of a future conflict, and did not merely fish in the small pool of Christians and socialists who were drawn to an ultra-exacting interpretation of their creeds. Some traditional pacifists were suspicious of it for that very reason: for example, three Christians published a book in order to warn of the 'danger . . . that true Pacifism is being heavily diluted with such non-Christian elements as personal selfishness and cowardice'.[69] Because of its broader kind of appeal the PPU also attracted young activists of a more apolitical and bohemian kind, such as David Spreckley and Nigel Spottiswoode, than those of the First World War generation, such as Allen and Brockway. This too worried some traditionalists. The sexual mores of certain members of the PPU's staff caused the London Quaker community to distance itself from it. Moreover, during the Second World War, when a Congregationalist minister took over as secretary, he objected to the PPU employing 'persons with irregular marital relations', and was backed by Hudson and Alfred Salter, elderly representatives of the Nonconformist conscience, who resigned their joint treasurerships when they failed to get their way on this issue.[70]

The PPU's comparative popularity can also be attributed to the optimistic orientation which its majority initially favoured. Most Sponsors began by presenting pacifism as a policy worth trying because all others had failed. Huxley claimed: 'Pacifism is . . . good policy—the only sensible policy that anyone has suggested in the circumstances of modern life.'[71] And Murry believed that it was 'probably as near to a certainty as human reckoning can attain that, against a Pacifist England, Fascist Germany would be completely

---

[68] B. Russell, *Which Way to Peace?* (1936), 151, 211–12.

[69] A. Dimond, E. B. Storr, and A. D. Belden, *Three Views of Pacifism* (1937), flyleaf (see also p. 39).

[70] *Vera Brittain: Wartime Chronicle: Diary 1939–1945*, 235 (entry for 15 Sept. 1943). Bennett, 'Testament of a Minority in Wartime', fo. 274. Brockway, *Bermondsey Story*, 236.

[71] *Nash's Pall Mall Magazine* (July 1936), 77.

incapable of making war'.[72] Both were influenced by Gregg's belief that Gandhi's approach could be developed into a 'moral jiu jitsu' which would deter or defeat international aggression: 'The psychological forces in non-violent resistance would operate in different ways in different nations, but they will operate effectively against them all, as sure as violent war has operated against them all.'[73] After Gregg's *The Power of Non-Violence* was described by Sheppard as 'the text book of our movement',[74] it was dutifully taken up by many groups. In practice, however, the esoteric exercises recommended by Gregg as a preparation for Gandhi-style resistance were not to everyone's taste: Crozier, for one, felt that 'the Gregg cranks' made the PPU appear 'faddist'; and another member complained that, as a result of their efforts, the union had 'gossiped about vegetarianism and knitting and Indian ahimsa' when it should have 'pondered economics and Parliament and Spain'.[75] In May 1937 the PPU made clear that 'Greggism', as it had come to be called, was not official policy, although groups were still free to explore it if they wished.

But despite having thus had to change its emphasis, and despite the fact that its membership had entered a plateau stage at which new pledges did little more than compensate for the weeding out of ones which had never been followed up, the PPU still exuded an engaging confidence that pacifism was practical politics and that the pacifist movement could be a significant force in British politics. By contrast, the other new pacifist organizations tended to rely more heavily on peaceful change, a policy which could be supported on *pacificist* grounds and therefore gave little incentive for going all the way to absolutism.

Admittedly, many of the PPU's most thoughtful members always favoured a more quietist approach. Plowman was particularly committed to this view, as will be seen. So, of course, was the FoR, especially after hiving off its war-preventing effort as the Embassies of Reconciliation. And Martin Wight, in later life a prominent academic student of international relations, insisted that for a Christian such as himself 'pacifism is not a psychological technique or a set of social reformist principles, but something inseparable from his religion, part of a life that can only be lived through divine grace'.[76]

The final group within the anti-containment coalition were socialist *pacificists* who argued for war resistance. Unlike socialist pacifists, they were

[72] J. Middleton Murry, *The Necessity of Pacifism* (1937), 26, 114.
[73] R. B. Gregg, *The Power of Non-Violence* (1936 edn.), 90.
[74] *PN* (25 July 1936).
[75] Crozier to Ponsonby, 7 Jan. 1937: Ponsonby papers. *PN* (17 Apr. 1937).
[76] M. Wight, 'Christian Pacifism', *Theology: A Monthly Journal of Historic Christianity*, 33 (July–Dec. 1936), 12–21 at 21.

committed to opposing capitalist conflicts only, and could consistently support military resistance to Franco as a people's war. Even so, the Spanish Civil War weakened support for war resistance. For example, it caused the volatile Brailsford, who had been reconverted to war resistance as recently as the Rhineland crisis, to renounce it again. Declaring that people 'who will not fight for what they hold dear deserve to go under', he tried to join the International Brigade, thirty-nine years after having enlisted in the Philhellenic Legion, but, being deemed too old to be a soldier and too independent-minded to be a political commissar, had to settle for being a recruiter.[77] He also came out in favour of a peace front linking the Soviet Union with countries such as Britain and France which could now be regarded as at least potentially peace-loving and democratic rather than imperialist and capitalist.

Yet, weakened though it was, war resistance continued to receive some support from the far left, other than the Communists. Most notably, the ILP endorsed the general strike against war at its conferences of 1935–7 and never subsequently rescinded this policy.[78] This was despite its support for the Spanish government's resistance to Franco's rebellion, a cause in which the ILP member George Orwell, himself a supporter of war resistance until ten days before the outbreak of the Second World War, was seriously wounded.[79]

In addition, a contingent form of war resistance found favour with some leading members of Labour's left wing: they supported a peace front in principle but could not trust the National government with the armaments necessary to carry it out in case they used them not to contain Hitler but to deflect his aggression eastwards towards the Soviet Union. Cripps, who refused to accept that it 'would be a bad thing for the British working class if Germany defeated us',[80] took this view. So did Harold Laski, who in March 1937 insisted that 'by its inherent nature this government cannot make any war which is not an imperialist war'.[81] The logic of Cripps's and Laski's position was that a peace front against the dictators could not be offered until after a change of government in Britain: until then, they were in effect war resisters.

The appeal of contingent war resistance within the Labour Party was sufficient to make the leadership careful about how it presented its own support for a peace front. For example, when in 1937 it stopped voting against the

[77] Leventhal, *The Last Dissenter*, 251–2.
[78] P. J. Thwaites, 'The Independent Labour Party 1938–1950', Ph.D. thesis (LSE, 1976), fo.101.
[79] See his book *Homage to Catalonia* (1938).
[80] *The Times* (15 Nov. 1936), cited in K. Middlemas, *Diplomacy of Illusion: The British Government and Germany 1937–39* (1972), 106.
[81] Cited in Thwaites, 'Independent Labour Party', fo. 91.

arms estimates in parliament, it decided to abstain rather than vote in favour. And in a book published that same year Attlee thought it expedient to express support for 'the general proposition that there is no agreement on foreign policy between a Labour Opposition and a Capitalist Government'.[82]

Despite being challenged by this diverse coalition, the LNU's leaders did not waver from their support for collective security. The hardening of Angell's views in 1936 was characteristic of their resolve. He stopped claiming to be a pacifist in his private beliefs. Since the central argument of *The Great Illusion* had been that additional territory did not bring with it additional welfare, he became a leading scourge of the view that the acquisition of colonies could solve the problems of the 'have-not' nations.[83] And he responded to the Rhineland crisis by arguing that 'the place to defend Abyssinia was on the Rhine'.[84]

However, because this resolute approach was unacceptable to many of its members, the LNU experienced serious internal divisions for the first time. In February 1936 the correspondence column in *Headway* began debating whether pacifists still had a place in the union. The following month, when the executive committee first discussed the remilitarization of the Rhineland, its chairman identified two distinct schools of thought: 'One stressed the impossibility of condoning Germany's flagrant breach of her freely negotiated treaty; the other was eager to explore the opportunity of general appeasement apparently offered to us by Herr Hitler's proposals.'[85] In May Captain Philip Mumford, a former RAF officer who advocated an international police force, urged 'the two main branches of the Peace Movement', the 'pacifists' and his fellow 'sanctionists', to renew their efforts to 'discover what they hold in common'; but his letter was dismissed by another reader as an 'unconvincing' though 'gallant attempt to postpone the pain of parting'.[86] Indeed, Mumford himself was shortly to convert to pacifism and become a Sponsor of the PPU.

A few LNU members were disaffected because they had wanted an even more forthrightly sanctionist policy: one threatened resignation because he was 'sick with disgust' at the league's betrayal of Abyssinia.[87] But, as Garnett acknowledged, many more were driven by the imposition of sanctions to 'complain that, instead of increasing international goodwill and removing

---

[82] C. R. Attlee, *The Labour Party in Perspective* (1937), 227.

[83] See N. Angell, *This Have and Have-Not Business: Political Fantasy and Economic Fact* (1936).

[84] Minutes, LNU executive, 2 Apr. 1936. *Report, LNU General Council June 1936* (1936), 54.

[85] Minutes, LNU executive, 12 Mar. 1936.

[86] *HW* (May 1936), 86–7; (June 1936), 116.   [87] *HW* (July 1936), 136.

obstacles to trade, the League has of late been making trouble between nations and creating new obstacles'; and since these complainants included 'a number of commercial firms and wealthy business men',[88] and even the LNU's treasurer, Lord Queenborough,[89] donations dropped sharply. The effectiveness of its appeals department had previously allowed the LNU to live well beyond its subscription income; and, despite an enlarged deficit because of the Peace Ballot, Cecil had only recently boasted that it had 'never been in serious difficulties over money'.[90] Yet in May it was forced to cut salaries by 10 per cent and reduce the size of its staff;[91] and the following month the chairman of its finance committee, Herbert Syrett, warned the general council: 'The day of big cheques is over; the sooner we realize that the better.'[92] The fall in the LNU's membership was also gathering pace: subscriptions dropped by 6.4 per cent in 1936, almost double the previous year's decline, and by a further 11.0 per cent in 1937.

The LNU did all that it could reasonably do to persuade anti-sanctionists to remain within its ranks. Mumford thus retained a connection with it for a while after joining the PPU, on the grounds that 'there are many pacifists still in it and I still approve of a great part of its work'.[93] For Eleanor Rathbone, indeed, it propitiated the opponents of sanctions too much. At the December 1936 general council she condemned Russell in particular for having adopted 'a spirit of cynical pessimism' towards the league in his writing, and proposed a resolution which condemned pacifists for encouraging aggression. And although she allowed the leadership to substitute a characteristically tactful motion which merely emphasized that the personal refusal of military service was not a practical method of war prevention,[94] she criticized the LNU in the pro-collective-security book which she wrote during 1937 for the inconsistency of professing 'fidelity to League obligations' whilst refusing 'to part company' with those advocating 'policies completely incompatible with such fidelity'.[95]

In particular, the LNU encouraged Allen to campaign for peaceful change as part of an official dual policy. He did so at the 31st International Peace Congress at Cardiff in mid-June 1936, thereby drawing attention to an event

---

[88] *HW* (July 1936), 140.

[89] Queenborough to Cecil, 27 Apr. 1936: Cecil Papers Add. MSS 51136.

[90] H. A. L. Fisher (ed.), *Essays in Honour of Gilbert Murray* (1936), 85.

[91] Minutes, LNU executive, 14 May 1936.

[92] *Report, LNU General Council June 1936* (1936), 28–9. See his earlier warning: *Report, LNU General Council Dec. 1935* (1936), 24.

[93] Mumford to Brittain, 3 Nov. [1936]: copy from Brittain Papers shown to me by Mark Bostridge.

[94] *Report, LNU General Council Dec. 1936*, 24–9.

[95] E. Rathbone, *War can be Averted: The Achievability of Collective Security* (1938), 14.

which was generally ignored by the mainstream of the British peace movement and whose archaic quality was symbolized by the fact that delegates attended an unveiling in nearby Neath Abbey of a plaque to Joseph Tregelles Price, who had co-founded the Peace Society 120 years previously.[96] Allen's argument was that there was 'no alternative to the League, the whole League and nothing but the League, with its full scheme of collective security as originally intended' but that in addition peaceful change must 'simultaneously' be provided. Although he complicated his message by repeating his claim still to be 'an unrepentant pacifist' who would personally prefer to see his country 'leading the world disarmed', his speech was thought worthy of publication as a pamphlet.[97] A week later Allen addressed the LNU's general council on behalf of the executive committee, once again defending the league but also insisting that it be seen 'as an instrument of mutual service and aid, and not merely as an instrument of force', urging that an international fact-finding commission be established to examine access to raw materials, and emphasizing: 'Germany will never reveal her *bona fides* unless we first reveal ours.'[98]

However, after he accepted Hitler's invitation to attend the Nuremberg rally in September,[99] Allen's dual policy tilted perceptibly in the direction of the accommodation of German demands: he began to argue that 'setting up the machinery for peaceful change should be a few inches ahead of pressure to improve the working of collective security'.[100] And although at the general council in December 1936 he still claimed to be offering a 'joint method', and tried to distance himself from the advocates of a world conference as well as from those of regional security pacts,[101] his emphasis had changed. He had begun working on a manifesto intended to revive the League of Nations in the same way as his fourteen-point plan of October 1933 had been intended to revive the World Disarmament Conference: it proposed fact-finding commissions to examine the problems associated with raw materials, population movements, colonies, and borders. The LNU's executive committee, all too conscious that its critics were constantly asking, as *Headway* put it, 'why not a League busy only with peace, with mediation, conciliation, the remedy of grievances, the friendly settlement of disputes?',[102] endorsed Allen's manifesto. When he presented it to the general council in June 1937 it was therefore as an

---

[96] *The Times* (15 June 1936), 14.

[97] Lord Allen of Hurtwood, *Peace in our Time: An Appeal to the International Peace Conference on June 16, 1936* (1936), 5, 21.

[98] *Report, LNU General Council June 1936*, 41–2.

[99] Marwick, *Clifford Allen*, 163, 175. See also Allen to Arnold-Forster, 8 Sept. 1936, in Gilbert, *Plough my own Furrow*, 377, and Allen's article, 'The Meaning of Nuremberg', *Spectator* (23 Sept. 1936), 487–8.

[100] *HW* (Dec. 1936), 231.   [101] *Report, LNU General Council Dec. 1936*, 14–15.

[102] *HW* (May 1937), 82.

official LNU document. His speech received 'prolonged applause' from the assembled delegates,[103] the next annual report acknowledging that this 'proof that the Union, while calling for the defence of peace, insists equally on a just peace was an influential factor preventing defections'.[104]

Although skilful in minimizing the loss of pacifists and accommodationists, the LNU proved much less effective in uniting sanctionist opinion during 1936–7. In May 1936 alarm at the prospect of 'a regular stampede away from the League such as is indicated by a stream of defeatist letters in *The Times*' prompted Murray to wonder 'whether all the League forces in the country should not unite at any rate temporarily to prevent such a collapse' and to raise the idea with Davies.[105] In the event, however, the LNU faced not only a revival of the minor friction with the New Commonwealth Society but a new and much more serious diversion of energies caused by the launching of a new European collective-security movement known in Britain as the International Peace Campaign.

The New Commonwealth Society stole a march on the LNU when on 5 June 1936 Churchill agreed to become president of its British section.[106] On 15 July he duly addressed one of its meetings. The acknowledged leader of defencism's pro-containment minority against the pro-appeasement majority led by Neville Chamberlain, Churchill had been working with the Anti-Nazi Council, a behind-the-scenes group funded mainly by Jewish businessmen. In April 1936, when he had been privately urged by some Foreign Office officials to take the lead in a collective-security campaign, he had told the cabinet secretary that he was conscious that 'the British people will not take rearmament seriously except as part of the League policy'.[107] It was, of course, a tribute to the strength of liberal *pacificism* in Britain that defencists should thus invoke it, rather than rely on their own rhetoric of king and country, to boost support for containment. Apparently untroubled by the utopian aspects of the New Commonwealth Society which had previously upset his fellow Conservatives, Churchill later explained that he had accepted its presidency because it was 'one of the few Peace Societies that advocates the use of force, if possible overwhelming force, to support public international law'.[108] It may be presumed that he also liked the fact that it was a small, leader-dominated body, without the constraints of the large and distinguished

---

[103] *Report, LNU General Council June 1937*, 50–1.

[104] *LNU Year Book 1938*, 11.

[105] Murray to Davies, 23 May 1936: Davies of Llandinam Papers.

[106] Churchill to Davies, 5 June 1936: Davies of Llandinam Papers.

[107] M. Gilbert, *Winston S. Churchill*, v (1976), pp. xx–xxi, 721–6. S. Roskill, *Hankey: Man of Secrets* (3 vols., 1970–4), iii. 239.

[108] Gilbert, *Winston S. Churchill*, v. 747–8, 763. *New Commonwealth* (June 1937), 146.

executive committee and sturdily democratic general council which Austen
Chamberlain had so disliked about the LNU.

Churchill had already accused the LNU publicly of 'inexhaustible gullibility' and privately of disarming the country;[109] and he therefore declined its
invitation of 24 July 1936 to join its executive committee.[110] This spared him
some irritation when its general council blocked an official pro-rearmament
resolution in December 1936, on the grounds that the National government
had not pledged never to use its armaments in a manner which contravened
the League Covenant—a decision which was to be reversed with only one
dissentient six months later.[111] However, he did not seek to favour one association at the expense of its rivals as much as to mobilize as broad a movement for collective security as possible.

It was therefore as 'a focus bringing together these various forces'[112] that
Churchill helped the Anti-Nazi Council launch a 'Defence of Freedom and
Peace' campaign in October. He not only addressed a New Commonwealth
Society luncheon at the Dorchester Hotel on 25 November, paid for by
Montagu Burton,[113] where Kingsley Martin 'seemed to see every public
person I knew',[114] but was principal speaker at the 'Defence of Freedom of
Peace' rally in the Albert Hall on 3 December 1936 which was organized by
the LNU. Churchill was also a co-signatory of the 'Save the League—Save
Peace' declaration which appeared in the press on 1 January 1937 and was to
be renamed the 'War Can Be Averted' declaration in the course of a follow-
up campaign in its support. However, he declined Davies's suggestion that he
embark upon a long speaking campaign using either the New Commonwealth
Society, the Defence of Freedom and Peace campaign, or the LNU 'as a vehi-
cle', arguing that it could have little effect on opinion compared with 'access
to the broadcast'.[115] Even apart from the fact that he became distracted by his
ill-fated attempt to save Edward VIII from abdication, he regarded his 'arms
and the covenant'[116] campaign as an uphill task.

Even so, his name on the New Commonwealth Society's letterhead was, as
Garnett acknowledged to Davies, 'a great coup on your part',[117] and helped

---

[109] Hansard, 272 HC col. 84 (23 Nov. 1932). Gilbert, *Winston S. Churchill*, (1976), 696
[110] Minutes, LNU executive, 24 July, 17 Sept. 1936.
[111] LNU, *General Council Report Dec. 1936*, 29, 32–6. *Report, LNU General Council June
1937*, 47.
[112] Cited in Gilbert, *Winston S. Churchill*, v. 799.
[113] Minutes, British executive, New Commonwealth, 15 July 1936.
[114] *New Statesman* (28 Nov. 1936), 843.
[115] Gilbert, *Winston S. Churchill*, v. 835.
[116] This was the title given to the edn. of his collected (mainly parliamentary) speeches which
his son Randolph Churchill issued in 1938.
[117] Garnett to Davies, 15 June 1936: Davies of Llandinam papers.

its membership to pass the 2,000 mark for the first time.[118] It also encouraged the society to revive its demand for a 'a pre-organized system of sanctions, including the creation of an International Police Force', at the LNU's December 1936 general council, thereby abandoning the compromise reached by Allen and Austen Chamberlain during the final stages of the Peace Ballot. Cecil refused to accept such a force except to deter the misuse of civil aviation as part of a disarmament agreement which seemed further off than ever; and the Earl of Lytton, who though not a politician was emerging as the leading Conservative within the LNU, successfully moved that the matter be postponed until the following summer while talks between the two associations were held.[119] At the June 1937 general council the New Commonwealth Society withdrew its motion because these talks were continuing;[120] but the fact that Allen, now identified primarily with peaceful change, was its spokesman considerably obscured the sanctionist message which it was mainly trying to convey.

Whereas the New Commonwealth Society was irritating for the LNU, the International Peace Campaign (IPC) was disruptive. Indeed, instead of harnessing the left-wing support for a peace front which was partially compensating for a declining liberal belief in the league, this new initiative further divided it: the problem was that though it engaged Cecil's stubborn loyalty, it was widely thought to be both unnecessary and a Communist manœuvre.

The IPC had emerged in France during September 1935[121] under the name Rassemblement universel pour la paix, abbreviated to RUP, and was ostensibly the brainchild of Pierre Cot, a prominent member of the Radical Party who had served as Air Minister from January 1933 to February 1934 and was president of the French section of the New Commonwealth Society.[122] RUP's aim was to provide a counterpart to the LNU in the different political conditions of continental Europe, where existing League associations were notoriously weak and the International Federation of league of Nations Societies

[118] Minutes, British executive, New Commonwealth, 17 Dec. 1936.

[119] *Report, LNU General Council Dec. 1936*, 20–2.

[120] *Report, LNU General Council June 1937*, 46.

[121] This date is given in International Peace Campaign, *World Peace Congress, Brussels 3–6 Sept. 1936* (Paris and Brussels, 1936), 7. For the RUP generally see E. Hermon, 'Une ultime tentative de sauvetage de la Société des Nations: La Campagne du Rassemblement Universel pour la Paix', in M. Vaïsse (ed.), *Le Pacifisme en Europe des années 1920 aux années 1950* (Brussels, 1993), 193–221.

[122] For Cot, see P. Cot, *The Triumph of Treason* (1944), 356; P. J. Larmor, *The French Radical Party in the 1930s* (Stanford, Calif., 1964), 54, 174, 188, 193, 207; R. Griffiths, *Marshal Pétain* (1979), 104, 134, 146–7, 181–5; and M. S. Alexander, *The Republic in Danger: General Maurice Gamelin and the Politics of French Defence, 1933–1940* (Cambridge, 1992), 150–66.

was 'fundamentally rotten', as Cecil later put it.[123] RUP put forward a four-point programme:

1. Recognition of the sanctity of treaty obligations.
2. Reduction and limitation of armaments by international agreement and the suppression of profit from the manufacture and trade in armaments.
3. Strengthening of the League of Nations for the prevention and stopping of war by the organization of collective security and mutual assistance.
4. Establishment within the framework of the League of Nations of effective machinery for remedying international conditions which might lead to war.

Despite the optimistic reference to disarmament in the second point and the prudent dual-policy concession to peaceful change in the fourth, it was an endorsement of collective security, as the third point—which, significantly, Britain's National Peace Council was never to accept—made clear. On 17 January 1936 RUP sent a request to the LNU asking for British assistance in promoting these four points.

However, when the executive committee discussed RUP at its next meeting, Austen Chamberlain immediately put his finger on a major drawback: although there was a strong case for it in other countries, no new association was needed in Britain.[124] Indeed, with the LNU starting to face serious difficulties, any competition for finance would cause it problems; and its staff also saw a new body as an implicit criticism of their own previous efforts. Soon afterwards a second serious flaw was identified: 'grave doubts on the part of members of the Executive Committee as to whether the whole of Cot's plan is not communism in disguise', as Cecil angrily informed Angell.[125] Cecil's inexperience of left-wing politics caused him to underestimate the significance of RUP's Communist links until the Molotov–Ribbentrop pact belatedly opened his eyes to 'what some Communists and their friends think fair and loyal'.[126] RUP had been launched almost immediately after the Comintern had decided at its August 1935 congress to try to form a popular front with socialists and liberals. Its principal organizer, Louis Dolivet, had simply transferred from the Movement Against War and Fascism, which was being allowed to fade away; and even Cecil described Dolivet as 'a Communist of a kind'.[127] Pierre Cot himself was not only a secret Communist but,

---

[123] Cecil to Noel Baker, 26 Aug. 1937: Noel-Baker Papers 5/134.
[124] Minutes, LNU executive, 23 Jan. 1936.
[125] Cecil to Angell, 21 Feb. 1936: Cecil Papers, Add. MSS 51140.
[126] Viscount Cecil, *A Great Experiment* (1941), 285.
[127] 'Copy of a Statement by M. Louis Dolivet, Paris, 18 January 1938': Cecil Papers Add. MSS 51143. Cecil to Noel Baker, 23 Dec. 1936: Noel-Baker Papers 5/51.

later at least, a Soviet agent too.[128] He became Air Minister again in the popular-front governments of June 1936 to January 1938, his role in nationalizing France's aircraft industry being particularly controversial; and in September 1940, by which time he was in exile and supporting de Gaulle, he was stripped of his citizenship by the Vichy regime. After 1945, when he was expelled by the Radicals for being too pro-Communist, he was blatantly a fellow-traveller.[129]

RUP was sufficiently tarred with the Moscow brush to be anathematized by Britain's trade unions, Roman Catholics, and Conservatives. The LNU's executive committee was warned as early as February 1936 that Sir Walter Citrine, general secretary of the Trades Union Congress and president of the International Federation of Trade Unions, would not endorse RUP because of Dolivet's former association with Münzenberg.[130] This was a significant setback because Citrine's devotion to the cause of containment could not be faulted: he was for example a leading member of the Anti-Nazi Council.[131] The most bitter opponent of RUP on the LNU's staff, John Eppstein, was an active Roman Catholic who had published a book on his church's approach to international law and was to write anti-Soviet articles for its religious press.[132] Eppstein too was a resolute supporter of containment, his 'untiring support' of the Defence of Freedom and Peace campaign being acknowledged by its historian.[133] Neville Chamberlain used his acceptance of the honorary presidency of the LNU offered to him when he took over as Conservative leader from Baldwin to lecture it on its pro-left bias; and he complained particularly about its links with RUP.[134]

However, Cecil refused to take these objections seriously. He became co-president with Cot of RUP, and insisted that a British section should be launched, under the name International Peace Campaign, despite the fact that of the LNU's heavyweights only Noel Baker and to a lesser extent Angell were enthusiastic about it, though Murray was as loyal as ever. Initially the LNU's overseas committee opposed the IPC on the grounds of duplication of effort and probable Communist links; but on Cecil's insis-

[128] C. Andrew and O. Gordievsky, *KGB: The Secret History* (1990), 370–1, 635. C. Andrew and V. Mitrokhin, *The Mitrokhin Archive; The KGB in Europe and the West* (1999), 143, 162–3.

[129] T. Wolton, *Le KGB en France* (Paris, 1986), 337, 352–3.

[130] Minutes, LNU executive, 13 Feb. 1936.

[131] Gilbert, *Winston S. Churchill*, v. 726 n., 739.

[132] J. Eppstein, *The Catholic Tradition of the Law of Nations* (1935). For his claim that Soviet membership of the League 'has greatly diminished confidence in the Council and Assembly', see *Blackfriars*, 17 (1936), 918–19.

[133] E. Spier, *Focus: A Footnote to the History of the Thirties* (1963), 44.

[134] Chamberlain to Cecil, 24 June 1937 (see also 30 June, 25 July 1937; 26 Jan., 9 and 15 Feb. 1938): Cecil Papers Add. MSS 51087.

tence its recommendation was not accepted.[135] Cecil wrote a memorandum claiming that, because the IPC would not have its own branches or members and would merely seek to promote collective security among organizations not currently taking an interest in the issue, it would not compete with the LNU but build up a secondary movement in its support. Despite Lytton's worry that the IPC would none the less 'require funds to the Union's detriment and in competition with it in order to do work which is already being effectively done by the Union', the LNU's executive committee agreed to participate in an *ad hoc* IPC committee to organize the British delegation to the international congress which would formally launch RUP as a mass movement. Meanwhile, the question of the LNU's exact relationship to the IPC was referred to a special subcommittee. The remilitarization of the Rhineland increased Cecil's determination to proceed; and on 13 March he held an international meeting 'of the Rassemblement universel pour la paix' in his home.[136]

Four days later Cecil attended the subcommittee which had to consider whether the union should take full responsibility for the British IPC or keep it arm's length. At this stage he preferred the latter option, believing that a British IPC outside the LNU's organizational structure would more easily raise money 'from some of the great American charitable funds'. Noel Baker agreed, arguing that, since the IPC's 'real purpose' was to 'stimulate the movement for peace through the League of Nations in Europe', and since on the continent 'co-ordinating committees were being formed outside the League of Nations societies', it would be most helpful 'if their opposite number in England were also a co-ordinating committee of the same kind'. But with Murray warning of the divisive potential of an independent IPC, the subcommittee recommended a compromise whereby the British section should be 'an autonomous committee of the League of Nations Union reporting its minutes for the approval of the League of Nations Union Executive'. Having clarified that 'autonomous' meant having 'a special office and special funds', and that the IPC would fund itself and seek the LNU's approval before launching a financial appeal, the executive committee ratified this decision on 26 March.[137] When this arrangement was reported to the first meeting of an organizing committee for a British IPC on 23 April, other participating peace associations expressed concern that the LNU 'was being unduly privileged'; but the counter-argument was advanced that the LNU was uniquely influential in Europe and would give

---

[135] Minutes, LNU executive, 13 Feb. 1936.

[136] The report of the meeting is in Noel-Baker Papers 5/46.

[137] Minutes, Subcommittee to consider the relationship of the RUP to the LNU, 17 Mar. 1936. Minutes, LNU executive committee, 26 Mar. 1936.

special assistance to the new body, notably by seconding Dame Adelaide Livingstone as an organizer.[138]

The IPC's British National Committee began operating the following month under Cecil's chairmanship.[139] Its first recorded income was a 'Donation from America'—in fact from the Rockefeller Foundation—of £1,861 on 28 May.[140] It took offices at 27 Chester Square, close to the LNU's premises. In July it launched a periodical, which appeared weekly until the autumn and monthly thereafter. With Livingstone, who was given the title of vice-chairman, soon succumbing to a breakdown of health, Communist sympathizers provided much of the organizational drive: for example, a future circuit-court judge, R. G. ('Dick') Freeman, who had been a founder of the (Marxist) October Club at Oxford, a temporary tractor driver on a Soviet collective farm, and the organizing secretary of the Communist-controlled Student Movement for Peace, Freedom and Cultural Progress,[141] was a crucial full-time employee; the fellow-travelling crystallographer J. D. Bernal was an influential committee member; and Bernal's lover Margaret Gardiner,[142] prominent in several front organizations, was a loyal activist. But its Communist links were the major reason why, despite justifying itself as 'the Continent's reply to the Peace Ballot',[143] the British IPC made only modest progress in persuading organizations, other than fellow-travelling ones, to cooperate. Prevented by its assurances to the LNU from creating its own branches, it therefore began creating local 'peace councils' to boost its numbers of affiliates. By mid-July, when the British IPC publicized its first eighty-six affiliations, the largest category consisted of such bodies.[144]

The national committee's initial purpose was to send a strong delegation to the World Peace Congress at Brussels on 3–6 September 1936 which RUP hoped would spark its campaign into life. Staged with the care that characterized all Communist-controlled events, it reinforced Cecil's confidence in the IPC: on his return he told the LNU's executive committee that it had 'manifested a passionate feeling, such as he had never seen in any other international gathering, that peace was essential and that the only possible peace was through the League'.[145] Since the British delegation had promised an

---

[138] Minutes of British IPC, 23 Apr. 1936, in Noel-Baker Papers 5/45.

[139] The minutes of a meeting on 14 May 1936 are in the Noel-Baker Papers 5/46.

[140] Unlike its minute books, which are missing, two IPC account books covering the period from May 1936 to January 1940 survive: Bodleian Library MS Eng misc c. 745–6.

[141] See his contribution to Foot *et al.*, *Young Oxford and War*, and *IPC Weekly Bulletin* (3 Sept. 1936)

[142] See M. Gardiner, *A Scatter of Memories* (1988).

[143] *IPC Weekly Bulletin* (23 July 1936), 3.

[144] *IPC Weekly Bulletin* (15 July 1936), 3–6.

[145] Minutes, LNU executive, 17 Sept. 1936.

annual contribution of £1,200 to RUP, Cecil asked the LNU make a substantial financial contribution. He also wanted it to have a closer relationship with the British national committee of the IPC. Having experienced the British IPC's organizational and financial fragility, he had come to see the advantages to it of full integration into a more powerful body. When some of his colleagues suggested that the IPC become wholly independent, Cecil argued that it would be 'absurd for it to run without regard to the immense organization possessed by the League of Nations Union'.[146] While the LNU's financial responsibility for and constitutional relationship to the IPC were being reconsidered by a subcommittee, LNU employees who had accepted a salary cut on the grounds that their employer had no spare money protested about so large a proposed donation to the IPC: after a unanimous staff meeting on 29 September Eppstein sent an unauthorized anti-IPC letter to the LNU's regional employees for which he was later made to apologize.[147] Cecil's proposal was also opposed by those whose suspicions of the IPC had been confirmed by what *Headway* described as a 'vocal and energetic and recalcitrant' red presence at Brussels:[148] for example, Citrine was still reminding colleagues more than a year later what a 'Communist nest' the trade-union section at that congress had been.[149]

None the less, Cecil's authority was such that the subcommittee supported his new proposal. Moreover, its recommendation was accepted by the executive committee, which had by then found a way of restoring staff salaries.[150] However, while waiting for the general council to give its approval at its December meeting, several members of the executive committee grew uneasy; and at Lytton's insistence the matter was referred back to a subcommittee.[151] Cecil complained to Noel Baker that 'the attack against the I.P.C. is clearly developing. Its features appear to be total untruthfulness and great passion. Evidently, it is inspired by the Roman Church.'[152] This attack became so strong that Cecil decided to compromise rather than face a divisive challenge to the executive committee's decision at the general council. His retreat took place while preparations were being made for Churchill's Albert Hall meeting and was attributed by his kinswoman Blanche Dugdale to 'Winston's persuasion'.[153] Cecil conceded that the British national

---

[146] Minutes, LNU executive, 24 Sept. 1936.
[147] Minutes, LNU executive, 1 Oct. 1936. Eppstein to Cecil, 12 Nov. 1936: Cecil Papers Add. MSS 51174.
[148] *HW* (Oct. 1936), 187.
[149] Citrine to Dalton, 28 Jan. 1938: copy in Cecil Papers, Add. MSS 51175.
[150] Minutes, LNU executive committee, 15 and 22 Oct. 1936.
[151] Minutes, LNU executive, 29 Oct., 5 Nov. 1936.
[152] Cecil to Noel Baker, 9 Nov. 1936 (copy): Cecil Papers Add. MSS 51108.
[153] Minutes, LNU executive, 19 Nov. 1936. Dugdale, *Baffy*, 31 (entry for 18 Nov. 1936).

committee of the IPC should become an independent body, and in return obtained agreement for the LNU to be represented on it, albeit merely on the same basis as every other affiliated body.[154] Lytton disliked even this decision, having consistently opposed the creation of a separate organization. However, at the general council the compromise had a fairly easy passage: Cecil publicly admitted that the idea of 'a special contribution to the British Committee had been abandoned'; Noel Baker reiterated the argument that 'the I.P.C. movement was like the Peace Ballot—the co-ordination of organizations for a special purpose'; and an amendment urging the LNU not to affiliate at all to a Communist-influenced body was thrown out.[155]

However, the compromise failed to bring harmony to the collective-security movement. Indeed, it brought organizational chaos, as Lytton had warned, without allaying fears of Communism. There was some friction at the national level: the IPC's first appeal for funds provoked complaints from the LNU's finance committee that it had not been notified; and an Albert Hall meeting on 30 April 1937 to promote the 'War Can Be Averted' declaration initially generated rivalry about who was to take responsibility and credit for it. These incidents prompted Murray to call for a reconsideration of the relationship between the two bodies; but all that emerged was a small coordinating committee.[156]

There was also serious institutional confusion at the local level, where many more peace councils were being formed, usually in order to organize 'peace weeks'. Having held a successful trial at Bolton in late September 1936, the IPC made great efforts to stage such events across the country as a way of spreading its message: indeed, apart from the standard Communist attempt to create 'vocational associations'—based on trade unions, professions, youth groups, and women's organizations—peace weeks were to be the IPC's major form of campaigning.[157] Concern that local peace councils were being used 'by political bodies in order to take the leadership of the peace movement out of the hand of the L.N.U.'[158] led Garnett to complain about the IPC's regular sending of Freeman, Bernal, and other left-wing speakers 'to address the new Local Peace Committees now being set up, mostly for the purpose of conducting peace weeks'.[159] The LNU decided early in 1937 to hold its own 'peace weeks', though it was later to admit that 'League of Nations Peace Weeks' would have been a more helpful title for them.[160] In

---

[154] Minutes, LNU executive committee, 5 Nov. 1936.
[155] LNU, *General Council Report Dec. 1936*, 53–7.
[156] Minutes, LNU executive, 4 Feb., 18 and 23 Mar. 1937.
[157] See, e.g., International Peace Campaign, *The Peace Week Handbook* (n.d. [1937]).
[158] Minutes, LNU administration committee, 3 Dec. 1936.
[159] Garnett to Lytton, 2 Feb. 1937 (copy): Davies of Llandinam Papers.
[160] *HW* (Feb. 1937), 40. Minutes, LNU executive, 10 June 1937.

addition, the reinvigorated National Peace Council had engaged an organizer to establish local affiliates of its own,[161] and was gratified by the resultant jump in the number of peace councils from the spring of 1936 onwards.[162] And in some places pacifists and other activists had formed similar bodies on their own initiative.

By October 1936 Kathleen D. Courtney was thus warning that 'the National Peace Council seems to be very busy forming local Peace Councils' which mostly promoted 'its policy or lack of policy'; that 'in other places, there are local Peace Councils which do not seem to be connected with any national organization'; and that, as an unsurprising consequence of such remarkable diversity, 'confusion is very great'.[163] In the same month two LNU activists from Finchley, one of them Angell's niece Barbara Hayes, objected to the widespread use of 'peace', as for example in the phrase 'peace week', which obscured the difference between 'exactly contrary' approaches to war prevention.[164] Members of the PPU felt no less misled: one who went unsuspectingly to an IPC-dominated meeting organized by the London Federation of Peace Councils late in 1936, and had to listen to speakers such as John Strachey calling for an anti-fascist front, complained that he had 'never attended a peace conference so misnamed'.[165]

However, what seemed like obfuscation to sanctionists and pacifists alike was hailed by Gerald Bailey, the ever hopeful directing secretary of the National Peace Council, as a sign that common ground was returning: he even claimed that 'the historical controversies of the peace movement have become largely theoretical'[166] and that cooperation between its two wings could therefore be achieved. At the end of 1936 he secured a provisional understanding with Garnett as to the relationship between the LNU and the National Peace Council at the local level: its basis was that the union's branches would be cooperative towards local peace councils, provided that the latter held back from recruiting individual members.[167] And, more ambitiously, in mid-June 1937 Bailey tried to bring together his council, the various collective-security associations, and the PPU at national level.[168] Some members of the LNU were already of the view that the peace movement had

---

[161] This organizer, G. James Joyce, described his work in *Peace News* (27 June 1936), 4, and *Peace* (Sept. 1936), 93–5.

[162] Minutes, NPC council, 5 June, 16 July, 24 Sept. 1936. *Peace* (Oct. 1936), 111. *Peace Year Book 1937*, 114.

[163] K. D. Courtney to Murray, 3 Oct. 1936: Murray Papers.

[164] Memorandum dated 27 Oct. 1936 by E. Cooper and B. Hayes: Murray Papers.

[165] *PN* (26 Dec. 1936), 8.

[166] *PN* (19 Dec. 1936), 8.

[167] Minutes, LNU executive, 18 Dec. 1936.

[168] Minutes, NPC executive, 17 June 1937.

become too fragmented: one complained at the general council that the existence 'of so many "Peace" organizations caused confusion', and called for their reduction to two, which between them were 'sufficient . . . to serve all points of view', namely the 'pacifist' PPU and the 'sanctionist' LNU.[169] But Murray opposed Bailey's attempt at coordination on the grounds that the dominant elements within the National Peace Council 'go wholeheartedly against rearmament and lay all their emphasis on constructive conciliation. Most of our left wing members will, I fear, prefer their policy to ours[170]—a revealing recognition that accommodation was more popular than containment even among socialists. Thus, although Bailey held talks with Cecil,[171] he got nowhere.

Within the collective-security wing of the peace movement, the obvious rationalization, the absorption of the IPC by the LNU, was made difficult by continuing anti-Communist feeling and resentment on the part of Garnett and his staff. On 18 January 1937 Cecil complained to Dalton that even though the British IPC had scrupulously excluded from membership 'a body calling itself the Friends of the Soviet Union', Citrine and the trade-union leadership refused to relax their opposition to it.[172] On 22 January 1937 eleven prominent league supporters in Scotland published a letter arguing that to avoid Communist influence the LNU should not be represented on the IPC.[173] Cecil hinted to Garnett that, if such attacks persisted, he might go over to the new body altogether: 'If I had to choose between the L.N.U. and the I.P.C., which heaven forbid, I should be in a great difficulty.'[174] Major A. J. C. Freshwater, the LNU's long-serving deputy secretary and a loyal and tactful man, was privately distressed that seventeen years of LNU activity 'almost seems to count for nothing' with Cecil because 'he is so eaten up with the IPC idea'.[175] Garnett composed a formal letter of complaint about the IPC to Cecil, but was dissuaded from sending it by Murray and Lytton.[176] Even the National Peace Council complained in its annual report of the 'regrettable dissipation of time and energy' caused by the IPC.[177] However, though temperamentally drawn to resignation because of the extent of opposition to his policy, Cecil knew that if he relinquished his power-base in the LNU he would be in a worse

[169] LNU, *General Council Report June 1937*, 23, 24

[170] Murray to Cecil, 7 June 1937: Murray Papers.

[171] Bailey to Cecil, 5 July, and telephone note 6 July 1937: Cecil Papers Add. MSS 51176.

[172] Cecil to Dalton, 18 Jan. 1937 (copy): Cecil Papers Add. MSS 51175.

[173] Minutes, LNU executive, 28 Jan. 1937. *IPC Monthly Bulletin* (10 Feb. 1937), 4.

[174] Cecil to Garnett, 18 Feb. 1937 (copy): Cecil Papers Add. MS 51136.

[175] Freshwater to G. Davies, 1 Mar. 1937 (marked 'personal and confidential'): Gwilym Davies papers.

[176] Freshwater to G. Davies, 7 Mar. 1937: Gwilym Davies Papers.

[177] NPC, *Annual Report for the Year Ending April 1937* (1937), 1.

position to help the IPC, which, although its analysis was being confirmed by Italian and German assistance to Franco in the Spanish Civil War and renewed Japanese aggression against China in the summer of 1937, was making little impact. For example, although its first national congress on 22-4 October 1937 claimed 783 delegates from 396 organizations,[178] it received very little publicity.

Immediately after that congress, Cecil proposed that the IPC be reabsorbed into the LNU. He asked that the latter's executive committee take financial responsibility and run it 'as one of the Committees of the L.N.U. on the lines of the National Youth Committee'.[179] The LNU's youth section was a more appropriate model than he perhaps realized: it too contained several influential Communists, notably Gabriel Carritt, who having become its secretary at the end of 1935 had been rebuked for unauthorized campaigning on behalf of the Spanish government the following summer.[180] This was no accident: Communists had been instructed not merely to promote the IPC but to create or infiltrate similar organizations. Thus in this period Vincent Duncan Jones was listed as secretary of a newly formed British Youth Peace Assembly: that he was a Communist is apparent from the fact that, during the cold war, his name was to appear as secretary of the Moscow-controlled British Peace Committee. Jenifer Fischer Williams, daughter of the prominent international jurist, was told to conceal her Communist Party membership and be active in the LNU; and almost half a century later her short-lived phase as a secret party member was to arouse a flurry of interest because her husband, Professor H. L. A. Hart, worked in British intelligence during the Second World War.[181]

Cecil's request that the LNU reabsorb the IPC ended in a humiliating retreat: after even Mrs Dugdale advocated 'friendly independence' for the IPC rather than reintegration with the LNU, he withdrew his proposal.[182] However, he was growing increasingly resentful: he had already privately complained that 'Citrine and Bevin . . . have both got Communism on the brain',[183] and was soon even to allege that criticism of the IPC 'was started by Goebbels when he began to see the strength of the movement'.[184] When in November 1937 Cecil won that year's Nobel Peace Prize, he took pleasure in observing: 'The award has probably something to do with the International

---

[178] *IPC Monthly Bulletin* (Nov./Dec. 1937), 4.
[179] Minutes, LNU executive, 25 Oct. 1937.
[180] Minutes, LNU executive, 19 Dec. 1935. Birn, *League of Nations Union*, 185.
[181] J. Hart, *Ask Me No More* (1998), 62, 70, 79. For her contribution see, e.g. LNU, *General Council Report June 1937*, 16, 25–6.
[182] Minutes, LNU executive, 28 Oct. 1937.
[183] Cecil to H. Syrett, 30 Sept. 1937 (copy): Cecil Papers Add. MSS 51137.
[184] Cecil to Dolivet, 22 Jan. 1938 (copy): Cecil Papers Add. MSS 51143.

Peace Campaign.'[185] The discomfiture of the LNU's anti-IPC faction at this claim was evident from *Headway*'s response: 'The plain man is not impressed by the claims of this movement or that, of one organization or another, but sees only a tribute to Lord Cecil himself.'[186] Organizational rivalry thus significantly reduced the effectiveness of the collective-security movement from the beginning of 1936 to the autumn of 1937.

BIFURCATION AND SUBORDINATION, AUTUMN 1937–MARCH 1939

The last months of 1937 and early months of 1938 marked an important further stage in the clarification of the peace-or-war debate. On the accommodationist side, the PPU tacitly accepted that it would not grow big enough to convert Britain to non-violence. This left it with peaceful change as the only policy compatible with pacifism which stood a chance of being implemented. However, the likelihood that either economic concessions or the transfer of colonies to international trusteeship would satisfy Hitler diminished markedly after he tightened his control within Germany from the autumn of 1937 onwards, annexed Austria in March 1938, and, in line with the agreement which Neville Chamberlain persuaded him to accept at the Munich conference in September 1938, took over part of Czechoslovakia. As peaceful change came to be understood as requiring territorial transfers to Germany, it became difficult to distinguish from appeasement as practised by Chamberlain. On the containment side of the debate, the LNU realized that the dual policy was unworkable and that it stood for a policy of collective security which was difficult to distinguish from a traditional concern for the balance of power. The idealist content of peace thinking was thus leaking away as each wing of the peace movement found itself not only aligned with but subordinated to realists—either those arguing for the appeasement of Germany, or those arguing for its encirclement.

Dick Sheppard's sudden death on 31 October 1937, immediately after being elected by the students of Glasgow University as their rector in preference to Churchill, brought an outpouring of grief unprecedented in the history of the peace movement, and marked the end of the PPU's initial, hopeful phase. The loss of a inspirational leader obliged it to proceed with the formalization of its procedures: at its first annual general meeting on 2–3 April 1938 it adopted a constitution, appointed Morris to the key post of chairman

[185] *IPC Monthly Bulletin* (Nov./Dec. 1937), 3.
[186] *HW* (Dec. 1937), 221.

(though in effect he did the work of general secretary as well) and Lansbury to the honorific one of president, and issued a policy manifesto.

This change brought to the surface a split within the PPU between those who wanted it to be a larger and more secular version of the FoR and those who wanted it to be a larger and less left-wing version of the NMWM. The former tendency was led by Plowman, who argued that, being 'a minority movement' which objected conscientiously to its country's defence policy, the PPU was based upon 'unanimity of conviction' not 'majority rule' and could not consistently adopt democratic procedures. Privately resentful of 'the small-time politicians' of the NMWM,[187] he resigned as general secretary in protest, though he remained a Sponsor and was put on the new management committee (which replaced the executive committee). A perceptive debate between what became known for a time as 'Plowman pacifists' and 'politicals'[188] developed in the correspondence columns of *Peace News*.

The Plowman pacifists regarded their absolutism as a faith rather than a practical policy.[189] Their approach had already gained ground among the PPU's leading intellectuals. For example, six months after withdrawing to the United States in April 1937 Huxley published a book which, without retracting his previous support for the 'short-term policy ... of war-resistance', emphasized that for pacifism to be effective 'there must be more than a mere deflection of evil; there must be a suppression at the source, in the individual will'; and he therefore concentrated on the need for a 'long-term' policy of pursuing, through meditation, the oriental goal of 'non-attachment', as the sole means by which the necessary awareness of 'oneness with ultimate reality' could be achieved.[190] Similarly, Murry was moving towards the quietist view: 'The pacifist cause will be won, if it is won, only by those who have come to see that winning is a secondary affair. What matters is that men and women should bear their witness—and bear it, if need be, to the end.' As he moved from an optimistic to a pessimistic orientation, he also adopted a Christian inspiration, noting approvingly that in Huxley's case too a 'previous scepticism has completed changed, under the urgency of Pacifism, to a religious mysticism',[191] and joining the Anglican Pacifist Fellowship. Indeed, only an irregular marital situation—his liaison with Mary Gamble, a Labour parliamentary candidate and notable PPU activist—prevented him from seeking ordination as a clergyman. Although the intellectually volatile Murry was later to swing briefly back to a belief in practical pacifism, he and other PPU

---

[187] Plowman to Murry, 8 Mar. 1938: Plowman Papers.   [188] *PN* (28 May 1938), 13–14.

[189] See M. Plowman, *The Faith Called Pacifism* (1936).

[190] A. Huxley, *Ends and Means: An Inquiry into the Nature of Ideals and into the Methods Employed for their Realisation* (1937), 24, 151, 298.

[191] J. M. Murry, *The Pledge of Peace* (1938), 9, 12.

intellectuals began thinking about creating communities in which they could nurture pacifism as a long-term social ideal within a political world which they knew to be far from ready for it. By March 1938 the FoR's journal was noting: 'Community is becoming one of those hard-worked words'.[192]

Quietism became more attractive as the prospects of the PPU developing into a politically significant force had faded. Just days before Sheppard's death the LNU was being reassured that its pacifist rival 'seems to be somewhat losing its attraction'.[193] Although the PPU stressed the growing number of local groups, which numbered 715 when Sheppard died, this represented the success of the inexhaustibly cheerful John Barclay, once a member of his father-in-law Basil Martin's Unitarian congregation in Finchley, in bringing scattered members together rather than an expansion of overall numbers. 'We haven't a million pacifists yet', Plowman acknowledged at the very end of 1937.[194] A discussion by the author Susan Miles, the pen-name of Sponsor Ursula Roberts, of why only 20,000 women had signed the pledge revealed that in the spring of 1938 overall membership stood at a fractionally lower level, approximately 117,000,[195] than that claimed at the end of 1936, presumably because of the weeding out of pledgers with whom the PPU had lost touch. And it was suggestive of unvoiced worries about stagnation that a *Peace News* editorial felt obliged to deny in May 1938 that the issuing of a manifesto was 'a device for waking up a flagging movement'.[196] By the beginning of 1939 Spottiswoode was willing to be blunt about the PPU's declining momentum: 'As a political factor in the affairs of this country, the Peace Pledge Union just doesn't count. Don't let's have any illusions about that.'[197]

In addition, non-violent resistance was losing such attraction as it had possessed. Even in the early years of the PPU many of those who advocated it may have done so as a thought-experiment rather than as a considered commitment. Indeed, Sybil Morrison, whose pacifist career ran from the late 1930s to the 1970s, was later to assert: 'No-one really believed that Hitler could be stopped by non-violent resistance.'[198] In particular, as a devout Christian *pacificist* pointed out, it was 'not easy to see how an air raid or gas attack can be passively resisted'.[199] Thus although it was increasingly accepted that 'the wars in Spain and China' had turned out 'nothing like' the armageddon 'so often' predicted for the era of air

---

[192] *Reconciliation* (Mar. 1938), 79.

[193] Memorandum by Courtney and Arnold-Forster, 25 Oct. 1937: Cecil Papers Add. MSS 51141.

[194] *PN* (1 Jan.1938), 4.   [195] *PN* (16 Apr. 1938), 7.

[196] *PN* (21 May 1938), 8.   [197] *PN* (27 Jan. 1939), 9.

[198] *Pacifist* (June 1974), 8.   [199] Beevor, *Peace and Pacifism*, 103.

power,[200] they had none the less reduced enthusiasm for Gandhian methods. When David Spreckley reported from Canton that by enduring Japanese air-raids 'the people of this city have practised a partial non-violent resistance—*and it works!*',[201] he was resorting to a much more modest criterion for the success of that policy than had been implied in the PPU's early literature, namely the avoidance of panic rather than the disabling of the attacker. Those who went on emphasizing its potential, such as Maurice Rowntree, now made clear that they were 'not claiming that the non-violent method always succeeds at once',[202]

As the early hopes for non-violence as an immediately effective technique faded, a few PPU members wavered in their commitment to pacifism. Rose Macaulay resigned as a Sponsor after the *Anschluss*, for example, though she was not to recant her pacifism until the summer of 1940.[203] However, many more simply transferred all their hopes from non-violence to peaceful change. Announcing the manifesto on which it was to base a national campaign during the spring and early summer of 1938, the PPU stated: 'The pledge to renounce war . . . leads inevitably to the necessity for a new foreign policy, based on economic appeasement and reconciliation.'[204] It thereby switched from the optimistic orientation to one of collaboration. This transition was later criticized by Spottiswoode for causing the union to forget its roots in non-resistance: ' "I renounce war." That is our pledge—not "I want a World Conference please, at which a lot of old gentlemen sitting round a table will produce the millennium out of a top hat." '[205] But it enabled the PPU to compensate for its modest size by joining forces with the much larger *pacificist* contingent that supported peaceful change.

For their part, these *pacificist* advocates of peaceful change found themselves working alongside the more numerous group of defencists that backed Chamberlain's policy of appeasement. As already noted, the accommodationist wing of the peace movement saw its own principled call for a new peace settlement as qualitatively different from a prudential attempt to propitiate the aggressors. During the crisis over Czechoslovakia, for example, *Peace News* distinguished between 'bargaining at the expense of the weak', which it opposed, and 'shaping relations now on a basis of international co-operation for the good of all', which it favoured.[206] And a later generation of activists

---

[200] E. C. Shepherd, 'Can the Bomber Get Through?', *Listener* (15 Sept. 1937), 541–3.

[201] David Spreckley, in *PN* (16 Oct. 1937), 1.

[202] M. L. Rowntree, *Mankind Set Free* (1939), 110.

[203] Minutes, PPU Sponsors, 14 Mar. 1938. Ceadel, *Pacifism in Britain 1914–1945*, 214–5. J. Emery, *Rose Macaulay: A Writer's Life* (1991), 251.   [204] *PN* (12 Mar. 1938), 1.

[205] *PN* (27 Jan. 1939), 9.   [206] *PN* (17 Sept. 1938), 1.

was no less keen to claim that, during the 1930s, 'appeasement had nothing to do with peace movements let alone with pacifism'.[207]

Yet in reality many members of the peace movement went beyond peaceful change and endorsed appeasement as a step in the right direction. By the end of 1937 Allen's partiality for Germany was becoming apparent even when he was trying his best to be even-handed: for example, at the LNU's general council in December of that year he commented that Germany might not come out 'much better' from a critical examination of the Treaty of Brest-Litovsk than Britain and France would come out from a critical examination of the Treaty of Versailles, it apparently not occurring to him that it might come out much worse.[208] During 1938, perhaps as a result of worsening health, he increasingly failed to see the difference between peaceful and coerced change, and became in effect an appeaser in search of any war-avoiding deal: he made an urgent goodwill visit to Germany in August 1938 during which he saw Ribbentrop; and he supported the Munich settlement. He also resigned from the LNU's executive, though he gave illness as the reason.[209]

Joad made the same transition from idealist to realist arguments at this time. As already noted, he had been one of the few pacifists still prepared to collaborate with collective security after the triple crisis of 1936. However, in 1938 he apparently arrived at the view that for the foreseeable future a collective-security bloc would lack the military preponderance necessary to deter aggression, and that in any case the status quo which it would be defending was flawed. In March he thus justified the National government's acquiescence in the *Anschluss* on the ground that unforeseeable eventualities— 'Germany may explode internally, Italy go bankrupt, Hitler be bitten by an adder'—made it possible that 'a war postponed may be a war averted'.[210] Even so, in the last week of May he told the National Peace Congress that 'the clear-headed pacifist' did not claim that 'the pacifist policy constitutes for the moment a practical method of avoiding war',[211] which indicated that he was still unprepared to advocate non-violence as a technique. He thus remained a collaborative pacifist but had transferred his practical hopes from collective security to peaceful change. However, it soon became clear that even he did not really believe, as the policy of peaceful change implied, that a just and pacific settlement could be constructed in central Europe. He had become an appeaser who simply wanted to keep Britain out of war. This became clear

[207] University Group on Defence Policy, *The Role of Peace Movements in the 1930s* (pamphlet no. 1; Jan. 1959), 7. See also *Pacifist* (Sept. 1971), 12.

[208] LNU, *General Council Report Dec. 1937*, 12–13.

[209] Marwick, *Clifford Allen*, 175–7, 182–4. Minutes, LNU executive, 15 Dec. 1938.

[210] *New Statesman* (26 Mar. 1938), 516–17.

[211] *Peace* (July/Aug. 1938), 31.

when in the aftermath of Chamberlain's Munich agreement he privately informed a disapproving Hardie that 'whether Sudeten Germans belong to Germany or Czechoslovakia is a matter not worth the life or even suffering of a single Englishman'.[212] And when on 10 November he returned to the Oxford Union to speak against the motion 'That war between nations can sometimes be justified', this time losing by 145 votes to 176, it was reported that his source of support had changed since the 'King and Country' debate, coming now from 'as Tory-looking a bunch as the Union could produce'[213]— in other words, from appeasers rather than peace activists.

Soon afterwards Joad embarked on a popular paperback, *Why War?*, to explain his support for 'Mr Chamberlain's courageous intervention' at Munich.[214] He claimed that a '*real* League' remained his ideal, thereby offending some members of the PPU, a body from which he still kept his distance.[215] Yet he also insisted that the present league was 'simply an alliance of Powers engaged in the old game of Power politics'.[216] A war against Germany would be 'the worst of all evils', an argument mainly derived from 'the principle of Utilitarianism' as applied to the extreme destructiveness of aerial warfare. However, he supplemented these arguments with humanitarian ones ('It is not death that is dreadful, but pain'[217]) of the kind that he had highlighted during 1932-3. And he presented his pacifism in a tone which was both flippant and self-consciously realist, as in his justification of Britain's policy of appeasement with the allusive quip: 'Ce n'est pas magnifique, mais ce n'est pas la guerre.'[218]

It was almost certainly Joad's style of exposition which his former tutor at Balliol, A. D. Lindsay, had in mind when he complained about the emergence of 'sham' pacifism. Now Master of the college, Lindsay became a public figure when the Labour and Liberal candidates stood down at a much publicized by-election in Oxford on 27 October 1938[219] to allow him a free run as an anti-appeasement 'independent progressive' against the Chamberlainite Conservative candidate (who, ironically, was Quintin Hogg, Joad's principal defencist adversary in the 'King and Country' debate). A few months later Lindsay gave a lecture in which he argued:

Sham pacifists have lately held that war in China or Abyssinia or Spain is not our business, and thank goodness for that. That is to go from thinking war the most evil thing

---

[212] Joad to Hardie, 3 Oct. 1938: Hardie Papers.
[213] *Isis* (16 Nov. 1938), 5.
[214] C. E. M. Joad, *Why War?* (Harmondsworth, 1939), 14.
[215] See the letter by J. Norbury, *PN* (14 Apr. 1939), 4.
[216] Joad, *Why War?*, 166, 178. [217] Ibid. 25, 48, 58, 60. [218] Ibid. 33.
[219] See I. McLean, 'Oxford and Bridgwater', in C. Cook and J. Ramsden (eds.), *By-elections in British Politics* (2nd edn., 1997), 112–29.

in the world to thinking that our suffering from war is the most evil thing in the world, quite different from other people suffering.[220]

Joad himself, though sincere in his pacifism, was guilty of resorting to isolationist and exemptionist arguments of the kind Lindsay despised.

Other pacifists accompanied Allen and Joad across the fine line separating peaceful change from appeasement. Russell criticized Eden, who resigned as Foreign Secretary in February 1938 after a disagreement with Chamberlain, for favouring a policy of unnecessary risk, whereas 'the Prime Minister's policy at least postpones the issue for a number of years, during which there is a possibility of changes that will at least prevent a first-class conflict'.[221] *Peace News* carried with seeming approval an article by a Hungarian which questioned the claim of 'Czecho-Germano-Slovako-Hungaro-Polono-Ruthenia' to true statehood; and it offered editorial support for Germany's claim on the Sudetenland as 'a just demand and a condition of peace'.[222] Royden finally left the LNU in September 1938 and joined the PPU, a step she had refused to take only a month before but which she took now 'in the belief that you were really backing up Chamberlain', as she afterwards explained to Morris.[223] Bishop Barnes also supported the Munich agreement.[224] The art critic Clive Bell, a PPU supporter, favoured 'uniting the continent under German leadership', by which he meant that the Nazis should 'absorb' other countries.[225] And the PPU offered to send 5,000 pacifists to the Sudetenland 'to practise non-violent methods' following its handover, suggesting that whereas non-violence had once been expected to disable aggression it was now seen as at best a means of oiling the wheels of coerced change. Its pro-appeasement stand helped the PPU grow a little faster: having acquired fewer than a thousand members over the previous three months it gained 1,330 in September, 1,146 in October, and 949 in November 1938.[226]

In addition, some members of the ILP went beyond war resistance and proclaimed their support for Chamberlain. The rump party had on 25 September 1938 declared, predictably, that a war for Czechoslovakia would be an imperialist one; but early in October two of its MPs, James Maxton and John McGovern, went further and explicitly congratulated Chamberlain on the

[220] A. D. Lindsay, *Pacifism as a Principle and Pacifism as a Dogma* (1939), 19–20.
[221] *PN* (5 Mar. 1938), 8.
[222] *PN* (13 Aug. 1938), 1; (17 Sept. 1938), 8.
[223] *PN* (13 Oct. 1939), 5. See also Royden to Cecil, 8 Aug. and 20 Sept. 1938: Cecil Papers Add. MSS 51181.
[224] Barnes, *Ahead of his Age*, 350.
[225] C. Bell, *Warmongers* (PPU, 1938), 14, cited in M. Gilbert, 'Pacifist Attitudes to Nazi Germany', *Journal of Contemporary History*, 27 (1992), 493–511 at 499.
[226] Figures from minutes, PPU Sponsors.

Munich agreement.[227] Brockway criticized them for this, and attempted to construct an explicitly progressive peace coalition instead: during 'the crisis of September' he took part in 'a meeting of members of the I.L.P., the P.P.U., the No More War Movement Trustees, the Society of Friends, and a section of the Labour, Trade Union and Co-operative movements which were opposed to war' that issued a collective statement in favour of peace; and he made some efforts to reactivate this coalition in subsequent months.[228] Brockway's attempt to distance his own policy of war resistance from Chamberlain's policy of appeasement later prompted McGovern to sneer that, even where 'there were only two roads Fenner was always looking for a third, and one that would establish him as a revolutionary force'.[229] However, Maxton tacitly recognized the force of Brockway's criticisms when, under the emotional strain of justifying his pro-Chamberlain policy to the ILP's national administrative council, he broke down and wept, although he was later exonerated by the party conference. In practice, the ILP was in an ideological muddle: it had supported war resistance because it believed a war supported by the National government would by definition be capitalist; yet logically the same guilt by association applied equally to an act of appeasement promoted by the same set of capitalist politicians. The ILP had thus failed to anticipate that it could be presented with, in its historian's words, 'a situation in which the choice was simply between capitalist peace and capitalist war'.[230]

The accommodationist wing of the peace movement was more embarrassed at seeming to support Chamberlain than at seeming to favour Germany. It prided itself on showing a proper scepticism towards anti-Nazi propaganda. Rose Macaulay still 'disbelieved all atrocity stories', partly because of her own experience as a British propagandist during the First World War.[231] Pacifists thought it bellicose to denounce foreigners. *Peace News* responded to the Japanese 'bombing terror' in China by asserting: 'Clearly you cannot condemn Japan. It is *war* that is to be condemned.'[232] And in a PPU pamphlet Clive Bell denounced critics of Hitler and Mussolini as 'warmongers' whose views should be censored.[233] Those of left-wing opinions believed that capitalist and imperialist Britain was socially and internationally as flawed as the fascist states. Wellock expounded this view

[227] Thwaites, 'Independent Labour Party 1938–1950', 78–81.
[228] F. Brockway, *Pacifism and the Left Wing* (1938), 16, 20.
[229] J. McGovern, *Neither Fear Nor Favour* (1960), 127–9.
[230] Thwaites, 'The Independent Labour Party 1938–1950', 82.
[231] Emery, *Rose Macaulay*, 250.
[232] *PN* (2 Oct. 1937), 6.
[233] Gilbert, 'Pacifist Attitudes to Nazi Germany, 1936–45',499.

with monotonous regularity in his *Peace News* column. And those who were Christians believed it was their religious duty to see the other point of view. Corder Catchpool, who spent most of the 1930s as a Quaker representative in Berlin, was an incorrigible apologist for Germany, claiming for example in 1937 that National-Socialist philosophy 'definitely repudiates' world-imperialist ambitions.[234]

These well-meaning attitudes sometimes produced a worrying gullibility in respect of fascism, particularly among pacifists. For example, Canon Morris joined The Link, an organization sympathetic to Nazism, soon after its foundation in July 1937 by Admiral Sir Barry Domvile, a Jew-hating former Director of Naval Intelligence.[235] Morris's decision was naïve rather than sinister; but a few Christian pacifists were led by the intensity of their religious convictions to extreme positions: as a historian of Jewish attitudes towards pacifism has noted, as the Second World War approached 'the word Christian' in this context could 'also be read as meaning "not Jewish" '.[236] This was most conspicuously true of the Marquess of Tavistock, who now supported the PPU. A painfully withdrawn and unhappy man, his miserable private life had become public knowledge when his wife, whom he had left in 1934 because of her close friendship with their children's tutor, unsuccessfully sued him for restitution of conjugal rights;[237] and his son and heir, no admirer of 'his many cranky notions', was later to offer the harsh observation: 'I don't think that all his life he really knew what it was to give affection to anybody, though he demanded it from others.'[238] Conversion to the Social Credit movement reflected a dislike of orthodox finance which reinforced Tavistock's dislike of Jews and his admiration for Hitler. Although overt connections of this kind with the far right were rare, the tone of certain columns in *Peace News* was such that in the aftermath of Munich a young pacifist who was to become a notable political theorist in later life, Maurice Cranston, complained that they were 'becoming increasingly sympathetic to Nazism'.[239]

None the less, most peace activists felt some guilt about Munich: thus despite defending it, Joad acknowledged a feeling of 'shame'.[240] They therefore called for an international conference which would legitimize the unilateral sacrifice imposed on Czechoslovakia by making it the prelude to a

---

[234] *PN* (4 Sept. 1937), 10.

[235] *PN* (18 Aug. 1939), 7. R. Griffiths, *Patriotism Perverted: Captain Ramsay, the Right Book Club and British Anti-Semitism 1939–40* (1998), 39–42.

[236] E. Wilcock, *Pacifism and the Jews* (Stroud, 1994), 134.

[237] *The Times* (14 Nov. 1935), 4.

[238] John, Duke of Bedford, *A Silver-Plated Spoon* (1959), 3, 33.

[239] *PN* (15 Oct. 1938), 13.   [240] Joad, *Why War?*, 12.

general revision of the Versailles order in which other countries would pay their share of the price of peace. Any transfer of territory to the dictatorships as part of a comprehensive settlement would therefore become legitimate peaceful change, not mere appeasement. On 18 October 1938 the National Peace Council decided to launch a national petition in support of 'a new Peace Conference', an initiative which 'brought the Council nearer to a substantial unity than at any time in recent years', as Bailey observed, and was a brave effort in view of its paralysed condition as recently as mid-decade. A target of between three and six million signatures was soon being talked of;[241] and a respectable tally of a million was in fact achieved in exactly five months. The LNU left a decision on whether to support the petition 'to individual members and Branches'; and some—for example, in Southampton—chose to do so.[242] The PPU and the Friends' Peace Committee promoted it with enthusiasm, as did the FoR, whose journal, renamed *Christian Pacifist* at the beginning of 1939, declared its 'hearty support' for 'appeasement', though conscious that this word had 'recently been given a new and less favourable content by its opponents'.[243]

As well as thus being a turning-point for the peace movement's accommodationists, the autumn of 1937 was a watershed for its containment wing. Socialists who favoured a peace front became increasingly impatient with left-wing colleagues who argued that this must await a change of government in Britain. In the aftermath of the *Anschluss*, for example, Kingsley Martin informed Cripps that whereas previously he had 'always tried to make a distinction' between a war in the interests of socialism and one in the interests of the British empire, it was 'now, I am afraid, obvious that they would be the same thing . . . I found this an almost intolerable position to take up, but I saw no alternative.'[244] Moreover, except for brief but famous vacillations—for example, during August 1938 and September 1940[245]—Martin was to stick to his anti-fascist guns. Even so, he failed to persuade Cripps, who still regarded it as 'a strange idea that we should accept a class Government such as our own as the champions of the workers' cause against Fascism!'[246] However, the tide was turning against Cripps's brand of contingent war resistance, as was apparent from a declining emphasis by the left on the economic causes of war. For example, when Brailsford's book *Why*

[241] Minutes, NPC council, 18 Oct. 1938. Bailey to Noel Baker, 25 Oct. 1938: Noel-Baker Papers 2/36. *Peace* (Nov. 1938), 58. *PN* (2 Dec. 1938), 7; (9 Dec. 1938), 5.
[242] Minutes, LNU executive, 3 Nov. 1938. Minutes, Southampton LNU, 24 Jan. 1939.
[243] *PN* (13 Oct. 1939), 5. Minutes, FPC, 3 Nov. 1938. *Christian Pacifist* (May 1939), 115.
[244] Martin to Cripps, 18 Mar. 1938: Cripps Papers.
[245] Rolph, *Kingsley*, 240–1, 244–6
[246] B. Russell *et al.*, *Dare We Look Ahead?* (1938), 121.

Capitalism Means War, which had been commissioned by Victor Gollancz in the summer of 1936 and written a year later, was finally published in August 1938, it no longer found a receptive audience.[247]

For its part, the LNU had to stop pretending that it could advocate peaceful change as part of a dual policy with collective security. At its December 1937 general council Cecil lost patience with Allen's demand for 'negotiations for an all-round peace settlement', and spoke out against 'the belief that you can secure peace by international discussions and nothing else'.[248] Its leaders were now prepared to admit, as Murray did to Cecil: 'We are no longer a peace party, opposing a Jingo party, we are a "League and Collective Security" party, opposing pacifists, isolationists, pro-Germans, etc. We are actually for a "spirited foreign policy".'[249] Murray developed this theme in a memorandum to the executive committee, which also acknowledged that the LNU had

lost the support of great numbers who no longer believe in collective security: e.g. the pure Pacifists, most Conservatives, and many influential writers and teachers who used formerly to support us, such as the Lothian group, Sir J. Fischer Williams, and all the holders of the special League of Nations Professorships, Zimmern, Manning, Carr and their numerous pupils.[250]

Having fully faced up to its unpopularity, the LNU discovered the courage to ignore it. When Eden resigned Murray immediately sent him a telegram conveying 'warmest sympathy and admiration from the L.N.U.'.[251] When Hitler annexed Austria, the LNU summoned an extraordinary meeting of its executive committee and a special session of the general council in protest,[252] its new resolve prompting Vera Brittain to note in her diary: 'L.N.U., Labour Party and all the so-called peace lovers (except the P.P.U.) are shouting war!'[253] When Hitler menaced Czechoslovakia, the LNU called for firm resistance. And, although when Chamberlain secured an agreement at Munich on 29 September 1938 it accepted Lytton's view that 'it would be suicidal to take action at the moment which would run counter to the universal sense of relief and joy that existed throughout the country that the danger of war had been averted',[254] it clearly identified itself with the Churchillian alternative.

---

[247] It was delayed because Gollancz disliked its criticisms of the Soviet Union: Leventhal, *Last Dissenter*, 248–9.
[248] LNU, *General Council Report Dec. 1937*, 13, 47.
[249] Murray to Cecil, 27 Dec. 1937 (copy): Murray Papers.
[250] Memorandum, 29 Dec. 1937: Murray Papers.
[251] Minutes, LNU executive, 22 Feb. 1938.
[252] On 15 Mar. and 1 Apr. 1938 respectively.
[253] Brittain, *Chronicle of Friendship*, 321 (entry for 14 Mar. 1938).
[254] Minutes, LNU executive, 29 Sept. 1938.

The LNU knew that this resolutely pro-containment stand would lose it further support: membership fell by another 16 per cent in 1938 and 26 per cent in 1939; and donations continued to dry up. When it was forced to slash its spending by a third in the summer of 1938, Murray pointed to the fact that it 'had been of late opposing the Government's policy, which had been that of the majority of the country';[255] and *Headway* offered the explanation: 'Evil days for the League are evil days for the Union.'[256] That the Genevan ideal was much less inspiring than formerly even to the non-pacifist young was illustrated by the paucity of references to it in the contributions both to a series of *Spectator* articles in which men under thirty were asked 'What Should We Fight For?'[257] and to a book in which a selection of recent Oxford graduates answered a similar question.[258]

The LNU made subtle changes to its propaganda, placing much less emphasis on the league as an institution essential to the organization and validation of collective security and more on the joint contribution which countries could, by their own unmediated efforts and on their own authority, make to the maintenance of international order. Its dropping of the slogan 'Save the League—Save Peace' in favour of 'War Can Be Averted' was symptomatic of this new approach, as was its occasional use of the terms 'peace front' and 'peace bloc' which had previously been associated with socialists.

Advocates of collective security also made unprecedented use of explicitly power-political language. As early as 1937 Angell had suggested that it was worth 'calling the political principle of collective defence, which underlies the League's efforts, by some other name' if this helped to win over the 'realist' who currently regarded collective security as dangerously 'sentimental' and therefore overlooked the fact that the vital interests of the British empire were also at stake. Angell explained his abandonment of *The Great Illusion*'s thesis that imperial possessions did not matter by claiming that he was now concerned with 'the preservation of order' rather than, as formerly, with material benefits only: 'Arguments which are entirely valid if our object is prosperity and welfare in peace-time lose their weight if our real object is power for war.'[259] In 1938 R. W. Seton-Watson told the National Peace Congress: 'Speaking as a hundred per cent League man, I am forced to admit that for the moment Italy and Germany have driven us off the basis of Geneva and

---

[255] Minutes, LNU executive, 2 June 1938.   [256] *HW* (July 1938), 124.

[257] Contributors to this series included William Armstrong, a future head of the home civil service, and Alastair Cooke, later a celebrated broadcaster: see respectively *Spectator* (1 July 1938), 15; and (22 July 1938), 142.

[258] K. Briant and L. Wilkes (eds.), *Would I Fight?* (Oxford, 1938).

[259] N. Angell, *The Defence of the Empire* (1937), 30, 40, 214–15.

forced us back to this basis of Balance of Power.'[260] And the military intellectual Captain B. H. Liddell Hart, whose appointment to the LNU's executive committee was further evidence of its closeness to Churchillian
defencists, suggested that the union ceased to define itself with reference to
'something which was so obviously beyond restoration in its existing form'
as the League of Nations and redefine itself as an association 'for the Defence
of Freedom in this country', though Cecil pointed out that this was precluded
by its royal charter.[261]

However, the LNU's executive committee, which had failed in renewed
efforts to secure the attendance of Churchill himself,[262] agreed that what he
had called his 'focus', the Defence of Freedom and Peace group, should take
control of its periodical in a bid to reach a wider public including defencists.
A 'Focus Company' was formed for the purpose, in which the Shell executive
Sir Robert Waley Cohen took a prominent part and Angell represented the
LNU's interests.[263] *Headway: Towards Freedom and Peace* made its first
appearance in October 1938 with an unmistakably Churchillian agenda:

The peace-loving Powers standing together and calling into co-operation all their
natural allies in the defence of the rule of law and their own safety and independence,
maintaining a united armed strength at the necessary level until respect for treaties
and covenants has been re-established, must be the nucleus of all nations bent on
peace.[264]

When it realized that this robust new tone 'perplexed' many readers, the
revamped periodical tried to claim historical legitimacy for its realism-tinged
brand of internationalism: 'The original idea that lay behind the League of
Nations was a "League of Free Nations Union". Under this name a group was
founded during the Great War, and from this group the League of Nations
Union proceeded.'[265] Presumably, Wickham Steed, a founder of the League
of Free Nations Association as well as an active member of the Defence of
Freedom and Peace group, was responsible for this rewriting of history so as
to omit the prior contribution of the League of Nations Society.

However, while the league movement was thus trying to adapt its tactics so
as to cope with a deteriorating international situation, it continued to be
plagued by quarrels with the New Commonwealth Society and, much more
seriously, the IPC. At the December 1937 general council, the advocates of an

---

[260] *Peace* (July/Aug. 1938).
[261] Minutes, LNU executive, 10 Nov. 1938.
[262] Minutes, LNU executive, 14 and 21 July, 22 Sept. 1938.
[263] See E. A. Risinger, jun., 'Sir Norman Angell: Critic of Appeasement 1935–1940', Ed.D.
thesis (Ball State University, 1977), fo. 210.
[264] *HW* (Oct. 1938), 3.   [265] *HW* (Mar. 1939), 1.

international police force had accepted a further postponement of the issue, but only grudgingly. Allen privately warned that the New Commonwealth Society might 'now have to form a rank and file organization with branches etc.' Vyvyan Adams, one of the few Conservative MPs genuinely interested in the peace movement, informed Garnett of his opinion that the LNU's behaviour had been 'humiliating and distressing' for a supporter of the New Commonwealth Society such as himself. And the society's periodical complained that the LNU 'stands today where it did in 1934. It still refuses to make up its mind.'[266] However, Davies and his colleagues did not have sufficient support to press the issue, which in any case seemed more abstract than ever after Hitler annexed Austria. In June 1938 they therefore reluctantly accepted what was in effect a return to the compromise of 1935.[267]

The IPC controversy took a turn for the worse in December 1937 when at the LNU's staff Christmas party Cecil took deep personal offence at a satirical sketch written and produced by Eppstein which depicted him as not only an IPC fanatic but a senile one at that.[268] The author apologized, professing to have been 'shocked' by a colleague's 'overacting';[269] but Noel Baker claimed that Eppstein, whom he in any case held 'primarily responsible for the Secretariat's constant thwarting and sabotage of I.P.C. policy', had for some time been 'saying freely that Lord Robert was too old'.[270] Cecil was reduced to near-despair, admitting to Noel Baker that he found 'this I.P.C.–L.N.U. controversy . . . *insufferable.* Everyone or almost everyone is perverse, and I am much too old to deal with them, and owing to circumstances I can't resign. It is just damnable . . . I intend to withdraw as much as possible.'[271]

In the event, however, Cecil determined to use the incident to bring the LNU's officers to heel. He eventually conceded that Eppstein could keep his job, partly because he had an invalid wife and lacked private means, though his behaviour would be strictly monitored in future. Cecil's anger came principally to be vented upon Garnett, not only because the general secretary was formally responsible for his staff but also because he had a long record of interference on matters of policy. Despite his intellectual ability, Garnett had failed to learn from the mistakes which had led the LNU's leadership to try to get rid of him during the 1920s. For example, a reiteration of his view that the

[266] LNU, *General Council Report Dec. 1937*, 11. Allen to Cecil, 18 Dec. 1937: Cecil papers Add. MSS 51178. Adams to Garnett (copy), 18 Jan. 1938: Adams Papers. *New Commonwealth* (Jan. 1938), 67.

[267] LNU, *General Council Report June 1938*, 51–3.

[268] Cecil to Murray, 17 Dec. 1937: Murray Papers.

[269] Eppstein to Cecil, 22 Dec. 1937: Cecil Papers Add. MSS 51178.

[270] Noel Baker to Cecil, 31 Dec. 1937: Cecil Papers Add. MSS 51108.

[271] Cecil to Noel Baker, 6 and 10 Jan. 1938 (copies): Cecil Papers Add. MSS 51108.

union was 'more concerned with far-reaching principle than immediate policies'[272] was not what most activists had wanted to hear in the crisis summer
of 1936. (Even so, the LNU's continued emphasis on its educational role had
the incidental benefit of enabling promising schoolchildren, such as Nora
Beloff, Iris Murdoch, and Raymond Williams, to win essay competitions at
this time.[273]) Garnett's allusion in his *Headway* column to the willingness of
the Roman Catholic Church and the Trades Union Congress to cooperate with
the LNU but not with the IPC[274] was tactless in the circumstances. He was
also alleged to have 'expressed the view that it would be better for all if the
"Left" were to cease co-operation with the Union and devote all their efforts
to the National Peace Council', as a result of which Noel Baker drafted a furious letter accusing him of wanting only 'to avoid offending the rich', though
he thought better of sending it.[275] Cecil was convinced that Garnett had even
'persuaded himself that the Union is his child for which he is fighting against
iniquitous persons like myself'.[276]

On 27 January 1938 the LNU's executive committee, meeting without any
officers in attendance, approved administrative changes designed to end staff
obstruction of the IPC, which Cecil had persuaded himself was exhibiting a
'buoyancy' that contrasted with the LNU's 'serious signs of loss of vitality'.[277] When an executive committee member asked if this action 'went
further in the direction of amalgamation with the I.P.C.' than was envisaged
in the general council's decision of December 1936, he was assured by
Murray that it involved 'no change in the policy laid down by the Council, but
made provision for carrying out with less friction such co-operation as may
be approved by the Executive'.[278]

At the same time the executive committee instructed Garnett to take sick
leave for six months. Soon afterwards Garnett confided to a colleague in the
Welsh LNU that his heart had been weakened by the strain of preventing the
executive committee 'falling under the control of the faction who run the
IPC', and that Lytton shared these concerns.[279] However, shortly before
Garnett was due to return, the executive committee called for, and obtained,

[272] *HW* (Aug. 1936), 160
[273] *HW* (Mar. 1937), 48–9; (Feb. 1938), 28–9. In addition, R. M. Hare won a New Commonwealth Society boys' competition, although surprisingly Harold Wilson failed to gain a Cecil
Peace Prize while an Oxford undergraduate: see New Commonwealth, *Annual Report 1936-37*,
49; and P. Foot, *The Politics of Harold Wilson* (Harmondsworth, 1968), 32.
[274] *HW* (Oct. 1936), 220.
[275] Noel Baker to Garnett, 29 Jan. 1937 (marked 'not sent'), 29 Jan. 1937: Noel-Baker Papers
5/142.
[276] Cecil to Lytton, 19 Dec. 1937 (copy): Cecil Papers Add. MSS 51139.
[277] Cecil to Murray, 30 Dec. 1937: Murray Papers.
[278] Minutes, LNU executive, 27 Jan. 1938.
[279] Garnett to G. Davies, 5 Feb. 1938 (marked 'private'): Gwilym Davies Papers.

his resignation. It did so by a narrow majority; and some of those who voted to force him out did so less on the grounds that he had behaved improperly than on the grounds that he was not the right sort of general secretary for an organization in such straitened circumstances. By then Cecil as well as Murray and Lytton considered this decision harsh: the three of them therefore paid tribute to him in *Headway*, and eventually secured a generous annual pension of £500 for him.[280] On leaving the general secretaryship, Garnett issued an unrepentant statement claiming to have been resented by his opponents 'as the principal obstacle to the Union's being used as an instrument of political propaganda'.[281] In an attempt to mollify him, he was given membership of the executive committee in his own right, which he took up the following April. His successor as general secretary was his assistant, Freshwater, who had been on the staff since 1920: though less brilliant than Garnett he had exceptional social skills, being credited in his obituary tributes with 'almost every quality which one could wish for', including 'very exceptional moral gifts'.[282]

In addition, Livingstone, who had returned to the British IPC after her illness but possessed a reputation for 'intrigue' and was regarded by Noel Baker as being 'in a state of mental collapse', was persuaded to take sick leave, Cecil having privately joked that it was 'a pity' that Garnett could not be married off 'to the Dame—that would keep both of them quiet!'[283] And Murray, who at nearly 72 was growing too frail for the demanding job of chairman,[284] agreed to stand down in Lytton's favour with effect from the general council's meeting in June 1938, when he was promoted into a co-presidency with Cecil.

Cecil and Noel Baker hoped that these changes would revive the collective-security movement in 1938. But the IPC continued to disappoint their high expectations. It attempted to repeat the success of the National Declaration Committee by establishing a National Boycott Committee on 18 February to organize a public refusal to buy Japanese goods.[285] But, despite

[280] Minutes, LNU executive, 14 and 21 July, 13 Oct. 1938. Cecil to Lytton, 8 July 1938 (copy): Cecil Papers Add. MSS 51139. *HW* (Aug. 1938), 142. The pension was ended by the LNU's financial difficulties at the outbreak of war but restored at the rate of £250 per annum in 1943: see Minutes, LNU executive, 4 Nov. 1943.

[281] Garnett to Lytton, 14 July 1938 (copy), in Minutes, LNU executive, 21 July 1938.

[282] Minutes, LNU executive, 15 July 1943 (a special meeting called to pay its respects). *HW* (Aug. 1943), 2. Birn wrongly gives him the initials 'J.G.': *League of Nations Union*, 181.

[283] Sir A. A. Howarth to Cecil, 19 July 1938: Cecil Papers Add. MSS 51180. Noel Baker to H. L. Nathan, 10 Feb. 1938: Noel-Baker Papers 5/137. Cecil to Noel Baker, 6 Jan. 1938 (copy): Cecil Papers Add. MSS 51108.

[284] Dugdale, *Baffy*, 69 (entry for 2 Dec. 1937).

[285] Minutes of a Conference called by Lord Cecil to consider the establishment of a National Boycott Committee, 18 Feb. 1938: Noel-Baker Papers 5/142.

unexpected early support for a boycott from the National Peace Council and—after much discussion and on the understanding that pacifists need not support it—from the WIL,[286] this was a failure: public faith in economic pressure had declined; and the Labour Party suspected that the IPC was implicated in a campaign by Cripps for a 'united front' between Labour and other socialist parties which it had proscribed as a fellow-travelling manœuvre.[287] An even more quixotic scheme to create a volunteer international air force to defend the Chinese against Japanese attacks also came to nothing in the summer of 1938, despite capturing the imagination of Lord Davies who tried interest the American tycoon Howard Hughes in it.[288] Moreover, Cardinal Hinsley was still 'disturbed' by the IPC and its connection with the LNU:[289] after Munich he was to resign his vice-presidency; and the Catholic representatives were to withdraw from the union's Christian organizations committee.[290]

In January 1939 Cecil felt unable to continue his efforts on behalf of the British IPC, resigning as its president, though retaining his position on RUP. However, with the British IPC 'facing a grave financial situation', its officers were even 'considering the whole problem of their future work' when they met their LNU counterparts on 16 February. Cecil still favoured an LNU takeover;[291] but the decision taken was that the IPC would carry on as a completely independent body. The LNU's executive committee agreed to this a fortnight later, although in response to a question Cecil admitted that it was 'not unlikely that the I.P.C. would wish to have affiliated committees in some of the larger towns'.[292] In reality, however, despite A. D. Lindsay's willingness to take over as president, the British IPC was too weak and the political climate too unhelpful for its new freedom to form local groups and raise funds entirely as it chose to be of significant advantage to it. Even Cecil was to admit to the LNU's July 1939 general council, which approved the divorce between the two bodies, that 'the actual work of the I.P.C. in Britain was not of the first importance'.[293]

Between the autumn of 1937 and the spring of 1939 the peace movement's

---

[286] Bailey to Noel Baker, 30 Sept. 1937: Noel-Baker Papers 2/36. Minutes, WIL executive, 12 Oct., 9 Nov., 14 Dec. 1937.

[287] Minutes, Labour NEC, 26 Jan. 1938 (Harvester microfiche 235). J. S. Middleton to Cecil, 17 Feb. 1938 (copy): Noel-Baker papers 5/142.

[288] Long and Wilson (eds.), *Thinkers of the Twenty Years' Crisis*, 65–6.

[289] Hinsley to Cecil, 13 Apr. 1938: Cecil Papers Add. MSS 51179.

[290] Hinsley to Cecil, 13 Dec. 1938: Cecil Papers Add. MSS 51182. Minutes, LNU executive, 12 Jan. 1939.

[291] Cecil to Murray, 9 Feb. 1939: Murray Papers.

[292] Minutes, LNU executive, 16 Feb., 2 Mar. 1939.

[293] Minutes, LNU general council, 7–10 July 1939 (fo. 12): LNU papers.

position had thus altered in two subtle ways. First, its polarization had been all but completed: Kingsley Martin noted that the 1938 National Peace Congress 'ended in a sharp split between the Pacifists and the apostles of Collective Security'—the latter rejecting the proposed communiqué by 105 votes to 73—and wondered how such an outcome 'has so long been avoided' in view of the fact that the 'difference in philosophy is fundamental'.[294] Secondly, each wing had found itself the junior partner in an alliance with a strand of defencist opinion: advocates of peaceful change were aligned with and subordinated to Chamberlainites; and advocates of collective security or a peace front were in the same position in respect of Churchillians. Yet, remarkably, the peace movement retained some sense of common purpose. Despite his support for the peace front and surprise that polarization had not occurred sooner, Martin still claimed to be 'on the same side as the pacifists'.[295] Similarly, the Ealing branch of the LNU accepted an invitation to a debate with the local PPU group because 'not . . . to do so might suggest a divergence of principle which did not necessarily exist'.[296] And in the policy statement which it issued as soon as the first euphoria over the Munich settlement had passed, the LNU's executive committee explained its support for containment in terms which were clearly *pacificist* rather than defencist: it reaffirmed its commitment to peace, as 'the positive process of substituting security for anxiety and goodwill for hatred' rather than in 'the negative meaning of not being at war', and noted that 'positive peace represents a spiritual ideal which, however paradoxical it may seem, men will defend, if need be, with their lives'.[297]

A deteriorating international situation had further increased the salience of the peace issue but had begun to starve the peace movement of the optimism necessary to give its ideas credibility. However, for a while non-violent resistance and peaceful change were promoted as the last untried policies. Thanks largely to Sheppard, the PPU mobilized support for pacifism with unprecedented flair; and the National Peace Council managed a creditable recovery to promote a new peace conference. On the other side of a deepening ideological chasm, the LNU showed resilience when its hopes for effective non-military sanctions were undermined. However, much of its good work on the Peace Ballot was undone by the IPC fiasco, which significantly reduced the effectiveness of its campaign for collective security.

---

[294] *New Statesman* (4 June 1938), 946. *Peace* (July/Aug. 1938), 12.
[295] *Political Quarterly*, 9 (1938), 172.
[296] Minutes, Ealing and District LNU, 16 June 1938: Ealing Public Library.
[297] Minutes, LNU executive, 6 Oct. 1938.

11

Retreat,
March 1939–August 1945

shift to containment
15 Mar 1939

In respect of thinking about international relations the German seizure of the non-Germanic rump of Czechoslovakia on 15 March 1939 ended the inter-war period. The *New Statesman* immediately observed: 'While the Führer was "righting the injustice of Versailles" and "unifying the German people", a gullible Britain could be persuaded that his actions were based on, and limited by, the morals of nationalism. These pretences are no longer neces-sary.'[1] Because Hitler had thus exposed himself as an imperialist, the balance of British opinion tipped sharply in favour of containment. Even Chamberlain changed tack: on 31 March he issued a guarantee to Poland; and on 26 April he announced Britain's first ever peacetime conscription, of men aged 20 and 21. Such moves were widely seen as preparations for war rather than as cred-ible acts of deterrence. Much of the idealism which had previously been focused on peaceful change, or on the belief that collective security could be achieved without the encirclement of Germany, was redirected into the longer term goal of federalism, which enjoyed a remarkable though little-remem-bered boom from the spring of 1939 onwards.

3 Sept 1939

Compared with the Prague crisis, Britain's actual entry into war on 3 September 1939 was a minor watershed, being greeted with a calm resigna-tion that contrasted with the febrile enthusiasm of August 1914. Of much greater intellectual impact was Hitler's military breakthrough in the summer of 1940, after which only the most obdurate or the most apolitical could support non-resistance, and only the most optimistic or gullible could expect a satisfactory negotiated peace. A more gradual change of mood occurred after the Soviet Union and the United States entered the war during the second half of 1941, and thereby improved the prospects of military victory.

FROM PRAGUE TO DANZIG, MARCH–AUGUST 1939

The seizure of Prague brought home a truth from which many had been shying away, particularly since the cession of the Sudetenland—namely, that

---

[1] *New Statesman* (18 Mar. 1939), 409.

Hitler was not appeasable. As Mary Agnes Hamilton later put it: 'After Munich we knew this in our bones: after March 1939 we spoke of it.'[2] In consequence, the accommodationist cause suffered a rebuff. Allen's death just twelve days before the Prague crisis thus spared him the disillusioning experience which prompted Lansbury to send Hitler a telegram of reproach.[3] C. R. Buxton was forced to 'admit that we have reached the lowest depth (so far) in international relations, and that everybody must be prepared to . . . *revise their opinions*'.[4] The Marquess of Tavistock acknowledged that Hitler's move was a 'grave disappointment to those who had hoped that he might confine his territorial ambitions to the people of the German race', though his son later observed that this was the 'maximum note of disapproval he could bring to bear after the Czechoslovakian *coup*'.[5] And some pacifists accepted the need for 'a reorientation of our views and policy towards German fascism' in view of the fact that there was 'no shadow of excuse for the virtual annexation of the rump of Czecho-Slovakia'.[6]

The National Peace Council had particular cause to be upset with Hitler. Both an Albert Hall meeting to conclude its peace-conference petition and a deputation to present the 1,062,000 signatures to Chamberlain had been arranged for 18 March, and were therefore, as Vera Brittain recorded in her diary, 'spoiled of what would have been their overwhelming effect by Hitler's last coup'.[7] At the Albert Hall the Bishop of Chelmsford did his best to keep up hopes for peaceful change, but felt obliged to point out that the German government's breach of faith three days before 'has almost universally destroyed confidence in its pledged word, has undermined the moral basis of its claims on other nations and has therefore made infinitely more difficult negotiations between the nations for the just and general peace which we and you desire and for which we shall continue to labour'.[8]

The Prague crisis prompted the far right to play the anti-war card which the non-pacifist left, with a rare exception such as the ILP, had abandoned. Just as radicals had twenty-five years previously blamed Anglo-German antagonism on the machinations of secret diplomacy, so right-wing extremists now blamed it on a Jewish conspiracy. A public characterized by 'a casual anti-semitism . . . at all levels', in a leading social historian's words,[9] offered some leverage for such a conspiracy theory. For example, the ILP's

---

[2] Hamilton, *Remembering my Good Friends*, 304.
[3] R. Postgate, *The Life of George Lansbury* (1951), 315.
[4] Memorandum dated 17 Mar. 1939: C. R. Buxton Papers, box 3(4). Emphasis in original.
[5] Bedford, *A Silver-Plated Spoon*, 155. [6] *PN* (24 Mar. 1939), 4.
[7] *Vera Britain: Chronicle of Friendship*, 346 (entry for 18 Mar. 1939).
[8] *Peace* (Apr. 1939), 100.
[9] McKibbin, *Classes and Cultures* 56.

journal *Forward* attacked 'Jewish control' of British foreign policy at this time.[10]

To argue this line more systematically, a British People's Party was formed in April 1939 by John Beckett, who as already noted had been a member of the ILP and an organizer of No More War demonstrations before becoming a fascist. His principal collaborator was Ben Greene, a conspicuous figure in the Society of Friends and the PPU in virtue of his gigantic physical stature, and also well known in the Labour Party, until his resignation in October 1938, both as a champion of the rights of constituency associations against the controlling trade-union section, and as a defender of Germany.[11] Another founder member of the British People's Party, though he recorded in his diary that its launch proved 'a bigger flop than I had imagined', was the writer and Labour constituency activist Hugh Ross Williamson. He too was anti-trade union and pro-German, and having publicly argued in the spring of 1939 that Britain should not go to war 'on behalf of the great capitalists, the Communists, and the Jews', was obliged to resign as a parliamentary candidate.[12]

The British People's Party tried to avoid being seen as pro-Nazi and anti-Jewish, as distinct from opposed to 'war and usury', and persuaded *Peace News* to carry an advertisement for it.[13] Tavistock, who was an active member, tried to rebut the charge of anti-Semitism by claiming to 'have heard Mr Beckett say at a public meeting that if he found an Englishman and a Jew exploiting the people of this country unfairly he would consider the Englishman deserving of the heavier punishment because he was injuring his fellow-countrymen'.[14] However, by thus showing that its leaders assumed that a Jew could not also be an Englishman, Tavistock gave the game away.

In addition, Greene established a Peace and Progressive Information Service, which issued a *Bulletin* full of pro-German propaganda. More significantly, Mosley's British Union of Fascists, which had long argued that there need be no quarrel between a Germany that dominated Europe and a Britain that concentrated on its empire, also launched an anti-war campaign. Though it thereby lost the support of a few old-style patriots, it won that of a larger number of ultra-appeasers, thereby enabling it after March 1939 to enjoy a limited revival.[15] On 22 July, for example, it staged the country's largest

---

[10] R. Skidelsky, *Oswald Mosley* (1975), 439.

[11] Minutes, Labour Party National Executive Committee, 6 Oct. 1938 (Harvester microfiche 248). B. Pimlott, *Labour and the Left in the 1930s* (1977), 116–40.

[12] H. R. Williamson, *The Walled Garden: An Autobiography* (1956), 104, 189, 192. See also *Spectator* (4 Aug. 1939), 184.

[13] Griffiths, *Patriotism Perverted*, 57.

[14] *Tribune* (7 July 1939), 14.

[15] R. Thurlow, *Fascism in Britain: A History, 1918–1985* (Oxford, 1987), 116–7.

indoor political meeting, at Earls Court in London, at which Mosley told an audience of 20,000: 'We fight for Britain, yes, but a million Britons shall never die in your Jews' quarrel'.[16]

For the PPU, Hitler's *démarche* of 15 March 1939 produced a net gain in membership but a loss in cohesion. It coincided with an important stage in its institutional consolidation. Just twelve days previously it had taken possession of 6 Endsleigh Street, a freehold property close to Friends' House in London, which it named Dick Sheppard House in recognition of the fact that much of the purchase price had been raised as a result of an appeal in its founder's memory. In April 1939 it completed its democratization process: its second annual general meeting reduced the Sponsors to an honorific category and handed their powers to an elected national council which included regional representatives. In May this new body formalized Morris's administrative role by appointing him general secretary as well as chairman. He was thereby enabled to give up his canonry at Birmingham, though he was embarrassed at reports which interpreted this simply as a protest against the Church of England's views on war, since, as he later made clear, he also had 'a personal reason' for doing so.[17] This was a reference to his affair with a married woman—Dr Kathleen Rutherford, who chaired the PPU's Harrogate group—of which a number of colleagues were aware.[18]

The PPU's new democratic structure was intended to enable it to decide policy on contentious issues. For example, its inability to commit itself to oppose compulsory military service at the end of 1938 had led to the launching of the No-Conscription League. Admittedly the leaders of this new body had mostly kept their distance from the PPU: its chairman was Cecil H. Wilson of the Parliamentary Pacifist Group; its secretary was Rose Simpson of the Women's Co-operative Guild; and its treasurer was Brockway, who, though no longer a pacifist, was still a war resister active in the ILP.[19] However, its vice-chairman was Hudson, who resigned his Sponsorship on joining the new league.[20] (After the No-Conscription League failed in its purpose, Hudson was to re-establish relations with the PPU and serve as its co-treasurer.)

Hitler's seizure of Prague produced the first significant batch of repudiated peace pledges, which *Peace News* blamed on 'people dropping back into a

[16] Cited in Skidelsky, *Oswald Mosley*, 440.

[17] Minutes, PPU national council, 20 May 1939. *PN* (21 Apr. 1939), 2; (20 Oct. 1939), 12.

[18] *Vera Brittain: War Time Chronicle: Diary 1939–1945* 32, 38 (entries for 22 Sept., 5 and 6 Dec. 1939).

[19] *PN* (13 Jan. 1939), 7. See also A. Rigby, 'The Response of British Pacifists to World War II', in G. Grünewald and P. van den Dungen (eds.), *Twentieth-Century Peace Movements: Successes and Failures* (Lampeter, 1994), 145–59 at 146–7.

[20] Minutes, PPU sponsors, 6 and 21 Jan. 1939.

belief in "collective security" '.[21] But it also brought a significantly larger number of new pledges from those fearful of war and conscription. Sales of *Peace News* also rose, as interest in the prospects for would-be conscientious objectors increased, reaching 20,000 in mid-1939.

However, the Prague crisis also exacerbated the long-standing tension between 'Plowman pacifists' and 'politicals'. The former wanted the PPU to be 'frank and realist, and confess that *we* aren't going to prevent the great catastrophe from happening by persuading the world to accept our programme, even if we have one': members should instead act 'as living witnesses' to their long-term values.[22] Even the non-Christians among them accepted that their absolutism was ethical or even religious rather than political. They thus found themselves adopting a similar approach to the FoR, whose quietism had enabled it to expand modestly in face of political adversity, reaching 9,813 members by the outbreak of war. This approach seemed vindicated when the conscientious-objection rate for the pre-war batch of conscripts, those asked to register on 3 June 1939, turned out to be only 1.8 per cent: though higher than in the First World War, this stood no chance of threatening the country's defence effort. In addition, the Fellowship of Conscientious Objectors which was established in June 1939[23] was not a publicity-seeking body.

Political pacifists favoured a more absolutist and militant response to conscription, which with characteristic overstatement Barclay denounced as 'a form of fascism'.[24] They also believed that war could still be prevented. Thus, after further deliberation, Lansbury concluded that 'it was not *our* policy of appeasement through conference and mutual concessions which has failed. It is appeasement plus the mailed fist which has failed.'[25] But looking so doggedly on the bright side led them into morally dangerous territory. A reader of *Peace News* defended the paper's determination 'to concentrate on the positive side—creating a friendly spirit and seeing the thing from the other man's point of view', while admitting that its contributors 'certainly do sometimes appear to be almost as "pro-German" as Goebbels himself'.[26] They could also seem hostile to Jews. Thus Ethel Mannin imported the ILP's anti-Semitism into her pacifism, arguing in *Peace News* that 'Jewish racial feeling in partnership with Jewish financial interests' was doubly 'dangerous'.[27] And Royden joined the council of the British People's Party, although, as a leading authority on the pro-Nazi movement has pointed out, she 'can

---

[21] *PN* (21 Apr. 1939), 10. [22] *PN* (24 Mar. 1939), 9.
[23] *PN* (17 Sept. 1939), 3. [24] *PN* (2 June 1939), 10.
[25] *Christian Pacifist* (May 1939), 115.
[26] *PN* (30 June 1938), 8.
[27] *PN* (4 Aug. 1939), 6; (11 Aug. 1939), 11.

hardly have been unaware of the company she was keeping'.[28] In addition, an overlap of membership developed between the British Union of Fascists and the PPU despite the fact that fascism was 'not, I suggest, a peace mentality in the sense that pacifists think of such', in the tactful words of Andrew Stewart, the PPU activist who had masterminded Sheppard's election to the rectorship of Glasgow University.[29]

Understandably, therefore, the PPU found its motives called into question for the first time in the spring and summer of 1939. Criticized for having drawn Greene's Peace and Progressive Information Service 'to the notice of its members', it had to argue that it 'in no way supported' that body.[30] It was also condemned for including The Link as an association working for peace and international friendship in the *Peace Service Handbook* which it published in response to the introduction of conscription. During the resulting press controversy, moreover, Morris's membership of that body came to light. His defence was that he had joined in the belief that it was a goodwill organization and had never been to any of its meetings. But he unwisely allowed himself to be quoted as being personally in favour 'of giving a great deal more away [to Hitler]. I don't think Mr Chamberlain has really started yet on any serious appeasement.'[31]

The PPU's insistence that it wanted only peace and reconciliation and condoned neither fascism or anti-Semitism was sincere. It can thus be acquitted of undergoing the 'moral collapse' following Sheppard's death of which Orwell, with the zeal of a late convert to the causing of fighting Hitler, was soon to accuse it.[32] But its members were often guilty of special pleading on Germany's behalf. For example, Bing claimed that it was wrong of those who had never met Hitler to criticize him, prompting Rose Macaulay, whose resignation as a Sponsor has already been noted, to expostulate that 'the system of tyranny, violence and injustice that he has devised and enforces wherever he rules' sufficed for an adverse judgement of his character.[33] She had already wondered whether it might be worse to condone 'a régime more brutal than any we have had in Europe since Alva' than to fight 'a horrible and inhuman war'.[34] However, few other pacifists were prepared to admit that they faced a choice of evils.

The containment wing of the peace movement felt that the Prague crisis had removed all doubt regarding Hitler's evil intentions. Commenting on the 'hurricane of moral indignation' generated by the stamping out of Czechoslovakian independence, William Brown, an Oxford psychologist, noted that

[28] Griffiths, *Patriotism Perverted*, 57.
[29] *PN* (11 Aug. 1939), 1; (18 Aug. 1939), 12.
[30] *PN* (21 July 1939), 5.
[31] *PN* (18 Aug. 1939), 7.
[32] Orwell, *Collected Essays*, ii. 69.
[33] *PN* (1 Sept. 1939), 9.
[34] *PN* (19 May 1939), 4.

'we now have complete certainty in matters where anything short of certainty must have paralysed action'.[35]

However, advocates of containment had no message of hope to offer. Even with Churchill as the speaker, the New Commonwealth Society had difficulty in getting its supporters to come to a meeting in the aftermath of Prague, Harold Nicolson inferring: 'They simply do not wish to hear what they fear will be painful things.'[36] The society, which believed its 'effective member-ship' to be 2,974, was facing 'a serious decline' in its momentum which it largely attributed to 'the lethargy or "hopelessness" of the general public about the international outlook'.[37] The LNU was also in difficulty: its membership fall in 1939 has alrady been noted; and after the Prague crisis the Focus Company lost interest in the new-format *Headway*, which had sold only 8,000 copies to members of the general public, and allowed control of the paper to pass back to the LNU, although the legal aspects of this reversion had not been tidied up by the outbreak of war.[38]

League supporters did their best to portray the commitment to Poland as a belated espousal of the policy of collective security, but not always with conviction. When shortly before Prague Murray had talked of a 'Peace Bloc', Cecil had privately retorted that it was 'in fact only a counter-alliance called by another name'.[39] Afterwards Angell tried to represent the Polish guarantee in a positive light by exhorting *Headway* readers to 'realise how great a vindi-cation of the L.N.U. policy is the recent change of attitude on the part of the British Government';[40] but a book he completed at this time also warned that, since a 'whole political philosophy . . . separates such a policy as the Balance of Power from the policy of concentrating power behind a law of peace', the government's intellectual conversion might be incomplete. He therefore acknowledged the 'danger that . . . under the guise of collective security we may slip back into what is virtually the pre-war policy of alliances erected for the maintenance of the so-called "Balance of Power." '[41] Similarly, the *Spectator* argued that 'at least in a mutilated form' the government had returned to 'the conception of collective security which inspired idealists to strengthen and develop the League of Nations, which has been mocked at by so-called "realist" statesmen';[42] but the veteran journalist J. A. Spender retorted that collective security had until recently been understood to require economic

---

[35] W. Brown, *War and Peace: Essays in Psychological Analysis* (1939), 5. The preface was dated Apr. 1939.
[36] H. Nicolson, *Diaries and Letters 1930–39* (1966), 393 (entry for 30 Mar. 1939).
[37] Minutes, British executive, New Commonwealth, 29 June 1939.
[38] Minutes, LNU executive, 9 Mar., 20 Apr., 14 and 21 Sept. 1939.
[39] Cecil to Murray, 9 Feb. 1939: Murray papers.
[40] *HW* (May 1939), 7.
[41] Angell, *Must it be War?*, 22–3, 30.   [42] *Spectator* (21 July 1939), 81.

sanctions only, and had therefore been 'proposed and defended . . . as the absolute antithesis of the alliance and balance-of-power system which prevailed before the war, and into which we have unfortunately been compelled to return, at all events for the time being'.[43] It was ironic that one of the fathers of the league movement, W. H. (now Lord) Dickinson, was present at the LNU executive committee's discussion of the policy conse-quences of the Prague crisis, and therefore able to witness the extent to which that movement had now reversed its views. Virtually all members accepted that 'some definite action in the form of military alliance' was inevitable, the only disagreement being whether it should be organized through Geneva or not. Lytton thought it would have 'a vastly greater effect' if it were so orga-nized. But another Conservative member, Captain Cazalet, argued that a league connection merely 'signified delay and excuses for evading obliga-tions'.[44]

In addition, internationalists were having to confront the mature version of E. H. Carr's theory of realism. He unveiled this during the 29th National Peace Congress on 7–9 July, arguing in an iconoclastic speech that the 'most shattering feature of the past twenty years has been the cruel and abrupt descent from the Utopia of the first post-war years to the reality of to-day'. He insisted that the widespread belief 'in a natural harmony of interests' among states had been shown to be 'simply not true', as a consequence of which a 'hurricane force' was shaking the world, namely 'the recognition of a real conflict which cannot be moralised or rationalised by a formula of the general good'.[45]

Carr's speech prompted the LNU's leaders to worry further about their previous neglect of issues of power which, as already noted, they had been privately acknowledging since 1933.[46] Even so, they did not accept the way in which he applied his own realist principles. As Angell pointed out in a review of *The Twenty Years' Crisis*, the book-length exposition which appeared shortly after the outbreak of war and later established itself as a clas-sic: 'If Chamberlainite "appeasement" had succeeded and we had maintained peace, there would have been a certain plausibility in many of the theories Professor Carr expounds.' As things had turned out, Angell insisted, it was the policy of collective security favoured by many supposed 'utopians' which had been shown to be more realistic.[47]

After Prague, moreover, socialists became increasingly reconciled to power politics. John Wilmot, who had lost East Fulham at the 1935 general

---

[43] *Spectator* (28 July 1939), 149 (see also Angell's reply: Spectator (11 Aug. 1939), 220).
[44] Minutes, LNU executive, 23 Mar. 1939.   [45] *Peace* (Aug./Sept. 1939), 19.
[46] e.g. Murray to Cecil, 22 Aug. 1939: Murray Papers.   [47] *HW* (Jan. 1940), 4–5.

election, returned to the Commons at a by-election for Kennington in May 1939 after a campaign in which his propaganda had been diametrically opposed to that of October 1933. One of his posters in Kennington thus read: 'MAKE BRITAIN SAFE: 1.   SPEED UP DEFENCE.   2.   REAL AIR-RAID PRECAUTIONS WITH BOMB-PROOF SHELTERS.   3.   UNITE ALL PEACEFUL NATIONS AGAINST WAR THREATS.'[48]

However, the slow progress of negotiations for an alliance with the Soviet Union meant that the hoped-for peace front did not materialize. Communists became increasingly impatient: for example, the LNU's youth groups embarrassed their parent organization by calling for Chamberlain's resignation;[49] and they urged the National Peace Congress to concentrate on 'the rebuilding of collective security on the lines of the "peace bloc"' to the exclusion of other issues.[50]

The Molotov–Ribbentrop pact of 22 August 1939 transformed the diplomatic situation. It caused Orwell to reject the ILP's continuing policy of war resistance and accept that a confrontation with Hitler would qualify as a people's war.[51] And it threw the Communist Party into turmoil, though for the time being it continued with its anti-fascist line.

After Prague, a vast reserve of peace sentiment—which had been displaced from policies such as peaceful change, collective security, and the peace front, now that they seemed to have little chance of preventing war in the short term—was suddenly in search of a cause which offered some hope of abolishing war in the longer term. It alighted on federalism, despite 'difficulties, geographical, political, and economic' which, as the *New Statesman* put it, 'would at any other time have been enough to laugh the proposal out of court'.[52] Although offering a plausible general diagnosis of the failure of the league—namely that, having been merely a confederation, it had allowed its member states to retain too much power—federalism too readily assumed that they could be persuaded to give up more. As Leonard Woolf was to observe, a federation assumed 'a much greater uniformity of communal organization and of "international" psychology than a confederal system like that of the League'.[53]

For those reasons, federalism had previously attracted only a small following in Britain. As already noted, some radicals had favoured it during the First World War; and Lord Davies had devoted himself to an institutionally selective version of it throughout the 1930s.

---

[48] I am grateful to Lady Wilmot for giving me photographs of billboards her husband used in this campaign.

[49] Birn, *League of Nations Union*, 208.   [50] *Peace* (Aug./Sept. 1939), 34.

[51] B. Crick, *George Orwell: A Life* (1980), 247.   [52] *New Statesman*, (1 July 1939), 3.

[53] L. Woolf, *The War for Peace* (1940), 204.

A handful of intellectuals had also taken the idea up. The Marquess of Lothian and his friend Lionel Curtis of All Souls College, who had originally seen federalism as a means of strengthening the British empire, came to see it as having wider applications too. They jointly expounded the superiority of federations over confederations in the early 1920s;[54] and both explored the issue further during the 1930s. Between 1934 and 1937, Curtis, a visionary, published a complex three-volume treatise about how constructive religion might bring about a world commonwealth. During May 1935 Lothian, essentially an appeaser, argued for 'a true Federation (not a League) of Nations',[55] in a lecture which, despite having only a modest impact at the time, was to acquire the status of a seminal text in the European integration movement after being read by Altiero Spinelli and Ernesto Rossi during their imprisonment by Mussolini.[56] Lothian increasingly saw federalism as necessary for peaceful change: frustrated that the league was 'utterly unable to revise the fundamental discriminations against Germany', as he told the 1936 National Peace Congress,[57] he concluded that only a federation could have the strength and authority to induce the 'have' powers to make concessions. In addition, in the mid-1930s the academic economist Lionel Robbins became interested in a federation as a way of maintaining an international financial order in the absence of a benign hegemon such as pre-1914 Britain had supposedly been.[58]

Moreover, in the summer of 1938 the looming crisis over Czechoslovakia brought a small federalist group, to be known as Federal Union, into existence. Its two founders were in their late twenties, had both been educated at Eton and Oxford, and had not previously taken an interest in the peace question: Derek Rawnsley was an exuberant entrepreneur, and Charles Kimber a gentle idealist of private means and the heir to a baronetcy. In July 1938 they had become convinced that 'an ideal is necessary to provide a horizon more remote than the next few weeks'.[59] Shortly before Munich they had set up an informal group, which met on 14 September 1938 and was joined on 10 October by Patrick Ransome, a severely disabled barrister who had been recruited for his greater knowledge of international affairs and duly informed them that

[54] P. Kerr and L. Curtis, *The Prevention of War* (New Haven, Conn., 1923).

[55] Lord Lothian, *Pacifism is Not Enough Nor Patriotism Either* (1935), 30.

[56] The lecture was published as *Pacifism is Not Enough*. See also J. Turner (ed.), *The Larger Idea: Lord Lothian and the Problem of National Sovereignty* (1988), 116, 149–50.

[57] *Peace* (July/Aug. 1936), 59–61.

[58] L. Robbins, *Economic Planning and International Order* (1937), based on a lecture given at Geneva in 1935; *Economic Causes of War* (1939); and *Autobiography of an Economist* (1971), 159–62. See also F. Rossosolillo, 'British Federalism in the Thirties', *New Europe* (Autumn 1976), 41–54 at 48–50.

[59] Draft statement 'Pax—Union': Federal Union papers.

the approach they were adopting was federalism.[60] The three of them held their first open meeting on 24 November—their ideas being 'greeted with derision by the majority', though the first members were also recruited[61]— and their first 'Members' Meeting' on 20 December.[62] Before the end of the year they were discovered by Gerald Bailey, who noted that they were 'young people and their work is not very experienced' and drew them to Lothian's attention, though he was leaving for the United States and unable to see them until February.[63] In late January 1939 they issued a manifesto which had gone through six drafts since October: successive versions referred to their new association as 'Pax', 'Pax Union', and 'Federal Union'.[64] However, they experienced 'an arduous struggle for recognition. The project was ridiculed by nine out of ten people talked to; the tenth expressed sceptical sympathy.'[65]

What transformed Federal Union's prospects was the publication in March 1939 of the British edition of a work by an American journalist, Clarence K. Streit, a former Rhodes Scholar at Oxford who had contributed to the UDC's periodical as early as 1920–1,[66] and had been employed as Geneva correspondent of the *New York Times* since 1929. Streit had come to believe that the league would deter aggression more effectively if it were replaced by a federal union in the same way that the United States had enjoyed greater political stability after the articles of confederation had been replaced by a federal constitution in 1787. Membership of the federation would be confined to the democracies, namely the United States, the British Dominions, France, Netherlands, Scandinavia, and Switzerland. Streit first set out his ideas in a newspaper article in 1933, and gave lectures at Geneva in 1935 and 1936 which, though later published, 'hardly stirred a ripple'.[67] Only after Munich did he expand them into a book, *Union Now*, which attracted considerable attention in the United States on its publication early in 1939.[68]

---

[60] See B. Wootton, *In a World I Never Made: Autobiographical Reflections* (1967), 97–9, for a description of the founders of Federal Union.

[61] *Federal Union News* (Dec. 1944), 13.

[62] Federal Union papers. R. Mayne and J. Pinder with J. C. de V. Roberts, *Federal Union: The Pioneers. A History of Federal Union* (1990), 5–10.

[63] A. Bosco, 'Lothian, Curtis, Kimber and the Federal Union Movement (1938–40)', *Journal of Contemporary History*, 23 (1988), 465–502 at 478.

[64] Federal Union papers.

[65] *Federal Union News* (Dec. 1944), 13.

[66] See *Foreign Affairs* (Aug. 1920), 20–3; (Sept. 1920), 42–5; (Oct. 1920), 60–4; (Jan. 1921), 110–12; (Feb. 1921), 127–8.

[67] C. K. Streit, *Union Now: A Proposal for a Federal Union of the Democracies of the North Atlantic* (1939), 9. Geneva Institute of International Relations, *Problems of Peace*, 10th series (1936), 216–51, and 11th series (1937), 213–32. *Friend* (19 May 1939), 411–12.

[68] *The Times* (24 Feb. 1939).

One reason for its even greater popularity when soon afterwards it appeared in Britain was, as Angell noted, 'that it comes from America'.[69] Davies also took the view that 'it was imperative that the book should have been written by an American, because the plan is still-born unless it is sponsored by Mr Streit's fellow countrymen'.[70] And Lothian, who privately admitted that he did not think Streit's 'plan will work, or anything like it', supported it because 'it approaches the problem from the right angle from the American point of view'.[71] In other words, Streit's scheme offered some hope that the United States might belatedly emerge from isolation and take an interest in the European situation.

However, the most obvious reason for the appeal of Streit's book was its timing. Even before Germany took Prague the peace movement was sufficiently in need of inspiration for the PPU Sponsor Storm Jameson to claim, presumably on the basis of the American edition, that it could 'do more for the hope of peace in our time than pacifism has been able to do'.[72] After Hitler's thunderbolt, the need for a new ideal was even greater. 'It is just because the ruin of our hope seems so nearly complete that it is of such vital importance to come to grips with first principles', a reviewer of the British edition observed, pointing out that as regards the European situation 'either there will be a relaxation or the catastrophe. In either event the chance may recur of beginning to rebuild.'[73] Lothian, both predisposed towards federalism and shocked by the failure of appeasement, was in his biographer's words 'carried off his feet by Clarence Streit's book . . . making the most extravagant claims for it, speaking of it as perhaps destined to be epoch-making like *The Wealth of Nations* or *The Origin of Species*'.[74] Although his notice criticized Streit for 'rather naively' implying that federalism was 'his own peculiar discovery', it welcomed 'a book which a weekly reviewer cannot possibly do justice to'.[75] Although the LNU disliked Streit's rejection of the league, it too believed that he had written a work 'which may well influence world history',[76] and gave it unprecedented exposure in *Headway*.

Streit's best-seller proved to be a windfall for Federal Union. Casting around for help, Rawnsley, Kimber, and Ransome had consulted Harold Butler, just retired from the International Labour Office, who told them of Streit's forthcoming book and agreed to give them advice, though he was later to dismiss their ideas as 'inconsistent with the facts of national life as they

---

[69] Angell, *Must it be War?*, 249.   [70] *New Commonwealth* (June 1939), 164–5.
[71] Lothian to Cecil, 1 May 1939: Cecil Papers Add. MSS 51183.
[72] *PN* (10 Mar 1939), 6.   [73] *HW* (May 1939), 17.
[74] J. R. M. Butler, *Lord Lothian* (1969), 243.   [75] *New Statesman* (18 Mar. 1939), 434–5.
[76] *HW* (Apr. 1939), 18.

exist today'.[77] They had also contacted Curtis, who, having recently met Streit in the United States, also knew about his book.[78] Thus forewarned, they approached Streit's British publisher and were allowed to insert a flier in each copy. This gave them their publicity breakthrough, and was therefore well worth the slight distortion of their thinking which hitching Federal Union to Streit's band-wagon necessitated. Their previous thinking had been directed towards a federation of Europe; but they now emphasized the globalist and Atlanticist approaches favoured by Streit, as well as Lothian and Curtis.

Just a week after Hitler's seizure of Prague, Federal Union was able to issue a circular to members announcing that it was 'a great deal more firmly established' than previously and had assembled a distinguished panel of advisers including Barbara Wootton, a specialist in social administration who was to become an enthusiastic activist, and Arnold Toynbee, a historian employed at Chatham House, as well as Butler, Curtis, and Steed.[79] By mid-April it had received about 800 expressions of interest from a broad cross-section of progressive opinion, including Attlee, Bevin, Joad, Kingsley Martin, Leyton Richards (whose daughter Margaret became a long-serving worker in Federal Union's office[80]), and Sir William Beveridge, the Master of University College, Oxford, where Rawnsley had been a student.[81]

From the outset, however, Federal Union had its critics. Perhaps feeling that his role as supranationalist prophet had been usurped by Streit, H. G. Wells dismissed its 'pseudo-practical short-sightedness' and its failure to realize that its constitutional proposals were unworkable 'without a preliminary mental cosmopolis'.[82] Socialists were offended by its failure to indict capitalism as the cause of war; and Communists were further outraged by its exclusion of the Soviet Union from the proposed union. Privately, the leaders of the LNU were also critical, Angell regarding it as 'too remote from present urgencies' and Cecil as 'fantastic and dangerous',[83] though they publicly claimed that there was 'no difference in our ultimate aims', from fear that

---

[77] Interview with Sir C. Kimber, 28 July 1977. H. Butler, *The Lost Peace: A Personal Impression* (1941), 202.

[78] D. Lavin, *From Empire to International Commonwealth: A Biography of Lionel Curtis* (Oxford, 1995), 282–5.

[79] Copy of letter to members, 22 Mar. 1939: Federal Union papers.

[80] 'Notes from memory of Margaret Richards', kindly shown to me by Mrs Sheila Barton, for whom they were compiled.

[81] J. Harris, *William Beveridge: A Biography* (rev. edn., Oxford, 1997), 355.

[82] H. G. Wells, *The Fate of Homo Sapiens* (1939), 52–4. This book appeared in August.

[83] Angell to Cecil, 16 May 1939: Cecil Papers Add. MSS 51140. Cecil to Murray, 26 Sept. 1939: Murray Papers.

many LNU members would prefer Federal Union if told they must choose between the two.[84]

Failing to understand that they were beneficiaries of an almost-freakish coincidence—*Union Now*'s publication at a psychologically propitious moment—Federal Union's leaders not only ignored these criticisms but expected their ideas to have immediate influence. Well into the summer of 1939, for example, Kimber was hoping for an immediate conference of European states, including Germany and Italy, at which at least some of them would agree to form a federation.[85]

By July Federal Union had 'caught on' as an association and began an 'impressive, almost triumphal march' that was to carry on well into the war.[86] On the first two days of that month it held its first conference in London, by which time it claimed to have 2,000 members. The following week its agenda dominated the National Peace Congress: indeed, with Streit sending a message of support and Carr making the influential speech which has already been mentioned, this gathering indicated how federalism was pulling one section of the peace movement in the direction of utopianism at precisely the moment when realism was exerting a countervailing attraction on another. Federal Union's new enthusiasts were unmoved by Carr's thesis. For example, in a book written during July and August the future diplomat Duncan Wilson and his wife Elizabeth insisted that federal union 'cannot be dismissed as a mere Utopian speculation, and it should not be grasped in blind desperation as a last, even if hopeless refuge'. They argued that, previous federations having been created because of 'the fear of danger from foreign powers' and 'the inconvenience of economic separation', the prevailing 'fear of the Totalitarian Powers' and 'discontent with existing economic conditions' made present circumstances 'only too favourable to the beginnings of a Federal system'.[87] The implication of the Wilsons' argument was that war would improve the prospects of federalism still further: this proved to be the case.

PHONEY WAR, SEPTEMBER 1939–APRIL 1940

Both the peace movement and defencists had for the most part been expecting hostilities for the previous five months. Britain's declaration of war on 3 September 1939 therefore constituted much less of a watershed for public

[84] G. Murray, 'L.N.U. and Union Now', *HW* (July 1939), 16–17. See also Viscount Cecil, *A Great Experiment* (1941), 345–8.

[85] Bosco, 'Lothian, Curtis, Kimber', 494.

[86] *Federal Union News* (Dec. 1944), 13.

[87] D. and E. Wilson, *Federation and World Order* (1939), 23–4, 160–1.

opinion than either the Prague crisis had been or the fall of France would be. Admittedly, Mrs Swanwick, depressed at the collapse of the isolationist *pacifism* which she had strenuously advocated, took her own life on 16 November. And some pacifists recanted. A young Welsh schoolteacher previously active in the War Resisters' International, George Thomas, 'went through an agonizing period of self-examination and decided not to go to a tribunal as a pacifist but to join one of the armed forces'.[88] Royden resigned from the PPU in September,[89] a mere year after joining and five months after accepting election to its national council. And Sassoon quietly severed a connection which had become increasingly nominal.[90] However, in most cases the outbreak of war was merely the moment at which a decision made earlier was either acted upon or announced. Thus a former activist in the Woodcraft Folk and the NMWM, Leslie Paul, later admitted that he had merely 'discarded the remnants of my pacifism' at the outbreak of war, having been practising self-deception for several years.[91] The same was true of Lucy Cox, who had taken no part in the pacifist movement after leaving the secretaryship of the NMWM and, having married the secretary of the Labour Party, had come to accept orthodox Labour policy.[92] Similarly, although Leslie Weatherhead made public his rejection of pacifism early in the war, he had not proceeded from his early membership of the Sheppard Peace Movement to a prominent role in the PPU because he was already having misgivings.[93] And when Hugh Martin, a Baptist who had been active in the FoR, announced in a pamphlet published in November 1939 that the 'development of events' had compelled him to reject pacifism, he specified that this change of heart had happened 'several years ago'.[94]

The Second World War did not raise the emotional temperature to the extent that the First had done. Returning to the Commons chamber after sheltering during the first air-raid alert, Lansbury was impressed by 'the calmness of the people and the feeling that, anyhow, the Government of the country were in the right'.[95] A supporter of the conflict offered an explanation for this serenity in a private letter to a pacifist friend:

Remember this war is quite different from the last . . . See how reluctantly we've gone into it: see how little hate, how little enthusiasm there is for the actual war itself.

[88] G. Thomas, *Mr Speaker: The Memoirs of the Viscount Tonypandy* (1985), 43, 46.
[89] Minutes, PPU national council, 23 Sept. 1939.
[90] Roberts, *Siegfried Sassoon*, 276.
[91] L. Paul, *Angry Young Man* (1951), 204, 284.
[92] Interview with Mrs L. Middleton (née Cox), 23 Apr. 1975.
[93] Weatherhead, *Thinking Aloud in War Time*, pp. v, 19–20, 22.
[94] H. Martin, *The Christian as Soldier* (1939), 5.
[95] Hansard, 351 HC col. 298 (3 Sept. 1939).

Plenty of enthusiasm for the end; but none for the means. And there's no flag-wagging to speak of, no 'King and Country' stuff. It's a rotten job that's been thrust upon France and us as the adult powers who have grown out of the childish delight in fighting for its own sake, so that we can forcibly persuade the half-baked clique who run Germany that it's time they grew up too.[96]

Carl Heath also contrasted the situation in 1939 with the 'wholly unexpected' outbreak of the First World War, when the National Peace Council of which he had then been secretary 'went largely to pieces', and confidently predicted: 'The Peace Council will not go to pieces for pacific ideas are strong. People view this war with a sort of calm horror. There is none of the wild enthusiasm of 1914–15.'[97]

This calm can be attributed to three differences from the situation at the outbreak of the First World War. First, the geo-strategic case for war was now almost universally understood, despite the fact that the *casus belli* was located as far away as east–central Europe. In the words of G. D. H. Cole, who had now stopped claiming to be a pacifist in his personal views: 'If the man in the street is asked why Great Britain went to war with Nazi Germany, he will probably answer "To stop Hitler" or, just possibly, "To stop aggression." . . . "I reckon we've got to stop that —— somewhere", fairly summed up the attitude of a large section of the British people.'[98]

Secondly, the war had arisen out a commitment to a country which, unlike Belgium in 1914, had little appeal to progressive opinion. As Cole's wife and partner in socialist endeavour put it privately: 'I don't care a damn about Poland or Rumania or whatever unpleasing object Mr Chamberlain has decided to guarantee; I did care about the Spanish Republic and less poignantly about the Czechs, but that has gone.'[99] There was thus little crusading zeal, despite the obnoxiousness of the Third Reich.

Thirdly, a Conservative-dominated government was in power, because Labour declined Chamberlain's invitation to form a genuine coalition in September 1939. Progressive opinion undoubtedly supported the war, liberals seeing it as the defence of international law against criminality, radicals as the defence of popular rule again authoritarianism, and socialists as the defence of social justice against reaction. But it also maintained a slight detachment from it. This was evident not only in Cripps's hopes for a peace 'with the German people'[100] but in the letter which Harold Laski, one of Labour's leading intellectuals, wrote on the second day of the war to President Roosevelt,

---

[96] R. Tomlin to C. Ure, 19 Sept. 1939: J. and P. Ure Papers. I am grateful to Ms J. Ure for showing me these.

[97] *Peace* (Oct. 1939), 41.

[98] G. D. H. Cole, *War Aims* (1939), 3.

[99] M. Cole to Murray, Oct. 1939: Murray Papers.

[100] Burgess, *Stafford Cripps*, 130.

urging him 'to keep America out. At some early stage we must have vital mediation, and no one but yourself will be in a position to suggest terms consistent with international decency.'[101] Keynes therefore had some justification for his complaint in the *New Statesman* on 14 October that, having been 'loudest in demanding that Nazi aggression be resisted at all costs', the 'intelligentsia of the left' was now 'leaving the defence of civilization to Colonel Blimp and the Old School Tie'—a recognition of the fact that defencists were initially showing greater stomach for the fight than *pacificists*.

A consequence of progressive opinion's sense of detachment was a paucity of 'war to end war' rhetoric compared with the previous conflict. Instead, there was a widespread demand for 'peace aims' to be specified. William Brown thought it psychologically understandable that 'idealistic plans and visions of the after-war world' should occupy people's thoughts 'as some relief from the repulsive business of supporting even righteous war'.[102] However, 'peace aims' proved an ambiguous concept: as well as being a euphemism for victory aims, which was how it was understood by most people, it could be a way of implying that the war could be ended by negotiation, a possibility which Hitler sought to encourage by making a peace offer on 6 October. Understandably, this ambiguity increased its appeal to the National Peace Council, ever striving to reconcile pacifists and *pacificists*. It therefore launched a 'State Britain's Peace Terms' campaign, with the endorsement of the Chief Rabbi amongst others.[103] Similarly, when a handful of Labour MPs led by the Roman Catholic industrialist R. R. Stokes launched a negotiated-peace campaign, in consultation not only with Greene but also with Mosley and von Papen, the German former Chancellor who was now his country's ambassador to Turkey, they called themselves the 'Peace Aims Group'.[104]

The WIL's insistence that a negotiated peace was a realistic possibility helped it avoid either endorsing or condemning the war at this time. Its executive committee stated in November 1939 that 'though we may not see the next step to take at the moment we must never forget the aims for which we have always stood and we must try to keep our light burning. Our aim now is to get constructive proposals across to the German people.'[105] However, some of its members grew uneasy about seeking to bargain with Hitler, as became apparent at the beginning of April 1940 when the association's

[101] K. Martin, *Harold Laski* (1953), 140.
[102] M. Chaning-Pearce (ed.), *Federal Union: A Symposium* (1940), 83.
[103] *Peace* (Nov. 1939), 47.
[104] Griffiths, *Patriotism Perverted*, 201–4, 211–12.
[105] Minutes, WIL executive, 14 Nov. 1939.

Quaker chairwoman, Mrs Duncan Harris, announced that she would stand for re-election only if the membership understood that she personally 'was not prepared to wait for the banishment of Hitler before pressing for negotiations'. When asked by a *pacificist* member of the executive committee, Dr Hilda Clark, if she therefore supported 'the kind of resolution that is being passed by various organisations that the war ought to be stopped and that peace can be made *now*', she replied that 'a Stop the War campaign first was unreal but she was not prepared to rule out the possibility of finding means of negotiating'. And to Dr Clark's further remark that negotiating with Hitler would at best produce another Munich, she retorted that 'Hitler was shrinking in the picture'[106]—an assessment which Germany's attacks on Norway and Denmark a mere six days later were to expose as singularly ill-judged. As yet, however, the WIL's opponents of peace negotiations were not prepared to press their objection to the point of resignation.

Eleanor Rathbone, though latterly a standard-bearer for the collective-security movement, also hoped for peace negotiations at this time,[107] as less surprisingly did the Buxton brothers.[108] Lloyd George, who when Prime Minister during the latter part of the First World War had opposed a compromise peace, now wanted to explore one.[109] Lord Beaverbrook, soon to be Churchill's minister for aircraft production, backed Stokes and discussed with the ILP the possibility of funding peace candidates at by-elections.[110] And R. A. Butler, a Conservative junior minister who in his biographer's words 'had not entirely succeeded in shaking off the influence of the appeasement school in which he had been trained', kept in touch with a group of Quakers interested in peace talks, including Corder Catchpool.[111]

The British Union of Fascists and other far-right groups overtly condemned the conflict, holding a series of private meetings in an attempt to overcome their many personal and ideological rivalries in the interests of a united anti-war campaign. The leaders of the British People's Party established a British Council for a Christian Settlement in Europe: at its first public meeting on 14 October Greene asserted that Hitler had been right to invade Poland; a member of the audience likened Hitler's treatment of the Jews to Christ's treatment of the money-changers in the Temple; and—surprisingly in view of his previous work for the Garton Foundation, the UDC, and the

---

[106] Minutes, WIL executive, 3 Apr. 1940.
[107] Stocks, *Eleanor Rathbone*, 276.
[108] M. Anderson, *Noel Buxton: A Life* (1952), 149.
[109] P. Addison, 'Lloyd George and a Compromise Peace', in A. J. P. Taylor (ed.), *Lloyd George: Twelve Essays* (1971), 366–71.
[110] A. J. P. Taylor, *Beaverbrook* (1972), 403–4. J. McGovern, *Neither Fear Nor Favour* (1960), 133–5. Griffiths, *Patriotism Perverted*, 226–8.
[111] A. Howard, *Rab: The Life of R. A. Butler* (1987), 100. Hughes, *Indomitable Friend*, 164–5.

National Council for Civil Liberties—B. N. Langdon-Davies also spoke.[112] This new organization published a document which Tavistock had obtained from a German diplomat in Dublin which it believed to contain genuine peace terms. It also held a large public meeting in Kingsway Hall on 3 April 1940 to publicize it: those taking part included Hugh Ross Williamson, who now supported Mosley and wanted to become an Anglo-Catholic priest, and John McGovern of the ILP. Later, frustrated by the British government's refusal to take his document seriously, Tavistock published his correspondence with the Foreign Secretary on the subject even though this drew attention to his own references to 'objectionable' Jews.[113]

On the left, the ILP also opposed the war, and contested a number of by-elections, though it was too weak to have much impact. Somewhat more significantly, its great rival, the Communist Party, decided to do the same. On 2 October 1939 it ended six weeks of uncertainty about the implications of the Molotov–Ribbentrop pact by switching to war resistance on instructions brought directly from Moscow by the British representative to the Comintern, Dave Springhall, who was later imprisoned for spying for the Soviet Union.[114] This change of policy resulted in the sacking of the party's general secretary, Harry Pollitt, who had been unwilling to abandon his support for the war, and his replacement by R. P. Dutt, who from the start had welcomed the pact of 22 August as 'the logical and inevitable' response to the 'sabotage of the Peace Front' by both the National government and the Labour Party, and now condemned what he called 'the second imperialist war'.[115] The party issued a manifesto with the message, 'Stop the War! The people must enforce the terms of a lasting peace'.[116]

This abrupt change of tack had a demoralizing effect on those sections of the collective-security movement which Communists had penetrated. On 22 October 1939 a subcommittee of the British IPC which had been instructed to produce a 'statement of peace aims' failed to agree one because of Communist obstruction. In particular, Carritt wanted to include a demand for an international peace conference, but was defeated at the national committee four days later. At an acrimonious meeting of the executive committee on 16 November Carritt complained that 'he had been charged as being a Moscow agent and a Goebbels agent' and insisted that 'the views he held were

---

[112] *Tribune* (27 Oct. 1939), 2. Griffiths, *Patriotism Perverted*, 180–1.

[113] Griffiths, *Patriotism Perverted*, 213–14.

[114] K. Laybourn, ' "About Turn": The Communist Party of Great Britain and the Second World War, 1939–41', in K. Dockray and K. Laybourn (eds.), *The Representation and Reality of War: The British Experience* (Stroud, 1999), 218–34.

[115] *Labour Monthly* (Sept. 1939), 516; (Oct. 1939), 581.

[116] E. Trory, *Imperialist War: Further Recollections of a Communist Organizer* (Brighton, 1977), 45, 59.

endorsed by members of the peace movement and many other people'. And at the LNU's general council a fortnight later he insisted that the war could not be one for collective security and democracy since the National government had missed so many previous opportunities of fighting for these causes. Communist obstructiveness was so serious that Lindsay believed the British IPC should be closed down, though Noel Baker considered that it could carry on if those who 'derived their policy from Moscow' were purged. On 14 December the executive committee backed Lindsay's more pessimistic view, a decision confirmed by the national committee on 18 January 1940, when what Arnold-Forster called the 'my Stalin right or wrong' group failed in its bid to capture and perpetuate the IPC.[117] Cecil persuaded a reluctant LNU to create an advisory committee which would substitute for the British IPC in maintaining contact with countries such as Sweden, Switzerland, China, the United States, and the British Dominions, where effective IPC committees still existed;[118] but in practice nothing was done; and in September 1940 the executive committee of the British IPC met again in Balliol to reaffirm that it 'ought to be wound up'.[119]

Though thus thwarted in the IPC, the Communists managed to capture the LNU's National Youth Group Council in March 1940, provoking Lytton to a denounce Carritt's ' "Stop the War" group' as 'an organisation within an organisation which was working definitely in opposition to the policy of the whole Union', and causing the LNU to suspend its entire youth operation.[120] However, the Communist Party stopped short of sabotaging the war effort. It instructed its members to enter the armed forces rather than claim conscientious objection. It also found it expedient to highlight economic grievances instead, because, in the words of a party historian: 'Building an anti-war movement among ordinary people was proving to be uphill work. By contrast, developing struggle on bread and butter issues offered quite new opportunities.'[121]

The most influential dissent from the war came from conscientious objectors and pacifists, who, because 'the life and campaigns of George Lansbury, Dick Sheppard and others had made their impression',[122] constituted a more

---

[117] Statement by Mr G. Carritt for 26 Oct. 1939 meeting; Minutes, British national committee of IPC, 26 Oct. 1939, 18 Jan. 1940; Minutes, executive committee of British IPC, 16 Nov., 14 Dec. 1939; W. Arnold-Forster to F. D. Williams, 19 Jan. 1940: Noel-Baker Papers 5/141. Minutes, LNU general council 30 Nov.–1 Dec. 1939 (fos. 52–5): LNU papers.

[118] Minutes, LNU executive, 4 July, 1 Aug., 19 Sept. 1940.

[119] Minutes, executive committee of British IPC, 12 Sept. 1940: Noel-Baker Papers 5/142.

[120] Minutes, LNU general council 19–20 June 1940 (fos..6–7): LNU papers.

[121] N, Branson, *History of the Communist Party of Great Britain 1927–1941* (1985), 281.

[122] D. Hayes, *Challenge of Conscience: The Story of the Conscientious Objectors of 1939–1949* (1949), p. xiii.

substantial minority than during in the First World War. Approximately 60,000 claims of conscientious objection were to be made during 1939–45, 1.2 per cent of those called up;[123] and the PPU alone claimed almost exactly 130,000 members as the war began. The government had therefore been careful, on reintroducing conscription, to avoid the mistakes of 1916. Having in any case improved prison conditions, it placed the military-service tribunals under civilian control from the outset, and appointed judges as chairmen to ensure a better understanding of the law. The 'great respect and even kindness' shown to objectors was acknowledged soon after the first batch met their tribunals.[124] Even after the war began tribunals made many generous decisions: for example, they exempted Gerald Bailey and Charles Kimber, provided only that they continued working for their respective peace associations.[125] The appellate tribunal also made a significant concession in allowing a few non-pacifists to be exempted. For example, it allowed the objection of an Indian nationalist who admitted that he would fight for an independent India; and it did the same for Hugh Ross Williamson, despite the fact that he did not claim to be a pacifist but instead insisted, partly because of evident prejudice towards Poland, that Britain's declaration of war had failed the traditional Christian test of a just war.[126]

Surprisingly, in view of the more sensitive behaviour by the tribunals, a higher proportion (29.7 per cent) were initially refused recognition than in the First World War. One explanation is that in the more hostile atmosphere of 1916–18 only the most committed of objectors had put themselves forward. By contrast, in 1939 the public offered much less 'scorn and hatred': indeed an 'almost complete absence of anything of the sort' was soon commented upon.[127] Even though Mass Observation estimated in March 1940 that for every registered objector there were two 'latent' ones deterred from applying by social pressure,[128] this ratio must have been significantly shorter than in the earlier conflict.

A provision for objectors who had been imprisoned for more than three months to have a second hearing from the appellate tribunal reduced the suffering of those unable to accept their original decisions. However, the main reason why only 3 per cent of objectors saw the inside of a prison, compared with about 30 per cent in the First World War, was that most objectors felt

---

[123] R. Barker, *Conscience, Government and War: Conscientious Objection in Great Britain 1939–45* (1982), 121.

[124] *Christian Pacifist* (Aug. 1939), 199.

[125] Interviews with G. Bailey, 18 Dec. 1970 and Sir C. Kimber, 28 July 1977.

[126] Hayes, *Challenge of Conscience*, p. xiii. Williamson, *Walled Garden*, 132–6.

[127] *PN* (3 Nov. 1939), 8.

[128] Hayes, *Challenge of Conscience*, 7.

uncomfortable about adopting an intransigent position. The courage shown during the First World War by the likes of Allen, Brockway, Corder Catchpool, and Stephen Hobhouse had meant that many pacifists had viewed absolutism as the right position to adopt: for example, in 1925 a Quaker conference had, after reviewing the positions taken by the objectors of 1916–19, endorsed the 'ideal that every man of military age . . . should be an absolutist' in a future conflict.[129] But in 1939 the government had seized the moral high ground by embarking upon a war which in political terms was as just as could reasonably be expected and by improving the treatment of those who none the less felt unable to fight.

From the outset it was clear that more pacifists wished to serve their fellow citizens than to defy their state. Even before Britain declared war, the revival of the Friends' Ambulance Unit, which was to cater for 1,314 non-combatants, was in hand.[130] And as early as the first week of the conflict the PPU's postbag revealed 'two views': the 'humanitarian'—a significantly more positive label than 'alternativist', the term used in the First World War—and the 'absolutist'.[131] From October 1939, when the first wartime batch of conscientious objectors registered (comprising 2.2 per cent of those called up, the highest proportion in any batch of conscripts in Britain's history), it was clear that the former was by far the more popular. Indeed, whereas the NCF had favoured the absolutist position, its equivalent in the Second World War, the Central Board for Conscientious Objectors, insisted: 'So far from pressing men to take the absolutist position . . . we should never encourage anyone to claim an exemption beyond the minimum which his inner compulsion can accept.'[132] Unlike the quarrelsome NCF, moreover, the Central Board 'worked with the most complete harmony' that its chairman, Brockway, had 'ever known'.[133]

Humanitarian objectors were mostly 'Plowman' pacifists, and absolutists mostly 'politicals'. War deepened this long-standing cleavage to such an extent that a member of the PPU soon warned of the 'danger of the division between "absolutists" and "humanitarian" pacifists becoming acute'.[134] At its meeting on 18 September the PPU's national council tried to be even-handed, creating a Pacifist Service Bureau to meet 'the demand of members for opportunities of service to their fellows, under pacifist auspices', yet deciding that the PPU should also work at 'bringing the war to an end'.[135] But the division

---

[129] Percy Bartlett, in Friends' Peace Committee, *Friends of International Peace* (1925), 29.
[130] L. Smith, *Pacifists in Action: The Experience of the Friends Ambulance Unit in the Second World War* (York, 1998), 4–6.
[131] *PN* (8 Sept. 1939), 1. [132] CBCO, *Bulletin*, 25 (Mar. 1942), 3.
[133] F. Brockway, *Outside the Right: A Sequel to 'Inside the Left'* (1963), 26.
[134] A. Lewis (letter), in *PN* (22 Sept. 1939), 7. [135] *PN* (22 Sept. 1939), 6.

became ever more apparent as pacifists had to decide whether to campaign in support of Hitler's peace offer of 6 October 1939 and objectors had to decide whether to accept non-combatant or civilian service. By November, the PPU official David Spreckley was offering a perceptive analysis of the two camps:

The first group regards this war as the inevitable outcome of a thoroughly immoral order of society . . . This war, then, is but a boil on a diseased body politic . . . To this first group the war is incidental: the varying degrees to which they will or will not compromise with the war machine is unimportant . . . They argue, logically, that one cannot escape the war machine, so why quibble? . . . The second group feel that their principal duty now is to Stop the War, the war time equivalent of renouncing war being to denounce it. . . The extremists of the first group either tend to become monastic . . . or else they throw themselves so wholeheartedly into ambulance work, & c., that they become a definite help to the war machine. Their opposite numbers, realizing that the stopping of this war is a question of immediate politics, have . . . descended to the depths of present day politics, using an expediency and small-talk argument in their scramble for peace. The result is misunderstanding and some questionable allies.[136]

The outlook of the first group was exemplified by Vera Brittain, who insisted: 'Great qualities, such as consistent pacifism requires, are slow growers in both individuals and nations.'[137] With the approval of both the PPU and the FoR, she expounded her message in a 'Letter to Peace-Lovers', sent to private subscribers from 4 October 1939 to the end of the war.[138] It was also given organizational expression by the formation in November of a Forethought Committee—a strongly Christian group which resembled a reconstituted meeting of Sponsors—within the PPU. In January 1940, moreover, the Methodist minister Henry Carter launched the forerunner of what with the support of the Council of Christian Pacifist Groups soon became the Christian Pacifist Forestry and Land Units: this organization was to provide work and opportunities for social service for 1,392 Christian objectors during the course of the war.[139] That this first group was in a majority was shown by the fact that on 28 January 1940 the PPU's national council adopted four 'affirmations' as optional glosses on the pledge: these placed emphasis on 'the integrity of the individual', a 'right relationship with others', an 'apprehension of the increasing power of the existing social order to destroy the

---

[136] *PN* (10 Nov. 1939), 9.

[137] *PN* (8 Sept. 1939), 3.

[138] Berry and Bostridge, *Vera Brittain*, 386–9. A selection has been published as *Testament of a Peace Lover: Letters from Vera Brittain*, ed. W. and A. Eden-Green (1988).

[139] L. Maclachlan, *C.P.F.L.U.: A Short History of the Christian Pacifist Forestry and Land Units* (1952), 27.

individual', and 'creative and constructive action in the face of existing circumstances'.[140]

The second group was typified by Barclay, who insisted: 'The only sane thing to say at this mad moment is "STOP THE WAR!" '.[141] Another exemplar was Andrew Stewart, who contested a by-election in Stirlingshire East and Clackmannan on 13 October 1939 on behalf of the PPU and the Scottish Anti-War Council, though his failure to poll more than 1,060 votes (6.3 per cent) provided 'a cold douche to pacifists everywhere', as *Peace News* admitted.[142] The PPU's political pacifists launched a Women's Peace Campaign under Sybil Morrison's direction following a meeting at Central Hall, Westminster, on 16 December.[143] They also formed a Forward Movement to press their own approach in competition with that of the Forethought Committee. Some political pacifists were, as Brittain later complained, 'belligerent pacifists . . . incorrigible minoritarians with a passion for unpopularity' who felt 'that the sole source of their sincerity is the extent to which they can embarrass the government'.[144] Some, moreover, acquired the 'questionable allies' mentioned by Spreckley: for example, on 13 February 1940 Morris attended a private meeting with the founders of The Link and the British Council for Christian Settlement in Europe to promote Tavistock's peace proposals; and PPU members constituted an estimated 40 per cent of the audience at the public meeting organized by the latter body on 3 April.[145] The fact that political pacifists were understood to be a minority must explain why they did not bring the PPU more into disrepute.

In addition to experiencing this acute cleavage, the PPU was embarrassed by Morris's resignation from the chairmanship.[146] This was mainly because of his impending divorce, although there was in any case a wish to separate the representative position of chairman from the functional one of general secretary, which he retained. The damage to the PPU caused by Morris's personal circumstances was limited by the willingness of the highly respected Cambridge don Alex Wood to take over the chairmanship in January 1940.[147]

Despite these difficulties, the PPU's membership made modest but steady

---

[140] I am grateful to Jan Melichar of the PPU for checking this date for me. The affirmations appeared in full in S. Morrison, *I Renounce War: The Story of the Peace Pledge Union* (1962), 101–2.

[141] *PN* (22 Sept. 1939), 6.   [142] *PN* (20 Oct. 1939), 9.

[143] *PN* (22 Dec. 1939), 5.

[144] V. Brittain, *Humiliation with Honour* (1942), 49. See also Ceadel, *Pacifism in Britain 1914–1945*, 303–4.

[145] Griffiths, *Patriotism Perverted*, 201, 208, 225.

[146] Minutes, PPU executive committee, 18 Nov. 1939.

[147] Minutes, PPU national council, 21 Jan. 1940.

progress during the phoney war, peaking at 136,000 in April 1940. However, a sufficient number of these wartime recruits were suspected of joining in order to improve their credentials as conscientious objectors for a reader of *Peace News* to warn other 'long-standing members of the Peace Pledge Union to show tolerance towards newcomers. They are not necessarily using the PPU as a cloak to get out of it.'[148] *Peace News* was also a beneficiary of the phoney war, building up its print run to 42,000 copies.[149]

For supporters of the war, as well as some opponents, the dominant peace aim was a federation, which—as was widely remarked upon[150]—enjoyed the same support during the early years of the Second World War that a league of nations had during the First. In October 1939 George Catlin, a political scientist with a serious interest in internationalism who had previously supported the LNU, now hailed federalism as

one of the few constructive ideas that have emerged since the fading out of collective security . . . Federal Union meets the constructive demand for law and order. It meets the old revolutionary demand for 'the withering away of the state'. It meets the pacifist demand that war must be abolished as uncompromisingly as slavery.[151]

On 8 November 1939 the Labour leader, Attlee asserted: 'Europe must federate or perish.[152] (This was to be much quoted back at him when as post-war Prime Minister he refused to respond to the federal initiatives of Jean Monnet and others.) The left-Labour paper *Tribune* admitted that 'most of us' wanted 'a federation of all the countries of Europe', provided that it had the right economic system.[153] The support of 'a large body of pacifists' for federal union was acknowledged by a reader of *Peace News*; and a member of a local FoR group in Bradford reported that federalism was 'taking hold of the imagination' of many of its members.[154] Joad, who had for years claimed to be in favour of a genuinely international organization, 'jumped at' Federal Union, admitting later that 'during those first few months of the war when the tide was running so strongly with us', he sometimes permitted himself 'to think that a Federation might emerge from the war'.[155]

Admittedly, Communists and fellow-travellers maintained an implacable

---

148 *PN* (20 Oct. 1939), 9.
149 *PN* (17 Nov. 1939), 2.
150 W. B. Curry, *The Case for Federal Union* (1939), 119; J. Strachey, *Federalism or Socialism?* 7; H. G. Wells, *The Rights of Man or What are We Fighting For?* (1940), 11; Harris, *99 Gower Street*, 129.
151 *Peace* (Oct. 1939), 39.
152 Cited in K. Harris, *Attlee* (1982), 168.
153 *Tribune* (10 Nov. 1939), 1.
154 *PN* (15 Dec. 1939), 8. Dorothy Gill to C. J. Cadoux, 8 Feb. 1940: Cadoux Papers.
155 *Federal Union News* (June 1944), 1–2.

objection to a scheme which professed 'to offer permanent peace without Socialism', in the words of a pamphlet published in 1940 by D. N. Pritt, a barrister who was expelled from the Labour Party in March of that year for endorsing the Soviet Union's attack on Finland.[156] Moreover, some liberals continued to have doubts about the practicality of Federal Union's thinking: J. A. Spender protested at the legalist fallacy whereby intellectuals produced 'paper constitutions . . . apparently supposing that they have only to make them logical and water-tight and consistent to make them work';[157] and Wells remained disdainful of 'the magic word "Federation" ', attempting to focus public discussion on 'the rights of man' instead.[158]

Yet progressives generally accepted Beveridge's view, put forward in February 1940 in the first of a series of 'Federal Tracts', that, when faced with a choice 'between Utopia and Hell',[159] one should try for the former. In consequence, at the outbreak of war, 'support for Federal Union changed abruptly from a mere polite interest into an active desire to help the movement', as Kimber acknowledged.[160] Being himself a conscientious objector, unlike the vast majority of his Federal Union colleagues, Kimber had particular reasons to hope that a 'peace movement which has hitherto been divided between pacifist and sanctionist could unite in support of Federal Union'.[161]

Kimber's association was at the peak of its influence. After briefly being evacuated to Kimber's country home at Lulworth Cove on the declaration of war, it returned to London and grew rapidly. It was boosted by a periodical, *Federal Union News*, which appeared from 5 September 1939 under Kimber's editorship; by a Streit-influenced 'Penguin special', *The Case for Federal Union*, written by the headmaster of Dartington School, W. B. Curry, in the last months of peace, which sold 100,000 copies in six months during the phoney war; and by its Federal Tracts. It established a Research Department—after March 1940 a Research Institute—in Oxford under Ransome's direction: its expert committees included Harold Wilson (the future Prime Minister), Evan Durbin (a rising Labour politician who was to die prematurely), Roy Harrod, Friedrich von Hayek, and Lionel Robbins (all celebrated economists), as well as Beveridge, who hosted a series of conferences in the Master's Lodgings during 1939–41.[162] But perhaps the best indicator of the association's fashionability during the early months of the war even among

---

[156] D. N. Pritt, *Federal Illusion* (1940), 10.
[157] Spender to W. Harris, 28 Jan. 1940 (copy): Spender Papers Add. MSS 46395.
[158] Wells, *The Rights of Man or What are We Fighting For?*, 11.
[159] Sir W. Beveridge, *Peace by Federation?* (Federal Union, 1940), 31.
[160] 'CDK draft for F[ederal] U[nion] N[ews], not used, Dec. 10, 1939': Federal Union papers.
[161] *Peace* (Dec. 1939), 56.
[162] Federal Union Research Institute, *First Annual Report 1939–40* (1940).

the previously apolitical was the establishment of a Federal Union club in central London by Robert Byron, an old Etonian, travel writer, and sometime friend of Evelyn Waugh. On 24–5 February 1940, by which time Federal Union claimed 263 branches and 10,000 members, it held its first delegate conference, elected its first national council, and committed itself to employ five full-time salaried officials.[163]

Federalist thought had subtly altered since the outbreak of war. With the United States not 'yet ready to take her place alongside European nations in establishing the reign of law and order', as Lord Davies put it,[164] and with Britain and France being military allies and even taking the 'first steps towards an economic union' in Duncan Wilson's words,[165] it became less globalist and Atlanticist in its focus and more regional and European. This made it more acceptable to some of its critics. While reiterating his view that Streit's proposals were 'fantastic and dangerous', Cecil accepted that there might be 'some kind of closer union between European states'.[166] Similarly, Angell, though still loyal to the LNU, wanted to 'build up a real federal unity with France; to make of the French and British Empires a unit'[167]—a suggestion which anticipated Churchill's offer of union with France, made in a last effort to keep that country fighting, on 16 June 1940. The LNU itself attached great significance to its own meeting with its French counterpart on 9 March. Moreover, European federalism, which John Strachey came to call 'the second version of Federal Union',[168] acquired its own Streit-equivalents when W. Ivor Jennings, a distinguished constitutional lawyer, and R. W. G. ('Kim') Mackay, a solicitor raised in Australia who became a Labour MP, both drafted blueprints for a federation of western Europe.[169]

The New Commonwealth Society had its thunder stolen by the popularity of Federal Union, and was able to issue its periodical only intermittently. The LNU, which left its 'large and costly office' at 15 Grosvenor Gardens for more modest premises at 60 St Martin's Lane on the outbreak of war,[170] was also thrown onto the back foot. It still felt obliged to mute its reservations about federalism, this time for fear of 'destroying the great force of peace at

---

163 Mayne *et al.*, *Federal Union*, 17–18, 24–5.
164 *New Commonwealth* (Feb. 1940), 5.
165 Chaning-Pearce (ed.), *Federal Union*, 56.
166 Cecil to Murray, 26 Sept. 1939: Murray Papers.
167 N. Angell, *For What Do We Fight?* (1939), 269.
168 Strachey, *Federalism or Socialism?*, 43.
169 W. I. Jennings, *A Federation for Western Europe* (Cambridge, 1940). R. W .G. Mackay, *Federal Europe: Being the Case for European Federation Together with a Draft Constitution of a United States of Europe* (1940). See also Lord Davies, *A Federated Europe* (1940), which was also published at this time.
170 *HW* (Oct. 1939), 3.

a time of almost complete darkness as to the future', in Murray's words.[171] It therefore acknowledged 'the important psychological change' which had made federalism more appealing than its own more modest programme, and invited Kimber to meet its executive committee; but it drew the line at issuing a joint statement of peace aims with Federal Union.[172]

BRITAIN ALONE, MAY 1940–JUNE 1941

The phoney war ended with Hitler's successful onslaught on western Europe, starting with Norway and Denmark on 9 April. Winston Churchill became Prime Minister of a new coalition government, which included Labour, on the day of German's attack on the Low Countries, 10 May. The British Expeditionary Force was evacuated from Dunkirk between 29 May and 3 June. France received a last-ditch offer of union with Britain on 16 June, but made peace with Germany instead six days later. Hitler prepared an invasion of Britain in July, and mounted an aerial bombardment of London and other British cities from September 1940 to May 1941.

The blitz exacerbated the peace movement's organizational difficulties: for example, the Council of Christian Pacifist Groups, the Embassies of Reconciliation, and the FoR's international organization lost their records when the building they shared was wrecked by a bomb.[173] (Admittedly, for the WIL, being 'bombed out' of 55 Gower Street and forced to operate from private houses and borrowed offices proved a blessing in disguise, because it reduced rental outlay.[174]) Not only collecting subscriptions and holding public meetings but even bringing small groups together became problematical. Cecil and Kathleen D. Courtney both missed the same session of the LNU's executive committee because they had to attend to the bomb damage at their respective homes.[175] And a member of the FoR walked out early from a local group meeting, during which 'the gun-fire was going all the time and we could hear the bombs dropping', because she 'couldn't stand it any longer', only to be faced with a long and dangerous walk home because the 'trains and buses had stopped'.[176]

The military emergency caused government and public to harden their previously tolerant attitudes towards the peace and anti-war movements. On

[171] *HW* (Dec. 1939), 5–6.
[172] Minutes, LNU executive, 23 Nov. 1939, 11 Jan. 1940.
[173] On 16 Apr. 1941: see Wallis, *Valiant for Peace*, 140.
[174] WIL, *25th Yearly Report, Mar. 1940–Mar. 1941*, 11.
[175] Minutes, LNU executive, 9 Nov. 1940.
[176] D. Gill to C. J. Cadoux, 18 Dec. 1940: Cadoux Papers.

22 and 25 April, the police collected evidence that the PPU was displaying the poster 'WAR WILL CEASE WHEN MEN REFUSE TO FIGHT. WHAT ARE *YOU* GOING TO DO ABOUT IT?'; on the day of Lansbury's funeral— he had died on 7 May—Barclay, Morris, Rowntree, Wood, and two local activists were brought to court; and on 6 June they were fined. It was a sign of how seriously the government had taken the case that, exceptionally, both the Attorney General and the Director of Public Prosecutions had appeared in Bow Street Magistrates' Court to press the charges. The defendants had been very conciliatory, admitting that the two-year-old poster should not have been reprinted because it was inappropriate to wartime conditions.[177]

Moreover, on 22 May the government interned almost all the leading fascists and anti-Semites who had opposed the war, including Beckett, Greene, and Mosley; and although the British Union of Fascists now called on its followers to resist invasion, it was declared illegal on 10 July.[178] The government also denied Brittain an exit visa to visit the United States, whereas it positively encouraged Angell, a reliable supporter of the war, do so.[179] Because of the blitz, moreover, it made fire-watching compulsory in urban areas with effect from January 1941, and, insisting that this was a wholly civilian activity, did not offer a conscience clause: 475 absolutists were to be prosecuted for resisting such compulsion.[180]

Tribunals were generally believed to have toughened their attitude towards objectors when the phoney war ended. The BBC, which had allowed Leyton Richards to broadcast a pacifist sermon on 11 February, banned pacifists from the microphone on 6 June.[181] In addition, many local authorities and private firms sacked their pacifist employees: for example, it was in the summer of 1940 that a London telephone-rentals firm dismissed John Ure, whose pacifist views it had previously tolerated even though he had refused any part in the company's lucrative work on munitions-related contracts, because he would not relinquish the secretaryship of the PPU's Putney group.[182] And the National Association of Wholesale Newsagents stopped handling *Peace News*.

Britain's military ordeal confirmed defencists in their pessimistic philosophy of international relations. In a book 'written in great part . . . during the

[177] PPU, *Pacifists at Bow Street: A Full Report of Proceedings Under the Defence Regulations Against Officers and Members of the Peace Pledge Union May–June 1940* (1940).

[178] R. Thurlow, *Fascism in Britain: A History, 1918–1985* (1987), 198.

[179] Bennett, 'Testament of a Minority in Wartime', fo. 189. F. R. Jewell, 'Sir Norman Angell: The World War II Years, 1940–1945', Ed.D. thesis (Ball State University, 1975), fo. 5.

[180] Barker, *Conscience, Government and War*, 109

[181] K. M. Wolfe, *The Churches and the British Broadcasting Corporation 1922–1956: The Politics of Broadcast Religion* (1984), 178, 181–3.

[182] Information from the J. and P. Ure Papers, in the possession of Ms J. Ure.

bombardment of London', the philosopher R. G. Collingwood insisted: 'The Yahoo is always with us; that is why hopes for the abolition of war are vain.'[183] It also increased the commitment of *pacificists* to the war effort. Federal Union acknowledged that the military setbacks had persuaded 'a growing body of opinion' that the conflict was 'one of principle';[184] And most socialists took for granted that a 'people's war' was now being fought.

One *pacificist* who abandoned his reservations at this time was John Strachey, who signalled his rejection of the Communist line in the *New Statesman* on 27 April.[185] Having previously regarded the 'Imperialist' character of the Second World War as 'decisive', Strachey now argued that 'this inter-Imperialist aspect of the struggle was subsidiary to the necessity to prevent a Nazi world-conquest'.[186] He thereby embarked on the process of conversion into an orthodox Labour politician which after a decade had transformed the ex-treasurer of the British Anti-War Movement into the British Minister for War—responsible, ironically, for resistance to the Communist invasion of South Korea in 1950.

Although the Communist Party was not yet prepared to abandon its opposition to the conflict, it further toned it down. In June it began calling for a people's government in Britain on the grounds that this would lead the German workers to overthrow Hitler and make peace.[187] And in July it launched a new front organization, the People's Vigilance Committee, which in addition to demanding a more left-wing government called for friendship with the Soviet Union and better living standards, but said little about the war.[188] This policy of prudence won support from those denied a more orthodox outlet for their wartime grievances by Labour's participation in Churchill's coalition. When therefore a People's Convention was held in London on 12 January 1941—switched from Manchester after the Free Trade Hall was bombed—it attracted the surprisingly large total of 2,234 delegates. However, many of these later felt they had been duped. For example, the actor Michael Redgrave, a socialist, discovered that the Convention had been controlled by Communists and was therefore linked with revolutionary defeatism only when the BBC dropped him for taking part in it.[189] And the future television scriptwriter Ted Willis, an activist in the Labour Party's

---

[183] R. G. Collingwood, *The New Leviathan or Man, Society, Civilization and Barbarism* (Oxford, 1942), pp. v, 241.

[184] 'Draft Report No. 1' [Nov. 1940]: Federal Union papers.

[185] Thomas, *John Strachey*, 190–7.

[186] J. Strachey, *A Faith to Fight For* (1941), 121.

[187] Branson, *History of the Communist Party of Great Britain 1927–1941*, 288–91.

[188] D. N. Pritt, *A Call to the People: A Manifesto of the People's Vigilance Committee* (People's Vigilance Committee, n.d. [c. Aug. 1940]).

[189] M. Redgrave, *In my Mind's Eye: An Autobiography* (1983), 135–41.

League of Youth who had joined the army, later described his decision to make a speech to the Convention as 'almost the only political decision in my life which I regret'.[190] The government responded to the success of the Convention by immediately banning the Communist newspaper *Daily Worker*.

For pacifists the late spring and summer of 1940 were a uniquely testing time. Admittedly, Corder Catchpool persuaded himself that the fall of France was to be welcomed for reducing the number of nations at war, telling an astonished fellow Quaker on 22 June: 'This is the happiest day of my life.'[191] But most pacifists were alarmed by the military situation: Vera Brittain thought an attempted invasion 'almost certain'.[192] With the security of the British Isles more obviously in jeopardy than ever before, they could not escape the truth articulated by Horace G. Alexander: 'Refusal of the weapons of war means that we are prepared to see England under foreign domination . . .'[193] Some of them discovered that they had all along been isolationists rather than non-resisters. In May 1940, therefore, the PPU for the first time lost more members than it gained. Mumford, Storm Jameson, and Russell resigned as Sponsors; other leading pacifists, including Joad, Macaulay, and A. A. Milne, made highly publicized recantations;[194] and 'a drastic reduction of staff' at Dick Sheppard House became necessary.[195] The rate of conscientious objection dipped sharply, falling below 1 per cent for the first time in June 1940.

Even so, while acknowledging that 'this possibility of military defeat . . . has come as a terrible shock to so many people', Murry argued that the real surprise was 'not that so many but that so few have recanted'.[196] He took over the editorship of *Peace News*, which built up its own distribution network and survived the war. The PPU avoided collapse, still having 98,414 pledges in its 'live' file in the summer of 1945.[197] The offsetting of defections from pacifism by continued loyalty to it was exemplified by the responses to the fall of France of two close friends who were later to become notable literary scholars: Frank Kermode withdrew his claim for conscientious objection and joined the Royal Navy; but his fellow PPU member Peter Ure (younger brother of the secretary of the Putney PPU whose loss of his job at this time has been mentioned) sustained his to the

---

[190] T. Willis, *Whatever Happened to Tom Mix? The Story of one of my Lives* (1970), 192–3.
[191] F. R. Davies, *Some Blessed Hope: Memoirs of a Next-to-Nobody* (Lewes, 1996), 34.
[192] Brittain, *Wartime Chronicle*, 43 (entry for 21 May 1940).
[193] *Friend* (30 Aug. 1940), 505.
[194] Ceadel, *Pacifism in Britain 1914–1945*, 296–7.
[195] *PN* (7 June 1940), 2.   [196] *PN* (14 June 1940), 3.
[197] Morrison, *I Renounce War*, 62.

extent of twice going to prison.[198] The FoR even managed a small net expansion every year—including 1940, despite a record number of resignations—and ended the war with 12,902 members.[199]

A further sign of pacifism's refusal to buckle in the face of defections was that it remained the official policy of the Women's Co-operative Guild and ~~WIL~~ became that of the WIL. The former had long been controlled by a pacifist leadership which had no difficulty in having its 'traditional' policy reaffirmed at the guild's diamond jubilee congress.[200] The latter was obliged by the 'critical and insistent' military situation of 1940 to resolve its long-standing ideological ambivalence. At the start of July Dr Clark, the leader of the WIL's *pacificists*, insisted that it was 'no longer possible to evade an attitude to the resistance of the German attack' and claimed that the executive committee should endorse armed opposition to Hitler because: 'Absolute pacifism . . . was never the basis of the W.I.L.' She was supported by Mary Sheepshanks, the daughter of an evangelical bishop and a long-standing Christian pacifist who now reluctantly concluded: 'Our freedom is as important as peace.' However, the pacifist chairwoman, Mrs Harris, ruled that in specifying that 'war is a crime' the WIL's objects made support of the military effort impossible. Dr Clark retorted that the league 'had failed for a long time to distinguish between the crime of an aggressor entering into war and the crime of defence' and argued that the latter was much less serious.[201] Two months later, she insisted on a showdown, on the grounds that 'the absolute pacifist position applied to politics' was disastrous, and that 'the sloppy sentimentality in some people and the selfishness in others' had been responsible for 'the appeasement front'. This time she also received support from former NCF organizer Catherine Marshall; but their efforts to overturn Mrs Harris's previous ruling were defeated by eight votes to five.[202] Clark resigned from the WIL, as eventually did Sheepshanks and Royden, whereas Mrs Harris remained in the chair until 1946 when she was promoted to the presidency. Thus pacifists won control of a weakened though still durable association.

One of these pacifists, Kathleen Innes, shrewdly observed that the 'difficulties of the W.I.L. largely arose from the fact that it did not adopt the—in a

---

[198] F. Kermode, *Not Entitled: A Memoir* (1996), 69–70. F. Kermode, 'Peter Ure, 1919–1969', in C. J. Rawson (ed.), *Yeats and Anglo-Irish Literature: Critical Essays by Peter Ure* (Liverpool, 1974), 1–39. J. and P. Ure Papers.

[199] Figures were given monthly in the General Council minutes.

[200] As was noted with pleasure in *PN* (9 July 1943), 4.

[201] Minutes, WIL executive, 3 July 1940.

[202] Minutes, WIL executive, 4 Sept. 1940. This vote runs counter to the claim by Sheepshanks's biographer that 'most of her colleagues in the WIL' shared her renunciation of pacifism: see S. Oldfield, *Spinsters of this Parish: The Life and Times of F. M. Mayor and Mary Sheepshanks* (1940), 285.

sense—easier, and strictly logical path of complete non-resistance, but sought ways of overcoming evil by a positive policy'.[203] She was aware that the pessimistic orientation was now less vulnerable to criticism than the optimistic one. Indeed, many of those who remained pacifists were willing to admit that in political terms the war was justified. One was C. J. Cadoux, who had previously seemed confident in his absolutism: in 1934, for example, he had warned his sons—who were to serve, as conscientious objectors, in the Friends' Ambulance Unit during the Second World War—that those adopting his interpretation of Christianity 'must, if needful, face martyrdom';[204] and he had not only continued to be active in the FoR but had supported the Oxford University Pacifist Association. However, conscious that the government was 'treating Pacifists very fairly' and thereby making it hard for them 'to follow the logical non-possumus attitude', as a pacifist acquaintance put it,[205] Cadoux spent the first nine months of the war writing a book which argued that British intervention was 'relatively justified' and therefore better 'victoriously carried through' than 'discontinued before the undertaking is completed'.[206] Just as many pacifists had once been prepared to support League of Nations sanctions as a step in the right direction, he was prepared to adopt a collaborative orientation towards the war effort. Cadoux's book was ready in June, but, despite its major intellectual concession to pro-war opinion, was held back by its publisher until September, on account of the military emergency.[207]

Understandably, many pacifists suffered from acute self-doubts at this time. Maurice Rowntree warned his colleagues: 'Until we have proved ourselves ready to make sacrifices as great as, or even greater than, [the armed forces] are making we should be extremely modest in our manner of advocating the truth we see.'[208] Such doubts would have been worse had it not been for the blitz, which not only provided conscientious objectors with an opportunity for social service but enabled them to claim, as Brittain did in her 'Letter to Peace-Lovers' of 2 January 1941, that the opponent of the war was 'as liable as its most convinced advocate to the loss of his home, the breakup of his family, and the death or injury by aerial bombardment of those whom he loves best'.[209]

The crisis of 1940 posed particular problems for political pacifists. It

---

[203] Minutes, WIL executive, 6 Nov., 10 Dec. 1940, 5 Mar. 1941, 4 Mar. 1942.
[204] Cited in Kaye, *C. J. Cadoux*, 167.
[205] E. Whittaker to Mrs Cadoux, 26 Feb. 1940: Cadoux Papers.
[206] C. J. Cadoux, *Christian Pacifism Re-Examined* (Oxford, 1940), 216.
[207] Kaye, *C.J. Cadoux*, 167.
[208] *PN* (14 June 1940), 1.
[209] *Testament of a Peace Lover*, 59–60.

brought the Women's Peace Campaign to a halt, Sybil Morrison acknowledging late in April that the invasion of Scandinavia had 'made it much more difficult to approach people about signing an appeal for negotiations because opinion is hardening against the pacifist'.[210] And it ensured the supremacy of the pessimistic orientation within the PPU. On 1 July an official statement acknowledged that 'there is no immediate political action' which the union could presently take', and that its priority would therefore be to help its members cope with 'a sense of isolation from society'.[211] On 18–19 July the Forethought Committee concluded that, although 'the cessation of war upon ignominious terms, or from motives which we condemn, would be preferable to a prolongation of the war', it would not be 'a veritable peace'. The committee further insisted that 'the idea of "a technique of non-violent resistance" is apt to be misleading. Gandhi has not produced some cut-and-dried method resisting armed invasion which the PPU is refusing to employ, as some criticisms would suggest.'[212]

Furthermore, the blitz increased the attraction of social service even among political pacifists. When the Forward Movement assembled 350 members at the Conway Hall in London on 10 November 1940, the majority opinion seemed to be that PPU members should undertake relief work whilst simultaneously trying to publicize their case against the war.[213] By the spring of 1941 Roy Walker thought it 'clear to everyone that we have cut down public work almost to nothing and widened our social service work'.[214] Even so, a minority felt obliged to keep agitating for a negotiated peace. For example, Morris did so by standing at a by-election in the King's Norton division of Birmingham on 8 May 1941, though this was in Donald Soper's view 'a mistake'.[215] He received only a fractionally larger percentage of the vote (6.3 per cent) than Andrew Stewart had nineteen months previously.

For the LNU, already shaken by the popularity of Federal Union, the blitz exacerbated a crisis of morale. At the general council in June 1940 'a few fainthearts ... wondered whether any useful purpose would be served' by such a meeting; and by the autumn a larger number of members were querying whether there was 'any point in carrying on'.[216] By the end of the year, when it was apparent that a further 45 per cent of subscriptions had been lost, *Headway* noted that 'the demands of war service, the black-out, and the bombing naturally make it extremely difficult to keep a movement such as ours in good health'.[217] Early in 1941 its leadership decided that a reconstructed League of Nations should have an 'inner ring' consisting of 'the few

---

[210] *PN* (26 Apr. 1940), 1.   [211] *PN* (5 July 1940), 1.   [212] *PN* (2 Aug. 1940), 3.
[213] *PN* (27 Nov. 1940), 4.   [214] *PN* (14 Mar. 1941), 2.
[215] Brittain, *Wartime Chronicle,* 84 (entry for 2 May 1941).
[216] *HW* (July 1940), 2; (Nov. 1940), 8.   [217] *HW* (Dec. 1940), 11.

powerful nations who are willing to accept the responsibility attached to their strength for maintaining the peace of the world', but was aware that such a concession to realists did nothing to counteract 'the flight to federalism' among idealists.[218] The only boost to the LNU's morale in this period was Churchill's prompt and gracious acceptance of an honorary presidency on his appointment as Prime Minister.

By contrast, Federal Union's ambitious thinking was initially rendered more plausible by Churchill's offer of Anglo-French Union on 16 June 1940 and the collapse of several European states. Alluding to Streit's book, Strachey noted in the late summer of 1940: 'The Nazis have made a union of Western Europe, and they have made it now.' And, dropping his previous reservations about federalism along with his Communism, he now argued that 'the Fall of France has made it clear that the day of the independent, completely sovereign, nation-state is over'.[219] Similarly, Davies called for the creation of 'a European Federal Council' made up of the national leaders who found themselves exiled to London.[220]

However, with western Europe unable to liberate itself and the United States starting to supply Britain from September 1940, the Atlanticist strand of federalism revived and mounted a challenge to Europeanism. During the spring of 1941 Streit wrote a second book, *Union Now with Britain*, which called for an immediate union of the English-speaking democracies, with provision for other states to join after the war. In addition to this ideological divergence, Federal Union faced financial problems. As it had grown in size, apparently to 12,000 members at its peak, its inexperienced organizers had overcommitted themselves by employing a staff of twenty. When the blitz made it hard for the association to retain its support, it ran into debt. It sent out 8,000 circulars asking members to make a special donation of £1 each, but received only 850 contributions (and only 472 normal subscriptions) by December 1940.[221] The association was saved from bankruptcy only by Mackay, who drastically pruned the staff and, to protect its executive committee from financial liability, converted Federal Union into a company limited by guarantee with effect from January 1941. It rebuilt its membership to 2,000 by the spring, but was no longer being swept effortlessly along on a current of uncritical public support.

[218] *HP* (Apr. 1941), 2; (May 1941), 13,
[219] Strachey, *Federalism or Socialism?*, 8, 10.
[220] *New Commonwealth* (Oct. 1940), 34.
[221] Mayne *et al.*, *Federal Union*, 30–2. Minutes, FU executive, 10 Dec. 1940.

FROM ALLIANCE TO VICTORY, JUNE 1941–AUGUST 1945

Germany's invasion of the Soviet Union on 22 June and Japan's bombardment of Pearl Harbour on 7 December 1941 turned the future superpowers
into Britain's allies. Despite continued military setbacks for a while, particularly in the Far East, the acquisition of allies against Hitler inexorably turned
the tide of the war. Before the end of 1942 the British public had begun to
anticipate victory: the remarkable enthusiasm with which it greeted the publication on 1 December of *Social Insurance and Allied Services*, a dry official
report by Beveridge, indicated that it was already thinking ahead to a new
social order. The peace movement's predicament was thus greater than in the
First World War: there was to be no repeat of the war-weariness which had
helped it in 1917; and domestic reform was increasingly to distract attention
from the peace question. Even after it became apparent that the United States
and Britain favoured a reformed version of the League of Nations, to be called
the United Nations, a decision for which the peace movement deserves some
credit,[222] there was much less internationalist enthusiasm than during
1917–18.

Predictably, Hitler's incursion into Russia prompted the Communists to
endorse the war effort wholeheartedly.[223] The LNU immediately recognized
this as 'good news for the youth movement', which, having been exhorted to
'forget past differences',[224] was rapidly reconstituted. Significantly, however,
there was no talk, even from Cecil, of reviving the IPC.

Only the ILP was left officially favouring war resistance. Ideological
purism being by now its sole *raison d'être*, it felt unable to abandon this position but promoted it an increasingly desultory fashion. For example, when
Brockway stood at by-elections in December 1941 and April 1942 he 'did not
come out for "Stop the War" ' but merely urged that 'the war be ended by a
people's revolution across the frontiers and not by military victory'.[225]

Hitler's onslaught on the Soviet Union even discouraged some members of
the PPU from calling for an immediate peace on the grounds that this would
now be at the expense of a socialist state.[226] Mary Gamble, the pacifist
activist who was to become Murry's third wife, claimed late in the summer of
1941 that whereas 'six months ago, certainly a year ago' the vast majority of
PPU members would have supported 'an offer of peace' from Hitler, this was

---

[222] As is argued by Lynch, *Beyond Appeasement*, ch. 7.

[223] J. Hinton, 'Killing the People's Convention: A Letter from Palme Dutt to Harry Pollitt',
Bulletin of the Society for the Study of Labour History, 39 (Autumn 1979), 27–32.

[224] *HW* (Aug. 1941), 16.

[225] Brockway, *Outside the Right*, 31.

[226] *PN* (29 Aug. 1941), 3.

'not so today'—a development she found 'disturbing'.[227] Moreover, even those pacifists who accepted that their faith required them always to prefer peace to war became more critical of 'glib and all-too-reassuring talk of the possibility of attaining the sort of peace we all instinctively desire by *any* sort of conference between *any* sort of statesmen, backed by *any* sort of public opinion now', as Stewart put it.[228] Spreckley concluded that the PPU should not call for peace negotiations unless it was also prepared to renounce imperial and social exploitation: he therefore not only resigned from the national council on the grounds that it was 'worse that useless for a movement to say: "Stop the War—negotiate now," unless it has an agreed policy which goes far beyond that' but even suggested that the union be wound up so that 'those who realize the implications of their pledge would be freed from those who don't'.[229] A major discussion at the PPU's national council in the autumn of 1941 accepted that, although 'any kind of negotiation is better than none', it was not then prudent 'to campaign on it'.[230] In July 1942 even the committee set up to consider an armistice campaign decided that this would 'require more agreement than is possible in the Union at the moment'.[231]

A further sign of a declining belief in the practicality of pacifism was the decision of the Congregationalist minister A. D. Belden to promote it in an 'ultimate' as distinct from 'immediate' form: he called for Christians to register a willingness to renounce war 'when called upon by the Churches to do so'; and for that purpose attempted in 1942 to start a League of Ultimate-Pacifism.[232] As left-wing sentiment gained ground, moreover, an increasing number of pacifists became reluctant to 'press for an armistice if it would not result in a "socialist peace" '.[233] The apolitical approach thus grew more dominant than ever, despite the fact that Plowman, its most committed exponent, had died suddenly in June 1941. By the summer of 1942 a member who diagnosed the PPU as suffering from a 'split personality'—split, that is, between those who 'would have it a semi-religious body, founding fellowship' and those who 'envisage it as an incipient political party, founding "cells" '—was in no doubt that 'the former are in the majority'.[234] And early the following year Sybil Morrison, herself still anxious for an armistice campaign, admitted that 'few pacifists, if any' believed that 'stopping the war' was feasible.[235]

[227] *PN* (22 Aug. 1941), 3.
[228] *PN* (11 July 1941), 2: for very similar opinions from Murry and Walker, see *PN* (10 Oct. 1941), 1, 3.
[229] *PN* (11 July 1941), 4.   [230] *PN* (17 Oct. 1941), 1.
[231] Cited in Bennett, 'Testament of a Minority in Wartime', fo. 316.
[232] A. D. Belden, *Pax Christi: The Peace of Christ* (1942), 65, 71.
[233] *PN* (9 Oct. 1942). 3.   [234] *PN* (31 July 1942), 3.
[235] *PN* (29 Jan. 1943), 3.

However, a minority was as willing as ever to advocate a deal with Hitler. Tavistock, who had inherited the dukedom of Bedford from his father in August 1940, believed that Hitler's trust could be won. Confident that 'God in His mercy has given me some share of His own divine understanding', he interpreted the German Führer as 'an "untested" man of mixed attributes whom it is neither necessary, sensible nor right to quarrel with until he has been tested by the one test which is worth anything, that of wise, practical, genuine friendliness'.[236] The new Duke of Bedford was also prepared candidly to invoke 'the very serious provocation which many Jews have given by their avarice and arrogance when exploiting Germany's financial difficulties, by their associations with commercialized vice, and by their monopolization of certain professions' as a justification for Hitler's aggressiveness.[237] Despite—or perhaps because of—these views he not only had his articles published regularly in *Peace News* but was elected to the PPU's national council in 1943 (being renominated in 1944, moreover, though he declined to stand again).

Although most PPU members probably conceded that an immediate peace would 'be a fascist peace', they were committed by their pacifism to preferring this to 'a fascist war'.[238] The PPU's annual general meeting in April 1943 therefore endorsed an armistice campaign by 1,410 to 759 in a card vote. However, it did so only after incorporating a reference to the four affirmations 'in order that there should be no misinterpretation of our motives and that the movement should not be associated with any elements which may desire peace from ulterior motives'.[239] And in practice, despite the best efforts of Sybil Morrison who chaired it, the armistice campaign committee, relabelled the negotiated peace committee in the autumn of 1943, experienced 'ever present and growing hindrance' even from PPU members and in practice produced 'little campaigning'.[240] When the renewal of the campaign was proposed at the 1944 annual general meeting, Morrison warned: 'Unless the movement was prepared to work harder it should vote against the resolution.' This it duly did,[241] thereby belatedly abandoning the pretence of campaigning against the war effort.

The pacifist movement thus had energy to spare for its internal problems. In June 1942 it dismissed its hearty but inefficient local organizer after five and a half years of service. This prompted many protests: for example,

---

[236] *PN* (31 Oct.1941), 1.
[237] *PN* (30 October 1942), 1; see also (17 Dec. 1943), 2; (21 Apr. 1944), 1).
[238] *PN* (25 Dec. 1942), 3.
[239] *PN* (7 May 1943), 4.
[240] *PN* (24 Sept. 1943), 3; (31 Dec. 1943), 3.
[241] *PN* (28 Apr. 1944), 6.

Spreckley called for his reinstatement, though he had resigned from the PPU and admitted having found Barclay's 'boundless optimism . . . too much' whilst working alongside him in Dick Sheppard House. After 'endless discussion' at the executive committee, which vexed Brittain, Barclay was later found a job on *Peace News*.[242] The PPU also faced financial difficulties over outstanding bank loans on its new headquarters, but these were satisfactorily resolved by November 1942.[243]

A much more worrying problem occurred just before Christmas 1942, when Morris, who had also been active in the Indian Freedom Campaign, was arrested along with a civil servant who had been supplying him with secret details about how Britain would respond to a serious challenge to its position in India. The PPU's executive committee panicked, holding an emergency meeting at 'Maurice Rowntree's house in a room without a telephone and the doors and windows shut' for fear of governmental surveillance, and initially suspecting that Morris had been the victim of an *agent provocateur*. When it realized that Morris was guilty as charged and faced imprisonment for nine months, it voted by seventeen votes to thirteen to accept his resignation. After a number of PPU members complained, the executive committee decided to refer the issue to the national council, thereby causing Alex Wood to resign as chairman, though he agreed to continue when the national council finally decided in April 1943 that Morris had to go.[244] (In 1946, however, he was to return to the post and serve until 1964.)

The new general secretary, who was to serve only three years, was the Revd Patrick Figgis, who had been a peace candidate at a by-election the previous year. He was himself a cause of internal controversy: as already noted, his Congregationalist conscience started off a controversy about the private lives of PPU employees which led the PPU's joint treasurers to resign. Maurice Rowntree stepped into the breach; but in August 1944 he died in a blackout-induced accident while attending a PPU summer school.[245] Corder Catchpool became treasurer in his place, despite his record as an apologist for Germany.

Communal living gave rise to additional disputes among pacifists, particularly where the need for agricultural productivity conflicted with the anarchical life styles of many conscientious objectors. The pacifist writer Ronald Duncan's farm community, set up shortly before the war, had already failed

---

[242] *PN* (15 June 1942), 3; (25 Sept. 1942), 3; (9 July 1943), 3. Bishop and Bennett (eds.), *Wartime Chronicle*, 158 (entry for 30 June 1942).

[243] *PN* (24 July 1942), 1; (6 Nov. 1942), 1.

[244] Brittain, *Wartime Chronicle*, 200–1, 204, 209, 218, 226 (entries for 22 Dec. 1942, 5 and 23 Jan., 5 Mar., 10 Apr. 1943).

[245] S. Smith, *Spiceland Quaker Training Centre: Cups without Saucers* (York, 1990), 216–17.

by the autumn of 1942 when Murry embarked on his own, similarly disillu-sioning, experiment.[246] As Maurice Rowntree commented sagely, pacifists were 'bitten by the idea of community, yet our individualism persists in stick-ing out at every odd corner, and some of these are very odd'.[247] Explicitly religious groups, such as the Christian Pacifist Forestry and Land Units and the Friends' Ambulance Unit, suffered least from such angularity.

By the last phase of the war pacifist morale was at a low ebb. C. Paul Glid-don of the Anglican Pacifist Fellowship wondered in 1943 if the movement 'has passed its zenith and is now entering into the familiar period of decline'.[248] The following year Murry not only bemoaned the lack of 'a simple form of pacifist action, such as existed in 1914–18, in the refusal of conscription and the acquiescence in imprisonment for the duration', but also claimed that a 'quick victory is now the best hope of a quick end to this massive suffering'. Predictably this prompted one pacifist to argue: 'Unless we are hypocrites we cannot hope for a victory without refusing to fight for it', and Corder Catchpool to make clear: 'I cannot pray for an Anglo-Ameri-can victory, not even for a quick one.'[249] Many pacifists found their greatest satisfaction in activity that was not exclusively pacifist, such as the food relief campaign, to which Roy Walker in particular devoted himself, and the Bomb-ing Restriction Committee, which was founded by Corder Catchpool in April 1942 and in which a number of absolutists felt able to collaborate, in Brit-tain's words, 'with the more humanitarian supporters of "legitimate" war, such as the Bishop of Chichester and Professor Stanley Jevons'.[250] The conscientious-objection rate continued to slide, so that by the end of the war only 0.2 per cent of conscripts—less than a tenth of the proportion at the start of the war—were taking this stand. It seems that many pacifists lapsed quietly from their faith rather than recanting volubly as in 1940. Early in 1945 the PPU admitted that it was in touch with at most 19,000 of its supporters, and that only 2,000 of these worked actively on its behalf.[251]

Pacificist associations fared somewhat better as the tide of the war turned. Federal Union managed to collect more subscriptions in the easier, post-blitz conditions, its membership recovering to 4,500 by 1944. Even so, the 'People's Poll for a People's Peace' which it launched late in 1942 proved a

---

[246] They described their experiences in R. Duncan, *Journal of a Husbandman* (1944), and J. M. Murry, *Community Farm* (1952).

[247] *PN* (17 Dec. 1943), 3.

[248] Cited in Wallis, *Valiant for Peace*, 143.

[249] *PN* (24 Mar. 1944), 2; (9 June 1944), 1; (23 June 1944), 2; (30 June 1944), 3..

[250] Brittain, *Testament of a Peace Lover*, 199 (newsletter for 1 June 1944). Bennett, 'Testa-ment of a Minority in Wartime', fos. 326–40. See also V. Brittain, *Seeds of Chaos: What Mass Bombing Really Means* (1944).

[251] *PN* (16 Feb.1945), 3; (30 Mar.1945), 3.

flop; and a round table which it tried to hold in Oxford a year later had to be abandoned because few of the invited participants were prepared to attend. The association's founders departed: Ransome resigned as a director in 1942; Rawnsley, who had joined the Royal Air Force, was killed in 1943; and Kimber withdrew early in 1944, having obtained his tribunal's permission to set up as a market gardener.[252] From the mid-point of the war the organization's most active figure was Miss F. L. ('Jo') Josephy, a Young Liberal whose interest in the peace movement dated back to the mid-1930s[253] and who chaired the board of directors with great vivacity from August 1941 onwards.

Ideologically, Federal Union suffered further fragmentation. It still attracted Europeanists, including Josephy, who called for 'a federation of the whole of Europe up to the borders of the Soviet Union'.[254] After the United States entered the war, Atlanticism revived: one of its leading advocates was Catlin, who dismissed European federation as 'secondary and contingent'.[255] In addition, with the Soviet Union bearing the brunt of the land war, an all-inclusive federalism attracted support. A prominent exponent was the Scottish nutritionist Sir John Boyd Orr, who claimed:

Since the United States entered the War, the idea of a British and United States English-speaking federation has been canvassed. This looks too much like the British Empire writ large with its capital transferred to Washington. There is much to be said for an English-speaking federation, but a federation which leaves out the U.S.S.R. and the great Asiatic nations will have little hope of maintaining world peace . . . Some form of world government has become a necessity.[256]

Similarly, Wells believed that it would 'be far easier to create a United States of the World . . . than to get together the so-called continent of Europe into any sort of unity'.[257] And Henry Usborne, after the war a Labour MP and founder of the Crusade for World Government, committed himself to this cause.[258] LNU supporters responded to calls for a world federation by noting: 'Whatever attraction this scheme may have for the theorist, it has little basis in practical politics.'[259] Some world federalists therefore suggested that it could be achieved organically, through an extension of the practical services

---

[252] Interview with Sir C. Kimber, 28 July 1977.

[253] e.g. she had attended the 1936 National Peace Congress: see NPC, *Annual Report for the Year Ending Apr. 1936*, 5.

[254] F. L. Josephy, *Europe: The Key to Peace* (Federal Union, n.d. [1944]), 16.

[255] G. Catlin, *One Anglo-American Nation* (1941), 31.

[256] Sir J. Orr, *Fighting for What?* (1942), 17.

[257] H. G. Wells, *The Outlook for Homo Sapiens* (1942), 224.

[258] *Federal Union News* (May 1944), 14.

[259] *HW* (Nov. 1943), 10.

already provided by international agreement in a world made increasingly interdependent by scientific progress. Orr argued that developments in finance, trade, health control, postal systems, science, the arts, and sport were 'already phases of a world government', though he also suggested that the winning side in the war would 'become the world government'.[260] A Romanian-born lecturer at the London School of Economics, David Mitrany, systematized a theory of 'functionalism', which established itself a distinct strand within Federal Union.[261]

A further source of ideological differentiation arose from the new primacy of domestic politics which followed the publication of the Beveridge Report. Ironically in view of the fact that it was one of Federal Union's early enthusiasts whose work had done much to bring this about, progressive opinion largely switched its attention from federalism to social reform. Mackay became active in Common Wealth, a party which acted as a surrogate for Labour during the electoral truce; and in December 1942 Attlee and Bevin asked that their names be withdrawn from Federal Union's notepaper.[262] During 1943–4 it became 'a common experience at a Federal Union meeting' to have 'a Labour man' in the audience accuse the organization of 'dragging a red herring across the plain Socialist trail'.[263] To pre-empt this objection, a 'Federal Union Plus' faction developed which wished to graft social welfare or even overt socialism onto the federalist programme. Its leaders were Wootton, who had long claimed that 'socialism and federation are complementary parts of the same whole', and Philip Edwards, an Anglican curate who had served as Federal Union's membership secretary during its heyday of 1939–40.[264]

Further intellectual fragmentation occurred in the form of demands for imperial federation and even British federation as starting-points.[265] In 1942 Federal Union resolved that world federation was the ultimate goal but that it should not commit itself to any particular 'nucleus federation'. Because of mounting discontent with this wait-and-see policy, it was reconsidered at an emergency general meeting on 15–16 January 1944. A majority of the 150

[260] Orr, *Fighting for Peace?*, 18.

[261] D. Mitrany, *A Working Peace System: An Argument for the Functional Development of World Organisation* (1943): a clear analysis of his views is provided by C. Navari, 'David Mitrany and International Functionalism', in Long and Wilson (eds.), *Thinkers of the Twenty Years' Crisis*, 214–46. See also J. A. Joyce (ed.), *World Organization—Federal or Functional?: A Round-Table Discussion* (1945).

[262] Minutes, FU directors, 4 Dec. 1942.

[263] J. S. Hoyland, *Federate or Perish* (1944), 178.

[264] B. Wootton, *Socialism and Federation* (Federal Union, 1941), 28. *Federal Union News* (Jan. 1945), 17. Interview with Sir C. Kimber, 28 July 1977.

[265] *Federal Union News* (Jan. 1944), 14; (June 1945), 15–16.

members present wanted to make an interim commitment; but because they held 'mutually incompatible opinions as to just which countries should or should not be included', Federal Union decided to remain on the fence, a decision which caused Kimber, Ransome, Margaret Richards, and Wootton to resign. It was not until 21 April 1945 that Federal Union's national council belatedly endorsed 'a Democratic Federation of European countries as a first step to ultimate world federation'.[266]

Whereas Kimber had resigned because he had concluded Federal Union should become an educational body only, Wootton had done so because she believed 'nothing short of world federation' was 'worth working for', whilst none the less accepting that it was 'unattainable as part of the peace settlement'.[267] Both understood that Federal Union had been weakened not only by fragmentation but by the steady fading of the near-apocalyptic hopes which had arisen during the most anxious phase of the war. With the allies moving towards victory, a restoration of the pre-war system of states became more likely than its replacement. The LNU's Kathleen D. Courtney was one of those emphasizing that this was what the defeated countries wanted: 'Invaded, occupied, tortured as they are, their first desire is to re-establish their own national identity—their "nationhood," as it is described by President Benes.'[268] And even Beveridge, once a European federalist and still strongly attracted to world federalism, settled for 'a system of compulsory arbitration' rather than 'a World-State'.[269] As was to be noted in an analysis of opinion on this issue commissioned by the New Commonwealth Society after the war: 'Hopes of a radical change in attitude at the world leadership level, of a continuing sense of national and international purpose extending into peace, ran high in the dark days of 1940–41. After that they weakened steadily.'[270]

An important cause of this weakening was that the United States sought a liberal but not a federal world order, as had been apparent when Roosevelt and Churchill signed the Atlantic Charter on 14 August 1941. This document was insufficiently internationalist even for non-federalists, its lack of 'a definite repudiation of the central proposal of the Nazi philosophy—the uncontrolled sovereignty of the State' being criticized by Cecil.[271] Admittedly, Churchill's appetite for supranationalist gestures, already apparent in his acceptance of the presidency of the New Commonwealth Society and his

[266] *Federal Union News* (Feb. 1944), 10–11; (June 1944), 11; (June 1945), 13.
[267] *Federal Union News* (June 1944), 11
[268] *HW* (Nov. 1943), 10.
[269] Sir W. Beveridge, *The Price of Peace* (1945), 62.
[270] Mass Observation, *Peace and the Public* (1947), 10.
[271] *HW* (Sept. 1941), 1–2.

offer of union to France, acted as a countervailing influence for a while: a statement he made in Washington on 15 June 1943 about a post-war international organization was described by an alarmed British official as 'a mixture of Cripps and Lord Davies'.[272] The death of Lord Davies in 1944 further weakened the movement for a fundamental reform of the international system.

This emergence of more modest internationalist goals vindicated the LNU's long-standing scepticism about the likelihood of fundamental change. As a contributor to *Headway* had argued in the autumn of 1941: 'This talk about the end of little States is not only nonsense but dangerous nonsense. It is the precise opposite of the facts. Victory must bring freedom and independence to the small nations. We have sworn it in the Atlantic Charter.'[273] This had not been what most internationalists had then wanted to hear; and that year's recruitment of new subscribers proved to be, at 1,190, the lowest ever, overall membership falling sharply from 100,088 to 69,354.

In 1942 the LNU still felt itself to be on the defensive. During the spring of that year, for example, its pre-war record suddenly came under attack from speakers 'who appeared to reflect the views of the Government' and alleged that the LNU 'had brought about unilateral disarmament and was therefore responsible for the present state of affairs'.[274] Like the allegation, which Churchill himself was to endorse, that the 'King and Country' debate had encouraged Hitler,[275] this was political scapegoating on the part of Conservatives embarrassed about their support for Neville Chamberlain and appeasement. However, Cecil had partly brought it upon himself when he had told the general council in December 1941 of his 'regret' that 'in the early days of the League' he 'did not sufficiently emphasize' the need for force.[276] It would have been more prudent for him to have followed the example of the perpetually doubt-free Noel Baker, who had told the previous meeting of the general that 'the main lesson of the past is that . . . the "appeasers", pacifists, Communists and so-called realists were wrong and that we were right'.[277] By the time of the Beveridge Report, moreover, the LNU faced pressure to espouse a left-wing domestic programme which was incompatible with its all-party tradition. At the second general council of 1942 Cecil robustly refused to turn 'the

---

[272] P. A. Reynolds and E. J. Hughes, *The Historian as Diplomat: Charles Kingsley Webster and the United Nations 1939–1946* (1976), 20.

[273] *HW* (Nov. 1941), 1–2.

[274] Minutes, LNU executive, 19 Mar., 2, 16 and 30 Apr. 1942. See also *HW* (July 1942), 1.

[275] W. S. Churchill, *The Second World War*, i. *The Gathering Storm* (1948), 66–7, 131. For a full discussion of this charge and the lack of evidence in its support, see Ceadel, 'The "King and Country" Debate, 1933', 397–9, 419–22.

[276] Minutes, LNU general council, 10–11 Dec. 1941 (fo. 7).

[277] Minutes, LNU general council, 26–7 June 1941 (fo. 43).

L.N.U. into an organization for general reform', and insisted that its duty was to remove the principal obstacle to any social improvement, namely war.[278] And Zilliacus was obliged to defend himself and other socialists against the charge of proposing that the LNU adopt 'technically unsound and vastly bold' domestic policies.[279]

It was in the summer of 1943 that the LNU began to rediscover some of its optimism. In June Kathleen D. Courtney told the general council: 'We are not a back number. We are a present number, and we mean to be a future number.'[280] By the autumn she was emphasizing that the 'ideological basis popularized by Mr Clarence Streit . . . has receded somewhat into the background'.[281] And at the December meeting of the general council Murray emphasized the 'immense rise' in the LNU's fortunes which had taken place since the final session of the League of Nations which he had attended four years to the day previously.[282] Although the LNU was conscious of ageing, and had lost Freshwater to a heart attack after a day in the office and an evening in the Home Guard,[283] it believed that it was starting to win back some of the generation it had lost to federalism: indeed, a journalist commented on the fact that 'the average age of the audience' at the December 1943 general council was 'twenty years younger' than usual.[284]

In 1944 the LNU benefited from the congruence between its own thinking and the United Nations Organization which the wartime allies were planning to create. Its rate of decline slowed significantly as it attracted 2,402 new subscribers in that year, making 53,032 in all, and planned to relaunch itself as the United Nations Association. Cecil, who was cheered by Churchill's warm tribute to him on his eightieth birthday, would have preferred to call it the 'Society for the International Organization of Peace', so as not to 'focus people's minds of any particular form of organization'[285]—an indication of prescient doubts about the capacity of the United Nations itself to arouse enthusiasm. In public, however, the LNU put a brave face on current international realities. For example, it accepted that the Polish frontier had to be where the Soviet Union wanted it to be, causing Corder Catchpool to complain of unfairness to the Germans.[286] Despite some misgivings about the veto power, it put a favourable gloss on the Dumbarton Oaks proposals, hailing them as evidence that 'the Great

[278] *HW* (Dec. 1942), 3.
[279] Minutes, LNU executive, 10 Dec. 1942.
[280] *HW* (July 1943), 4.
[281] *HW* (Nov. 1943), 10.
[282] Minutes, LNU general council 9 Dec. 1937 (fo. 1): LNU papers.
[283] *HW* (Aug. 1943), 1.
[284] *HW* (Jan. 1944), 1.
[285] Minutes, LNU executive, 23 Nov. 1944.
[286] *HW* (Sept. 1944), 13.

Powers were putting forward a Charter along the lines of the Covenant and in a spirit exactly like the Covenant'.[287] And Cecil sent a message to his 'old comrades' which boasted: 'We have striven for a revolution in international relations and all our main principals [sic] have been accepted.'[288]

The LNU thus played down the weaknesses of the United Nations just as it had played down those of the League of Nations twenty-five years previously. Other peace associations were much more critical: for example, the National Peace Council, which had held regular 'Peace Aims Conferences', normally at St Hilda's College, Oxford, throughout the war, suspected that it would prove little more than a revived Concert of Europe.[289] However, there was no repeat of progressive opinion's worries about the post-war settlement which the UDC had mobilized at the end of the previous conflict. Indeed, the National Petition for a Constructive Peace, which the National Peace Council launched in the spring of 1944, secured only 85,000 signatures instead of 'at least a million' as had been hoped.[290] Rather than hostility there was apathy. Murray was to tell the LNU's last major gathering that, whereas 1919 had seen 'a great wave of enthusiasm and much scepticism', in 1945 there was 'no enthusiasm but little opposition'.[291]

The two-and-a-half years between the turning of the military tide and final victory had seen a steady erosion of international (as distinct from domestic) idealism, of which the lack of excitement about a United Nations was but one symptom. As the war ended, this disillusion was exacerbated by three major shocks.

The first was the discovery of the Holocaust in the spring of 1945 which falsified the view to which Murry had clung in 1940: 'Personally I don't believe that a Hitlerian Europe would be quite so terrible as most people believe it would be.'[292] As early as December 1942 reports of Nazi maltreatment of Polish Jews began appearing in the press. Brittain, who believed that 'Jewish suffering has been extended by war' and could have been greatly limited even by 'the worst peace', thought these reports 'more and more fantastic' and recorded her husband's theory that they were appearing in order to subdue the public and thereby discourage it 'from spending much money' over the Christmas period.[293] Murry argued that 'a great generous offer of asylum would make it hard even for Hitler to reject it';[294] but most pacifists simply avoided the subject.

---

[287] *HW* (Jan. 1945), 3.
[288] *HW* (May 1945), 3.
[289] *Peace* (Oct.–Dec. 1944), 1.
[290] *PN* (27 Oct. 1944), 1; (27 Apr. 1945), 1.
[291] *HW* (Oct. 1945), 3.
[292] *PN* (9 Aug. 1940), 1.
[293] Brittain, *Wartime Chronicle*, 198, 200 (entries for 11 and 20 Dec.1942).
[294] Ibid. 200 (entry for 20 Dec. 1942). *PN* (1 Jan. 1943), 2.

When in the final weeks of the war this could no longer be done, Corder Catchpool wondered privately to Brittain 'whether the revelation of conditions in the Camps has not come as a godsend to our authorities just at this juncture, and that the most is being made of them', though he admitted that the revelations had to be believed and could not be condoned.[295] Brittain agreed, suggesting in her letter to peace-lovers of 3 May 1945 that the camps were being publicized 'partly, at least, in order to divert attention from the havoc produced in German cities by Allied obliteration bombing'.[296] And Soper and others tried to argue that 'Auschwitz was produced by the war', in the sense that it was only after the conflict began that Hitler embarked on the Holocaust.[297]

Such suggestions created a bad impression. *Peace News* felt obliged to deny 'the assumption . . . that pacifists are, as a body, sceptical of the full depth of Nazi depravity'.[298] There was no disguising the fact that the discovery of the Holocaust had dealt pacifism a devastating blow. In addition, after Germany's surrender on 7 May it suffered from the same psychological letdown it had experienced in the immediate aftermath of the Crimean and First World Wars. When soon after the war Murry repudiated the PPU in order to 'enter the political era', he did so in scathing terms: 'The disintegration of the pacifist movement (which I have witnessed at close quarters) has been a significant and creative process. Much *soi-disant* "conscience" has been revealed by it as retarded moral development; much as ignominious self-preservation.'[299]

The second major shock was the dropping of atomic bombs on the cities of Hiroshima and Nagasaki on 6 and 9 August, thereby causing Japan to sue for peace on 14 August. Though the significance of this revolution in the technology of war was immediately understood, the use of nuclear weapons received little initial criticism. Even Victor Gollancz, who had once described himself as a pacifist 'to the point of extreme bitterness', defended the use of the atomic bomb in the context of 'a just, defensive war'.[300] Referring to the pen-name under which he had written many of his contributions to *Peace News*, Murry admitted within days of Japan's surrender: 'The atomic bomb has scattered among other things Observer's wits'; and he identified the possible need to threaten the Soviet Union with nuclear attack 'for the sake of

---

[295] C. Catchpool to Brittain, 25 Apr. 1945, cited in Bennett, 'Testament of a Minority in Wartime', fo. 323.
[296] Brittain, *Testament of a Peace Lover*, 254.
[297] Cited in Purcell, *Odd Man Out*, 136.
[298] *PN* (4 May 1945), 2.
[299] J. M. Murry, *The Free Society* (1948), 160. This book was completed in 1947.
[300] R. Dudley Edwards, *Victor Gollancz: A Biography* (1987), 207, 405.

world-peace' if it attempted to manufacture its own nuclear weapons rather than join 'a world organization'.[301]

The third exacerbating factor was the rapid onset of the cold war. In October 1945 Murry was to tell a peace meeting: 'Visibly the United Nations are not united; we suspected that years ago. To the short-term vision the prospects of future peace look about as black as human imagination can conceive. That would have been so, even without the spectre of the atomic bomb.'[302] In the same month Russell suggested that a crusade might be needed to force the Soviet Union into confederation of nations, a position he sustained, despite subsequent denials, for at least three years, as did Murry.[303] The United Nations Association, which built the LNU's 46,607 subscribers of 1945 into 87,000 by mid-1947, found work thereafter 'unbelievably difficult'[304] because of the cold war. As a result, its sustainable membership proved to be not more than about 60,000. Federalism found it less easy than in 1939–40 to benefit from the difficulties of confederalism: its world-government strand was as damaged by the cold war as the United Nations was; and its European strand turned increasingly into a campaign for a regional bloc. Belief in the possibility of a profound reform of the international system as a whole had been seriously weakened.

The peace movement had improvised enterprisingly by mounting a federalist campaign in the aftermath of the Prague crisis when neither peaceful change nor collective security offered much prospect of preventing war. During the Second World War, it showed tenacity in dealing with unprecedented organizational difficulties. However, its ideas had generally fared badly. Pacifism, as Murry put it in June 1945, 'assumes an irreducible minimum of human decency ... which no longer exists'.[305] *Pacificism* required a degree of reformist optimism but faced 'majority passivity' instead, as a post-war survey soon pointed out in the particular context of attitudes to the United Nations.[306]

---

[301] *PN* (17 Aug. 1945), 1, 4.
[302] J. M. Murry, *The Third Challenge* (NPC Peace Aims pamphlet, 3; 1945), 3.
[303] See Ceadel, *Thinking about Peace and War*, 52–3.
[304] United Nations Association, *Annual Report 1947*, 3.
[305] *HP* (22 June 1945), 2.
[306] Mass Observation, *Peace and the Public*, 44.

12

Conclusion

By the end of the Second World War the British peace movement had lost a little of its detachment, Vera Brittain observing during the blitz: 'Our island is no longer a detached unscarred participant, sharing in the conflict only through the adventures of masculine youth.'[1] Its idealism had also abated somewhat, Murry commenting at the beginning of 1945: 'As the war draws on to its uncertain end, a black fog of disillusion, cynicism and gloom settles over the whole world.'[2] Even so, its sense of special mission remained undiminished: in 1958 CND was to be launched with the expectation that, if Britain renounced nuclear weapons, other countries would 'follow our moral lead'—an assumption which A. J. P. Taylor was later to describe as a 'last splutter of imperial pride'.[3]

By 1945 the Crimean War seemed a remote era. It had of course slipped beyond the reach of personal memory, though Joseph Sturge's daughter Sophia had remained an indomitable pacifist until her death aged 87 in 1936, the year which also saw the decease of the last surviving founder of the Workmen's Peace Association in 1870,[4] and Cecil H. Wilson, who just outlasted the Second World War, traced his own 'out-and-out pacifism . . . back to the bombardment of Alexandria by the British fleet in 1882'[5] when Henry Richard had still been leading the peace movement. It was also outside the scope of institutional memory ever since the demise of the Peace Society.

But although the peace movement's major reconstruction in 1914–15 had marked a significant break in its organizational continuity, it had been exploring the same intellectual agenda throughout the 1854–1945 period. Above all, it had been continuously posing two questions. Might not reforms of domestic politics or interstate relations be achievable which would eventually abolish war? Might not an absolutist rejection of war bring about this abolition more directly?

---

[1] V. Brittain, *England's Hour* (1941), p. xiii.   [2] *PN* (5 Jan. 1945), 1.
[3] A. J. P. Taylor, 'Accident Prone, or What Happened Next', *Historical Journal*, 49 (1977), 1-18 at 13.
[4] Hughes, *Sophia Sturge*, 179. *Arbitrator* (Oct./Nov. 1936), 43.
[5] *PN* (13 Nov. 1937), 9.

After at least ninety years, however, this agenda had worn thin. For example, liberal *pacificists* had explored a succession of strategies for curbing the irrational preoccupation with national or state prestige which since at least the 1840s they had identified as the cause of war. But after suggesting free trade, arbitration, confederalism, and federalism, they had become aware how deeply rooted nationalism and state sovereignty were. Similarly, radicals had discovered the limitations of democratic control as a panacea; socialists were already less confident than formerly that the abolition of capitalism was the solution to the problem of war; and pacifists had been brought up short by the 'evidences of demonic evil' to which the clerk of the London Yearly Meeting of the Society of Friends drew the attention of members in May 1945.[6]

Defencism therefore still reigned supreme. Admittedly, it faced a new and major difficulty: how to define a role for nuclear weapons, whose destructiveness threatened not only a potential aggressor but also the country supposedly being defended. This difficulty for defencism was to stimulate two phases of significant CND activity, in 1958–64 and 1980–83;[7] but these were notable for being challenges to a particular weapon rather than to defencism as an ideology. Moreover, they constituted the only vigorous and sustained peace-related activism seen in Britain between the end of the Second World War and the end of the twentieth century.

Yet although neither structural reform nor moral revolution seemed any closer in 1945 than it had in 1854, there had over the intervening period been significant intellectual change. Warfare had forfeited respect as an institution, to the extent that major war—other than in a defensive last resort—was believed by some to be on the way to obsolescence.[8] The resort to armed force had been subjected to legal constraints by the League of Nations Covenant, the Kellogg–Briand pact, and the United Nations Charter. Militarism had disappeared, except at an individualistic level where a cult of the guerrilla warrior was briefly to appear in the 1960s.[9] Crusading had been much diminished, despite Murry's and Russell's conversion to it in 1945 and the increased calls for humanitarian intervention which were to come after the end of the cold war. In addition, defencism had made significant concessions. It had accepted not only conscientious objection but the need for an international organization with greater legitimacy than a concert of great powers.

[6] Maude Brayshaw, epistle to London Yearly Meeting, 23 May 1945: *Friend* (25 May 1945), 321.

[7] See R. Taylor, *Against the Bomb: The British Peace Movement 1958-1965* (Oxford, 1988). P. Byrne, *The Campaign for Nuclear Disarmament* (1988). A. Mattoo, 'The Campaign for Nuclear Disarmament: A Study of its Re-emergence, Growth and Decline in the 1980s', D.Phil. thesis (Oxford University, 1992).

[8] J. Mueller, *Retreat from Doomsday: The Obsolescence of Major War* (1989).

[9] Ceadel, *Thinking about Peace and War*, 42.

Thus although the United Nations aroused 'nothing like the same enthusiasm' as the League of Nations, as Murray admitted to Lytton's widow in 1955, this was 'largely because it is now an accepted idea and no one is against it'.[10]

These changes had largely occurred for three reasons unconnected with peace activism. First, the powerful ideas of nationalism and democracy had combined to create a widespread belief that in principle there was a legitimate international order, arranged into nation-states and grounded upon popular consent. Military aggression might very occasionally be justified in giving a more complete expression to this order, but never in subverting it. Second, economic, social, and political progress had made the fruits of peace more attractive, at least in advanced states, than those to be expected from conquest. Third, developments in military technology had raised the costs of war dangerously high.

Yet the peace movement had made a contribution too. For example, it was not only the much greater apprehension about the damage to be expected from war which explains why the visits by Lansbury, Allen, and others to Germany in the late 1930s provoked less criticism than that of Sturge, Charleton, and Pease to Russia in 1854. Successive goodwill initiatives, such as those by J. Allen Baker and W. H. Dickinson which resulted in the creation of the World Alliance for Promoting International Friendship Through the Churches in 1914, had made them more acceptable. Politically, too, the movement had enjoyed moments of real importance: for example, in 1857 Cobden's outrage at the *Arrow* war had been crucial in forcing Palmerston into a general election; in 1878 the WPA had demonstrated through its Workmen's National Anti-War and Arbitration Conference of 10 April that working-class support for jingoistic intervention could not be taken for granted; during the First World War Angell, G. L. Dickinson, and others had helped to set President Wilson's internationalist agenda; and in 1934–5 the LNU's Peace Ballot had affected the government's tactics during the Abyssinia crisis. Although its influence as a pressure group should not be exaggerated, it had established itself as a player in the political game.

In addition, the primary and secondary associations had chipped away at the social obstacles to *pacificism* and pacifism. The economic and philanthropic contribution of the Quakers had done something to overcome society's instinctive feeling that conscientious objectors were parasites. The Nonconformist denominations had done much to spread values that were conducive to a questioning of traditional nostrums, as also had the Liberal and Labour Parties. And both the Peace Society, in virtue of a longevity which excused its ultimate senility, and more especially the League of Nations

---

[10] Murray to Lady Lytton, 5 Oct. 1955: Lytton Papers.

Union, in virtue of a social reach which was unprecedented, had made dissent from conventional 'King and Country' chauvinism respectable.

Above all, as the pages of this book have tried to show, the peace movement had sustained a relentless intellectual conversation—normally with defencists but intermittently with crusaders and occasionally with militarists—about the causes of, and cures for, international conflict. Between the Crimean War and the Second World War, its ideological vision had been sufficiently sharp to require its interlocutors to engage with it, and in various subtle ways to adapt to it. The metaphor for the cumulative effect of the peace movement's ideological protagonism during this period that Henry Richard offered in the Peace Society's annual report for 1858-9 cannot be bettered:

The little insects that build up the beautiful islands which stud the face of the Southern seas work for ages, we are told, in the 'dark unfathomed caves of ocean,' myriads of them perishing in obscurity long before their graceful architecture even begins to peep above the surface of the waters, but each content to contribute its tiny labours to hasten on the final glittering like a gem on the bosom of the deep, crowned with verdure and fertility, and teeming with life and abundance. So it is with those who labour . . . for the accomplishment of some remote good. They may be destined to work on for generations in obscurity and contempt, conscious only that . . . they are helping, in however feeble a degree, in bringing to pass those scenes of blessedness and peace, upon which humanity, even in its darkest moments, has loved to repose in hope.[11]

[11] *HP* (June 1859), 209.

APPENDIX 1

National Peace Congresses

1904	1st	Manchester (22–3 June)
1905	2nd	Bristol (28–9 June)
1906	3rd	Birmingham (17–18 June)
1907	4th	Scarborough (27–8 June)
1908		[Universal Peace Congress in London]
1909	5th	Cardiff (29–30 June)
1910	6th	Leicester (13–15 June)
1911	7th	Edinburgh (13–15 June)
1912	8th	London (14–18 May)
1913	9th	Leeds (10–13 June)
1914	10th	Liverpool (9–12 June)
1915		[no congress]
1916		[no congress]
1917	11th	London (30–1 January)
1918	12th	London (30–1 May)
1919	13th	Manchester (25–7 June)
1920	14th	Glasgow (17–20 June)
1921	15th	Birmingham (16–19 June)
1922		[International Peace Congress in London]
1923	16th	Leeds (6–8 June)
1923	17th	London (10 November)
1924	18th	London (10–13 December)
1925	19th	Bristol (11–13 November)
1926	20th	York (11–13 November)
1927	21st	Manchester (2–3 December)
1928	22nd	London (6–7 July)
1929		[no congress]
1930		[no congress]
1931		[no congress]
1932		[no congress]
1933	23rd	Oxford (7–10 July)
1934	24th	Birmingham (22–5 July)
1935	25th	London (28 June–2 July)
1936	26th	Leeds (26–9 June)
1937	27th	London (28–31 May)
1938	28th	Bristol (27–9 May)
1939	29th	London (7–9 July)

APPENDIX 2

British Peace Associations

Anglican Pacifist Fellowship: established August 1937 by Revd C. Paul Gliddon and Revd R. H. Le Messurier. Soon acquired 400 members. Christian pacifist.

Anti-Aggression League: established by Herbert Spencer, who had first discussed it in the autumn of 1879; launched on 22 February 1882. Because of the Egyptian crisis it had collapsed by August 1882. Liberal *pacificist*.

British Anti-War Movement: established, following the World Anti-War Congress in Amsterdam, 27–9 August 1932, by Communists. It held a national congress in Bermondsey Town Hall on 4–5 March 1933, but was weakened by Labour Party ban. Renamed British Movement Against War and Fascism after the Soviet Union joined the League of Nations, it was allowed to fade away after 1935. No individual membership was reported. Socialist *pacificist*.

British Commonwealth Peace Federation: established by W. H. Ayles in 1932 after his dismissal from the No More War Movement. A pseudo-association. Ostensibly *pacificist*.

British and Foreign Arbitration Association: established in 1886 by Lewis Appleton after the non-renewal of his contract as secretary of the International Arbitration and Peace Association. A pseudo-association. Ostensibly *pacificist*.

British Neutrality Committee: established by J. A. Hobson and Graham Wallas. It sent a letter to the press on 2 August 1914; formally constituted itself on 4 August; and dissolved itself the following day. Radical *pacificist*.

Central Board of Conscientious Objectors: established 1939 as a welfare agency for objectors, run by Denis Hayes from Dick Sheppard House. Mainly pacifist.

Christian Pacifist Party: established in October 1936 by Howard Ingli James, a Baptist minister in Coventry, as a single-issue party. It had a negligible impact. Christian pacifist.

Church of England Peace League: established in 1910, and acquired about 100 members, including Canon W. L. Grane. It was apparently short-lived. *Pacificist*.

Council of Christian Pacifist Groups: established late in 1933 to coordinate the work of the denominational fellowships and the Fellowship of Reconciliation. Christian pacifist.

Crusader Group: established March 1916 by Wilfred Wellock around his magazine, originally called *New Crusader*, and backed by Theodora Wilson Wilson. It collected 558 signatures for an 'Affirmation against War', thereby helping to create the No More War Movement on 24 February 1921. Socialist (and Christian-socialist) pacifist.

Federal Union: established in November 1938 by Derek Rawnsley, Charles Kimber, and Patrick Ransome. It adopted its name in January 1939 but made progress only after the publication of Clarence K. Streit's *Union Now*. It apparently had 12,000 members at its peak in 1940, but suffered from ideological fragmentation thereafter. Liberal *pacificist*.

Fellowship of Conscientious Objectors: established in June 1939, as conscription was reintroduced, but had little public impact. Pacifist, all inspirations.

✓*Fellowship of Reconciliation*: established 28–31 December 1914 at a conference in Cambridge following an initiative by Henry Hodgkin. It held its first meeting on 13 January 1915, and had 6,983 members in 1918, though weeding reduced it to 3,000 in the 1920s. It expanded in the late 1930s, reached 9,813 members at the outbreak of war, and 12,902 by the end. Christian pacifist and quietist.

✓*Friends' Peace Committee*: established in May 1888 on the initiative of George Gillett following a Quaker conference in the United States. It was intended to bolster an ebbing peace commitment within the Society of Friends. Quaker pacifist.

Friends' Service Committee: established May 1915 to help Quakers of military age. It worked closely with the No-Conscription Fellowship, and terminated in May 1920. Quaker pacifist.

✓*International Arbitration and Peace Association*: established, after preliminary meetings beginning on 16 August 1880, as a non-absolutist body aiming to offer substantive solutions to international issues. Its founding secretary, Lewis Appleton, departed in July 1885. Its leading member was Hodgson Pratt. It moved left under the influence of J. Frederick Green, who was appointed secretary in 1886 and held that post for the rest of its existence. After hesitating for three months it supported the First World War, and thereafter became moribund, winding itself up in 1925. Liberal, later socialist, *pacificist*.

✓*International Arbitration League*: see Workmen's Peace Association.

International Crusade of Peace: launched by W. T. Stead at a public meeting on 18 December 1898 to welcome the first Hague Conference. Its provisional committee first met on 21 December. It published *War Against War!*, between 12 January and 31 March 1899, and held a National Convention on 21 March 1899. Allowed a diversity of opinions.

International Peace Campaign: British section of the Rassemblement universal pour la paix, which emerged in France late in 1935. Promoted by Cecil and Noel Baker in 1936, it was controversial on account of its Communist influence and duplication of the activities of the LNU, with which it never established a satisfactory relationship. Its British national committee decided in September 1940 to close down because of Communist obstruction. Liberal and socialist *pacificist*.

League of Free Nations Association: established on 24 June 1918 by David Davies, after failing to capture the League of Nations Society at its annual meeting ten days before. It acquired 987 members; but a merger with the League of Nations Society, under discussion from 26 July, was agreed on 10 October and resulted on 8 November 1918 in the creation of the League of Nations Union. Liberal *pacificist*.

League of Nations Society: established on 3 May 1915 (after preliminary meetings beginning on 5 February), it had 148 members by the time of its first general meeting on 29 November 1915. It held no public meeting until 14 May 1917, and had 2,230 members at the time of its merger with the League of Free Nations Association to produce the League of Nations Union on 8 November 1918. Liberal *pacificist*.

League of Nations Union: established on 8 November 1918 by combining the League of Free Nations Association and the League of Nations Society. It was led by Lord Robert Cecil and Gilbert Murray, with Maxwell Garnett as its general secretary, 1920–38. The world's largest peace association, it peaked at 406,868 annual subscriptions in 1931, which had declined to 46,607 subscribers by 1945, when it was succeeded by the United Nations Association. Liberal *pacificist*.

League of Universal Brotherhood: established on 29 July 1846 by Elihu Burritt. It claimed to have collected 10,000 pledges in Britain. Losing momentum after 1848, it merged with Peace Society in May 1857. Pacifist.

League to Abolish War: established on 18 May 1916 by F. Herbert Stead to promote a league of nations equipped with its own armed forces, but had only 170 adherents. It affiliated to the National Peace Council in the 1920s, and was still in nominal existence in 1932. Liberal *pacificist*.

National Declaration Committee: established by League of Nations Union to run the Peace Ballot of 1934–5. It met first on 11 April 1934 and concluded its work in the summer of 1935. Its principal organizer was Dame Adelaide Livingstone. Liberal *pacificist*.

National Defences Committee: established in January 1848, during a short-lived invasion scare, partly to attract Chartist and other *pacificist* support. Allowed a diversity of opinions.

National Peace Council: established on 9 February 1904 as a committee to organize a National Peace Congress at Manchester in June. It was kept in being thereafter as a National Council of Peace Societies. It acquired a full-time secretary in 1908, and met as the National Peace Council for the first time on 5 August 1908. Its function was to coordinate the peace movement, but it had an anti-sanctionist bias from the First World War onwards. From February 1924 to November 1931 it was known as the National Council for the Prevention of War. Its major venture was a petition for a new peace conference between October 1938 and March 1939, which attracted 1,062,000 signatures but was overtaken by the Prague crisis. Allowed a diversity of opinions.

Neutrality League: established on 31 July by Norman Angell with Dennis Robertson as secretary; published a manifesto on 3 August 1914. Radical *pacificist*.

New Commonwealth Society: established in October 1932 by Baron (David) Davies of Llandinam to campaign for an International Police Force and International Equity Tribunal. It had nearly 3,000 members in 1939. Liberal *pacificist*.

No-Conscription Fellowship: established by Lilla and Fenner Brockway after an appeal in the ILP weekly *Labour Leader* on 12 November 1914. It claimed a membership of 5,000 in October 1915, and after the introduction of compulsory military service in 1916 became a welfare organization for conscientious objectors, with Bertrand Russell and Catherine Marshall playing prominent roles after the original organizers were imprisoned as absolutists. It was disbanded on 29 November 1919, though some of its members helped to found the No More War Movement. Socialist pacifist.

No-Conscription League: established late 1938 because of the Peace Pledge Union's reluctance to mount a political campaign against conscription. It had little impact and was short-lived. Socialist (and Christian-socialist) pacifist.

No More War Movement: established on 24 February 1921 as the No More War International Movement by former members of the No-Conscription Fellowship and the Crusader Group. It dropped 'International' from its name in 1923 on becoming the British section of the War Resisters' International. It claimed 3,000 members at its peak, and, hit hard by the Spanish Civil War, merged with the Peace Pledge Union in February 1937. Socialist (mainly ILP) pacifist.

Northern Friends' Peace Board: established in 1913 by Robert J. Long to supplement work of the Friends' Peace Committee in the north of England. Quaker pacifist.

Parliamentary Pacifist Group: established in the summer of 1936, recruiting approximately twenty Labour MPs, plus some peers. It issued a National Manifesto for Peace and Disarmament in September, and held a number of 'pacifist conventions'. Socialist (and Christian-socialist) pacifist.

Pax: established around September 1936 for Roman Catholics by Edward Ingram Watkin. It condemned all wars 'for national ends'. Near-pacifist.

Peace Congress Committee: established 31 October 1848 to organize international congresses. It linked Richard Cobden with the Peace Society and League of Universal Brotherhood. It was renamed the Peace Conference Comittee in 1853 and acquired a Manchester offshoot in the same year which lasted until 1858. Its final meeting was on 14 October 1859. Allowed a diversity of opinions.

Peace Letter: a petition, launched in 1925 by Arthur Ponsonby, which pledged those endorsing it to 'refuse to support or render war service to any Government which resorts to arms'. It was promoted at an Albert Hall rally on 5 December 1926. On 8 December 1927 Ponsonby presented 128,770 signatures to the Prime Minister. Utilitarian pacifist.

Peace of Nations Society: established in December 1847 with the aspiration to be international. It was still in nominal existence in 1851, but had achieved very little impact. Liberal *pacificist*.

Peace Pledge Union: established 22 May 1936, a relaunch of the Sheppard Peace Movement, with a distinguished array of Sponsors, including Brittain, Huxley, Murry, and Russell. Swallowed No More War Movement in February 1937. Membership peaked at 136,000 in April 1940. Still in existence with 1,100 members but moved out of Dick Sheppard House in 1995. Humanitarian and Christian pacifist.

Peace Society (full name Society for the Promotion of Permanent and Universal Peace): established on 14 June 1816 by William Allen and Joseph Tregelles Price (after preliminary meetings beginning on 7 June 1814); steady membership, mainly Quaker, of 1,500; became moribund in First World War; last recorded meeting in July 1939. Christian pacifist, but latterly only formalistically so, and always allowed *pacificists* as rank-and-file members.

Rationalist Peace Association: established in 1910 by Hypatia Bradlaugh Bonner. A small body whose members included Norman Angell and Edward G. Smith. Mainly *pacificist*.

Sheppard Peace Movement: established at an Albert Hall meeting on 14 July 1935 called by Dick Sheppard for those who had responded to his request of 16 October 1934 for peace pledges. It was relaunched as the Peace Pledge Union in May 1936. Humanitarian and Christian pacifist.

Society for Abolishing War: established on 20 March 1816 by Unitarian publisher Sir Richard Phillips; failed to establish itself. Radical-*pacificist*.

Society for the Promotion of Permanent and Universal Peace: see Peace Society.

South Africa Conciliation Committee: established on 1 November 1899; issued a public declaration on 17 January 1900; campaigned for a just peace with the Boers; its leader was Leonard Courtney. Liberal and radical *pacificist*.

Stop-the-War League: established on 24 October 1855 by John Hamilton, F. W. Chesson, and other London radicals to oppose the Crimean War; ended operations in February 1856. Allowed a diversity of opinions.

Stop-the-War Movement: established by Silas K. Hocking and W. T. Stead to oppose the Boer War; asked for signatures on 10 November 1899; held meetings on 11 January and 24 May 1900. Issued *War Against War in South Africa* between 29 October 1899 and August 1900. Mainly radical and socialist *pacificist*.

Union of Democratic Control: established by C. P. Trevelyan, with Angell, MacDonald, Morel, who held meeting on 10 August 1914, and were joined shortly afterwards by Ponsonby. Its existence was leaked on 10 September and it announced its policy on 17 September. Claimed 100,000 members (probably an exaggeration) by end of First World War. At peak of influence in the early 1920s, but declined sharply in the second half of that decade, though it stayed in nominal existence until 1967. Isolationist. Radical *pacificist* until it fell under Communist influence in the 1930s.

United Socialist Committee: established on 31 March 1917 in response to that month's Russian revolution; dominated by the ILP and the British Socialist Party; organized the Leeds Convention on 3 June 1917. Socialist, mainly *pacificist*.

War Resisters' International: established March 1921 at The Hague under name 'Paco'; moved to Enfield and changed name in 1923, becoming a socialist-pacifist information service about conscientious objectors. Socialist pacifist.

Women's International League: established on 30 September/1 October 1915, to follow up the 27–30 April 1915 Hague conference which launched an International Committee of Women for Permanent Peace (after 1919 the Women's International League for Peace and Freedom). It soon attracted 3,000 members. It attempted to reconcile both *pacificists* and pacifists, but in 1940 the latter got the upper hand. It added 'for Peace and Freedom' to its name in 1950.

Workmen's Peace Association: established as Workmen's Peace Committee on 21 July 1870; institutionalized as Workmen's Peace Association on 10 September 1870, formally adopting its rules on 3 December 1870. Its secretary (1870–1908) was Sir Randal Cremer. It held an important Workmen's National Anti-War and Arbitration Conference on 10 April 1878. It renamed itself 'Workmen's Peace Association and International Arbitration League' on 13 October 1886 and 'International Arbitration League' on 13 June 1888. Supported the First World War; thereafter moribund, though issued publications until 1956. Merged with Mondcivitan Republic in 1963. Originally pacifist, then radical *pacificist*.

World Alliance for Promoting International Friendship Through the Churches: established 1 August 1914, having grown out of Associated Council of Churches in the British and German Empires for Fostering Friendly Relations between the Two Peoples, established in 1910 by J. Allen Baker and W. H. Dickinson. *Pacificist*.

SELECT BIBLIOGRAPHY

This is confined to works cited in the text or notes. The place of publication is given only for books not originally published in London.

PRIMARY SOURCES

Unpublished material

Archives of associations

Anglican Pacifist Fellowship: St Mary's Church House, Bayswater Road, Oxford
British and Foreign Anti-Slavery Society: Rhodes House Library, Oxford
Federal Union: in the possession of Mr O. Adler
Fellowship of Reconciliation: British Library of Political and Economic Science, London
Friends' Peace Committee: Friends' House Library, London
Friends' Service Committee: Friends' House Library, London
International Arbitration League: in the possession of Mr P. Deed
International Peace Campaign (account book): Bodleian Library, Oxford
League of Nations Union: British Library of Political and Economic Science, London
League of Nations Union Ealing and District Branch: Ealing Public Library
League of Nations Union Hampshire Federation, Southampton Branch, and Swinton and Pendlebury Branch: shown to me by Professor D. Waley
National Peace Council: British Library of Political and Economic Science, London
New Commonwealth Society: with Davies of Llandinam Papers
No More War Movement: in the possession of Mrs M. Eyles Monk
Peace Pledge Union: consulted at Dick Sheppard House, London
Peace Society (including Peace Conference Committee, Peace Congress Committee, Peace Union, and Peace Negotiations Committee): in the possession of Mr C. R. Dunnico
Union of Democratic Control: Brynmor Jones Library, Hull
Women's International League: British Library of Political and Economic Science, London

Personal papers

Adams, V.: British Library of Political and Economic Science, London
Baldwin, S.: University Library, Cambridge

Bridgeman, R.: in the possession of Mrs O. Bridgeman
Bright, J.: British Library, London
Broadhurst, H.: British Library of Political and Economic Science, London
Burritt, E.: New Britain Public Library, Connecticut
Buxton, C. R.: Rhodes House Library, Oxford
Cecil of Chelwood, Viscount: British Library, London
Cadoux, C. J.: Bodleian Library, Oxford
Chesson, F. W.: John Rylands Library, Manchester
Cobden, R.: British Library, London
Cripps, S.: Nuffield College Library, Oxford
Davies, Revd G.: with Davies of Llandinam Papers
Davies of Llandinam, Baron: National Library of Wales, Aberystwyth
Dickinson, W. H.: Bodleian Library, Oxford
Ellis, H. J.: British Library, London
Gainford, Lord (Pease, J. A.): Nuffield College Library, Oxford
Hardie, F.: Bodleian Library, Oxford
Jones, A. C.: Rhodes House Library, Oxford
Lansbury, G.: British Library of Political and Economic Science
Lytton, 2nd Earl: in the possession of Lord Cobbold
Martin, K: University of Sussex Library
Murray, G.: Bodleian Library, Oxford
Noel-Baker, P.: Churchill College, Cambridge
Plowman, M.: University College, London
Ponsonby, A.: Bodleian Library, Oxford
Richard, H.: National Library of Wales, Aberystwyth
Smith, R.: Bodleian Library, Oxford
Smith, R. A.: Friends House Library, London
Spender, J. A.: British Library, London
Sturge, J.: British Library, London
Thompson, G.: John Rylands Library, Manchester
Ure, J. and P.: in the possession of Ms J. Ure
Wilson, G.: Manchester Public Library
Woolf, L. S.: University of Sussex Library

Published material

Periodicals of peace associations

[Central Board for Conscientious Objectors] *Bulletin*
[Federal Union] *Federal Union News*
[Fellowship of Reconcilation] *Reconciliation; Christian Pacifist*
[International Arbitration and Peace Association] *International Arbitration and Peace Association Monthly Journal; Concord*
[International Arbitration League/ Workmen's Peace Association] *Arbitrator*

[International Crusade of Peace] *War Against War!*
[International Peace Bureau, Berne] *The Peace Movement*
[International Peace Campaign] *IPC Weekly Bulletin*
[League of Peace and Freedom] *The Flame*
[League of Universal Brotherhood] *Bond of Brotherhood*
[Ligue internationale de la paix et de la liberté] *États-Unis d'Europe*
[National Peace Council] *[International] Peace Year Book; News Bulletin; Monthly Circular; Peace Review; Peace*
[New Commonwealth Society] *New Commonwealth*
[No More War Movement] *No More War; New World*
[Norman Angell Movement] *War and Peace: A Norman Angell Monthly*
[Peace Pledge Union] *Peace News; Pacifist*
[Peace Society] *Herald of Peace*
[Society of Friends] *Friend; British Friend*
[Stop-the-War Movement] *War Against War in South Africa*
[Union of Democratic Control] *The U.D.C.; Foreign Affairs*
[United Nations Association] *United Nations News*
[World Alliance for the Promotion of Peace and Friendship Through the Churches] *Peacemaker*

Other periodicals

Aborigines' Friend; Adelphi; Blackfriars; British Quarterly Review; Christian Commonwealth; Colosseum; Echo; Edinburgh Review; Empire; English Republic; Essential News; Fraser's Magazine; International Affairs; Isis; Labour Leader; Labour Monthly; Listener; Manchester Examiner; Manchester Guardian; Nash's Pall Mall Magazine; New Clarion; New Leader; New Oxford Outlook; New Statesman; Nonconformist; Oldham Chronicle; Political Quarterly; Review of Reviews; Speaker; Spectator; The Times; Tribune; Truth

Other published works

A Clergyman of the Church of England, *Thoughts on the Lawfulness of War* (Philadelphia, 1796).
A Clergyman of the Church of England, *Notes from France on the War with Russia* (1855).
A Member of the Establishment, *Thoughts on the Lawfulness of War* (1796).
Alexander, H. G., *Joseph Gundry Alexander* (1920).
Allen of Hurtwood, Lord, *Britain's Political Future* (1934).
—— *Peace in our Time: An Appeal to the International Peace Conference on June 16, 1936* (1936).
Angell, N., *Europe's Optical Illusion* (1909).
—— *The Great Illusion* (1910 and Sept. 1912 edns.).
—— *Peace Theories and the Balkan War* (1912).
—— 'War as the Failure of Reason', in J. M. Robertson, *et al.*, *Essays Towards Peace* (1913), 65–75.

——, Lord *Prussianism and its Destruction: With which is Reprinted Part II of the 'The Great Illusion'* (1914).

—— *The Foundations of International Polity* (1914).

—— *The Peace Treaty and the Economic Chaos of Europe* (1919).

—— *The Fruits of Victory: A Sequel to 'The Great Illusion'* (1921).

—— 'War and Peace, 1914', in J. Bell, (ed.), *We Did Not Fight* (1935), 43–60.

—— *This Have and Have-Not Business: Political Fantasy and Economic Fact* (1936).

—— *The Defence of the Empire* (1937).

—— *For What Do We Fight?* (1939).

—— *Must it Be War?* (1939).

—— *After All* (1951).

Angus, H. F., *The Problem of Peaceful Change in the Pacific Area* (1937).

Appleton, L., *Henry Richard: The Apostle of Peace* (1889).

Attlee, C. R., *The Labour Party in Perspective* (1937).

—— *As It Happened* (1954).

Baker, E. P. and P. J. N, *J. Allen Baker Member of Parliament: A Memoir* (1927).

Baldwin, S., *This Torch of Freedom: Speeches and Addresses* (1935).

Ballard, F., *The Mistakes of Pacifism or Why a Christian can have Anything to Do with War* (n.d. [1915]).

Ballou, A., *Christian Non-Resistance in All Its Important Bearings* (London edn., 1848).

Barnes, G. N., *From Workshop to War Cabinet* (1923).

Bartlett, V., *This is my Life* (1937).

Bassett, A. T., *The Life of the Rt. Hon. John Edward Ellis, M.P.* (1914).

Bedford, J., Duke of, *A Silver-Plated Spoon* (1959).

Belden, A. D., *Pax Christi: The Peace of Christ* (1942).

Bell, J. (ed.), *We Did Not Fight: 1914–18 Experiences of War Resisters* (1935).

Beveridge, Sir W., *Peace by Federation?* (Federal Union, 1940).

—— *The Price of Peace* (1945).

Birch, L., *The Demand for Colonies: Territorial Expansion, Over-Population, and Raw Materials* (LNU, Jan. 1936).

Blanchard, J., *Preparations for War: being one of the papers presented to the Peace Convention in 1843* (Peace Society, n.d. [1843]).

Bloch, I. S., *Is War Now Impossible?* (1899).

[Bowring, J.] *Detail of the Arrest, Imprisonment and Liberation of an Englishman by the Bourbon Government of France* (1823).

—— *The Political and Commercial Importance of Peace: A Lecture Delivered in the Hall of Commerce, London* (n.d. [1846]).

—— *Autobiographical Recollection of Sir John Bowring* (1877).

Brailsford, H. N., *The War of Steel and Gold: A Study of the Armed Peace* (1914 and June 1915 edns.).

—— *A League of Nations* (1917).

—— *After the Peace* (1920).

—— *Property or Peace* (1934).
Briant, K., and Wilkes, L. (eds.), *Would I Fight?* (Oxford, 1938).
Bright, J., *Speeches on Parliamentary Reform, & c.* (Manchester, n.d. [1866])
Brinton, H. (ed.), *Does Capitalism Cause War?* (n.d. [1935])
Brittain, V., *England's Hour* (1941).
—— *Humiliation with Honour* (1942).
—— *Seeds of Chaos: What Mass Bombing Really Means* (1944).
—— *Testament of Experience* (1957).
—— *The Rebel Passion: A Short History of Some Pioneer Peace-makers* (1964).
—— *Vera Brittain: Chronicle of Friendship: Diary of the Thirties 1932–1939*, ed. a. Bishop (1986).
—— *Vera Brittain: Wartime Chronicle: Diary 1939–45*, ed. A. Bishop and Y. A. Bennett (1989).
Brockway, F., *Pacifism and the Left Wing* (1938).
—— *Inside the Left* (1942).
—— *Socialism over Sixty Years: The Life of Jowett of Bradford (1864–1944)* (1946).
—— *Bermondsey Story: The Life of Alfred Salter* (1949).
—— *Outside the Right: A Sequel to 'Inside the Left'* (1963).
Brown, J. H., *Frances E. Brockway* (1905).
Brown, W., *War and Peace: Essays in Psychological Analysis* (1939).
Brown, W. J., *What have I Got to Lose?* (1941).
Burrage, E. H., *J. Passmore Edwards: Philanthropist* (1902).
Burt, T., *An Autobiography with Supplementary Chapters by Aaron Watson* (1924).
Butler, H., *The Lost Peace: A Personal Impression* (1941).
Buxton, C. R. (ed.), *Towards a Lasting Settlement* (1915).
Cadoux, C. J., *Christian Pacifism Re-Examined* (Oxford, 1940).
Campbell Johnson, A. (ed.), *Peace Offering* (1936).
Carnegie, A., *War as the Mother of Valour and Civilization* (Peace Society, 1910).
Carr, E. H., 'Public Opinion as Safeguard of Peace', *International Affairs* (Nov./Dec. 1936), 846–62.
—— *The Twenty Years' Crisis: An Introduction to the Study of International Relations* (1939).
Catchpool, E. St J., *Candles in the Darkness* (1966).
Catlin, G., *One Anglo-American Nation* (1941).
—— *For God's Sake, Go! An Autobiography* (Gerrard's Cross, 1972).
'Cato', *Guilty Men* (1940).
Cecil of Chelwood, Viscount, *Peace and Pacifism* (Oxford, 1938).
—— *A Great Experiment* (1941).
—— *All the Way* (1949).
Chamberlain, A., *The Austen Chamberlain Diary Letters: The Correspondence of Sir Austen Chamberlain with his Sisters Hilda and Ida, 1916–1937*, ed. R. C. Self (Camden 5th series 5; Cambridge, 1995).
Chaning-Pearce, M. (ed.), *Federal Union: A Symposium* (1940).
Charques, R. D., *The Soviets and the Next War* (1932).

Chesterton, G. K., *Autobiography* (1936).

Churchill, W. S., *The Second World War*, i. *The Gathering Storm* (1948).

Cobden, R., *What Next—and Next?* (1856).

—— *The Three Panics* (1862).

Cobden, R., *Speeches on Questions of Public Policy by Richard Cobden, MP*, ed. J. Bright and J. Thorold Rogers (2 vols., 1870).

Cole, G. D. H., *The Simple Case for Socialism* (1935).

—— *War Aims* (1939).

Collingwood, R. G., *The New Leviathan or Man, Society, Civilization and Barbarism* (Oxford, 1942).

Conwell-Evans, T. P., *Foreign Policy from a Backbench 1904–1918: A Study Based on the Papers of Lord Noel-Buxton* (1932).

Cooper, T., *The Life of Thomas Cooper, Written by Himself* (1872).

Corder, P., *The Life of Robert Spence Watson* (1914).

Cot, P., *The Triumph of Treason* (1944).

Coulton, G. G., *A Victorian Schoolmaster: Henry Hart of Sedbergh* (1923).

Creighton, L., *Life and Letters of Thomas Hodgkin* (1917).

Cruttwell, C. R. M. F., *A History of Peaceful Change in the Modern World* (1937).

Curry, W. B., *The Case for Federal Union* (1939).

Dale, A. W., *The Life of R.W. Dale of Birmingham* (1898).

Dalton, H., *Towards the Peace of Nations* (1928).

—— *Call Back Yesterday: Memoirs 1887–1931* (1953).

—— *The Fateful Years: Memoirs 1931–45* (1957).

Darby, W. E., *Beneath Bow Bells: Addresses on International Peace* (1909).

—— *The Claim of 'The New Pacificism': A Paper Read at the Autumnal Conference of the Peace Society, Dundee, October 14th, 1912* (1912).

Davidson, S., *The Autobiography of Samuel Davidson, D.D., Ll.D. Edited by his Daughter* (Edinburgh, 1899).

Davies, D., *The Problem of the Twentieth Century* (1930).

—— *An International Police Force* (1932).

—— 'Robert the Peeler', *Letters to John Bull and Others* (1932).

Davies, Lord, *Force* (1934).

—— *Nearing the Abyss: The Lesson of Ethiopia* (1936).

—— *A Federated Europe* (1940).

Davies, F. R., *Some Blessed Hope: Memoirs of a Next-to-Nobody* (Lewes, 1996).

Day Lewis, C., *We're Not Going to Do Nothing: A Reply to Aldous Huxley* (1936).

—— *The Buried Day* (1969).

Dickinson, G. L., *After the War* (1915).

—— *The War and a Way Out* (1915).

—— *The European Anarchy* (1916).

—— *The International Anarchy 1906–1914* (1926).

—— *The Autobiography of G. Lowes Dickinson and Other Unpublished Writings*, ed. D. Proctor (1973).

Dorling, W., *Henry Vincent: A Biographical Sketch* (1879).

Duckers, J. S., '*Handed Over': The Prison Experiences of Mr J. Scott Duckers, Solicitor of Chancery Lane, under the Military Service Act* (n.d. [1917]).

Dudley, J., *The Life of Edward Grubb 1854–1939: A Spiritual Pilgrimage* (1946).

Dugdale, B. *Baffy: The Diaries of Blanche Dugdale 1936–1947*, ed. N. A. Rose (1973).

Duncan, D., *The Life and Letters of Herbert Spencer* (1908).

Duncan, R., *Journal of a Husbandman* (1944).

Durant, R., *Watling: A Survey of Social Life on a New Housing Estate* (1939).

Durbin, E. F. M., and Catlin, G. (eds.), *War and Democracy: Essays on the Causes and Prevention of War* (1938).

Dyer, G. H., Catchpool, W., and Dyer, A. S., *Six Men of the People* (n.d. [1882]).

Eastern Question Association, *Report of Proceedings of the National Conference at St James's Hall London December 8th 1876* (n.d.).

Edwards, G., *From Crow-Scaring to Westminster: An Autobiography* (1922).

Eppstein, J., *The Catholic Tradition of the Law of Nations* (1935).

Evans, H., *Sir Randal Cremer: His Life and Work* (1909).

—— *Radical Fights of Forty Years* (1913).

Federal Union Research Institute, *First Annual Report 1939–40* (1940).

Field, G. C., *Pacifism and Conscientious Objection* (Cambridge, 1945).

Fisher, H. A. L., (ed.), *Essays in Honour of Gilbert Murray* (1936).

Foot, M., Freeman R. G., Hardie F., and Steel-Maitland, K., *Young Oxford and War* (1934).

Forster, E. M., *Goldsworthy Lowes Dickinson* (1934).

Fothergill, S., *Essay on the Society of Friends: Being an Inquiry into the Causes of their Diminished Influence and Numbers* (1859).

Fox, A. F., *Memoir of Robert Charleton* (1873).

Friends' Peace Committee, *Friends of International Peace* (1925).

Fry, A. R., *A Quaker Adventure: The Story of Nine Years' Relief and Reconstruction* (1926).

Fry, J. M., (ed.), *Christ and Peace: A Discussion of Some Fundamental Issues Raised by the War* (n.d. [1915]).

Gardiner, M., *A Scatter of Memories* (1988).

[Garrison, W. L.], *Selections from the Writings and Speeches of William Lloyd Garrison* (Boston, Mass., 1852).

Geneva Institute of International Relations, *Problems of Peace*, 9th series (Geneva, 1935).

—— *Problems of Peace*, 10th series (1936).

Gibbs, P., *Ordeal in England* (1937).

Gladstone, W. E., *The Gladstone Diaries*, ed. M. R. D. Foot and H. C. G. Matthew (14 vols., Oxford, 1968–94).

Gooch, G. P., *Life of Lord Courtney* (1920).

—— (ed.), *In Pursuit of Peace* (1933).

—— *Under Six Reigns* (1958).

Graham, J. W., *War from a Quaker Point of View* (1915).
—— *Conscription and Conscience: A History 1916–1919* (1922).
Grane, W. L., *The Passing of War: A Study in Things that Make for Peace* (1912).
Graves, R., and Hodge, A., *The Long Week-End: A Social History of the Great Britain 1918–1939* (1940).
Gregg, R. B., *The Power of Non-Violence* (1936 edn.).
Grigg, Sir E., *The Faith of an Englishman* (1936).
Hall, B. T., *Our Fifty Years: The Story of the Working Men's Club and Institute Union* (1912).
Hall, N., *An Autobiography* (1898).
Hamilton, M. A., *Remembering my Good Friends* (1944).
Hammond, F., *War—and the Average Man* (1914).
Haraszti Taylor, E., *My Life with Alan* (1987).
Harris, W., *99 Gower Street* (1943).
—— *Life So Far* (1954).
Harrison, F., *Autobiographic Memoirs* (2 vols., 1911).
Hart, J., *Ask Me No More* (1998).
Harvey, O., *The Diplomatic Diaries of Oliver Harvey 1937–49*, ed. J. Harvey (1970).
Heath, C., *Pacifism in Time of War* (n.d. [1915]).
Henderson, A., *Labour's Foreign Policy* (1933).
Heyworth, L., *Glimpses at the Origin, Mission, and Destiny of Man* (1866).
Hirst, F.W., *The Six Panics* (1913).
—— *Armaments; The Race and the Crisis* (1937).
Hirst, M. E., *The Quakers in Peace and War: An Account of their Peace Principles and Practice* (1923).
Hobhouse, L. T., *The World in Conflict* (1915).
—— *Questions of War and Peace* (1916).
—— and Hammond, J. L., *Lord Hobhouse: A Memoir* (1905).
Hobhouse, S., *Margaret Hobhouse and her Family* (privately printed, Rochester, 1934).
—— *Forty Years and an Epilogue* (1951).
Hobson, J. A., *The War in South Africa: Its Causes and Effects* (1900).
—— *The Psychology of Jingoism* (1901).
—— *Imperialism: A Study* (1902).
—— *The Importance of Instruction in the Facts of Internationalism* (1912).
—— *Richard Cobden: The International Man* (1919).
Hobson, S. G., *Pilgrim to the Left: Memoirs of a Modern Revolutionist* (1938).
Hocking, S. K., *My Book of Memory: A String of Reminiscences and Reflections* (1923).
Hodder, E., *The Life of John Morley* (3rd edn., 1887).
Holland, Sir T., *The Mineral Sanction as an Aid to International Security* (1935).
Horner, A., *Incorrigible Rebel* (1960).
Hoyland, J. S., *Federate or Perish* (1944).
Huddleston, S., *War Unless* (1933).

James Hinton, *Protests + Visions: peace politics in twentieth century Britain*, Hutchison Radius, UK ?

CND member, socialist — Victorian times → 1980

—— In my Time (1938).

[Hughes, D. P.], The Life of Hugh Price Hughes by his Daughter (1904).

Hughes, W. R., Sophia Sturge: A Memoir (1940).

Huxley, A., What are You Going to Do about it? The Case for Constructive Peace (PPU, 1936).

—— Ends and Means: An Inquiry into the Nature of Ideals and into the Methods Employed for their Realisation (1937).

Hyams, E., Few Men are Liars (PPU, 1937).

—— The New Statesman: The History of the First Fifty Years (1963).

Ingram, K., Fifty Years of the National Peace Council 1908–1958 (n.d. [1958]).

International Peace Campaign, World Peace Congress, Brussels 3–6 Sept.1936 (Paris and Brussels, 1936).

—— The Peace Week Handbook (n.d. [1937]).

International Working Men's Association, General Council of the First International 187071 (Foreign Languages Publishing House, Moscow, n.d.).

Inwards, J., The Life and Labours of Jabez Inwards (n.d. [1860]).

James, W., Memories and Studies (1911).

Jennings, W. I., A Federation for Western Europe (Cambridge, 1940).

Jerrold, D., 'The League and the Future', Nineteenth Century and After (Dec. 1935), 657–74.

—— They That Take The Sword: The Future of the League of Nations (1936).

—— Georgian Adventure (1937).

Joad, C. E. M., Why War? (Harmondsworth, 1939).

Jones, T., A Diary with Letters 1931–1950 (1954).

—— Thomas Jones: Whitehall Diary, ed. K. Middlemas (3 vols., 1969–71).

Jones, W., Quaker Campaigns in Peace and War (1899).

Josephy, F. L., Europe: The Key to Peace (Federal Union, n.d. [1944]).

Joyce, J. A. (ed.), World Organization—Federal or Functional?: A Round-Table Discussion (1945).

Kell, E., Peace, the Gift, the Injunction of Our Holy Redeemer: The Paramount Obligation of Immediate Peace (1855).

Kermode, F., Not Entitled: A Memoir (1996).

Kerr, P., and Curtis, L., The Prevention of War (New Haven, Com, 1923).

Labour Party, Labour Party Conference Reports (1917–40).

—— National Executive Committee Minutes (Harvester Microfiches).

—— Labour and the Nation (1928).

—— For Socialism and Peace (Dec. 1934).

Lane, R., Patriotism under Three Flags: A Plea for Rationalism in Politics (1903).

Layton, Lord, Dorothy (1961).

League of Nations Union, The League, Manchuria and Disarmament (Dec. 1931).

—— The Churches' Call for International Disarmament (Jan. 1932).

—— Economic Sanctions (Aug. 1934).

—— The Problem of the Air (1935).

—— The League and the Crisis: Making Collective Defence Effective (Sept. 1936).

League of Peace and Freeedom, *Towards Ultimate Harmony: Report of Conference on Pacifist Philosophy of Life, Caxton Hall, London, July 8th and 9th, 1915* (1915).

Lefebure, V., *Common Sense about Disarmament* (1932).

Levi, L., *The Story of my Life: The First Ten Years of my Residence in England, 1845–1855* (privately published, 1888).

Lewis, S., 'Why we Burnt the Bombing School', in R. Reynolds, (ed.), *British Pamphleteers* (2 vols., 1951), ii. 287–300.

Lindsay, A. D., *Pacifism as a Principle and Pacifism as a Dogma* (1939).

Livingstone, A., *The Peace Ballot* (1935).

Lothian, Lord, *Pacifism is Not Enough Nor Patriotism Either* (1935).

Lovelock, E. H., *The Penitent's Confession and Plea for Mercy and the Christian's Duties in the Present Crisis* (1854).

McCallum, R. B., *Public Opinion and the Last Peace* (1944).

McCurdy, C. A., *Freedom's Call and Duty: Addresses Given at Central Hall, Westminster, May and June 1918* (1918).

MacDonald, J. R., *National Defence: A Study in Militarism* (1917).

McGovern, J., *Neither Fear Nor Favour* (1960).

Macgregor, G. H. C., *The New Testament Basis of Pacifism* (1936).

—— *The Relevance of the Impossible: A Reply to Reinhold Niebuhr* (1941).

Mackay, R. W. G., *Federal Europe: Being the Case for European Federation Together with a Draft Constitution of a United States of Europe* (1940).

Maistre, J. de, *The Works of Joseph de Maistre*, ed. J. Lively (1965).

Manning, C. A. W. (ed.), *Peaceful Change: An International Problem* (1937).

Martin, B., *An Impossible Parson* (1935).

Martin, H. (ed.), *The Ministry of Reconciliation* (1916).

—— *The Christian as Soldier* (1939).

Martin, K., *Editor: A Second Volume of Autobiography, 1931–45* (1968).

Marvin, F. S. (ed.), *The Evolution of World Peace* (1921).

Marx, K., and Engles, G., *Karl Marx and Friedrich Engles: Writings on the Paris Commune*, ed. H. Draper (New York, 1971).

Mass Observation, *Peace and the Public* (1947).

Maxwell, Sir H., *The Life and Letters of George William Frederick Fourth Earl of Clarendon* (2 vols., 1913).

Mellor, S. A., *Five Sunday Evening Addresses delivered in Hope Street Church Liverpool, November 8th to December 6th 1914* (Liverpool, 1914).

Miall, C. S., *Henry Richard, MP* (1889).

Mitchison, G. R., *The First Workers' Government* (1934).

Mitrany, D., *A Working Peace System: An Argument for the Functional Development of World Organisation* (1943).

Morel, E. D., *Morocco in Diplomacy* (1912).

—— *Ten Years of Secret Diplomacy: An Unheeded Warning (Being a Reprint of 'Morocco in Diplomacy'* (1915).

Morley, J., *The Life of Richard Cobden* (2 vols., 1881).

—— (ed.), *Early Life and Letters of John Morley*, ed. F. W. Hirst (2 vols., 1927).

Moscheles, F., *Fragments of an Autobiography* (1899).

Morrison, H., *An Autobiography* (1960).

Morrison, S., *I Renounce War: The Story of the Peace Pledge Union* (1962).

Murray, G. M., *The League of Nations Movement: Some Recollections of the Early Days* (1955).

—— *The League of Nations and the Democratic Idea* (1918).

—— *The Ordeal of this Generation: The War, the League, and the Future* (1929).

—— *An Unfinished Autobiography with Contributions by his Friends* (1960).

Murry, J. M., *The Necessity of Pacifism* (1937).

—— *The Pledge of Peace* (1938).

—— *The Third Challenge* (NPC Peace Aims pamphlet no. 3, 1945).

—— *The Free Society* (1948).

—— *Community Farm* (1952).

National Declaration Committee, *The National Declaration on the League of Nations and Armaments: Results in each Constituency of the United Kingdom* (1935).

National Reform League, *The War with Russia: An Address of the Council of the National Reform League to the People of Great Britain and Northern Ireland* (n.d. [1855]).

National Reform Union, *Report of the Great Meeting in Support of Mr Gladstone's Government and Non-Intervention in the Free Trade Hall on Wednesday Evening, February 1st, 1871* (Manchester, 1871).

Neal, J., *Wandering Recollections of a Somewhat Busy Life: An Autobiography* (Boston, Mass., 1869 [facsimile edn., Ann Arbor, Mich., 1976]).

Nichols, B., *Cry Havoc!* (1933).

—— *The Fool hath Said* (1936).

—— *News of England or A Country without a Hero* (1938).

—— *Men Do Not Weep* (1941).

—— *All I could Never Be: Some Recollections* (1949).

Nicolson, H., *Diaries and Letters 1930–39* (1966).

Nicolson, W., *The Theory of a Universal Peace Critically Investigated* (1862).

Noel Baker, P., *The Private Manufacture of Armaments*, i (1936).

Norman, C. H., *A Searchlight on the European War* (1924).

Novikow, J., *Les Luttes entre sociétés humaines et leurs phases successives* (Paris, 1893).

—— *War and its Alleged Benefits* (1912).

Orr, Sir J. B., *Fighting for What?* (1942).

Orwell, G., *Homage to Catalonia* (1938).

—— *The Collected Essays, Journalism and Letters of George* ed. S. Orwell and I. Angus (4 vols.; Penguin edn., Harmondsworth, 1970).

Parliamentary Papers, *Report for the Select Committee on Newspaper Stamps* (n.d.).

Parmoor, Lord, *A Retrospect: Looking Back over a life of more than Eighty Years* (1936).

Passy, F., *Pour la paix* (Paris, 1909).

Paul, L., *Angry Young Man* (1951).

Peace Pledge Union, *Pacifists at Bow Street: A Full Report of Proceedings under the Defence Regulations Against Officers and Members of the Peace Pledge Union May–June 1940* (1940).

Peace Society, *Proceedings of the 10th Universal Peace Congress, St Andrew's Hall, Glasgow, 10–13 September 1901* (1901).

Pease, Sir A. E., *Elections and Recollections* (1932).

Pease, M. H., *Henry Pease: A Short Story of his Life* (1897).

Percy, Lord E., *Some Memories* (1958).

Perris, G. H., *Our Foreign Policy and Sir Edward Grey's Failure* (1912).

—— *The War Traders: An Exposure* (1913).

Petrie, Sir C., *A Historian Looks at his World* (1972).

Phillips, W., *Sixty Years of Citizen Work and Play* (n.d. [1910]).

Playne, C. E., *The Pre-War Mind in Britain: An Historical Review* (1928).

Plowman, M., *The Right to Live* (1918).

—— *The Right to Live* (1942).

—— *War and the Creative Impulse* (1919).

—— 'Mark VII', *A Subaltern on the Somme in 1916* (1927).

Pollard, F. E., *Pacifism and the League of Nations* (Friends' Peace Committee, May 1925).

Pollard, W., 'The Peace-at-Any-Price Party', *Fraser's Magazine*, 22 (1880), 490–500.

Ponsonby, A., *Democracy and the Control of International Affairs* (1912).

—— *Democracy and Diplomacy: A Plea for Popular Control of Foreign Policy* (1915).

—— *A Basis of International Authority* (Peace and Freedom Pamphlet no. 10, 1915).

—— *Now is the Time: An Appeal for Peace* (1925).

Porter Goff, E. N., *The Christian and the Next War* (1933).

Postgate, R., *The Life of George Lansbury* (1951).

Pritt, D. N., *A Call to the People: A Manifesto of the People's Vigilance Committee* (n.d. [1940]).

—— *Federal Illusion* (1940).

Ram, J., *The Philosophy of War* (1878).

Rathbone, E., *War can be Averted: The Achievability of Collective Security* (1938).

Raven, C., *Is War Obsolete? A Study of the Conflicting Claims of Religion and Citizenship* (1935).

—— *The Theological Basis of Christian Pacifism* (1952).

Redgrave, M., *In my Mind's Eye: An Autobiography* (1983).

Richard, H., *Memoirs of Joseph Sturge* (1864).

Richards, E. R., *Private View of a Public Man: The Life of Leyton Richards* (1950).

Richards, L., *The Christian's Alternative to War: An Examination of Christian Pacifism* (1928).

—— *The Christian's Contribution to Peace: A Constructive Approach to International Relationships* (1935).

—— *Economic Planning and International Order* (1937).

—— *Economic Causes of War* (1939).

—— *Autobiography of an Economist* (1971).

Robertson, J. M., *et al.*, *Essays Towards Peace* (1913).

Romilly, E., *Boadilla* (1937).

Romilly, G. and E., *Out of Bounds* (1935).

Roscoe, W., *Occasional Tracts Relative to the War between Great Britain and France* (1810).

Rowan-Robinson, H., *Sanctions Begone!: A Plea and a Plan for the Reform of the League* (1936).

Royal Institute of International Affairs, *The Future of the League of Nations* (1936).

—— *What Should We Fight For?* (1936).

—— *International Sanctions* (1938).

Royden, A. M., *The Great Adventure: The Way to Peace* (1915).

—— 'War and the Woman's Movement', in C. R. Buxton, (ed.), *Towards a Lasting Peace Settlement* (1915), 131–41.

Russell of Killowen, Lord, *Arbitration: Its Origin, History, and Prospects* (1896).

Russell, B., *Which Way to Peace?* (1936).

—— *et al.*, *Dare We Look Ahead?* (1938).

—— *The Autobiography of Bertrand Russell* (3 vols, 1967–78).

—— *Prophecy and Dissent, 1914–16: The Collected Papers of Bertrand Russell*, xiii (1988).

—— *Pacifism and Revolution, 1916–18: The Collected Papers of Bertrand Russell*, xiv (1995).

Scott, I., *War Inconsistent with the Doctrine and Example of Jesus Christ* (1796).

Scott, J. R., *Memorials of the Family of Scott, of Scott's-Hall in the County of Kent* (1876).

Schwabe, S., *Reminiscences of Richard Cobden* (1895).

[Seebohm], *Private Memoirs of B. and E. Seebohm, Edited by their Sons* (1873).

Sefton-Jones, H., *German Crimes and our Civil Remedy* (1916).

Seton-Watson, R. W., *Britain and the Dictators: A Survey of Post-War British Policy* (Cambridge, 1938).

Shee, G. F., *The Briton's First Duty: The Case for Conscription* (1901).

Soutter, F. W., *Fights for Freedom* (1925).

Spencer, H., *An Autobiography* (2 vols., 1904).

Spier, E., *Focus: A Footnote to the History of the Thirties* (1963).

Stanley, E. H., *A Selection from the Diaries of Edward Henry Stanley Earl of Derby (1826–93) between September 1869 and March 1878*, ed. J. Vincent (Camden 5th series 4; 1994).

Stead, F. H., *To Abolish War: At the Third Hague Congress: An Appeal to the Peoples* (Letchworth, 1916).

Stead, W. T., *Always Arbitrate before You Fight: An Appeal to English Speaking Folk* (1896).

Stephen, C. E., *Quaker Strongholds* (1890).

Stoddart, A. M., *Elizabeth Pease Nichol* (1899).

Strachey, J., *Federalism or Socialism?* (1940).

—— *A Faith to Fight For* (1941).

Streit, C. K., *Union Now: A Proposal for a Federal Union of the Democracies of the North Atlantic* (1939).

—— *Union Now with Britain* (1941).

Summerskill, E., *A Woman's World: Her Memoirs* (1967).

Swanwick, H. M., *Builders of Peace: Being Ten Years' History of the Union of Democratic Control* (1924).

—— *Frankenstein and his Monster: Aviation for World Service (A Sequel to 'New Wars for Old')* (1934).

—— *New Wars for Old (A Reply to the Rt. Hon. Lord Davies and Others)* (1934).

—— *Pooled Security: What does it Mean?* (1934).

—— *I have been Young* (1935).

Taylor, A. J. P., 'Accident Prone, or What Happened Next', *Historical Journal*, 49 (1977), 1–18.

The Czar's Manifesto on Disarmament and Peace: Great Town's Meeting in the Winter Gardens, Harrogate, September 18th 1898 (Harrogate, 1898).

Thomas, G., *Mr Speaker: The Memoirs of the Viscount Tonypandy* (1985).

Thompson, G. C., *Public Opinion and Lord Beaconsfield* (2 vols., 1886).

Trevelyan, G. M., *Life of John Bright* (1913).

Trory, E., *Imperialist War: Further Recollections of a Communist Organizer* (Brighton, 1977).

University Group on Defence Policy, *The Role of Peace Movements in the 1930s* (pamphlet no. 1, Jan. 1959).

Vigilantes, *The Dying Peace* (New Statesman pamphlet, 29 Sept. 1933).

—— *Why the league has Failed* (1938).

—— *Between Two Wars?* (1939).

Walker, F. A., *The Blunder of Pacifism* (1940).

Ward, H., *A Venture in Goodwill* (1925).

Waugh, E., *Brideshead Revisited* (1945).

Weatherhead, L., *Thinking Aloud in War Time* (1939).

Wellock, W., *Off the Beaten Track: Adventures in the Art of Living* (Tanjore, 1961).

Wells, H. G., *Mr Britling Sees it Through* (1916).

—— *The Fate of Homo Sapiens* (1939).

—— *The Rights of Man or What are We Fighting For?* (1939).

—— *The New World Order* (1940).

—— *The Outlook for Homo Sapiens* (1942).

WheelerBennett, J. W., The Disarmament Deadlock (1934).

Whyte, F., *The Life of W. T. Stead* (2 vols., 1925).

Wight, M., 'Christian Pacifism', *Theology: A Monthly Journal of Historic Christianity*, 33 (July–Dec. 1936), 12–21.

Wilkinson, M., *E. Richard Cross* (1917).

Wilks, W., *Edward Irving: An Ecclesiastical and Literary Biography* (1854).

Williams, A., 'Proposals for a League of Peace and Mutual Protection among Nations', *Contemporary Review* (Nov. 1914), 628–36.

Willis, I. C., *England's Holy War: A Study of English Liberal Idealism during the Great War* (New York, 1929).

Willis, T., *Whatever Happened to Tom Mix? The Story of one of my Lives* (1970).

Wilson, D. and E., *Federation and World Order* (1939).

Wilson,W. E., *Christ and Peace: The Reasonableness of Disarmament on Christ, Humanitarian, and Economic Grounds: A Peace Study Text-Book* (1913).

Wood, H. G., *Henry T. Hodgkin: A Memoir* (1937).

Woolf, L.S., *International Government* (1916).

—— *The War of Peace* (1940).

—— *Beginning Again: An Autobiography of the Years 1911–1918* (1964).

Wootton, B., *Socialism and Federation* (Federal Union, 1941).

—— *In a World I Never Made: Autobiographical Reflections* (1967).

Woolf, V., *Diaries of Virginia Woolf*, ed. A. O. Bell (5 vols., 1977–84).

Workmen's Peace Committee, *The Workman's [sic] Peace Committee to the Working Men of Great Britain and Ireland* (leaflet: n.d., 1870).

Yeats-Brown, F., *Bengal Lancer* (1930).

—— *Dogs of War!* (1934).

SECONDARY SOURCES

Unpublished works

Abrams, I. M., 'A History of European Peace Societies 1867–1899', Ph.D. thesis (Harvard University, 1938).

Bell, A. D., 'The Reform League from is Origins to the Reform Act of 1867', D.Phil. thesis (Oxford University, 1961).

Bennett, Y. A., 'Testament of a Minority in Wartime: The Peace Pledge Union and Vera Brittain 1939–1945', Ph.D. thesis (McMaster University, 1984).

Berkman, J. A., 'Pacifism in England 1914–39', Ph.D. thesis (Yale University, 1967).

Buzan, B. G., 'The British Peace Movement from 1919 to 1939', Ph.D. thesis (London School of Economics, 1973).

Ceadel, M., 'Pacifism in Britain, 1931–1939', D.Phil. thesis (Oxford University, 1976).

Cecil, H. P., 'The Development of Lord Robert Cecil's Views on Securing a Lasting Peace 1915–19', D.Phil. thesis (Oxford University, 1971).

Croucher, B. C., 'British Working Class Attitudes to War and National Defence, 1902–1914', Ph.D. thesis (Swansea University, 1992).

Davis, S., 'The British Labour Party and British Foreign Policy 1933–1939', Ph.D. thesis (London University, 1950).

Fielding, R. J., 'The Elimination of War: An Examination of the Work of Sir Norman Angell', Ph.D. thesis (Sussex University, 1967).

Frick, S., 'Joseph Sturge, Henry Richard and the *Herald of Peace*: Pacifist Response to the Crimean War', Ph.D. thesis (Cornell University, 1971).

Gavigan, P. J., 'Ralph Norman Angell Lane: An Analysis of his Political Career, 1914 to 1931', Ph.D. thesis (Ball State University, 1972).

Hafer, P. C., 'Two Paths to Peace: The Efforts of Norman Angell 1914–1918', Ed.D. thesis (Ball State University, 1972).

Hines, P. D., 'Norman Angell: Peace Movement 1911', D.Ed. thesis (Ball State Teachers' College, 1964).

Jackson, C. F., 'The British General Elections of 1857 and 1859', D.Phil. thesis (Oxford, University, 1980).

Jewell, F. R., 'Sir Norman Angell: The World War II Years, 1940–1945', Ed.D. thesis (Bell State University, 1975).

Kyba, J. P. 'British Attitudes toward Disarmament and Rearmament 19325', Ph.D. thesis (London University, 1967).

Laity, P., 'The British Peace Movement 1896–1916: Ideas and Dilemmas', D.Phil. thesis (Oxford University, 1995).

Marwick, A., 'The Independent Labour Party (1918–32)', B.Litt. thesis (Oxford University, 1960).

Mattoo, A., 'The Campaign for Nuclear Disarmament: A Study of its Re-emergence, Growth and Decline in the 1980s', D.Phil. thesis (Oxford University, 1992).

Phillips B. D., 'Friendly Patriotism: British Quakerism and the Imperial Nation, 1890–1910', Ph.D. thesis (Cambridge University, 1989)

Pugh, M. C., 'British Public Opinion and Collective Security 1926–1936', Ph.D. thesis (University of East Anglia, 1975).

Risinger, E. A., jun., 'Sir Norman Angell: Critic of Appeasement 1935–1940', Ed.D. thesis (Ball State University, 1977).

Robbins, K. G., 'The Abolition of War: A Study of the Organisation and Ideology of the British Peace Movement, 1914–19', D.Phil. thesis (Oxford University, 1964).

Sager, E. W., 'Pacifism and the Victorians: A Social History of the English Peace Movement 1816–1878', Ph.D. thesis (University of British Columbia, 1975).

Schneider, E., 'What Britons were Told about War in the Trenches', D.Phil. thesis (Oxford University, 1997).

Shepherd, G. W., 'The Theory and Practice of Internationalism in the British Labour Party (with Special Reference to the Inter-War Period)', Ph.D. thesis (London University, 1951).

Thwaites, P. J., 'The Independent Labour Party 1938–1950', Ph.D. thesis (London School of Economics, 1976).

Weinroth, H., 'British Pacifism 1906–1916: A Study of the Ideology and Organisation of the British Peace Movement during the Early Years of the 20th Century', Ph.D. thesis (Cambridge University, 1968).

Published works

Abrams, I., 'Disarmament in 1870', *Die Friedenswarte*, 54 (1957), 57–68.

Addison, P., 'Lloyd George and a Compromise Peace', in A. J. P. Taylor, (ed.), *Lloyd George: Twelve Essays* (1971), 366–71.

Alexander, H., 'A Nearly Forgotten Chapter in British Peace Activity—1915', *Journal of the Friends' Historical Society*, 55 (1983–9), 139–43.

Alexander, M. S., *The Republic in Danger: General Maurice Gamelin and the Politics of French Defence, 1933–1940* (Cambridge, 1992).

Allen, V. L., 'The Origins of Industrial Conciliation and Arbitration', *International Review of Social History*, 9 (1960), 237–54.

Allott, S., *John Wilhelm Rowntree 1868–1905 and the Beginnings of Modern Quakerism* (York, 1994).

Anderson, M., *Noel Buxton: A Life* (1952).

Anderson, M. S., *War and Society in Europe of the Old Regime 1618–1789* (Leicester, 1988).

Andrew, C., and Gordievsky, O., *KGB: The Secret History* (1990).

—— and Mitrokhin, V., *The Mitrokhin Archive; The KGB in Europe and the West* (1999).

Ayerst, D., *Garvin of the Observer* (1985).

Barker, R., *Conscience, Goverment and War: Conscientions Objection in Great Britain 1939–45* (1982).

Barnes, J., *Ahead of his Age: Bishop Barnes of Birmingham* (1979).

Bartle, G. F., 'Jeremy Bentham and John Bowring: A Study of the Relationship between Bentham and the Editor of his *Collected Works*', *Bulletin of the Institute of Historical Research*, 36 (1963), 27–35.

Beales, A. C. F., *A History of Peace: A Short Account of the Organized Movements for International Peace* (1931).

Beales, D., *England and Italy 1859–60* (1961).

Beckett, I. W. F., *Riflemen Form: A Study of the Rifle Volunteer Movement 1855–1908* (Aldershot, 1982).

Bellamy, J., and Savile, J. (eds), *Dictionary of Labour Biography* (9 vols., 1972–93).

Berry, P., and Bostridge, M., *Vera Brittain: A Life* (1995).

Biagini, E. F., and Reid, A. J. (eds.), *Currents of Radicalism* (Cambridge, 1991).

Birn, D. S., *The League of Nations Union 1918–1945* (Oxford, 1981).

Bisceglia, L. R., *Norman Angell and Liberal Internationalism in Britain 1931–1935* (New York, 1982).

Blake, R., *Disraeli* (1966).

Blamires, D. M., 'Towards a biography of William Pollard', *Journal of the Friends' Historical Society*, 55 (1983–9), 112–23.

Bosco, A., 'Lothian, Curtis, Kimber and the Federal Union Movement (1938–40)', *Journal of Contemporary History*, 23 (1988), 465–502.

Boulton, D., *Objection Overruled* (1967).

Bourne, K., *The Foreign Policy of Victorian England 1830–1902* (Oxford, 1970).

Bradshaw, D., 'The Flight from Gaza: Aldous Huxley's Involvement in the Peace Pledge Union in the Context of his Overall Intellectual Development', in B. Nugel (ed.), *Now More than Ever: Proceedings of the Aldous Huxley Centenary Symposium Münster 1994* (Berlin, 1996), 9–27.

Bramsted, E., 'Apostles of Collective Security: The LNU and Its Functions', *Australian Journal of Politics and History*, 13 (1967), 347–74.

Branson, N., *History of the Communist Party of Great Britain 1927–1941* (1985).

Brock, P., *Pacifism in the United States: From the Colonial Era to the First World War* (Princeton, 1968).

—— *The Quaker Peace Testimony 1660–1914* (York, 1990).

Brown, G., *Maxton* (Edinburgh, 1986).

Brown, K. D., *John Burns* (1977).

Bullock, A., *The Life and Times of Ernest Bevin* (2 vols., 1960–7).

Burgess, S., *Stafford Cripps: A Political Life* (1999).

Bussey, G., and Tims, M., *Women's International League for Peace and Freedom 1915–65* (1965).

Butler, J. R. M., *Lord Lothian* (1969).

Byrne, P., *The Campaign for Nuclear Disarmament* (1988).

Carlton, D., *MacDonald versus Henderson: The Foreign Policy of the Second Labour Government* (1970).

Ceadel, M., *Pacifism in Britain 1914–1945: The Defining of a Faith* (1980).

—— 'Popular Fiction and the Next War, 1918–1939', in F. Gloversmith (ed.), *Class, Culture and Social Change: A New View of the 1930s* (Brighton, 1980), 161–84.

—— 'The First British Referendum: The Peace Ballot, 1934–5', *English Historical Review*, 95 (1980), 810–39.

—— 'Christian Pacifism in the Era of Two World Wars', in W. J. Sheils (ed.), *The Church and War* (Studies in Church History, 20; Oxford, 1983), 391–408.

—— 'Between the Wars: Problems of Definition', in R. Taylor and N. Young (eds.), *Campaigns for Peace: British Peace Movements in the Twentieth Century* (Manchester, 1987), 73–99.

—— *Thinking about Peace and War* (Oxford, 1987; OPUS paperback edn., 1989).

—— 'La Campagne pour le désarmement nucléaire (CND) et l'approche britannique des relations internationales', *Relations internationales* (Paris), 53 (Spring, 1988), 83–91.

—— 'Britain's Nuclear Disarmers', in W. Lacqueur and R. Hunter (eds.), *British Peace Movements and the Future of the Western Alliance* (New Brunswick, NJ, 1988), 218–44.

—— 'The First Communist "Peace Society": The British Anti-War Movement 1932–5, *Twentieth Century British History*, 1 (1990), 58–86.

—— 'Supranationalism in the British Peace Movement in the Early Twentieth Century', in A. Bosco (ed.), *The Federal Idea, i.: The History of Federalism from the Enlightenment to 1945* (1991), 169–91.

—— 'Attitudes to War: Pacifism and Collective Security', in P. Johnson (ed.), *Twentieth-Century Britain: Economic, Social and Cultural Change* (1994), 221–41.

—— 'Sir William Randal Cremer', in K. Holl and A. Kjelling (eds.), *The Nobel Peace*

Prizes and the Laureates: The Meaning and Acceptance of the Nobel Peace Prize in the Prize Winners' Countries (Frankfurt, 1994), 167–92.

—— *The Origins of War Prevention: The British Peace Movement and International Relations, 1730–1854* (Oxford, 1996).

—— 'Interpreting East Fulham', in C. Cook and J. Ramsden (eds.), *By-elections in British Politics* (2nd edn., 1997), 94–111.

—— 'A Legitimate Peace Movement: The Case of Interwar Britain, 1918–1945', in P. Brock, and T. Socknat, (eds.), *Challenge to Mars: Essays on Pacifism from 1918 to 1945* (Toronto, 1999), 134–48.

Cecil, Lord D., *The Cecils of Hatfield House* (1973).

Chamberlain, M. E., 'British Public Opinion and the Invasion of Egypt, 1882', *Trivium*, 16 (1981), 5–28.

Chickering, R., *Imperial Germany and a World without War* (Princeton, 1975).

Claeys, G., 'Mazzini, Kossuth and British Radicalism', *Journal of British Studies*, 28 (1989), 225–61.

Clarke, I. F., *Voices Prophesying War 1763–1884* (1966).

Clarke, P. F., *Liberals and Social Democrats* (1978).

Cline, C. A., *E. D. Morel 1873–1924: The Strategies of Protest* (Belfast, 1980).

Cole, M., *The Life of G. D. H. Cole* (1971).

Collins, H., and Abramsky, C., *Karl Marx and the British Labour Movement* (1965).

Conacher, J. B., *Britain and the Crimea, 1855–1856: Problems of War and Peace* (1987).

Connon, B., *Beverley Nichols: A Life* (1991).

Conway, S., 'Bentham on Peace and War', *Utilitas*, 1 (1989) 82–101.

—— 'John Bowring and the Nineteenth-Century Peace Movement', *Bulletin of the Institute of Historical Research*, 64 (1991), 344–58.

Cookson, J. E., *The Friends of Peace: Anti-War Liberalism in England 1792–1815* (Cambridge, 1982).

Cooper, S. E., *Patriotic Pacifism: Waging War on War in Europe, 1815–1914* (New York, 1991).

Cory, H. M., *Compulsory Arbitration of International Disputes* (New York, 1932).

Cowling, M., *The Impact of Labour 1920–1924* (Cambridge, 1971).

Crick, B., *George Orwell: A Life* (1980).

Crook, P., *Darwinism, War and History* (Cambridge, 1994).

Cunningham, H., 'Jingoism in 1877–78', *Victorian Studies*, 14 (1970–1), 429–53.

Curti, M., *The American Peace Crusade 1815–60* (Durham, NC, 1929).

Davey, A., *The British Pro-Boers 1877–1902* (Cape Town, 1978).

Donoughue, B., and Jones, G.W., *Herbert Morrison: Portrait of a Politician* (1973).

Douglas, J., *Parliament Across Frontiers: A Short History of the InterParliamentary Union* (1975).

Dowse, R. E., *Left in the Centre: The Independent Labour Party 1893–1940* (1966).

Dubin, M. D., 'Toward the Concept of Collective Security', *International Organization*, 24 (1970), 288–318.

Dudley Edwards, R., *Victor Gollancz: A Biography* (1987).

Egan, D., 'The Swansea Conference of the British Council of Soldiers' and Workers' Deputies, July 1917: Reactions to the Russian Revolution of February 1917, and the Anti-War Movement in South Wales', *Llafur*, 1/4 (1975), 12–37.

Egerton, G. W., *Great Britain and the Creation of the League of Nations: Strategy, Politics, and International Organization* (1979).

Emery, J., *Rose Macaulay: A Writer's Life* (1991).

Estorick, E., *Stafford Cripps: A Biography* (1949).

Finn, M. *After Chartism: Class and Nation in British Radical Politics, 1848–1874* (Cambridge, 1993).

Fisher, J., *That Miss Hobhouse* (1971).

Fletcher, S., *Maude Royden: A Life* (Oxford, 1989).

Foot, M., *Aneurin Bevan* (2 vols., 1962).

Foot, P., *The Politics of Harold Wilson* (Harmondsworth, 1968).

Frick, S., 'The *Christian Appeal* of 1855: Friends' Public Response to the Crimean War', *Journal of the Friends' Historical Society*, 52 (1968–71), 203–10.

—— 'Henry Richard and the Treaty of Paris of 1856', *National Library of Wales Journal*, 17 (1971/2), 299–313.

Gaffin, J., and Thoms, D., *Caring and Sharing: The Centenary History of the Co-operative Women's Guild* (1983).

Gilbert, M., 'Pacifist Attitudes to Nazi Germany, 1936–45', *Journal of Contemporary History*, 27 (1992), 493–511.

Gilbert, M. S., *Plough my own Furrow: The Life of Lord Allen of Hurtwood* (1965).

—— *Winston S. Churchill*, v (1976).

—— *Winston S. Churchill*, v *Companion Part I* (1979).

Goldman, L., 'The Social Science Association, 1857–1886: A Context for Mid-Victorian Liberalism', *English Historical Review*, 100 (1986), 95–134.

—— 'Exceptionalism and Internationalism: The Origins of American Social Science Reconsidered', *Journal of Historical Sociology*, 11 (1998), 1–36.

Golant, W., 'The Emergence of C. R. Attlee as Leader of the Parliamentary Labour Party in 1935', *Historical Journal*, 13 (1970), 318–32.

Goodall, F., *A Question of Conscience: Conscientious Objection in the Two World Wars* (Thrupp, Glos., 1999).

Griffiths, R., *Marshal Pétain* (1979).

—— *Patriotism Perverted: Captain Ramsay, the Right Book Club and British Anti-Semitism 1939–40* (1998).

Grossi, V., *Le Pacifisme européen 1889–1914* (Brussels, 1994).

Hamer, D. A., *John Morley: Liberal Intellectual in Politics* (Oxford, 1968).

Hanak, H., 'The Union of Democratic Control during the First World War', *Bulletin of the Institute of Historical Research*, 36 (1963), 167–80.

Hannam, J., *Isabella Ford* (Oxford, 1989).

Harris, J., *William Beveridge: A Biography* (rev. edn., Oxford, 1997).

Harris, K., *Attlee* (1982).

Harrison, B., *Prudent Revolutionaries: Portraits of British Feminists between the Wars* (Oxford, 1987).

Harrison, R., *Before the Socialists: Studies in Labour and Politics 1861–1881* (1965).

Hayes, D., *Challenge of Conscience: The Story of the Conscientious Objectors of 1939–1949* (1949).

Hazlehurst, G. C. L., *Politicians at War July 1914–May 1915: A Prologue to the Triumph of Lloyd George* (1971).

Henderson, G. B., 'The Pacifists of the Fifties', *Journal of Modern History*, 9 (1937), 314–41.

Hermon, E., 'Une ultime tentative de sauvetage de la Société des Nations: La Campagne du Rassemblement Universel pour la Paix', in M. Vaïsse, (ed.), *Le Pacifisme en Europe des années 1920 aux années 1950* (Brussels, 1993), 193–221.

Hewison, H. H., *Hedge of Wild Almonds: South Africa, the 'Pro-Boers' and the Quaker Conscience* (1989).

Hinton, J., 'Killing the People's Convention: A Letter from Palme Dutt to Harry Pollitt', *Bulletin of the Society for the Study of Labour History*, 39 (Autumn 1979), 27–32.

——— *Protests and Visions: Peace Politics in Twentieth-Century Britain* (1989).

Hirschfield, C., 'The Anglo-Boer War and the Issue of Jewish Culpability', *Journal of Contemporary History*, 15 (1980), 19–31.

Howard, A., *Rab: The Life of R. A. Butler* (1987).

——— *Crossman: The Pursuit of Power* (1990).

Howell, D., *British Workers and the Independent Labour Party 1888–1906* (1983).

Hughes, W. R., *Indomitable Friend: The Life of Corder Catchpool 1883–1952* (1956).

Ingram, N., *The Politics of Dissent: Pacifism in France 1919–1939* (Oxford, 1991).

Isichei, E., *Victorian Quakers* (1970).

Jenkins, R., *Mr. Attlee: An Interim Biography* (1948).

Jones, E. H., *Margery Fry: The Essential Amateur* (1966).

Jones, R. A., *Arthur Ponsonby: The Politics of Life* (1989).

Jordan, G., and Malone, W. A., *The Protest Business? Mobilizing Campaign Groups* (Manchester, 1997).

Kaye, E., *C. J. Cadoux: Theologian, Scholar and Pacifist* (Edinburgh, 1988).

Kennedy, T. C., 'Fighting about Peace: The No-Conscription Fellowship and the British Friends' Service Committee, 1915–1919', *Quaker History*, 69 (1980), 3–22.

——— *The Hound of Conscience: A History of the No-Conscription Fellowship 1914–1919* (Fayetteville, Ark., 1981).

Kermode, F., 'Peter Ure, 1919–1969', in C. J. Rawson (ed.), *Yeats and Anglo-Irish Literature: Critical Essays by Peter Ure* (Liverpool, 1974), 1–39.

Kirby, M. W., *Men of Business and Politics: The Rise and Fall of the Quaker Pease Dynasty of North-East England, 1700–1943* (1984).

Larmor, P. J., *The French Radical Party in the 1930s* (Stanford, Calif., 1964).

Lavin, D., *From Empire to International Commonwealth: A Biography of Lionel Curtis* (Oxford, 1995).

Laybourn, K., ' "About Turn": The Communist Party of Great Britain and the Second World War, 1939–41', in K. Dockray and K. Laybourn (eds.), *The Representation and Reality of War: The British Experience* (Stroud, 1999), 218–34.

Lee, A. J., 'Franklin Thomasson and the *Tribune*: A Case-Study in the History of the Liberal Press, 1906–1908', *Historical Journal*, 16 (1973), 341–60.

Leventhal, F. M., *The Last Dissenter: H. N. Brailsford and his World* (Oxford, 1985).
—— *Arthur Henderson* (Manchester, 1989).

Liddington, J., *The Long Road to Greenham: Feminism and Anti-Militarism in Britain since 1820* (1989).

Lloyd, L., *Peace through Law: Britain and the International Court in the 1920s* (1997).

Lowe, B., *Imagining Peace: A History of Early English Pacifist Ideas* (University Park, Penn., 1997).

Lubenow, W. C., *Parliamentary Politics and the Home Rule Crisis: The British House of Commons in 1886* (Oxford, 1988).

Lukowitz, D. C., [articles on the early history of the PPU] *Pacifist* (June/July 1971), 15–17; (Aug. 1971), 10–12; (Sept. 1971), 10–12; (Nov. 1971), 7–9; (Feb. 1972), 7–9.

—— 'British Pacifism and Appeasement: The Peace Pledge Union', *Journal of Contemporary History*, 9 (1974), 115–27.

—— 'Percy W. Bartlett', *Journal of the Friends' Historical Society*, 55 (1983–9), 175–7.

Lynch, C., *Beyond Appeasement: Interpreting Interwar Peace Movements in World Politics* (Ithaca, NY, 1999).

McCarthy, F., *Eric Gill* (1989).

Macfarlane, L. J., 'Hands off Russia: British Labour and the Russo-Polish War, 1920', *Past and Present*, 38 (Dec. 1967), 126–52.

Macintyre, S., *Little Moscows: Communism and Working-Class Militancy in Inter-War Britain* (1980).

Macleod, E. V., *A War of Ideas: British Attitudes to the Wars Against Revolutionary France 1792–1802* (Aldershot, 1998).

MacKenzie, N. and J., *The Time Traveller: A Life of H. G. Wells* (1973).

McKibbin, R., *Classes and Cultures: England 1918–1951* (Oxford, 1998).

Maclachlan, L., *C.P.F.L.U.: A Short History of the Christian Pacifist Forestry and Land Units* (1952).

McLean, I., 'Oxford and Bridgwater', in C. Cook and J. Ramsden (eds.), *By-elections in British Politics* (2nd edn., 1997), 112–29.

Marquand, D., *Ramsay MacDonald* (1977).

Marrin, A., *Sir Norman Angell* (Boston, Mass., 1979).

Martin, D. A., *Pacifism: An Historical and Sociological Study* (1965).

Martin, K., *Harold Laski* (1953).

Martin, L. W., *Peace without Victory: Woodrow Wilson and the British Liberals* (New Haven, Conn., 1958).

Marwick, A., *Clifford Allen: The Open Conspirator* (Edinburgh, 1964).

Marx, S., 'Shakespeare and Pacifism', *Renaissance Quarterly*, 45 (1992), 49–96.

Matthew, H. C. G., *The Liberal Imperialists: The Ideas and Politics of a Post-Gladstonian Elite* (1973).

—— *Gladstone 1809–1898* (Oxford, 1997).

Mayne, R., and Pinder, J., with Roberts, J. C. de V., *Federal Union: The Pioneers. A History of Federal Union* (1990).

Middlemas, K., *Diplomacy of Illusion: The British Government and Germany 1937–39* (1972).

—— and Barnes, J., *Baldwin* (1969).

Miller, J. D. B., *Norman Angell and the Futility of War: Peace and the Public Mind* (1986).

Monk, R., *Bertrand Russell: The Spirit of Solitude* (1997).

Moorehead, C., *Troublesome People: Enemies of War 1916–1986* (1987).

Morris, A. J. A., *Radicalism Against War, 1906–1914: The Advocacy of Peace and Retrenchment* (1972).

Mowat, C. L., *Britain between the Wars 1918–1940* (1955).

Mueller, J. D., *Retreat from Doomsday: The Obsolescence of Major War* (New York, 1989).

Navari, C., 'David Mitrany and International Functionalism', in D. Long, and P. Wilson, (eds.), *Thinkers of the Twenty Years' Crisis* (Oxford, 1995), 214–46.

Naylor, J. F., *Labour's International Policy: The Labour Party in the 1930s* (1969).

Newton, D., *British Labour, European Socialism, and the Struggle for Peace 1889–1914* (Oxford, 1985).

Oldfield, S., *Spinsters of this Parish: The Life and Times of F. M. Mayor and Mary Sheepshanks* (1984).

—— *Women Against the Iron Fist: Alternatives to Militarism* (Oxford, 1989).

Orr, E. W., *The Quakers in Peace and War 1920 to 1967* (Eastbourne, 1974).

Patterson, D. S., *Toward a Warless World: The Travail of the American Peace Movement 1887–1914* (Bloomington, Ind., 1976)

Pease, J. A., *A Liberal Chronicle: Journals and Papers of J. A. Pease, Lord Gainford, 1908 to 1910*, ed. C. Hazlehurst and C. Woodland (1994).

Pimlott, B., *Labour and the Left in the 1930s* (1977).

—— *Hugh Dalton* (1988).

Porter, B., 'David Davies and the Enforcement of Peace', in D. Long, and P. Wilson, (eds.), *Thinkers of the Twenty Years' Crisis* (Oxford, 1995), 58–78.

Postgate, R.W., *The Builders' History* (1923).

Price, R., *An Imperial War and the British Working Class* (1972).

Prochaska, F. K., *Women and Philanthropy in Nineteenth-Century England* (1980).

Pugh, M., *Women and the Women's Movement in Britain* (1992).

Rae. J., *Conscience and Politics: The British Government and the Conscientious Objector to Military Service 1916–1919* (1970).

Ramsden, J., *The Age of Balfour and Baldwin 1902–40* (1978).

Rempel, R. A., 'British Quakers and the South African War', *Quaker History*, 64 (1974–75), 75–95.

Rigby, A., *A Life in Peace: A Biography of Wilfred Wellock* (Bridport, 1988).

Rigby, A., 'The Response of British Pacifists to World War II', in G. Grünewald, and P. van den Dungen, (eds.), *Twentieth-Century Peace Movements: Successes and Failures* (Lampeter, 1994), 145–59.

—— 'The Peace Pledge Union: From Peace to War, 1936–1945', in P. Brock, and T. Socknat, (eds.), *Challenge to Mars: Essays on Pacifism from 1918 to 1945* (Toronto, 1999), 169–85.

Robbins, K. G., 'Lord Bryce and the First World War', *Historical Journal*, 10 (1967), 255–78.

—— 'Morgan Jones in 1916', *Llafur*, 1/4 (1975), 38–43.

—— *The Abolition of War: The 'Peace Movement' in Britain 1914–1919* (Cardiff, 1976).

—— *John Bright* (1979).

Roberts, J. S., *Siegfried Sassoon (1886–1967)* (1999).

Rolph, C. H., *Kingsley: The Life, Letters and Diaries of Kingsley Martin* (1973).

Roskill, S., *Hankey: Man of Secrets* (3 vols., 1970–4).

Rossosolillo, F., 'British Federalism in the Thirties', *New Europe* (Autumn 1976), 41–54.

Ruston, A., 'Unitarian Attitudes to World War 1', *Transactions of the Unitarian Historical Society*, 21 (1995–8), 269–84.

Ryan, A., *Bertrand Russell: A Political Life* (1988).

Sager, E. W., 'The Working-Class Peace Movement in Victorian England', *Histoire sociale–Social History*, 12/23 (May 1979), 122–44.

—— 'The Social Origins of Victorian Pacifism', *Victorian Studies*, 23 (1979/80), 211–36.

Samuel, R. (ed.), *Patriotism: The Making and Unmaking of British National Identity* (3 vols., 1989).

Savile, J., *Ernest Jones: Chartist* (1952).

Schuker, S., *The End of French Predominance in Europe* (Chapel Hill, NC, 1976).

Shannon, R. T., *Gladstone and the Bulgarian Agitation* (1963).

Shepherd, J., 'Labour and parliament: The Lib.-Labs as the First Working-Class MPs, 1885–1906', in E. F. Biagini, and A. J. Reid, (eds.), *Currents of Radicalism* (Cambridge, 1991), 187–213.

Skidelsky, R., *Oswald Mosley* (1975).

Smith, L., *Pacifists in Action: The Experience of the Friends Ambulance Unit in the Second World War* (York, 1998).

Spall, R. F., 'Free Trade, Foreign Relations, and the Anti-Corn-Law League', *International History Review*, 10 (1988), 405–32.

Spear, S., 'Pacifist Radicalism in the Post-War British Labour Party: The Case of E. D. Morel, 1919–24', *International Review of Social History*, 23 (1978), 224–41.

Stargardt, N., *The German Idea of Militarism: Radical and Socialist Critics, 1866–1914* (Cambridge, 1994).

Stocks, M., *Eleanor Rathbone: A Biography* (1949).

Suganami, H., *The Domestic Analogy and World Order Proposals* (Cambridge, 1989).

Swartz, M., *The Union of Democratic Control in British Politics during the First World War* (Oxford, 1971).

—— *The Politics of British Foreign Policy in the Era of Disraeli and Gladstone* (1985).

Tatham, M., and Miles, J. E., *The Friends Ambulance Unit 1914–1919: A Record* (n.d.[1919]).

Tarrow, S., *Power in Movement: Social Movements, Collective Action and Politics* (Cambridge, 1994).

Taylor, A., 'Palmerston and Radicalism, 1847–1865', *Journal of British Studies*, 33 (1994), 157–79.

Taylor, A. J. P., *The Trouble Makers* (1957).

—— *Beaverbrook* (1972).

Taylor, M., 'The Old Radicalism and the New: David Urquhart and the Politics of Opposition, 1832–67', in E. F. Biagini, and A. J. Reid, (eds.), *Currents of Radicalism: Popular Radicalism, Organised Labour and Party Politics in Britain, 1850–1914* (Cambridge, 1991), 23–43.

—— *Decline of British Radicalism 1847–1860* (Oxford, 1995).

Taylor, R., *Against the Bomb: The British Peace Movement, 1958–1965* (Oxford, 1988).

Temperley, H., *British Antislavery 1833–1870* (1972).

Thompson, J. A., 'Lord Cecil and the Pacifists in the League of Nations Union', *Historical Journal*, 20 (1977), 949–59.

—— 'The "Peace Ballot" and the "Rainbow" Controversy', *Journal of British Studies*, 20/2 (Spring 1981), 150–70.

Thorne, C., *The Limits of Foreign Policy* (1972).

Thurlow, R., *Fascism in Britain: A History, 1918–1985* (Oxford, 1987).

Tolis, P., *Elihu Burritt: Crusader for Brotherhood* (Hamden, Conn., 1968).

Touraine, A., *Anti-Nuclear Protest: The Opposition to Nuclear Energy in France* (Cambridge, 1983).

Trebilcock, C., 'Radicalism and the Armament Trust', in A. J. A. Morris (ed.), *Edwardian Radicalism 1900–1914* (1974), 180–201.

Troyat, H., *Tolstoy* (New York, 1967), tr. N. Amphoux from the French original (Paris, 1965).

Turner, J. A. (ed.), *The Larger Idea: Lord Lothian and the Problem of National Sovereignty* (1988).

Tyrrell, A., 'Making the Millenium [sic]: The Mid-Nineteenth Century Peace Movement', *Historical Journal*, 21 (1978), 75–95.

—— *Joseph Sturge and the Moral Radical Party in Early Victorian Britain* (1987).

van der Linden, W. H., *The International Peace Movement 1815–1874* (Amsterdam, 1987).

Vellacott Newbury, J., 'Anti-War Suffragists', *History*, 62 (1977), 411–25.

Vellacott, J., *Bertrand Russell and the Pacifists in the First World War* (Brighton, 1980).

Vellacott, J., *Liberal to Labour with Women's Suffrage: The Story of Catherine Marshall* (Montreal, 1993).

Villiers, G., *A Vanished Victorian: Being the Life of George Villiers Fourth Earl of Clarendon 1800–1870* (1938).

Vogeler, M., *Frederic Harrison: The Vocations of a Positivist* (Oxford, 1984).

Wall, J. F., *Andrew Carnegie* (New York, 1970).

Wallis, J., *Valiant for Peace: A History of the Fellowship of Reconciliation 1914 to 1989* (1991).

Weber, T., 'From Maude Royden's Peace Army to the Gulf Peace Team: An Assessment of Unarmed Interpositionary Peace Forces', *Journal of Peace Research*, 30 (1993), 45–74.

Weinroth, H., 'Left-Wing Opposition to Naval Armaments in Britain before 1914', *Journal of Contemporary History*, 6 (1971), 93–120.

—— 'Norman Angell and *The Great Illusion*: An Episode in Pre-1914 Pacifism', *Historical Journal*, 17 (1974), 551–74.

—— 'Peace by Negotiation and the British Anti-War Movement, 1914–1918', *Canadian Journal of History*, 10 (1975), 369–92.

Weisser, H., *British Working-Class Movements and Europe 1815–48* (Manchester, 1975).

Weller, K., *'Don't be a Soldier': The Radical Anti-War Movement in North London 1914–1918* (1985).

White, H. C., *Willougby Hyett Dickinson 1859–1943: A Memoir* (Gloucester, 1956).

White, S., 'Soviets in Britain: The Leeds Convention of 1917', *International Review of Social History*, 19 (1974), 165–93.

Whittaker, D. J., *Fighter for Peace: Philip Noel-Baker 1889–1982* (York, 1989).

Wilcock, E., *Pacifism and the Jews* (Stroud, 1994).

Wilkinson, A., *The Church of England and the First World War* (1978).

—— *Dissent or Conform? War, Peace and the English Churches 1900–1945* (1986).

Wilson, D., *Leonard Woolf: A Political Biography* (1978).

—— *Gilbert Murray OM 1866–1957* (Oxford, 1987).

Wiltsher, A., *Most Dangerous Women: Feminist Peace Campaigners of the Great War* (1985).

Wiltshire, D., *The Social and Political Thought of Herbert Spencer* (Oxford, 1978).

Winkler, H. R., *The League of Nations Movement in Great Britain, 1914–1919* (New Brunswick, NJ, 1952).

—— 'The Emergence of a Labour Foreign Policy in Great Britain, 1918–1929', *Journal of Modern History*, 28 (1956), 247–58.

—— *Paths Not Taken: British Labour and International Policy in the 1920s* (Chapel Hill, NC, 1995).

Winslow, B., *Sylvia Pankhurst: Sexual Politics and Political Activism* (1996).

Winter, J. M., *Socialism and the Challenge of War* (1974).

Wolfe, K. M., *The Churches and the British Broadcasting Corporation 1922–1956: The Politics of Broadcast Religion* (1984).

Wolton, T., *Le KGB en France* (Paris, 1986).

Wrench, J. E., *Francis Yeats-Brown 1886–1944* (1948).

Wright, A. W., *G. D. H. Cole and Socialist Democracy* (Oxford, 1979).

Yearwood, P., ' "On the Safe and Right Lines": The Lloyd George Coalition and the Origins of the League of Nations, 1916–1918', *Historical Journal*, 32 (1989), 131–55.

Zarjevski, Y., *The People have the Floor: A History of the Inter-Parliamentary Union* (Aldershot, 1989).

Richard Taylor + Nigel Young, eds.
Campaigns for Peace, Manchester UP, 1988
(Rev Am Jrnl of Sociology Robert D Benford (1989)
12 original essays — 10 peace traditions
6 cycles
Josephine Eglin — women 1915-present

INDEX

Aberdeen, Lord 37, 46, 47
Aborigines' Protection Society 51–2
Abrams, Irwin 1
absolutism, distinguished from reformism 7
Abyssinia 319–22, 324–5, 327–8, 343, 361–6, 426
Adams, Vyvyan 371
Afghanistan 24, 77, 108–9
Alabama case 74, 84, 96
Albright, Arthur 106–7
Alexander, Horace G. 406
Alexander, Joseph Gundry 197
Allen, Clifford: (1914–18) 212–13, 218, 222–3, 227, 232–3, 397; (1919–31) 244, 277; (1931–5) 285–6, 300–1, 306–7, 309, 313, 315; (1936–9) 340, 344–6, 348, 364, 368, 377, 397, 426
Amberley, Lord 89
American Civil War 15, 33, 65, 68–71, 74
American Peace Society 69–71, 79, 96, 338
anarchism 25, 43, 212–13
Anderson, M. S. 12–13
Anderson, W. C. 176
Angell, Norman: (1898–1914) 151, 167–8, 177–81, 184–5; (1914–18) 188, 199, 202–3, 226, 426; (1919–31) 240, 258–60, 265–6; (1931–5) 293 (n. 57), 294, 300–1, 308, 314–15; (1936–9) 343, 350, 355, 369–70; (1939–45) 383, 387–8, 402, 404
Anglicans 14, 19–20, 22, 42, 69, 82, 95, 132, 141, 149, 157, 174, 176, 195, 215, 234, 325, 417
Anglican Pacifist Fellowship 337, 359, 415
Anglo-American Arbitration Committee 149
Anglo-American Arbitration Treaty 118, 133, 144–5
Anglo-German Fellowship 327
Anglo-German Friendship Committee 167
Anti-Aggression League 109–10, 115–17, 119–21, 154
Anti-Corn-Law League 25–6, 47, 272

anti-semitism 52, 121, 155, 366, 377–81, 393
Anti-Nazi Council 346–7, 350
appeasement 8, 167, 293, 297, 307, 324, 326–87, 332–3, 343, 346, 358, 361–7, 378, 380–1, 383, 385, 387, 407, 419–20; distinguished from peaceful change 167
Appleton, Lewis 73, 75, 83, 111–15, 117, 122, 126, 129–30, 289
Arbitration Alliance 119, 149
arbitration: of international disputes 15, 20, 26–8, 31, 35, 37, 44, 53–4, 65, 67, 69, 71–2, 93–9, 123, 128, 130, 133, 135–6, 144, 148, 166, 169, 169, 173, 178, 203, 250, 262, 418; of labour disputes 86, 92
Arch, Joseph 92, 106–7
Archer, William 236
Armenian massacres (1895–6) 142–3, 145, 149, 162, 328
arms trade 183, 310
Arnaud, Émile 14, 158
Arnold-Forster, Will 256, 275, 304, 395
Arrow war 57–8, 76, 97, 426
Artingstall, Leslie 337
Asquith, H. H. 172, 176, 222, 240
Associated Council of Churches in the British and German Empires for Fostering Friendly Relations between the two Peoples 167
Association de la paix par le droit 139
Association des jeunes amis de la paix 139
Association for the Reform and Codification of International Law, 98, 107, 127; renamed International Law Association (1894) 96
atomic bomb, 1, 422–3
Attlee, Clement 246–7, 257, 305, 332, 343, 388, 400, 417
Attlee, Thomas 305
Australian Defence Act (1910) 191, 213
Ayles, Walter 191, 212–13, 225, 267, 289
Ayrton-Gould, Barbara 239–40

What about Ireland? India?